The **Rough G**

Tasmania

written and researched by

James Stewart and Margo Daly

ROUGH GUIDES

NEW YORK • LONDON • DELHI

www.roughguides.com

Contents

Colour section — 1

Introduction 6
Where to go 8
When to go 10
Things not to miss 11

Basics — 17

Getting there 19
Getting around 25
Accommodation 33
Food and drink 36
The media 39
Festivals 40
Sports and outdoor activities ... 42
Culture and etiquette 49
Shopping 49
Travelling with children 51
Travel essentials 52

Guide — 61

❶ Hobart and around 63
❷ The southeast 119
❸ Central Tasmania 143
❹ The east coast 173

❺ The northeast 209
❻ The northwest 249
❼ The west and southwest ... 291
❽ Bass Strait Islands 333

Contexts — 349

History 351
Flora and fauna 364
Books 369
Australian English 372

Travel store — 375

Small print & Index — 381

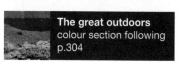

Food and drink colour section following p.112

The great outdoors colour section following p.304

◀◀ Retro Café, Salamanca Place, Hobart ◀ Painted cliffs, Maria Island

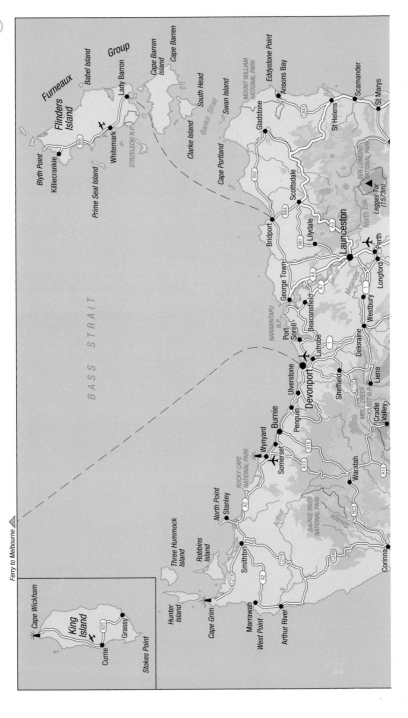

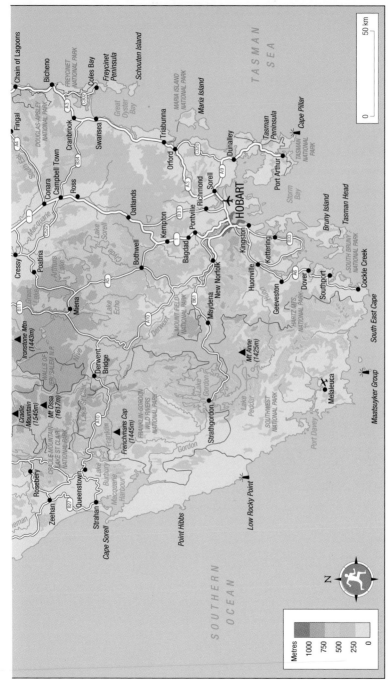

0   50 km

Metres
1000
750
500
250
0

N

Introduction to

Tasmania

Tasmania has always been a land apart from Australia. As Van Diemen's Land during its colonial past, then in the twentieth century as the nation's bucolic kitchen garden, it was separated by an island mentality as much as by the Bass Strait. But since the 1990s, Tasmania has captured the imagination of Australians and international visitors alike. In its home country, "Tassie" now means an adventure playground with a laid-back lifestyle; a small-town throwback in an increasingly suburban nation. For overseas visitors, it means wilderness, activities and penal history. That the convict clichés and chintz are being ditched in favour of sophisticated tourism infrastructure is just one sign of Tasmania's new-found self-assurance.

Once its bane, remoteness is now Tasmania's trump card. Even the erratic economy has had its benefits: though it has stymied modernization, it has also preserved the island's phenomenal natural beauty. If Australia is known for its vast skies and cinnamon-red earth, the quintessential Tasmanian **landscape** is of temperate rainforest, buttongrass plains and glacial mountains. Yet the real ace up its sleeve is diversity. Only one percent of Australia's area, Tasmania packs in more variety than anywhere else in the country: it has some of the most pristine **wilderness** on Earth, comprising over a fifth of the island; its **coastline** is longer than that of New South Wales and Victoria combined, yet is largely undeveloped; it has historic colonial **architecture** that could have been beamed in from Georgian-Victorian England; and there are bizarre **wildlife** species such as the Tasmanian Devil that only survive through being adrift on this geographical Noah's Ark.

6

Small wonder, then, that Tasmanians are quietly, defiantly proud of their state. If "mainlanders", as Tasmanians call all other Australians,

Fact file

• Tasmania is 68,331 square kilometres in **area**. The **coastline** is 3000km long.

• The state **population** in March 2008 was 494,520, of whom 203,600 lived in the Hobart area. The next largest urban centres are Launceston, with 98,500 people, Devonport (25,000) and Burnie (18,000).

• Tasmania protects more of its land than any state in Australia. Around forty percent of the total area is set aside as the **Tasmanian World Heritage Area**, national parks and in state and coastal reserves.

• The $60-million worth of **apples** exported by the "Apple Isle" each year represents sixty-five percent of Australia's total. Tasmania also grows eighty percent of Australia's **hops** and forty percent of the world's pharmaceutical **opium**.

• Tasmania has the world's only scheduled air service to **Antarctica** (one a week in summer from Cambridge Airport) and is the only exporter of commercial igloos in the world.

have only just caught on, it is because the islanders add under-statement and self-reliance to the New World virtues of hard work and vitality. A beach lifestyle and the backyard "barbie" are as much a part of Tasmania as the mainland. But without the waves of foreign immigration, Tasmania is noticeably more Anglocentric than its neighbour states.

More then anything, it is the **great outdoors** that defines the state both physically and mentally. A fierce debate rages within Tasmania about how to manage the **environment**: on one side are conservatives who fear for jobs founded on natural resources; on the other are liberal progressives who aspire to a clean green island. Both would probably celebrate that in just over two centuries Tasmania has gone from being seen as a brooding outcast to a paragon of pure wilderness. As the **economy** outperforms every other in the country, Tasmania doesn't look to the mainland for approval anymore. But having embraced its past, the challenge now is to reconcile the opposing visions for its future.

Where to go

veryone underestimates the size of Tasmania. Though tiny by Australian standards – it is roughly the size of Ireland – with only two or three weeks, you'll still be forced into making choices about what to see. The classic Tasmania circuit spins around the poster-places: **Hobart** and **Port Arthur**, **Freycinet National Park**, **Cradle Mountain** and **Strahan**. This ticks many boxes – the maritime capital, convict past, a postcard-perfect beach and **World Heritage wilderness** – but you'll still come away with a feeling that you've barely scratched the surface. Many of the most memorable areas are not destinations so much as landscapes; places you travel through not to. They're also far less crowded in high summer.

For most visitors, the journey begins at **Hobart**, the state capital and its wellspring, whose blend of maritime and mountains, historic streetscape and swish restaurants is as good an introduction to Tasmania as any. Within an hour's drive is a summary of Tasmania's appeal: mountain and coastal wilderness in **Mount Field National Park** and **Bruny Island** respectively,

Forestry: conservation vs. exploitation

No issue defines – or divides – Tasmania like forestry. Timber has been central to the economy since colonial settlement. But with industrial logging since the 1960s, clearance has accelerated. Conservationists estimate that only a fifth of the pre-colonial forest – the "old-growth" that covered most of the island – now remains, much of it unprotected in areas like the Tarkine, the Northeast or Southern Forests. Even ardent "greenies" concede that Tasmania needs a forestry industry. What infuriates is the practice of clear-felling native old-growth forest and replacing it with fast-growing plantation forest – and only once the area is cleared by napalm-fired burn-offs. The switch to single-species forest and removal of the understory is catastrophic for biodiversity, never mind that ninety percent of the trees are milled into cheap woodchips to serve a declining Asian market. State department Forestry Tasmania and the logging industry have taken steps to counter the critics: a flurry of "forest playground" attractions, for example, or the road-side arboreal "modesty strips" that screen the clear-felling. But the faultline over forests is not

simply about power and money. It is also ideological: about jobs versus conservation, with each side deriding the other as rednecks and greenies. Don't expect a resolution anytime soon.

the bucolic southeast, heritage villages like **Richmond** and the convict penitentiary of **Port Arthur**. **Launceston**, the only other true city, is the state's second gateway, with the **Tamar Valley** wine country in its backyard. The easiest way to sample these is along the **Midlands Highway** – places such as Ross, Oatlands and Campbell Town, or Evandale and Longford, the latter renowned for Georgian manor estates.

For most visitors, however, Tasmania's towns are less compelling than its scenery. The **east coast** teeters on the tropical, with kilometres of white sands and aquamarine seas. **Swansea**, **Coles Bay** and **Bicheno** are the main resorts, all fairly low-key places, though such is the fame of **Wineglass Bay** in the **Freycinet National Park** that Coles Bay can get hectic in summer. Crowds are thinner on dream-like **Maria Island** and St Helens, gateway to the white-powder beaches of the **Bay of Fires**.

The **central north** is densely populated by Tasmanian standards, with a string of so-so urban centres along its coast – Devonport, Burnie, Ulverstone and Wynyard – and a profusion of **farming villages** in the hinterland. By contrast the tips are startlingly empty and there's plenty of scope to get away from the crowds. The **northwest** remains one of the state's best-kept secrets, with a rugged coastline backed by ancient forests and **Stanley**, the historic centre of the Van Diemen's Land Company.

More isolated still is the **west**. Civilization only arrived in the late 1800s as mining towns like Zeehan, Rosebery and Queenstown were scratched out of the bush. Most of the area is the acclaimed World Heritage Area wilderness: **Cradle Mountain** (actually in the central north) and erstwhile fishing village **Strahan** on the west coast are the premier access points. The **south- west**, on the other hand, is pure wilderness: bar one road and a dirt track which circuit its fringe, you either have to walk in or fly to Melaleuca, a one-hut settlement near the great bowl of Bathurst Harbour.

One step removed even from Tasmania, **King** and **Flinders islands** in the Bass Strait operate at a slower pace still.

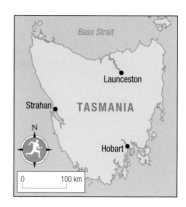

When to go

The common perception of Tasmania as a cold, rain-sodden island doesn't stand up to scrutiny: Hobart is the second-driest Australian state capital after Adelaide. Midwinter in Europe is high summer in Tasmania, and conversely, July and August are the coldest months of the year. Unlike much of Australia, Tasmania has four clearly defined seasons akin to those in northern Europe.

In general the **best time to visit** is during **summer**, from late November until March, though Christmas to January is noticeably more crowded and more expensive for accommodation. **Spring** from September to October is fairly unpredictable in terms of weather. Snow is common in **winter** (June– August) and puts many areas off-limits; it's not unknown even in midsummer in the highlands. Due to prevailing weather patterns, the island gets progressively drier as you move east. It is also progressively warmer as you go north: Launceston is closer to Melbourne than Hobart in terms of climate. That said, the weather is notoriously fickle. In the central highlands and southwest especially, there's much truth in the old cliché about four seasons in one day.

Average temperatures (°C) and rainfall (mm)

	Jan/Feb		Mar/Apr		May/Jun		July/Aug		Sept/Oct		Nov/Dec	
Hobart												
Max temp	22	22	20	17	14	12	12	13	15	17	19	20
Rainfall	48	43	45	51	47	54	53	53	53	55	54	57
Launceston												
Max temp	24	25	22	19	15	13	12	13	16	18	21	23
Rainfall	43	39	40	57	69	78	80	76	69	60	48	52
Strahan												
Max temp	20	21	20	17	15	13	12	13	14	16	18	19
Rainfall	104	105	105	150	154	167	180	188	164	138	115	124

things not to miss

It's not possible to see everything that Tasmania has to offer on a short trip – and we don't suggest you try. What follows is a selective taste of the state's highlights: national parks, outdoor activities and spectacular beaches. They're arranged in five colour-coded categories, which you can browse through to find the very best things to see and experience. All highlights have a page reference to take you into the guide, where you can find out more.

01 **Cradle Mountain and the Overland Track** Page **311** • The most accessible wilderness of the World Heritage Area not only has fantastic glaciated landscapes, it is the start of Australia's greatest trek.

02 **Mount Strzelecki National Park and Trousers Point** Page **341** • Rugged mountain scenery is a backdrop to this impossibly pretty corner of Flinders Island.

03 **Diving** Page **43** • Come face to face with curious creatures in the underwater wilderness that lies off the east coast.

05 **Bruny Island** Page **126** • Travel an hour from Hobart to reach an idyllic, little-developed island steeped in the history of early European explorers.

04 **Abseiling the Gordon Dam** Page **329** • The world's highest commercial abseil is a must-do for adrenaline junkies.

06 Surfing Page **42** • The compensations for cold water are uncrowded line-ups and friendly locals. Head to King Island and Marrawah for seriously big waves.

07 Salamanca market Page **77** • A historic streetscape, a convivial atmosphere and stalls of crafts and tasty food – this Saturday market is Hobart in a nutshell.

08 Port Arthur penitentiary Page **112** • These sandstone ruins provide a thought-provoking insight into the infamous convict era. A haunting one too on a night-time ghost tour.

09 Freycinet National Park Page **186** • The hike to exquisite Wineglass Bay is one of the best walks in Freycinet National Park.

10 Food and drink Page **36** • Superb local produce and first-class chefs make Tasmania a rising star of gourmet Australia, with cool-climate wines to taste in the Coal and Tamar valleys.

11 The Tarkine Page **285** • The last wilderness secret in Australia is characterized by one of the oldest rainforests on Earth and a rugged coastline pounded by waves that have rolled all the way from Patagonia.

12 Maria Island Page **179** • A hauntingly beautiful world of its own just twenty minutes off the east coast, packed full of wildlife and with easy trails to explore.

13 The Franklin River Page **321** • Whitewater rafting is the best way to experience one of the greatest, wildest rivers in Australia.

14 See a Tasmanian Devil
Page **284** • Go west or to wildlife parks to see the most iconic and beleaguered of Tasmania's unique species.

15 The Tasman Peninsula
Page **107** • Take a hike or a boat trip to see the highest sea-cliffs in Australia, not to mention sun-bathing seals and whales in season.

17 Bushcamping
Page **35** • The birth-right of every Tasmanian, the treat for every visitor, is to camp in scenic splendour, usually without forking out a cent.

16 Southwest National Park
Page **323** • Jagged mountains draped in primeval rainforest, buttongrass plains and not a single town in sight – this is as remote as it gets.

18 **Kayaking** Page **43** • Dip a paddle from Coles Bay or Hobart, or make longer excursions to the Tasman Peninsula or Bathurst Harbour to see Tasmania's impressive coastline at its best – afloat.

19 **Arthur River cruise** Page **286** • Visit the "End of the World" to embark on a great five-hour river trip that's refreshingly free of commercial gloss.

20 **The Bay of Fires** Page **204** • With dazzling white sands and aquamarine seas, there's a touch of the tropical about these pristine beaches. Great camping and a superb café-restaurant too.

21 **Bushwalking** Page **45** • Whether you go for two hours or two weeks, this is the only way to experience some of the purest landscapes in the world.

Basics

Basics

Getting there 19

Getting around 25

Accommodation.. 33

Food and drink 36

The media 39

Festivals 40

Sports and outdoor activities... 42

Culture and etiquette 49

Shopping.. 49

Travelling with children 51

Travel essentials.. 52

Getting there

It will come as no surprise to learn that almost every visitor flies to Tasmania. No international airlines go directly to the state, so overseas visitors will need to enter mainland Australia first and then pick up an ongoing connection – whether a second flight (see p.21) or a ferry across the Bass Strait (see p.24). The principal Australian gateways to Tasmania are Sydney and Melbourne; these are also the most convenient for overseas visitors due to the frequency of flights from Europe, North America and Singapore. However, you could also enter at Adelaide to hook up with flights to Hobart with a couple of budget operators.

The highest **air fares** are charged for the two weeks either side of Christmas – Christmas Day itself is the only chance to snap up a bargain. Fares drop in the shoulder months – September to November and February to March, while the low season is generally from April to August. Bear in mind that many flights omit **airport taxes**, which can add around £25–50/€34–66/$48–98.

Specialist flight agents or discount agents, which may also offer student or youth fares as well as travel insurance and car rental, are one way to cut costs. Charter flight specialists are also worth a look and are often cheaper than scheduled operators; the downside is less flexibility in terms of changing your flights. **Fly-drive packages** that include accommodation can provide good deals if you are prepared to determine a route in advance; ask at travel agents. **Round-the-world tickets** offer great value for visitors from Europe and North America who have a few months to spare (see p.22).

Note too that open-jaw tickets (flying into one city and out of another) usually cost no more than an ordinary return and can help with touring the state. Because some of the big-name Australian scheduled carriers let you alter the return date for free for within a year, and the maximum visa time is also a year (and that only for limited working visas), one-way tickets are not worth considering unless you're an Australian or New Zealand citizen.

Flights from the UK and Ireland

Fierce competition between operators ensures that the prices between Britain and the east coast of Australia stay low except when prices sky-rocket over the Christmas period. Major route operators such as Qantas and Virgin have already ordered fleets of a new Boeing aircraft that will make the London–Sydney voyage non-stop in seventeen hours. For the moment, however, standard flights take a minimum of 21 hours to reach the east coast, which includes a stopover in Southeast Asia or North America, so you're looking at a total journey time to Tasmania of at least 25 hours and often up to 34 hours, depending on the waiting time to transfer onto domestic flights to Tasmania from Australian gateway destinations.

There are two **routes** from the UK – east via Asia or west via the USA and Pacific. The former has the most competitive deals. Most direct scheduled flights go from London's two major airports, Gatwick and Heathrow. With Qantas you can fly from regional airports at Aberdeen, Belfast, Edinburgh, Glasgow, Manchester or Newcastle to connect with your international flight in London. The cheapest **fare** is likely to be in the region of £600 return, available during the low season with Middle Eastern and Asian airlines such as Emirates, Gulf Air and Japan Airlines. During the peak period from mid-December, you'll be lucky to find anything under £1000 – and to have any chance at all, you'll need to book around six months in advance. For the same sort of price you can buy multi-stopover or slightly more expensive round-the-world tickets (see p.22) via tantalizing destinations such as Africa, Asia or South America. A good agent comes into its own here, able to devise a travel plan pieced together from various airlines with Tasmania as its ultimate goal. Prices for the traditional London–Bangkok–Sydney–Auckland–Fiji–LA–London itinerary start from as little as £700. It's also possible to add in substantial overland segments into the journey.

No flights go direct to Australia from Ireland. Instead, most routes involve a transfer in London to one of the major airlines. That said, Singapore Airlines and Malaysian Airlines have ticketed flights from all three Irish airports via London. BA and Qantas do the same with an added Dublin–London fare included in the price.

Flights from the US and Canada

From Los Angeles, you can reach the east coast gateways of Sydney and Melbourne in fourteen hours. Qantas is the biggest provider of direct flights, with 38 scheduled flights a week, followed by United and Air New Zealand. If not originating in LA, most flights are from San Francisco or from New York via LA, though United flies from Chicago daily to both Sydney and Melbourne and Qantas flies to Sydney direct from Honolulu a few times a week. Flying with one of the Asian airlines will usually involve a stopover in the operator's capital city (Singapore, Tokyo, Hong Kong, Kuala Lampur, etc) or in the Pacific Rim. Air Canada flies nonstop from Vancouver. You'll have to connect with an ongoing domestic flight in Sydney, Melbourne or Adelaide to get to Tasmania itself.

Unlike the UK, there's not a great deal of variation between the **prices** for low and high season. For a direct flight to Australia from the west coast, you're looking at an average return fare of around $2000–2600. If you book far enough in advance or take a non-direct flight you can pick up a deal of around $1400–$1600. Both direct and non-direct fares from Canada are similar, with

those for Toronto being a couple of hundred dollars more expensive.

Flights from South Africa and New Zealand

Getting to Tasmania from **South Africa** can prove a long-winded process. Qantas schedules a handful of direct flights to Sydney, but the majority of flights arrive at Perth, on Australia's west coast, from where you have to take an onward domestic flight to Sydney and Melbourne (typically around four hours), then connect to an onward link to Tasmania itself. Some Asian carriers such as Singapore Airlines fly to their home bases for connecting flights to the east coast. Either way, flights depart from Johannesburg – national carrier South African Airlines, which also acts as an agent for some Qantas flights, can add flights from other national airports into the ticket price. Journey times for a direct flight to Sydney are around twelve hours, while for those with domestic connections you're looking at travel times of around nineteen hours. As an idea of prices, return fares, without taxes, are around R8000.

New Zealand–Australia routes across the Tasman Sea are busy and subject to fierce price wars between the major carriers: Air New Zealand, Virgin offshoot Pacific Blue and Qantas. Air New Zealand and Qantas schedule regular direct flights from Auckland, Wellington and Christchurch to Sydney and Melbourne, while Pacific Blue operates out of Christchurch only. At the time of writing, it was not possible to get a direct flight from New Zealand to Tasmania, so you'll have to catch a domestic flight from Sydney, Melbourne or Adelaide. That said, it's worth checking the schedules of budget carriers, which can change rapidly. In addition, budget carrier Freedom Air flies from Hamilton to Sydney and from Dunedin to Sydney and Melbourne; it goes from other airports to the Gold Coast or Brisbane should you fancy a road trip down to Tasmania. Flight times for all carriers are three to four hours, and standard prices start at around NZ$800 return. But so long as you are flexible about your travel plans, you can often pick up a promotional or discounted fare that will reduce the price by around a

Fly less – stay longer! Travel and climate change

Climate change is the single biggest issue facing our planet. It is caused by a build-up in the atmosphere of carbon dioxide and other greenhouse gases, which are emitted by many sources – including planes. Already, flights account for around 3–4 percent of human-induced global warming: that figure may sound small, but it is rising year on year and threatens to counteract the progress made by reducing greenhouse emissions in other areas.

Rough Guides regard travel, overall, as a global benefit, and feel strongly that the advantages to developing economies are important, as are the opportunities for greater contact and awareness among peoples. But we all have a responsibility to limit our personal "carbon footprint". That means giving thought to how often we fly and what we can do to redress the harm that our trips create.

Flying and climate change

Pretty much every form of motorized travel generates CO_2, but planes are particularly bad offenders, releasing large volumes of greenhouse gases at altitudes where their impact is far more harmful. Flying also allows us to travel much further than we would contemplate doing by road or rail, so the emissions attributable to each passenger become truly shocking. For example, one person taking a return flight between Europe and California produces the equivalent impact of 2.5 tonnes of CO_2 – similar to the yearly output of the average UK car.

Less harmful planes may evolve but it will be decades before they replace the current fleet – which could be too late for avoiding climate chaos. In the meantime, there are limited options for concerned travellers: to reduce the amount we travel by air (take fewer trips, stay longer!), to avoid night flights (when plane contrails trap heat from Earth but can't reflect sunlight back to space), and to make the trips we do take "climate neutral" via a carbon offset scheme.

Carbon offset schemes

Offset schemes run by Ⓦ**www.climatecare.org**, Ⓦ**www. carbonneutral.com** and others allow you to "neutralize" the greenhouse gases that you are responsible for releasing. Their websites have simple calculators that let you work out the impact of any flight. Once that's done, you can pay to fund projects that will reduce future carbon emissions by an equivalent amount (such as the distribution of low-energy lightbulbs and cooking stoves in developing countries). Please take the time to visit our website and make your trip climate neutral.

Ⓦ**www.roughguides.com/climatechange**

third. Be careful about the restrictions which hedge the cheapest deals, however.

Flights from Australia

The majority of domestic flights to Tasmania leave from Sydney and Melbourne and arrive at the state's principal airports, Hobart and Launceston. Both are served by frequent flights a day. However, you can also enter Tassie at the minor airports of Devonport, Burnie (Wynyard) and King Island, all departing from Melbourne. Although the nitty-gritty of who flies where can change, the following information has been consistent for the last few years:

Qantas's budget airline **Jetstar** operates daily services from Melbourne and Sydney to Hobart and Launceston, and from Adelaide to Hobart; **Qantas** itself flies daily to Hobart from Melbourne and Sydney, and daily into Launceston from Melbourne, while subsidiary airline **Qantaslink** flies Melbourne to Devonport. **Tiger Airlines**, a budget offshoot of Singapore Airlines, flies from Melbourne to Hobart and Launceston a couple of times a day; **Virgin Blue** provides daily flights to Hobart and Launceston from Sydney and Melbourne and less frequent services from Adelaide to Hobart; and **Regional Express** (Rex) goes from

Melbourne to King Island daily and to Burnie several times a day. Qantas and Virgin Blue have connecting flights with other airports in Australia, often without any significant difference in price.

Fierce competition between budget airlines means price discounting is the norm – most airlines have a quota of promotional fares and there are superb deals of up to fifty percent off if you book in advance, ideally at least four weeks. The shorter flight from Melbourne to Launceston is generally the cheapest, and the budget operators (Jetstar, Virgin Blue and Tiger Airlines) provide the keenest fares. Obviously **prices** change, but as a rough idea of one-way prices for a standard seat, you'll pay between $50 and $110 for a one-way fare from Sydney or Melbourne to Launceston or Hobart. Fares from Adelaide to Tasmania cost between $120 and $150, and from Brisbane around $150 to $180. Note that some budget operators such as Jetstar reserve the cheapest fares for passengers with hand-luggage only – a problem for international visitors unless you travel light. Another caveat with budget flights is that you will incur fees for any changes to flight details and tickets are non-transferable and usually non-refundable.

Round-the-world flights

Because of the distances involved, Australia is a standard inclusion in **round-the-world tickets**. These only come into their own if you are travelling for at least a couple of months. Stopovers are usually in Asia, the Pacific and North or South America, through you can pretty much devise your own itinerary, opening up the possibility of combining overland routes for substational segments of the journey. A good **agent** comes into their own here – reputable outfits such as STA will also let you redeem the ticket value for another flight should your plans change en route. Prices increase with the number of destinations. Keep your itinerary down to three continents, however, and you can get a basic London–Bangkok–Sydney (then Tasmania)–Fiji–LA–London deal for around £700. A simple LA–Fiji–Sydney–Paris–LA route starts at $1400.

Airlines, agents and operators

Online booking and general travel sites

ⓦ **www.cheapflights.com** Flight search engine with access to third-party search engines, daily deals and also hotels. Handy for specific routes.

ⓦ **www.expedia.com**. Discount airfares, an all-inclusive airline search engine and daily deals.

ⓦ **www.flyaow.com** An online information source with an air fares search engine.

ⓦ **www.hotwire.com** US-only bookings with last-minute bargains but no refunds, transfers or changes allowed. Users must be over 18 and log-in is required.

ⓦ **www.kelkoo.co.uk** A useful price comparison search engine that covers all things travel – flights, car hire, holidays, etc.

ⓦ **www.lastminute.com** A good choice for last-minute flights and holiday packages.

ⓦ **www.priceline.com** Name-your-price non-transferable, non-refundable flights from a US-based website, which promises no booking fees and savings of up to 40 percent.

ⓦ **www.opodo.co.uk** Popular and reliable source of UK air fares, car rental and deals. Owned and run by a conglomerate of nine European airlines.

ⓦ **www.orbitz.com** Comprehensive US web-based travel service renowned for its customer support.

ⓦ **www.skyauction.com** Auction site for flight bookings from the US only – works like eBay, so place your highest bid, since the final price is only that which beats all other competitors.

ⓦ **travel.yahoo.com** Incorporates some Rough Guides material in the coverage of destinations, with information and user reviews about where to eat and sleep.

ⓦ **www.travelocity.com** (in US)

ⓦ **www.travelocity.co.uk** (in UK)

ⓦ **www.tripadvisor.com** Less useful for its flights search engine than its user-driven content about destinations, with over ten million opinions voiced about hotels, sights, restaurants, bars and activities. Beware of bias, however.

ⓦ **www.zuji.com.au** (in AUS)

ⓦ **www.zuji.co.nz** (in NZ). A handy one-stop shop for everything holidays – flights, hotels, cars, package holidays and insurance.

International airlines

Aerolineas Argentinas US ☎1-800/333-0276, Canada ☎1-800/688-0008, UK ☎0800/096 9747, New Zealand ☎09/379 3675, Australia ☎02/9234 9000; ⓦwww.aerolineas.com.

Air Canada ☎1-888/247-2262, UK ☎0871/220 1111, Republic of Ireland ☎01/679 3958, Australia ☎1300/655 767, New Zealand ☎0508/747 767; ⓦwww.aircanada.com.

Air China US ☎1-800-9828/802, Canada ☎416-581/8833, UK ☎020/7744 0800, Australia ☎02/9232 7277; ⓦwww.airchina.com.cn.

Air New Zealand ☎0800/737000, Australia ☎0800/132 476, UK ☎0800/028 4149, USA ☎1800-262/1234, Canada ☎1800-663/5494; ⓦwww.airnz.co.nz.

Asiana Airlines US ☎1-800/227-4262, UK ☎0207/514 0201/8, Australia ☎02/9767 4343; ⓦwww.flyasiana.com.

British Airways US and Canada ☎1-800/AIRWAYS, UK ☎0870/850 9850, Republic of Ireland ☎1890/626 747, Australia ☎1300/767 177, New Zealand ☎09/966 9777, South Africa ☎114/418 600; ⓦwww.ba.com.

Cathay Pacific US ☎1-800/233-2742, Canada ☎1-800/2686-868, UK ☎020/8834 8888, Australia ☎13 17 47, New Zealand ☎09/379 0861, South Africa ☎11/700 8900; ⓦwww.cathaypacific.com.

China Airlines US ☎1-917/368-2003, UK ☎020/7436 9001, Australia ☎02/9231 5588, New Zealand ☎09/308 3364; ⓦwww.china-airlines.com.

China Eastern Airlines US ☎1626-1583/1500, Canada ☎1604-6898/998, UK ☎0870/760 6232, Australia ☎02/9290 1148; ⓦwww.chinaeastern.co.uk.

China Southern Airlines US ☎1-888/338-8988, Australia ☎02/9231 1988; ⓦwww.cs-air.com.

Emirates US and Canada ☎1-800/777-3999, UK ☎0870/243 2222, Australia ☎03/9940 7807, New Zealand ☎05/0836 4728, South Africa ☎0861/363 728; ⓦwww.emirates.com.

Etihad Airways US ☎1-8888/ETIHAD, Canada ☎1-416/221-4744, UK ☎0870/241 7121, South Africa ☎11/3439 140; ⓦwww.etihadairways.com.

EVA Air US and Canada ☎1-800/695-1188, UK ☎020/7380 8300, Australia ☎02/8338 0419, New Zealand ☎09/358 8300, ⓦwww.evaair.com.

Freedom Air ⓦwww.freedomair.com.

Garuda Indonesia US ☎1-212/279-0756, UK ☎020/7467 8600, Australia ☎1300/365 330 or 02/9334 9944, New Zealand ☎09/3661862; ⓦwww.garuda-indonesia.com.

Hawaiian Airlines ☎1-800/367-5320, Australia ☎02/9244 2377; ⓦwww.hawaiianair.com.

Korean Air US and Canada ☎1-800/438-5000, UK ☎0800/413 000, Republic of Ireland ☎01/799 7990, Australia ☎02/9262 6000, New Zealand ☎09/914 2000; ⓦwww.koreanair.com.

JAL (Japan Air Lines) US and Canada ☎1-800/525-3663, UK ☎0845/774 7700, Republic of Ireland ☎01/408 3757, Australia ☎02/9272 1111, New Zealand ☎09/379 9906, South Africa ☎11/214 2560; ⓦwww.jal.com or ⓦwww.japanair.com.

Malaysia Airlines US ☎1-800/5529-264, UK ☎0870/607 9090, Republic of Ireland ☎01/6761 561, Australia ☎13 26 27, New Zealand ☎0800/777 747, South Africa ☎11-8809 614; ⓦwww.malaysia-airlines.com.

Philippine Airlines US ☎1-800/435-9725, Canada ☎604/276 6075, UK ☎01293/596 680, Australia ☎612/9279 2020, New Zealand ☎09/308 5206; ⓦwww.philippineairlines.com.

Qantas Airways US and Canada ☎1-800/227-4500, UK ☎0845/774 7767, Republic of Ireland ☎01/407 3278, Australia ☎13 13 13, New Zealand ☎0800/808 767 or 09/357 8900, SA ☎11/441 8550; ⓦwww.qantas.com.

Singapore Airlines US ☎1-800/742-3333, Canada ☎1-800/663-3046, UK ☎0844/800 2380, Republic of Ireland ☎01/671 0722, Australia ☎13 10 11, New Zealand ☎0800/808 909, South Africa ☎11/880 8560 or 11/880 8566; ⓦwww.singaporeair.com.

South African Airways ☎11/978 1111, US and Canada ☎1-800/722-9675, UK ☎0870/747 1111, Australia ☎1800/221 699, New Zealand ☎09/977 2237; ⓦwww.flysaa.com.

Thai Airways US ☎1-212/949-8424, UK ☎0870/606 0911, Australia ☎1300/651 960, New Zealand ☎09/377 3886, South Africa ☎11/455 1018; ⓦwww.thaiair.com.

United Airlines US ☎1-800/UNITED-1, UK ☎0845/844 4777, Australia ☎13 17 77; ⓦwww.united.com.

Vietnam Airlines US ☎1-415/677-0888, Canada ☎1-416/599-2888, UK ☎0870/224 0211, Australia ☎02/9283 9658; ⓦwww.vietnamairlines.com.

Virgin Atlantic US ☎1-800/821-5438, UK ☎0870/380 2007, Australia ☎1300/727 340, South Africa ☎11/340 3400; ⓦwww.virgin-atlantic.com.

Domestic airlines

Jetstar Australia ☎131 538, ⓦwww.jetstar.com.

Regional Express (aka Rex) ☎13 17 13, ⓦwww.regionalexpress.com.au.

Tiger Airlines ☎03/9335 3033, ⓦwww.tigerairways.com.

Virgin Blue ☎13 67 89, ⓦwww.virginblue.com.au.

International agents and operators

Audley ☎01993 838 810, ⓦwww.audleytravel.com. Tailor-made journeys for the discerning traveller, booked by agents with experience of the country.

Austravel ☏ 0870 166 2020, ⊚ www.austravel .com. Tasmanian options as part of an Australasia specialist.

Australian Pacific Tours UK ☏ 020 8879 7444, US and Canada ☏ 1-800 298 8687, New Zealand ☏ 09/302 5780; ⊚ www.aptouring.com.au. An international area specialist. General interest tours along with stopover packages to King Island.

Destination World ☏ 1-888-345-4669, ⊚ www.destinationworld.com. US operator with a Tassie programme among its wide variety of Australian tours, including off-the-beaten track adventures.

ebookers UK ☏ 0800/082 3000, Republic of Ireland ☏ 01/488 3507; ⊚ www.ebookers.com, ⊚ www.ebookers.ie. Low fares on an extensive selection of scheduled flights and package deals.

North South Travel UK ☏ 01245/608 291, ⊚ www.northsouthtravel.co.uk. Friendly, competitive travel agency, offering discounted fares worldwide. Profits are used to support projects in the developing world, especially the promotion of sustainable tourism.

Qantas Holidays/Qantas Vacations UK ☏ 020/8222 9125, ⊚ www.qantasholidays.co.uk; US ☏ 866 914 4359, ⊚ www.qantasvacations.com. Holiday packages from the Australian state airline.

STA Travel US ☏ 1-800/781-4040, UK ☏ 0871/2300 040, Australia ☏ 134 STA, New Zealand ☏ 0800/474 400, SA ☏ 0861/781 781; ⊚ www.statravel.com. Worldwide specialists in independent travel; also student IDs, travel insurance, car rental, rail passes and more. Good discounts for students and under-26s.

Tailor Made UK ☏ 0800 988 5887, ⊚ www .tailor-made.co.uk. Bespoke holidays provided by a small operator with a good selection of activities, gourmet and nature tours.

Tas Vacations Australia ☏ 1800 030 160, international ☏ 61 3 6234 4666; ⊚ www .tasvacations.com. Package holidays from the state's largest independent travel agent: flights, accommodation, vehicle hire, park passes and bespoke special interest holidays.

Trailfinders UK ☏ 0845/058 5858, Republic of Ireland ☏ 01/677 7888, Australia ☏ 1300/780 212; ⊚ www.trailfinders.com. One of the best-informed and most efficient agents for independent travellers.

Turquoise Holidays ☏ 01494 678400, ⊚ www .turquoiseholidays.co.uk. High-end UK operator that specializes in quality, tailor-made trips, with wildlife trips, private guides, unique accommodation, food and wine, etc.

Ferries from Australia

If you are travelling from Australia with a car, ferries operated by **TT-Line** (☏ 1800 634 906 in Australia, ☏ +61 3 6421 7209 international calls; ⊚ www.spiritoftasmania.com.au) can make savings on the cost of hiring a vehicle in Tasmania. One *Spirit of Tasmania* ferry sails each night at 8pm between Melbourne and Devonport year-round (although there is often a reduced Sunday service in winter months). Additional ferries sail at 9pm in peak season and at 9am on weekends from late December to mid-April, often with the occasional Monday or Tuesday thrown in. The **ferry terminals** are at Station Pier and Waterfront Place, Melbourne; and The Esplanade, East Devonport.

The **crossing** takes nine to eleven hours, which you can spend in the onboard restaurants, bars, gaming room, kids' playroom, Tourism Tasmania centre and free cinema. For overnight sailings you also need to book **accommodation**, which ranges in luxury and price from recliner seats in the lounge to deluxe en-suite cabins with a queen-size bed and a free bottle of fizz. Day-ticket passengers are allowed to roam the decks. Cots are also available for free.

Prices vary by season: peak from mid-December to late January; the shoulder season from late January to early May; and early September to mid-December; and off-peak at all other periods. Standard fares for passengers are poor value compared with airlines. Depending on the season, you'll pay one-way: from $120 to $170 for a recliner seat; $220 to $240 for a bed in a shared four-bunk cabin; $250 to $290 for an inside twin cabin; and $320 to $420 for a deluxe cabin. A quota of non-refundable discount fares provided for advance bookings reduce the price by around $20 to $30, and there's usually a promotional deal.

Where the ferry service trumps the airlines is the one-way rate for cars of $61 – roughly the cost of car hire for a day in high season. Campervans cost from $79 each way, while charges for motorbikes are $50, and $8 for a bicycle. If you're coming as a foot passenger, Tasmanian coach operators Tassielink and Redline (see p.30) meet all ferries at Devonport with express services to Launceston and Hobart.

Getting around

The flip side to Tasmania's appeal as a small-town and wilderness destination is a so-so public transport system (which is all by bus or coach). While suburban bus transport is good around the cities of Hobart and Launceston, and regular on arterial routes or to the major tourist destinations, getting to the lesser national parks and even some holiday resorts can prove an intensely frustrating experience. Many schedules only operate a few days a week, especially up the east coast, or only during weekdays – timetable details are at the end of each chapter. To see some of Tasmania's more far-flung destinations, therefore, you will either need a car, a tour, or plenty of time, patience and a head for timetables. Cycling is also worth considering in summer, provided you're keen and realistic about how far you'll travel in your allotted holiday period. However you travel, don't underestimate the length of time involved. Tasmania is pocket-sized by Australian standards, but the standard Tassie road is a winding single carriageway that bumps up journey times – 260km from Hobart to Queenstown by coach takes at least five hours, for example.

By car or motorbike

By far the most practical and rewarding way to see Tasmania is with your own vehicle: no more being held hostage to the whims of bus timetables, a chance to access the remote beaches and national parks, tiny towns and bushcamps that make the state so special. If your trip is a long one – around two to three months or more – then buying a vehicle makes sense (see box, p.28). For shorter trips you're looking at renting. Most foreign driving licences are valid for a year in Australia, though an **International Driving Permit** (IDP) is recommended if your licence is not in English or does not have a photo. It is issued by your home licencing authority and is valid for a year.

Vehicle rental

All the international players are represented in the two big cities and operate bureaux at the airports. Fly-drive deals booked when you buy a flight provide lower prices, and online rates are lower still. YHA members can buy a one-, two- or three-week Tasmania Adventure Freedom Pass package with a car from Europcar and hostel accommodation ($365; $714 and $1042 respectively). Ensure Tasmania's few YHA hostels fit in with your travel plans before you go ahead,

however. Standard **prices** of the major agencies typically range from $40 to $70 a day depending on the model and the season of hire. Smaller local outfits in the cities are always better value, and the bottom-line agencies can go as low as $30 for a basic runaround – some are named in the Listings sections of Hobart and Launceston, others are in free tourism newspaper *Tasmania Travelways* (also ⓦ www.tasmaniatravelways .com.au) or look for flyers in the visitor centre. Bear in mind that those bargain $22 rentals don't include **insurance**. Many companies have an insurance excess charge of around $1000; you'll have the option of paying a daily premium to reduce this. Double-check, too, that the price includes breakdown cover and that there is no limit on the mileage. And check the small print to determine your insurance status when driving off sealed roads. Not a problem if you don't have it, but something to be aware of as you're bound to go onto gravel a few times in Tasmania.

Rental of **four-wheel drives** (listed throughout the book as 4WD) is expensive and only worth considering if you intend to drive on specific areas such as beaches and the more remote off-road tracks. With the exception of a few named beaches, all destinations in this book are accessible by

Driving distances

Bicheno	Burnie	Campbell Town	Coles Bay	Cradle Mtn	Devonport	Dover	Hobart
301							
91	194						
38	301	107					
318	110	227	334				
252	49	145	252	85			
257	405	210	273	438	355		
178	325	130	194	359	277	79	
156	148	66	173	180	100	276	199
425	139	334	440	245	189	544	465
208	164	117	225	197	115	210	130
221	419	224	236	453	371	171	94
353	176	262	370	131	192	340	260
76	290	119	114	325	242	345	265
344	447	253	352	425	331	238	160
43	261	67	59	295	212	215	134

a standard 2WD, even if the going on unsealed roads is pretty rough at times.

Campervans and motorhomes are more popular than ever as people cotton on that they are the perfect way to experience Tasmania – this is a state tailored towards touring, which revels in the big outdoors and has plentiful bushcamps, many in awesome locations and most free. Moreover, considering that the daily price for a two-person van is $80 to $250 (according to model and season), which includes accommodation, it can represent excellent value. Campervans come in two forms: basic vans with a couple of bench beds and high-tops that allow you to stand up. The latter are preferable to save you getting a bad back or cranky after a couple of weeks. Vehicles sleep two to four – bear in mind that the upper capacity is a maximum and space is always tight – and are designed with a sink, stove or microwave and a fridge. Motorhomes are larger, usually sleeping up to six and often with separate living and sleeping areas and an onboard shower and toilet. The compromise is between comfort and access – more remote locations are off-limits to large vehicles and you may require an external power source for some onboard equipment. Prices are around $100 per day more than for a basic van. Whatever you choose, double-check that the agency includes cooking equipment and bedding if you require it – they should do, though the latter may come with a small charge. And again, check the small print about travel on unsealed roads.

Motorbike rental is still in its infancy in Tasmania – there are currently only two rental agencies (see opposite). Large-capacity all-purpose bikes are best for extended touring; comfortable, economical and a pleasure to ride when loaded up (though they weigh a ton and need thought about tyres for off-road driving). The Tasmanian Motorcycle Council (ⓦ www.tasmanianmotorcyclecouncil.org.au) publishes a *Ride Tasmania Safely* pamphlet, also available as a download from its website.

Car-rental agencies

Avis US and Canada ☏ 1-800/331-1212, UK ☏ 0870/606 0100, Republic of Ireland ☏ 021/428 1111, Australia ☏ 13 63 33 or 02/9353 9000, New Zealand ☏ 09/526 2847 or 0800/655 111; ⓦ www.avis.com.
Budget US ☏ 1-800/527-0700, Canada ☏ 1-800/268-8900, UK ☏ 0870/156 5656, Australia ☏ 1300/362 848, New Zealand ☏ 0800/283 438; ⓦ www.budget.com.
Europcar US and Canada ☏ 1-877/940 6900, UK ☏ 0870/607 5000, Republic of Ireland ☏ 01/614 2800, Australia ☏ 393/306 160; ⓦ www.europcar.com.
Hertz US and Canada ☏ 1-800/654-3131, UK ☏ 020/7026 0077, Republic of Ireland ☏ 01/870 5777, New Zealand ☏ 0800/654 321; ⓦ www.hertz.com.
Holiday Autos UK ☏ 0870/400 4461, Republic of Ireland ☏ 01/872 9366, Australia ☏ 299/394 433,

Launceston							
287	**Marrawah**						
110	302	**Miena**					
291	559	223	**Port Arthur**				
251	299	139	354	**Queenstown**			
162	431	215	298	430	**St Helens**		
319	586	213	252	286	372	**Strathgordon**	
134	401	183	178	396	119	295	**Swansea**

US ☎ 866-392/9288, South Africa ☎ 11/2340 597; ⓦ www.holidayautos.co.uk. Part of the LastMinute.com group.

Lo-Cost Auto Rent ☎ 1800 647 060, ⓦ www .locostautorent.com. Cheap used car rentals from a Tassie operator with bases in Hobart, Launceston and Devonport.

Rent-a-bug ☎ 03/6231 0300, ⓦ www.rentabug .com.au. New, classic and prestige VW Beetles. Bases in Hobart, Launceston and Devonport.

Rent For Less ☎ 1300 883 728, ⓦ www .rentforless.com.au. Good-value new vehicles from an Aussie operator with bases in Hobart, Launceston and Devonport.

Selective ☎ 1800 300 102, ⓦ www .selectivecarrentals.com.au. A Tasmanian outfit with bases in Hobart and Launceston.

Thrifty US and Canada ☎ 1-800/847-4389, UK ☎ 01494/751 500, Republic of Ireland ☎ 01/844 1950, Australia ☎ 1300/367 227, New Zealand ☎ 09/256 1405; ⓦ www.thrifty.com.

Campervan- and motorhome-rental agencies

Unless stated, all agencies are based at Hobart airport or its adjacent town, Cambridge.

Autorent Hertz Campervans ☎ 1800 030 500, ⓦ www.autorent.com.au. Bases in Cambridge and Launceston.

Backpacker Sleeper Vans Tasmania ☎ 1800 627 074, ⓦ www.tasmania-sleepervans.com.au.

Britz Campervan Rentals ☎ 1800 331 454, ⓦ www.britz.com.au.

Cruisin' Tasmania ☎ 1300 664 485, ⓦ www .cruisin-tasmania.com.au.

Devil Campervans ☎ 03/6248 4493, ⓦ www .devilcampervans.com.au

Maui Motorhomes ☎ 1300 363 800, ⓦ www .maui.com.au.

Tasmania Campervan Rentals ☎ 03/6248 5638, ⓦ www.tasmaniacampervanrentals.com.au.

Motorbike-rental agencies

Moto Adventure Tasmania ☎ 0447 556 189, ⓦ www.motoadventure.com.au. Powerful BMW 650cc bikes and BMW's flagship 1200cc all-rounder.

Tasmania Motorcycle Hire ☎ 03/6391 9139, ⓦ www.tasmotorcyclehire.com.au. An agency in Evandale with the cheapest hire in Tassie – the all-Honda fleet ranges from 250cc to 800cc and includes a Harley-style tourer.

Driving practicalities

Australia drives on the left, with right of way given to vehicles approaching from the right (as in Britain). Seatbelts are compulsory for all passengers. It is also illegal to use a mobile phone while driving unless with a hands-free kit. **Speed limits** are 50kmph in built-up areas (if there is no sign assume this is the limit), 100kmph on non-urban roads unless indicated, and 110kmph on major highways. Due to Tassie's meandering roads, common sense dictates that non-urban speeds are a limit rather than a challenge. The legal **alcohol limit** for drivers is 0.05g/100ml, which in practice means no

27

Buying a car

Powerful, mid-1980s **station wagons** ("panel vans") make good travellers' cars – they are cheap, reliable, mechanically basic and durable, and roomy enough to convert the rear into a temporary bed with a foam mattress. Holden Kingswoods and especially Ford Falcons are cultural icons of Australia, affectionately known as "sin-bins" or "shag-wagons". At the lower end of the market, $1500 should get you a basic tatty vehicle that runs reliably; the chances are that if it's lasted this long, it'll keep going for a couple more months. Ideally, though, you should plan to spend around $2500 for a solid model. Manual transmission models are cheaper than old automatics. If you are less fussed about storage volume, mid-1990s Japanese runarounds such as the Toyota Corolla and Mistubishi Magna are more modern and ubiquitous, which means spares are widely available – expect to pay from $2500 for a good model. Look, too, at the remaining length of vehicle registration – any car with only a month or so to go is probably a rust-bucket. Vehicle registration also provides the minimum third-party insurance.

Dealers may offer extended warranties, but tend to be more expensive. Real bargains are sometimes available through hostels from other travellers. Otherwise look at local newspapers *The Mercury* (Hobart and the south) and *The Examiner* (Launceston and the north), both of which have motoring supplements. Online **search engines** are a handy source that crawl through dealer vehicles as well as private newspaper classifieds: try Ⓦwww.autotrader.com.au, Ⓦwww.autoguide .com.au or Ⓦwww.carsguide.com.au. As ever, shop around.

Unless you know your axles from elbows, get a professional mechanic to double-check the roadworthiness of a vehicle. The RACT (Royal Automobile Club of Tasmania; ☏13 27 22, Ⓦwww.ract.com.au) is a good bet, and also provides more comprehensive insurance to protect against theft and breakdown cover. In any case, you'll need a roadworthiness certificate when you transfer car ownership to your name through the Department of Transport – its website, Ⓦwww.transport.tas .gov.au, has details on this. For more general advice on buying, check out the Justice Department's consumer advice website Ⓦwww.consumer.tas.gov.au.

alcohol at all – police are authorized to stop and breath-test any vehicle and routinely perform random tests in rural areas, especially around the Christmas period. One rule that routinely catches out visitors is that roadside parking must be in the same direction as the traffic – either to stop you crossing a lane of oncoming traffic or because it keeps the streets looking neat. Parking is free in all towns except central Hobart, Launceston and Burnie, and major tourism centres such as Strahan and Cradle Mountain.

Fuel prices in Tasmania are around $1.45 per litre for standard unleaded petrol – diesel is a few cents more expensive – and prices are up to 20¢ a litre higher in remote destinations. Be aware, too, that garages in the country – often just a pump in front of a general store – are only open from 8am to 6pm weekdays and Saturday, and may shut on Sunday. "Servos" in urban centres operate longer hours, and there are 24-hour outlets in Hobart and Launceston. To be safe it's best to fill up whenever you drop to a quarter-tank.

The main **hazards** of driving in Tasmania are excess speed and fatigue. Narrow, usually winding roads frequently throw up corners without much warning and extend driving times. Distances look short, but unless you are travelling on the main Hobart–Launceston and Launceston–Devonport motorways, do not underestimate the times involved – assume driving speeds of around 60kmph and take a break every two hours. In any case, Tasmanian scenery and lifestyles warrant a slower pace of travel.

Unsealed dirt roads are common throughout the state (they are marked on most commercial maps in yellow, as opposed to orange sealed routes) and can appear without warning beyond a stretch of smooth bitumen. Frequently potholed, they vary in quality, though teeth-jarring severe corrugation usually only lasts a few kilometres at a stretch. The best advice is to slow down to at least 80kmph and to 50kmph if conditions dictate, and use a low gear as road conditions deteriorate. To save windscreens being shattered by flying stones, give passing traffic plenty of room. Another tip is to keep windows closed unless you like a light coat of persistent dust that defies every attempt at cleaning. On all types of road, never discard cigarette butts out of the window – bushfires are a constant threat, especially on the dry east coast.

Beware of heavy logging **trucks** on all roads, especially in the forestry regions of the northeast, northwest and in the south and southwest. Might is right – and lorry drivers know it – so always pull aside if there's the slightest doubt, and do not overtake unless you can see well ahead. Another concern is **wildlife**, especially from dusk to dawn, as witnessed by the high volume of road-kill throughout the state – as the joke goes, if you want to see wildlife in Tasmania, get a glass-bottomed car. Over fifty percent of animals killed on the roads are hit between 6pm and midnight, so try to avoid driving in remote areas at night, or at least slow down if you have to drive and scan the verges – remember, this can damage your car too. If you do hit something, stop if you can, and if the animal is injured keep it in a warm, dark place and seek advice from Parks & Wildlife Service (℡03/6223 6556) as soon as possible. Advice on 4WD tracks is published on its website (Ⓦwww.parks.tas.gov.au) under "Outdoor Recreation".

By air

Tasmania's size means the few scheduled air routes within the state are only of interest to reach otherwise inaccessible destinations or if you are seriously pressed for time. The most useful flights are those to the Bass Strait Islands and the bushwalkers' service into the Southwest National Park – schedules are published online on the airlines' websites or in state tourism freesheet *Tasmanian Travelways*, available at visitor centres throughout Tasmania. All prices quoted below are one way – returns cost double.

Domestic airlines

Airlines of Tasmania ℡1800 144 460, Ⓦwww.airtasmania.com.au. Daily flights from Launceston to Flinders Island ($155) and Cape Barren Island ($240). It also incorporates Par Avion Tours (℡03/6248 5390), which provides daily bushwalker flights to Melaleuca and a couple of flights a week from Cambridge (Hobart) to Strahan (both $160).

Tasair ℡1800 062 900 (Tasmania only) or ℡03/6248 5088, Ⓦwww.tasair.com.au. Daily scheduled services between King Island and Devonport and Burnie (Wynyard); plus a limited weekday service between Hobart and Devonport, and Hobart and Burnie (Wynyard). All flights $198. Also offers bushwalkers' pick-ups and drop-offs to Cox Bight and Melaleuca (both $176).

By boat

A daily car and passenger **ferry** (℡03/6273 6725) shuttles frequently between Kettering and Bruny Island in southeast Tasmania; there are at least ten services a day except on Sunday, when there are nine. The trip takes thirty minutes and reservations are not generally required outside peak times in high summer. Standard **prices** are $25 for a car, $3.50 for a bicycle. A passenger-only ferry contracted by Parks & Wildlife Service operates to Maria Island from Triabunna twice a day in summer and once a day in winter. Bicycles are allowed on board for a small fee. At the time of writing the contract was out to tender, with a stop-gap service provided by eco-tour operator Sea Wings; up-to-date information is published on the Parks & Wildlife Service website, Ⓦwww.parks.tas.gov.au. The only other car ferry service, Bridport-based Southern Shipping Co (Mon departures, times depend on tides; ℡03/6356 3333, Ⓦwww.southernshipping.com.au) provides links to Cape Barren Island, Flinders Island then on to Port Welshpool in Victoria. **Prices to Flinders Island** are steep for vehicles ($515 return) though good value for foot-passengers ($96.50 return) and reservations are required at all times, and at least a month in advance from November to February.

By coach

Almost all your long-distance public transport will be by coach. Hobart and Launceston are the two transport hubs, with routes fanning

See Tasmania by tour

If time is tight, take a bus tour. Usually lasting a week or more, these minimize the hassle of organizing transport and accommodation, thereby allowing you to see more, they also include national park passes and a few activities. Most operators are geared towards the backpacker market, with appropriate budget style and easy-going vibe. Excellent Tassie operator **Under Down Under Tours** (℗03/6362 2237 or 1800 064 726, ⓦwww.underdownunder.com.au) is a small-group ecotourist outfit aimed at independent-minded travellers. Trips usually depart from Launceston or Devonport and include bushwalking and wildlife-spotting, hostel accommodation (which can be upgraded), and some but not all breakfasts and lunches. A five-day tour ($645) does a loop of the island including Cradle Mountain and the Freycinet Peninsula, while a two-day Tarkine tour ($275) of the northwest includes the Arthur River cruise. Both can be combined into a seven-day trip ($745). Another five-day tour focuses on the wild west coast ($625). The "Bloomin Lot" eight-day ($925) or nine-day ($950) versions can be treated as a tour pass with the components done at your leisure. It also runs Walk & Cycle Tours up the east coast from Hobart that last three days ($495) and four days ($650).

Nationwide operator **Adventure Tours Australia** (℗1300 654 604, ⓦwww.adventuretours.com.au) runs a range of small-group trips; again, meals and hostel or motel accommodation are included. There are three-day tours from either Hobart or Devonport via Cradle Mountain (from Hobart; $440) or the East Coast (from Devonport or Launceston; $425). These can be combined as a six-day loop around the island from Hobart ($795), or done in seven days from Devonport by adding an extra day in Hobart ($810).

Pepperbush Adventures (℗03 6352 2263, ⓦwww.pepperbush.com.au) provides high-end 4WD nature-based tours from Launceston, led by charismatic bush expert Craig "Bushie" Williams. Eight-day "Best of Tassie" and eleven-day "Mild, Wild & Untamed" tours take in the highlight destinations of the state as well as interesting sidetracks. Luxury accommodation, fine food and interesting tours such as a Freycinet cruise, Devil-watching at Marrawah or Craig's own "Quoll Patrol" wildlife-spotting are included in the price. It also has a six-day gourmet tour. All are highly recommended. Prices are on application.

Activities operators such as Island Cycle Tours and Tasmanian Expeditions also run longer island tours (see p.44).

out from each to most tourist destinations, plus a few villages on the way. As ever, a rough rule of thumb is that the denser the settlement, the better the coach service, so things become tricky on the east and west coasts. A second truism is that services are reasonable during the week, when daily schedules operate along most routes, while weekends see a drastically reduced timetable – services often stop altogether on Sundays. In winter and spring, services are further reduced.

Almost all coach routes are divided between two companies. The largest operator, **Tassielink** (℗03/6230 8900 or 1300 300 520, ⓦwww.Tassielink.com.au), provides comprehensive transport along major highways from terminals at Hobart and Launceston. Tassielink also operates two bushwalker services to the Southwest National Park from late October to the end of March; information on both is provided in the relevant sections in the Guide. **Redline Coaches** (℗03/6336 1446 or 1300 360 000, ⓦwww.tasredline.com.au) focuses on the north and northeast, while small operator **Bicheno Coach Service** (℗03/6257 0293) connects with both operators' east coast schedules to go to Coles Bay and the Freycinet National Park. It's worth making reservations for all three operators – indeed, Redline will only stop at some smaller destinations if you've made a reservation. Timetable information is published on the operator websites – Tassielink as pdf downloads, Redline via a search page. Some timetables are also printed in free state tourism newspaper *Tasmanian Travelways*, available in visitor centres.

Supplementary coach services in the Hobart area are operated from Monday to Saturday by Hobart Coaches (☏03/6233 4232, ⓦwww .hobartcoaches.com.au) – useful routes from Hobart include services east to Richmond, west to New Norfolk, and a southern service to Kingston, Snug, Kettering, Woodbridge and Cygnet.

Fares and passes

Prices are generally fairly reasonable and set by the distance. As a gauge, Tassielink's express service from Hobart to Launceston takes two hours thirty minutes and costs \$30.20; Hobart to St Helens is four hours and \$46; and Hobart to Queenstown is five hours and \$58.50. Buying a Tasmania-wide **pass** with either of the two main operators, both of which offer unlimited travel, can be one way of cutting costs – but study timetables carefully before you buy. In general you'll have to travel fairly fast to make either pay their way, and spend only a day or two at each destination. Redline's Tassie Pass comes in seven-, ten-, fourteen- and 21-day versions (\$135/\$160/\$185/\$219), starting from the first day of use. Tassielink's Explorer Bus Pass has several formats: a seven-day pass valid for travel over ten days for \$189; a ten-day pass for fifteen days for \$225; a fourteen-day pass for twenty days for \$260, or a 21-day pass for thirty days for \$299. You can buy passes at city visitor centres and at the transport terminals in Hobart and Launceston. A **YHA or backpacker VIP Card** (see p.52) will give you minor savings on bus tickets and activities, but since the number of affiliated hostels in Tasmania is limited, it's not worth buying into either scheme solely for cheaper travel.

Cycling

With relatively few cars and distances short between diverse landscapes, cycling in Tasmania can be a good option – it is certainly a great way to explore the landscapes. At its best it provides blissful days of coastal vistas. At its worst, you face gruelling pedals uphill in driving rain. The east

---

Bushwalkers' bus services

As well as the walkers' timetables scheduled by Tassielink, a number of private operators provide minibus charters to and from national park trails. Prices are far from cheap if you are alone – Launceston to Cradle Mountain or the Walls of Jerusalem costs around \$240, for example – but are reasonable if you can split the cost between a group, generally of up to ten people. The operators below are based in the Launceston area and provide a pick-up-and-return service, so you don't have to finish where you started.

Maxwell's ☏03/6492 1431. A charter service, based on a minimum of four passengers from Devonport and Launceston to and around the Cradle Mountain–Lake St Clair area and the Walls of Jerusalem National Park.

Outdoor Recreational Transport ☏03/6391 8249, ⓦwww.outdoortasmania.com .au. Minibus transport for walkers, canoeists and cyclists based in the Launceston area, but travelling anywhere in Tassie. Charter fares are priced by distance and group size (two people \$0.76 per km, three people \$0.54 per km, etc), with cash discounts available. An online message board is useful to tag along with other walkers.

Tasmanian Tour Company ☏1300 659878, ⓦwww.tasmaniantourcompany.com .au. Bushwalking charter service from Devonport to Cradle Mountain, Frenchmans Cap and the Walls of Jerusalem National Park.

Tiger Wilderness Tours ☏03/6394 3212, ⓦwww.tigerwilderness.com.au. Launceston-based transport to and from: the Walls of Jerusalem National Park, Dove Lake, Lake St Clair and between any mix of the three. Plus online message board that publishes available spaces on confirmed journeys.

coast, the southeast and the centre are the driest and flattest areas of the state, so, arguably, the best options, though there's also lovely cycling through the Derwent Valley to Mount Field, and in the farmland around Sheffield and Deloraine. The caveat for the east coast as Tasmania's greatest cycle route is that the Tasman Highway is busy in summer, and, like all major highways in the state, it does not have a cycle lane. For this reason, you're best to avoid the Midlands Highway – central Tasmania is best tackled on the 480-kilometre Tasmanian Trail (see p.258) that stretches from Devonport to Hobart.

Helmets and front and rear lights are compulsory – failure to comply risks an on-the-spot $80 fine. Cycle advocacy group Bike Tasmania (ⓦwww.biketas.org.au), a local arm of national pressure group Bike Federation of Australia (ⓦwww.bfa.asn.au), is your best source of advice. Its Giro Tasmania page (ⓦwww.biketas.org.au/giro.php) has general advice on equipment, details of state cycle shops and an itinerary for an eighteen-day circuit. The site also has links to local groups that hold open cycling meets.

Air carriers vary in their attitudes towards transporting bicycles – most charge a fee of around $5 per kilo, though some may take it as part of your overall baggage allowance. Spirit of Tasmania ferries from Melbourne charge $8 per bike. **Long-term hire** of touring bikes with paniers is available at Hobart and Launceston; details are provided in the listings of each chapter.

Organized cycle tours simplify matters by providing a bike, food and accommodation and back-up. Island Cycle Tours leads multi-day trips throughout the state that can be combined into a ten-day tour around the island with a discount, while Tasmanian Expeditions has six-day tours in the north, centre and down the east coast; see p.45 for details of both.

Metropolitan buses

State-owned urban transport provider Metro Tasmania (☏03/6233 4232, ⓦwww .metrotas.com.au) operates comprehensive daily **bus** schedules around Hobart, Launceston and Burnie, often taking in small towns in the vicinity; Bothwell with Metro Hobart, or Penguin with Metro Burnie, for example. Merseylink (☏1300 367 590, ⓦwww .merseylink.com.au) is the metropolitan bus service for the Devonport area. Bus services generally operate from 7am until 8pm (later on Fridays) with reduced services at weekends. That said, arterial routes such as Central Hobart to Glenorchy run until 10pm and until midnight on Friday and Saturday nights. **Timetables** and route maps are published on the website of each operator and are available free from the transit centres of each town. Single **tickets** can be bought from the driver and must be validated in machines on the bus; prices start at $2 and rise to $4.50 depending on the distance travelled. Children pay $1.20 for all journeys. Day-Rover travel passes ($5) and ten-pack "Metro Tens" ($16) provide savings.

Accommodation

Compact and laid-back, Tasmania is the ideal freewheeling holiday destination. A good spread of accommodation across the state means you can generally just sort out a bed on the day. Even in the most remote settlements, there's usually something close by – indeed, the rise of those buzz terms in Tasmanian tourism, "wilderness-retreat'" and "eco-resort", has introduced a growing number of upmarket lodges whose stock in trade is isolation.

Once a land of chintz and doilies that traded on heritage, Tasmania has bought into boutique in a big way, and your options now range from good camping and hostels all the way up to sophisticated five-star hotels. Overseas visitors also need to watch out for the word **hotel**, which in Australia can denote a pub as well as the usual hotel. The facilities can be far from luxurious, but if you don't mind dated decor and amenities, hotels are good sources of a cheap bed – valuable considering that the hostel scene in Tasmania is still in its infancy.

The step up from the hostel (or "backpackers") and the pub is the **B&B**. Something of a catch-all term, a B&B can be anything from a spare room in a private house to places that border on small personal hotels. **Camping** is excellent throughout the state, either in a "holiday park" with full facilities or in dedicated bushcamps. The former generally have good-value self-contained units, which are worth considering if you're in a group and on a tight budget. Elsewhere, you're never far from self-contained accommodation in a cottage or lodge.

On the east coast and in premier resorts such as Cradle Mountain and Strahan it's a good idea to **book ahead**. This is essential for the Christmas and summer holiday periods (January), for the Easter holidays and for long weekends. Throughout Tasmania rates rise in high summer, generally from mid-December to mid- or late January – all prices quoted in this book are for peak season. Conversely, prices fall in shoulder months and drop substantially in winter. Be aware too that some providers in popular resorts require a minimum stay of two or three nights in high season.

Hotels and motels

Hotel accommodation (in the usual sense rather than pubs) tends to be in cities or resorts and is geared towards the business traveller or high-end tourist. Most are comfortable though fairly anonymous places,

Accommodation price codes

All the accommodation listed in this book is categorized into one of eight price codes, as set out below. These represent the cost of the cheapest double room in high season, quoted at the official rack rate – walk-up rates are usually cheaper, and single rooms are about two-thirds the price of doubles. In hotels with a wide spread of accommodation, prices are listed as a range. Effectively, this means that anything in the ❶ category and most places in ❷ will be basic rooms without a bath. By category ❹ you can expect private amenities except in the cities, where you're likely to pay in the region of ❺. For ❻ upwards, you're moving into the luxury market, something that's guaranteed at ❽. Alongside price codes for double rooms in hostels, we've also provided the specific price of beds in dormitories.

❶ $35 and under   ❹ $81–110   ❼ $201–250
❷ $36–55   ❺ $111–150   ❽ $251 and upwards
❸ $56–80   ❻ $151–200

with a restaurant, bar and the usual creature comforts. True-blue Tassie chains include Federal Resorts (@www.federalresorts.com .au), a high-end provider focusing on signature destinations; and The Innkeepers Collection (@www.innkeeper.com.au), the state's largest group. In broad terms, you'll pay between $110 and $160 for a basic double room, depending on its location and luxury – those in the cities are more expensive and modern in interior style. All provide breakfast, generally buffet-style, though some charge up to $20 for it, so check before you tuck in. Generally speaking, walk-in rates are lower than official rack rates in many hotels, so sometimes it pays not to book ahead.

More interesting than the usual hotel fare is a growing quota of small luxury **boutique hotels** – the best hotel in Australia award went to Tasmania twice in recent years. Standouts include: *Henry Jones Hotel* and *The Islington* in Hobart; *Hatherley House* in Launceston; *Peppers Calstock* near Deloraine; and *Tarraleah Lodge* in Tarraleah.

Though often stuck in a 1970s timewarp of wood panelling and pastel hues, **motels** often represent better value for money if you're only after a comfy room for the night. You can usually expect a cubby-sized en-suite bathroom and a TV, possibly satellite. Average prices for a double start at around $80 and go up to $140. Reliable Aussie chain Budget (@www.budgetmotelchain .com.au) manages seventeen motels state-wide.

Self-contained accommodation

Most "holiday homes" in Tasmania are self-contained **cottages or apartments**. A mainstay of tourist accommodation throughout the state, they are rented by the night or week and generally provide a good deal for a group or families. At the very bottom of the price range, you are looking at basic trailer-style units in caravan parks (see opposite). At the top end are luxury, serviced apartments, a few of which are pretty glamorous affairs with walls of glass to frame their views. The majority lie somewhere in between, either as appealing lodge-style cabins in the bush or historic cottages – the

latter are especially prevalent in the heritage villages of Richmond, Ross and Westbury. Self-contained units have some sort of cooking facilities, usually a small kitchen and an en-suite bathroom. Most have a TV and often a DVD with a library of films for hire. Linen is usually provided, as are breakfast provisions for the first night. All prices in this book are quoted for two people – each extra person costs around $25.

B&Bs and guesthouses

The **bed-and-breakfast** rules supreme in Tasmania. Many lay on the heritage clichés a bit thick, but there's a move towards relaxed contemporary style within historic properties. Consequently, interiors vary from the simple to the sumptuous, as do prices – the lowest you'll pay for a double room is around $80, the highest around $240. All prices in this book are quoted for two people; each extra person in the same room (where possible) generally costs an extra $30. Upper and mid-range properties have en-suite rooms, while rooms in budget places share bathrooms. Continental breakfasts have replaced the traditional cooked breakfast in most properties, except in those that trade on their heritage. Isolated establishments also offer evening meals with advance notice. Bed & Breakfast and Boutique Accommodation of Tasmania (☎1800 673 388, @www .tasmanianbedandbreakfast.com) is a central reference and bookings agency that lists over a hundred properties state-wide. It also produces an excellent B&B booklet, available at larger visitor centres.

Hostels and pubs

Unlike on the mainland, **budget hostels** are not widespread in Tasmania. Hobart and Launceston have a decent selection, as does Devonport. Outside of these cities, you're struggling. At the time of writing, the official **YHA** only has ten youth hostels in the state. The association's properties are dependable if unexciting, though at least they have dropped the regimental rules of old. Filling the gap are independent hostels or **backpackers'**; both names are widely used and imply accommodation type rather than affiliation. At their best, these offer good value, an escape from hotel anonymity and a chance to meet other travellers. At their worst, hotels can be just shabby pubs with grubby rooms. There's usually a choice of dormitories, typically from four- to eight-bed, as well as double or twin rooms, a handful of singles, a communal room and a kitchen. Many hostels rent bikes and have noticeboards that advertise work and cheap activities. Staff are generally young, well-travelled and sympathetic to the needs of budget travellers – you can expect to pay around $18–26 for a dorm bed and around $50–60 for a double room. Most hostels ban guests from using sleeping bags on hygiene grounds, in which case they rent linen for around $5 a sheet.

Pubs (often known as hotels) are the fallbacks for budget accommodation. There's one in every small town or oversized village, usually the focus of its community, and almost all with basic double rooms for the same price as you'd pay in a hostel. Generally small, pub rooms tend to be dated in decor and fairly basic in terms of facilities – a TV and a washbasin in the room is usually the best you can hope for. Amenities amount to a shared bathroom further down the hall. However, most are clean enough and some have smartened up their acts to suit their historic buildings. Because many pub rooms are on the upper storey above the bar, they can be noisy on Friday and Saturday nights – more reason to go for a beer yourself – while reception is the bar itself. Some places provide a continental breakfast for around $5.

Youth hostel associations

UK and Ireland

Youth Hostel Association (YHA) England and Wales ☏ 0870/770 8868, ⊛ www.yha.org.uk. Annual membership £15.95; 16–25s £9.95; family £22.95.
Scottish Youth Hostel Association ☏ 01786/891 400, ⊛ www.syha.org.uk. Annual membership £8; under 16s free; over 60s £6; family £12.
Irish Youth Hostel Association Republic of Ireland ☏ 01/830 4555, ⊛ www.irelandyha.org. Annual membership €20; under 18s free; family €40.
Hostelling International Northern Ireland ☏ 028/90324733, ⊛ www.hini.org.uk.

US and Canada

Hostelling International–American Youth Hostels US ☏ 1-301/495-1240, ⊛ www.hiusa .org. Annual membership $28; under 18s free; over 55s $18.
Hostelling International Canada ☏ 1-800/663-5777, ⊛ www.hihostels.ca. Annual membership $35; under 18s free.

Australia, New Zealand and South Africa

Australia Youth Hostels Association ☏ 02/9565 1699, ⊛ www.yha.com.au. Annual membership $42; under 26s $32.
Youth Hostelling Association New Zealand ☏ 0800/278 299 or 03/379 9970, ⊛ www.yha .co.nz. Annual membership $40; under 18s free.

Camping and caravan parks

Tasmania is one of the last states in Australia with an abundance of free **bushcamping**. The majority are in reserves or conservation areas, often just behind the beach or beside mountains. Facilities almost always include a composting pit toilet, and sometimes water, fireplaces, a picnic shelter and tables (possibly with a barbecue) and rubbish bins. Many sites provide firewood, others operate a BYO ("bring your own") policy – don't degrade the local environment by scavenging if not. Similarly, keep fires small and under no circumstances light a fire when a fire ban is in force. For free sites, the length of time you can stay is restricted, albeit to up to four weeks. If not free, the cost is a minimal fee of around $5 a night, usually payable by honour system. Campsites in national parks typically cost $12 a night on top of your park pass – a bargain considering their location. Parks & Wildlife Service (⊛ www.parks.tas.gov.au) maintain the majority of bushcamps, though Forestry Tasmania (⊛ www.forestrytas.com .au) has a few on its forest reserves. Both publish site locations on their websites, or you can pick up a copy of *Free-Camping In Tasmania* ($14.95), a handy booklet though a little sketchy in places, or *Camping Guide to Tasmania* ($14.95), which focuses more on paying sites.

For more facilities, head to a **caravan park**, usually called a holiday park or tourist park. Generally well-maintained, these are as cheap as it gets in Tasmania – a tent-pitch for two people costs around $18–26, or around $10 more for a powered site. (Prices listed in this guide are for unpowered sites.) Most parks also offer budget cabins or vans (caravans), typically priced ❷ or ❸ and with a simple kitchenette. A couple also have a bunkhouse with dorms. On-site facilities include shared kitchen blocks, washrooms with hot showers and usually a laundry. Be aware that some places charge for showers, so it's worth keeping some spare change handy and confirming as you check in because you may need to buy shower tokens. Note, too, that while most sites are close to the centre, those in Hobart and Launceston are in the suburbs. Your best reference is Tourism Tasmania's free booklet *Caravan and Holiday Park Guide to Tasmania* (Ⓦ www.caravantasmania.com.au), available at visitor centres throughout the state.

Food and drink

Tasmania prides itself on the quality of its produce. As well as fruit, the "Apple Isle" has an abundant larder of fresh ingredients, nearly all of which are produced through small-scale, non-industrial farming methods. In recent decades, a food and wine culture has swept across the Bass Strait to introduce a sophisticated dining scene into larger towns and resorts. Gourmet Tasmania has most definitely arrived – indeed, some mainland visitors only come to pay homage to chefs who create dishes as good as anything you'd eat in the elite restaurants of Sydney and Melbourne. Rural regions remain bastions of the no-nonsense, meat-and-three-veg school of cookery rooted in traditional British cuisine. Usually rustled up in the local pub, it's not particularly exciting but any chef could produce something palatable given the quality of local ingredients.

Tasmanian cuisine has also been saved from the culinary wilderness by immigration. Mainlanders and a minority of non-British immigrants have had a profound effect on local tastes by introducing ethnic flavours and contemporary Australian cuisine. "**Modern Australian**" food is a slippery term that changes definition according to trends. A constant is that it blends influences from the major immigrant populations to Australia, principally Asian and Mediterranean. Tastes come and go – the current shift seems to be away from the complex dishes of a few years ago to simpler flavours that let the quality of the ingredients shine through. Like Californian New World cooking, Modern Australian cuisine is healthy, eclectic and, above all, fresh.

Specialities

Anything that comes from the sea is excellent. White **fish** includes trevalla (blue-eye cod), flathead and flake (shark). Salmon reared in the D'Entrecasteaux Channel and Macquarie Harbour is superb, as is fish and chips, a dish that's more ubiquitous than in Britain and certainly healthier. Elsewhere, make sure you're getting fresh not frozen when you order. **Seafood** is among the best in Australia: crayfish (rock lobster), mussels, oysters, scallops and abalone are all reliable if fresh. Note that prawns have always been imported. Plentiful and cheap, steak is a staple of pub menus and the barbecue – every picnic ground has a gas or electric barbie, and heading to the beach with a full esky (insulated food holder) is a ritual at summer weekends. **Beef** is superb due to a natural grass-fed (as opposed to grain-fed) production system – Tasmania is the only Australian state that bans antibiotic supplements and growth hormones in the cattle industry. King Island beef is the highest quality, but local meat is always reliable, especially in the rain-soused northwest. Tassie **lamb** is good too, and Flinders Island lamb is a fixture on top-end menus. **Game** pops up now and then – quail principally, but also farm-reared venison and wallaby, a low-fat meat with a light flavour.

Cool-climate **fruits** – apples, pears and cherries – are plentiful, especially in the southeast, and Tasmania is a key grower of berries: strawberries, raspberries, blueberries plus red- and blackcurrants. These are fresh from early summer to early autumn – many places will let you pick your own (PYO). Fresh and cheap, **vegetables** include all the usual European varieties – note that red and green peppers are known as capsicums, aubergine as egg-plant, and courgette as zucchini. Local dairy produce is turned into highly rated **cheeses** which tend to be in the cheddar vein, though the state's most acclaimed dairy producer, King Island Dairy, produces a delicious creamy brie. As an aside, it's worth hunting out the unique leatherwood **honey** produced from flowers of trees in the World Heritage wilderness. There are a few manufacturers in the Deloraine area.

Vegetarians are better served than you might think in meat-loving Tasmania, and most small towns have a café serving healthy dishes. Out in the sticks you'll struggle, however, and can only expect one non-meat dish on the menu. Vegans will often have to put their principles on hold.

Places to eat

Tasmania's foodie scene is centred on Hobart and Launceston. However, most moderate towns, and also a fair few villages in tourist areas, have good **restaurants**. A main dish in a moderate restaurant will cost around $20, and even gourmet places (which are markedly less stuffy than in Europe) only charge prices in the high twentys. A few of the cheaper restaurants allow BYO (bring your own); you can buy your own wine and bring it with you to the place, which will charge a fee for corkage, usually around $2–5.

The mainstay of everyday eating in Tasmania is the **pub** meal, generally known as a counter meal. You'll always find steak and some sort of fish on the menu, and usually a roast, especially on Sundays – vegetarians are often poorly served. Quality varies enormously. At its best, the counter meal approaches restaurant quality, at its worst it is school-dinner stodge. In small towns it is often all that's available, however, in which case get there on time – lunch is usually served from noon until 2pm and dinners from 6 until 8pm. Prices average out at around $17 a main, though daily roasts can be as low as $12. Be aware that many hotels don't serve food on Mondays.

Bistros are more upmarket. They tend to sit somewhere between the pub and the restaurant – many are in smarter hotels, others are really upmarket cafés – and prepare healthy light meals, typically simple Modern Australian fare, with several daily specials. Prices are usually slightly higher than the counter meal.

Cafés open from 8am until 5pm and move from breakfasts to freshly prepared wholesome lunches – they are always a good bet in the cities. Most also have sandwiches, pastries and home-made pies for around $5: look for slow-cooked beef pies or, that most Tasmanian invention, the scallop pie with a hint of curry. Rural places will probably have home-made cakes and Devonshire teas (an English cream tea). **Takeaways** are many and varied. There's a fair sprinkling of roadside joints selling greasy chicken or burgers, plus there's always a Chinese or pizza place in every small town. Fish and chips takeaways are a better bet, especially on the coast where they are reliable sources of cheap and tasty fillers. Some in Hobart are must-dos of the city.

Excellent resources for foodies are the state tourism booklet *Cellar Door & Farm Gate Guide* from visitor centres, and *A Guide to Tasting Tasmania* ($19.95) by local food and wine writer Graham Phillips.

Drink

Considering the abundance of fruit in the state, there's far too much **juice** made from concentrate in the supermarkets. This might explain why many cafés press their own in-house. Tasmania shares the national taste for Bundaberg ginger beer and flavoured milk. Though yet to reach the obsessional levels seen in the metropolitan mainland, **coffee culture** is spreading in Tasmania. The style is rich Italian and the best is in Hobart and Launceston, but you'll also find good coffee in rural towns with aspirations to tourism. **Tea** is the usual strong British-style brew, complemented with a few fruit teas.

Beer is the alcoholic drink of choice in Tasmania. Which one is a matter of allegiance: Cascade, brewed in Hobart, is most prevalent in the south; Launceston-brewed Boag's is the beer of the north. Ask for either in the pub and you'll get a standard pilsner-style draught lager. The two companies also brew a premium lager and specialized beers, including a low-alcohol ("Light") beer at around 2% alcohol. They are also starting to dabble in English-style real ales, which – shock horror – are intended to be drunk at just below room temperature. Craft breweries to look out for are Two Metre Tall, Hazards Ale and organic beer Moo Brew, produced by Hobart wine estate Moorilla. They are generally only available in smarter bars and restaurants. Guinness, or in fact anything foreign, is only on-tap in Irish-style bars in the cities. Standard pub servings for beer are the half-pint and pint, or sometimes ten-ounce and schooners, which are half-pints and fifteen-ounce respectively. Unless you say otherwise, you'll always be given the smaller size. Pubs also sell stubbies (short-necked bottles).

Tasmania's history of **wine** goes back to colonial days. Cuttings from Sydney vines were planted in Hobart as early as 1818, but most of today's wineries date from the 1950s and are in the Tamar Valley. Smaller wine-growing regions are the Coal River Valley south of Richmond, on the east coast between Swansea and Bicheno, and in the southeast in the Huon Valley. Whatever you drink, Tassie wines are cool-climate varieties: well-structured whites such as riesling, chardonnay, gewürztraminer, sauvignon blanc and pinot gris; sensual reds such as cabernet sauvignon, merlot, a few shiraz varieties and a rich earthy pinot noir that's probably the star performer. However, sparkling wines have been taking the wine gongs in recent years, especially those produced by Tamar Valley wine estates Jansz and Bay of Fires. Details of wine routes for **tasting and sales** at estates, both known as "cellar door" in Australia, are in the relevant chapters and at state tourism site ⓦ www.tasmanianwineroute.com.au.

The media

Tasmania is too small to support a large media, though it has a voice through the local press. The combined circulation of Tasmania's three regional newspapers is only around 200,000 copies, yet they are the first choice of reading material for most. For outsiders, local news can be fairly parochial stuff, but newspapers are useful as an insight into the mentalities of the regions, especially regarding coverage of touchstone issues like forestry and conservation. For more rigorous coverage you'll have to turn to the nationwide media sources. International media is thin on the ground in Tasmania.

Newspapers and magazines

Two centuries after *The Derwent Star* and *Van Diemen's Land Intelligencer* hit Hobart's news-stands in 1810, Tasmania has three tabloid-sized **newspapers** peddling a similar diet of local outrage, gossip and small ads. Hobart's *The Mercury* has the largest circulation and focuses on southern Tasmania. *The Examiner* is the daily of Northern Tasmania, operating from an HQ in Launceston, which leaves smaller *The Advocate* to report on Burnie, Devonport and the state's northwest. All are conservative in stance. At a push, *The Mercury* is the most liberal, with *The Examiner* and especially *The Advocate* espousing the traditional views of regions involved in primary industries such as forestry.

For comprehensive international coverage and more sophisticated news media look to the mainland: left-leaning broadsheet *The Australian* is Australia's only national daily (Mon–Sat only); sister paper the *Australian Financial Review* has some news amid its business coverage; while Melbourne's venerable *The Age*, focusing on Victoria, is widely available in Tasmania. All syndicate a handful of news and feature stories from British and US nationals. One or two British and US newspapers are stocked by larger newsagents in Hobart and Launceston, but international media is not widely available.

Tassie **magazine** *Tasmania 40° South* is a quarterly that unashamedly celebrates local culture and landscapes. Photography is excellent throughout. Smaller *Tasmanian Life*, a sort of local Tatler, is a bi-monthly for Tasmanian high society – expect a lead interview with an island personality, features about country life, aspirational homes and photos of smart society bashes. A full portfolio of Australian magazines is widely available in Tasmania. The best current affairs publications are news weeklies *The Bulletin* and *Time Australia*. *Australian Geographic* has excellent photographs to accompany well-researched travel features, while quarterly wilderness adventure magazine *Wild* focuses on home trails, with at least one Tassie feature per issue.

Television and radio

The Australian Broadcasting Corporation (ABC) runs the only advert-free national **television** channels, ABC and ABC2, and is the heavyweight for world news, drama and sport. Commercial broadcasters Southern Cross and WIN Television programme a diet of light news, human interest "docos" (documentaries), sports events, comedy, movies and chat-shows, in between frequent advert breaks. Mid- and upper-range hotels have cable TV.

Tasmania's mountainous terrain forces you to retune frequently – some stations have twelve different broadcast frequencies in Tasmania. The best **radio** stations are those provided by the ABC. Amped-up youth station Triple J (Hobart 92.9FM, northeast 90.9FM, Queenstown area 88.9FM) playlists Aussie rock. Australia-wide Radio National FM (Hobart 585AM; east coast 88.9FM, 107.7FM, 91.3FM & 96.1FM; northeast 94.1FM; Strahan 105.9FM) provides arts and intellectual programmes, as well as occasional news features syndicated from international media, including the BBC World Service. Classic FM (Hobart 93.9FM, northeast 93.3FM) has non-stop classical music. ABC NewsRadio (Hobart 747FM, northeast 92.5FM, Burnie 90.5FM) is the station for news junkies, with rolling coverage and regular sport updates. Local radio for Hobart is 107.3FM, for the northeast is 91.7FM.

Festivals

The major festivals listed here celebrate the mainstays of contemporary Tasmania: agriculture, forestry, the outdoors, food and the arts. The Tassie festival is a good-natured, laid-back beast, generally alcohol-fuelled but without the excessive beer-swilling that characterizes other states in Australia. The agricultural show is the bastion of local culture: alongside traditional livestock-judging, dog-handling and sheep-shearing competitions, there's always a wood-chopping event – a sight in itself – a sprinkling of local food and crafts stalls and usually a fashion show or dollop of low-key entertainment.

Most festivals are staged over summer, several of the main ones straddling the Christmas and New Year period. Easter holidays are also marked by celebrations, as are national events such as Australia Day. State tourism website ⓦwww .discovertasmania.com has a searchable database of events.

January

King of the Derwent, Hobart. January 2. A traditional yacht race that sees Sydney–Hobart competitors (see Dec) go head-to-head on the river.
Cygnet Folk Festival, Cygnet. Second weekend. Country weekender of world music and folk acts. ⓦwww.cygnetfolkfestival.org.
Australia Day. January 26. A national knees-up to celebrate the founding of the country with events state-wide. ⓦwww.australiaday.gov.au.

February

Australian Wooden Boat Festival, Hobart docks. Every odd-numbered year. The largest celebration of traditional boats in the southern hemisphere. ⓦwww.australianwoodenboatfestival .com.au.

Festivale, Launceston. Second weekend. Gourmet food, wine, arts and general merriment in City Park. ⓦwww.festivale.com.au.
Clarence Jazz Festival, Hobart. Third week. Tasmania's premier jazz festival, with six days of swing by the river in the suburb of Bellerive. Evening and twilight events.
Evandale Village Fair and the National Penny Farthing Championships, Evandale. Late weekend. International riders and lots of lycra on one big wheel. ⓦwww.evandalevillagefair.com.

March

Taste of the Huon, Ranelagh. Second weekend. A regional counterpart to the Taste of Tasmania that showcases the food and crafts of the southeast, plus live jazz. ⓦwww.tasteofthehuon.com.
Ten Days on the Island. Late Mar–early Apr. The state's biggest cultural bash. A biennial (next 2009) celebration of island identity throughout the state. ⓦwww.tendaysontheisland.org.

April

Targa Tasmania. Mid-Apr. One of Australia's top motoring events spread over six days: around three hundred cars, many vintage, go on a 2000km rally around the island. ⓦwww.targa.org.au.

May

Agfest, Carrick. Early May. Tasmania's leading agricultural festival, held over three days. ⓦ www .agfest.com.au.

June

Suncoast Jazz Festival, St Helens. Penultimate weekend in June. Mainstream, Dixieland and New Orleans sounds on the east coast.

September

Blooming Tasmania. Sept–May. A showcase of Tasmanian horticulture that runs until autumn; typically floral festivals and open gardens. A dedicated state brochure available in visitor centres lists what's on where.

October

Royal Launceston Show, Launceston. Early weekend. Celebration of primary industries plus agricultural competitions, fashion shows and entertainments.
Royal Hobart Show, Hobart. Last weekend. All the fun of the rural fair in the capital. ⓦ www .hobartshowground.com.au/rhs.

November

Tasmania Craft Fair, Deloraine. Last weekend. Australia's largest crafts event is a get-together for the island's artisans, with around two hundred exhibitors spread over twelve venues. ⓦ www .tascraftfair.com.au.

V8 Supercar Championships. Symmons Plain Raceway, near Launceston. End November. Round 14 of the V8 world championships on a notoriously tight racecourse – petrol-heads' paradise. ⓦ www .v8supercarevents.com.au.

December

Sydney–Hobart Yacht Race and Melbourne– Hobart Yacht Race. Dec 26–Jan 2. The former is one of the most celebrated yacht races in the international fixture list, the latter battles down Tasmania's west coast. Both climax in Hobart to bring a festive air to the waterfront – arguably the biggest bash in Tassie.
Hobart Summer Festival, Hobart. End Dec–first week Jan. The capital's all-embracing celebration of summer: two weeks of arts, music, entertainments and just good-natured fun. Coincides with the yacht races and is centred on the waterfront. ⓦ www .hobartsummerfestival.com.au.
Taste of Tasmania (aka "The Taste"). Dec 28–Jan 3, Hobart. Part of the summer festival but now big enough to stand alone, this is a showcase for gourmet food and wine. Among Australia's best food festivals.
The Falls Festival, Marion Bay near Dunalley. Dec 29–January 1. Tasmania's biggest outdoor rock festival offers two huge days and nights of major-name bands, including international acts, DJs, comedy and cinema. Advance tickets are a must. ⓦ www.fallsfestival.com.

Sports and outdoor activities

Australians and sport were made for each other, and a proud young nation breeds an intensively competitive nature. The main spectator sports are, in order of popularity, Australian Rules football, cricket, then soccer, once derided as a wimps' game but increasingly popular thanks to the success of the national side. On top of their love of spectator sports, Tasmanians are among the most active Australians. They do not pursue a love of the outdoors so much as take it for granted, and at summer weekends, half the state seems to load up a car and head for the hills and beaches.

Spectator sports

Aussie Rules football is the greatest source of sporting pride. Tasmania was the first state to play the sport outside its Victoria homeland, and only the Northern Territories beats its 5 percent amateur participation level. A breathless, brawling rip-roarer of a game, "footy" most closely resembles Gaellic football and commands the same sort of passion as soccer in Europe. Until the Australian Football League (AFL) heeds a petition to grant Tasmania its own club, the state's "home" teams are Melbourne-based football clubs St Kilda and Hawthorn. The latter – "The Hawks" – play four home games at the Aurora Stadium in Launceston (ⓦwww.aurorastadiumlaunceston.com.au), during a season that runs from March to September. All are big events – Ticketmaster (ⓣ13 61 00, ⓦwww.ticketmaster.com.au) handles tickets, which cost around $23 a game. The state's regional leagues are the Northern Tasmania Football League (ⓦwww .ntfl.com.au) and Southern Football League (ⓦwww.southernfootball.com.au); each of the cities has a stadium and you can pick up tickets on the gate. Most matches are played on Saturdays, with a few Sunday and public holiday games.

When the Grand Final brings the AFL season to a close at the end of September, attention shifts to the **cricket** season throughout summer. State team the Tasmanian Tigers competes in interstate competitions at the Bellerive Stadium in Hobart. This also hosts international fixtures of the national squad and visiting international teams, which makes for a great day out. Again, tickets are bought through Ticketmaster. At other times, the stadium hosts club cricket. The eight-strong league is managed by the Tasmanian Cricket Association (ⓦwww.tascricket.com.au).

Water sports

Tasmania has a coastline of 5400km and you're never more than two hours' drive from ocean. **Swimming** is possible all over the coast, but with precaution – even in summer the sea temperature catches the breath. Rips – sea currents caused by waves and tides – are a real danger for those who do not have sea-sense; see "Safety outdoors" box opposite. Wherever possible you should only swim on beaches patrolled by lifeguards or in sheltered areas and within your depth. Do not ignore signs that warn of rips. Swimming on the west coast can be dangerous due to heavy waves.

The most convenient locations to **surf** are around South Arm near Hobart, Bruny Island, the Tasman Peninsula, and along the upper east coast from Bicheno to Eddystone Point. The west coast around Marrawah and Arthur River has the most consistent surf. King Island is as consistent but you're usually surfing alone. There's no equipment rental in Tasmania (though Stranger Surfboards in Rokeby is open to negotiation; see Hobart Listings on p.96), so you'll have to buy or bring your own kit. New boards start at around $350. You'll also need a good wetsuit: 3mm in summer, the most inconsistent season; 4mm or 5mm plus boots in spring and autumn, and a balaclava and gloves in mid-winter. Daily surf forecasts and surfcams are at ⓦ www.coastview.com.au and ⓦ www.tassiesurf.com.

Hailed by *National Geographic* magazine as the most accessible underwater wilderness in the world for **scuba-diving**, Tasmania's coastal seas have visibility from 12m in summer to 40m in winter. Highlights of surprisingly colourful cold-water diving include giant kelp forests with weedy seadragons and seahorses; whales, bottlenose dolphins and fur seals; and historic shipwrecks. The Tasman Peninsula concentrates some of the best dive sites in one area, while other sites – a marine nature reserve at Bicheno, for example – are marked on a *Dive Trail* leaflet stocked in visitor centres (and downloadable from ⓦ www.discovertasmania.com), which also lists dive operators and shops. Good diving elsewhere is off Low Head in the Tamar River, at Rocky Cape National Park and on the Bass Strait islands. Rewarding spots to snorkel are Tinderbox Marine Nature Reserve, south of Hobart, and Maria Island. You'll need a wetsuit if snorkelling outside of high summer.

White-water rafting on Franklin River is one of the signature experiences of Tasmania, involving several days paddling through rapids of the last wilderness river in Australia. Gentler day-trips are on the Derwent River near New Norfolk and on the Picton River, west of Geeveston. Tour outfits lead **sea kayaking** trips down the Derwent River near Hobart, around the awesome coastline of the Tasman Peninsula, around Kettering to Bruny Island, and at Freycinet National Park – a great way to arrive at Wineglass Bay. For wilderness adventure, investigate kayaking expeditions in the Southwest National Park in summer. (If you're planning your own trip, Parks & Wildlife publishes advice on its website.) You can also hire a canoe for a lazy paddle throughout the state; two of the best areas are George Bay (St Helens) and Arthur River.

Tasmania has more boats per head of population than any other Australian state, but little opportunity to go **sailing** – such are the dangers of its coastline for novices. Strahan-based West Coast Yacht Charter has skippered charters on Macquarie Harbour and the Gordon River, or you can bareboat charter from Hobart with Yachting Holidays (Ⓣ 03/6224 3195; ⓦ www.yachtingholidays .com.au) to access the D'Entrecasteaux Channel and Bruny Island. For spectators, the premier event in the yachting calendar is the arrival of the Sydney–Hobart fleet up the Derwent River around two days after it sets out from Hobart on Boxing Day. Sandy Bay is the traditional spot to watch the

Safety outdoors

Wilderness does not suffer fools. Weather conditions change rapidly and summer blizzards are not unknown in the mountains and central highlands. As ever, be prepared. Bushfire warnings in summer should be taken seriously. Fires can spread at frightening pace, so do not walk in any region affected. If you are caught out, open spaces are the safest areas, forests the most dangerous. If you are driving, pull over and remain in the car with your headlights on. It goes against all instincts, but you are safest within the car - lie on the floor and cover exposed skin, ideally with a blanket. Under no circumstances flout a fireban if it is imposed - and that includes using a fuel stove.

On the coast, rips (currents caused by wave action) are far more dangerous than scare-stories about white pointers (great white sharks). Rips either sweep across a beach (parallel to the shore) or, more commonly, go out to sea - they often appear as trails of foam. Signs at popular beaches alert you to severe rips and wherever possible you should only swim on beaches patrolled by lifeguards or in sheltered areas and within your depth. Swimming on the west coast is not advisable. If you are caught by a rip while swimming, fight a natural reaction to paddle against it because this will only exhaust you. Instead, paddle across the rip's current to escape its stream, then you can swim back to shore.

front-runners power upriver. Yachting Tasmania (@www.tas.yachting.org.au) is the umbrella body.

Outdoor activities

Without doubt, the landscape remains Tasmania's greatest asset. Tasmanians are passionate about the outdoors, and the sheer diversity of landscapes is astonishing: within a couple of hours' drive from the capital there's the glacial mountain scenery of Cradle Mountain, unspoilt east coast beaches which raise an eyebrow even among Australians, and some of the most remote places on Earth. This permits an enormous variety of outdoor activities; bushwalking, of course, but also fishing, diving, surfing, abseiling, white-water rafting, kayaking, climbing, hang-gliding, even skiing. Small wonder that Australians increasingly see Tasmania as a sort of activities adventure playground in their backyard.

A superb resource for all activities is the **Parks & Wildlife Service** (☎1300 135 513, @www.parks.tas.gov.au). This government body manages all national parks as well as reserves, conservation and recreation areas and a few marine reserves. All are detailed throughout this guide and on its useful website (which also has downloadable handouts, plus details of campsites and major walking trails), or you can pick up local information at ranger stations and visitor centres. The head office is in Hobart at 134 Macquarie St (Mon–Fri 9am–5pm).

Numerous operators lead **organized activities**. As well as providers who operate state-wide, we have listed local outfits throughout this Guide. For other listings, Tourism Tasmania (@www.discovertasmania.com.au) and free-sheet *Tasmania Travelways* (@www.travelways.com.au), stocked in visitor centres, are good resources.

Tasmania's trails make it superb **mountain-biking** country. Bike rental is available at most of the major tourist centres and from some hostels. A couple of niche specialists lead organized trips lasting several days (see below) and also thrilling mountain descents of Mount Wellington (Hobart) and Ben Lomond (Launceston). More traditional trail-riding is on **horseback**. A handful of operators lead groups for anything from a couple of hours to multi-day expeditions with camping in the bush: look in "Activities" boxes in the Tasman Peninsula, Cradle Mountain and Tullah sections.

Fluted dolerite columns and high sea cliffs provide excellent **climbing**. There are cliffs on Mount Wellington (Hobart) and death-defying stack- and cliff-climbing on the Tasman Peninsula, where you ascend as massive swells crump below – not for the faint-hearted. You'll have to bring your own equipment or hook up with a local climber for the latter. Organized climbing is in the Freycinet National Park and in the Cataract Gorge, Launceston. Adrenaline-junkies might like to know that the Gordon Dam near Strathgordon is the highest commercial abseil in the world (and feels it). One of the more unusual activities to appear in recent years is **hang-gliding**, albeit on cabled gliders at the Tahune AirWalk near Geeveston and in Launceston. A new addition is a flying-fox cable ride through the treetops at Hollybank Forest, northeast of Launceston.

Finally, you may not associate Australia with **skiing**, but there's a small ski culture during winter (July–mid Sept) – erratic, certainly, and no great shakes compared to the pistes of Europe or Canada, but gentle fun if you're in the area. The two resorts (actually just a few huts) are at Ben Lomond, which has the best pistes, and Mount Field National Park, near Hobart, where there are cross-country routes and a couple of downhill runs. Details of ski rental are provided in each section.

Tasmanian tour operators

Aardvark Adventures ☎03/6273 7722, @www.aardvarkadventures.com.au. Multi-activity provider offering abseiling, caving, rafting and mountain-biking.
Bottom Bits Bus ☎03/6234 5093 or 1800 777 103, @www.bottombitsbus.com.au. Fun, budget, small-group tours from Hobart and Launceston to major Tassie sights.
Craclair Tours ☎03/6339 4488, @www.craclairtasmania.com. "Lightweight bushwalking" and "Challenging treks" in the World Heritage Area, including some of Tassie's toughest hikes, plus some cabin-based walks.
Island Cycle Tours ☎03/6234 4591 or 1300 880 334, @www.islandcycletours.com. Recommended tours based on mountain-biking and walking: trips to

Mount Field, Freycinet, the northeast and the west can be combined for a ten-day Tassie tour by bike.

Rafting Tasmania ☎03/6239 1080, ⓦwww .raftingtasmania.com. Gentle rafting trips on the Picton and Derwent rivers as well as on the rapids of the wild Franklin River.

Roaring 40s Ocean Kayaking ☎03/6267 5000, ⓦwww.roaring40skayaking.com.au. Tassie's leading sea-kayaking operator offers an excellent programme around the southeast – including Bruny Island and the Tasman Peninsula – plus inspirational multi-day expeditions in the Southwest National Park.

Tarkine Trails ☎03/6223 5320, ⓦwww .tarkinetrails.com.au. Coast and forest expeditions by foot and 4WD into the remote Tarkine from an area specialist. Also leads bushwalks to the Overland Track and the Walls of Jerusalem.

Tasmanian Expeditions ☎1300 666 856 or 03/6339 3999, ⓦwww.tas-ex.com. Cycle, walk, raft, kayak, climb – a Launceston-based outfit that has a huge range of activities. All the usuals alongside interesting trips such as walking in the northeast or a six-day cycle through the centre of the state.

Tasmanian Wilderness Experiences ☎03/6261 4971, ⓦtwe.travel. A small Glenorchy team that leads bushwalks in most national parks; remote groups in the southwest as well as day-hikes around Mount Field and Mount Wellington.

Tassielink ☎1300 300 520, ⓦwww.tassielink .com.au. Daytours by coach from Hobart and Launceston to main destinations.

Fishing

Fishing is a Tassie obsession, conducted on lakes and rivers, from beaches, in tinnies (small aluminium dinghies) and, if your bank balance is up to it, on ocean-going fishing boats. Trout fishing is among the best anywhere in the world, focused at Arthurs Lake and the Great Lake in the central highlands. The best game-fishing is from St Helens – the quarry is ocean species such as marlin, shark, tuna or swordfish. Operators at both locations lead half- and day-trips that include equipment, tuition, fishing licence, transport and usually lunch, but they're not cheap – alone, you'll pay around $600 a day, less if in a group. Without this you'll need to hire a rod (around $20 a day) and buy a fishing licence. These cost from $18 for 24 hours to $59 for a year and can be bought from tackle shops or Service Tasmania centres. Most waters are open year-round, but check the regulations for details and

gear restrictions. Visitor centres stock angling guides and a government sea-fishing guide that lists hotspots and seasonal restrictions on catch size.

Bushwalking

The variety and purity of landscapes make Tasmania among the top bushwalking destinations in the world. Notwithstanding the abundance of short easy trails, you'll need to be properly equipped to tackle any walk longer than half a day, and good **maps** are essential. State cartographer Tasmap produces comprehensive hiking maps of all national parks. There's a fair spread of walking **guidebooks**, many of which are dedicated to popular routes such as the Overland Track. Recommended general titles include: *120 Walks in Tasmania*, by Tyrone T. Thomas ($32.50), the best overview of walks in the state; and *Day Walks Tasmania*, a full-colour book by acclaimed bushwalkers John and Marie Chapman ($34.95). Both have sketch maps and gradient profiles. In Hobart, try the Tasmanian Map Centre at 100 Elizabeth St (☎03/6231 9043, ⓦwww.map-centre .com.au), which also posts abroad.

Where to go is a matter of preference – you could stay in Tasmania for years and still not exhaust its possibilities. The *60 Great Short Walks* booklet from visitor centres is a good source of ideas, and every national park has a short walk from the car park. The premier extended walk is the Overland Track from Cradle Mountain to Lake St Clair, though access is restricted in summer, and many experienced local walkers now prefer the Walls of Jerusalem National Park. For accessible coastal scenery, head to the Tasman Peninsula, known for its cliff walks and abundance of day-walks, or the east coast national parks of Maria Island or Freycinet National Park. There are great beach walks in the Bay of Fires/Mount William National Park, and rugged coastal scenery south of Arthur River. Experienced hikers looking for a challenge go south and west: Frenchmans Cap is a tough four- or five-day hike; Federation Peak is the ultimate summit to bag for Aussie adventurers; and the South Coast Track is ten days of pristine coastal scenery, climactic contrasts, isolation and, above all, mud. Parks & Wildlife Service is the best reference, though conservation campaigner the Wilderness Society (ⓦwww.wilderness .org.au) produces free guides to threatened areas such as the Tarkine and Styx Valley, available as downloads or from its campaign headquarters in Hobart (130 Davey St) and Launceston (174 Charles St). For nervous novices or just to reduce the hassle of organization, there are plenty of companies that lead organized bushwalks, most taking in remote hikes as well as the obvious highlights. These are listed in relevant sections and under tour companies on p.44.

Tasmania's national parks

Mount Field came first in 1916, and by voting to nominate the Tarkine for World Heritage status in September 2007, the Australian Senate may have brought the tally to twenty.

For now, nineteen national parks make Tasmania the prize of Australian natural environments. Comprising just over 21 per cent of the state's 68,400 square kilometres, most of which is within the World Heritage Area, they are some of the most pristine places on Earth.

Two of the national parks – Savage River in the Tarkine area and Bass Strait islets the Kent Group – are inaccessible to visitors. Of the others, only the Walls of Jerusalem cannot be accessed directly by car – the car park is 30min from the park boundary – although you'll have to hike or fly in to get the best out of the Southwest National Park.

Regardless of which park you go to, you'll need a **national parks pass**. Prices per person are: $11 for a 24-hour pass or $28 for an eight-week "Holiday pass". Passes are

Bushwalking essentials

Safety For health and safety advice relevant to bushwalks, see the sections on p.43 and p.55. Wilderness does not suffer the foolhardy and the old scout motto of "Be prepared" rings true in Tasmania's fickle climate. Do not cut corners on equipment, research your route and if possible schedule to avoid times of high track use. Avoid walking alone and always inform someone where you are going and for how long, even if you are in a group. Similarly always register in and out of trails using books provided at the start and end of the route. Always get a weather forecast before you go and be prepared to turn back if conditions dictate. Popular tracks are well-marked and well-maintained, but a map and compass is still a must for anything over a few hours. Be aware too that less-popular routes are often "tagged trails", which means that they are indicated with coloured tags rather than demarcated by a path. On these it is essential to tag-hop from one marker to the next rather than trust your instincts about what may be the route.

Minimal impact In a nutshell, take only photographs and leave only footprints. Rule one: pack it in, pack it out. That includes all rubbish and waste food – do not burn or bury anything. Wash up at least 50m from water sources and ideally use hot water rather than detergents, which are banned in the World Heritage Area anyway. If there are no toilets, urinate (and bury excrement) at least 100m from campsites and water sources. When walking, stick to tracks (however muddy) to minimize damage to the habitat, and remember that campsites are found, not made – altering a site is not necessary. If you use rocks to secure a tent, return them when you leave. The entire World Heritage Area and many national parks are fuel-stove only; fuel stoves are best practice for all natural areas. If you light a fire (where permitted) use fireplaces provided and keep it small. Under no circumstances ignore fire bans and note that these also apply to fuel stoves. On a similar note, never discard cigarette butts. However cute, wildlife should not be fed as it causes debilitating "lumpy jaw" disease and creates dependency.

Bushwalker's checklist
Equipment hire is available in Hobart, Launceston and Devonport (see relevant Listings). As a rule of thumb, a third of your own bodyweight is the maximum comfortable load.

also payable for a vehicle of up to eight people at a cost of $22 (24 hours) and $56 (eight weeks). Annual vehicle passes cost $66 or $99 depending on whether they are bought in low or peak season. All passes are sold at park visitor centres, visitor information centres or Service Tasmania shops. (You can also buy them aboard Bass Strait ferries to Tasmania.) The longer pass makes economic sense if you intend to visit iconic landscapes such as Cradle Mountain or Wineglass Bay.

As well as excellent extended bushwalking, the parks are geared towards **day-trippers** who just want to stroll or experience the abundant wildlife. All parks have short walking tracks with information boards on habitat, flora and fauna. Larger parks – Cradle Mountain, Lake St Clair, Mount Field, Freycinet, Narawntapu and Maria Island

– have a visitor centre within the park area. These are excellent sources of free information on habitats and walking, all manned by friendly rangers who lead nature walks in peak season. Camping is possible in all parks except the Hartz Mountains, Mole Creek and Rocky Cape, either for free or for a minimal charge of up to $12. All parks have toilets and usually a picnic site at the car park.

The telephone numbers on p.48 are for local ranger offices or visitor centres as appropriate. For all parks, the website of Parks & Wildlife Service is a goldmine for planning. Another excellent introduction is Greg Buckman's comprehensive guidebook *A Visitor's Guide to Tasmania's National Parks* ($27.50), available from major bookshops, including Tassie independent retailer Fullers (Ⓦ www.fullers bookshop.com.au) in Hobart and Launceston.

Hygiene essentials
• Toilet paper and steel hand-trowel (for burying faecal waste)
• Fuel stove, fuel, waterproof matches or lighter
• Plastic bags to carry out all rubbish
• Water carrier, so you can camp and wash at least 50m from streams and lakes

Safety and comfort essentials
• Good-quality tent
• Warm sleeping bag (with means to keep it dry)
• Sleeping mat
• Waterproof jacket and trousers
• Warm clothing in layers (fleece, thermals, etc)
• Spare set of clothes, kept dry
• Sturdy boots, woollen socks and gaiters
• Gloves and warm hat
• Sunhat, sunscreen and sunglasses
• First aid kit
• Map, compass, whistle
• Torch and batteries
• Lightweight, nutritious food

Optional gear
• EPIRB (Emergency Position Indicating Radio Beacon) and GPS (Global Positioning System) for remote treks
• Satellite phone
• Rope or elastic cord
• Notebook and pencil
• Books or field guides
• Camera (always in a waterproof container)
• Camp shoes
• Playing cards

Ben Lomond National Park ☎03 6336 5312. Spectacular alpine plateau with rugged walks and the best skiing in Tasmania; see p.238.

Cradle Mountain-Lake St Clair National Park ☎03/6492 1110 (Cradle Mountain) & 03/6289 1172 (Lake St Clair). Two conjoined national parks linked by one iconic walk, the Overland Track. Glaciated Cradle Mountain and Lake St Clair bookend a region of buttongrass plains, ancient forests and alpine heath; see p.311.

Douglas-Apsley National Park ☎03 6256 7000. Dry eucalyptus forest, river gorges, a waterhole for a dip and remote walking within a little-visited park; see p.197.

Franklin-Gordon Wild River National Park ☎03/6471 2511 or 03/6472 6020. Outstanding white-water rafting, rugged river valleys cloaked in rainforest, plus the hike to Frenchmans Cap; see p.320.

Freycinet National Park ☎03 6256 7000. Wineglass Bay is the big ticket, but there's also exhilarating coastal scenery, a great three-day hike and activities galore; see p.186.

Hartz Mountains National Park ☎03/6264 8460. A remote alpine highland: waterfalls, glacial lakes and a mountain summit that provides a window into the southwest; see p.137.

Maria Island National Park ☎03/6257 1420. Historic ruins, sweeping bays, rugged cliffs and mountains, and abundant wildlife: a little piece of paradise; see p.179.

Mole Creek Karst National Park ☎03/6363 5182. The only subterranean park to protect the finest cave systems in the state; see p.168.

Mount Field National Park ☎03/6288 1149. A favourite of Tasmanians near Hobart, with diverse scenery - Russell Falls, giant trees, remote subalpine walking, and lovely picnic grounds - and a small ski scene; see p.99.

Mount William National Park ☎03/6376 1550. Long powder beaches and idyllic coves at the north of the Bay of Fires. Renowned for mobs of Forester kangaroos; see p.246.

Narawntapu National Park ☎03/6428 6277. A popular coastal park whose mazy wetlands and grassy plains teem with wildlife. Great beaches and camping too; see p.261.

Rocky Cape National Park ☎03/6452 4997. Small but diverse park, with many interesting corners: Aboriginal heritage, slanted rock formations and hills speckled with wildflowers. Excellent possibilities for diving; see p.274.

South Bruny National Park ☎03/6293 1419. An island with high sea cliffs and coastal heathland, dramatic short walks and powerful surf beaches; see p.132.

Southwest National Park ☎03/6288 1283 (north); ☎03/6264 8460 (south). Not just an epic area of forests and peaks, but one of the greatest wilderness regions in the world. As grand and as remote as it gets in Tasmania. Isolated bushwalks, scenic flights, abseiling, outstanding kayaking; see p.323.

Strzelecki National Park ☎03/6359 2217. The mountainous southwest corner of Flinders Island whose endemic fauna is a crossover of mainland and Tasmanian species; see p.341.

Tasman National Park ☎03/6214 8100. One of Australia's most spectacular coastlines, ranging from the drama of the nation's highest sea cliffs to idyllic bays. Exhilarating cliff-walks, wildlife trips by boat; see p.110.

Walls of Jerusalem National Park ☎03/6363 5133. The flip-side of Cradle Mountain, with remote hiking through a fragile glaciated habitat. A favourite of Tassie bushwalkers, but notorious for extreme weather; see p.169.

Culture and etiquette

Tasmania's remoteness and isolation has inculcated in Tasmanians a strong sense of community that celebrates small-town virtues such as unhurried lifestyles and easy-going attitudes. It also means getting things done takes a little more time. Friendly and reserved in equal measure and known for a quirky, gentle sense of humour, Tasmanians are a largely conservative bunch with a soft spot for tradition, self-reliance and sincerity, and a distaste of showing off.

Yet Tasmania is increasingly polarized between its liberal progressives and the traditionalists in areas of primary industries (broadly, the west and northwest). The most obvious example of this is the conservation debate. Everyone you meet will be passionate about it, so refrain from leaping in with black-and-white opinions – it is never as clear-cut as it seems to outsiders.

Dress codes are casual and modest – flamboyant dress will always provoke a wry comment – and for dinner jeans and a T-shirt are usually fine in all but the smartest places. Thongs (flip-flops) and shorts are frowned on in restaurants. Greetings, while warm, are restricted to handshakes rather than metropolitan cheek-kissing. Tasmania has some of the most progressive gay rights in Australia (see p.54) but public displays of affection are inadvisable outside of Hobart and Launceston.

Smoking has been banned in enclosed areas since 2006, including pubs and restaurants. In the pub, Tasmania follows the British system of buying drinks in a round – if you are bought one, you'll be expected to offer to reciprocate. **Tipping** is not expected except in upmarket restaurants, where a rate of ten percent applies. In cafés, leave a few coins to round up to the nearest dollar, and a dollar or two in standard restaurants. Taxi drivers and bar staff do not expect tips.

Shopping

No clichéd boomerangs and fluffy koalas in the souvenir shops of Tasmania. The speciality wares of the state are the wide range of handicrafts produced by Tasmania's thriving artistic community. These range from twee mementoes to more contemporary designs. Alongside dedicated outlets, local markets are good hunting grounds: the best is Hobart's Salamanca market on Saturday; others are held in Penguin, Evandale and Latrobe.

Woodcraft is a Tasmanian speciality – this is, after all, a state that celebrates wood-chopping and chainsaw-carves spare tree stumps. You can pick up sculpture, homeware and smart contemporary furniture made of local timbers such as myrtle, Huon pine and blackwood. Launceston's design museum and Geeveston are among the best places to look. **Painting** is less widespread; try Salamanca Arts Centre in Hobart, or Thistle Gallery in Ross for kitsch-free work. **Aboriginal fine art** is the stock in trade of Art Mob (@www.artmob.com.au) on Hunter Street, Hobart. It also has exquisite shell

Clothing and shoe sizes

Women's dresses and skirts

American	4	6	8	10	12	14	16	18
Australian/British	8	10	12	14	16	18	20	22
Continental	38	40	42	44	46	48	50	52

Women's blouses and sweaters

American	6	8	10	12	14	16	18
Australian/British	30	32	34	36	38	40	42
Continental	40	42	44	46	48	50	52

Women's shoes

American	5	6	7	8	9	10	11
Australian/British	3	4	5	6	7	8	9
Continental	36	37	38	39	40	41	42

Men's suits

American	34	36	38	40	42	44	46	48
Australian/British	34	36	38	40	42	44	46	48
Continental	44	46	48	50	52	54	56	58

Men's shirts

American	14	15	15.5	16	16.5	17	17.5	18
Australian/British	14	15	15.5	16	16.5	17	17.5	18
Continental	36	38	39	41	42	43	44	45

Men's shoes

American	7	7.5	8	8.5	9.5	10	10.5	11	11.5
Australian/British	6	7	7.5	8	9	9.5	10	11	12
Continental	39	40	41	42	43	44	44	45	46

necklaces, a speciality of Tasmanian Aborigines crafted today on Cape Barron Island. Mother-of-pearl maireener shell necklaces are fantastic – you'll pay $1000–2000 for a good one. Sources of **general crafts** include Hunter Street and Salamanca Place in Hobart; Deloraine; and Tamar Valley villages Rosevears and Gravelly Beach. Merino wool knitwear is excellent in the sheep-farming centre – head to Oatlands and Ross, but think cosy rather than high fashion. Heritage towns on the Midlands Highway are also your best source of antiques. The most memorable source of Tasmanian wines is direct from the wine estates after tasting. For all shopping, haggling is not common, but is worth a go in markets if you use a cheeky smile.

Travelling with children

Children and Tasmania are a good match. This is a gentle, small-town state with an indulgent attitude towards youngsters. It has one of the most pristine environments in the world, with abundant organized activities to entertain young thrill-seekers alongside sedate countryside pursuits. Traffic outside the cities is minimal and travelling times between destinations are rarely more than an hour so long as your plans are not too ambitious.

Getting around and practicalities

All means of **public transport** – Airporter shuttle buses, the major coach companies and Metro city services – provide discounts for children under sixteen. Infants under four years old travel free of charge, so long as they are not occupying a seat. Given the vagaries of Tasmania's bus timetables, it makes sense to self-drive. Distances are short and there are free public toilets at regular intervals in bushcamps or small towns. All hire companies can provide child seats on request for an extra charge: as an idea of prices, Hertz charge $8.80 a day, capped at $62. It's definitely worth considering a campervan or motorhome. These dispense with the daily ritual of loading and then unloading the car every day and add the frission of adventure when you bushcamp; all kids – big and little – are thrilled by a wallaby loping around the van at dusk. Hobart and Launceston provide dedicated baby-changing areas in public amenities. In rural Tasmania you'll have to make do with a fold-down bed in the public toilet.

Accommodation

Hotels and motels are child-friendly. Most can rustle up a cot and have family rooms with a double bed and two singles. Larger hotels may allow children to go free; otherwise you're looking at the standard discount of thirty to fifty percent. Large or resort hotels often have a swimming pool and playground. The best option for kids is self-contained accommodation – with young children, it means you can relax and just let them run around. This is especially true on farms – endless space to romp around and perhaps livestock to pet. Babysitters are a rarity even in large hotels. Backpackers' hostels are welcoming to children – some offer family rooms – but a baby will be frowned on. B&Bs are full of things to break so are best avoided; many at the top end market themselves as child-free in any case.

Eating out and activities

Cafés and standard restaurants are relaxed about kids in their premises and often provide cheaper child menus. Easy-going high-end rural restaurants are usually blasé about kids, but it's worth double-checking, and definitely ask first in the top city restaurants. Unless you're eating, taking the kids into the pub is not common.

Concessions are standard practice for sights, tours and travel passes – expect around thirty to fifty percent off. Every national park and most forest reserves have a short, board-walked route often accompanied by kiddie-friendly interpretive boards, while boat-trips at Tasman Peninsula, Bruny Island and Triabunna are excellent. Wildlife parks and aquariums let kids see the state's fauna up close. Ghoulish convict memorabilia always fascinates – Port Arthur is entertaining and thought-provoking – and there are numerous ghost tours at dusk. Beaches are of the spectacular, empty variety, often with a rookery of Fairy Penguins that waddle ashore to roost at dusk. There are always plenty of organized activities (kayaking, abseiling, rafting, hang-gliding, game fishing; quad-biking); the best range is in Strahan and Coles Bay.

For information about children in Hobart, pick up *It's a Kid's Life! Hobart*, by Wendy Nielsen and Avril Priem. General travel advice is in the *Rough Guide to Travel With Babies & Young Children*.

Travel essentials

Costs

Tasmania has the lowest cost of living in Australia. In broad terms you can expect similar or slightly cheaper prices to those in continental Europe and the US. Your biggest expense is liable to be travel – not just getting there, but the hire of a car, which is the best way to see the state; budget for at least $30 a day. Accommodation is most expensive in Hobart and Launceston, but prices hike throughout the state from mid-December to the end of January. They will also be more expensive if you are travelling alone, as single rooms cost around two-thirds the price of doubles. For day-to-day spending, Goods and Services Tax (GST – an Australian equivalent to Britain's VAT) of ten percent is added to most products. See p.49 for advice on tipping.

Travelling as a couple, assuming three meals a day and an occasional paid attraction, your **daily budget** could be as little as $70/£33/US$66 per person a day if you're prepared to stay in hostels or pubs and stick to basic bar meals. Staying in hostel dorms where possible will save money, as will cooking your own meals. You could shave off up to $30/£14/US$28 a day if you take advantage of free bushcamps throughout the state, though you'll need your own transport to reach them. Upgrade the accommodation to a mid-range hotel or B&B and splurge on a good meal now and then, and you're looking at daily costs of around $100/£48/US$95. With a daily spend of $140/£72/US$142, you're having a fine old time, with fine food and upper-mid hotels. For luxury, set aside $180/£86/US$170 a day. Tours and organized activities will increase these guideline figures.

Due to a nascent hostel scene, backpacker **discount cards** favoured on the mainland don't cut the mustard in Tasmania. A VIP card, available through travel agents or online (annual membership $43; ⓦwww.vipbackpackers.com) may pay its way thanks to a ten percent cut on the price of organized tours and activities, but check the website for an up-to-date list of current operators before you splash out. More useful, perhaps, is the See Tasmania Smartvisit Card (☎1300 661 711, ⓦwww.seetasmaniacard.com) available online or at visitor centres in Hobart, Launceston and Devonport. It provides discounts or free entry to attractions, plus reduced rates on a select list of tours and restaurants. Even with a discount of $20 for online purchase it is far from cheap, however – $159 for three consecutive days, $229 for seven days, $299 for ten days. You'll have to travel fast to make a card pay, so, again, visit the website for a list of current participants and do the maths.

Crime and personal safety

Tasmania has the lowest crime rates in Australia and most of the statistics are confined to Hobart and Launceston. For overseas visitors, roads, wilderness and weather are far more dangerous – see p.27 for advice on safe driving and p.46 for bushwalking tips. That said, the usual precautions apply. Do not leave valuables on display in cars or carry large quantities of cash with you. All recreational drugs are illegal in Tasmania. Drink-driving is taken extremely seriously and random breath-tests are common, especially around Christmas, so don't risk it.

Drinking areas in cities and untouristed towns can get a little rough on Friday and Saturday night and disputes may escalate into the traditional pub "blue". **Single women** may provoke comments in country pubs, usually just a bit of banter rather than anything aggressive, and may attract predatory drunks, though no more so than anywhere else in small-town Australia. Tasmanian police (ⓦwww.police.tas.gov.au), all armed, keep a low profile but are helpful when you need them. For non-emergencies call ☎131 444; for **emergencies** call ☎000.

Though Tasmania has lost a tag of "Bigot's Island" from the 1980s, **racism** is not unknown. The state remains almost exclusively white European and other ethnicities can experience prejudice from rednecks. Black travellers may attract attention when they do not want it (and not get any when they do). Asian visitors are more accepted as a result of widescale immigration from Southeast Asia, though those from the Indian subcontinent are a minority. Australia has powerful anti-discrimination laws – you can make a complaint to the Human Rights and Equal Opportunity Commission (☎1300 656 419, ⊛www.humanrights.gov.au). Unfortunately there is not much you can do about overt racism on the ground.

Electricity

Supply is 240/250V, 50Hz AC. British appliances work with an adaptor for the Australian three-pin plug; American and Canadian 110V appliances require a transformer.

Emergencies

Dial ☎000 for all emergency services.

Entry requirements

All visitors except New Zealanders require a **visa** or an Electronic Travel Authority (ETA) to enter Australia. Both must be obtained before arrival in the country – applications can be made up to a year before entry, either online or from the Australian high commissions, embassies or consulates.

For nationals of the UK, Ireland, most European countries (including Scandinavia and Iceland), the US, Canada, Malaysia, South Korea, Singapore and Brunei who are coming for a short-term visit, it is simplest to get an **ETA**. Applied for online on the immigration department site ⊛www.immi .gov.au, these are effectively computerized visas that replace the stamp in your passport. They allow multiple three-month stays for up to twelve months, so long as your passport remains valid. Many travel agents and airlines issue an ETA for free when you book your flight – some add on a handling charge of around £15/US$30 – or you can buy one online for a AUS$20 administration charge. You'll need to have details

of your travel itinerary and passport when you apply, plus a credit card to pay for the ETA. Confirmation of the pass is instant.

Non ETA-approved passport-holders – the full list is published on the department website – and those intending to stay in Australia for longer will need a **tourist visa**. Like ETAs, standard-issue visas are valid for a year and permit multiple three-month visits. You can also apply for up to six months – both cost $75/£35/US$70. Again, applications can be made online, or you can download application forms from the website or pick them up from Australian high commissions, embassies or consulates, listed on p.54. All fees are non-refundable regardless of the outcome of an application. If you need a visa extension, you simply apply for a new tourist visa within Australia. So far so simple, but bear in mind when applying that a visa within Australia costs $215/£100/US$205, so it's best to go for a longer visa if you're in any doubt about how long you will stay. Remember, too, that your passport must remain valid for the entire extension period. If you are refused a further visa, you must leave Australia before the original expires. If you're visiting immediate family who live in Australia – parents, spouse, child, brother or sister – you can apply for a **Sponsored Family Visitor visa** ($65/£30/ US$60; three- and six-month, or one year) with fewer restrictions.

Year-long **Working Holiday Maker (WHM) visas** are easily available for visitors between 18 and 30. Open to passport-holders from Britain, Ireland, most European countries, Canada and Japan, WHMs allow you to work for up to six months for a single employer, though they are geared towards casual jobs of a month or so – which is all the fruit-picking that most people can take. The visas also permit four months of study. They cost $190/£90/US$180 and are valid for a year after being granted, so you can use one aged 31 so long as you apply aged 30. Three-quarters of applications made online are processed within two days, or you can go through travel agents such as Trailfinders and STA. A limited number of WHMs are available for US citizens (US$170).

A visa is not a guarantee that you'll be permitted into the country, however.

Immigration officers may check that you have sufficient funds to cover yourself while in Australia and that you have a return ticket. Quarantine regulations are similarly strict: fresh fruit and vegetables, packaged and dried foodstuffs, seeds and nuts, animal products and plant materials (including some wood crafts, souvenirs and unlacquered ceramics), firearms, steroids and drugs except with a prescription are just a few of the generic items on the banned list. Camping and sports equipment, including hiking boots, must be clean (ie free of all dirt) and may be confiscated if it fails to meet rigorous hygiene standards. Visit ⓦwww .daff.gov.au if you're in any doubt.

Australian embassies and consulates

For the full list visit ⓦwww.dfat.gov.au.

UK and Ireland

London Australian High Commission, Australia House, Strand, London WC2B 4LA ⓣ020/7379 4334, ⓦwww.uk.embassy.gov.au.
Dublin Australian Embassy, Seventh Floor, Fitzwilton House, Wilton Terr, Dublin 2 ⓣ01/664 5300, ⓦwww.ireland.embassy.gov.au.

US and Canada

Washington Australian Embassy, 1601 Massachusetts Ave, Washington DC NW 20036-2273 ⓣ202/797 3000, ⓦwww.usa.embassy .gov.au.
Consulates in New York, Seattle, Chicago, Boston, Honolulu, Houston, Los Angeles, Denver & Atlanta
Ottawa Australian High Commission, Suite 710, 50 O'Connor St, Ottawa ON K1P 6L2 ⓣ613/236 4376, ⓦwww.canada.embassy.gov.au.

New Zealand and South Africa

Wellington Australian High Commission 72-76 Hobson St, Thorndon, Wellington ⓣ04/473 6411, ⓦwww.newzealand.embassy.gov.uk.
Pretoria Australian High Commission 292 Orient St, Arcadia, Pretoria ⓣ012/423 6000, ⓦwww .southafrica.embassy.gov.au.

Gay and lesbian travellers

Acts of male homosexuality were still a criminal offence in Tasmania until 1997. Founded in 1988, the Tasmanian Gay and Lesbian Rights Group (TGLRG) put persistent pressure on the government. Led by spokes-person Rodney Croome, their rally cry "We're here, we're queer, and we're not going to the mainland" certainly shook up conservative Tasmania; thousands signed the petition to urge the reform of the law. The federal government and the UN Human Rights Commission also pressed for change, and Tasmania's Upper House finally cracked, changing the law on May 1, 1997. Ironically, Tasmania now has Australia's best legislation to protect gay and lesbian rights. In 2004, it became the first state in Australia to allow same-sex couples to register their relation-ships. The heart of the gay scene is Hobart, which has a decent spread of gay-friendly bars. Outside the capital, with the exception of Launceston, there is less acceptance of gay couples. Displays of intimacy such as holding hands in public will provoke comment. Gay-friendly accommodation options usually display a sticker of a rainbowed Tasmania in the window. Far easier is to source information from Gay and Lesbian Tourism Australia (ⓣ03/6264 2233; ⓦwww.galta.com.au) and Rainbow Tourism (ⓦwww.rainbowtourism.com). Both list gay-friendly outlets in Tasmania, including hire companies, tour operators, etc. Gay Info Line (ⓣ03 6234 8179) has up-to-date details of community events.

Health

Australian healthcare is excellent. Hygiene standards are high and there are no diseases to worry about. Even if it has a tinge of yellow due to local tannins, tap water is safe to drink everywhere. The Australian government has reciprocal agreements with the United Kingdom, Sweden, the Netherlands, Finland, Norway, Malta and Italy that entitles visitors to **free medical treatment** with national healthcare provider Medicare (ⓦwww .medicareaustralia.gov.au). The exceptions are those visitors who enter with a student visa. For everyone else, healthcare is free at the point of treatment in hospitals – ie casualty departments, which operate 24 hours a day. Note that visitors end up paying for an ambulance. Local doctors charge for their services, either a local health authority or else you directly for a sum that you can reclaim at a Medicare Centre. Either way, you'll need to present a **Medicare Card**, which is available from any Medicare Centre in Australia. You'll need a passport and valid visa, and in some cases National Health documents of your home provider when you enrol. Do this early on if you're staying for any length of time. Dental treatment is not provided by Medicare. Pharmacies can handle minor illness and can provide medicines if you get the prescription endorsed by a local doctor.

The biggest health problem in Tasmania is the **weather**. Even though you are 40 degrees south, the Australian sun is ferocious and ultra-violet light can penetrate on cloudy days. When it's sunny, follow "Slip, Slop, Slap" – a government approved catchphrase of old to slip on a T-shirt, slop on a water-resistant cream of at least SPF15 and slap on a hat. **Heat exhaustion** can be an issue when bushwalking in high summer – as a rule of thumb, carry at least half a litre of water per hour's walking. **Hypothermia** is a danger when bushwalking in mountainous regions – even in summer, you cannot rule out a blizzard, and heavy rain and high winds are a recipe for losing body heat. Go prepared for the worst.

Despite the fearsome reputation of Australian fauna, wildlife actually poses far less of a threat than the environment or other people. All three **snake** species in Tasmania are poisonous. None will attack unless provoked (ie trodden on or poked) – in fact you're unlikely to see any. Snakes are most active from October to March and on warm nights. If scrambling on rocks or poking around in forests to collect firewood, bear in mind that they inhabit holes and crevices. When walking, remember that snakes often bask in sunshine on open ground (ie paths and boardwalks) until mid-morning. Wearing thick socks and covered shoes will minimize the danger, which is most prevalent in areas of bushland scrub. Use a torch when walking at night. Also bear in mind that the fangs of a dead snake can still carry crystallised venom. Funnelweb and redback **spiders** have a highly toxic bite. Because identification is beyond most overseas visitors, seek medical attention for all spider and snake bites.

In summer, **mosquitoes** are irritating around lake shores – standard advice of long-sleeves and repellent applies – and

mites are annoying on your ankles. It's a fair bet that you'll encounter **leeches** on longer bushwalks in the centre and west. Use a lighter or salt to remove them – pulling off leeches can cause infection. **Ticks** are the bane of bushwalkers, especially in the northeast. They lurk in areas of long grass and bushes and attach themselves to passing animals – ie you – causing allergic reactions and irritation. Check yourself over after a trek. Look for a pea-sized blob in areas of local swelling or stinging and gently pull out the animal with tweezers – be careful not to use too much force or you'll just inject more venom. Spraying insect repellent on your shoes and leggings helps keep both leeches and ticks at bay.

Medical resources for travellers

UK and Ireland

British Airways Travel Clinics ☎0845/600 2236, ⓦwww.britishairways.com /travel/healthclinintro/public/en_gb for nearest clinic.
Hospital for Tropical Diseases Travel Clinic ☎0845/155 5000 or 020/7387 4411, ⓦwww .thehtd.org.
MASTA (Medical Advisory Service for Travellers Abroad) ⓦwww.masta.org or ☎0870/606 2782 for the nearest clinic.
Travel Medicine Services ☎028/9031 5220.
Tropical Medical Bureau Republic of Ireland ☎1850/487 674, ⓦwww.tmb.ie.

US and Canada

CDC ☎1-877/394-8747, ⓦwww.cdc.gov/travel. Official US government travel health site.
International Society for Travel Medicine ☎1-770/736-7060, ⓦwww.istm.org. Has a full list of travel health clinics.
Canadian Society for International Health ⓦwww.csih.org. Extensive list of travel health centres.

Australia, New Zealand and South Africa

Travellers' Medical and Vaccination Centre ⓦwww.tmvc.com.au, ☎1300/658 844. Lists travel clinics in Australia, New Zealand and South Africa.

Insurance

Thanks to fierce competition, travel insurance is not just a wise precaution but

Rough Guides travel insurance

Rough Guides has teamed up with Columbus Direct to offer you travel insurance that can be tailored to suit your needs. Products include a low-cost backpacker option for long stays; a short break option for city getaways; a typical holiday package option; and others. There are also annual multi-trip policies for those who travel regularly. Different sports and activities (trekking, skiing, etc) can usually be covered if required.

See our website (Ⓦwww.roughguides.com/website/shop) for eligibility and purchasing options. Alternatively, UK residents should call ℡0870/033 9988; Australians should call ℡1300/669 999 and New Zealanders should call ℡0800/55 9911. All other nationalities should call ℡+44 870/890 2843.

an inexpensive one. The standard policy covers the expenses of lost luggage and accommodation if flight plans change beyond your control. It will also cover theft – in the unlikely case of stolen property, you'll need a written statement from the police – and emergency dental coverage. As ever, check the small print. Also check the extent of accident or medical coverage to complement that of Medicare (where applicable). Make sure that a policy's maximum per article for lost baggage, typically around £500, covers the most expensive item in your luggage. And before you agree, double-check the extent of any home insurance policy and also theft/damage insurance on purchases made by credit card – you may already be covered without realizing it. Most policies have exemptions for "high-risk" sports such as skiing, surfing, rock-climbing, sometimes hiking and always diving. It's easy enough to obtain extra cover for these at an additional cost.

Internet

Thanks to the Tasmanian Communities Online programme, 66 **Online Access Centres** are scattered throughout Tasmania, usually in the library or a local school. They are available for visitors' use at a cost of around $2.50–$3 per half-hour. Details are printed throughout the guide or you can search for a centre at Ⓦwww.tco.asn.au. Dedicated cybercafés are in the cities, larger towns and in some tourist resorts, plus in some cafés that act as community hubs. Most are able to burn digital photographs to a disk for a few dollars. Most

hostels – plus larger hotels – provide Internet access using pre-paid scratchcards with a quota of credit; enter the code and off you go. Be aware that many cards are non-transferable, so only work on the computer on which you first used it – the best policy is to ask when you buy. For details of Internet information resources see "Tourist information" on p.59.

Laundry

Known as "laundromats", these are rare outside large towns and cities. Even there they're hard to find. Most caravan parks ("tourist parks" or "holiday parks") and hostels have laundry facilities for guests, as do a few of the larger hotels. Five-star joints will do it for you at a price. Washing machines and tumbledryers are coin-operated, usually costing a couple of dollars a go.

Living in Tasmania

Assuming you have a work visa, the easiest casual work for backpackers to pick up is **fruit-picking**, though you're certainly not going to make a fortune doing it. Hours are long and the pay is low – it's best seen as a subsistence existence. If that hasn't put you off, look in orchards around Huonville and, to a lesser extent, the Tamar Valley from January to April. Ask at visitor centres and hostels for what's available. In Hobart and Launceston, you may strike it lucky and find a short-term contract through a **human resources agency**. Jobs are typically temporary administrative and hospitality contracts, though sometimes there are construction and specialized administrative roles such as accountancy on offer. The state's largest agency, Searson Buck (Ⓦwww.searsonbuck.com.au), has bureaux in Hobart, Launceston, Devonport and Burnie. Other good resources for job hunting are: Internet-based agency Tasmanian Jobs (Ⓦwww.tasmanianjobs.com); CareerOne (Ⓦwww.careerone.com.au); and government site Ⓦwww.jobsearch.gov.au. The website of the guidebook *Work About Australia* ($29.95; Ⓦwww.workaboutaustralia.com.au) is worth a look for its overview of work possibilities.

If you're less fussed about money than getting under the skin of Tassie culture, look into a **farmstay** through Willing Workers on Organic Farms (Ⓣ03 5155 0218, Ⓦwww.wwoof.com.au). Pioneered as a sustainable living concept in the early 1970s, the programme provides a cultural exchange in which WWOOFers live and work as a family with host farms in exchange for a few hours' work a day. Idealistic workers should note that not all farms listed on the site are organic, however. Conservation Volunteers (Ⓣ03/6334 9985 Ⓦwww.conservationvolunteers.com.au) is a rewarding short-term option for eco-minded visitors. Workers are involved in hands-on management or repair of historic sites and wilderness habitats; typically planting and weed removal, fencing or track maintenance. Transport to the site and meals are provided, but you may have to pay for bunkhouse accommodation on some overnight contracts – jobs last from one day to three. A nationwide outfit, Conservation Volunteers, has an office in Launceston at 49 Elizabeth St.

Mail

Australian Post (Ⓦwww.auspost.com.au) provides a fast, reliable mail service. Outlets are widespread throughout the state, either in dedicated branches or the general store of a village. Opening times for post offices are Mon–Fri 9am–5pm. **Postage cost** for a small letter or postcard of up to 125g will be around 50¢ within Australia. International deliveries for a letter up to 50g cost $1.30 to the Asia-Pacific region, or $1.95 to the rest of the world. Domestic delivery costs for small parcels up to 500g are $5.20 – heavier parcels are priced by weight and distance from the state. Delivery costs of international parcel deliveries vary, though sea deliveries cost about 40 percent less than air. Airmail takes around a week to reach Europe and the US/Canada – the most expensive service, Express Post International (EPI), reduces this to around five days – and sea mail can take a month or even two. As a gauge of prices, a package of 250–500g costs $13.90 to the US/Canada or $16.95 to the rest of the world by air and $9.75 for both by sea. Prices are lower to New Zealand and Asia-Pacific, and delivery times faster. Australia Post has an international courier service with the usual price hike. All post offices can receive mail for visitors – the general post offices in Hobart and Launceston have post restante rooms.

Maps

Tourism authority Tourism Tasmania produces an excellent 1:100,000 **visitors map** that marks national parks, differentiates between sealed and unsealed roads, has tourist attractions and some campsites and includes city maps on the reverse. It is available from large visitor centres for $5.95. Royal Automobile Association of Tasmania (RACT, Ⓦwww.ract.com.au) produces an almost identical touring map at 1:500,000 scale – you can pick one up for a similar price at RACT Travelworld offices: in Hobart, on the corner of Murray and Patrick streets; in Launceston, at the corner of York and George streets.

State cartographer Tasmap publishes **hiking and national park maps.** Scaled at 1:50,000 or 1:100,000, these topographic maps include notes on walking trails alongside general information on flora, fauna and history where relevant. Prices range from $4.50 for localized maps to around $9.95 for those that cover an entire national park. Tasmap brings similar rigour to topographical maps of the state: these come in scales of 1:25,000; 1:100,000 (though this series is being phased out); and 1:250,000 that divide the state into quarters, roughly corresponding to the area divisions of chapters five, six, and seven of this guide. All their maps cost $9.95.

Maps are available at outdoors shops throughout the state, while those for national parks are also stocked in that park's visitor information centre or Parks & Wildlife visitor centres where relevant. You can also pick them up direct from the Hobart base, Service Tasmania at 134 Macquarie St (☎1300 366 773 or 03/6233 3382). Another outlet in Hobart is the excellent Tasmanian Map Centre at 100 Elizabeth St (☎03/6231 9043, ⓦwww.map-centre.com.au), which takes international orders online.

Money

Each Australian dollar is divided into one hundred cents. Waterproof plasticized notes come in denominations of $5, $10, $20, $50 and $100; coins come in 5¢, 10¢, 20¢, 50¢, $1 and $2. Even though prices in shops come in single cents, bills are rounded up or down to the nearest 5¢. At the time of publication, $1 was worth 48p, €0.61 or US$0.96.

The four banks in Australia are ANZ, Commonwealth, National and Westpac. Their **ATMs** accept major credit cards such as Visa and Mastercard – American Express and Diners Card are not as widespread – plus standard international bank networks such as Cirrus, Maestro, Plus and Eurocard. No banks charge for withdrawals, making the ATM by far the easiest way to access money, but your home bank certainly might, often at a rate of 1 percent of the amount withdrawn. Check before you go – it's worth opening up a dedicated travel account with a free provider if you're staying for any length of time. A few villages or small towns have a

Commonwealth ATM in a general store rather than a branch, but be aware that ATMs dry up in less populated areas. **EFTPOS** (Electronic Funds At Point Of Sale) fills in some of the gaps between ATMs. EFTPOS allows you to pay for goods and services using a credit or debit card and often lets you withdraw small amounts of cash. Participants in the scheme are widespread: pubs, newsagents, general stores and petrol stations are reliable sources. Most smaller businesses – as well as many small B&Bs – only accept cash.

If you're still carrying them, **traveller's cheques** can be cashed at banks and hotels. Banks offer the best rates but charge a small fee. Banks in the cities and larger towns have a foreign exchange. There are also exchange bureaux – and ATMs – at Hobart and Launceston airports.

Opening hours and holidays

The standard **working hours** in Tasmania are Mon–Fri 9am–5.30pm. Banks close at 4pm, except on Friday when they also stay open until 5.30pm. Shops open on Saturdays, though many in rural areas only for half a day, while commercial shopping high streets in Hobart and Launceston open for business on Sundays, as will a general store in most small towns. Large supermarkets operate from around 8am until 9–10pm, though may close early on Sunday outside of the cities. In addition, large towns have late-night trading on Friday (until 9pm).

Restaurants open for lunch from noon and may remain operational throughout the

---

Public and school holidays

Treat public holidays like a Sunday – shops and many attractions shut, and bus services are, at best, reduced to a skeleton service or cease entirely.

1 January New Year's Day
26 January Australia Day
Second Monday in March Eight Hours Day
March/April Good Friday and Easter Monday
25 April Anzac Day
10 June Queen's Birthday
25 December Christmas Day
26 December Boxing Day

Calling home from abroad

Note that the initial zero is omitted from the area code when dialling the UK, Ireland, Australia and New Zealand from abroad.

UK international access code + 44 + city code.
Republic of Ireland international access code + 353 + city code.
US and Canada international access code + 1 + area code.
Australia international access code + 61 + city code.
New Zealand international access code + 64 + city code.
South Africa international access code + 27 + city code.

afternoon. Otherwise, they reopen for dinner at around 6pm – most Tasmanians eat around 7pm – and close around 9–10pm. As ever, city establishments open longer. Cafés generally operate daily from 8am to 5pm.

School holidays transform the state. The bucket-and-spade brigade descends on the beaches, campsites fill and hotels get booked up as Australian families take their family fortnight. The coach companies also reschedule their timetables for popular routes such as the east coast. The busiest times are the eight-week summer holidays from mid-December to mid-February and a week-long break over Easter. There are also two-week holidays in early June and early September.

Phones

Mobile phone coverage is good in the major urban centres, patchy in rural areas and non-existent in the wilderness. Overseas visitors need to check that their mobile phone network is compatible with that in Australia and also the price of overseas calls. Companies in Hobart and Launceston hire phones on short-term contracts – see Yellow Pages for listings. It may just be easiest to buy a **local SIM card**. These cost around $20 and include some credit. You then buy credit as you need it, either via a credit card or in newsagents and post offices. Telstra has the widest coverage by far of the three mobile networks – that for Optus and Vodafone is limited to the main urban areas. You can select a package of call charges according to how you intend to use your phone. A head-spinning number of **callcards** reduce the cost of international calls – again, you buy credit from a newsagent or post

office, then make calls through a local access telephone number. Because calls via a callcard are as low as 2¢ per minute and some mobile network packages let you select a few freecall local numbers, you can reduce calls to a minimal cost with careful planning.

Time

Tasmania is on Eastern Australian Standard Time, ten hours ahead of Greenwich Mean Time and fifteen hours ahead of New York. The clocks get pushed forward an hour for daylight from the first Sunday in October – a week before the other states in Australia – until the last Sunday in March.

Tourist information

The co-ordinator of state tourism is Hobart-based Tourism Tasmania. Its website (ⓦwww.discovertasmania.com) is the most comprehensive resource before you arrive. There are also state-run Tasmanian Travel Centres in Sydney (60 Carrington St; ☎1300 655 145) and Melbourne (259 Collins St; same tel). Once you've arrived in Tasmania, head to a visitor information centre; all 21 are central and demarcated with a yellow italicised "i" on a blue sign. The standard varies hugely according to the size of the destination. The biggest centres in state gateways Hobart, Launceston and Devonport cover the entire state and are good resources from which to begin any visit. Those in smaller towns are usually volunteer-run, so information is more sketchy and opening times erratic. Either way, they're a good first port of call upon arriving in a town. You'll find them well stocked with free town maps and brochures for the surrounding area, as well as leaflets for attractions and accommodation. In this guide, details are provided for each destination under "Information" or "Practicalities". It's also worth visiting to pick up a copy of *Tasmanian Travelways* (see below), a free bi-monthly newspaper with comprehensive listings.

Tasmanian tourism sites

Parks & Wildlife Service ⓦ www.parks.tas .gov.au.
Service Tasmania ⓦ www.service.tas.gov.au.
Tasmania Online ⓦ www.tas.gov.au.
Tasmanian Travelways (listings) ⓦ www.tasmaniantravelways.com.
T-change (relocation advice) ⓦ www.tchange.com.au.
The Mercury (newspaper) ⓦ www.news.com.au/mercury.
Tourism Tasmania ⓦ www.discovertasmania .com, ⓦ www.tastravel.com.au.
Wilderness Society (conservation) ⓦ www.wilderness.org.au.

Government travel sites

Australian Department of Foreign Affairs ⓦ www.dfat.gov.au, ⓦ www.smartraveller.gov.au.
British Foreign & Commonwealth Office ⓦ www.fco.gov.uk.
Canadian Department of Foreign Affairs ⓦ www.dfait-maeci.gc.ca.
Irish Department of Foreign Affairs ⓦ www.foreignaffairs.gov.ie.
New Zealand Ministry of Foreign Affairs ⓦ www.mft.govt.nz.
US State Department ⓦ www.travel.state.gov.

Travellers with disabilities

Recent legislation has increased awareness about the needs of the disabled and elderly. Buses and major tourist destinations are wheelchair-friendly, as are many public toilets, and boardwalks permit access to many of the national parks. The best reference is national awareness organization the National Information Communication Awareness Network (☎ 1800 806 769, ⓦ www.nican.com .au), whose website provides a searchable database of accessible sights, accommodation, information resources and community groups. The Paraplegic and Quadriplegic Association of Tasmania (also known as Prequad Tasmania; ☎ 03/6272 8816, ⓦ www .paraquadtas.org.au) has similar listings for tourist operators, including details of wheelchair-friendly wineries, toilets and taxis. Its office is at 26–28 Tolosa St, Glenorchy (Hobart); call before you head out there.

Even if you have sourced a hotel through the organizations' websites, it's worth calling ahead to ensure the facilities meet your needs. To check which national parks and reserves are accessible – and there are more than you might think considering the rugged terrain – either consult the Parks & Wildlife website (ⓦ www.parks.tas.gov.au/recreation /disabled) or pick up its *Parks for all People* brochure. Guide-dogs are permitted into the national park areas if rangers are forewarned. The Red Cross in Hobart, at 110 Elizabeth St (☎ 03/6231 3719, ⓦ www.redcross.org .au) provides hire of wheelchairs and electric scooters.

Guide

Guide

1 Hobart and around... 63

2 The southeast 119

3 Central Tasmania... 143

4 The east coast 173

5 The northeast 209

6 The northwest 249

7 The west and southwest... 291

8 Bass Strait Islands 333

Hobart and around

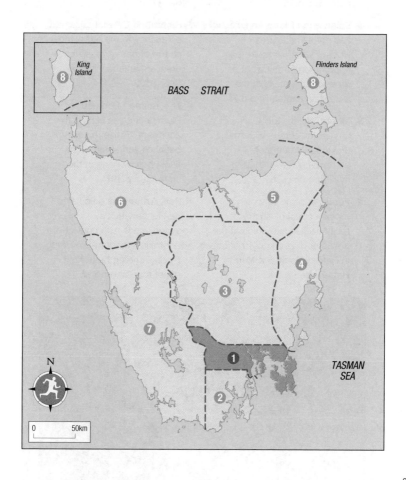

CHAPTER 1 # Highlights

* **Derwent River cruises** See what Mark Twain and Agatha Christie raved about – get afloat to see the city at its best. See p.75

* **Salamanca Place** An eclectic and charismatic area of Hobart, whether you're bar-hopping on Friday night or browsing the stalls of the Saturday market. See p.75

* **Mount Wellington** A slice of the southwestern wilderness on Hobart's doorstep; astounding views, thrilling cycling. See p.86

* **Food** Welcome to a rising foodie capital of Australia – tuck into fish and chips at the docks or dine on gourmet fare in Battery Point and North Hobart. See p.89

* **Mount Field National Park** Waterfalls, giant gum trees and extended treks in an untamed alpine environment. See p.99

* **Richmond** Convict tales add poignancy to the old-world charm of one of Tassie's premier heritage villages. See p.102

* **The Tasman Peninsula** Plummeting sea cliffs with abundant wildlife, haunting beaches and some of the finest bushwalking in the state. See p.107

* **Port Arthur** The colonial penitentiary that's synonymous with convict-era Australia – thought-provoking by day, chilling by twilight ghost tour. See p.112

▲ Richmond Church

Hobart and around

Though a metropolis by local standards and home to over half the state's population, Hobart is typically Tasmanian. Its inhabitants have the same state-wide attitudes of self-reliance and steadiness, and like Tasmanian towns everywhere, Hobart is defined by sea and mountains. It's a city in awe of its environment rather than imposed on it and the approach from any direction is exhilarating: speeding across the expressway on the Tasman Bridge you cross the wide **Derwent River**; swooping up the Southern Outlet you enter to a view of the harbour, docks and green-and-red tin roofs strung out along the estuary. And from whichever direction you arrive, there is the backdrop of **Mount Wellington**, snow-topped for two or three months a year.

For all the mountain's visual impact, Hobart's focus is its **waterfront**, as it has been since its foundation in 1804, making it Australia's second-oldest city after Sydney. Uniquely among Australian capitals, a fishing fleet moors within a few minutes' walk of the city centre and the day's catch can be eaten fresh off the boat from fish-and-chip punts at adjacent Constitution Dock. Nearby on **Salamanca Place**, the dockside warehouses of Georgian merchants now back a famous **Saturday market**, a Hobart highlight. Yacht races and local regattas keep the water abuzz, especially on summer weekends; you can choose any type of craft for a **cruise**, from a replica of the first settlers' brig to a sleek catamaran. The climate is fairly obliging too: in the rain-shadow of Mount Wellington, Hobart is the second-driest state capital after Adelaide.

Hobart has always had the richest streetscape of colonial **Georgian architecture** in the antipodes, but to this asset it can now add an increasingly sophisticated **restaurant and hotel scene**, evidence that the city is shedding a parochialism that made it the butt of mainland jokes even into the early 1990s. Despite all the newly acquired cosmopolitan gloss, Hobart remains a touchstone of Tasmania. In part, this is due to the city's status as the administrative and political hub of the state. But perhaps just as important is that only in Hobart do politicos rub shoulders with fishermen in the pub, and city commuters share their thoroughfares with logging trucks. It is never going to feel like a major city when compared to those in mainland Australia, and it may even appear a little thin on sights. Yet Hobart is a place that has come of age: unpretentious and easy-going, where art galleries sit comfortably alongside a fishing fleet, and the sense of history is constant. Simply loafing around is an essential part of Hobart's greatest pleasures. When that loses appeal, there are also some superb landscapes in its backyard.

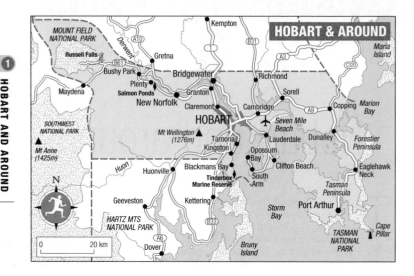

A short history

The early history of Hobart is very much that of white Tasmania. The Mouhenener Aborigines foraged for seafood in the area until they were displaced by the British who sailed up the Derwent in September 1803. They founded a settlement at Risdon Cove, on the east bank of today's Bowen Bridge. Within a year, **Lieutenant-governor David Collins** shifted the encampment 10km downriver to take advantage of the freshwater Hobart Rivulet that ran into today's Sullivans Cove. Some soldiers remained at Risdon Cove and on May 3, 1804, massacred an indigenous hunting party – the first chapter in what would be a sorry tale for the island's Aborigines.

Collins went on to serve as lieutenant-governor of the fledgling capital for six years. Under his rule, the most southerly settlement in the world developed from tented community to wattle-and-daub township – the government and church dwellings on what is now Franklin Square, those of convicts on the banks of the Hobart Rivulet. Hobart Town, as the settlement was known until 1882, found its stride in the 1820s under teetotal disciplinarian **Lieutenant-governor Arthur**. A new stone wharf built in 1821 boosted activity in the deep-water port and a burgeoning whaling industry in the estuary. And the creation of New Wharf alongside Salamanca Place in 1832 permitted larger ships to dock, consolidating Hobart Town's position as an exporter of merino wool, wheat, cattle hides, sealskins, timber and whale oil to Sydney, then to Batavia (now Jakarta), India, China and home to England.

Though Hobart Town remained a rough frontier, growing prosperity ushered in a golden age of architecture during which government architect **John Lee Archer** designed many of the city's finest Georgian buildings. Yet even though it won city status in 1842, alongside an elite of officials and merchants lived an underclass of poor settlers and ticket-of-leave convicts in **slums** as squalid as any in Victorian London. Most notorious of all was Wapping, piled up behind the docks. One resident was ex-convict Isaac "Ikey" Solomon, a fence from London's East End on whom Charles Dickens is said to have modelled Fagin. The slum burnt down in 1890.

The end of transportation in 1853 emboldened a more respectable class of settler and coincided with a boom in agricultural and timber exports, largely to New South Wales and Victoria. Served by the abundant timber, shipbuilding boomed, too – in the 1850s Hobart Town produced more ships than the combined output elsewhere in Australia. Stability also encouraged the first **tourism** from the 1860s, and by the early 1900s, Hobart was on the cruise itineraries of the P&O, Orient and Blue Star lines. Industry was a hostage to changing trade, however. Shipbuilding petered out with the shift from wood to steel, and after World War I Hobart was forced to diversify into light industry, served by cheap hydroelectricity from power plants in the central lakes. Over following decades, Hobart settled into suburban living and sprawled steadily north along the river. The integrity of the city centre suffered from haphazard development – the ugly architecture on the water-front in the 1980s was surely a mistake – but without the spurt of growth post-World War II that propelled other Australian capitals upwards, the city remained as low-rise as it was low-key.

Hobart's maritime role sputters on, too. The city is growing as a port-of-call for cruiseships and a supply centre for Antarctic research vessels, one facet in its emergence as a leader in South Polar research. Several international scientific bodies are headquartered here, and in early 2008 Hobart became the first city in the world with a scheduled air service to Antarctica.

Arrival, information and city transport

Hobart **airport** is 17km east of the city near Seven Mile Beach. Redline's **Airporter Shuttle Bus** ($12 one way, $20 return; bookings ☎0419 383 462 or 0419 382 240), meets all flights and stops throughout central Hobart as well as going north to New Town and south to Sandy Bay. A **taxi** into the city centre costs around $32. Redline **coaches** arrive from northern Tasmania at the **Transit Centre** at 199 Collins St (☎1300 360 000; left-luggage $1.50 per item per day; their airport service also drops off and picks up here). Tassielink disembarks from destinations state-wide at the **Hobart Bus Terminal** at 64 Brisbane St (☎1300 300 520), where there's a free short-term left-luggage service for passengers (or $10 per bag for several days if you are going on a bushwalk) and a cafeteria. **Hobart Coaches** from destinations south of Hobart arrive and depart from a stop at Murray Street, just up from Davey Street.

Information

The first stop for general information is the **Tasmanian Travel and Infor-mation Centre** at 20 Davey St, on the corner of Elizabeth Street (Mon–Fri 8.30am–5.30pm, Sat & Sun 9am–5pm; ☎1300 655 145 or 03/6230 8102; Ⓦwww.hobarttravelcentre.com.au). Although it functions mainly as a travel, car-rental and accommodation agency, it also has city maps and walk leaflets as well as the usual array of flyers. The **National Trust Shop**, in the Penitentiary Chapel at the corner of Brisbane and Campbell streets (Mon–Fri 10am–2.30pm; ☎03/6231 0911), displays charts detailing a bewildering range of listed buildings. The **Tasmanian Environment Centre**, at 102 Bathurst St (Mon–Fri 9am–5pm; ☎03/6234 5566, Ⓦwww.tasmaniaenvironmentcentre .org.au), is a relaxed resource space with books about Tassie's flora and fauna and information on environmental events. For **bushwalking information**

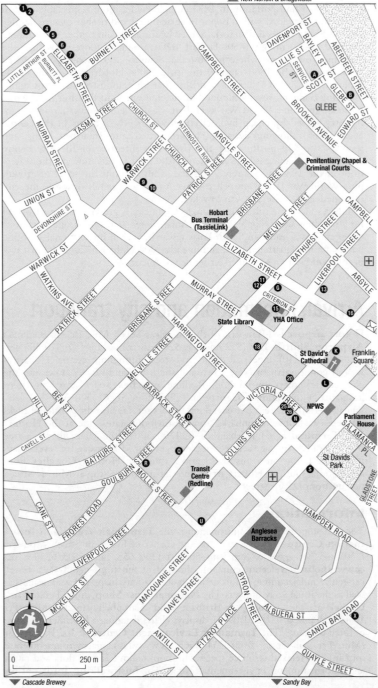

New Norfolk & Bridgewater

Cascade Brewey

Sandy Bay

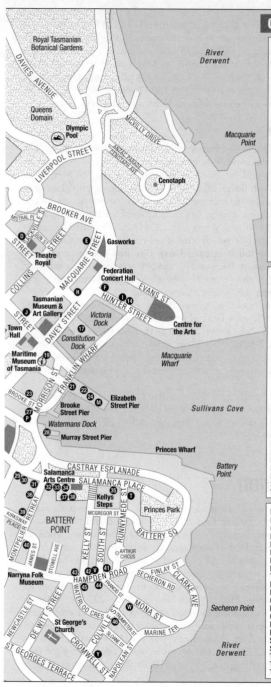

CENTRAL HOBART

ACCOMMODATION

Astor Private Hotel	N
Battery Point Manor	Y
Central City Backpackers	K
Colville Cottage	W
Corinda's Cottages	B
Customs House Hotel	P
Edinburgh Gallery B&B	U
Grand Chancellor	H
Hadley's Hotel	L
Henry Jones Art Hotel	I
Hobart Hostel	O
Lenna	T
The Lodge on Elizabeth	C
Mantra One	S
MidCity	G
Montgomery's Private Hotel & YHA	J
Narrara Backpackers	R
The Old Woolstore	E
The Pickled Frog Backpackers	Q
Prince of Wales	V
St Ives Hotel Apartments	X
Somerset on the Pier	M
Theatre Royal Hotel	D
Wellington Lodge	A
Zero Davey	F

RESTAURANTS & CAFÉS

Amulet	6
Annapurna	7
Ball & Chain Grill	35
Criterion Street Cafe	15
Da Angelo Ristorante	42
Drifters Internet Cafe	36
Fish 349	5
Fish Frenzy	21
Francisco's	45
Jackman & McRoss	25, 43
Jam Packed	14
Kelly's	40
La Cuisine	12
Magic Curries	41
Maldini	33
Marque IV	22
Monty's	39
Mures Fish Centre	17
Piccalilly	44
Quarry	30
R Tagaki Sushi	18
Restaurant 373	1
Retro Café	31
Shu Yuan	13
Sirens	26
Sugo Shop	38
Vanidol's	4

PUBS, BARS & CLUBS

Bar Celona	37
Grape	34
Halo	16
Irish Murphy's	29
Isobar	27
Kaos Cafe & Soak Lounge Bar	9
Knopwood's Retreat	32
The Lark Distillery	19
Lizbon	10
New Sydney Hotel	11
Observatory	28
Proller	20
Queen's Head Cafe & Wine Bar	3
Republic Bar & Café	8
Rockerfeller's	23
Shipwright's Arms Hotel	46
Syrup	32
Telegraph Hotel	23
Trout Bar and Cafe	2
T-42°	24

and a full range of Tasmap hiking maps, head for the Service Tasmania Shop at 134 Macquarie St (Mon–Fri 8.15am–5.30pm; ☎1300 135 513). The Parks and Wildlife Service has an unmanned desk (same hours and number) here with information sheets and a phone (☎03/6233 6191) to talk to a parks officer for advice; other maps are stocked at the Tasmanian Map Centre at 100 Elizabeth St (☎03/6231 9043). The Wilderness Society also has information on walks in its conservation campaign areas at its office at 130 Davey St (☎03/6224 1550, ⓦwww.wilderness.org.au/tas) and a shop at 33 Salamanca Place.

City transport

Although Hobart is a walkable city, **buses** run by **Hobart Metro** (information ☎132 201, ⓦwww.metrotas.com.au) are useful to reach less central accommodation, sights in the suburbs and the base of Mount Wellington. The Metroshop, inside the GPO on Elizabeth Street, sells Metro Tens (a pack of ten tickets gives a twenty percent saving) and provides timetables, as do several newsagents. Tickets can also be bought on boarding: a single fare costs $2 (valid for 1hr 30min); a Day Rover (all-day) ticket is $4.80 and Metro Tens are $15.20. The main bus interchange is outside on Elizabeth Street, or around the corner on Macquarie Street for buses south. The handy yellow-painted **Busy Bee bus** does a circuit from Franklin Square through Battery Point and up Sandy Bay Road to the casino and back again. Timetables with route maps are available from the Metroshop or can be downloaded as pdfs from the Hobart Metro website.

As well as buses, you can cross the Derwent River on a morning and evening commuter **ferry** run by Captain Fell's Historic Ferries (☎03/6223 5893, see p.75) from Brooke Street Pier, south of Elizabeth Pier, to Bellerive on the eastern shore (Mon–Fri 7.50am & 5.25pm from Sullivans Cove, 8.15am & 5.40pm from Bellerive; $4; 20min). Alternatively, the dinky Hobart Yellow Water Cab (☎0407 036 268) has an on-call service (9am–8pm) priced from only $10 per person.

You can hail a **taxi** on the street, or there are stands around the city; the most central one is outside the Town Hall on Elizabeth Street. For advance taxis try City Cabs (☎131 008), Taxi Combined Services (☎132 227) or Hobart and Southern Maxi Taxis (☎03/6227 9577).

Accommodation

There's plenty of **accommodation** in Hobart, but during the peak season from late December to the end of January, prices shoot up and places can be hard to find, especially from Boxing Day to the first week of January, when the yachties hit town for the Sydney–Hobart race. Be aware, too, that some hotels charge high-season rates until the end of March. City and dockside **hotels** are the best option for clean, affordable private accommodation, and there are an increasing number of **hostels**; in summer, student rooms are available for extended stays at Jane Franklin Hall in South Hobart (☎03/6223 2000). Battery Point has a decent quota of **B&Bs**, most on the pricey side, and several self-catering holiday **apartments**, with costs comparable to a medium-range motel. Most **motels** are south of here along Sandy Bay Road, or north of the city centre along the Brooker Highway, but are only worth considering for their convenience if you are arriving late by car – B&Bs and guesthouses tend to offer better value.

The city centre

Hostels and budget accommodation

Central City Backpackers 2nd Floor, 138 Collins St, entrance off Imperial Arcade ☏03/6224 2404 or 1800 811 507, ⓦwww.centralbackpackers .com.au. One of Hobart's best hostels – friendly, efficiently run and in the spacious quarters of a once-grand hotel. All dorms (three- to eight-bed, no bunks), singles ($49), twins and doubles are heated; linen rental is extra. Well-set-up kitchen, pleasant dining area, satellite TV and games rooms, Internet access and bike rental. No parking. Dorms $22–26, rooms ❸

Hobart Hostel Corner of Barrack and Goulburn streets ☏03/6234 6122, ⓦwww.hobarthostel .com. Created from a pub just down the road from *Narrara Backpackers*, this has a colourful spacious lounge and decent kitchen. Also has laundry, Internet access, luggage storage and bike hire. Simple clean dorms (ten- to twelve-bed) plus rooms, some en suite. Dorms $21, doubles ❸–❹

Montgomery's Private Hotel & YHA 9 Argyle St ☏03/6231 2660, ⓦwww.montgomerys.com.au. Not as spacious as *Central City* nor as good value, but a decent hostel in the central business district nevertheless, with YHA discounts. Six-, eight- and twelve-bed dorms and rather pricey doubles, some en suites and disabled-friendly. Small kitchen and laundry, bike and luggage storage. Dorms $23–29, rooms ❹–❺

Narrara Backpackers 88 Goulburn St ☏03/6231 3191, ⓦwww.narrarabackpackers.com. A small hostel with an amiable live-in manager and a communal vibe. The snug common room has a big table and comfy sofas, and there's a decent, well-equipped kitchen. Dorms, twins, doubles and triples are all very clean. Internet access and off-street parking. Dorms $19, rooms ❷

New Sydney Hotel 87 Bathurst St ☏03/6234 4516, ⓦwww.newsydneyhotel.com. Clean, central and small backpackers' hostel above a pub with kitchen facilities and guest lounge, plus Internet access. Always lively, though noisy when bands play downstairs. Budget pub meals are also available. Parking $2 per day. Dorms $20, rooms ❷

The Pickled Frog Backpackers 281 Liverpool St ☏03/6234 7977, ⓦwww.thepickledfrog.com. Large hostel with young staff and a lively feel. The extensive communal area includes a bar/café, sofas, pool table, a wood fireplace, Internet access and kitchen. Simple, clean dorms (four- to eight-bed) and rooms; all have sinks and heating, though no storage. Light breakfast and linen included,

bedding extra. Bike rental. Parking available. Dorms $23–25, rooms ❸

Hotels and motels

Astor Private Hotel 157 Macquarie St ☏03/6234 6611, ⓦwww.astorprivatehotel.com.au. Central, old-fashioned, family-run hotel established in the 1920s. Rooms are comfy rather than classy, but are good value for location, especially if you opt for shared facilities. ❹–❺

Battery Point Manor 13-15 Cromwell St, Battery Point ☏03/6224 0888, ⓦwww.batterypointmanor .com.au. Rather pricey considering its somewhat old-fashioned flowery rooms, but you do get sea views and heritage appeal in a Georgian manor house dating from 1834. Good value in off-season too. ❻

Customs House Hotel Corner of Murray and Morrison streets, opposite Watermans Dock ☏03/6234 6645, ⓦwww.customshousehotel.com. A waterfront pub of 1846, stylishly modernized to provide all en-suite rooms. Excellent value for the location, though it is noisy at weekends, when bands often play in the pub downstairs. ❺

Grand Chancellor 1 Davey St ☏03/6235 4535 or 1800 753 379, ⓦwww.ghihotels.com. Ugly exterior but a great waterfront location and international four-star standards – you pay extra for harbour views, though those at the back look to the city centre and Mount Wellington. Facilities include two restaurants, two bars and a health club. ❻–❽

Hadley's Hotel 34 Murray St ☏03/6223 4355 or 1800 131 689, ⓦwww.hadleyshotel.com.au. National Trust-listed hotel in the central business district, well placed for the docks and Salamanca Place. A traditional old-fashioned feel complements four-star facilities: in-house restaurant, café, bistro and bar, room service, 24hr reception and free parking. ❻–❽

🏃 **Henry Jones Art Hotel** 25 Hunter St ☏03/6210 7700, ⓦwww.thehenryjones .com. Australia's most awarded hotel and a showpiece of Hobart's renaissance, a revamp of a nineteenth-century waterfront warehouse into a luxury hotel-cum-art gallery. Expect timber beams, sandstone walls, sensuous lighting, huge beds draped in silks, stunning wet-room bathrooms, and immaculate service everywhere. The restaurant, *Henry's*, and *IXL Long Bar* are very New York in feel. ❽

Lenna Corner of Salamanca Place and Runnymede streets ☏03/6232 3900, ⓦwww.lenna.com.au. Although not all rooms are in the National Trust-listed manor of a shipping magnate – most are in an adjacent modern block – all are elegant and modern, some with harbour views, and the location is superb. Also has slick contemporary penthouses for a splurge. ⑦–⑧

MidCity Corner of Elizabeth and Bathurst streets ⑦03/6234 6333, ⑩www.hobartmidcity.com.au. Bland chain hotel that's a reliable fallback nevertheless, reasonably priced for four-star standards and relatively central. ⑤

Prince of Wales 55 Hampden Rd, Battery Point ⑦03/6223 6355, ⑩www.princeofwaleshotel.net .au. An ugly modern pub in a great location, whose motel-style rooms (no phones) have views of the water or Mount Wellington. Guest laundry and parking. ⑤

Theatre Royal Hotel 31 Campbell St ⑦03/6234 6925, ⑩www.theatreroyalhotel.com. A basic hotel, but in a good position, with plain but presentable rooms, some en suite. Some singles are available, and a light breakfast is included. Excellent bar and bistro downstairs. ⑤

B&Bs and guesthouses

Colville Cottage 32 Mona St, Battery Point ⑦03/6223 6968, ⑩www.colvillecottage .com.au. Peaceful, Victorian weatherboard B&B, with a lovely garden and chintz-free period charm in en-suite rooms. The most charming address in Battery Point. ⑥

Edinburgh Gallery B&B 211 Macquarie St ⑦03/6224 9229, ⑩www.artaccom.com.au. Retro furniture and modern art lend a laid-back, funky vibe to this spacious historic house, which has an excellent communal kitchen and Internet access. Front rooms can suffer from traffic noise. ⑥

The Lodge on Elizabeth 249 Elizabeth St, corner of Warwick St ⑦03/6231 3830, ⑩www.thelodge .com.au. Delightful guesthouse in an elegant National Trust-listed 1829 mansion; guest lounge with fireplace, games and complimentary port. All rooms en suite, some with spa. Also offers a self-contained cottage with spa (min two nights). Rooms ⑤–⑥, cottage ⑥

Wellington Lodge 7 Scott St, Glebe ⑦03/6231 0614. A Victorian-era weatherboard B&B (cooked breakfast served) classified by the National Trust, close to Queens Domain and the city centre, and with a pretty rose garden. All rooms either en suite or with own private bathroom nearby. ④–⑤

Outside the centre

Hostels and budget accommodation

Adelphi Court YHA 17 Stoke St, New Town ⑦03/6228 4829, ⓔadelphi@yhatas.org.au.

Caravan parks and self-catering apartments

Corinda's Cottages 17 Glebe St, Glebe ⑦03/6234 1590, ⑩www.corindascottages .com.au. Probably the most enchanting address in Hobart – three convict-built servants' cottages around the cobbled yard of an Italianate manor whose old beams, antiques and bric-a-brac have bags of country character. Hard to believe central Hobart is only ten minutes away. ⑦–⑧

Mantra One Sandy Bay Road 1 Sandy Bay Rd ⑦03/6221 6000, ⑩www.onesandybayroad.com .au. Built in late 2007, these modern open-plan apartments have kitchenette and laundry plus Internet access. Great value considering the location near Salamanca Place. ⑤–⑥

The Old Woolstore 1 Macquarie St ⑦1800 814676, ⑩www.oldwoolstore.com.au. Well placed near the waterfront, close to major transport routes and with ample parking space. Has executive-friendly, hotel-style studios and apartments (one- to three-bed), a little bland but all with flat-screen TV, DVD, laundry and fast Internet access. ⑤–⑧

St Ives Hotel Apartments 67 St Georges Terrace, off Sandy Bay Rd, Battery Point ⑦03/6224 1044, ⑩www.stivesmotel.com.au. Two-level two-bedroom apartments with full kitchen, TV/dining room, and bathrooms with tubs. Generally, the decor is motel-style – some apartments are like standard motel rooms, but with full kitchen. All have balconies with water views. Rooms ④, apartments ⑤–⑥

Somerset on the Pier Elizabeth St Pier ⑦03/6220 6600 or 1800 766 377, ⑩www .somersetonthepier.com. Sea views guaranteed in a dockside apartment hotel – gorgeous split-level, spacious and light-flooded studio and one-bedroom apartments. Some have balconies, all have kitchen and laundry, and there's a gym and sauna. Similar in style and price is *Somerset on Salamanca*, above Salamanca Place. Both ⑧

Zero Davey Corner of Hunter and Davey streets ⑦03/6270 1444 or 1300 733 422, ⑩www .escapesresorts.com.au. Slick modern apartments, from studios to three-bedroom, with bright acid-drop colour accents, hi-tech toys, and a superb location by the waterfront; some have balconies over Victoria Dock. ⑦–⑧

Modern, motel-like hostel and guesthouse arranged around a courtyard, with the usual facilities. In the suburbs 2.5km north of the city, though a 10min walk to North Hobart's restaurant strip and with plenty of parking. Buses #15 or #16 from Argyle Street, or #25–42, #100 or #105–128 from Elizabeth Street. Dorms $21–28, rooms ❸–❹

Hotels and motels

Clydesdale Manor 292 Sandy Bay Rd, Sandy Bay ☏03/6223 7289, ⓦwww.clydesdalemanor.com.au. No children are allowed in this smart four-star manor in salubrious Sandy Bay. The style is heritage without the chintz – spa rooms have balconies onto the garden. Charming owners, too. ❻–❼

🏃 **Islington Hotel** 321 Davey St ☏03/6220 2123, ⓦwww.islingtonhotel.com. A luxury boutique hotel in an 1840s manor that simply oozes class. The sumptuous style is an effortless blend of eclectic modern design and colonial antiques and the views of Mount Wellington from the modern conservatory are jaw-dropping. Less a hotel than an aristocratic retreat and the most glamorous address in Hobart. ❽

Wrest Point Hotel 410 Sandy Bay Rd, Sandy Bay ☏03/6225 0112, ⓦwww.wrestpoint.com.au. Attached to the casino, this upmarket hotel has riverside rooms, heated indoor pool, sauna and 24hr room service. Luxury tower or cheaper motel section. ❻–❽

Caravan parks and self-catering apartments

Graham Court Apartments 15 Pirie St, New Town ☏03/6278 1333, ⓦwww.grahamcourt.com.au. Comfortable, well-equipped one- to three-bedroom self-contained apartments set in a pleasant garden, but 2.5km north of the city centre. Disabled access. ❹–❺

The Pavilions Moorilla, 655 Main Rd, Berriedale ☏03/6277 9900, ⓦwww.moorilla.com.au. Coastal style in a city location. Luxury one- and two-bed units of this prestigious wine estate have cantilevered balconies that hang over the river, while inside are artwork or antiquities, Smeg applicances and vast spa bath. Think coastal style in a city location. Effortless indulgence. ❽

Treasure Island Caravan Park 671 Main Rd, Berriedale ☏03/6249 2379. The best site in the Hobart area is this large park 14km northwest of the centre on the banks of the Derwent River; there's a camp kitchen and pool. Vans ❷, en-suite cabins ❸

Central Hobart

The focus of Hobart is **Sullivans Cove**, once a bay thick with teatree scrub and towering eucalyptus where the settlement was established in 1804, now fronted by harbours whose crayfishing fleets lend a down-to-earth tang to some increasingly flash development. The original shoreline of the cove runs roughly beneath the east end of Macquarie Street, angling onto Davey Street by **Constitution Dock**, while **Hunter Street** more or less follows a sandbar that ran from the Hobart Rivulet mouth to Hunter Island. It served as foundations for the colony's first sandstone wharf, created by convict labour in the early 1820s.

The docks makes for a logical place to start an exploration of Hobart. Just loafing around with a drink or a plate of fish and chips is one of Hobart's great pleasures. South of the docks, **Salamanca Place** is a charismatic strip of galleries, restaurants and pubs in a Georgian setting, and behind is the nineteenth-century "village" of **Battery Point**. The commercial centre is rather tawdry by comparison, at its best around historic **Franklin Square** and the excellent **Tasmanian Museum and Art Gallery**.

Along Hunter Street

Hobart Town made its debut on Hunter Street. Brass medallions embedded in the street mark the path of the sandbar along which settlers disembarked and the first wharf was built. More than 65,000 convicts stepped ashore here and murderers swung from a gallows erected by the dock. It was also the base for the town's first pioneer merchants – contemporary sketches depict the **Drunken Admiral** restaurant as one of the original warehouses to appear on the wharf in the 1820s. But as the colony grew wealthier and the New Wharf freed up land, these were replaced by flour mills and factories. Largely derelict in the late 1990s, these have been renovated to create a complex of stylish **bars and galleries** of Aboriginal art and wood design, whose centrepiece is the luxury *Henry Jones Art Hotel*, formerly a jam factory of Henry Jones & Co's IXL company. Its name is derived from the jam magnate's motto "I excel at everything I do" and Jones capped an already considerable fortune by producing apricot jams for ANZAC rations – apparently much of the land behind the warehouses was reclaimed using millions of discarded apricot stones. A **hotel tour** that includes a free glass of champagne (5.30pm Fri; free) explains the renovation process, or you can ask the concierge for permission to ascend a blackwood staircase that led up to Jones's offices, where you can see 3D stereoscopic images of the renovation process.

A clincher in the planning authority's decision to grant the renovation tender to a local development team was its pledge to display the work of students at the University of Tasmania's **Centre for the Arts** just along from the hotel. In a courtyard beyond the original facade is the art school (daily 8.30am–5pm; free), an architecturally striking factory conversion which is flooded with light, carved up by beams and has the odd flywheel and pulley embedded in the ceiling. Also here is the **Sir James Plimsoll Gallery** (daily noon–5pm when there is an exhibition; free), which has several shows a year of contemporary Tasmanian artists.

Around the docks

Just as Hunter Street is still thriving, so are its docks. Crayfishing boats are moored in **Victoria Dock**, named in 1840 to honour the new queen of England, albeit not actually formed as a separate harbour for another fifty years. The bronze at its back commemorates Belgian-born, Tassie-raised **Louis Bernacchi**, the first Australian to over-winter in the Antarctic and the chief scientist on Captain Scott's *Discovery* expedition to the South Pole – he wisely declined the offer to join Scott's subsequent ill-fated 1906 adventure, citing family duties. Adjacent **Constitution Dock** is a local institution for fish and chips, eaten at punts moored alongside – relics of those from which fishermen sold their catch – or at *Mures* restaurant complex. It also holds a small fleet of historic craft, the most impressive of which is the *May Queen*, Australia's oldest existing sailing trader (1867), which transported timber from logging settlements on the Huon River. The stately sandstone building opposite is the former **Customs House**, a Neoclassical pile from the early 1900s whose statues at either end salute exports of Tasmanian merino wool and grain. Now holding a wing of the Tasmanian Museum and Art Gallery (see p.80), the building envelops an original brick **bond store** (1824), which is only visible in the rear courtyard and houses temporary exhibitions.

On the corner of Davey Street opposite Constitution Dock, the modest **Maritime Museum of Tasmania** (daily 9am–5pm; $6; Ⓦwww.maritimetas .org), in the red-brick Carnegie Building, provides a fairly engaging introduction to Hobart's maritime heritage – taking in whaling, shipbuilding and Naval duties once you get past some dull information boards. Themed displays feature an enjoyable clutter of memorabilia and photographs, with some excellent model boats (the most impressive is a third-scale model of an open whaling boat), although there's also the companionway hatch of the *Otago*, which ended as a hulk near Risdon Cove and whose master, Captain Korzeniowski, is better known as author Joseph Conrad.

Back at the docks, the **Lark Distillery** (Ⓣ03/6231 9088, Ⓦwww .larkdistillery.com.au) offers tastings and sales of its single-malt whiskies plus intermittent cellar tours, while further south, **Elizabeth Street Pier** has been jazzed up with some stylish bars, eateries and hotel-apartments. As such the

Hobart looks its best from the water. "The voyage up the Derwent displays a grand succession of fairy visions in its entire length unequalled", Mark Twain wrote, and Agatha Christie's daydreams of emigrating to "incredibly beautiful Hobart" were founded on "its deep blue sea and harbour". As well as the cruises listed here, shorter cheap trips are available on commuter ferries, by chartering a water taxi (see p.70), or on organized kayak trips (see p.94).

Captain Fell's Historic Ferries Brooke St Pier ☏03/6223 5893, ⊛www.captain fellshistoricferries.com.au. A range of good-value harbour cruises on the *MV Emmalisa*, all of which include meals of some kind ($17–30). Also has a combined double-decker bus and harbour cruise (return leg) tour to the Cadbury's factory in the suburb of Claremont for $50 (departs Mon–Fri 10am or noon), which includes lunch and wine.

The Cruise Company Brooke St Pier ☏03/6234 9294. Their Cadbury's Cruise heads upriver on a ferry to the chocolate factory (Mon–Fri 10am; 4hr; $50 includes factory tour).

Lady Nelson Elizabeth St Pier ☏03/6234 3348, ⊛www.ladynelson.org.au. This replica of the brig in which Lieutenant John Bowen brought the first European settlers into the Derwent in 1803, is a sail-training vessel, but also offers bargain pleasure-trips most weekends year-round (usually 11am and 4.30pm; 1hr 30min; $10).

Navigators Brooke St Pier ☏03/6223 1914, 03/6224 0033 or 1300 134 561, ⊛www .navigators.net.au. Two historic boats and two state-of-the-art catamarans run a variety of coastal and harbour cruises. Short cruises start from $22; a trip to Moorilla Estate Winery costs $35. The trip to Port Arthur travels along the stunning, rugged coastline on the *MV Marana*, a 25-metre fast catamaran (departs 8am Wed, Fri & Sun, no service June–Sept; 2hr 30min cruising, 3hr 30min at Port Arthur; site entry fee and return coach to Hobart leaving at 4pm included, plus morning tea; $150, without return coach $70).

The Peppermint Bay Cruise Brooke St Pier ☏1300 137 919, ⊛www.hobartcruises .com.au. Spectacular cruise on a luxury catamaran (May–Sept Mon, Wed & Fri–Sun 11.30am; Oct–April daily noon; from $78; gourmet-platter lunch included), south along the Derwent River and the D'Entrecasteaux Channel past Bruny Island to Woodbridge, where there's a shore excursion to the stylish *Peppermint Bay Hotel*.

Wild Thing Adventures ☏03/6224 2021, ⊛www.wildthingadventures.com.au. Options for harbour and coastal cruises priced from $25 to $165 on a Ferrari-red powerboat include a tour of Moorilla Estate Winery and a Monday-only circumnavigation of Bruny Island (Oct–April; dress warmly whatever the weather).

Windeward Bound Elizabeth St Pier ☏0418 127243 or 0409 961327, ⊛www .windewardbound.com.au. Stately three-hour lunch cruises aboard Tassie's largest tall ship, a 33-metre brigantine (Thurs–Sun; $60). A volunteer-run charity organization, with all profits going to disadvantaged young people.

pier provides a quintessentially Hobart blend of contemporary sophistication and working fishing port – a drink or meal here is a classic modern Hobart experience. Unless out on a cruise, the *Lady Nelson*, a replica of the brig that brought the first settlers, is moored alongside. Brooke Street Pier and Watermans Dock further south are more traditional affairs, backed by the four-square buildings of the former Marine Board and the embarkation points for many **harbour cruises**.

Salamanca Place

Renowned for its galleries and good eating and drinking, not to mention a Saturday market, **Salamanca Place** is Hobart at its best, comfortably knotting together the threads of colonial heritage, arts and a quirky individuality in a convivial unpretentious setting. The street was laid to celebrate England's naval victory against Spain in 1812, but it took another two decades before the parade of Georgian buildings began to go up. They were created as merchant warehouses and shipping offices to service the New Wharf (now **Princes Wharf**), which itself was built to service a booming whaling industry and boost the export trade. Frequented by volatile frontiersmen, the area soon became notorious for grog and brawls. A near-riot erupted when a hundred single women (in short supply in the new colony) were disembarked in 1832 on a half-day holiday for convicts – probably not the wisest day for it.

▲ Salamanca Place

With the wane of the port in the 1950s, the warehouses became rundown and depressed. There were plans to raze the lot, until proposals were made for their restoration in the 1970s as a complex of arts-and-crafts galleries, speciality boutiques and cafés. A couple of good pubs keep things down to earth – *Knopwood's Retreat* pub is probably as popular today as it was in the 1830s, when it was a boozer for whalers and sailors. The strip also hosts the open-air **Salamanca Market** on Saturday (8am–3pm), arguably Hobart's biggest single attraction and an excellent spot to browse for crafts, particularly woodwork using Tasmanian timber (often recycled). There are also lots of bric-a-brac and secondhand books and clothes, and wonderful food stalls.

It's worth exploring the narrow lanes and arcades off Salamanca Place to hunt out the less obvious arts-and-crafts outlets, and find the **Salamanca Arts Centre** (Ⓦwww.salarts.org.au), the base for a diverse range of arts-based organizations in a former jam-canning factory. Downstairs is the Peacock Theatre, and upstairs are galleries (daily 10am–5pm), with emerging Tassie artists in the Long Gallery and smaller displays in adjacent gallery Sidespace. Bands play in the rear courtyard on Fridays (from 6pm), making it a popular spot to start the weekend. Woobies Lane, off Salamanca Place, leads to **Salamanca Square**, a rather bland space with luxury apartments strung along the quarry where convicts hewed the stone that built the warehouses. This is prime retail (and recently office) space, and as such is mostly taken by modern shops and café-bars, with a few chains; worth checking out is the Hobart Bookshop, which has an excellent array of books on Tasmania old and new.

State parliament and St David's Park

Heading west uphill on Salamanca Place, the **state parliament** built by colonial architect John Lee Archer was intended as Hobart's first Customs House; when built on reclaimed marshland in the late 1830s, ships tied up beneath the balustrade at the bottom of what is now Parliament Square. Guided tours (Mon & Fri, 10am & 2pm; free) go into the debating hall when parliament is not in session and descend to a museum, whose exhibits on Tasmanian politics are less interesting than the vaulted brick room that was once the bond store. Local historians are divided on whether a tunnel that runs between the store and the *Customs House Hotel* opposite was for smuggling or convenience. Security guards will usually escort you to the museum at other times if they are free. Opposite the parliament is **St David's Park**. The hillside expanse originated as the colony's first cemetery, but by the mid-1800s it had become an odious, weed-choked place into which criminals bolted to evade the police, some even by hiding in collapsed graves. Grave slabs of early settlers, which were rescued during the transformation of the cemetery into a late-Victorian park, are mounted in a remembrance wall at the bottom of the park. A large sandstone memorial uphill commemorates Hobart founder Lieutenant-governor David Collins. Although the first church on the spot was blown away in a gale in 1811, he still lies beneath in a near-imperishable casket of Huon pine.

Through the park's northeast gate on Davey Street is Australia's oldest **real tennis court**, built in 1875, which a settler created from the stables behind his house. With luck, you might catch a game of the arcane tennis-squash hybrid that predates tennis in play (9am–4pm Mon–Sat; free) – you sit in netted galleries as players bounce a ball off the side and back walls. You can also book a lesson with the club pro (Ⓣ03/6231 1781; racket hire available).

Battery Point

The cat's cradle of streets above Salamanca Place is **Battery Point**, a quaint inner-city village with an enduring bygone atmosphere. Though occupied early by Reverend "Bobby" Knopwood (see box below), the low hillside was not

Colonial characters of Battery Point

During the colony's formative years, Battery Point was known as Knopwood's Point after its owner, **Reverend Robert Knopwood**. One of Hobart Town's most colourful figures in what was a highly colourful era, "Bobbie" arrived in Tasmania with Lieutenant David Collins in 1804. His diary explains that "having been sixteen months three weeks and five days exposed to the inclemency of all weathers and continual robberies by convicts and servants" in a tent, he was granted a house on the low headland. Here he tended orchards and a vegetable garden – "the talk and envy of all colonists" he wrote – when not ministering to his flock or handing down notoriously severe sentences on convicts as the first magistrate. By 1824, he was forced to sell the headland at a knock-down rate to **Lieutenant-governor Arthur**. "Be it so known I was harshly and fraudulently deprived of this my garden and home by that blackguard Colonel George Arthur, who through the whiles of his toady solicitors acted to rob me under pretence of law", Knopwood railed in a protest pinned to a pub on Salamanca Place (and reproduced outside the *Knopwood's Retreat* pub). In truth, Knopwood could only blame himself for his financial ruin. Renowned as a sportsman cleric even while studying in the English ministry, he had a weakness for tobacco and liquor, and his bills suggest he was fond of entertaining. In addition, a churchman who paraded on a white horse wearing a scarlet dresscoat and cocked hat was anathema to an evangelical disciplinarian such as Arthur. A prima donna in the larrikin early years of the colony, Knopwood had been overtaken by events and became a victim of attempts to bring the early colony to heel by reducing the excesses of its garrulous settlers. Knopwood died bitter and penniless in 1838 on the east bank, and was buried in St Matthew's Church, Rokeby.

It's probable that Knopwood knew **James Kelly**. A first-generation Australian, born in Paramatta, near Sydney, in 1791, Kelly was apprenticed on a ship from the age of 13 and became Australia's first Master Mariner in 1809. He captained Bass Strait sealing expeditions and was wrecked for eighteen months on Macquarie Island before he washed up in Hobart Town. It was the making of him. In December 1815, he rowed down the Derwent and into history on a **circumnavigation of Tasmania** in a 25-foot whaling boat named *Elizabeth* after his wife. In theory, the swashbuckling trip was a prospecting expedition for Huon pine on behalf of a timber merchant. But with the insouciance of a 24-year-old at the top of his game, Kelly scattered names of governors and friends behind him – the first European to enter Macquarie Harbour, he named the Gordon River after his friend who loaned him the boat, James Gordon. Thanks to Kelly, the west coast was opened up to pioneers – and convicts – with catastrophic results for the indigenous Aborigines.

Back in Hobart Town, Kelly cut a dashing figure: he was a whaling captain and master sailor who hunted down escaped convicts in his brig *Sophia*, or transported prisoners to the new penitentiary on Maria Island. He drew up a small fleet and served as the pilot and harbourmaster of the Derwent River, based at Battery Point; later he built Kellys Steps as a short cut home from the quay. Though his name is recalled by that staircase off Salamanca Place, as well as Kelly Point (Bruny Island) and Kelly Basin (Macquarie Harbour), he is a forgotten character today. Family tragedies and economic depression in the 1830s and 1840s forced him to sell up and he become just another employee of the port authorities. Worse, he watched as peers reaped the gains of the industry he had founded. He died suddenly in 1859 and was buried in a family vault in today's David's Park.

settled until the late 1820s, thanks to a legal sleight of hand that delivered the area to Lieutenant-governor Arthur. He advertised "delectable building sites that will inevitably become the resort of the Beau Monde". Paintings of the early 1850s depict a few manor houses, St George's Church and a windmill, but with the boom in trade on the New Wharf came a rollicking community of dockers, sailors and whalers, making Battery Point synonymous with brawls and robbery. At the same time, the area acquired its engaging mix of port workers' cottages and fine merchants' and sea captains' houses. Inevitably the area is gentrifying rapidly, and the cottages now command the highest prices per square metre in Tasmania.

The quickest access from Salamanca Place is by **Kellys Steps**. The staircase was built by Captain James Kelly (see box opposite) as a short cut between his home and the wharf. You can also follow the road east around to **Princes Park**, where there's a lone fruit tree in the car park in honour of Reverend Knopwood. The raised bluff was the site of gun emplacements that give Battery Point its name and were upgraded whenever the isolated colony got the jitters about invasion by Britain's contemporary enemies – French and American whalers in 1841, Russians during the Crimean campaign of 1854. All defences were lambasted as "next to useless" by the itinerant lieutenant-governor, not helped by the forts' commanders spending more money on uniforms, pay and prizes than on guns. The squat white house downhill in the park, the oldest remaining building in Battery Point (1818), was the signalman's residence for the adjacent semaphore, the last node in a relay chain that stretched to Port Arthur via Mount Nelson.

The kernel of Battery Point, where Lieutenant-governor Arthur sold his first plots of land, is **Arthurs Circus**, a miniature England realized as a twee village green ringed by tiny cottages. It opens on to the village high street **Hampden Road**, lined with fine nineteenth-century houses and a growing number of smart restaurants. Off its west end, De Witt Street leads to Cromwell Street and **St George's Church,** the finest Greek Revival church in Australia. The church was an exercise in solidity by the early colony's star architects: John Lee Archer completed the nave in 1838; convict James Blackburn added the octagonal belltower in 1847. Another early building – one of the first in the Salamanca area – is the **Georgian manor** further west at 103 Hampden Road. It was built in 1836 by a Scottish sea captain who used ship's ballast as facing stone. As **House-Museum Narryna** (Mon in summer & Tues–Fri all year 10.30am–5pm, Sat & Sun 2–5pm; $6; ☎03/6234 2791), it is furnished with a collection of colonial antiques and *objet d'art* donated by members of Tasmania's pioneer families.

Turn left at the end of Hampden Street and it's a 500-kilometre walk to **Anglesea Barracks**, the oldest still in use in Australia (since 1814) and whose jail (Tues 9am–1pm, Thurs 9am–noon; $5; free tour of barracks from entrance gate Tues 11am) holds a museum of military history in Tasmania.

Around Franklin Square

Leafy **Franklin Square** is the civic heart of Hobart, a function unchanged since Lieutenant-Colonel David Collins established the first officers' encampment on its low hill above Sullivans Cove. A parade ground and muster point for convicts in early years, the square had its military past air-brushed out with the establishment of a park here in the late 1800s as the colony stabilized. At the same time it was boxed in by the slab-sided Italianate government offices to the south and the Town Hall to the north, the latter on the site where the ever-present Bobbie Knopwood conducted the colony's first church service on

February 26, 1804. The square's name derives from the imposing statue of Sir John Franklin, governor of Van Diemen's Land between 1837 and 1843, although more famous posthumously as an Arctic explorer whose ill-fated expedition in 1845 vanished while trying to find the Northwest Passage.

A short way west on Macquarie Street is **St David's Cathedral**. Built in the 1860s using local sandstone and native stringy bark, Huon pine and blackwood timbers, its design – arguably the most perfect neo-Gothic church in Australia – is from the drawing board of George Frederick Bodley, the architect behind the cathedrals of Liverpool, San Francisco and Washington DC. He also designed the intricate oak rood screen that divides choir from congregation. Beyond a small display of Boer War colours and historical records in the cloisters is the belltower. If inspecific plans to open it up to visitors come to anything, it will provide great views of Hobart's roofscape.

Going the other way from Franklin Square you pass the **post office**. In 1912, **Roald Admundsen** stood beneath its clocktower to announce his conquest of the South Pole to a largely unimpressed local crowd. It was just the latest insult from Hobartians to the Norwegian explorer. A few days earlier he had returned triumphant from the South Pole only to get the cold shoulder from the receptionist at *Hadley's Hotel* on Murray Street – "Treated like a tramp… given a miserable little room", he chuntered in his diary.

A little further, on the corner of Macquarie and Argyle streets, **Ingle Hall** is the only Georgian townhouse to survive in the city centre and one of the few left in Australia, built by an anonymous but evidently successful merchant in 1814.

The Tasmanian Museum and Art Gallery

Behind the Town Hall on Macquarie Street is the excellent **Tasmanian Museum and Art Gallery** (daily 10am–5pm; free but charges for some exhibitions; free guided tours Wed–Sun 2.30pm and audio guides available; Ⓦwww.tmag.tas.gov.au). As the name suggests, its collection is a mixed bag of Tasmaniana that takes in the tragic history of penal cruelty and persecution of the Aborigines, alongside light relief of native fauna, colonial art and South Polar research. It is also subject to a rolling $30 million redevelopment programme.

Downstairs, a dull taxidermy display of native species is enlivened by video footage of the last captive **Tasmanian tiger** (thycaline), which died in captivity in Hobart's Beaumaris Zoo in 1936. There's also a stuffed example and, occasionally, a unique, eight-skinned **thylacine rug** made in the late 1890s and purchased in a share-deal with Launceston's Queen Victoria Museum and the Federal Hotels chain. The museum is scheduled to shift its **Tasmanian Aboriginal exhibits** to an adjacent room by late 2008, to provide more insight into the Aborigines' traditional and contemporary practices, tragic near-extermination and modern land-rights campaigns. Upstairs there's an excellent section on **convicts** – a decent overview if you're not going to Port Arthur – and a fine collection of donated **Chinese art and porcelain**. Beyond is a gallery of **colonial art**: Benjamin Duterrau's famous depiction of tubby negotiator George Augustus Robinson greeting a tribe, *The Conciliation*, is here, as are portraits of the infamous "final" Aborigines, including Manalargenna and Truganini, and there are superb images of Tasmanian scenery and early Hobart Town by the nineteenth-century artists John Glover and W.C. Piguenit, who are indebted to English Romantic landscape painting and French Impressionism respectively. Don't miss, too, an excellent room on Tasmania's South Pole connections, "Islands to Ice", that takes in Antarctic ecology and exploration.

A little further along Macquarie Street, the **Hope & Anchor** has a good claim to being the oldest continuously open pub in Australia. That the pub opened its doors just three years after the longboats were first hauled out of the Hobart Rivulet nearby (and which still runs beneath the pavement) speaks volumes about local priorities.

North of Macquarie Street

There are a handful of worthwhile sights behind the centre of town on the ruler-straight streets that head uphill from the harbour. The **Theatre Royal**, on Campbell Street at the corner of Sackville Street, is Australia's oldest surviving theatre, opened in 1837 to great fanfare in the *Hobart Mercury* newspaper. Nöel Coward, who called it "a dream of a theatre", and Laurence Olivier performed in the intimate Regency-style auditorium, which was meticulously rebuilt after a fire in 1984, albeit without an original pub beneath the stalls whose boozy maelstrom of freed convicts, sailors and prostitutes once appalled theatre-goers. It is best seen during a performance (see "Listings", p.91), though the staff might let you in for a peek. Further up, at the corner of Brisbane Street, the **Penitentiary Chapel and Criminal Courts** (daily tours except Aug 10am, 11.30am, 1pm & 2.30pm; 1hr; $8; ☎03/6231 0911, ⓦwww.penitentiarychapel.com) is another creation of colonial architect John Lee Archer, its complex of court-rooms, tunnels and solitary confinement cells buried in the foundations of the

---

Beaches in the Hobart area

The various beaches are ordered here by distance from the centre; none is more than an hour's drive away. Note that only skeleton bus services run on Sundays, if at all, and that Clifton Beach requires careful planning or a two-kilometre walk from the turn-off. Bus services to the Tasman Peninsula enforce an overnight stay for Pirates Bay, while you'll need your own transport for Fortescue Bay.

Bellerive A passable crescent on the east bank if you're desperate for sand between your toes, though water quality can be poor – make a day of it by travelling across by commuter ferry; see p.85.

Kingston and Blackmans Bay A coastal vibe with an urban buzz in the southern commuter belt, which means good bus services, good eating and a couple of smaller coves if you're prepared to walk; see p.102.

Snug A mellow village-resort south of Margate. Gets busy in the school summer holidays but its long stretch of silvery sands is never crowded; see p.123.

Seven Mile Beach At the head of Storm Bay and as long as its name suggests; good for idle weekend strolls and prime dog-walking territory; see p.107.

Clifton Beach Closed by cliff headlands, this long beach, the local surf break for Hobartians, is patrolled by lifeguards at summer weekends. Calverts Beach in a reserve further south is wilder. No amenities, so bring a picnic; see p.107.

South Arm and Opposum Bay Two mellow villages on the hook east of Hobart and two pretty arcs of sheltered sand, though both reduce to a sliver at high tide. Less developed South Arm has a general store to hand, while Opposum Bay, backed by holiday homes, is more protected; see p.107.

Pirates Bay, Eaglehawk Neck Silky sands enclosed by bush-cloaked hills, turquoise water, penal history to ponder, and sea caves and rock formations a short stroll away; see p.110.

Fortescue Bay In the national park and perfect for an overnighter. A hauntingly beautiful crescent of bleached sand and pristine sea, with wildlife scampering in the bush and a handful of short walks to pass an afternoon. Tassie in a nutshell; see p.112.

best-preserved convict building in Hobart. When completed in 1831, the complex's church was intended for use by free settlers, but they objected to the sounds of cursing and chains beneath the floorboards. It's worth saving a visit for the **ghost tour** (nightly 8pm or 8.30pm depending on season; $10; 1hr; bookings essential on ☎0417 361392).

Three blocks behind Macquarie Street, on the corner of Murray and Bathurst streets, the **State Library** (Mon–Thurs 9.30am–6pm, Fri 9.30am–8pm, Sat 9.30am–12.30pm; ⓦwww.statelibrary.tas.gov.au) holds the **Allport Library and Museum of Fine Arts** (Mon–Fri 9.30am–5pm, last Sat of month 9.30am–2.30pm, until 12.30pm in Jan; free). A local family's private collection of eighteenth- and nineteenth-century furnishings, ceramics, silver and glass, paintings, prints and rare books relating to Australia and the Pacific, it was given as a bequest to the library in 1965. The library also has a great little café at ground level.

Queens Domain and the Royal Tasmanian Botanical Gardens

A former hunting ground of the Mouhenener Aborigines, **Queens Domain** is a sparse, bush-covered hill just north of the centre traversed by walking and jogging tracks. Unfortunately, "the Domain" is also sandwiched between two busy highways, although its width means you may only suffer one at a time. At the base of the hill on the Derwent, where the trees suddenly become lush and green near the Tasman Bridge, are the **Royal Tasmanian Botanical Gardens** (daily Oct–Mar 8am–6.30pm, Sept & Apr 8am–5.30pm, May–Aug 8am–5pm; free; ☎03/6236 3075, ⓦwww.rtbg.tas.gov.au), a formal collection of flowers and manicured borders with the usual arboretum, lily pond and conservatory, and also a unique house of sub-Antarctic plants. Pick up a leaflet of the gardens' features at the north or south entrance, or from the **Botanical Discovery Centre** at the main entrance on the west side of the park (same times; free), where you'll find interactive exhibits as well as an **information centre**, café and restaurant with lovely views. There's a secondary entrance on the north of the gardens by the river.

Follow Domain Road south of the gardens and you pass the iron gates of Beaumaris Zoo, where the last captive Tasmanian tiger died in 1936. From here you'll get a good view of the neo-Gothic **Government House** (1858), which locals claim is Queen Elizabeth's favourite government building. Fans of Battery Point should also detour west of the Domain to **Glebe**, another villagey corner of the city with fine nineteenth-century architecture.

It's an easy walk to the Domain via Davey Street or through a rose garden beyond Liverpool Street, but the gardens are deceptively far inside: allow thirty minutes to get from the city centre to the gardens. A dedicated Metro bus (stop F on Elizabeth St) goes direct, or bus #17 or any of those for the Eastern Shore will drop you at Government House, though they do not make the return journey.

The suburbs

Steep surrounding hillsides pool Hobart's suburbs into a red-and-green-roofed sea alongside the Derwent estuary. Beyond a vibrant nightlife strip in North Hobart, **Glenorchy** is a heartland of Tasmanian suburbia; a forgettable sprawl of residential housing and light industry with only a few sights to quicken the pulse en route to a chocolate factory at Claremont. The mellow east-bank suburbs around **Bellerive** are not especially memorable either, but provide a

HOBART SUBURBS

ACCOMMODATION
Adelphi Court YHA	D
Clydesdale Manor	F
Graham Court Apartments	C
Islington Hotel	E
The Pavilions	B
Treasure Island Caravan Park	A
Wrest Point Hotel	G

RESTAURANTS
Cornelian Bay Boathouse	1
Flathead	3
Lebrina	2
Macquarie Street Foodstore	4
The Metz	5
Prosser's on the Beach	6
The Source	B

Cadbury Chocolate Factory

RIVER DERWENT

New Norfolk & Bridgewater

Mount Direction

Ridson Brooke Reservoir

Moorilla Estate Winery & Museum

Ellis Point

Otago

Meehan Range Recreational Park

RISDON VALE

Bowen Bridge

Risdon

Dowsings Point

B35

Royal Showground

GLENORCHY

B32

LUTANA

GEILSTON BAY

Cambridge

WEST MOONAH

cycle track

Selfs Point

cycle track

LINDISFARNE

Runnymede

Cornelian Bay

Lindisfarne Bay

ROSE BAY

A3

LENAH VALLEY

NEW TOWN

B36

Tasman Bridge

ROSNY

NORTH HOBART

Royal Tasmanian Botanical Gardens

Kangaroo Bay

BELLERIVE

See Central Hobart map

HOBART

Kangaroo Bluff Battery

Wellington Park

The Springs and Mount Wellington walks

Cascade Brewery

Female Factory

SOUTH HOBART

SANDY BAY

Sandy Bay

RIVER DERWENT

Tours to Tasman Peninsula and Bruny Island

Sandy Bay Point

Waterworks Reservoirs

LOWER SANDY BAY

Ridgeway Park

Fern Tree

Mount Nelson Signal Station

B68

Truganini Conservation Area

A6

N

0   2 km

Kingston

Taroona

pleasant cycle ride along the foreshore to a beach – or cricket match. Things get smarter when you go south of the centre into South Hobart, gateway to the Cascade brewery, or salubrious **Sandy Bay** spread along the waterfront beneath Mount Nelson. Behind both is **Mount Wellington**, an exhilarating slice of wilderness on Hobart's doorstep.

North of the centre: North Hobart to Claremont

The old colony's route north, Elizabeth Street heads up out of the centre into **North Hobart**, a laidback locals' hangout with an excellent strip of restaurants and one of the city's best live music pubs, the *Republic Bar*. In New Town beyond, marooned among bland residential housing, you'll come across the elegant Georgian manor of **Runnymede** (Mon–Fri 10am–4.30pm, Sat–Sun noon–4.30pm; $8). The rambling pile set in mature gardens was built by the colony's first lawyer, Robert Pitcairn, a Scotsman who led the push to end transportation. After a brief stint in the hands of the colony's first Anglican bishop, whose liberal attitudes were frowned on by civic authorities, the house came to Charles Bayley, a whaling magnate rumoured to dabble in opium-running, and who renamed the manor after his favourite ship. His heirlooms and family portraits furnish the rooms to provide an image of aspirational colonial life in the mid-1800s. Buses #15 and #20 from central Hobart stop nearby. You could also **cycle** on a bitumen track alongside the **Derwent River**: it begins at the south end of the Domain by the Aquatic Centre and passes under the Tasman Bridge to pretty Cornelian Bay, before it cuts in towards Runnymede.

A couple of kilometres beyond New Town in Glenorchy, the **Royal Showground** hosts a large general goods and a secondhand market – worth a visit if you're passing on Sunday (8am–2pm), though not a special trip. Beyond is Berriedale and the **Moorilla Estate Winery**. Although the headland was planted with vines in 1958 – just what any Italian immigrant would do, founder Claudio Alcorso said – the current glamorous mix of Old World values and New World aesthetics is from owner David Walsh, a reclusive millionaire and ex-professional gambler whose skill is blackjack and passion is art. Rotating exhibits of his collection of Roman and Egyptian antiquities, ethnographic artefacts from Africa, and largely Australian modern art are displayed in a striking glass-and-steel building and are scheduled to be collated as the **MONA** (Museum of New Art) by 2009. Above the museum, you can taste the vineyard's fine cool-climate wines or a recent sideline into organic beers under the Moo Brew brand, and eat in a wonderful restaurant, *The Source*, with superb river views. Bus #X1 passes the estate or a cruise (see box, p.75) from Hobart centre allows a short stop.

Beyond Berriedale lies Claremont and the riverfront **Cadbury's Factory**, dating from 1921, when Hobart began to turn to light industry. Factory tours here were understandably popular (they included lots of chocolate tasting) but as this Guide went to press, tours were stopped due to health and safety concerns. For the latest information call ☎03/6249 0333. Buses #37, #38 or #39 go direct to the factory, as do two harbour cruises (see box, p.75). Signposted off the main road nearby in Claremont, **Alpenrail** (daily 9.30am–4.30pm; $12; ☎03/6249 3748, ⊚www.alpenrail.com.au) is a truly bizarre homage to Switzerland through model railway; it is on the route of bus #42.

East of the centre: Bellerive

The eastern side of the river is almost entirely residential – looking across the water you see bush-clad hills swell above a modest line of homes. The link between the two is the **Tasman Bridge**, an impressive span that's exhilarating to cross on a walkway. For over two years from January 1975, the bridge was put out of action after a twenty-thousand-tonne tanker bound for the zinc-smelting works crashed into it and destroyed two pylons. The *Lake Illawarra* is still at the bottom of the river, with its cargo of zinc concentrate, as are the bodies of the twelve victims, seven crew and five people who plunged off the bridge in their cars. The disaster not only cut the city in two, it forced east-bank commuters to make a fifty-kilometre drive into work until a Bailey bridge was completed at Risdon that December. The bridge was fully reopened in 1964 – unsurprisingly, a pilot is now a requisite for all shipping.

From Rosny on the east bank, a walking and cycling track hugs the shore to **Bellerive** (pronounced "Bell-*reev*-ee") 3km southeast. The suburb is nothing special, but the views from Kangaroo Bay across the river to Hobart and Mount Wellington behind are superb – unsurprisingly, it was a favourite location for colonial painters. The bay's yachtclub bar is also a pleasant spot for a break. There are more good views on the two-kilometre path south to **Kangaroo Bluff Battery**, the hilltop fort that was created in response to a Russian scare in the late nineteenth century – it was located to create a triangular crossfire with its counterparts at Sandy Bay (Alexandra Battery) and Battery Point. Like them, it never saw active service, but it alone retains the fortifications, including cannon from the Sandy Bay emplacement.

A little further south, there's a long, sandy **beach** at the Esplanade; some swim from it, although the water is somewhat polluted. The suburb is an occasional host to international test cricket (usually mid-Nov) at the modern **Bellerive Oval** on Derwent Street (tours Tues 10am; $7; ☏03/6282 0400, ⓦwww.tascricket.com.au), where there's also a museum on Tassie cricket (Tues–Thurs 10am–3pm, Fri 10am–noon; $2).

Commuter ferries from Brooke Street Pier to Kangaroo Bay (see box, p.70) provide an enjoyable alternative to the frequent buses for Bellerive from stands A and B on Elizabeth Street.

South of the centre: Sandy Bay and Mount Nelson

Leafy, well-heeled **Sandy Bay** is a pleasant riverfront twenty-minute walk south of Battery Point. Coming downhill, you cross the **Errol Flynn Reserve**. The Hollywood heartthrob was brought up in the suburb of South Hobart and fondly recalled its "apples, jams and rose-cheeked girls" in his memoirs. However, his reputation as something of a scoundrel meant civic authorities procrastinated until long after he was famous before they acknowledged him, and even then only with this picnic area. Further south is the Royal Yacht Club (where visitors can take a drink) and marina, which fills to capacity during the annual weekend **Sandy Bay Regatta** in January, when the river fills with boats and a funfair decamps to the waterfront. Beyond rises the incongruous 1970s high-rise of **Wrest Point**, whose casino (Fri–Sat 2pm–4am, Sun–Thurs 2pm–2am) and hotel complex has a rather dated idea of glitz, not helped by a clientele of older tourists who hog the slot machines. However, a revolving restaurant, *The Point*, offers stupendous views of the river and city – at the time of writing, one of Tasmania's most brilliant chefs, Luke Stepsys, was due to take charge – and on the water's edge bar-restaurant *Pier One* is a great place for a sundowner. Several buses go to Sandy Bay from the city centre, among them #52–56 and #60, #61 and #94.

South of Sandy Bay rise the thickly wooded slopes of **Mount Nelson** (340m). A signal station was established on its summit in 1811 to announce ships in Storm Bay and the D'Entrecasteaux Channel to the station at Battery Point, and also relay messages from Port Arthur. The signalman's residence has been converted into a café-restaurant (daily lunch and dinner) that provides an outstanding panorama of sea and hills – a great choice for a lazy lunch. To get to Mount Nelson, take buses #57, #58 or #157.

Inland to Mount Wellington

Heading inland, the route southwest towards Mount Wellington via Davey and Macquarie streets takes you through **South Hobart** – whose colonial mansions lure an upmarket professional set – and on to Cascade Road. Around 500m along it you come to pretty **Cascade Gardens** and nearby, on Degraves Street, the **Cascades Female Factory Historic Site**. A sandstone shell is all that remains of the prison complex built in 1827 to house recidivist convict women, who were set to work washing and sewing or unthreading old rope for ships' caulking. Interpretive boards tell their story and that of the Flash Mob, a renegade gang said to have hoisted their skirts during a visit of the governor's wife, Lady Jane Franklin. **Tours** to fund conservation (Mon–Fri 9.30am, plus Dec–April Mon–Fri 2pm; $10; 1hr 15min; bookings ℡03/6233 1559, ⓦwww .femalefactory.com.au) are available through the adjacent fudge factory and café (Mon–Fri Dec–Apr 9am–5pm or until 4pm May–Nov). You could also see the area via a theatre production, *Louisa's Walk*, performed as a walking tour (Sat–Mon 2pm; $22.50; booking essential; ℡03/6230 8233).

Beyond Cascade Gardens, the magnificent seven-storey **Cascade Brewery** is the oldest in Australia (1824). Grog was a problem in the early colony, yet Lieutenant-governor Arthur rubberstamped a brewery after founder Peter Degraves persuaded him that beer was a healthy alternative to strong spirits. The brewery still uses traditional methods and takes advantage of the pure spring water that cascades (of course) down Mount Wellington, channelled by a complex system of sluices and pipes after angry protests greeted Degraves's initial diversion of stream water. **Tours** (daily approx every hour summer, 10am & 1pm winter; $20; bookings essential on ℡03/6221 8300) are pretty active – there are 220 stairs and you're required to wear long trousers and enclosed shoes – but the reward is up to three glasses of draught beer in the renovated brewery manager's residence, where there's also a restaurant serving pub-style food. You can come for a drink without joining a tour, either at the bar or in a garden full of tree ferns – Degraves demanded that his drivers return from their West Coast deliveries with plants rather than empty lorries.

Buses #43, #44, #46, #47 or #49 (stop M from Elizabeth St) go to the brewery. Alternatively, you can walk or cycle to Cascades Gardens and past the Female Factory Historic Site along a path that follows the peaceful **Hobart Rivulet,** a two-kilometre route where you might see a platypus at dusk. The start is opposite the intersection of Collins and Molle streets; allow 45 minutes each way and be prepared for boggy conditions after rain.

Mount Wellington

In any image of Hobart, **MOUNT WELLINGTON** (1270m) looms in the background, a presence hardwired into the mindset of Hobartians, who know it simply as "the mountain" and gauge the day's weather by cloud cover on the summit. Its massive dolerite slab – Captain William Bligh named it Table Mountain before the name change to salute the duke who triumphed at Waterloo – also causes the rain-shadow that makes Hobart the second-driest

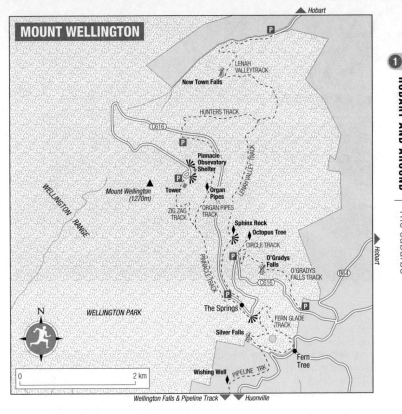

MOUNT WELLINGTON

Hobart

New Town Falls

LENAH VALLEY TRACK

HUNTERS TRACK

C616

Pinnacle Obsevatory Shelter

LEHAH VALLEY TRACK

Mount Wellington (1270m)

Tower

Organ Pipes

ZIG ZAG TRACK

ORGAN PIPES TRACK

WELLINGTON RANGE

Sphinx Rock

Octopus Tree

CIRCLE TRACK

O'Gradys Falls

O'GRADYS FALLS TRACK

B64

PINNACLE TRACK

C616

The Springs

Hobart

WELLINGTON PARK

N

FERN GLADE TRACK

Silver Falls

Fern Tree

0   2 km

Wishing Well

PIPELINE TRK

Wellington Falls & Pipeline Track   Huonville

state capital in Australia. Tourism has long been established on its slopes. In 1836 a young naturalist called Charles Darwin made the trek to its summit and in the 1930s bush lodge getaways were dotted throughout the temperate forest. Yet Hobartians remain highly protective of the wilderness so close to their city. The first summit road, a work-for-dole scheme cut during the depression of 1934, was derided as a "scar", and a new viewing shelter that added a tiny cube to the mountain's skyline in 1990 met with loud protests, as did two telecoms masts. More tellingly, a cablecar has been mooted for over twenty years and still hasn't overcome local opposition.

Car access is up Huon Road, via the semi-rural suburb of **Fern Tree**, most of which vanished in a bushfire in 1968. From here, Pillinger Drive turns into the steep and winding Pinnacle Road to the summit, with several lookouts on the nineteen-kilometre drive. A **walking route** goes right up the mountain via three trails: Fernglade Track, Pinnacle Track, then the stiff final push up Zig Zag Track (13km; 2hr 45min one way). The *Fern Tree Tavern* at the start offers teas, meals and views. There are also picnic grounds with barbecues, shelters, toilets and information boards at the beginning of the track at Fern Tree, and about halfway up at **The Springs**. Pure, drinkable water cascades from rocks as you climb and the thick bush begins to gradually thin; by the top it's alpine and bare. Here, the stone **Pinnacle Observatory Shelter** (daily 8am–6pm) has details of the magnificent panorama of the city and harbour spread before you, which takes in vast tracts of bush and grassplains, and stretches south to Bruny Island

▲ Fishing boats on Victoria Dock

and north as far as Maria Island. There are toilets but no refreshments at the top, and bear in mind it is always around 10°C colder than at ground level, and that conditions change quickly.

As well as the route to the summit, there's some great **walking** on the mountain slopes, with parking at The Springs if you're driving. **Organ Pipes Circuit** takes in most Mount Wellington landscapes, from wet forest to subalpine woods, boulder fields to soaring cliffs, on a nine-kilometre loop. From The Springs, you follow the flat Lenah Valley Track, which provides great views of Hobart from Sphinx Rock after 45 minutes, ascend on Hunters Track, then return beneath spectacular dolerite cliffs on Organ Pipes Track; the fluted cliffs, known as the "Organ Pipes", are a favourite for local climbers. Allow four hours for the full circuit. You also get a great view of the Organ Pipes on a gentle walk (45min return) to pretty waterfall **O'Grady Falls**; the track starts from a car park 1km north of Fern Tree via Pillinger Drive. There's also good (and easy) **mountain-biking** on the well-formed **Pipeline Track** from the Fern Tree car park; you'll have to walk the last 2km to Wellington Falls though. Allow three to four hours for the 25-kilometre return trip, less if you start further along Huon Road at Neika, which halves the distance. The Wellington Park Management Trust website (Ⓦ www.wellingtonpark.tas.gov.au) has downloadable information sheets and **maps**, details of other walks and links for weather conditions. You can also pick up the detailed *Mount Wellington Walks* ($9.20) walking map by Tasmap from the tourist information centre.

Island Cycle Tours operates an exhilarating three-hour Mount Wellington Descent by bike, Mount Wellington Walks and Tasmanian Wilderness Experiences offer guided bushwalks, while Aardvark Adventures leads abseiling expeditions on the mountain (see box, p.94). Metro buses #48 or #49 run to Fern Tree, or the Mount Wellington Shuttle Bus Service can get you to the summit (Mon–Fri 9.30am, noon & 2.30pm, Sat & Sun 9.30am & 1.30pm; $25; 2hr tour includes 30min on top; Ⓣ 0417 341 804), leaving from the Travel and Information Centre (see p.67), or picking up from accommodation in the city centre.

Eating and drinking

Once a solid meat 'n' veg city, Hobart has an increasingly sophisticated dining scene; the greatest diversity of restaurants and cafés is in North Hobart on Elizabeth Street. There's also a decent choice at Salamanca Place and Battery Point. For cheap eats, pubs rustle up the usual bar meals or there are inexpensive Asian eateries in the centre on Harrington Street, between Collins and Liverpool streets, and around the Liverpool Street corner. Superlative **seafood** can be had throughout the city, but especially on Victoria Dock and Elizabeth Street Pier, or from the punts moored in Constitution Dock. On Saturdays, the fresh produce and food stalls at **Salamanca Market** are excellent.

Cafés and takeaways

Criterion Street Cafe 10 Criterion St. A buzzy central café and organic foodstore for shoppers and workers. Breakfast fare includes Spanish omelette and gourmet bacon sandwich, and lunchtime blackboard specials include good soups, salad, risotto or savoury cheesecake and lots of vegetarian options; nothing on the main menu is over $12.50. Divine cakes and coffee, too. Mon–Fri 7.30am–5pm, Sat 8.30am–3pm.

Drifters Internet Cafe 33 Salamanca Place, off Montpellier Retreat. Cosy, long nook of a café, its walls covered with Errol Flynn paraphernalia. Soups, toasted sandwiches and nachos all come under $9. Great smoothies too and Internet access ($1 per 10min, $5 per hr). Mon–Sat 10am–7pm, Sun 11am–7pm.

Jackman & McRoss 57–59 Hampden Rd, Battery Point, and 4 Victoria St. Always busy eat-in bakeries that serve excellent pastries and savouries such as gourmet baguettes and rolls, plus great pies. Mon–Fri 7.30am–6pm, Sat & Sun 7.30am–5pm.

Jam Packed 27 Hunter St. A more refined café in the impressive atrium of the former IXL jam factory. Serves great breakfasts until 3pm, as well as tasty lunches such as gourmet burgers, tarts, risottos and salads, plus daily specials for around $15. Daily 8am–5.30pm.

La Cuisine 85 Bathurst St. Café-patisserie serving excellent French-style pastries and mounds of delicious, healthy salads. Mon–Fri 7am–5pm, Sat 8am–1.30pm.

Retro Café 31 Salamanca Place. A Hobart institution, relaxed, light and airy, serving the best espresso in town plus wonderful breakfasts. Midweek sees politicians from the nearby State Parliament and high-flyers assemble here for coffee meetings, while outside tables are popular on market day (Sat). Mon–Sat 8am–6pm, Sun 8.30am–6pm.

R Tagaki Sushi 155 Liverpool Rd. Tiny and terrific café and takeaway that serves sensational sushi, always freshly made and with most portions costing under $9, in a Zen-like minimalist interior. Nori maki rolls and soups are always a good bet. Mon–Fri 10.30am–6pm, Sat 10.30am–4pm.

Shu Yuan Bank Arcade, 64 Liverpool St. This tiny vibrant place, little more than a takeaway, packs in the customers – many Asian – for delicious vegetarian food from a Taiwan-trained chef who mixes mushrooms, gluten and tofu into delicious, filling creations. A lunch special of three dishes on rice costs $8.50. Also serves fresh fruit drinks. Mon–Sat 10am–3.30pm.

Sugo Shop 9, Salamanca Square. Trendy café, with a dramatic red interior and big glass windows facing onto the square. Not as expensive as it looks: Italian-styled coffee and food is excellent, including gourmet pizza (from $13), focaccia, salads, pasta and risotto. Mon–Fri 8.30am–4.30pm, Sat & Sun 9am–4.30pm.

Restaurants: city centre

Ball & Chain Grill 87 Salamanca Place. Speciality steaks are charcoal-grilled in a reassuringly old-fashioned place of stone and wood, with a bar – wait there rather than go to the modern backroom. Good wine list, too. Moderate to expensive.

Da Angelo Ristorante 47 Hampden Rd, Battery Point ☎03/6223 7011. A great village spot for an upmarket, tasty and good-value Italian meal including gourmet pizzas; generous portions and good service. Licensed and BYO. Lunch Fri, dinner Mon–Sat.

Fish Frenzy Elizabeth St Pier. Nothing fancy, just the best fish and chips in the centre served in a quintessentially Hobart location. Expect big, cheap portions and bigger queues in early evenings. Licensed.

Francisco's 60 Hampden Rd, Battery Point ☎03/6224 7124. Reasonably priced tapas and larger plates – house special is *paella Valenciana* – in a classy bar-cum-restaurant or al fresco in the garden. Lunch & dinner Tues–Sat.

Kelly's 5 Knopwood St, Battery Point ☎ 03/6224 7225. A long-standing village favourite serving modern seafood dishes – the accidental occy (tenderized grilled octopus with orange and ginger glaze) is a local classic – and sushi in a small informal house. Bookings recommended at weekends. Dinner Tues–Sun.

Magic Curries 41 Hampden Rd, Battery Point. A great little Indian restaurant with bags of character, serving all the favourites plus dishes like Goan fish curry and house special mango chicken. Mains $15. BYO. Dinner only.

Maldini 47 Salamanca Place ☎ 03/6223 4460. Bustling and always busy, this is an old-hand on Salamanca Place that has survived because of reliable upmarket Italian cuisine. Strong on seafood – there's a good *risotto alla pescatore*. Bookings advisable at weekends. Moderate to expensive.

🏃 **Marque IV** Elizabeth St Pier ☎ 03/6224 4228. A slick modern restaurant whose dockside location and Asian-influenced gourmet cuisine epitomize Hobart's foodie renaissance: menus change daily but expect bold flavours and daring combinations in mains priced around $26. Also has eight- and ten-course degustation menus. Bookings essential weekends.

Monty's 37 Montpelier Retreat, Battery Point ☎ 03/6223 2511. Fine dining without the fuss: expertly cooked modern Australian cuisine and a friendly vibe in a small dining room that's always full. Bookings essential; expensive. Dinner Tues–Sat.

🏃 **Mures Fish Centre** Victoria Dock. Set among yachts and fishing boats, this two-level food centre houses three restaurants, a fishmonger, a bakery (great scallop pies) and a café. *Mures Upper Deck* (☎ 03/6231 1999) is an upmarket restaurant that has lovely harbour views; *Mures Lower Deck* (☎ 03/6231 2121) has bistro food, with cheaper prices; *Orizuru* (☎ 03/6231 1790; closed Sun) serves the finest Japanese in Tassie, with superb sushi – their salmon is delicious.

🏃 **Piccalilly** Corner of Hampden Rd and Francis St, Battery Point ☎ 03/6224 9900. In a snug cottage, this has mix-and-match menus of entrée-sized plates that are creative without showing off. A four-plate meal costs $75, and Tasmanian wines are available by the glass. Bookings essential. Dinner only.

Quarry 27 Salamanca Place. Light contemporary cuisine and metropolitan decor in a sandstone Georgian warehouse, beautifully lit in the evenings. Mains start at around $18.

Sirens 6 Victoria St. Upmarket but moderately priced vegetarian/vegan restaurant serving subtle Middle Eastern/North African-inspired food in a lovely plant-filled, high-ceilinged space that's a cross between Gothic and Ottoman. Licensed. Mon–Sat from 5.30pm.

Restaurants: outside the centre

Amulet 333 Elizabeth St, North Hobart ☎ 03/6234 8113. By day a laid-back café-bistro, by night an understated restaurant serving modern Australian cuisine that's strong on European flavours, and is made using organic local ingredients where possible. Good wine list too. Bookings essential in evenings; moderate to expensive.

Annapurna 305 Elizabeth St, North Hobart. Original characterful outlet of a casual restaurant serving North and South Indian food – a more modern second restaurant is at 93 Salamanca Place (lunch Wed–Sun & dinner daily). The *masala dosa* is legendary, plus there are lunch specials for under $10. Closed lunch Sat & Sun.

Cornelian Bay Boathouse Queen's Walk, Cornelian Bay. Aussie fusion dishes from a French-trained, Asian-influenced chef. Lots of moderately priced seafood, all served in a glass-walled place on the bay. A great spot for lunch. Lunch daily, dinner Mon–Sun summer or Fri–Sat winter.

Fish 349 349 Elizabeth St, North Hobart. A minimalist, modern fish café where the food is cheap and always fresh ($10–24). Licensed.

Flathead 3 Cascade St, South Hobart. En route to the Cascade Brewery, this fishmonger-cum-café is a local secret for superb fish dishes, many of them Asian, plus great fish and chips ($12–22). BYO. Lunch Tues–Sat, dinner daily.

🏃 **Prosser's on the Beach** Long Point Beach Rd, Sandy Bay ☎ 03/6225 2276. In a relaxing spot in extensive Long Beach Reserve on Little Sandy Bay overlooking the Derwent River, this is Hobart's – and probably Tasmania's – best contemporary seafood restaurant, using superb local fresh fish. Asian-influenced dishes vie with simple fish fillets on mash. Prices are very reasonable, with mains around $28–32. Licensed. Lunch Wed–Fri, dinner Mon–Sat from 6pm. Bookings essential.

Restaurant 373 373 Elizabeth St, North Hobart ☎ 03/6231 9031. Though bistro by appearance, this has decor as understated yet sophisticated as the modern dishes, largely European-influenced and created from Tasmanian ingredients. A favourite of local foodies. Bookings essential. Closed Sun.

🏃 **Lebrina** 155 New Town Rd, New Town ☎ 03/6228 7775. Long Hobart's temple of gastronomy and arguably still *the* address in town. The classic haute cuisine dining experience means a small menu of meticulously prepared

French- and Italian-influenced food served in elegant rooms of a cottage. One for a big occasion. Dinner Tues–Sat. Bookings essential.

The Source Moorilla, 655 Main Rd, Berriedale ☎03/6277 9900. Metropolitan glamour and contemporary Australian dishes with an Italian twist in the glass-walled restaurant of the Hobart wine estate, with great river views. Mains around $33. Bookings recommended at weekends. Lunch daily, dinner Fri & Sat.

Vanidol's 353 Elizabeth St, North Hobart. A popular veteran of the North Hobart strip, this casual, affordable place serves Thai, Indian and Indonesian food. BYO. Dinner Tues–Sun.

Entertainment and nightlife

A lively **nightlife**, albeit on a small scale, is centred on Salamanca Place and the pub *Knopwood's Retreat*, which attracts a large crowd on weekend nights and has a popular nightclub upstairs. To find out **what's on**, check the gig guide in Thursday's *Mercury* newspaper or pick up state-wide freesheet *Source* in bars, pubs and music shops. Alternatively, *Ruffcut Records*, at the south of Elizabeth Street Mall (no. 33A), and *Aroma Records*, at 323 Elizabeth St, North Hobart, have lots of flyers and info. Touring Aussie alt-rock acts visit regularly, but Hobart is too small to lure large touring bands on a weekly basis, so those that play the pubs are mainly local. There's free **live music** in the courtyard at Salamanca Place on Friday evenings, known as "Rektango" (5.30–7.30pm). For more compelling gigs, keep an eye on what's happening in the *Uni Bar* at the University of Tasmania campus at Sandy Bay (☎03/6226 2495). Berriedale wine estate Morrilla also hosts occasional outdoor gigs by the water in summer. **Classical concerts** by the Tasmanian Symphony Orchestra are at the Federation Concert Hall and by the Tasmanian Conservatorium of Music at the Conservatorium (5–7 Sandy Bay Rd; ☎03/6226 7306) or in churches around town. The Theatre Royal also hosts the odd lightweight classical concert. Most **tickets** can be booked via Centretainment, at 53 Elizabeth St Mall (☎03/6234 5998; ⓦwww.centretainment.com.au) or for gigs go to Ruffcut Records.

In general, Hobart prefers its dramatic arts to be racy, off-beat or entertaining rather than avant garde and challenging. The main venue in Hobart, the lovely **Theatre Royal**, hosts a varied programme of crowd-pleasers: modern Australian plays to comedy plus touring productions and occasional nights of popular opera or big-name jazz performers. The venue's second space, Backspace Theatre, hosted by Is Theatre company, offers more combative fare. Productions at the intimate **Peacock Theatre** in the Salamanca Arts Centre are also worth a look. The most interesting **cinema** is a repertory programme screened at State Cinema in North Hobart.

Pubs

Irish Murphy's 21 Salamanca Place. Live music and club nights, and Guinness on tap in a popular noisy pub on Hobart's nightlife strip.

Knopwood's Retreat 39 Salamanca Place. A favourite with students, yachties and just about everyone else, this pub has a relaxed feel, with plenty of magazines and newspapers inside, plus outside tables – the choice at summer weekends. Lunch served Mon–Fri; open until 1am on Fri, when the pavement outside is packed.

New Sydney Hotel 87 Bathurst St. Hobart's biggest Irish pub, featuring live music nightly except Mon – from traditional Irish to blues and folk. Twelve beers on tap, including Guinness, and decent pub meals (no lunch Sun).

Queen's Head Cafe & Wine Bar 400 Elizabeth St, North Hobart ☎03/6234 4670. Colourful, spacious and casual venue hosting free live music nightly except Sun (from 8.30pm Mon–Thurs, 9.30pm Fri & Sat), from pub rock to reggae and jazz. The menu ranges from a $5 soup to a $17 chargrilled steak or half a kilo of rib-eye for $22.

Republic Bar & Café 299 Elizabeth St ☎03/6234 6954. Hobart's best pub venue has a laid-back lounge atmosphere, funky decor and music six nights a week (except Mon) – free local rock or jazz bands plus touring Aussie alternative-rock acts around once a week. Always attracts a good crowd, including plenty of students. Also has excellent meals, with lots of seafood on the menu.

Shipwright's Arms Hotel Corner of Colville and Trumpeter streets, Battery Point. Hobart's most traditional English-style pub, affectionately dubbed "Shippies" and popular with yachties after the New Year race. Dishes up a legendary fresh seafood platter, though service can be a misnomer. Also has rooms (❹).

Bars and clubs

Bar Celona 24 Salamanca Square. Renovated sandstone warehouse turned into a slick and spacious café (by day) and bar on two levels. The light lunches (from $8.50 to $15) can also be eaten at tables on the square. On Fri and Sat nights DJs play laid-back lounge music on the mezzanine level (9pm–12.30am). Daily 9am–midnight, until 1am Fri & Sat.

Grape 55 Salamanca Place. Over six hundred wines in stock and a list that changes once a month and is strong on Tassie wine. Also has cheese platters, wine sales and tastings Tues 5.30–8pm and Sat 11am–2pm.

Halo Purdy's Mart (off Collins St, near Elizabeth St junction). Drum 'n' bass, techno and breaks spun by Australian and occasional international DJs. Fri–Sat only.

Isobar 11 Franklin Wharf. Young and packed, the *Isobar* (Wed 5pm–midnight, Fri 6pm–2am, Sat 7pm–2am) is a weekend favourite, with live music on Fri and Sat; Wed attracts a student crowd. At *The Club* upstairs (Fri & Sat 10pm–5am; Fri $5, Sat $7 or free before 11pm; happy hour 11pm to midnight) DJs play commercial dance on the main floor and there's also an R&B room and the quieter *Back Bar*.

Kaos Cafe and Soak Lounge Bar 237 Elizabeth St, North Hobart. Trendy, gay-friendly, late-night licensed coffee spot and café with its own funky bar room, *Soak*, that has plenty of lounge space, and on Fri and Sat nights a club atmosphere, with DJs spinning until the late hours. Mon–Thurs noon–midnight, Fri & Sat noon–2/3am.

The Lark Distillery 14 Davey St. A range of spirits made on the premises can be tasted for free ($4 for single malt whisky), plus a huge range of whiskies and an all-Tasmanian wine list. Cheese platters to snack on (and soup in winter), live folk music on Fri evenings (5.30–8pm; free). A cocktail bar operates nightly except Fri from 6pm to 2am. Mon–Thurs & Sun 10pm–2am, Fri 9am–10pm.

Telegraph Hotel 19 Morrison St ☎03/6234 6254. No cover charge and very popular with the young after-work crowd and uni students. DJ (Wed–Fri) and live band on Sat, plus tapas on Thurs & Fri.

Trout Bar and Cafe Elizabeth St, corner of Federal St, North Hobart ☎03/6236 9777. Relaxed pub that feels more like an arty café. Music, often jazz or blues, usually free (or around $7), Wed–Sat nights in a friendly, chatty atmosphere. Small menu of pasta, salads, steaks, chicken and Asian curries. Lunch Wed–Fri, Sun brunch 11am–3pm, dinner nightly.

Lizbon 217 Elizabeth St, North Hobart. Cocktails and spirits in a hip lounge bar that's favoured by a stylish crowd – think leather sofas, a stainless steel bar and an epic drinks menu. The sound-track is laid-back funk and jazz grooves, with live music at weekends. Tues–Wed until 11pm, Wed–Sat until 2am.

The Metz 217 Sandy Bay Rd. A café-bar and restaurant where DJs lay down house beats for Sandy Bay's style-concious crowd. Sunday sessions get notoriously messy. Breakast, lunch & dinner daily.

Observatory Murray St Pier. Known locally as "The O", this spacious retro-modern bar on the waterfront attracts a post-work drinks crowd on Fri nights, then dressed-up clubbers for clubnights of party house. Wed–Sun until late.

Proller 121 Collins St. Retro kitsch basement lounge-bar with a laid-back vibe and house and funk tunes spun by DJs at weekends. Wed–Sat 5pm–4am.

Rockerfeller's 11 Morrison St ☎03/ 6234 3490. Gay-friendly bar-restaurant. A fun atmosphere and a contemporary Australian menu, plus cocktails. Lunch Mon–Fri, dinner nightly. Live jazz Sun night.

Syrup 39 Salamanca Place ☎03/6224 8249. Often hosting international guest DJs, this trendy club is on two levels above *Knopwood's*. Anything goes on different nights and different floors, from retro to techno via house, drum 'n' bass and disco. Open from 9pm Thurs, 8pm Fri & Sat (until 6am) and with live bands on Sat afternoon 3–6pm.

T-42° Elizabeth St Pier ☎03/6224 7742. Stylish lounge bar in a great waterfront location – some tables on the pier – attracting a cross-section of trendies and young professionals. Half the place is an eating area serving well-priced modern Australian-style meals at lunch and dinner (mains from $18). Daily 11.30am–1.30am.

Gay and lesbian Hobart

Founded in 1988, the **Tasmanian Gay and Lesbian Rights Group (TGLRG)** put persistent pressure on the government. Led by spokesperson **Rodney Croome**, their rally cry "We're here, we're queer, and we're not going to the mainland" certainly shook up conservative Tasmania; thousands signed the petition to urge the reform of the law. The federal government and the UN Human Rights Commission also pressed for change, and Tasmania's Upper House finally cracked, changing the law on May 1, 1997. Ironically, Tasmania now has Australia's best legislation to protect gay and lesbian rights: it's the only state that allows same-sex couples to officially register their relationship to access the same rights as married couples under Tasmanian law.

The TGLRG can be contacted on ☏ 03/6224 3556 or via ⊛ www.tglrg.org. Working It Out (☏ 03/6231 1200, ⊛ www.workingitout.org.au) is a state-funded gay and lesbian support and health agency, and there's a social and support group Gay and Lesbian Community Centre (GLC Inc). GLC Inc publishes a monthly newsletter, *CentreLines*, which is sold from the TGLRG stall at Salamanca Market and details events and occasional dance parties around town that they organize, details of which are available on their recorded **Gay Information Line** (☏ 03/6234 8179, ⊛ www.glctas.org). A comprehensive **Tasmanian Gay and Lesbian Vistor's Guide** can be dowloaded from ⊛ www.discovertasmania.com. *GAY TAS*, a fold-out gay and lesbian visitor guide, is available from tourist offices. *The Trade Hotel*, at 24 Barrack St, is popular for its Saturday-night DJs (free) and so is the monthly **gay and lesbian club night**, La La Land Bar & Club at *Halo*, 37A Elizabeth St Mall, on the first Saturday of the month (10pm–5am; $10; ☏ 0408 328 456 to check details). Other gay-friendly places are *Kaos*, a café and cocktail lounge, *T-42°*, a restaurant, and the nightclub *Syrup*.

Film, theatre, concerts and cabaret

Federation Concert Hall 1 Davey St, bookings ☏ 1800 001 190, ⊛ www.tso.com.au. Striking brass-clad oval that's home to the Tasmanian Symphony Orchestra. Apparently has the best acoustics in Australia.

The Playhouse Theatre 106 Bathurst St ☏ 03/6234 1536, ⊛ www.playhouse.org.au. The Hobart Repertory Theatre Society, an amateur not-for-profit group established in 1926, puts on at least five plays a year here plus a popular Christmas panto. Premises are also rented out to travelling shows.

Salamanca Arts Centre 77 Salamanca Place ☏ 03/6234 8414, ⊛ www.salarts.org.au. The base of several performance companies, including the Terrapin Puppet Theatre, which puts on touring shows, among them a puppet picnic at the end of December in St David's Park. Puppeteers are welcome to come in and look around.

Specializing in contemporary works, the Peacock Theatre hosts performances by various local theatre companies.

State Cinema 375 Elizabeth St, North Hobart ☏ 03/6234 6318, ⊛ www.statecinema.com.au. Art-house and foreign films; reduced ticket prices Wed ($10). Licensed bar.

Theatre Royal 29 Campbell St ☏ 03/6233 2299, ⊛ www.theatreroyal.webcentral.com.au. This lovely old theatre is not too expensive or stuffy, offering a broad spectrum of entertainment from comedy nights to serious drama. Challenging or quirky smaller productions are staged in second space Backspace Theatre (⊛ www.istheatre.com). Tickets from $35.

Village Cinema Centre 181 Collins St ☏ 03/6234 7288, ⊛ www.villagecinemas.com.au. Seven screens showing mainstream new releases; discount day is Tues.

Festivals and events

Hobart's premier event is the last part of the **Sydney–Hobart yacht race**. The two hundred or so yachts, which leave Sydney on December 26, arrive in

HOBART AND AROUND | Festivals and events

The one-stop shop for activities is the Tasmanian Travel & Information Centre (see p.67), which has flyers galore and a booking centre. See the box on p.75 for details of harbour cruises, and "Listings" below for information about bike hire.

Aardvark Adventures see p.44. Tailored abseiling excursions in the Hobart area – locations include Mount Wellington and the cliffs of Blackmans Bay ($120; minimum three people). Includes lunch.

Blackaby's Sea Kayaks ☏0418 124 072, ⓦwww.blackabyseakayaks.com.au. The closest you can get to the Derwent River without getting wet. Tours in double kayaks let you dip a paddle at sunset and get fish and chips afloat, plus there are morning and afternoon trips ($50). Also runs pedal-and-paddle tours with Island Cycle Tours.

Bruny Island Charters see p.129. The thrilling trip along Bruny Island's coastline without the hassle of getting there – the day-trip by the island specialist includes transfers from Hobart, the three-hour boat trip and lunch (departs 8am Sun–Fri; $100).

Bruny Island Ventures ☏03/6229 7465, ⓔbrunyislandventures@hotmail.com. Small-group day-tours to Bruny Island led by a knowledgeable guide. Destinations include Adventure Bay, Mount Mangana and the Cape Bruny Lighthouse (Mon, Wed, Fri & Sat 8.30am, returning 5.30pm; $145 including meals).

Freycinet Adventures ☏03/6275 0500, ⓦwww.freycinetadventures.com.au. Kayaking trips run at morning, afternoon and dusk by an acclaimed activities organizer that has double-sea kayaks (Sept–June; 2hr; $65).

Ghost Tours of Hobart ☏0439/335 696. Spooky tales of skulduggery and murder in old Hobart Town, related on two-hour Battery Point tours from Salamanca Square at dusk ($25).

Hobart Explorer ☏03/6234 3336. Three-hour coach tram-tours around the city and suburbs, departing from the visitor information centre (Sun–Fri, 9.45am, Sat 1pm; $39).

Hobart Historic Tours ☏03/6278 3338, ⓦwww.hobarthistorictours.com.au. Themed 1hr 30min walking tours around the city (all $27); history walks around

Hobart around December 29, making for a lively New Year's Eve waterfront party complete with fireworks. The race coincides with the fortnight-long **Hobart Summer Festival** (Dec 27 to Jan 9; more information at ⓦwww .hobartsummerfestival.com.au), focused on waterfront Sullivans Cove. The major event is **The Taste of Tasmania** (daily 11am–11pm, Dec 28–Jan 3), a gourmet food-fest promoting Tasmanian food, wine and beer, held at Princes Wharf. The main festival features outdoor concerts in St David's Park (the kids' one is free), a circus, symphony concerts, children's theatre in the Botanical Gardens, the one-kilometre Pier-to-Pier River Swim, a Tasmanian film festival, buskers, and night-time gallery openings. The **Australian Wooden Boat Festival** runs over three days in early February in odd-numbered years, marked by a host of boats moored around the docks; activities include theatrical and musical performances and boat-building courses (☏03/6231 6407).

The week-long **Hobart Fringe Festival** in mid-February has visual arts, film and performance components (ⓦwww.hobartfringe.org; many events free). The city shuts down for four days to attend the **Royal Hobart Show** at the Glenorchy showground (ⓦwww.hobartshowground.com.au/rhs; Oct 23–26), a good-natured agricultural festival that has the staple woodchopping and best-in-show competitions and is as happy to stage pig-racing as fashion shows.

central Hobart and Battery Point, pub walks and tours that expand on Hobart and the South Pole.

Hobart Rivulet Tours ☏03/6283 2711. The most eccentric tour in Hobart (1hr; $19) follows the underground stream that flows beneath the city, with a commentary about its construction interwoven with tales of the city's convict history. Tours go from the information centre at 4pm on Thurs and also Tues in Jan & Feb.

Island Cycle Tours ☏0418/234 181 or 1300 880 334, ⓦwww.islandcycletours.com. An excellent operator that provides the exhilarating three-hour Mount Wellington Descent, which takes in the summit before a 20km downhill mountain-bike ride to Salamanca Place (9.30am & 1.30pm; $65). There are also options for a night-time descent in summer, plus various packages that tack on kayak trips on the Derwent River. Provides pick-ups in the centre and lunch.

Mount Wellington Walks ☏0439 551 197, ⓦwww.mtwellingtonwalks.com.au. Offers four-hour guided walks ($70) to the summit of Mount Wellington, plus several walk-cycle-kayak packages in conjunction with Island Cycle Tours. Provides pick-ups in the city centre and lunch.

Roaring 40s Kayaking see p.45. Tassie's premier sea-kayaking outfit runs day-trips from Hobart to Bruny Island (Mon–Fri; $155) and around the dramatic coastline of the Tasman Peninsula (Mon–Fri; $255). Both include transfers and lunch. It also leads a thrilling three-day kayak tour (Nov–Apr; $1150) around the Tasman Peninsula – the exact route varies according to conditions. The price includes transfers, food and accommodation.

Tasmanian Wilderness Experiences The national parks trekking operator (see p.45) runs two day hikes on Mount Wellington – one to the summit via the dramatic Organ Pipes Track, the other a more demanding three-peaks route that takes in Collins Bonnet, Trestle Mountain and Collins Cap (both $165). Includes transfers to walk start.

Tassielink The ubiquitous large-group bus tours (see p.45): its Hobart city centre and Mount Wellington tour covers the city, docks, Battery Point, Mount Wellington and the Royal Botanical Gardens (Tues & Thurs 2pm, Sun 9am; 3hr; $55).

Listings

Airlines Airlines of Tasmania ☏1800 144 460, ⓦwww.airtasmania.com.au; Jet Star ☏13 15 38, ⓦwww.jetstar.com.au; Par Avion Wilderness Tours, Cambridge Airport ☏03/6248 5390, ⓦwww.paravion.com.au; Qantas ☏13 13 13, or their travel centre at 130 Collins St; Tasair, Cambridge Airport ☏03/6427 9777 or 1800 062 900, ⓦwww.tasair.com.au; Virgin Blue ☏13 67 89, ⓦwww.virginblue.com.au; King Island Airways ☏03/ 9580 3777, ⓦwww.kingislandair.com.au.

Banks Branches of all major banks are on Elizabeth Street.

Bike rental Most central is Bike Hire Tasmania, 109 Elizabeth St (☏03/6234 4166, ⓦwww.bikehiretasmania.com.au), with hybrids, mountain bikes, tandems and touring bikes with paniers: prices from $25–35 per 24 hours ($55 for tandem). Derwent Bike Hire (☏03/6234 2910, ⓦwww.derwentbike hire.com) at the beginning of the bike track to Cornelian Bay, by the cenotaph in the Regatta Grounds, has the same plus recumbent and child bikes, as well as child trailers and baby seats: $7 per hour, $20–25 per day ($40 tandem), $125 per week.

Bookshops Ellison Hawker Bookshop, at 90 Liverpool St, has an excellent travel section upstairs. Fullers Bookshop, at 140 Collins St, and The Hobart Bookshop, at 22 Salamanca Square, are Hobart's two best literary bookstores; the former has its own café, while the latter has a great section of Tasmanian books old and new. For a fine range of secondhand books, try Rapid Eye Books, at 36–38 Sandy Bay Rd, Battery Point.

Bus companies Redline Coaches, Hobart Transit Centre, 199 Collins St ☏1300 360 000; Tassielink, Hobart Bus Terminal, 64 Brisbane St ☏1300 300 520.

Camping and outdoor equipment There is a concentration of camping-gear shops on Elizabeth

Street near Bathurst Street, including a big range at Jolly Swagman Camping World, at 107 Elizabeth St; Paddy Pallin, 119 Elizabeth St, has quality outdoor equipment, and provides bushwalking information; Mountain Creek Great Outdoors Centre, at 75–77 Bathurst St ☏03/6234 4395, has a big selection, from cheap to top of the range, and also rents out gear.

Car and campervan rental Autorent-Hertz, at the airport and 122 Harrington St (☏03/6237 1111 or 1800 030 222, ✎www.autorent.com.au), also has campervans; and Avis, at the airport (☏03/6248 5424), has similar rates. Lo-Cost Auto Rent, at the airport and at 225 Liverpool St (☏03/6231 0550 or 1800 647 060, ✎www.locostautorent.com), has older cars plus newer models; Devil Campervans (☏03/6248 4493, ✎www.devilcampervans.com.au), from $50 per day minimum five days rental. Tasmania Campervan Rentals (☏03/6248 5638, ✎www.tasmaniacampervanrentals.com.au), from $80 per day off-peak to $110 in summer, minimum five-day rental; Rent-A-Bug, at 105 Murray St (☏03/6231 0300, ✎www.rentabug.com.au), has low-priced VW Beetles.

Travellers with disabilities The Commonwealth Carelink Centre (☏1800 052 222) and the Aged and Disability Care Information Service, at 181 Elizabeth St (☏03/6228 5799, ✎www.adcis.org.au), are excellent sources of information, providing free mobility maps of Hobart. Hobart City Council produces a free *Hobart CBD Mobility Map*, available from their HQ on the corner of Elizabeth and Davey streets (☏03/6238 2711). City Cabs (☏131 008 or 03 6274 3103) has specially adapted vehicles.

Diving The Dive Shop, at 67A Argyle St (☏03/6234 3428), hires equipment and runs PADI certification courses.

Environment To find out about or volunteer for environmental conservation programmes, the Wilderness Society's campaign office is at 130 Davey St (☏03/6224 1550, ✎www.wilderness.org.au/tas); its shop is at 33 Salamanca Place.

Hospitals Royal Hobart Hospital, 48 Liverpool St ☏03/6222 8308.

Internet access As well as hostels, try: the State Library on the corner of Bathurst and Murray streets, with free access for Australian residents, $5.50 per 30min for overseas visitors; Pelican Loft at the south end of Elizabeth Street Mall ($2 per 10min, $4 per 30min; Mon–Fri 8.30am–7pm, Sat 10.30am–5pm, Sun 12–4pm); Drifters Internet Café ($5 per hour) off Montpellier Retreat pub, Salamanca Place.

Laundry 12 Salamanca Square is a combined café/laundry.

Pharmacy Macquarie Pharmacy, 180 Macquarie St (daily 8am–10pm; ☏03/6223 2339); North Hobart Pharmacy, 360–362 Elizabeth St (daily 8am–10pm; ☏03/6234 1136).

Post office GPO, corner of Elizabeth and Macquarie streets (Mon–Fri 8am–6pm). Poste restante: Hobart GPO, TAS 7000.

Surfing The factory outlet of Tassie surf chain Red Herring (☏03/6244 5866; ✎www.redherringsurf.com.au) at 1/2 Bayfield St, Rosny Park, stocks boards from around $400. For custom boards and a decent range of secondhand equipment head to friendly shapers Stranger Surfboards (☏03/6244 5866, ✎www.strangersurfboards.com) at 55 South Arm Rd, Rokeby, 7km southeast of the centre.

Swimming pool Hobart Aquatic Centre (☏03/6222 6999), corner of Liverpool Street and Davies Avenue (Mon–Fri 6am–10pm, Sat & Sun 8am–6pm; $5.30). Heated swim centre with 50m and 25m pools, waterslides and bubblejets. Also gym and fitness centre.

Taxis City Cabs ☏13 10 08; Combined Services ☏13 22 27.

Women Women Tasmania, at 140 Macquarie St (☏03/6233 2208, ✎www.women.tas.gov.au), provides information services. Hobart Women's Health Centre is at 25 Lefroy St, North Hobart ☏03/6231 3212, ✎www.hwhc.com.au.

YHA Tasmania Head Office, 28 Criterion St ☏03/6234 9617, ✎www.yha.com.au (Mon–Fri 9am–5pm).

Around Hobart

Hobartians flee the city at weekends to immerse themselves in the landscapes on their doorstep, and it's small wonder. In under an hour's drive in any direction there are golden beaches, alpine mountains and temperate rainforest that can hold their own against any in the state. Indeed, if only visitors stopped fixating on convict heritage they might realise that the Tasman Peninsula has one of the most dramatic coastlines in Australia. Everything within this part of the chapter can be done on a day–trip from the city, although some deserve an overnight stay to see them in any depth.

Because Hobart was the cradle of the colony, history is writ large whichever direction you go. The Derwent River permitted early exploration west of Hobart to found **New Norfolk** amid broad hop-growing country, while Tasmania's first national park (and its most popular), **Mount Field National Park**, is a pocket of the wilderness that lies further west. Going east of Hobart, there are ideal spots for lazing around, whether in the postcard-pretty colonial village of **Richmond**, the wine estates of the **Coal River Valley** or the good surf beaches of **South Arm** – an appealing mix whatever your taste. The **Tasman Peninsula** beyond has been on the day-tripper circuit for almost as long as there have been tourists. The cause is the convict penitentiary at **Port Arthur**, an attraction so captivating that most visitors overlook its spectacular coastal scenery or superb bushwalking, both just as compelling a reason to visit.

West of Hobart

New Norfolk is an urban anomaly among the rural hills inland from Hobart. The agricentre is the largest town west of Hobart until you hit Queenstown, a base for a couple of trips on the Derwent River with a modest tourist infrastructure. You'd barely know it today, but it's also one of the earliest settlements in Tasmania – the Derwent facilitated early settlement by the British, and pioneering navigator Lieutenant John Hayes explored upstream a decade before the birth of Hobart Town – with a colonial past centred on hop-growing.

Lines of poplar trees act as windbreaks in the surrounding fields, and wooden oasthouses and dilapidated warehouses are dotted alongside the road west. Cultivation today is at **Plenty** and **Bushy Park** – the family of nineteenth-century Derwent Valley hop pioneer Ebeneezer Shoobridge continues to farm the area. Nurtured by the pure air and rain blown from the pristine southwest, Tasmanian hops are reputed to be the finest in the world; German and Belgian brewers prize them and mainland Australians name hops after apples as the state's principal export. For those who want a change of scene from bucolic charm, there's the temperate rainforest and alpine wilderness of **Mount Field National Park**.

New Norfolk and around

Heading up the Derwent Valley, the A10 hugs the river along an initially scrubby riverbank whose looks are not helped by the industrial Norske Skog paper mill. Tours of the factory complex that produced Australia's first newsprint in 1941 – its 290,000-tonne output still represents forty per cent of Australian paper consumption – run a couple of times a week; book through the visitor information centre at New Norfolk (see "Practicalities", p.98). In **Granton** before you reach the factory, Stefano Lubiano Wines (☏03/6263 7457, ⓦwww.slw.com.au; 11am–3pm Sun–Thurs, closed June) is lauded among connoisseurs for crisp and nutty sparkling wines, and a well-structured pinot noir and pinot grigio, while nearby Derwent Estate Vineyard (☏03/6263 5802, ⓦwww.derwentestate.com.au; 10am–4pm daily except Sat, closed winter) offers tastings of cool-climate wines, including a great riesling, in an 1830s cottage.

Fifty kilometres west of Hobart, **NEW NORFOLK** has settled into a pleasant if anonymous agricentre after a promising start as one of the most prosperous rural towns in colonial Tasmania. Founded as Elizabeth Town in 1806, it was renamed when settlers from Norfolk Island were relocated in 1808–1814; the British planned to turn the island that was famous as the refuge of the *Bounty* mutineers into a penal colony. That saltwater did not seep this far up the tidal Derwent River even led to New Nrofolk being proposed as the capital of Van Diemen's Land. The town flourished later as the hub of the region's hop-growing industry. A kilometre east of the centre, off the Hobart road, the **Oast House Hop Museum** (daily 10am–5pm; free) in the belly of a mid-1800s building, details hop production in the brick kilns and drying room, although it exists more as a lure to the craftshop and café-restaurant above (same times, plus dinner Fri–Sat). It also sells the real ales of local producer Two Metre Tall – a boutique brewery west of town at 120 Hamilton Rd, which offers tastings with advance notice (☎03 6261 1930, ⓦ www.2mt.com.au).

New Norfolk's main drag (High Street) is nothing special despite a sprinkling of colonial buildings picked out in a historic walk leaflet available from the visitor information centre (see below). In truth, more heritage charm lies in the antique shops at the east end of the street. Nearby **St Matthew's Anglican Church** is nominated as the oldest church in Tasmania, although the original building has been much tinkered with since it was built in 1824. The nineteenth-century stained-glass windows are worth a look though.

New Norfolk is at its best by the broad Derwent River, which is clean and swimmable, and fringed by a strip of park. The gentle **rapids** just upriver from the town centre are highly prized by trout fishermen, or for more thrills the Devil Jet runs high-speed jetboat rides through the rapids (daily 9am–4pm, on the hour; 30min; $55 per person, minimum two people; ☎03/6261 3460), leaving from the Esplanade. Rafting tours over the grade 1–2 rapids are run year-round by Aardvark Adventures (☎03/6273 7722, ⓦ www.aardvarkadventures.com.au/aard; $130) and Rafting Tasmania (☎03/6239 1080, ⓦ www.raftingtasmania.com; $115), both based in Hobart. Just above the river at 49 Montagu St (the main road), the *Bush Inn* is another contender for Australia's oldest continuously licensed **hotel** (☎03/6261 2011; ❸) having served spirits since 1815. Its other claim to fame is as the site of the first trunk call in Australia, made by the landlord to the Hobart general post office on December 1, 1888.

From New Norfolk, you can continue west to visit the **Salmon Ponds** (daily 9am–5pm Oct–Apr, 10am–4pm May–Sept; $7), 18km west on the Glenora Road in Plenty. Established in 1861, its six stone pools are the wellspring of Australian salmon and trout fishing – the first fish transported from England to be released into the wild were released here. Among the site's formal English gardens is a **Museum of Trout Fishing** (same ticket) whose antique equipment is displayed in the cottage of the hatchery superintendent – clearly colonists took their fishing seriously. A licensed restaurant prepares savoury and sweet crepes.

Practicalities

Hobart Coaches operates a good **public transport** service from Hobart to New Norfolk on weekdays and a limited schedule on Saturday, leaving from Metro Hobart's Elizabeth Street terminus. Tassielink also goes to New Norfolk on its scheduled service to Queenstown. The **visitor information centre** (daily 10am–4pm; ☎03/6261 3700, ⓦ www.newnorfolk.org) is adjacent to the Art Deco town hall at the west of High Street and covers the entire Derwent Valley region. The Online Access Centre (10am–6pm Mon–Fri) is in the library on Charles Street, off High Street.

Accommodation

All Saints & Sinners 93 High St ☎1800 207 970, Ⓦwww.allsaintsandsinners.com.au. Central four-star B&B between the church and pub, a little pricey for its floral en suites, but homely and comfy. ❺

New Norfolk Caravan Park Esplanade ☎03/6261 1268, Ⓔvickev55@hotmail.com. Near though not on the river, this small but tidy site has tent pitches ($15), vans (❸) and cabins, some en suite (❸–❹).

Old Colony Inn 21 Montagu St ☎03/6261 2731, Ⓔmigloo30@hotmail.com. Restored one-bed cottage in the rose garden of a mock-Tudor hop store built in 1815. Decor full of bygones is a love or loathe affair. Good value though. ❸

🏃 **Stanton B&B** 504 Back River Rd, Magra, 3km north ☎03/6261 3290, Ⓦwww.stantonbandb.com. Lovely heritage en suites are full of character but free of cliché in this splendid country manor from 1817, raided by bushranger Martin Cash in 1843. Original detail abounds: carved fireplaces, a sandstone staircase and old eucalyptus floorboards. Also has a firetub in the cherry orchard. To get there, head left over the New Norfolk bridge, go towards Magra, then right at the T-junction. ❺

Tynewald Hobart Road 100m east of roundabout ☎03/6261 2667, Ⓦwww.tynwaldtasmania.com. Old-fashioned, Victorian-style hotel in a magnificent mansion (c.1830) by the river, with six antique-filled rooms and a self-contained cottage in a stone granary. Also has an outdoor heated pool and a tennis court set in 40 acres of grounds. ❺–❻

Willow Court Gardens 15 George St ☎03/6261 8783, Ⓕ03/6261 4291. A great backpackers' hostel one block from High Street, recently refurbished to provide bright, spotless rooms, all with TV. Laundry, billiards, Internet access and cheap meals in the attached bar. Dorms $25, rooms ❸

Woodbridge on the Derwent 6 Bridge St ☎03/6261 5566, Ⓦwww.woodbridgenn.com.au. A convict-built manor hotel (1825) renovated to offer a classy take on heritage: neutral and pastel shades with flashes of silk and rich fabrics, old wood and antique prints, and all rooms with river views. Currently, this is Tasmania's only member of the Luxury Small Hotels of the World group. ❽

Eating and drinking

Convivial café-restaurant *Verandahs* (☎03/6261 4461; closed Sun) at 21 Burnett St, off High Street one block from the council offices, has healthy salads and steak sandwiches for lunch, plus a tasty dinner menu strong on fish and seafood; mains average $20. The restaurants of Tynewald and Woodbridge on the Derwent are open to non-residents (reservations required) and serve respectively Provencal-style cooking with game specials, and creative modern cuisine. For cheap eats, there's rib-sticking stuff from $10 in the *Bush Inn*, where the dining room overlooks the river, and cheap steaks in the modern Willow Court Inn attached to *Willow Court Gardens*.

To Mount Field National Park

From New Norfolk to Mount Field National Park, it's 37km through pretty villages of hop fields and wooden barns. Fuel and a few provisions (mostly canned and dried) for camping are available in the largest village, **Westerway**. A few kilometres west, quirky animal sanctuary Something Wild (daily 9am–5pm summer, 10am–3pm winter; $13) specializes in the rehabilitation of injured and orphaned native wildlife prior to their release – expect Tasmanian devils, wombats, eastern quolls, pademelons, Bennetts wallabies and forester kangaroos; "Roo Food" bags ($1) are available for the latter.

MOUNT FIELD NATIONAL PARK is no stranger to tourism. A refuge of bushrangers in the 1840s, who sold possum skins in between raids on Bushy Park farmsteads, it was set aside as a tourist reserve in 1885, then protected as the state's first national park in 1916. No one saw the irony in celebrating its opening with a woodchopping match. Today, it vies with Cradle Mountain as Tasmania's most popular national park, its 160 square kilometres hugely popular with Hobartians for easy strolls and extended hikes in a rugged alpine country dotted with tarns – uniquely among Tassie parks, you can drive to the high country,

▲ Russell Falls, Mount Field National Park

saving yourself a one-kilometre-long slog uphill. The area also supports a small ski field in winter, although snowfall is rather erratic and the skiing is more of the cross-country than downhill variety. Ski equipment and car snowchains can be hired in Hobart from Skigia & Surf (123 Elizabeth St; ☎03/6234 6688).

Most visitors come to see the forty-metre **Russell Falls**, which were granted protected status in 1885. Their two-tier cascade remains impressive despite the tour groups, and the gush of one early visitor about "incomparably beautiful, strikingly romantic, purely Tasmanian" still rings true. The waterfall is close to the park entrance and can be reached on an easy thirty-minute circuit walk (wheelchair-accessible); visit at dusk and you might spot glow-worms in the forest beside the track and platypus in the creek. An extension of the track continues to **Horseshoe Falls** (1hr return). For a longer walk, the Lady Baron Falls Circuit (2hr return) takes in the Russell Falls and the eponymous waterfall, plus the **Tall Trees Track** (30min), which loops through a forest of massive old-growth swamp gums. These awesome trees are among the largest in Australia and frequently date back to the early nineteenth century. You can also access the track on a five-minute drive from Lake Dobson Road, uphill from the visitor centre.

To get away from the tour-group mob, there are several shorter walks off Lake Dobson Road: you'll see the flora change from open eucalyptus forest to closed mixed rainforest and then stunted subalpine woodland as you ascend. The easy Lyrebird Nature Walk (15min), around halfway along the road, goes through mixed forest and is children-friendly. After 16km the road emerges from the forest to cross alpine moorland and reach glacial **Lake Dobson**. Follow signs for "Alpine tracks" to access the **Pandani Grove Nature Walk** (information leaflets from visitor centre; see opposite), a forty-minute lake circuit that passes through pencil pines and a grove of tall **pandanus**, a striking plant whose crown of long fronds suggests a semitropical palm. Plenty of longer walks go from the lake car park, from day-hikes to treks along the tarn shelf that take several days, with huts to stay in along the way. The most rewarding day-walk is the Tarn Shelf Circuit (5-6hr return) along a ridge above a string of tarns, via **Twilight Tarn** (4hr return), where a historic hut has ski memorabilia.

Practicalities

Tassielink's summer bus service to Scotts Peak stops at Mount Field from late November to late March (Tues, Thurs & Sat only). At other times or to access the higher walks without your own transport, you'll need to join a **tour** from Hobart. Bottom Bits Bus (p.44) has small-group tours (daily except Sat; $105) and Island Cycle Tours (Sun; $120; see p.45) has day-trips that combine a short hike and mountain biking. Tasmanian Wilderness Experiences runs a one-day guided bushwalk on a less well-tramped route through subalpine forest to a high-altitude ridge ($165; see p.45). Tassielink (Mon, Wed, Fri; $120) tours give you a few hours at the lower areas of the park, calling at the Salmon Ponds and the Something Wild animal sanctuary en route.

The **Mount Field Visitor Centre** (daily 9am–4pm; ℡03/6288 1149) at the park's car park provides free sketch maps and sheets on the natural environment and walks, and sells a Tasmap hiking map ($4.50); you should also register here before tackling longer walks. The complex also houses a shop, an interpretive centre and a café serving the usual focaccias, burgers, and fish and chips.

Accommodation and eating

Within the national park, the *Land of Giants* Campsite (℡03/6288 1149; $8 per person) is a lovely spot with good facilities (including hot showers and a laundry) and abundant wildlife. It's also very popular, especially at weekends in summer. **Walkers' cabins** (same tel; ❶) at Lake Dobson are an excellent base to explore the alpine regions and make up in location for what they lack in amenities – you'll need to bring everything except your own bed and toilet.

Just outside the park entrance, *Russell Falls Holiday Cottages* (℡03/6288 1198; ❺), managed by Something Wild animal sanctuary, is well-located but pricey for its spartan self-contained chalets. Back on the main road in the tiny settlement of National Park, there's basic ground-floor accommodation at the *National Park Hotel* (℡03/6288 1103; ❸ including breakfast), which also prepares evening **meals** from Thursday to Saturday plus a roast for Sunday lunch. At the other end of National Park, alternative café *Celtic Dawn* (℡03/6288 1058) has healthy light meals, with lots of vegetarian options and fresh juices. A unit here is split to create a small double (❸) and a shared room ($30 per person) and there are plans to offer beds in a teepee. The most appealing options hereabouts are 5km east in Westerway. The postbox-red *Platypus Playground* (℡0413 833 700; ⓦwww.riverside-cottage .com; ❺) is a funky one-bed bolthole that opens onto a stream with a resident platypus. Cooking facilities are minimal – only a microwave, toaster and kettle – but there's a gas barbecue on the deck. The adjacent *Possum Shed* café (9am–6pm Wed–Sun) serves tasty lunches – such as baby smoked salmon with lemon stuffing or spinach and feta parcels – on a splendid riverside deck or in the arty café; it's excellent value at around $13 a main and does great coffee too.

South of Hobart

Swooping south through Hobart's suburbs, Sandy Bay Road becomes the Channel Highway (B68) to knit **TAROONA** ever tighter into the city. Its name refers to the "seashells" gathered by the Aboriginal Mouhenener tribe on the Derwent River banks, but its place in Tasmanian history is due to local girl **Mary Donaldson**. Four years after she got chatting to Denmark's Crown Prince Frederick in a Sydney pub in 2000, she was married in a lavish wedding in Copenhagen to become Australia's only homegrown royalty, Crown Princess Mary of Denmark. Princess Mary is now the subject of affection and scrutiny in her home state, with the local press obsessing over outfits and gossip about "Our Mary". At the southern end of the suburb, the chimney-like, sandstone **Shot Tower** (☎03/6227 8885; daily 9am–6pm summer, 9am–5pm winter; $5.50) was built by a Scottish engineer in 1870 for the manufacture of gun shot – droplets of molten lead poured from the top of the 58-metre tower solidified into perfect spheres by the time they reached the bottom. Its summit affords views down the Derwent River estuary and its café rustles up fine Devonshire teas.

KINGSTON, a few kilometres further on, is an overspill commuter town with little to recommend it except a decent urban beach and the headquarters of the **Australian Antarctic Division** (Mon–Fri 8.30am–5pm; ☎03/6232 3516; ⓦwww.aad.gov.au) on the southern fringes of the shopping thoroughfare. A foyer museum provides an overview of South Polar research, from clothing and tools from the 1911–14 Australasian Antarctic Expedition to webcams of current conditions on the ice. More interesting are its documentaries about ongoing science programmes, many focused on the ecological effects of climate change. East of the main drag via Beach Road, **Kingston Beach** is a good urban strand and a popular place to catch the last dash of the Sydney–Hobart yacht race in late December. **Boronia Beach**, is more secluded; it is located 1km south off the main road or via a footpath from the south end of Kingston Beach. **Blackman's Bay**, a further 2km south, has another strand – a popular spot for a lazy weekend brunch.

In Kingston, there's **accommodation** behind the beach on Osborne Esplanade in the homely *Kingston Beach Motel* (☎03/6229 8969; all units with kitchenettes; ❹) and at the *Beachside Hotel* (☎03/6229 6185; ❸). The latter serves good bistro **meals** and has bands on Thursday and Friday nights, or there are café dishes in the *Citrus Moon* (daily 9/10am–5pm, Fri until 9pm) nearby at 23 Beach Rd. However, the finest food in the area is at hip café-restaurant *The Beach* (daily 10am–late) at Blackman's Bay, with gourmet pizzas and smart bistro-style dishes of local produce, all served beachside.

South of Blackman's Bay, the C624 tracks around a thumb of land that pokes into the estuary to reach **Tinderbox**. A car park is the access point for a small **marine reserve** close to the shore. You can snorkel over a sandstone reef on the south side in up to three metres of water, or dive on the platform's deeper northern end, its more exposed aspect attracting leatherjackets and wrasse or the odd big-bellied seahorse wafting among the kelp. Underwater information displays on the sea-bed link up as snorkelling and dive trails.

East of Hobart

Take the Tasman Highway as it zips out of the suburbs and you're following the old colonial road. The area east of Hobart has rich layers of history, especially in the pretty heritage village of **Richmond**, a miniature England that was created as the route's principal staging post. However, there's also ample scope for uncomplicated hedonism: to sample cool-climate wines in the **Coal River Valley** or just kick back on golden sands at **South Arm**. For most day-trippers the big-ticket draw is the **Tasman Peninsula**, home to the finest convict-era site in Australia and one of its most stupendous coastlines. Though manageable in a whirlwind day, its bushwalks and beaches deserve more time if you can spare it.

Richmond

Set in the undulating hills of the Coal River valley, **RICHMOND** is a shining example of the village England the first settlers pined for. Its wealth of Georgian buildings, from solid sandstone manors to tiny timber cottages, makes it not only one of the oldest towns in Australia, but also one of the best-preserved, and it vies with Ross for the accolade of Tasmania's premier heritage village. Unsurprisingly, being just 25km from Hobart, it attracts tourists by the coachload, and in places its heritage appeal teeters on the mawkish. Yet it's a soul-soothing place, blessed with history, good looks and good eating, not to mention heritage accommodation and a string of wine estates nearby (see box, p.104).

A short history

Settlers received land grants in the area not long after the declaration of the colony in 1803, and in 1824 Lieutenant-governor Sorell founded the town on the route between Hobart and the east coast. Richmond Gaol was built in 1825, reflecting Richmond's strategic location, and five years later, traffic to the new penal settlement at Port Arthur began to pass through what was now an important military post and convict station; by the 1830s it was the third-largest town in Tasmania. But with the opening of the **Sorell Causeway** in 1872, a shortcut east from Hobart across Pittwater Bay, Richmond found itself bypassed, a mere rural community with little incentive for change or development. The upside of stagnation is the preservation of approximately fifty buildings from the 1830s and 1840s, many used as galleries, craft shops, cafés, restaurants and guesthouses; most are strung along Bridge Street.

Practicalities

Hobart Coaches runs four **coach** services a day from Hobart, and Tassielink drops off in Richmond on its weekday Hobart to Swansea service. The Richmond Tourist Bus (℡0408 341 804; $25) departs from the visitor information centre in Hobart twice daily (9.15am & 12.20pm) and leaves Richmond at 12.50pm & 3.50pm. Richmond has no visitor information centre, but local flyers are available at Oak Lodge, the model village and gaol; the village website Ⓦwww .richmondvillage.com.au is useful for planning. Guided 45-minute walking **tours** on Sunday (hourly 11am–4pm; $10) depart from Sweets & Treats sweetshop on Bridge Street in the village centre. Ghost tours at dusk are run on demand (℡0409 935 139; $25). A monologue play (daily except Tues, 3pm & 6pm; 45mins; $15) about the life of a transported convict, *Turn The Key of Time*, is performed at 23 Franklin St, Richmond's only cottage without mains water or electricity. The **Online Access Centre** is on Torrens Street (times vary).

Accommodation

If heritage cottage accommodation is your thing, you'll love Richmond. However, the options are limited if your budget is tight – more alternatives are published on the village website (see above) and it's always worth making reservations in summer.

Hollyhock Cottage 3 Percy St ℡03/6260 1079, Ⓦwww.hollyhockcottage.com.au. Small in size, big in bygone character, this is a snug cottage from 1830 with a spa bath. ⑥

Mrs Currie's House 4 Franklin St ℡03/6260 2766, Ⓔmrscurries@optusnet.com.au. Old-fashioned charm and an open log fire in a red-brick B&B with four en suites, formerly a Georgian pub. ⑤

Mulberry Cottage B&B 23a Franklin St ℡03/6260 2664, Ⓦwww.mulberrycottage.com.au. Modern rooms either in the style of French boudoir or

colonial English in a quirky B&B. Price includes theatre performance (see "Practicalities", above). ⑤

Prospect House 1km west of Richmond centre ℡03/6260 2207, Ⓦwww.prospect-house.com.au. The hayloft of this Georgian manorhouse in landscaped grounds has been converted into twelve hotel-style rooms with a heritage theme; comfy but not really as elegant as they should be. ⑥

Richmond Arms Hotel 42 Bridge St ℡03/6260 2109, Ⓦwww.richmondarmshotel.com.au. The cheapest beds in central Richmond are these modest

country-styled units for two to six people, housed in the former pub stables. That in the eaves is brightest, those below feature original sandstone walls. ④–⑤
Richmond Barracks 16 Franklin St ☏03/6260 2453, ⓦwww.richmondbarracks.com. Respite from the heritage aspic – though created from the military barracks, these three self-contained cottages (for two to four people) have modern furnishings and kitchens. ⑤–⑥
Richmond Cabin and Tourist Park Middle Tea Tree Rd, 1km west of Richmond centre ☏1800 116 699 or 03/6260 2192, ⓦwww.richmondcabins.com. A

small, pretty site that's family-friendly – there's an indoor pool, half-size tennis court, games room and a playground – plus it has plenty of shade. Campsites ($16), and cabins with shared facilities (③) or two-bed en suites (④).
Richmond Colonial Accommodation 4 Percy St ☏03/6260 2570, ⓦwww.richmondcolonial.com. Two conjoined one-bed cottages created from the residence of a convict-gang supervisor (1823) and an early 1900s home with a log fire that sleeps five. ⑤–⑥

The Town

A free information leaflet with a map, *Let's Talk About Richmond*, is available at the gaol and information points (see "Practicalities", p.103). The only Georgian manor open to the public is **Oak Lodge** (daily 11.30am–3pm; donation) at Bridge Street's west end. Most furnishings in the two-storey property (built in 1830) are those of the former spinster owners who gifted the house to the National Trust

Coal Valley Vineyards

Although not as famous as the Tamar Valley, the **Coal Valley** nurtures good cool-climate wines on its south-facing slopes. Producers range from boutique producers of 2.5 acres to large estates, most located on Richmond Road (the B31 south to Cambridge). The *Wine South* leaflet from Richmond or Hobart visitor information centres provides a map of all growers and has contact details and cellar door times, or visit ⓦwww.winesouth.com.au or ⓦwww.tasmanianwineroute.com.au.

Below is a list of some of the most noteworthy growers in Coal Valley:

Coal Valley Vineyard 257 Richmond Rd ☏03/6248 5367, ⓦwww.coalvalley.com.au; Thurs–Mon 10am–5pm, closed July. Chardonnay, ripe rieslings and Tasmania's only tempranillo, plus a lovely relaxed restaurant serving modern-rustic Italian-influenced cuisine on a large deck – idyllic. Lunch Thurs–Mon, dinner Fri Oct–Mar.

Craigow 528 Richmond Rd ☏03/6248 4210, ⓦwww.craigow.com.au; daily 11am–5pm, Jan–March. Rieslings, pinot noir and gewürztraminer get rave reviews; tastings are in a colonial farm-worker's cottage.

Hood Wines Corner of Denholms and Richmond roads ☏03/ 6248 5844, ⓦwww.hoodwines.com.au; Sat–Sun 10am–5pm. Wellington wines by Andrew Hood, one of the most respected winegrowers in Australia, plus affiliates the organic Frogmore Creek label and budget Roaring 40s.

Meadowbank 699 Richmond Rd ☏03/6248 4484, ⓦwww.meadowbankwines.com.au; daily 10am–5pm. One of Tasmania's larger wine estates in a glamorous modern tasting centre – upstairs is a display of Australia's oldest wines (mid-1800s), unearthed in a cellar in New Town, Hobart, and a quirky mosaic floor of wine cultivation in Tasmania by artist Tom Samick. As famous for a sophisticated restaurant whose entrée-sized gourmet plates are as delicious as the views over the vineyards. Reservation recommended. Lunch only.

Palmara Vineyard 1314 Richmond Rd ☏03/6260 2492, ⓦwww.palmara.com.au; daily noon–6pm mid–Sept to May. A tiny award-winning vineyard which produces elegant pinot noirs and intriguing boutique wines such as Exotica, an aromatic wine made from seigerrebe grapes.

Puddleduck Vineyard 992 Richmond Rd ☏03/6260 2301, ⓦwww.puddleduckvineyard.com.au; daily 10am–5pm. Small and unpretentious estate by a duck-filled lake; child-friendly and with lauded sparkling wines.

in 1998. However, rooms replicate its former uses as a school and the early 1900s surgery of Dr William Clark, a Harvard-educated American who was friends with Teddy Roosevelt and rented the house for forty years. The upstairs rooms display convict memorabilia, and behind is an English-style cottage garden.

Also on Bridge Street are the wooden **Richmond Maze** (daily 9am–5pm; $6.50) and the **Old Hobart Town Model Village** (daily 9am–5pm; $10), a large-scale outdoor model of Hobart in the 1820s. However, Richmond's most authentic draw is the sandstone, slate-roofed **Richmond Gaol** (daily 9am–5pm; $5.50), an intact example of an early colonial prison. It was erected to hold prisoners in transit or awaiting trial, or as accommodation for convict road gangs, rather than as a place of long-term incarceration. Famous lags who spent time behind its bars include bushranger Martin Cash (see box, p.111) and "Ikey" Solomon, a fence of London's East End on whom Dickens is said to have based the character Fagin in *Oliver Twist*. Displays inside explain the features of the gaol and you can enter a tiny solitary confinement cell measuring 1.8m by 0.9m. Just behind the jail, via a lane seemingly transposed from village England, the church of St Luke's was designed by colonial architect John Lee Archer. Lieutenant-governor Arthur himself laid the foundation stone in 1834; convict labour from the jail did the rest.

Richmond has the distinction of having not only Australia's oldest Roman Catholic church but also its oldest bridge, both at the far end of Bridge Street. **St John's church** dates in part from 1837 and has furnishings and stained glass by Augustus Pugin, the prodigious English architect responsible for the Gothic Revival decoration of London's Houses of Parliament. The stone **bridge** in front was built using convict labour in 1823. The story goes that it is haunted by the ghost of chain-gang master George Grover, a brutal overseer who raised his whip once too often during the construction, and was beaten to death and then thrown into the river by the convicts. Paradoxically, its span over a willow-fringed river is the most idyllic image in Richmond.

Eating

Richmond Bakery on Edward Street, off central Bridge Street, has an attached café for its pastries and pies, plus tables in the courtyard. For a stylish gourmet lunch, head south to the wine estates (see box opposite).

Abby's Prospect House, 1km west of Richmond centre ☎03/6260 2207. Richmond's fine dining address serves Asian and European-influenced cuisine in the Georgian-styled dining room of a manor house. Mains around $25, reservations recommended. Dinner only.

Anton's Best of Tasmania 91 Bridge St. Cheap but great thin-crust pizzas and pasta featuring local ingredients such as salmon and scallops. BYO. Lunch Tues–Sun, dinner Fri–Sun.

Ashmore on Bridge Street 34 Bridge St. This quietly stylish café-bistro rustles up tasty breakfasts, focaccias, salads and jacket potatoes, as well as mains like pan-seared tiger prawns in a creamy garlic sauce. BYO. Lunch daily, dinner Tues. Cheap to moderate.

Richmond Arms Hotel 42 Bridge St ☎03/6260 2109. All the usual pub grub plus upmarket specials – lamb in honey gravy, grilled quail or Tasmanian salmon with lemon salsa – in a characterful old pub. Last order 7.30pm Sun–Thurs, 8pm Fri–Sat.

Richmond Wine House 27 Bridge St. An upmarket café-restaurant in an old weatherboard cottage in pretty gardens. Moderately priced dishes make use of all-Tasmanian ingredients: quail in pinot noir sauce, speciality cheese and antipasto platters. Lunch daily, dinner Wed–Sat.

South Arm

SOUTH ARM, the small hook east of Hobart that hangs into Storm Bay, has the best **beaches** within striking distance of the capital. Although overlooked by most visitors, these are superb strands, largely protected from development by their reserve status. That said, the laid-back coastal villages are attracting a growing smattering of city-style development as commuters relocate for a beach lifestyle. The beaches are also popular with surfers for the wide choice of waves in southerly swells.

Travelling southeast of Hobart, beyond spillover suburb Rokeby, a signposted left turn five kilometres past Lauderdale goes to **Clifton Beach** village, where the beachpads behind the dunes get increasingly glamorous the further you go. The western end of the long strand is patrolled by lifeguards on summer weekends – beware rips if swimming at other times – and has toilets and a cold-water shower. It is also the most popular **surf** beach in the Hobart area; there's a passable beachbreak at its near end which works best from mid- to high-tide, although close-outs can be a problem. South Coast Surf School (☎03 6248 9895 or 0400 489 895, ⓦwww.southcoastsurfschool.com.au; one lesson $40, three lessons $100) provides surfing lessons – on demand during the week and three times a morning over summer weekends – on large soft boards.

More remote beaches – and better, less busy waves – can be found at the end of the dirt tracks off the main road south of the Clifton Beach turning. Just under 8km further, a track into the South Arm Nature Recreation Centre goes to **Calverts Beach**, a great undeveloped beach on the hook's south-facing shore. It has two decent surf breaks, Goats and Rebounds, the latter, beloved by kamikaze bodyboarders. Again, it works best upwards from mid-tide. Note that rips here make swimming dangerous and there is no shade. Continuing west around the hook, the long dune-backed stretch of **Hope Beach** has a decent right-hand break, though being fully exposed to the southerly swells it's also dangerous for swimming. For that, continue a few kilometres to the easygoing village of **South Arm**, whose protected bay is backed by a long arcing crescent of golden sand, albeit reduced to a sliver at high tide. At the end of the road, a shallow beach in front of mellow holiday village **Opposum Bay** receives even more shelter, so is always safe for a dip.

Activities on the Tasman Peninsula

The Tasman Peninsula is the overlooked prize of Tassie **bushwalking**. No other area of the state boasts so many day-walks and short hikes – 35 are listed in Peter and Shirley Storey's authoritative *Peninsula Tracks*. It and Tasmap's hiking map can be sourced in Hobart. Until the proposed 2009 launch of the Three Capes Track, a five-or six-day trail with hut accommodation that will be Australia's greatest coastal walk, the peninsula's superlative track is the **Tasman Coastal Trail**. Its 45-kilometre route (3–5 days one way) heads south from the Devils Arch near Doo Town through the Tasman National Park to the giddy sea-cliffs of Cape Pillar. The going is generally flat but there are a couple of steep ascents, especially that over Tatnell Hill on day one. Six bushcamps are en route, and walkers must carry all food. Track notes are published on the Parks & Wildlife website (ⓦwww.parks.tas.gov.au). Alternatively, Tasmanian Wilderness Experiences (see p.45) operates four guided tours each summer (four days; $982).

The main **surf** breaks are at Eaglehawk Neck, Maignon Bay and Roaring Beach, west of Nubeena. Premier sea-kayaking outfit Roaring 40s runs a great programme of day-trips and extended tours around the coastline from Hobart (see p.95).

Organized tour operators include:

Blackaby's Sea Kayaks ☎0418 124 072, ⓦwww.blackabyseakayaks.com.au. The Hobart-based operator also leads one-day kayaking trips in the Port Arthur bay, around the remote northwest coast and around the stupendous wildlife-rich sea cliffs around Fortescue Bay (all $195).

Eaglehawk Dive Centre 178 Pirates Bay Drive ☎03/6250 3566, ⓦwww .eaglehawkdive.com.au. Dive-boat charters (equipment included) to caves, shipwrecks,

Metro **bus** #294 runs from Hobart to Clifton Beach, then on to the turn-offs for Clarence Beach, and buses #196 and #X17 run all the way to Opossum Bay, bypassing Clifton Beach. In January to the first Friday in February, bus #299S does a morning beach-run from Hobart to Opossum Bay via Clifton Beach, returning in mid-afternoon. Bring a packed lunch – there's no food and only a shop selling takeaway snacks at South Arm.

Seven Mile Beach

East of the South Arm peninsula and 15km east of Hobart off the A3 highway, **Seven Mile Beach** is a favourite spot for Hobartians to take a weekend stroll. It has picnic areas with barbecues and tables, toilets with a cold-water shower and a Parks & Wildlife office (Mon–Fri 9am–4pm; ☏03 6214 8100) at its east end. The village itself has a general store and a small holiday park with backpacker accommodation, *Seven Mile Beach Cabin Park* (☏03/6248 6469, ℻03/6248 6846; sites $15, dorms $20; rooms ❸, self-contained units ❹, cabins ❺) – served by a regular bus service to the city centre (1hr), it makes an appealing beach alternative to the city camping in Claremont, Hobart. Back on the main road, *Barilla Bay* restaurant (☏03/6248 5458; lunch daily except July & Aug, dinner Tues–Sat) is famed for the oysters cultivated in adjacent Pittwater Bay; you can also sample them in its café. It is also worth a visit for its gourmet Tassie produce (daily 7.30am–6pm).

Seven Mile Beach is served by regular Metro buses #191, #192, #292 and #293 – allow 1hr from city to beach.

The Tasman Peninsula

The Tasman Peninsula should be one of Tasmania's premier destinations. Crammed onto its hook-shaped peninsula 100km east of Hobart are more short

kelp forests and nearby seal colonies with an underwater visibility of 15–30m; quality is world-class and dives are surprisingly colourful. Two boat-dive packages from $190, plus night dives, speciality courses and tuition (Discover Scuba $199, four-day PADI open-water $550). Also offers equipment hire and dorm accommodation for $25.

Personalised Sea Charters Pirates Bay, Eaglehawk Neck ☏03/6250 3370, ✉seachart@southcom.com.au. Game-, deep-sea-, reef- and bay-fishing trips on a 26ft boat, all gear and bait supplied, and a catch guaranteed. Half- and full-day. Also offers bespoke wildlife tours. Prices vary.

Sealife Experience Tasmania Eaglehawk Neck (booking office on main road, Dunalley) ☏03/6253 5325, ⓦwww.sealife.com.au. Operating from Pirates Bay, runs 3.5hr eco-tours of the rich seas of the east coast cliffs to a fur seal colony at Cape Pillar. The boat has an underwater camera to view wildlife below the waves and provides a gentler ride than that of Tasman Island Cruises. Daily 10am; $95.

Seaview Riding Koonya ☏03/6250 3110. Scenic trail-riding for all ages and experience levels, plus riding for the disabled. From $30 per hour.

Tasman Island Cruises Port Arthur ☏03/6250 2200, ⓦwww.tasmancruises.com.au. Eco-tours with adrenaline in a new venture by the Bruny Island Charters crew. Has the same 750hp speedboats, but now offers a more spectacular three-hour ride along the east-coast cliffs. Locations and embarkation point vary according to conditions, but the enthusiastic commentary and wildlife such as sea birds, fur seals and albatross – plus dolphins and whales (Nov–Dec) if you're lucky – are always the same. Highly recommended. Daily 10am, plus 2pm Dec–May; $100.

bushwalks than anywhere else in Tasmania, wilderness beaches, a decent array of activities, a couple of great bushcamping sites, virtually the full spotter's book of native wildlife, and the state's most spectacular coastline, featuring the highest sea-cliffs in Australia. Yet so famous – or perhaps infamous – is its principal sight, the convict settlement of **Port Arthur**, that the peninsula itself is, paradoxically, one of the state's hidden jewels.

It was ever so – the penal establishment became a ghoulish tourist attraction as soon as it was closed in 1877, and it remains Tasmania's most-visited site, as well as the most historic site from Australia's convict past. But the fact that your entry ticket is valid for 48 hours is just one more reason to explore away from the big-ticket draw. The eco-cruises along the east coast are reason enough to visit, the temperate-water diving is world-class, and if a proposed Three Capes Track gets the green light in 2009, its route along the staggering coastline of capes Hauy, Pillar and Raoul will become a multi-day classic to rival the famous Overland Track. It might even eclipse Port Arthur.

East to Eaglehawk Neck

The fastest route from Hobart heads east along the Tasman Highway and across the Sorell Causeway, laid in the 1870s as a short-cut across Pittwater Bay, to the nondescript small town of **SORELL**, which has largely rubbed out all evidence that it was once one of Tasmania's oldest settlements. However, it has the last good shopping before the peninsula, and, just east, the **Sorell Fruit Farm** (daily Oct–May 9am–5pm; ☎03/6265 2744, ⓦsorellfuitfarm.com) a local institution for pick-your-own fruit and berries with a good café. A useful stop for picnic provisions.

From Sorell, the Arthur Highway cuts 21km southeast to **COPPING**, where an automated mannequin waves you into the **Copping Colonial & Convict Collection** (9am–5pm daily; $8), more accurate in its subtitle a "living museum of fabulous junk" – three small warehouses of it, from knickers to numberplates via bygone sewing machines and farm machinery collected by a local resident. A few leg irons and manacles among the dotty horde permit the convict tag. An alternative route from Sorell tracks the coastline southeast via the small beach settlements of Lewisham and Dodges Ferry, with a decent surfbeach, Park Beach.

Both routes lead to **DUNALLEY** on an isthmus to the **Forestier Peninsula**; the connecting bridge opens regularly to let boats through. The area's moment in history occurred on December 3, 1624. In the late afternoon, a landing party piloted by Dutch navigator Abel Tasman beached 3km west of today's settlement and became the first Europeans on Tasmania. During three day's R&R after a storm-tossed week, Tasman recorded "fruitful timber in plenty… trees 2.5 fathoms [4.5m] thick" and stored samples of a strange square animal poo (a wombat's). He also heard a "trumpet", probably the call of a crow-like currawong, and saw smoke, though did not see any Aborigines. From the notches he saw carved into a tree trunk 1.5m apart, he deduced that the natives might be giants, a proposition that inspired Jonathan Swift's Brobdingnag, the land of giants in *Gulliver's Travels*. Near a waterfront memorial, signposted off the main road, the *Waterfront Café* (daily 10am–4pm) is a relaxing place with superb views of the fishing boats anchored just offshore. Further south near the bridge, the *Dunalley Fish Market* (9am–5pm daily, except Fri until 7.30pm) rustles up fresh fish and chips, and, just over the bridge, the *Dunalley Hotel* (☎03/6253 5101) prepares seafood specials. It also permits free camping in an adjacent field. It's a further 42km to **Eaglehawk Neck** – en route, a general store at the hamlet of **Murdunna** has tasty home-made scallop pies and local octopus marinated in

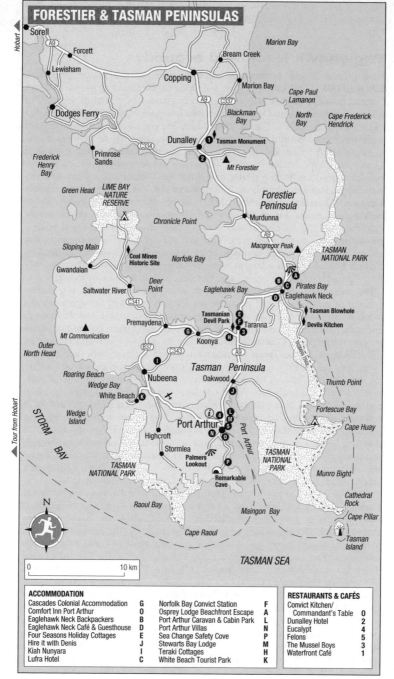

FORESTIER & TASMAN PENINSULAS

Orford

Hobart

Sorell
Forcett
Lewisham
Dodges Ferry
Primrose Sands
Frederick Henry Bay
Copping
Bream Creek
Marion Bay
Marion Bay
Cape Paul Lamanon
North Bay
Cape Frederick Hendrick
Blackman Bay
Dunalley ❶ Tasman Monument
❷
Mt Forestier
Forestier Peninsula
Green Head
LIME BAY NATURE RESERVE
Chronicle Point
Murdunna
Macgregor Peak
TASMAN NATIONAL PARK
Sloping Main
Coal Mines Historic Site
Norfolk Bay
Gwandalan
Saltwater River
Deer Point
Eaglehawk Bay
B A
C Pirates Bay
D Eaglehawk Neck
Tasman Blowhole
Devils Kitchen
Premaydena
Tasmanian Devil Park
E
F Taranna
3
H
Mt Communication
Koonya
Outer North Head
Roaring Beach
Nubeena
Oakwood
Tasman Peninsula
Thumb Point
Wedge Bay
White Beach
Wedge Island
K
Highcroft
Port Arthur
ℹ d
L M
5
N O
J
Fortescue Bay
Cape Huay
STORM BAY
Stormlea
Palmers Lookout
P
Port Arthur
TASMAN NATIONAL PARK
Munro Bight
Remarkable Cave
TASMAN NATIONAL PARK
Raoul Bay
Maingon Bay
Cathedral Rock
Cape Pillar
Tasman Island
Cape Raoul
TASMAN SEA

Tour from Hobart

N

0   10 km

ACCOMMODATION

Cascades Colonial Accommodation	G
Comfort Inn Port Arthur	O
Eaglehawk Neck Backpackers	B
Eaglehawk Neck Café & Guesthouse	D
Four Seasons Holiday Cottages	E
Hire it with Denis	J
Kiah Nunyara	I
Lufra Hotel	C
Norfolk Bay Convict Station	F
Osprey Lodge Beachfront Escape	A
Port Arthur Caravan & Cabin Park	L
Port Arthur Villas	N
Sea Change Safety Cove	P
Stewarts Bay Lodge	M
Teraki Cottages	H
White Beach Tourist Park	K

RESTAURANTS & CAFÉS

Convict Kitchen/ Commandant's Table	O
Dunalley Hotel	2
Eucalypt	4
Felons	5
The Mussel Boys	3
Waterfront Café	1

lemon as well as a few provisions; and the Tasman National Park Lookout 2km before the Neck provides a superb panorama over the eucalyptus crowns to Pirate Bay.

Eaglehawk Neck and around

Sited on the narrow isthmus that joins the Forestier and Tasman peninsulas, **EAGLEHAWK NECK** served as the door to Lieutenant-governor Arthur's "natural penitentiary" (see Port Arthur, p.112), guarded by a permanent watch of soldiers and the infamous Dog Line. This ferocious pack of mongrels, given pugnacious sobriquets such as Caesar, Ugly Mug, Tear'em and Jowler, were chained with sufficient scope to intercept any hopeful absconders where the Neck was at its narrowest. A bronze dog just south of the hut marks the position of the Dog Line. Later escape attempts across the bay (see box, opposite) even led to dogs being stationed on floating platforms. Of the area's substantial military base – a guardhouse, barracks, semaphore station, sentry box and jetty – only the timber **Officers' Quarters** dating from 1832 survives. Reputedly the oldest timber building in Australia, it is still the "rickety little wooden house" that one lieutenant described in 1835 (albeit a room or two longer after extensions), and holds a **mini-museum** on the Eaglehawk Neck site and early colonial history, including information on Aboriginal conflicts. Entry is free and the museum, managed by Parks & Wildlife, is open as long as the nearby *Officers Mess* café and takeaway (daily 9am–6pm). However, the café's future was uncertain at the time of writing.

The long beach on **Pirates Bay** that fronts Eaglehawk Neck is a superb crescent of powder sand and turquoise sea – it gets good surf in large south and southeasterly swells, especially wrapping around into its southern end. At its north end is the Tessellated Pavement, a rock shelf eroded into bizarre cobble-like blocks by salt crystallization. Grander natural features are at its southern end, reached by the road beyond **Doo Town** – a fisherman named the first shack here Doo-Us (as in "this will do us") in the 1950s, then a mate joined in with "I Doo Two" to set the course for today's hamlet filled with excruciating puns. By the car park, where a snack van (daily Oct–April) sells local oysters and seafood pies, ice cream and strawberries, a blowhole sprays whenever massive swells crump through its collapsed sea cave. An adjacent path makes a short circuit around the adjacent headland of **Fossil Bay** to a lookout, although a sidetrack that descends to a slab shelf in front of the cliffs should only be made in the calmest conditions. A secondary road south near the blowhole goes to **Tasmans Arch**, another collapsed sea cave with lookouts, and, a few hundred metres further, the **Devil's Kitchen**, a sheer cleft in the cliffs from where you can look down at the foaming sea.

Waterfall Bay Road as you enter Doo Town leads into the **Tasman National Park**, and after a few kilometres a small bay ringed by staggering cliffs. This is also the start of a number of **cliffside walks** through the bush: north to Paterson Arch (30min return) or back to Tasman Arch (1hr return); and south to Waterfall Bluff (2hr return), where you get great views of fluted dolerite cliffs towering 200m over swirling ocean. You can also follow the Tasman Coastal Track 16km south to the campground at Bivouac Bay (6.5hr one-way), north of Fortescue Bay (see p.112).

Heading southwest of Eaglehawk Neck, the road traces the shore of Norfolk Bay to **TARANNA**. From 1836, convicts hauled carriages of food, coal and even passengers from a terminus on the bay to Port Arthur on Australia's first railway, pushing the trucks uphill, then leaping aboard when they clattered down. The tracks were laid to save supply ships the perilous journey around the peninsula's southern coast, but were abandoned once the penal settlement became self-sufficient. Ask at the *Norfolk Bay Convict Station*, now a heritage B&B, to see a

Martin Cash, escapee extraordinaire

Neither the formidable security at Eaglehawk Neck nor rumours of shark-infested seas around the Tasman Peninsula deterred convicts from escape attempts. Many bolters starved in the dense bush or drowned while attempting a crossing on makeshift rafts. One, Billy Hunt, attempted to hop across the Neck disguised as a kangaroo, a ruse which only went awry when soldiers took potshots at the unusually large boomer, forcing the escapee to reveal himself. Punishment for those caught was severe – around fifty lashes, solitary confinement at Port Arthur, and possibly an assignment to the feared coal mines at the northern tip of the peninsula.

Yet a few attempts succeeded, garnering high prestige among the criminal under-world for those who made it. That **Martin Cash** slipped away twice helps account for his status as the most celebrated bushranger of Van Diemen's Land. A Wexford-born Irishman transported for shooting a man in 1827 – he argued he only fired because the victim was embracing his wife – and who had worked his ticket of leave in New South Wales, Cash was imprisoned in Port Arthur for larceny in 1839. He escaped and eluded the authorities for two years until recaptured and reincarcerated. This time he fell in with a pair of old-hand bushrangers, Lawrence Kavenagh and George Jones, also from New South Wales, and on Boxing Day 1842, the three bolted from a quarry chain-gang. Rather than flee immediately, the wily trio bided their time at Eaglehawk Neck – according to local folktale they hid out at Cash's Lookout, off the Blowhole road at the south end of Pirates Bay – until the guard was relaxed after three days, then swam quietly across the bay.

So began an eight-month spree during which the gang ranged southern and central Tasmania, robbing inns and the houses of moneyed settlers seemingly with impunity. However, they were far from the desperate absconders of the colony's infancy. Violence was avoided where possible, women were treated with the utmost respect, the poor were never robbed unless the need was dire, and raids were undertaken with such wit and daring that Cash acquired a reputation as a "gentleman bushranger" like some latter-day Robin Hood. Cheekily, the gang sent a letter from "Messrs Cash and Co" to Governor John Franklin, demanding the release of Cash's girlfriend, Bessie Clifford, from Hobart Town gaol on pain of "a wholesome lesson in the shape of a sound flogging, beginning with Sir John". But when Cash risked a trip to Hobart to spring Bessie, he was captured. At the last hour, his death sentence was reduced to transportation to Norfolk Island for ten years, and there Cash mellowed into a respectable character renowned as a fine milliner. He married an Irish ex-convict and returned to Hobart (ironically working initially as a constable) before he was granted a pardon in 1863 and died a free man in 1877.

His popular reputation as a cheerful scoundrel blessed with blarney and a rapscallion charm is largely due to a biography by author James Lester Burke published during his lifetime; it is unclear which of the two Irishmen dressed up his exploits with the rose-tinted detail of *The Adventures of Martin Cash* (1870). Writer Marcus Clarke turned to Cash for the swashbuckling convict John Rex in his romantic tragedy *For the Term of His Natural Life* and some reports claim that Aussie tennis hero Pat Cash is a descendant.

model of the carriages. A little further on is the **Tasmanian Devil Conservation Park** (9am–5pm daily; $22 unlimited entry day-ticket), a government-sponsored refuge for the threatened state icon. It's worth timing a visit with feeding displays (10am, 11am, 1.30pm & 5pm; 4.30pm May–Sept) to hear a talk about efforts to combat Devil Facial Tumour disease, a contagious cancer which has wiped out over sixty per cent of the population. You can also just wander around the park at other times to see its captive devils. The park also has the state's only raptor free-flight shows (11.15am & 3.30pm). Opposite, Federation

Chocolate (9am–5pm daily; free) has a room of bygone forestry and blacksmith tools to honour the former trades of a family now producing handmade chocs.

Fortescue Bay, Cape Hauy and Cape Pillar

Hauntingly beautiful **Fortescue Bay**, 12km along a bumpy track in the Tasman National Park (standard entry fees apply), is probably the most idyllic spot on the Tasman Peninsula. The former site of a whaling camp in the early 1800s, then a semaphore station and sawmill during the convict era, its white powder beach is exceptionally clean, its sheltered turquoise waters gin-clear. There's also great camping in several areas (see "Accommodation", p.116).

If you fancy doing more than loafing on the beach, a number of **bushwalks** head off into the national park. Note that bar a display board at Fortescue Bay, there's no walking information on the peninsula, so pick up hiking maps in Hobart – Tasmap publish three at 1:25,000 scale and a passable 1:75,000 of the park area, all with notes. An easy stroll goes north along the foreshore to a Fairy penguin rookery at Canoe Bay (2hr return) – visit at dusk to see the birds return to their roosts – and on to a remote campsite at Bivouac Bay (4hr return). From here you can join the Tasman Coastal Trail to Waterfall Bay (16km; 6.5hr one-way). A route of medium difficulty follows the bay east to reach the spectacular dolerite headland of Cape Hauy (4hr return), from where you get views of offshore rock columns The Lanterns and, close to the shore, The Totem Pole. The latter 65-metre sea-stack is one of Australia's most prestigious climbs, and one to tick off for any adrenaline-junkie in Tasmania. For information on the route, best made in four-strong groups and which requires a boat trip or a brave soul to swim across to the stack to create a traverse, pick up a copy of climbing guide *Craglets* ($4) in Hobart outdoors centres or at indoor climbing centre The Climbing Edge at 54 Bathurst Street (℡03/6234 3575).

For more experienced hikers, the Cape Pillar Track (30km; 2–4 days return) is a tough but spectacular bushwalk through temperate forest and grassplains to the dizzying, 300-metre sea-cliffs at the southeast tip of the peninsula, the highest in Australia. The cape's exposure to the full fury of the Southern Ocean means the wind can be extreme – names en route include Tornado Ridge and Hurricane Heath – so check the weather forecast and be prepared for all eventualities. That said, with the right equipment and sufficient care, a night spent here in a blow is as compelling as it is unnerving. You can also connect with the track via a trail off the Cape Hauy route, though this involves a slog over Mount Fortescue.

Port Arthur

The most unceasing labour is to be extracted from the convicts . . . and the most harassing vigilance over them is to be observed.

Lieutenant-governor George Arthur

Lieutenant-governor George Arthur interpreted Tasman Island as a "natural penitentiary", walled by cliffs and with an easily guarded "door" at Eaglehawk Neck. The disciplinarian also recognized it would be more practical to administrate from Hobart than the Sarah Island prison that his predecessor had established in Macquarie Harbour. However, the principles trialled at that west coast penal island would remain. **PORT ARTHUR** was to be a **prison settlement** for re-offenders who had committed serious crimes in New South Wales or Van Diemen's Land; men who were condemned as the worst of the worst, with no redeeming features. The regime was never

Food and drink

Local and pure are the watchwords of contemporary cuisine in Tasmania. There's still pub grub, but as superstar chefs do innovative things with the island's produce, the state now takes its food and drink seriously, albeit in a typically unpretentious New World way. The problem now is one of choice: go for fish and chips, Modern Oz, a scallop pie, succulent berries, the best steak in Australia or just throw a snag on the barbie?

Fish and seafood

Anything caught in the pristine seas that lap Tasmania is exceptionally good, and the state standard-bearer is **fish and chips**. A dish that's more ubiquitous than in Britain and far healthier, it features fish such as trevally, tuna, blue eye, stripey trumpeter and flake (shark), and comes battered, breadcrumbed or fried. Atlantic **salmon** farmed in the cold, nutrient-rich D'Entrecasteaux Channel and Macquarie Harbour is superb, as is **shellfish**, especially the plump oysters farmed at Bruny Island and Coles Bay. Blue mussels, wild abalone and crayfish are specialities – Bass Islanders would say theirs are the best crays in the world, though fishermen from Stanley might disagree. The main freshwater fish is **trout**, sourced from the lakes of the central highlands.

Cheese and fruits

At the last count, there were 150,000 dairy cows on 700 farms munching Tasmania's rich pasture. Their milk provides the raw material for **gourmet cheeses** that have become an island speciality. Most follow the mould of British varieties such as cheddar or Lancashire, often laced with island fruits, berries or walnuts. However, the state's premier producer, King Island Dairy, is renowned for creamy bries. Other award-winning cheese producers include Pyengana Cheese Factory, near St Helens, the Bruny Island Cheese Company, and sheep's-cheese specialist Grandvewe.

The "Apple Isle" still produces **apples**, but the orchard growers of the southeast have now branched out into cherries and pears. The cool climate is ideal for **berries** such as strawberries and blackcurrants: growers at Swansea and Scamander are not to be missed.

Apple sellers at Salamanca market, Hobart ▲

Lobster pots at Victoria Dock, Hobart ▼

Cake and bread stall at Salamanca market, Hobart ▼

Modern Australian cuisine

A shifting term if ever there was one. Once Modern Australian signified contemporary cooking that nodded towards Southeast Asia. Then it swung towards more Mediterranean flavours and now it often cherrypicks from the best of both. Perhaps the best definition of "**Mod Oz**" is as a fusion of cuisines from the largest immigrant groups of Australia. Tasmania has added its own twist by featuring the best **local produce**, which perhaps explains why many island chefs have turned away from fussy recipes to let the ingredients shine. Many also favour menus of tapas-style tasting plates over a larger single dish. Though Hobart and Launceston are the hubs of contemporary Mod Oz eating, vineyard restaurants such as those at Meadowbank or Coal Valley near Richmond, *Home Hill* at Ranelagh or *Daniel Alps* at *Strathlynn* in the Tamar Valley are among the best.

▲ Restaurant at Meadowbank vineyard, Cambridge

▼ Daniel Alps at Strathlynn restaurant, Rosevears

Steak

Tasmania is the only Australian state to ban the use of hormonal growth stimulants and antibiotics in the cattle industry. Factor in some of the purest air in the world and feed from the lushest pasture in Australia (rather than grain) and all the requirements are there for seriously good steak. The best of the best is cultivated on King Island, where juicy, fat T-bone steaks rule – almost no one on the island eats fillet. You'll also find it on many high-end menus throughout the state.

Wine and beer

Despite its relatively recent emergence onto the nation's **wine** radar, Tasmania has been producing it since 1823 – the acclaimed wine industries in South Australia and Victoria were established through cuttings from the other side of the Bass Strait. Today Tasmania has over two hundred **vineyards** and nearly thirty wineries. Most are in the Tamar Valley, the premier wine-growing region north of Launceston, followed by the Coal Valley, near Hobart, and a handful on the mid-east coast around Cranbrook and just west of Hobart. Each has its own wine route to taste and buy direct from the producer – called "cellar door", covered in relevant chapters – and restaurants always list a decent local range. It's the **cool-climate wines** that are best-known – pinot noirs, cabernet sauvignons, chardonnay, riesling – but the sparkling wines of Bay of Fires and Jansz near Pipers Brook also get the wine gongs. Tourism Tasmania promotes wine routes in all viticulture areas: details are in the relevant chapters and state tourism site Ⓦwww.tasmanianwineroute.com.au, which has map downloads, or from local visitor information centres.

All Tasmanians tell you their **beers** are the best in Australia. The disagreement is over which is better: Hobart-brewed Cascade or Launceston's Boag's. Just don't remind Hobartians that Boag's is the most awarded beer in brewing history – they'll probably counter that Cascade is the oldest brewery in Australia. Alongside the two beer giants is a growing number of craft breweries producing ales from local hops: Moo Brew, Dark Isle, Hazards Ale and Two Metres Tall are names to request.

Boag's beer ▲

Vineyard at Pipers Brook ▼

Picnic at Moorilla wine estate ▼

a subtle one. The goal was to reform or break habitual criminals and Arthur decreed a convict's "whole fate should be ... the very last degree of misery consistent with humanity". Yet the policy was less wilfully punitive than a flawed experiment in criminal reform; contemporary English prison reformer Jeremy Bentham conceived the penitentiary as "a machine for grinding rogues honest". And the provision of regular meals, free clothing and regular trade work meant some men lived better lives at Port Arthur than they had in the slums from which they had been transported.

The prison settlement opened in September 1830 and the first 150 convicts were worked like slaves to establish a timber industry in the surroundings of Eaglehawk Neck. Gradually, Port Arthur became a self-supporting industrial centre: the timber industry grew into shipbuilding, there was brickmaking and shoemaking, market gardening and wheat-growing, even a flour mill. There was also a separate prison for boys – the first in the British Empire – at **Point Puer**, where the inmates were taught trades for their rehabilitation after eventual release. From the 1840s until transport of convicts ceased in 1853, the settlement grew steadily, the early timber constructions later replaced by brick and stone buildings. The lives of the labouring convicts contrasted sharply with those of the prison officers and their families, who strolled ornamental gardens, performed in a drama club, and had a library and cricket fields.

In many ways, the years after transport ended were more horrific than those that preceded them, as physical beatings were replaced by psychological punishments; Victorian social theory had swung around to the argument that unrelenting discipline only hardened criminals, whereas solitary confinement would let them ponder their misdeeds in quiet. In 1849, the **Separate Prison** was opened, based on a new spoked-wheel design of Pentonville Prison, London. Here, prisoners were kept in total isolation and absolute silence in tiny cells for up to thirty days; they were referred to by numbers rather than names and wore hoods whenever they left their cells.

The prison continued to operate until 1877, unsurprisingly now incorporating its own **mental asylum** full of ex-convicts, as well as a geriatric home for ex-convict paupers. In 1870, Port Arthur was popularized by Marcus Clarke's novel *For the Term of His Natural Life* and the public showed a ghoulish fascination for its buildings and tragedies – soon after the prison closed, guided tours were provided by the same men who had been wrecked by the regime. When Tasmania faced up to the "convict stain" in the 1970s, a major restoration project began. Yet tragedy seems bound to the site: another horrific chapter in Port Arthur's history occurred in April 1996, when the **massacre** of 35 tourists and local people by lone gunman Martin Bryant made international headlines. The Broad Arrow Café where twenty people were killed has been partially dismantled and transformed into a memorial, with a garden and reflecting pool around the remaining walls. Understandably, the subject still touches a raw nerve – visitors are requested to act sensitively and not enquire about the tragedy.

Visits to the **Port Arthur Historic Site** (☎1800 659 101, ⓦwww.portarthur .org.au; ticket office ☎03/6251 2300; daily 8.30am–dusk; office 8.30am–11pm; $28 for 48hr pass, includes 40min tour and 20min harbour cruises; combined ticket with ghost tour $44; 1hr audio tours for $6) take in a huge area and more than thirty buildings, the most important of which are documented in an excellent guidebook provided free. Some, like the poignant **prison chapel**, are furnished and restored. Others, like the bar-windowed penitentiary or the **church** covered in ivy, are ruins in a picturesque landscape of green lawns, shady trees and paths that slope down to a cove. The beautiful setting – a paradox remarked upon even during penal days – makes it feel less a prison than a serene old-world campus. The site also has a good visitor centre – an entertaining "Lottery of Life" exhibit in which you follow an allocated character highlights the arbitrary fates of those who were transported – and a busy bistro. With such a lot to see, it's worth spreading a visit over the allotted two days, divided by a trip elsewhere on the peninsula.

Additional **tours** are also available: a cruise on the *MV Marana* to explore the boys' prison at Point Puer (daily except Aug; 2hr; $12); the **Isle of the Dead** (daily except Aug; 1hr; $10), Port Arthur's cemetery from 1833 to 1877, where you can view the resting places of 1100 convicts, asylum inmates, paupers and free men; and a hugely popular **Historic Ghost Tour** (daily at dusk; 1hr 30min; $20; bookings essential) conducted amid the ruins by lamplight. All tours are booked at the ticket office or on the main site telephone number.

The rest of the Tasman Peninsula

South of Port Arthur, rugged **Mango Bay** provides great views south to the dolerite stacks off Cape Raoul. An adjacent stairway descends to a platform positioned to watch the waves surge through **Remarkable Cave**; an atmospheric spot when swells surge through its slab-sided tunnel and foam just beneath your feet. There's a good right-hand surf break on the west side of the bay, although Southern Ocean swells here can be heavy. The main road (A9) from Port Arthur heads west. A turning after 10km heads south via the hamlet of Highcroft to a car park for the start of the walk to the 200m cliffs of **Cape Raoul** (5hr return). A sidetrack northwest of the route goes to **Shipstern's Bluff** (5hr return), renowned as the site of the heaviest surf break in Australia; an awesome, heaving monster-wave comparable to Teaupoo in Tahiti, it is impressive even for non-surfers, which only breaks in southerly swells over 5m. Unsurprisingly, "Shippies" is a break for kamikazee pros only. Some locals call it Fluffies.

A couple of kilometres beyond the turning is **Nubeena**, the Tasman Peninsula's commercial and administrative centre, where you'll find two good supermarkets with post office facilities and an ATM, fuel, a pharmacy, a bakery, and a couple of fish-and-chip takeaways. It also has a couple of pubs, both with bottleshops. A kilometre or so beforehand, there's a long sheltered beach at the minor resort of **White Beach**. Alternatively, a few kilometres on a dirt road west of Nubeena is **Roaring Beach**, pounded by heaving surf; from the car park go left alongside the lagoon then over the dunes to reach the beach.

North of Nubeena you pass through a string of farmholdings to reach **Premaydena**, where a general store sells fuel and basic supplies. About 6km beyond it is the **Coal Mines Historic Site**. Although less notorious than the Port Arthur penitentiary, the penal settlement mine was more feared by convicts, and a sentence here was reserved for the worst offenders. Opened in 1834, the mine was producing fifty tonnes of coal a day by 1847, extracted by gangs who toiled for sixteen hours in near-total darkness – in the oxygen-starved seams 90m down, lamps gave out very little light. Unsurprisingly, deaths among miners were common, although authorities were more vexed by rife homosexuality. Indeed, "moral grounds" were cited alongside financial for the mine's closure in 1848. The coal wasn't even of particularly high quality; one writer bemoaned its tendency to spit embers when hot, "to the detriment of carpets, ladies' gowns etc". The most impressive relics of the mining operation, which are scattered in the bush over a wide area and signposted off the main road, are the ruined sandstone buildings at the convict precinct. It

▲ Cliffs at Cape Raoul

retains the punishment cells and a corridor of single apartments erected to combat homosexuality, their windowless stone cubbies little different in terms of comfort.

A few kilometres beyond the site, **Lime Bay Nature Reserve** has a spacious bushcamp beside a bay, with lots of shade for the grassy sites and pit toilets. However, be aware that there is no drinking water.

Practicalities and tours

Tassielink has a single afternoon service to Port Arthur (Mon–Fri during school terms; Mon, Wed & Fri during school holidays), stopping en route at Eaglehawk Neck and all other destinations on an anticlockwise circuit of the peninsula. There are also plenty of day-tours run by private operators, most of which sample some of the Tasman Peninsula sights en route. Bottom Bits's small-group tours ($110; Sat only; see p.44) cover the Eaglehawk Neck area and the historic site, including a dusk Ghost Tour. Tassielink ($90; Tues–Fri & Sun; see p.45) runs similar daytime tours. Tasman Island Cruises ($220; see box, p.107) includes its exhilarating eco-cruise with a bus tour from Hobart to the Port Arthur site. Navigator Cruises go from Hobart (Sun, Wed & Fri; $149; see p.75) along the coast to the site, returning by coach. The **visitor centre** at Port Arthur is the best source of tourist information on the peninsula, or for planning visit regional tourism website ⓦwww .portarthur-region.com.au. Fuel and supermarkets with ATM and post office facilities are at Port Arthur and Nubeena, the latter with the best choice of produce.

Accommodation

As well as the campsites listed here, there's good **bushcamping** at idyllic Fortescue Bay (Ⓣ03/6250 2433, reservations recommended Dec–Jan; $6 per person), with toilets, cold-water showers and barbecues. You can also camp in the Tasman National Park north of Port Arthur, and at Lime Bay Nature Reserve (free; pit toilets; no water), 1km north of the Coal Mines Historic Site. At some point, the dated *Comfort Inn* at Port Arthur is due to make way for a glamorous heritage-styled luxury hotel by Federal Resorts, though the schedule is still to be confirmed.

Eaglehawk Neck, Taranna and Koonya

Cascades Colonial Accommodation Koonya Ⓣ03/6250 3873, ⓦwww.cascadescolonial .com.au. This is a National Trust-listed 1840s probation station, owned by a farming family for five generations, now converted into self-catering cottages in heritage style with a smattering of antiques, most with open fires and one with a spa. ⑤–⑦

Eaglehawk Neck Backpackers 94 Old Jetty, 1km west of Officers Mess, Eaglehawk Neck Ⓣ 03/6250 3248. A friendly, nonsmoking and green (in both senses) hostel, although it only has four beds, so reservations are essential. There are also a few tent pitches in the garden. Camping $8, dorm $20, rooms ②

Eaglehawk Neck Café & Guesthouse Arthur Highway, 500m south of Officers Mess Ⓣ03/6250 3331, ⓦwww.theneck.com.au. Above an excellent café, this has two pleasant en suites, wood-panelled

and coloured in warm shades of ochre and mustard. Good value. ④

Four Seasons Holiday Cottages Arthur Highway, Taranna Ⓣ0407/044 483, ⓦwww.fourseasons holidaycottages.com.au. An upmarket self-catering option geared towards families, this has spacious two-storey cottages on the bay, relaxed but stylish in modern décor and flooded with light. ⑥

Lufra Hotel Pirates Bay Drive, Eaglehawk Neck Ⓣ03/6250 3262, ⓦwww.lufrahotel.com. A member of the Best Western chain, this has above-average hotel-style rooms with three-star facilities. Although not in place at the time of research, it should now also offer new suites with great views across Pirates Bay. ⑤

Norfolk Bay Convict Station Arthur Highway, Taranna Ⓣ03/6250 3487, ⓦwww.convictstation. com. Patchwork quilts and quirky heritage character in five colourful suites of a convict-built former warehouse (1838), located by the jetty of the old railway terminus. Home-made jams and juices are provided for breakfast. ⑥

Osprey Lodge Beachfront Escape 14 Osprey Rd, Eaglehawk Neck ☎03/6250 3629. Fantastic views and hospitality in a comfortable B&B at the north end of Pirates Bay. Floral fabrics and ocean views in all en suites. ⑥

Teraki Cottages 19 Nubeena Rd, Taranna ☎03/6250 3436. Four fairly old-fashioned but clean rustic wooden cottages in the bush; one- and two-bed, all with kitchens, laundry facilities and a log fire. Call before you visit because the business was for sale at the time of research. ④

Port Arthur, White Beach and Nubeena

Comfort Inn Port Arthur 29 Safety Cove Rd, Port Arthur ☎1800 030 747, ⊛www.portarthur-inn .com.au. An unrivalled location overlooking the historic site, but let down by the tired motel-style rooms in a dated hotel. Overpriced and can be block-booked by tour groups. ⑤

🚶 **Hire it with Denis** Oakwood, 3km north of Port Arthur, ☎03/6200 9998, ⊛www .accommodationportarthur.com. A sort of private backpacker's, this snug settler's cottage for up to four is full of ramshackle charm. The affable owner sells fresh eggs, has the only Internet connection in the area, and can pick up guests from Port Arthur. No stove (though there is a mircowave), and own linen required, but a bargain. ③

Kiah Nunyara 2.5km northeast of Nubeena, off C343 to Koonya ☎03/6250 2281, ⊛www .kiahnunyara.com.au. The perfect rural retreat from summer crowds, this is a modern self-contained cottage on a fifty-acre farm. Hospitable owners, abundant wildlife, superb views and fresh bread baked for guests. ⑤

Port Arthur Caravan & Cabin Park Garden Point, 2km north of Port Arthur ☎03/6250 2340, ⊛www .portarthurcaravan-cabinpark.com.au. Bunkhouse

rooms and camping, with an excellent enclosed camp-kitchen, at a tree-filled site. Camping $20, dorms $18, en-suite cabins ④

Port Arthur Villas 52 Safety Cove Rd, Port Arthur ☎03/6250 2239, ⊛www.portarthurvillas.com.au. Better value than the *Comfort Inn* opposite, though still motel-style, this has comfy self-contained studios and two-bed rooms. ⑤–⑥

Sea Change Safety Cove 425 Safety Cove Rd, Port Arthur ☎03/6250 2719, ⊛www.safetycove.com. There are great views of sunsets and coastline in this friendly B&B beside a rarely visited beach. Two rooms have a choice of ocean or beach outlook and a self-contained apartment has a wood fire. All ⑥

Stewarts Bay Lodge Arthur Highway, Port Arthur ☎03/6250 2888, ⊛www.stewartsbaylodge .com.au. Above a bay where officers' wives swam at a safe distance from the convicts, just north of the historic site, this provides rather swish open-plan lodges that sleep two to seven, all with verandas. ⑥

White Beach Tourist Park White Beach, 10km west of Port Arthur, ☎03/6250 2142, ⊛www .familyparks.com.au. A mellow alternative away from the crowds, well-maintained and just behind a sheltered beach. Camping $25, cabins ④

Eating

Convict Kitchen/Commandant's Table 29 Safety Cove Rd, Port Arthur. Respectively the bar and the heritage-themed restaurant of the *Comfort Inn* hotel, serving pub grub (all year) and more formal dinners (summer only). The real draw, however, is the superb view over the historic site.

Eaglehawk Neck Café Arthur Highway, 500m south of Officers Mess, Eaglehawk Neck. An inviting lodge-styled café that prepares a tasty and reasonably priced menu (around $15 for mains), ranging from filled baguettes and platters of local produce to home-made pies (rabbit, venison, seafood), plus great coffee and cakes. Daily 9am–5pm.

Eucalypt Arthur Highway, Port Arthur. "Coffee, art, food" in a metropolitan-styled café in the village centre. Breakfasts, daily lunch specials for $15, gourmet burgers and tasty baguettes. Daily 8am–5pm, closed Tues.

Felons Port Arthur. "Dine with conviction" puns the restaurant at the historic site: wallaby burgers, grills and fish, with mains priced around $21. Busy in summer. Opening times as site.

Lufra Hotel Eaglehawk Neck. Basic bar meals, cheap and in rib-sticking portions – nothing special, but the only option for dinner at Eaglehawk Neck. Lunch & dinner daily.

🚶 **The Mussel Boys** Arthur Highway, Taranna ☎03/6250 3088. Not just the finest dining on the Tasman Peninsula, but some of the best café-bistro fare in Tassie. Contemporary cuisine features local produce – oysters, octopus, salmon, quail, venison, and, of course, mussels – plus there's a tasting menu to graze. Great coffee and a nice laid-back vibe too. Summer lunch & daily daily, winter times vary; call first. Moderate.

Travel details

Buses

Hobart to: Bothwell (Mon–Fri 1 daily; 1hr 30min); Devonport (1 daily; 4hr); Dover (Mon–Fri 1 daily; 1hr 50min); Eaglehawk Neck (Mon–Fri 1 daily; 1hr 30min); Hamilton (Tues & Thurs–Sun 1 daily, 1hr 10min); Kingston (Mon–Sat every 20min, Sun hourly; 25min); Lake St Clair (Tues & Thurs–Sun 1 daily, 2hr 40min); Launceston (Mon–Fri 4 daily, Sat 3 daily, Sun 5 daily; 2hr 30min–3hr 30min); Mount Field National Park (end Nov–end Mar Tues, Thurs & Sat; 1 daily; 1hr 20min); New Norfolk (Mon–Fri 8 daily, Sat 5 daily, Sun 1 daily; 55min–1hr 15min); Opposum Bay (Mon–Fri 6 daily, Sat 2 daily; 1hr); Port Arthur (Mon–Fri 1 daily; 2hr 15min); Queenstown (Tues & Thurs–Sun 1 daily, 5hr 30min); Richmond (Mon–Fri 4 daily; 20min); St Helens (Fri & Sun 1 daily; 4hr 30min); Seven Mile Beach (Mon–Fri every 30min–1hr, Sat hourly, Sun 9 daily; 1hr); Swansea (term time: Mon, Tues & Thurs 1 daily, Wed & Fri 2 daily, Sun 1 daily; school holidays Tues–Sun 1 daily; 2hr 15min–2hr 20min).
New Norfolk to: Hobart (Mon–Fri 8 daily, Sat 5 daily, Sun 1 daily; 55min–1hr 15min); Lake St Clair (Tues, Thurs–Sun 1 daily; 2hr); Queenstown (Tues, Thurs–Sun 1 daily; 4hr 30min).
Richmond to: Hobart (Mon–Fri 4 daily; 20min); Swansea (term time: Mon–Fri 1 daily; school holidays Tues, Thurs & Sat 1 daily; 2hr); Triabunna (same times as Swansea; 1hr).

Flights

Hobart to: Adelaide (1 daily; 1hr 15min); Brisbane (1 daily; 1hr 35min); Burnie (Wynyard) (Wed & Thurs 1 daily; 1hr 20min); Devonport (Mon 1 daily; 50min); Melbourne (12 daily; 1hr 10min); Sydney (5 daily; 1hr 50min).

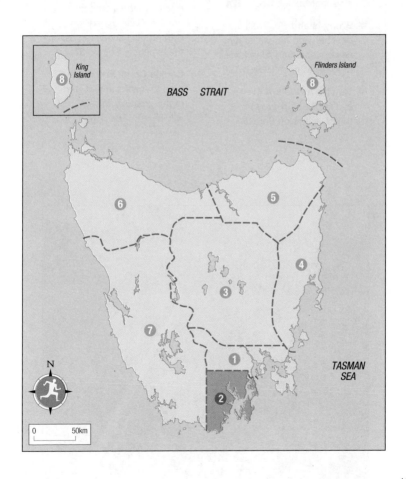

The southeast

King
Island

Flinders Island

BASS   STRAIT

6

5

4

3

7

N

1

TASMAN
SEA

2

0   50km

CHAPTER 2   # Highlights

✳ **Peppermint Bay, Woodbridge** One of Tassie's most revered gourmet temples, and not necessarily a budget-buster. See p.124

✳ **Bruny Island** Bushwalks, beaches and an exhilarating sea cruise on an island free of mass tourism. See p.126

✳ **Tahune AirWalk** A bird's-eye view of old-growth forest, either on Forestry Tasmania's showpiece attraction or a cable hang-glider. See p.136

✳ **Rafting the Picton River** A taste of the more famous Franklin River expedition without the serious rapids, or the expense. See p.137

✳ **Cockle Creek** End of the road in Australia, and start of the great southwest wilderness. See p.140

▲ Tahune AirWalk

The southeast

Hobart has an admirable back garden. Just thirty minutes' drive from the capital is a bucolic landscape of secluded bays, orchards and islands. Travel an hour further and the coast is backed by a more rugged terrain of forested hills and subalpine peaks, before Australia's most southerly road peters out in true wilderness. If one part of the appeal of the southeast is the diversity of landscapes that means a day-trip from Hobart can take in rolling, apple-blossomed hills and lonely, pristine bays, another is that this corner of Tasmania generally remains free of any major tourist development.

The names of the region's two main waterways, the D'Entrecasteaux Channel and Huon River, recall the **French explorers** who were first to survey the area in the late eighteenth century: Admiral Bruni D'Entrecasteaux, who lent his name to the area's largest island and a channel, and Huon Kermandec, after whom the river and, indirectly, the pine tree is named. Their ships *La Recherche* and *La Esperance* also gave their names to two of the southeast's most impressive bays. British penetration into the bush in the early 1800s led to a series of logging settlements on the arterial waterways to exploit eucalpytus forest and the Huon pine, whose resin-rich, rot-resistant timber was prized by architects and shipbuilders.

Today the southeast is Tasmania's premier **fruit-growing** district. Huon Valley orchards put the "Apple" into the "Apple Isle" tag that was routinely attached to Tasmania until the UK joined the European Community in the 1970s, effectively locking out Australian crops. With its major export market gone, two-thirds of the orchards were abandoned and growers diversified into cherries and berries or switched produce to join a sizable number of small growers specializing in **gourmet food**: crayfish, scallops, oysters and salmon reared in the cold, clear waters of the D'Entrecasteaux Channel, handmade cheeses from small farmholdings, tasty wild Huon mushrooms, and a select band of wineries famed for their spicy, berry-rich Pinot Noirs.

With more villages than small towns and distances between them short, the southeast is touring country. The Channel Highway (B68) hugs the upper reaches of the D'Entrecasteaux Channel past sleepy beach resort **Snug** to **Kettering**, which serves as the gateway to **Bruny Island**. This was the birthplace of the 'last' indigenous Tasmanian, Truganini (see box, p.356), and arguably Tasmania itself; the island is little-developed considering its outstanding coastal scenery and bushwalks. Elsewhere on the highway, **Woodbridge** has one of Tassie's best restaurants in the shape of Peppermint Bay. The B68 continues to arty apple town **Cygnet** and then **Huonville**, the southeast's fruit capital and its administrative centre. It is also the launchpad for the southeast's main arterial route, the Huon Highway (A6), which zips south through pretty

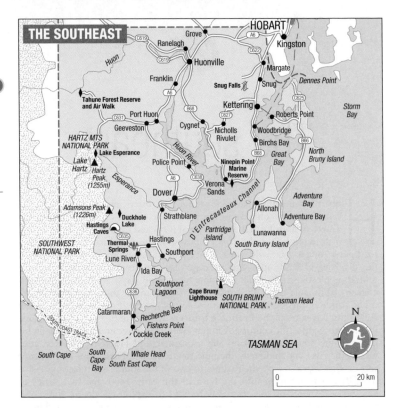

THE SOUTHEAST

Franklin to forestry town **Geeveston**, in the heart of the much-logged (and disputed) Southern Forests, managed by Forestry Tasmania – its **Tahune Forest AirWalk** through old-growth forest is fast becoming the region's main draw. For more remote walking, there's the subalpine **Hartz Mountains National Park**. From mellow **Dover**, caves and thermal springs are easily accessible as you head down the coast to **Cockle Creek**, literally the end of the road in Australia and the start of the South Coast Track into the great southwest wilderness.

Public transport to all destinations is good except at the far extremities and on Bruny Island, where you'll need your own vehicle or a tour.

The Channel Highway

As a route south, the single-lane **Channel Highway** (B68) makes for slower going than the Huon Highway (A6). But beyond Kingston it is a lovely drive, hugging the coastline of the D'Entrecasteaux Channel most of the way to Cygnet and passing through a series of small villages en route. Thanks to the relative proximity to Hobart, Hobart Coaches (Ⓦ www.hobartcoaches.com/au) also provides a regular bus service along the entire length of the route, albeit limited to weekdays only.

South of Kingston to Kettering

Once free of the dormitory suburb of Kingston, the Channel Highway heads south to **MARGATE** and its **steam train**. Imported from England and then beefed up to 825 horsepower to cope with the Tasmanian terrain, the train operated the state's last passenger train service, pulling *The Tasman* from Hobart to Launceston until 1975 when increased car ownership made it uneconomical. The train rusted in the possession of Hobart then Kingsborough councils until it was bought for $40,000 by a private buyer, who converted its carriages into today's craft, book and bric-a-brac shops. One carriage, finished in Queensland maple, serves teas and snacks as the *Pancake Café*. Just behind the train, the **Inverawe Native Gardens** (daily Sept–May 9.30am–6pm, June–Aug closed Mon; $8; ☎03/6267 2020, ⓦwww.inverawecom.au) has 95,000 landscaped square metres with views over the bay.

The next stop, **SNUG**, owes its name to the sheltered harbour favoured by early navigators rather than any inherent cosiness. It's a largely modern village, much of it rebuilt following a bushfire in 1967. The destruction is documented south of the centre in a **Heritage and Folk Museum** (Wed–Sun 10am–4pm; $5; ☎03/6267 9169), which also has displays on the timber and fishing industries that supported settlers. But Snug's real draw is its **beaches**: a long arc of sand in front of the village or a quieter small strand at the Conningham Beach Reserve 2km south. The **Snug Falls** are 4km inland, off the highway; not particularly high but a pretty torrent which plumes through a cleft in a cliff-face, a pleasant 40-minute return walk from the carpark. **Accommodation** is limited to the *Snug Beach Caravan Park* (☎03/6267 9138; ⓦwww.big4.com.au), which has tent pitches ($22) and cedar-clad cabins (❹), some with sea views. The only **meals** are available at the *Snug Tavern* (Wed–Sun only), but for self-catering, the Snug Butchery sells superb smoked salmon at bargain prices, plus good barbecue provisions.

More options can be found in **KETTERING**, 8km south, a sleepy village straggled along the road, strung behind a pretty gum-fringed bay which holds a local fishing fleet and one of the southeast's largest marinas. It also serves as the ferry terminal for Bruny Island (see p.126). At the back of the bay by the turn-off to the terminal, the unpretentious *Oyster Cove Inn* (☎03/6267 4446; rooms share bathroom; B&B ❸–❹) has fantastic views in a restaurant that specializes in seafood and local produce, and a quirky sculpture-cum-beer garden. More upmarket **accommodation** is available at *Herons Rise Vineyard* at the north end of the village (☎03/6267 4339, ⓦwww.heronsrise.com.au; ❻), whose spacious self-contained cottages have wood floors and stoves, with views over the vineyards. The *Mermaid Café* on the ferry quay is modern and bright, and rustles up good food and great coffee (daily 9am–5pm; licensed). It also has **Internet access** and holds the excellent **visitors' centre for Bruny Island** (daily 9am–5pm; ☎03/6267 4494, ⓦwww.tasmaniaholiday.com).

Kettering marina is also the base for Tassie's premier **kayaking** operator, Roaring 40s Ocean Kayaking (☎03/6267 5000, ⓦwww.roaring40skayaking.com.au). It rents sit-on kayaks ($15 hour, $40 per day) and single and double sea kayaks ($20 per hour, $55 per day), and on weekdays organizes morning paddles around Oyster Cove ($90) and day-trips to Bruny Island ($155). From November to April, it also schedules a programme of instruction courses from its base and longer trips to destinations such as Freycinet, Lake St Clair, Lake Peddar and the magnificent Port Davey harbour in the southwest.

Woodbridge

Most of the well-preserved buildings in **WOODBRIDGE** date from the late 1800s, built around sixty years after an English businessman bought thirteen acres of bush near a convict sawmill and named his residence after his hometown in Suffolk. Other settlers followed and his house name became that of the nascent farming and logging settlement. Woodbridge's biggest makeover since then was the arrival of the $10 million ⚓**Peppermint Bay** restaurant and bar complex in 2003 (lunch daily plus dinner Sat; ☎03/6267 4088, ⓦwww .peppermintbay.com.au). The sophisticated, modern-European cuisine on offer uses regional produce – local crayfish with smoked tomato, white wine and basil; Spring Bay scallops in truffle butter; or chargrilled quail with mushroom compote and hazelnuts, for example – and its enviable waterfront location makes it one of Tasmania's culinary highlights. A dedicated lunch cruise to the complex from Hobart (p.124) runs daily in summer; reservations are recommended. Less formal but almost as good is the *Local Bar* (lunch and dinner Tues–Sat), which opens onto a deck and prepares upmarket takes on pub classics, while a providore (daily 10am–5pm) sells local produce and bakes superb bread. Regnans Gallery (same times) retails modern art and crafts.

More food is on offer 3km south at the **Grandvewe Sheep Cheesery** (Sept–June daily 10am–5pm, July–Aug Mon & Wed–Sun 10am–4pm; ☎03/6267 4099; ⓦwww.grandview.au.com), where you can taste and buy organic cheeses and watch the flock being fed and milked (daily at 4pm Oct–Mar). The shop also sells wines and essential oils produced on the farm and there's unfussy Mediterranean cuisine, simply but perfectly prepared, and pastoral views in the on-site *Pecora Café* (lunch Fri–Sun).

In Woodbridge, you can **stay** at the *Old Woodbridge Rectory* (☎03/6267 4742, ⓦoldwoodbridgerectory.com.au; ❹), an attractive B&B with disabled access, or at *Telopea*, which has two modern self-contained cottages on a working farm, again both disabled-friendly (☎03/6267 4565; ⓦtelopea-accommodation .com.au; ❹). More spectacular are the straw bale-walled eco-lodges of

▲ Peppermint Bay restaurant, Woodbridge

⨀ *Peppermint Ridge Retreat* (☎03/6267 4192; ⓦwww.peppermintridge.com
.au; ❼), 3km west on the C267, with stunning views and organic fruit and
veggies grown on-site available for guests.

Two routes lead from Woodbridge to Cygnet. The first is to continue along
the coast on the Channel Highway. En route is *Fleurty's* farm at Birch's Bay,
which sells its highly rated Diemen Pepper products and also essential oils. It's
worth a visit as much for the good-value healthy fare and home-made ice
creams served on the deck of a cool café (lunch Wed–Sun). Three short trails
loop around the farm to walk them off. Further on is **Gordon**, where there's
free camping on the waterfront half a kilometre past the jetty reserve, and
Verona Sands, whose pretty, sheltered beach is undeveloped save for the
Applejack Resort Motel (☎03/6297 8177, ⓦwww.applejack.com.au; ❹), which
has tidy holiday units with cooking facilities and a small shop for basic supplies.
There's also good (if chilly) snorkelling 2km beforehand at the **Ninepin Point
Marine Reserve**, where the tanin-stained waters concentrate marine life into
the shallows.

Alternatively, a gorgeously scenic short cut heads uphill from Woodbridge on
the C627, hauling over Peppermint Ridge and affording superb views back
over the channel, before descending among hills and small farmholdings. After
5km you'll reach the **Hartzview Wine Centre** (daily 10am–5pm; ☎03/6295
1623, ⓦwww.hartzview.com.au; luxury three-bedroom homestead ❻), which
offers tastings of choice Pinot Noir wines (appointment preferred) and good
views of the Hartz mountains.

Cygnet

After a century of apple cultivation, **CYGNET** has finally begun to diversify.
It remains in the heart of a fruit-growing region – the population of around
nine hundred swells when transient workers arrive for the harvest of apples
(March–May), strawberries (Nov–May) or blueberries (Dec–Feb) – but its
dramatic location has also attracted a small community of artists, adding an
alternative bent to what at first appears a quaintly old-fashioned small town.
The **Cygnet Folk Festival** (ⓦwww.cygnetfolkfestival.org; tickets $70–80 for
the full weekend) in early January is Tasmania's principal folk, world and roots
music event.

The town's galleries and laid-back cafés occupy some of the red-brick
buildings on the main street and hint at Cygnet's prosperity in the nineteenth
century, while the **Cygnet Living History Museum** (Fri–Sun 12.30–3pm or
on request; donation; ☎03/6295 1602) beside the church has small displays on
local history. At the south end of the main street, Barton's Reserve is a key
wetland for waterbirds during the breeding season and usually has a few of the
black swans that inspired French navigator Bruni D'Entrecasteaux to name the
long inlet Port du Cygnes Noir. British settlers with lousy French subsequently
mistranslated it as Port Cygnet.

A further 5km south at Nicholls Rivulet (off Channel Highway), the
community-run **Living History Museum of Aboriginal Cultural
Heritage** (Sat–Sun 10.30am–2.30pm; $4.50) narrates the tale of the area's
first settlers through displays of tools and crafts of the Melukerdee tribe, a
part of the South East Nation group. There's also a small bush tucker garden.
While here, you can have a look in the nearby **Deepings Woodturner**
studio (Mon–Fri 9am–5pm, Sun noon–5pm; ☎03/6295 1398, ⓦwww
.deepingsdolls.com), which sells painted wooden figures but can be swamped
by summer coach tours.

Practicalities

The only **accommodation** option in central Cygnet is the *Cygnet Hotel* (℡03/6295 1267; ❹) at the north end of Mary Street, which has clean flowery rooms. It also has two- and three-bed dorms for $25 per person and manages the rather forlorn *Cygnet Holiday Park* opposite, where a camping pitch costs $25. Out of the centre, *Cygnet Bay Waterfront Retreat*, 2km south at Crooked Point (℡03/6295 0980, ⓦwww.cygnetbay.com.au; ❺) offers tranquillity and water views in a light-flooded, country-styled two-bed apartment. Four kilometres north at Cradoc, just off the Channel Highway, *Huon Valley Backpackers* (℡03/6295 1551, ⓦwww.huonvalleybackpackers .com; dorms $22, rooms ❷–❸; pick-ups from Hobart bus and shopping runs into town if arranged in advance), spread over several rural acres, has contacts for fruit-picking work.

An arty community has bequeathed a couple of good **eating** options. Café-bistro *Red Velvet Lounge* (Mon–Thurs 9am–5pm, Fri–Sun 9am–9pm) on Mary Sreet is a fulcrum of the arts community – check its noticeboard for details of local events – and serves good bistro-style cooking using organic ingredients and home-made cakes that are the stuff of local legend. The best food in town is from nearby ⚘ *Lotus Eaters* (Thurs–Mon 9am–5pm), which crafts superb globally inspired cuisine from the freshest regional produce: creamy Indonesian curries, pastas, tarts of Huon Valley mushrooms or spinach, pinenut and local cheese. Highly recommended and keenly priced at around $15 a dish. The cosy *School House Coffee Shop* across the road rustles up traditional Devonshire teas with scones, jam and clotted cream. For evening meals, although the three pubs on Cygnet's main drag prepare fairly standard meals, the chef of the *Commercial Hotel* offers local oysters, stir-fries and salads in a pleasant café-style dining room.

Moving on from Cygnet

From Cygnet to Huonville, the C639 heads south before it swings back and takes over twice as long as the Channel Highway, but it offers a great coast-hugger of a drive with views of Port Cygnet and then the mighty Huon River. Halfway along at Petchys Bay, **Welcome Swallow Cyderworks** (daily except Tues 11am–3pm; ℡03/6295 1214, ⓦwww.southcountrycyder.com) offers tastings of its organic ciders, while just before the Channel Highway junction, the tiny family-owned **Panorama Vineyard** (daily except Tues 9am–5pm; ℡03/6266 3409, ⓦwww.panoramavineyard.com.au) is renowned for an award-winning Pinot Noir.

Bruny Island

With its powder beaches, dolerite cliffs, abundant wildlife and isolated bushwalks, **BRUNY ISLAND** packs a lot of Tasmania's appeal into an area only 71km from tip to toe. Despite the name, it actually consists of two land masses – North Bruny and South Bruny – united by a sandy isthmus ("The Neck") but very different in character. The north is a pastoral region of rolling hills and small farms, while the south has dense wet eucalyptus forests, a dramatic coastline of cliffs and coves and most of the tourist infrastructure, all small-scale and low-key. It also has the majority of the island's population, although since Bruny Island's total headcount is only 650, overcrowding is hardly a problem until summer, when the population swells to around five

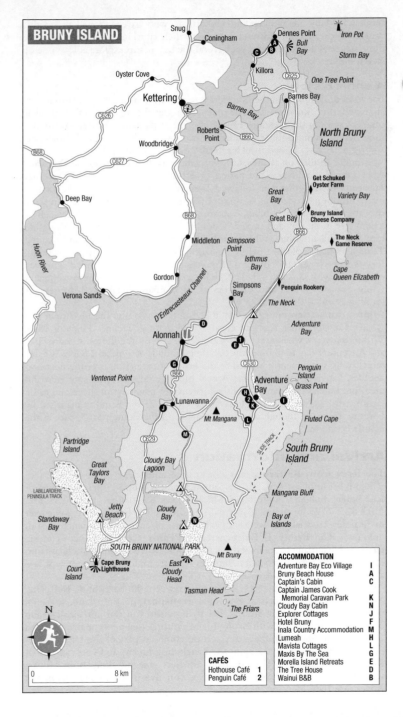

BRUNY ISLAND

Snug
Coningham
Dennes Point
Iron Pot
Bull Bay
Storm Bay
Killora
One Tree Point
Oyster Cove
Barnes Bay
Kettering
Barnes Bay
North Bruny Island
Roberts Point
C625
C626
B866
Woodbridge
B68
C627
Get Schuked Oyster Farm
Variety Bay
Deep Bay
Great Bay
Bruny Island Cheese Company
Huon River
Middleton
Simpsons Point
Great Bay
B866
The Neck Game Reserve
B68
Isthmus Bay
Gordon
Cape Queen Elizabeth
Verona Sands
Simpsons Bay
Penguin Rookery
D'Entrecasteaux Channel
Simpsons Bay
The Neck
Adventure Bay
Alonnah
D
C630
Penguin Island
Grass Point
E
Ventenat Point
G F
B866
Adventure Bay
Lunawanna
H
2 K
I
J
Mt Mangana
L
Fluted Cape
M
South Bruny Island
Partridge Island
C629
Cloudy Bay Lagoon
Great Taylors Bay
SLIDE TRACK
Mangana Bluff
LABILLARDIERE PENINSULA TRACK
Jetty Beach
Cloudy Bay
Bay of Islands
Standaway Bay
N
SOUTH BRUNY NATIONAL PARK
Mt Bruny
Cape Bruny Lighthouse
East Cloudy Head
Court Island
Tasman Head
The Friars

N

0   8 km

CAFÉS	
Hothouse Café	1
Penguin Café	2

ACCOMMODATION	
Adventure Bay Eco Village	I
Bruny Beach House	A
Captain's Cabin	C
Captain James Cook Memorial Caravan Park	K
Cloudy Bay Cabin	N
Explorer Cottages	J
Hotel Bruny	F
Inala Country Accommodation	M
Lumeah	H
Mavista Cottages	L
Maxis By The Sea	G
Morella Island Retreats	E
The Tree House	D
Wainui B&B	B

thousand. Many are weekending Hobartians, who have cottoned on to the pristine landscapes only forty minutes from their city. However, Bruny rewards those who stay for longer and get beyond the beaches to explore at least one of its ten bushtracks.

A short history

For around 35,000 years, the Nuononee people lived in small family groups on an island they knew as Lunnawunna-Allonnaa; the mounds of their shell middens still dot the coastline. One of the last of the tribe was **Truganini**, the most iconic indigenous Tasmanian, if not necessarily the last full-blooded Aborigine as was claimed in older history books (see box, p.356).

European history on Bruny starts with the very first **explorers** in Tasmania. Abel Tasman noted it as he passed in a gale in 1642, and in 1773 Tobias Furneaux of the *Adventure* followed Tasman's charts and became the first of many Europeans to land at Adventure Bay. Encouraged by Furneaux's reports of water and abundant timber, Captain James Cook moored the *Resolution* to a gum tree in the bay and carved "Cook 26 Jan 1777" into its trunk. Alongside him was William Bligh, who returned as master of the *Bounty* and planted Tasmania's first apple tree before embarking on his ill-fated journey to Tahiti. It was French admiral Bruni D'Entrecasteaux, who commanded a survey expedition with two ships in 1792, who gave the island its current name and wrote awe-struck accounts of "trees of an immense height and diameter… looking as old as the world".

European settlement of the island began in earnest after the adventurer and whaler Captain James Kelly received a land grant at Dennes Point in 1818. Within ten years, whaling stations had been set up on the shores of Storm Bay and Adventure Bay to plunder the breeding grounds of Southern Right Whales, which were subsequently hunted to the brink of extinction over the next two decades. Latter-century attempts at coal mining and quarrying sputtered and died, and instead the island established its current mainstays of sheep and cattle farming, fishing and logging. Today over a third of the island is managed by Forestry Tasmania, though tourism is playing an increasingly large part in the island's economy.

Arrival and information

The **ferry from Kettering** sails at least nine times daily (Mon–Sat 6.35am–6.30pm, Fri until 7.30pm, Sun 7.45am–6.30pm; 20min; $25 per car return or $30 public holidays, motorbikes $12.50, bikes $3.50, foot passengers free; ℡03/6273 6725 for times). If you're driving, it's best to book before going over in summer, especially at weekends when two or three-hour queues are not unknown. The **Bruny D'Entrecasteaux Visitor Centre** at the Kettering ferry terminal (daily 9am–5pm; ℡03/6267 4494, ⓦwww.tasmaniaholiday.com) can book island accommodation, supplies basic trail information and maps, and also sells national park passes.

Hobart Coaches operates services between Hobart and Kettering (Mon–Fri only) but there is no public **transport** on the island, so you'll need a car or bike to get around. For flying visits, you can join small-group day-tours from Hobart with Bruny Island Ventures (see p.94) or Bruny Island Charters (see opppsite); the latter's cruise comes as part of the trip (Hobart pick-up 8am, returning 5.15pm; $155 including lunch) and you can join at Kettering to save $40. The company also lets you tag along from Hobart without the cruise for $45, which gives you five hours in the vicinity of Adventure Bay.

Tours

The most popular organized tour on the island is run by Adventure Bay-based **Bruny Island Charters** (daily departure Oct–Apr at 11am; $95; ⓣ03/62933 1465, ⓦwww .brunyislandcharters.com.au), an exhilarating three-hour trip in speedboat-style cruisers that takes in the sensational cliffs, caves and bird rookeries on the east coast. In settled weather the cruise also circles a fur seal colony on The Friars at the south tip of the island. Even if conditions are rough, seals and bottlenose dolphins are often seen en route. Biologist and conservationist Tonia Cochran runs bespoke walking and 4WD wildlife tours, from half-days to extended customized trips, as **Inala Nature Tours** (ⓣ03/6293 1217, ⓦwww.inalabruny.com.au; prices vary) from a base on the Cloudy Bay road 2km south of Lunawanna. **Ol' Kid Fishing Charters** (ⓣ03/6293 1128, ⓦwww.capcookolkid.com.au; $90) operates out of *Captain Cook Caravan Park* in Adventure Bay and runs 3hr all-in trips, with a money-back guarantee if you don't catch anything. **Tassielink** (see p.45) also has scheduled day tours of the island from Hobart (Wed & Fri Aug–June, plus Sun Aug–April; $145).

As a gauge of driving times from the island ferry terminal, Roberts Point, allow 35min to get to Adventure Bay and 1hr 10min to Cape Bruny lighthouse. Petrol is available at Adventure Bay, Alonnah and Lunawanna, but prices are high, so it's worth filling up in Kingston or Margate. Whether you're driving or cycling, be aware that many roads are unsealed – smooth bitumen switches suddenly to dusty unsealed road for kilometres at a time.

Practicalities

There are **general stores** at Adventure Bay (daily 6am–9.30pm summer, 7am–6pm winter), Lunawanna (Mon–Fri 8am–7pm, Sat–Sun until 8pm) and Alonnah (daily 7am–7.30pm summer, until 6pm winter), all of which stock a limited choice of foodstuffs (including fresh groceries) plus the usual fishing tackle and hot snacks. All have **EFTPOS** facilties and the store at Adventure Bay has the island's only **ATM**. The Alonnah store has the only **post office**. The **police station** (ⓣ03/6293 2090) is in Alonnah and the island's only **mechanic**, Bruny Towing and Mechanical (ⓣ03/6293 1108), is based at Adventure Bay. **Internet facilties** are available at Adventure Bay in the *Penguin Café* (see p.133) and at Alonnah in the Online Access Centre (Mon & Wed 9am–noon & 1–4pm, Tues, Thurs & Sat 1–4pm, Fri 3–9pm; ⓣ03/6293 2036). **National park passes** are sold at the visitor centre in Kettering and at the general stores in Adventure Bay and Alonnah.

Accommodation

Most accommodation in Bruny is in the vicinity of Adventure Bay and in self-catering cottages. These aside, rental agency Bruny Island Accommoda-tion Services, based at the *Adventure Bay Eco Village* (ⓣ1300 889557, ⓦwww .brunyisland.net.au), has a range of properties on its books. You can **bushcamp** for free at the south end of The Neck and at three sites in the South Bruny National Park, where park passes are required. There are two spots at the north and south ends of Cloudy Bay (Pines Camp and Cloudy Corner) – the latter is gloriously remote and only accessible by walking along the beach or a 4WD track, and then making a short hike. You can also camp at a quiet shady site at Jetty Beach, 3km north of Cape Bruny lighthouse. All campsites have pit toilets, and those at The Neck and Jetty Beach have a tank of rainwater – in theory.

North Bruny

Bruny Beach House Dennes Point ☎ 03/5243 8486, ⊛ www.brunybeachhouse.com. Japanese-inspired minimalism meets coastal cabin chic in a two-bed house with great sea views. ❺

Captain's Cabin Blight Point, 2km west of Dennes Point ☎ 1300 889 557 or 03/6293 1511, ⊛ www .captainscabin.com.au. A luxury light-flooded

hideaway whose stylish deck is just 15m from 1.6km of private beach. ❼

Wainui B&B Dennes Point ☎ 03/6260 6260, ⊛ www.wainuibandb.com. Three en-suite rooms in an airy open-plan house with a laid-back vibe and a great position above the beach, though for sale at time of writing. ❺

South Bruny

Adventure Bay Eco Village Cookville, 2km south of central Adventure Bay ☎ 03/6293 1270, ⊛ www.adventurebayholidayvillage.com.au. Peace and abundant wildlife on the fringe of the national park in hostel-style rooms and cute cabins (❸), one- and two-bed cottages (❺), and powered sites for motorhomes ($20).

Captain James Cook Memorial Caravan Park centre of Adventure Bay ☎ 03/6293 1128, ⊛ www.capcookolkid.com.au. Friendly and tidy central site opposite the beach, with the only camping in Adventure Bay ($16), plus backpacker-friendly vans (❷) and cabins (❹).

Cloudy Bay Cabin Cloudy Bay ☎ 03/6293 1171, ⓔ dgregg1@bigpond.com.au. The getaway *par excellence*, a solar-powered log cabin with wood heater, hidden in the bush above the beach. ❺

Explorer Cottages 1km south of Lunawanna centre ☎ 03/6293 1271, ⊛ www.brunyisland.com. Comfy two-bed cottages on Daniels Bay, all with wood heaters and DVD players, plus use of a communal laundry. ❺

Hotel Bruny Alonnah ☎ 03/6293 1148. Basic motel-style units in Bruny's only pub, whose redeeming features are their uninterrupted water views. ❸

Inala Country Accommodation 3km south of Lunawana towards Cloudy Bay ☎ 03/6293 1271, ⊛ www.inalabruny.com.au. A family-friendly

three-bed cottage and modern one-bed spa cottage set in the private nature reserve of conservationist Toni Cochran. ❻

Lumeah 5 Lumeah Rd, Adventure Bay ☎ 03/6293 1265, ⊛ www.lumeah-island.com.au. At the north end of the village above Quiet Corner beach, this fully self-contained homestead has an outside spa and garden with bbq. ❺

Mavista Cottages 120 Resolution Rd, Adventure Bay ☎ 03/6293 2009, ⊛ www.storyshare.com.au /mavista. A studio apartment for two plus a country-styled house that sleeps up to ten, both full of rustic charm, four-star rated and five minutes' walk from the beach. ❻

Maxis By The Sea 1km south of Alonnah centre ☎ 03/6293 1271, ⊛ www.brunyisland.com. New in early 2008, these quietly stylish two-bed cottages all come with views over Sunset Bay. ❻

Morella Island Retreats 46 Adventure Bay Rd, 5km north of Adventure Bay ☎ 03/6293 1131, ⊛ www.morella-island.com.au. A lovely retreat with four smart lodges scattered around 25 acres of garden, most with stupendous views over The Neck all the way to Mount Wellington. ❻

The Tree House 1.5km north of Alonnah centre ☎ 0405/192892, ⊛ www.thetreehouse.com.au. A homely open-plan lodge with stilts below, high ceilings above and views over the gum trees to Sheepwash Bay. ❻

North Bruny: Dennes Point and Barnes Bay

There's no town at **Roberts Point**, where the ferry docks; just a phone box, a public toilet, a post box and occasionally a stall with cherries for sale. The main settlement on North Bruny is **Dennes Point** at the northern tip, although it consists of little more than a small jetty and a handful of beach houses, and only stirs to life when weekenders arrive to fish. However, as a favoured getaway for Hobartians, it features some excellent accommodation options and there are the gorgeous sands of Nebraska beach to stroll.

A detour on the way north, 3km off the main road along an unsealed road, lies the secluded settlement of **Barnes Bay**, where pretty Shelter Cove was the first "Black station" for the forced Aboriginal resettlement before the move to Flinders Island.

Treason and treasure on Nebraska Beach

The white strand of **Nebraska Beach** at Dennes Point has lured intermittent treasure hunters ever since a shipwreck in 1827. Bound for Hobart from Sydney, the *Hope* had grounded on South Arm opposite, carrying the military paychest for all Van Diemen's Land, and when the rumour got round that her pilot, who knew the waters well, ignored several warnings of breakers ahead, tongues began to wag in Hobart taverns. For three weeks, the *Hope* broke up in the shallows, during which, the story goes, her three guards conspired with whalers on North Bruny to ferry the loot across the channel and hide it beneath Nebraska's shifting sands.

The yarn continues that the guards' plan to recover the cash went seriously awry when they were reposted to India, then a British colony. A few years later, an educated Irishman arrived in Hobart, purchased a mining right and chartered a boat to land him on the beach. Eyebrows were raised in Hobart. Five days of fruitless pacing later, he left empty-handed. Apparently, he returned two years later with a better map than the sketch provided by one of the original guards of the *Hope* and the proceeds from selling the family farm in Ireland. The story goes that he ended as a penniless labourer in Hobart.

Head south from the T-junction after Roberts Point and you reach Great Bay, whose nutrient-rich shallows provide ideal conditions for the oysters sold at **Get Schucked Oyster Farm** (daily 10am–5pm; ☏0428 606250, ⓦwww .getschucked.com.au) midway around the bay. A little further on, where the bitumen road restarts, is the **Bruny Island Cheese Company** (daily 10am–5pm; ☏0428 606332), whose hand-crafted cow's and goat's cheeses rank high on gourmets' lists. You can sample squares in the farmhouse or in a café that also opens on Saturday nights in summer to serve wood-fired pizzas in the bush.

The northern end of the isthmus connecting the two islands is protected as the **Neck Game Reserve**, breeding ground for Little (or "fairy") Penguins and short-tailed shearwaters ("muttonbirds"). These return to the same rookery in the sand dunes each year from late October to February, or until April for the shearwaters, which arrive after a thirty thousand-mile migration from Alaska. A boardwalk descends to an observation platform to view the birds as they return to their burrows an hour or so after dusk; torches must be covered with red cellophane and flash photography is prohibited. Nearby, a stairway climbs Big Hummock dune to a small monument to **Truganini**, the Bruny Island-born indigenous Tasmanian who has become a symbol of Aboriginal genocide in Tasmania (see box, p.356). It's also a good spot to hunt a wave – Neck Beach picks up decent **surf** in southerly swells.

South Bruny: Adventure Bay

The principal tourist centre on Bruny Island is **ADVENTURE BAY** on the east coast. Its perfect crescent of sand also has a fair claim to the title of birthplace of Van Diemen's Land after Furneaux waded ashore in 1773, followed in quick succession by a roll call of illustrious names in European exploration – Cook and Bligh, D'Entrecasteux with naturalist Julien Houtou de La Billardière, and in 1802 Commodore Nicolas Baudin, who enjoyed several amicable contacts with the Nuononee. For all, the bay provided a safe refuge to replenish water and effect repairs after the arduous journey across the Southern Ocean. The eclectic **Bligh Museum of Pacific Exploration** (daily 10am–4pm summer, closed Tues winter; $4; ☏03 6293 1117) documents the period with a scattering of original charts and illustrations among the usual photocopies. It also has a large splinter of the gum tree that Cook moored against in 1772 – apparently it fell down in 1914, to much consternation. There are also a few display cases of aboriginal and Pacific island ethnology.

As the location of the captain's landfall, the far south end of the bay is officially **Cooksville**. It was here too that Bligh planted the apple tree he had nurtured from the Cape of Good Hope. Fifty years later, up to ninety men were employed in a whaling station behind the bay's small beach. Interpretation boards explain the few remaining ruins on an easy hour-return walk to **Grass Point** in the South Bruny National Park, which begins at the *Adventure Bay Eco Village* and follows the shore towards **Fluted Cape**; keep your eyes peeled for an endemic colony of white Bennett's wallabies. From here, a spectacular extension of the walk climbs steeply alongside high dolerite cliffs to the summit of Fluted Cape (2.5hr return), where white-breasted. A more serious walk is the ten-kilometre **Slide Track** along an old logging tramline though rainforest. The start is at the Adventure Bay bridge – allow seven hours return and be prepared for a slog uphill at the start followed by a steady ascent. Better still, get a lift for 10km along Lockleys Road and walk the track in reverse.

South Bruny: Alonnah, Lunawanna and the far south

The west coast that faces the D'Entrecasteaux Channel is the quieter side of South Bruny, whose villages only pay a passing nod to tourism. The island's administrative centre, **ALONNAH**, has a small **history room** (daily Mon–Fri 9am–4pm, Sat–Sun 10am–3pm; free) in its council offices with folders that archive the minutiae of the island's past, from Aboriginal life to logging practice via convicts, the Kettering ferry and whaling. A little further along Bruny Main Road, the island's only pub and bottle shop, Hotel Bruny, offers passable pub grub, while beyond Alonnah is the ramshackle village of **Lunawanna**, gateway for the routes south.

Turn right at the village's T-junction and a decent unsurfaced road takes you to the Labillardiere Peninsula that forms the western "hook" of South Bruny Island – it's in the South Bruny National Park, so entry fees apply. At the southern tip, Australia's second-oldest lighthouse, **Cape Bruny lighthouse** (guided tours by arrangement $8; ☎03/6298 3114), was built in 1836 by convicts after three successive wrecks spurred the Hobart government into action. It was manned until 1996, by then lit by electricity rather than a pint of whale oil an hour. Worth the trip alone are the views from its headland – a vast end-of-the-world panorama of high-fluted cliffs, lonely beaches and empty ocean, with only a few specks of land between you and Antarctica. Access to the gated area around the lighthouse is generally open daily 9am–5pm, although the exact times are posted at the Lunawanna T-junction.

A right turn before the lighthouse grinds along the island's first road to the pretty bushcamp above **Jetty Beach**, where keepers' supplies and convict workmen were once landed. This is also the start of one of the island's great walks, the seventeen-kilometre **Labillardiere Peninsula** track (5hr), which rolls north through undulating gum and teatree forest, then climbs Mt Bleak before a gentle descent to small beaches at the peninsula tip (a perfect lunch stop), before the return along the coast. The Luggaboine Circuit (1.5hr) initially follows the same route, but ducks off for the return after about 1.5km.

The right turn from the Lunawanna T-junction concludes at **Cloudy Bay**, the final chunk of the national park, with a great sweep of isolated **surf beach** – be warned, the swells here can pack a punch – and two bushcamping sites.

A ten-kilometre short cut back to Adventure Bay on the rough unsurfaced C629 slaloms uphill through a managed forestry reserve – beware of logging trucks. On the way are the **Clemments Top Mill**, a short boardwalked walk past the rusting machinery of an early-1900s logging operation, and a lay-by for the climb up **Mount Mangana** (1h 30m return), the island's highest peak. Neither are anything special, but the latter provide a great view to the south coast, depending on the height of eucalyptus around the 571-metre summit.

Eating and drinking

Your eating options are seriously limited on Bruny and largely restricted to the Adventure Bay area. Bar hot snacks from the general store, the only central **restaurant** is *The Penguin Café* in Adventure Bay (daily 10am–5pm plus dinner Sat; ⓣ03/6293 1352; licensed & BYO), which does tasty casseroles, vegetarian dishes, gourmet burgers and great coffee. The finest fare on Bruny is prepared at the *Hothouse Café* (lunch & dinner daily, bookings essential after 5.30pm) at Morella (see p.130), a quirky spot to sample a daily menu of seasonal home-cooking prepared from whatever's freshest. Great views, too. At Alonnah, *Hotel Bruny* prepares passable bar meals and has the island's only bottleshop.

If self-catering, be aware that the range of provisions in general stores is limited, especially for fresh produce – it may be worth stocking up in Hobart. Good options for picnic fodder are the superb oysters from Get Shucked and the cheeses and breads of Bruny Island Cheese Company, both on North Bruny (see p.131).

Down the Huon Highway (A6)

A dual carriageway that starts in central Hobart makes this the fast-track route to Tasmania's wilderness. However, away from poster-places such as the Tahune Forest AirWalk, the far southeast sees relatively few tourists and is perhaps better known among Tasmanians as a battleground between conservationists and the loggers who nibble ever deeper into the old-growth forest abutting the World Heritage Area. Tassielink has regular bus services as far as Dover and a summer schedule along Australia's most southerly road to Cockle Creek.

Huonville and around

Too large to be quaint, too small to be dynamic, **HUONVILLE** is the business end of the Huon Valley and the focus for the region's trade in apples and delicious Huon Valley mushrooms. Once a rather redneck place that emerged during the logging days of the mid-1800s, it is slowly edging upmarket to suit a pretty site on the Huon River. That said, the best to be said of its main drag is that it provides all you should need, and at no. 24 a **Parks & Wildlife Service information centre** and shop (Mon–Fri 9am–4.30pm; ⓣ03/6264 8460) that stocks information sheets and sells park passes, books, maps and basic walking gear. Aside from the accommodation and wines of nearby Ranelagh, Huonville's visitors usually arrive for **river cruises** aboard the *Huon Jet* (ⓣ03/6264 1838, ⓦwww.huonjet.com; every 45min from 9.15am–4.15pm; $62; reservations recommended) that skims upstream over rapids to a riverbank lined by young Huon pines. Trips depart from the **Huonville Visitor Information Centre** (daily 9am–5pm; same phone as Huon Jet) on The Esplanade, 1km from the Huonville bridge on the Cygnet road. You can also hire pedalos here ($14 per 30min).

To **eat**, there's an outlet of the *Banjo's* bakery chain at no. 8 or real café culture and home-made food, much of it veggie, at *Café Moto*, opposite the Environment Centre (Tues–Fri 8.30am–4pm). For larger meals, the *Huon Manor Bistro* (T03/6264 1311; closed Sun), in a colonial-style homestead by the bridge, is a noted address for fish and seafood, while just downriver the bring-your-own *Boat House Café* (T03 6264 1133; Wed–Thurs 10.30am–7.30pm, Fri-Sat until 8.30pm, Sun until 7pm), on a floating punt off The Esplanade, serves tasty fish and chips. The most convenient **Internet access** in the centre is at DS Café (daily 8am–6pm; $2.50 per 30min) near the Parks & Wildlife outlet, and at the visitor information centre ($2 per 30min).

At **GROVE**, 6km back towards Hobart on the Huon Highway (A6), the **Apple Heritage Museum** (daily Oct–Apr 8.30am–5pm; T03/6266 4345; $4.50) is far more interesting than it sounds. Hundreds of varieties of apple are on display in harvest season (March–May) and bizarre fruit paraphernalia such as the 1901-vintage "Slinky Apple" corer, peeler and slicer are displayed – and demonstrated – in a packing shed whose size says much about the industry's former size. Relief from apples comes via quirky dioramas of rural life at the turn of the nineteenth century. At the same site, *The Starving Artist Gallery* displays and retails local artists' work (same hours; free). **Accommodation** is in central Grove at *Crabtree River Cottages* (130 Crabtree Rd, T03/6266 4644, Wwww.crabtreerivercottages.com; ●), whose homely cottages and self-contained heritage suite are located beside a stream with a resident platypus.

Three kilometres northwest of Huonville via Wilmot Road, the picturesque hamlet of **RANELAGH** is home to the sleek winery/restaurant of *Home Hill* (wine tasting daily 10am–5pm; lunch daily noon–3pm, dinner Fri & Sat; Sun lunch bookings essential; T03/6264 1200). Their Pinot Noir is a regular among the wine gongs each year and their gourmet modern Australian cuisine showcases local ingredients – the Dover-farmed salmon is as exquisite as the backdrop of mountain peaks. **Accommodation** hereabouts is also impressive: *Matilda's of Ranelagh*, opposite St James's Church (T03/6264 3493, Wwww .matildasofranelagh.com.au; ●) provides B&B in a rambling National Trust-listed

▲ Home Hill winery

mansion set among English-style gardens. West of the centre on North Huon Road, then 3km up Browns Road, *Huon Bush Retreats* (🕾 03 6264 2233, 🖳 www .huonbushresretreats.com; ❻; camping $20) strives to take the wild out of wilderness in modern solar-powered cabins on a nature reserve. Its hosts also offer yoga, massage and meals.

Franklin

Though just an eight-kilometre drive southwest of Huonville along the west bank of the Huon, **FRANKLIN** oozes bygone bucolic charm on a high street lined with fine old buildings and cute weatherboard homes. Many date from when the town was founded in 1839 and named after Lady Jane Franklin, pious do-gooder wife of the colony governor and one of the first landowners in the area. She was also a keen sailor on the Huon River, the settlement's focus; all houses face the waterway along which barges transported timber and then apples to Hobart, and a few former store sheds dot the shores. The reach also doubles as a course for national championship rowing races. Appropriately, Franklin's chief sight is its **Wooden Boat School** (daily 9.30am–5pm; 🕾 03 6366 3586, 🖳 www.woodenboatschool.com; $6) which attracts students from worldwide for a year-long course on traditional boat-building and restoration, the only one of its type in the southern hemisphere. There's a small museum and you can view boats of up to 36ft built by students from Tasmanian timbers (Huon pine, celerytop pine, myrtle and blackwood). The school also runs **short courses** of one to seven weeks at a cost of $500 per week, open to allcomers.

As the prettiest village on this reach of the Huon, Franklin has a good range of **accommodation**. In the village centre, the colonial-era *Franklin Lodge* (🕾 03/6266 3506, 🖳 www.franklinlodge.com.au; ❺) has four en-suite rooms which lay on the heritage charm in antique and lacy style; *Huon Franklin Cottage* (🕾 03 6266 3040, 🖳 www.huonfranklincottage.com.au; ❺) is an upmarket B&B at the south end of the village whose owners also manage central *Cottage on Main* (🕾 03/6266 3080, 🖳 www.cottageonmain.com; ❺), a cute two-bedroom place that sleeps up to six. There's also self-catering accommodation in the friendly hilltop *Kay Creek Cottage* (🕾 03/6266 3524, 🖳 www.kaycreekcottage.com; ❺). The best **food** in town is the varied modern menu at the *Petty Sessions Gourmet Café* (daily dinner, plus lunch Thurs–Sun summer, Fri–Mon winter), a former courthouse that's now a vision of pastel blue on the waterfront, famed for its abalone chowder and steaks. For lighter bites, *Franklin Woodfired Pizza* (from 5pm Mon–Fri, from 4pm Sat & Sun) cooks them thin in a corrugated iron oven and offers takeaway, as does *Aqua Grill* opposite the fire station, which does fish and chips, delicious tempura Huon Valley mushrooms and sweet-potato cakes.

Geeveston and around

Sleepy and solid **GEEVESTON** in the heart of the Southern Forests plays up to its self-declared status of "Tasmania's Forestry Town". Massive logs form a gateway as you enter from the north, and chainsaw-carved Huon pine statues of local heroes furnish a tiny centre whose shop facades are planked in timber. Although diversification into logging has enabled the town to prosper while other fruit towns have withered – and it now benefits from being the launchpad for Forestry Tasmania's showpiece Tahune Forest AirWalk (see p.136) – the industry has put Geeveston on a frontline in the bitter war between conservationists and the timber industry; the "Battle of Farmhouse Creek" in 1986 was just the opening salvo in a dispute that continues to rage (see box, p.137). Some of the millions of dollars the Forestry Commission was awarded in compensation for losing in 1986 funded the **Forest and Heritage Centre** on Church Street (daily 8am–6pm summer, 9am–5pm winter; ☎03/6297 1836, ⓦwww .forestandheritagecentre.com.au; free), which sells tickets for the AirWalk, dispenses a map of walks and holds the town's **visitor information centre**. It can also advise on abseil and rafting trips in the Tahune Forestry Reserve. Beyond the desk, a fairly dull display ($5) explains native trees in the Southern Forests and offers a history of logging with an emphasis on sustainability – a resident woodturner chisels behind a screen on occasion. Upstairs is a gallery (free) of craftsmen's work fashioned from local timbers, most of which is for sale. More local woodcraft is sold in the design centre of **Southern Forest Furniture** on School Road, just south (daily 10am–5pm).

Despite an increasing visitor quota, **accommodation** in Geeveston is limited. On the main street, *The Bears Went Over The Mountain* (☎03/6297 0110, ⓦwww .bearsoverthemountain.com; ❺) provides rather chintzy four-star en suites in pastel shades, while *Cambridge House* (☎03/6297 1561, ⓔbjbone@bigpond .com; ❹), just south on the Huon Highway, has old-fashioned charm in a pretty colonial home. Opposite, backpacker's choice *Bob's Bunkhouse* (☎03/6297 1069, ⓦwww.bobsbunkhousegeevestonbackpackers.com.au; dorms $20; doubles ❷) is a laid-back, homely place with a woodheater whose owner can help find fruit-picking work. To **eat** head to the main street: there are simple good-value specials at the *Geeveston Bakery* (Mon–Sat 9am–5pm), while modern café *Kyari* (closed Tues) rustles up breakfast and lunch, and *The Contented Bear* (Tues–Fri lunch and dinner, Sat dinner only, Sun lunch only) prepares upmarket dishes using fresh regional produce and gourmet take-out pies.

The Tahune Forest Reserve

The Huon Valley's crowd-puller, the Tahune Forest AirWalk, is 29km southwest of Geeveston along the Arve Road, upgraded to a sealed route but still used by the occasional logging truck. Seven short trails break up the journey (you can get a map from Geeveston forestry centre): some of them are enchanting strolls into swamp gum and eucalyptus forest, others are more puff-pieces for Forestry Tasmania to argue its case for sustainable logging. Signs en route also date regrowth forest in a bid to placate visitors about the impact of clear-felling. At 7km, the **Look-in Lookout** walk follows the remnants of an early-1900s logging operation, and at 12.7km a path loops off **Arve River Picnic Ground** through a gorgeous mossy area canopied by manferns. The most popular walk is 2km further along **Keogh's Creek**, and is just before the turn-off to **Big Tree**, a 405-tonne, 87-metre giant that is dubiously declared as Australia's largest tree. Apparently, it was higher still until struck by lightening in 2005.

However, most visitors hurry straight to the $4.5 million **Tahune Forest AirWalk and Visitor Centre** (daily 9am–5pm; $22; ☎03/6297 0068, ⓦwww .tasforestrytourism.com.au), which was opened to great fanfare in 2001. Supported by twelve towers, this 600-metre, steel-framed walkway is suspended among the tree canopy to offer a bird's-eye view of mixed old-growth forest, climaxing at a cantilevered section that hangs 48m above the confluence of the Huon and Picton rivers – a spot to linger over magnificent views of the Hartz Mountains slopes. An easy walk (20min return) back at ground level circles through a forest of Huon pines, or you can embark on the **Swinging Bridges Circuit** (1hr 30min) along both banks of the river via the eponymous bridges. Most walks have interpretation displays, but better photocopied information sheets are available in the Bluestone Centre – it's adjacent to the ticket office

Battle for the Southern Forests

March 7, 1986: after months of standoff, **violence** flares as conservationists and the timber industry meet at the unspoken frontline of Farmhouse Creek deep in the Southern Forests. What begins as a protest over the building of a new logging road to open up virgin forest degenerates into a twenty-minute brawl as loggers manhandle the environmentalists away from machinery while police stand by. The confrontation had long been bubbling under, but the High Court's **Franklin River decision** (see p.360) had raised the stakes for both parties and fuelled feelings of resentment and vindication respectively. And like that dispute, the issue became a federal election issue after the brawl was broadcast nationwide. Again, the conservationists won the day in court – the forests were saved, some later awarded World Heritage listing, and a government inquiry prompted a rethink on the management of eucalyptus forest – although the Forestry Commission was awarded millions in compensation.

Yet the issue was far from settled. Instead, the focus shifted as loggers nibbled into new areas of the Southern Forests. Clear-felling of the Styx Valley south of Maydena has caused bitter confrontation since 2001, and in recent years the conservation battle has taken in the **Weld Valley**, just north of the AirWalk. In March 2007, to protest old-growth logging in the Weld, artist **Allana Beltram** blocked the way to the AirWalk as an angel on a log tripod. The striking image made frontpages around Australia and raised the hackles of forestry officials, who tried to hit Beltram with the $6,200 police costs incurred to remove her. The fine was reduced to $200 for causing a nuisance – authorities backtracked after it was pointed out that other criminals were not charged for police operations – but the bitter aftertaste of the battle is emblematic of the schism between conflicting interests: an obligation to protest, say conservationists, arguing a case about climate change and world heritage; only time before a protestor is killed by machinery, counters Forestry Tasmania, standing up for contractors who lose earnings due to disputes.

and visitor centre, where there's also a licensed café. There are also great picnicking facilities, with a shelter and gas barbecues, and **camping** (toilets, tables, fireplaces and wood) is permitted in the overspill car park for motorhomes or further upstream by the river for tents.

The latest addition to the tourist area is the **Eagle Glide** ($33), a cable-hang-glide that soars 400m over forest and river at 40kmph – twice. For more thrills in the Tahune Forest Reserve, there's **rafting** on the Picton River, which skirts the Hartz Mountains from its source deep in the Southwest National Park. The bouncy rapids (Grade 2/3), intermittent gentle sections and magnificent wilderness scenery make it a popular, short (and affordable) alternative to the Franklin River. Rafting Tasmania (℡03/6239 1080, ⓦwww.raftingtasmania.com) and Aardvark Adventures (℡03/6273 7722, ⓦwww.aardvarkadventures.com) both run year-round day-trips from Hobart for $115 and $130 respectively.

Public transport to the area is limited to day-tours from Hobart by Tassielink twice a week (currently Tues & Thurs 9am; $107).

The Hartz Mountains National Park

Though often overlooked by visitors, the rugged **Hartz Mountains National Park** (park fees apply) is acclaimed by Hobart bushwalkers as an accessible taster of Tasmania's great southwestern wilderness. Much of its 64 square kilometres falls within the World Heritage Area, and the subalpine and glacial scenery, and especially its flora – snow-gum forest, tall King Billy pines, alpine moorland knobbled by cushion-plants that take forty years to regenerate after a misplaced boot – possesses a similar remote appeal.

Access is via Hartz Road, 12km off the Arve Road, whose stony track winds for a further 12km with several stopping points. Two kilometres from the end there's a five-minute walk to **Waratah Lookout** – named for the flame-red waratah flowers that appear in early summer – which gives great views over the Huon Valley and Southern Forests; 1km further, a 20min return trip though alpine herbs and gum forest brings you to a view of the **Arve Falls**; or from the final car park there's a gentle ascent to **Lake Osbourne** (40min return).

There's also rewarding day-hiking from the car park. The easiest trail leads through forest to the high country around **Lake Esperance** (2hr return). Experienced bushwalkers could continue to tackle **Hartz Peak** (1225m, 5hr return), which comprises a stiff ascent to Hartz Pass – sometimes so windy that you are forced onto hands and knees – before a 45-minute push on an erratically marked path to the summit of the Hartz range, often snowcapped even in early summer. The view of forest peeling away southwest to the jagged edges of Federation Peak is outstanding.

Although most tracks are boardwalked, come prepared for rough, wet and boggy conditions underfoot, and for sudden rain, fog, icy winds and blizzards at all times of the year. Even the experienced should be careful: old-hand explorers the Geeves family (of Geevestown fame) were caught out on the return from prospecting on Federation Peak in late November 1897 and lost two sons to hypothermia. For the longer day-hikes a map is a must. Basic facilities – a toilet, shelter, picnic tables and a gas barbecue – are located by the start of the Waratah Lookout track.

Dover and around

Somnambulent **DOVER**, 21km from Geeveston, has no pretensions to being anything other than an attractive fishing village – a small fleet returns roughly every day with crayfish and abalone, and salmon is farmed in the cold clear waters off Esperance Point. But helped by a picturesque location on the bowl-like inlet of **Port Esperance**, it also doubles as a low-key resort from which to visit the handful of sites further south, or to walk the surrounding countryside. The almost perfectly triangular outline of **Adamsons Peak** (1226m) rises as a lure behind the village and you can climb to the summit – a tough day-long hike on a badly degraded track – by taking Old Hastings Road south of Strathblane, then turning right at the T-junction; as ever go prepared for all weathers at subalpine height. Turn left at the T-junction and it's a short drive to the path for **Duckhole Lake**, a picturesque flooded sinkhole that's an easy thirty minutes from the car park. For food, the *Dover Hotel* at the head of the bay has passable accommodation (℡03/6298 1210, ⓦwww.doverhotel.com; rooms ❸, motel units ❹) and a **restaurant** that serves adventurous pub-grub from local fish and seafood in an old-fashioned dining room. The only other option is the excellent *Dover Woodfired Pizza* (daily 4–10pm) a little way back up the Huon Highway, near the **Online Access Centre** ($3 for 30min; Mon–Fri, times vary), although the *Gingerbread House Café* serves tasty pastries and home-made pies.

For **accommodation** off the main road, *Driftwood* (℡03/6298 1441, ⓦwww.driftwoodcottages.com.au; ❻) has tasteful, modern studios whose large windows look out onto the bay, while beyond the jetty there's *Dover Beachside Tourist Park* on Kent Beach Road (℡03/6298 1301, ⓦwww.dovertouristpark .com.au; camping $20; vans ❷, cabins ❸–❹), a tidy site in front of a sliver of beach. Back up towards Geeveston, 12km north near Police Point, *Huon Charm*

(☎03/6297 6314, Ⓦwww.huoncharm.com; ❹) consists of two waterfront cottages and a houseboat beautifully sited on a small bay. The drive on the unsealed **C638** (shortlisted for upgrading) also makes a more picturesque route south from Geeveston, leaving the Huon Highway at Surges Bay, then looping around headlands where the Huon River meets the D'Entrecasteaux Channel, and passing deserted Roaring Beach three-quarters of the way along.

Six kilometres south of Dover, off the highway is **Strathblane** (Tassielink will drop you off), is the truly marvellous ⚡ *Far South Wilderness Lodge & Backpackers* (☎03/6298 1922, Ⓦwww.farsouthwilderness.com.au; dorms $25; double ❸; camping also available) on an inlet of the Esperance River in eighty acres of unspoilt forest. Its spotless modern rooms put those of some hotels to shame, and activities include a nightly campfire, guided walks, mountain biking ($10 half day; $15 full day) and kayak hire ($15 per hr; $45 per day) – all highly recommended, although the hostel was sold to new owners in late 2007, so there may be some changes ahead. It is also the base for **Glow Worm Adventure Caving** tours, offered as Southern Wilderness Eco Adventure Tours (☎03/6297 6368 or 0427 976368; 4hr; Sept–June, 1pm & 6pm; $65). On the same road, *Riseley Cottage* (☎03/6298 1630, Ⓦwww .riseleycottage.com; ❺; dinner by arrangement) is an elegant heritage house with upmarket country-styled en suites.

Although you can find fuel and supplies 20km south at **Southport** (the last place to get either), there's more choice and better value in Dover, and the town serves only as a launchpad to the Hastings Caves, in the foothills of Adamsons Peak, with the **Thermal Springs State Reserve** (☎03/6298 3209, Ⓦwww.parks.tas.gov.au; $5 or cave ticket includes pool entry) en route. The small, shallow springs, which range from 20–30°C and are channelled into a small swimming pool (28°C), are no great shakes, but the setting is lush and there are several wheelchair-accessible walks in the grounds, and also a pleasant café and visitor centre. Tickets to visit **Hastings Caves**, a few kilometres further on from the springs, must be bought from here. Newdegate Cave is the only one of this unusual dolomite system that is open daily for tours (hourly 11am–3pm, until 4pm Sept–April; 45min; $22); loggers stumbled upon the cave in 1917 during an illegal forestry expedition and had to rediscover it legally a few months later. The largest showcave in Australia, it has impressive stalactites and stalacmites in lofty caverns, especially in the fairytale Titania's Palace cavern. It's always cold inside, so bring something warm to wear.

South to Cockle Creek

The superlative "Australia's southern-most" is tagged to everything beyond Southport. Unsurfaced Cockle Creek Road is as far south as you can drive, and the **Ida Bay Railway** (☎03/6298 3110, Ⓦwww.idabayrailway.com.au) past Lune River is the nation's most southerly rail service, a miniature heritage bush train that trundles 7km through forest and over grassplain to Elliott's Beach on the Lune River Estuary. With notice the driver will stop at the heads of paths to Southport Lagoon or Southport Bluff for a walk before you catch a later return. Departures from the Lune River Station cost $25 and are daily except Friday from October to April, at 9.30am, 11.30am, 1.30pm, 3.30pm and 5.30pm; and on Wednesday, Saturday and Sunday from May to September at 10am, noon and 2pm. There's also a café and a campsite at the Lune River terminal.

The unsealed road south bumps past picturesque bays and coastal forests to the shackies' hamlet of **Catamaran**, scratched out between beach and bush. A trio of excellent bush campsites with pit toilets – the last site, Catamaran

Campsite, on an inlet is probably the prettiest – line the onward route through old-growth forest to **Cockle Creek**, literally the end of the road in Australia. These last few kilometres are beside the remote **Recherche Bay** (pronounced "research" by locals), named after the ship in which French admiral **Bruni D'Entrecasteaux** hunted the overdue *La Pérouse* expedition. *La Recherche* and its escort *L'Espérance* nosed into an inlet in the north of the bay to find water and effect repairs for four weeks in 1792, then again in 1793. The bay had "all we could wish for", wrote the admiral in his log, while naturalist Labillardière enthused about his botanical research and official expedition gardener Felix de la Haie planted celery, onions, cress, chevril and potatoes to create Australia's first vegetable garden. The French also enjoyed "cordial" meetings with Aboriginal people of a "peaceful disposition", and entered into a jovial beach tournament of spear-throwing and long jump – more "a reunion of friends" than a first contact, a lieutenant of *L'Espérance* marvelled, although the moustachioed face one sailor carved into a tree in 1792 was feared as an evil spirit for years afterwards.

Within thirty years of the French leaving, the bay held seven British whaling stations – "Our olfactory nerves were sorely disturbed by the effluvia of putrid whale carcasses on the sand", Lady Jane Franklin huffed after sailing past in 1838 – then developed as a logging and coal-mining settlement once the whales had been hunted to near-extinction. Now called Ramsgate after the English seaside town, the nascent town had its own hotel, a bank, and a streetplan was drawn up to organize the two thouand people straggled out in encampments along the bay. Only a small graveyard behind the beach and the odd relic of former industry remains.

Instead it is D'Entrecasteaux's description of "a lonely harbour at the end of the world" which rings true (although a long-stalled project for a 32-lodge eco-retreat by Hook Island entrepreneur David Mariner could change this). The only provision around the Recherche Bay Community Centre in the centre of Cockle Creek – just a few caravans inhabited semi-permanently by fishing-obsessed retirees after the abundant crayfish, cockles and fish – is an emergency phone. Beyond are a string of free camping spots set back from the beach (one-month limit), with pit toilets and water. A rickety wooden bridge over Cockle Creek crosses into the **Southwest National Park** (fees apply) where there's an informative history board and another emergency phone outside an erratically manned park office (to speak to a ranger, contact Huonville NPWS ☏03/6264 8460). The road leads past more camping spots to a seafront bronze of a baby southern right whale – so-called because a tendency to float once harpooned made them the 'right' quarry for whalers – which is the start for an easy **coast walk** to Fishers Point (4km round trip; up to 2hr). However, the finest walk in the area is a boardwalked but occasionally muddy route through mixed eucalyptus forest to the beach at South Cape Bay (4hr return; moderate difficulty), the first, more accessible section of the **South Coast Track** (see p.33) whose entire length is for experienced hikers only.

Tassielink runs a "Wilderness Link" service to Cockle Creek three times a week (currently Mon, Wed & Fri) from late November to late March.

Travel details

Buses

Cockle Creek to: Hobart (3 weekly late Nov–late April; 3hr 30min); Huonville (same times; 2hr 30min); Geeveston (same times; 2hr).

Cygnet to: Hobart (Mon–Fri 1 daily except Thurs 3 daily; 1hr 10min); Snug (Mon–Fri 1 daily except Thurs 3 daily; 20–30min).

Dover to: Franklin (Mon–Fri 1 daily; 40min); Geeveston (Mon–Fri 1 daily; 25min); Hobart (Mon–Fri 1 daily; 1hr 50min); Huonville (Mon–Fri 1 daily; 55min).

Franklin to: Dover (Mon–Fri 2 daily; 40min); Hobart (Mon–Fri 7 daily, Sat–Sun 1 daily; 50min–1hr 15min); Huonville (Mon–Fri 5 daily, Sat–Sun 1 daily; 10min); Geeveston (Mon–Fri 5 daily, Sat–Sun 1 daily; 15min).

Geeveston to: Cockle Creek (3 weekly late Nov–late Apr; 2hr); Dover (Mon–Fri 2 daily; 25min); Hobart (Mon–Fri 4 daily, Sat–Sun 1 daily; 1hr 10min); Huonville (Mon–Fri 4 daily, Sat–Sun 1 daily; 20min); Franklin (Mon–Fri 4 daily, Sat–Sun 1 daily; 15min).

Hobart to: Cockle Creek (3 weekly late Nov–late April; 3hr 30min); Cygnet (Mon–Fri 1 daily, except Thurs 3 daily; 1hr 5min); Dover (Mon–Fri 2 daily; 1hr 45min); Franklin (Mon–Fri 7 daily, Sat–Sun 1 daily; 55min–1hr 10min); Geeveston (Mon–Fri 5 daily, Sat–Sun 1 daily; 1hr 10min); Huonville (Mon–Fri 7 daily, Sat–Sun 1 daily; 40min–1hr 5min); Kettering (Mon–Fri 4 daily; 40min); Snug (Mon–Fri 7 daily except Thurs 9 daily & Sat 2 daily; 30–45min); Woodbridge (Mon–Fri 4 daily; 55min).

Huonville to: Cockle Creek (3 weekly late Nov–late April; 2hr 30min); Dover (Mon–Fri 2 daily; 45min); Geeveston (Mon–Fri 5 daily, Sat–Sun 1 daily; 20min); Grove (Mon–Fri 7 daily, Sat–Sun 1 daily; 10min); Hobart (Mon–Fri 7 daily, Sat–Sun 1 daily; 40min–1hr 5min); Franklin (Mon–Fri 5 daily, Sat–Sun 1 daily; 5min); Ranelagh (Mon–Fri 5 daily; 5min).

Kettering to: Woodbridge (Mon–Fri 3 daily; 15min); Hobart (Mon–Fri 4 daily; 50min).

Snug to: Cygnet (Mon–Fri 1 daily except Thurs 2 daily; 30min); Hobart (Mon–Fri 7 daily except Thurs 9 daily & Sat 2 daily; 30–40min); Kettering (Mon–Fri 4 daily; 10min).

Ferries

Kettering to: Bruny Island (Mon–Thurs & Sat 10 daily, Fri 11 daily, Sun 9 daily; 30min).

Central Tasmania

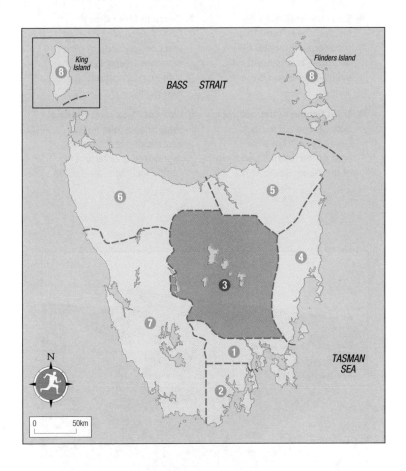

CHAPTER 3

Highlights

✳ **Ross** Soak up the old-world atmosphere in the best-preserved – and most idyllic – nineteenth-century village in Australia. See p.149

✳ **Brickendon Estate** A historic sheep farm that timewarps you back over a century – charming to visit, even better if you can stay. See p.154

✳ **Trout fishing in the central lakes** A chance to hook brown or rainbow trout against the tranquil backdrop of the lakes. See p.157

✳ **Bushwalks from Deloraine Rainforest** Waterfalls, sandstone gulleys and sheer craggy bluffs beneath the Western Tiers. See p.166

✳ **Caves at Mole Creek** Crystal-encrusted caverns and constellations of glow-worms in Tasmania's only subterranean national park. See p.168

✳ **Walls of Jerusalem National Park** Spectacular remote bushwalking in the much-overlooked counterpart to Cradle Mountain. See p.169

▲ Ross Bridge

Central Tasmania

T he move away from the coast is more marked than an absence of sea views. It's only a short drive before you enter a bucolic world characterized by Georgian coaching towns, rose bushes and hawthorn hedgerows, colonial estates and antique shops that declare your arrival not just in Tasmania's historic heartland but in the most "English" area of Australia. More than anything else this is sheep country, where some of the finest merino wool in the world is produced. Both the historic atmosphere and the agriculture are a legacy of early colonial settlement driven by efforts to tame the wilds where outlaw bushrangers roamed, a move which had dire consequences for Aboriginal communities who hunted the grasslands. Most visitors soak up the old-world atmosphere while zipping between Hobart and Launceston on the **Midland Highway** ("Heritage Highway") that more or less follows the first trans-state coach road. **Ross** could easily pass for a village in England's Cotswolds, and **Oatlands** and **Campbell Town** resemble working English agricentres. Clustered just off the highway south of Launceston are four of Australia's finest **Georgian estates**, whose scale bears testimony to the value of wool exports for the nascent colony. One, Brickendon near Longford, is still farmed by the descendants of its English settler.

There is, however, a great deal more to the region. Though less visited, the sleepy colonial towns of **Hamilton** and **Bothwell** have handsome Georgian architecture and, in the latter, a historic golf course. Beyond both lies the **Central Plateau**, a sparsely populated, lake-pocked upland at the heart of the state, known for its world-class trout fishing and fickle climate; the old cliché about four seasons in one day rings true here. Its northwestern corner provides superb remote hiking in the World Heritage-protected **Walls of Jerusalem National Park**. The plateau comes to an abrupt end as the **Great Western Tiers**, whose dolerite slab is a constant presence amid the pleasant farmland west of Launceston. Historic crafts hub **Deloraine** provides the ideal base in the area, whether for good daywalks in the foothills of the Tiers or excursions to colonial **Westbury** and the cave systems around **Mole Creek**.

Three **highways** fan out from Hobart to trisect the region: as well as the Midland Highway, the Highland Lakes Highway cuts off west onto the Central Plateau, and the Lyell Highway runs to the west coast. **Bus** services ply all routes except the Highland Lakes Highway, although Metro buses from Hobart go as far as Bothwell.

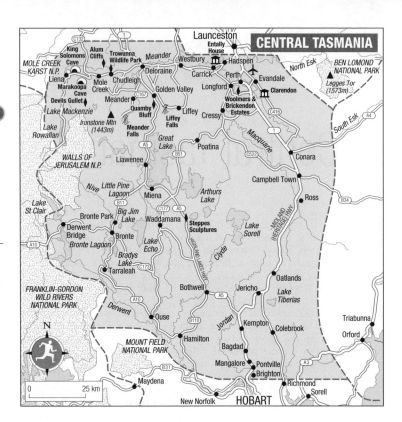

The Midland Highway

The spine of Tasmania is the dual carriageway which speeds traffic between Hobart and Launceston. The imperative of a road to connect the colony's principal settlements became apparent as each nascent city struggled to cope alone, and a positive preliminary was conducted by Governor **Lachlan Macquarie**. The Sydney-based "Father of Australia" embarked on a tour of Van Diemen's Land in 1811, christened the Macquarie River – a weakness for a legacy he repeated throughout the area by insouciantly throwing around the names of family and friends – and in 1812 commissioned a second survey to map out a carriage road and four military outposts. Convict work gangs had laid most of the cobblestones by 1821, but it took a successive colony governor, the ruthlessly efficient **George Arthur**, to upgrade and extend the route into a usable highway. Within a decade, coaches regularly made the run from Hobart Town to Port Dalrymple in fifteen hours, changing horses every twenty miles or so and turning the garrison settlements into towns. These early towns on "Main Road" not only served as staging posts for the first trans-state coach and post services: they were launchpads to tame an interior that was the refuge of outlaw bushrangers.

Travelling the Heritage Highway is an odd experience for Britons. Drenched in the luminous light of the southern hemisphere, the former coaching towns

Skulduggery on the Heritage Highway

The Midland Highway's success as a fast-track between Hobart and Launceston has proved detrimental in modern times. Once coaching centres to change horses, its towns are now places that many visitors go through not to. In an effort to make people slow down and explore the attractions between Hobart and Launceston – whether to discover the colonial architecture in the back streets or simply do a spot of shopping – regional tourism masterminds have come up with **"Skulduggery"**. This historical detective game requires players to piece together clues scattered throughout participating towns in order to solve a 170-year-old crime resurrected from the notebooks of John James, a convict-turned-constable who served in the local field police in the 1820s and 1830s. Currently available for Longford, Ross and Oatlands, interactive games can be purchased for $19.95 from visitor information centres in Hobart, Launceston, Sydney and Melbourne, as well as in retail outlets in participating towns. More details are available via a link on regional tourism website Ⓦwww.heritagehighway.com.au.

of **Kempton**, **Oatlands** and **Campbell Town** appear like a hyper-real Hampshire. Each has a sprinkling of antiques shops and heritage B&Bs, but the tourism infrastructure is centred at **Ross**. Alongside its perfect Old-World appearance, it has a good museum on the surrounding merino sheep industry, a handy foil to the Georgian mansion homesteads that were built through wool profits near **Evandale** and **Longford**, at the north end of the highway.

Being the main artery of Tassie transport, **coach** services along the highway are good. Redline schedules regular town and direct services; the former call at all destinations, the latter stop only at Oatlands and Campbell Town. Longford is accessed by daily services from Launceston, while you'll really need your own transport to visit Evandale.

North of Hobart

A series of over-sized villages breaks up the route to Oatlands, none particularly exciting but worth a stop if you have your own transport. Once across the Derwent River, the highway heads 27km north to the commuter town of **BRIGHTON**, a former garrison settlement that Governor Macquarie named after King George IV's favourite English seaside town. There's now little to suggest it was once mooted as a potential capital of Van Diemen's Land, and instead the interest is two kilometres east at the **Bonorong Wildlife Centre** (daily 9am–5pm; keeper tours 11.30am & 2pm; ☏03/6268 1184, Ⓦwww.bonorong.com.au). The centre specializes in the conservation and rehabilitation of native species, and lets visitors feed Forester kangaroos by hand. (Ironically, the area's kangaroo and emu were hunted to extinction when early food shortages wracked Hobart Town.)

Brighton's star waned as that of **PONTVILLE** rose to the north. The garrison waypoint peaked at two thousand people, but the arterial road which drip-fed wealth now cleaves the town with heavy traffic, to the detriment of its historic monuments. Most date from the 1840s, including **St Mark's Church**, an unusual Romanesque building of white ashlar designed by James Blackburn. The convict architect worked his ticket of leave and went on to mastermind the water system for Melbourne; city planners later named a suburb in his honour. According to Tasmanian folklore, the first surveys of the surrounding terrain were undertaken around 1805, during the hunting trips of Private Hugh Germain. Armed with copies of the Bible and the *Arabian Nights*, the Royal

Marine is said to have named his landmarks after his reading matter. So Pontville stands on the banks of the **Jordan River**. North is **Jericho** and **Lake Tiberias**, while **Colebrook** east of Kempton was originally christened Jerusalem. **Bagdad**, north of Pontville, is another one of Germain's. The locale prospered in the mid-1800s through apple-growing and wheat, which funded the handsome homesteads beside the highway – several are dotted south of the town around **Mangalore**. Signposted off the highway as "Chauncy Vale Road", Chauncy Vale Wildlife Sanctuary, 4km east of Bagdad (daily 9am–sunset; $2; ☎ 03/6268 6365, ⓦ chauncy-vale.tassie.org), is a private wildlife reserve in a valley. There are a couple of sandstone caves at the end of trails through the bush – used as shelters by Aborigines, they served as boltholes for bushrangers after colonization – and a pleasant picnic ground. The early 1900s cottage of its former owner, children's author Nan Chauncy, is open to the public on the first Saturday of the month (2–4pm; $2).

One of the most prosperous (and prominent) settlers of the fledgling colony was Anthony Fenn Kempton, a colourful chancer and racketeer whose cunning was matched only by his ego. **Kempton**, the bucolic small town named after him, is now bypassed by the highway, and many of its Georgian and Victorian cottages on Main Street house antiques shops. St Mary's Church midway along is another of Blackburn's designs.

Oatlands

Back on the Midland Highway, it's 10km north of Kempton to the turn-off for Bothwell, then a further 29km northeast to **OATLANDS**. Although less obviously appealing than neighbouring Ross, dedicated to its service role for the wool industry rather than tourism, Oatlands nevertheless boasts Australia's greatest concentration of colonial **Georgian buildings**: 140 in two square kilometres. Most were built by convicts and line the wide coaching thorough-fare that runs through the centre. The story goes that the road was planned ruler-straight but a shop owner bribed convict workmen to introduce its one bend so carriages would slow past her window. A decade after the founding of a military outpost at Oatlands in 1821 by Governor Macquarie, his successor Lieutenant-governor George Arthur kick-started development by ordering a town plan in 1832. Oatlands boomed during that decade thanks to the abundance of sandstone quarried from adjacent **Lake Dulverstone**, but never came close to the eighty kilometres of streets that its surveyor had planned for a prospective colony capital.

A *Welcome to Historic Oatlands* leaflet from the visitor information centre (see opposite) lists the historic buildings in town, most of them on High Street and many housing antique and bric-a-brac shops. On Gay Street, west of the bend in the centre, **St Paul's Church** is an idealized English village church by Augustus Pugin, the prolific architect who produced the designs for the interiors of the Houses of Parliament and Big Ben. Nearby **St Peter's Church** was part-designed by colonial architect John Lee Archer. On Mason Street, one block behind the other side of the main road, the substantial gaoler's residence suggests the scale of the military precinct that formed the heart of the early town. The most striking edifice is **Callington Mill** and its shingle-roofed outbuildings at the north end of the main street. The partially restored windmill, the only wind- and steam-powered mill in Australia, was built in 1837 and produced up to seven tonnes of flour a day until 1892. There are fine views of the town and surrounding countryside from the top (daily 9am–4pm; free).

The most entertaining way to see the town is on a one-hour **guided walk** conducted on demand by local historian Peter Fielding (☎03/6254 1135; $5). He also conducts evening ghost tours in spring and summer (1.5hr; $10). Both visit several buildings, including the old gaol and courthouse. For a stroll out of the centre, a path tracks the shore of Lake Dulverston just east; nothing spectacular, but a pleasant picnic spot and waterbird wetland.

Practicalities

The helpful **Central Tasmania Tourism Centre** (daily 9am–5pm; ☎03/6254 1212), beside the police station at 85 High St, houses a small colonial heritage museum (same times; free). It is also the place to book self-catering **accommodation**, much of which is in colonial-style B&Bs. The premier address is *Oatlands Lodge* at 92 High St (☎03/6254 1444, ✉oatlandslodge@bigpond .com; ❺), whose plush heritage-style en suites feature original Georgian sandstone walls. There are cheaper bright en suites, all with DVD players, in the *Kentish Hotel* at 60 High St (☎03/6254 1119; ❸) and free **camping** for up to three nights (barbecues; water; toilets) on the banks of Lake Dulverton. It's worth booking accommodation when the **Oatlands Spring Festival** – an enjoyable crossbreed of agricultural show and village fete – sets up its stalls on the third weekend in October.

For **food**, *The Stables* beside the information centre serves breakfasts, light lunches and afternoon teas. A bit smarter is the licensed café-restaurant of *Casaveen* at 44 High St (9am–5pm daily; ☎03/6254 0044, ⊛www.casaveen .com.au), a manufacturer and retail outlet of merino wool knitwear (daily factory tours; free). Expect risottos, gourmet pies and home-made soups served on the veranda. Surprisingly tasty pub grub is also rustled up in the *Kentish Hotel* (lunch and dinner daily).

Ross

Now bypassed by the Midlands Highway in prime sheep-grazing countryside, **ROSS** is Tasmania's – and arguably Australia's – premier heritage village, and makes a good base to explore the area. One of four garrison towns built in 1812, it was founded on a ford of the Macquarie River; the "beautiful and noble view" put Governor Macquarie in mind of the parliamentary seat of a friend, evidently untroubled that Mr HM Buchanan MP actually lived at Loch Lomond, Scotland. It developed in the early 1820s as a staging-post halfway up the new coach road, then blossomed a decade later as the flat land was put to sheep-grazing. Outlying farmsteads were prime targets for bushrangers despite the military garrison, leading to the establishment of militia groups that coalesced to form the first Light Horse Brigade in Australia. Today, regimental planning laws preserve Ross's tiny centre, a postcard-pretty distillation of the village England that early settlers hankered after. No modern building or chain store intrudes into the old-world atmosphere, and surrounding sheep paddocks nurture a serene rural feel. Despite the summer coach tours, the village ticks over at a more soporific pace than its rival Richmond, and the appeal is mainly soaking up the bygone bucolic atmosphere.

The village's most celebrated sight is the **Ross Bridge**, the third-oldest in Australia. Commissioned in 1831 as a replacement for a log bridge upstream, its aristocratic Georgian design was designed by John Lee Archer, but the carvings that adorn its three arches were the inventions of two convict stonemasons, highwayman Daniel Herbert and burglar James Colbeck. The stone squiggles are intended to represent Celtic deities, flora and fauna, and also weathered busts of the sculptors' mates (innkeepers and fellow convicts) and enemies (officers and governors). A bearded self-portrait of Herbert is on the central arch on the south side. Also depicted is Lieutenant-governor George Arthur, the disciplinarian who commissioned and then opened the bridge in October 1836. He wears a cocked hat on the north-facing arch by the west bank, an unflattering bust that is chiselled beside a pig's head. The governor either missed or overlooked the jibe, since the two stonemasons won a pardon for their efforts.

Church Street is the manicured core of the village, canopied by elm trees and lined with 22 listed buildings – the post office (1896) fronted by iron columns and mounting steps is an appealing slice of colonial Victoriana. At its central crossroads, there's a much-repeated joke about the four corners of Ross that were the frontier town's moral compass: the characterful sandstone *Man O'Ross Hotel* pub (temptation); the Roman Catholic church, adapted from a former general store (salvation); the town gaol (damnation), now a private residence; and the barn-like town hall where town festivities were held (recreation). The **Thistle Gallery** (daily 10am–5pm except Thurs from 1pm; closed June–Aug; free), at 36 Church St, is also worth a look for its high-quality exhibitions of contemporary Australian work, some by indigenous artists. The **Tasmanian Wool Centre** (summer daily 9am–6pm, winter Mon–Fri 9am–5pm, Sat–Sun 10am–4pm; entry by voluntary donation; ☎03/6381 5466, ⓦwww.taswoolcentre.com.au) uphill documents the wool trade that filled Ross's coffers. Its hands-on museum has boxes of graded wool samples sheared from local flocks – bales of extra-fine merino wool from Ross set world-record prices on several occasions. An adjacent history room has the usual miscellany of pioneering odds and ends culled from homesteads, and plaster casts of the bridge carvings, including Herbert and Arthur.

Further uphill past the Uniting Church, one of three pretty churches, you reach the optimistically titled **Heritage Walkway**, which leads past an uneven field that was the site of the **Female Factory**, actually a prison where women convicts worked on menial tasks such as the military laundry before being sent to properties as assigned servants. The overseers' cottages (same times as wool centre; free) house a few interpretative boards about convict life and a model of the prison, there's little to see. The trail concludes at the colonial cemetery where Herbert lies; having won his ticket of leave, he settled in a riverside cottage with his family and died aged 65.

Practicalities

The **information centre** in the Tasmanian Wool Centre on Church Street (same hours and contacts) hands out free booklets that list all historic buildings, and can book accommodation and guided walking tours (from $5, depending on group size). You'll also find **Internet** access here. Two recommended **cafés** are on Church Street: *Old Ross Bakery & Tea Rooms* (no. 31) has delicious pies filled with venison or slow-cooked steak and serves lunch specials in a stone-walled room; further down, the licensed *Ross Bakery* (no. 13–15) cooks breads and cakes in a wood-fired oven, and prepares the usual filled focaccias. Both open daily 9am–5pm. For dinner you are restricted to the *Man O'Ross Hotel* (lunch & dinner daily except Mon), no bad thing considering it has a garden and an affordable menu of pub favourites such as steaks and fish of the day.

Accommodation

Ross is well stocked with accommodation, though advance reservations are recommended throughout summer, especially in December and January.

Colonial Cottages of Ross 12 Church St ☎03/6381 5354, ⓦwww.rossaccommodation .com.au. A small agency with three historic cottages in the village centre, all self-catering with an open fire or wood heater. It also has two B&B en suites in a colonial house. ⑤–⑥

Man O'Ross Hotel Corner of Church and Bridge streets ☎03/6381 5445, ⓦwww.manoross.com .au. More pricey than most pub accommodation and with shared facilities, but the modern rooms are comfy and as central as it gets. ④

Ross Bakery Inn 15 Church St ☎03/6381 5246, ⓦwww.rossbakery.com.au. B&B in the period-styled en suites of a Georgian coaching inn, whose communal lounge has an open fire. Breakfasts feature fresh bread from the attached bakery. ⑤

Ross Caravan Park and Ross Motel Esplanade ☎03/6381 5224, ⓦwww.rossmotel.com.au. The small caravan park by the Ross Bridge has a laundry and barbecue, plus five basic rooms. A modern motel adjacent offers mock-Georgian units with four-star facilities, though decor is fairly bland. Campsites $17, rooms ❸, motel rooms ⑤

🏃 Somercotes Off Mona Vale Rd, signposted from Midland Highway 4km south of Ross ☎03/6381 5231, ⓦwww.somercotes.com. Unfussy and cliché-free heritage beds in four National Trust-listed settler cottages dating from 1823. They are set in the gardens of one of Tasmania's most historic estates – guests receive a guided tour of the fortified homestead which still bears the scars of a heist by bushranger Martin Cash (see box, p.111). ⑤

Campbell Town

Having nothing more prepossessing, **CAMPBELL TOWN** prides itself on bricks. Though one of Governor Macquarie's pioneering garrison settlements – named after his wife Elizabeth Campbell – it is a more prosaic prospect than Ross or even Oatlands. In part, this stems from its being the administrative hub of the Midlands, bisected by heavy traffic on the highway. But it is also reflected in the ubiquitous red brick that gives Campbell Town the flavour of a British rural town. At the south end of High Street, the three-arch **Red Bridge** is Australia's oldest convict-built bridge made of brick (1838), while at the other end of town, there's the red-brick **St Luke's Church** (1835). Between the two, a trail of 68,000 engraved bricks is set in the pavements in remembrance of the convicts transported to Australia and Norfolk Island; the still-incomplete project was launched in 2004 to commemorate the bicentenary of transportation. A **heritage museum** (in theory Mon–Fri 10am–3pm; free), in the old court-house at 103 High St, tells the story of local heroes such as Harold Getty, navigator for the first flight around the world in 1931, and Dr William Valentine, who held the first telephone call in Australia in 1874. The building also houses the **information centre** (same times; ☎03/6381 1283).

The town is worth a visit during the **Campbell Town Show** (also called the Midlands Agricultural Show), the oldest country fair in Australia, held over the weekend at the end of May or early June; check ⓦwww.campbelltownshow .com.au for dates.

Practicalities

Campbell Town is on the standard Midland Highway **coach** route plus Redline's Launceston–Bicheno East Coast service. For **accommodation**, there are modern four-star comforts and colonial features in the period en suites of the *Foxhunters Return* B&B (☎03/6381 1602, ⓦwww.foxhunters.com.au; ⑥). Signposted off the highway 500m north of the centre, *Ivy on Glenely* (☎03/6381 1228; ⑥) offers three self-contained options; all are elegant and open onto a garden, and the largest is worth the extra $20. For cheaper en suites, your best bet is the *Campbell Town Hotel* (☎03/6381 1158; ❸). City-style *Zep's* at 92 High St (daily 8.30am–8pm, later Sat–Sun) prepares tasty café fare such as bruschetta and toasted panini by day, then more substantial bistro dishes plus pasta and pizza in the evenings.

Evandale

Though public transport is very limited to **EVANDALE**, 5km east of Perth, the National Trust-classified town rewards a visit, especially when Tasmania's largest **country market** (Sun 8am–2pm) brings its convivial jumble of stalls to Falls Park. Like the heritage towns of the Midland Highway, it dates from the 1830s, and many of its Georgian buildings were erected by convicts, including John "Red" Kelly, father of Ned. But being on a road to nowhere special, Evandale is cocooned in a blissful village atmosphere that is only disturbed by the jets at Launceston airport just north. In late February, usually over the last weekend, Evandale hosts the **National Penny Farthing Championships** as part of its Village Fair festival (ⓦ www.evandalevillagefair.com); races of lycra-clad riders on antique bikes are not a sight you'll forget in a hurry.

Approaching from the west on High Street, you enter before a castellated turret built using penal labour – actually, the water tower of a failed scheme to channel river water to Launceston – and reach the **Evandale Tourism and History Centre** (daily Oct–Apr 9am–5pm, May–Sept 10am–3pm; ☎03/6391 8128; Internet access $2.50 per 15min), where you can pick up a *Heritage Walk* brochure ($2.20) and peruse displays of local history. Beyond two opposing **churches** to St Andrew (1840s), one neo-Gothic, the other with a Classical bell tower and Doric columns, lies the town's kernel on Russell Street. Here, **Brown's Village Store** (1834) is an attractive throwback with vintage shelving and counter, while the *Clarendon Arms* (1847), one of Tassie's more characterful pubs, built over the former convict station, has corniced ceilings and historical murals in a side room. Where Russell Street segues into Logan Road, there's a bronze of local resident **John Glover**, the club-footed colonial artist who fathered landscape painting in Australia. Adjacent to the statue is Falls Park, which hosts the long-running market, and, behind, a **miniature train** that operates on the second and last Sunday of the month (9.30am–1pm; $2; no flip-flops (thongs) or open-toed sandals).

▲ Clarendon Arms, Evandale

Clarendon Homestead

Eight kilometres south of Evandale via the C416 and C418, the National Trust-owned **Clarendon Homestead** (daily 9am–5pm, until 4pm June–Aug; $22), on the banks of the South Esk River is one of the great Georgian houses of Australia. The grand Neoclassical country house, fronted by a swaggering portico whose size trumps anything similar in the nation, was commissioned by merchant James Cox as a centrepiece to his merino wool estate. Built using stone from Ross, it was completed in 1838 for the princely outlay of £30,000 (approximately £2.5 million in today's money). The most valuable heirloom in the Georgian state rooms is an oil painting by John Glover in the drawing room. Painted from a sketch a decade after he emigrated in 1831, the depiction of an oak tree is a curious hybrid of European oak and Australian eucalyptus. There's also a lovely café at the site.

Practicalities

Redline's Launceston–Bicheno **coach** service calls at Evandale on Thursdays. Free overnight parking for campervans is at Falls Park (no facilities). The best **food** in Evandale is in the café-gallery *Ingleside Bakery* (licensed): all-day breakfasts, quiche and lunch platters baked in a wood-fired inglenook oven are on the menu, and there's a small garden. More substantial fare such as house special beef and Guinness pie is served at the *Clarendon Arms*.

Accommodation

Clarendon Arms 11 Russell St ☏ 03/6391 8181, ⒺClarendonarms@bigpond.com. Good value en-suite rooms in the village's historic pub. ❸
Greg & Gill's Place 35 Collins Street ☏ 03/6391 8248. Two self-contained units in a modern, split cottage in the gardens of the town's oldest houses. It's located near Falls Park. ❹
The Menzies ☏03/6398 6190. The Clarendon homestead manages three self-contained cottages on-site. The style is modern(ish) and not as charming as they should be, but there's no faulting the serenity of the location. ❹
🏃 **Solomon Cottage** junction of High Street and Russell Street ☏03/6391 8331, Ⓔsolomonhouseandcottage@hotmail.com. Sweet cottagey rooms in an antique-furnished former bakery from 1838 with two beds; it also has a self-catering cottage (same price). ❺
The Stables 5 Russell St ☏03/6391 8048. Comfy modern units carved from the former stables, set in a garden behind Brown's Village Store. ❺
Strathmore off the C416 past the turn for Clarendon ☏03/6398 6213. A grand rural homestead built by convicts in 1826 and located amid mature gardens, this is a traditional upmarket B&B that prepares meals for guests on request. ❺

Longford

"History and gardens entwined" is the epithet of **LONGFORD**, 6km southwest of Perth. The former refers to its status as a heritage town that was founded in 1807 by farmers resettled from Norfolk Island, which subsequently prospered as land grants were handed out for wool and dairy estates. The "gardens" refers to a famous rose garden south of town (see p.154) and, possibly, to an arboretum planted in front of the church by 1830s settlers. Contemporary buildings, most built by convict work gangs, are clustered at the town's central fork: the *Queen's Arms Hotel* (1835) and the adjacent Neoclassical **Town Hall**, erected as an entertainments adjunct to the pub; or the sandstone **Christ Church** (1839), which has impressive stained glass and a bell and clock gifted by King George IV. **Brown's Big Store** (1889) near the pub on Wellington Street is an enjoyable slice of colonial Victoriana. Longford has two other claims to fame: it hosts

Australia's oldest continually running **racecourse**, established in 1847 and whose country classic is the New Year's Day Longford Cup; and it was a venue for Australian Grand Prix races of the 1950s and 1960s. Racing memorabilia, including a glossy TR2 racer steered by the era's only female driver, Diane Leighton, are on display in the *Country Club Hotel* at 19 Wellington Rd.

Estates out of town

On the outskirts of town, 2km along Woolmers Lane (C521), **Brickendon Estate** (Tues–Sun 9.30am–5pm; closed July & Aug; $12; ℡03/6391 1251, ⓦwww.brickendon.com.au) was established on land granted to **William Archer** in 1824. Created as a model English farm, the estate is still run as a working sheep concern by seventh-generation Archers. More remarkable is that the Dutch-style barns built of pit-sawn timber or small buildings of hand-made bricks are largely true to William's originals – because of this, the estate was nominated for World Heritage status in 2007. The estate's rural charm can't have changed much either. Notable buildings include a tiny two-room cottage from which Archer established his farm for five years, an insight into the privations of pioneer settlers, and the granary barn, raised on mushroom-like pedestals to thwart rats (a cat-hole is included to be sure) and window bars to thwart the farm's convict workforce. The family home – a handsome Georgian manor reached on a driveway opposite the farm village – is closed to the public, but you are free to wander around idyllic **gardens** planted in rambling English style; these are less frequented but arguably more enchanting than the famous National Rose Garden nearby.

The spur for William to emigrate was his brother **Thomas Archer**, who established the **Woolmers Estate** (daily 10am–4.30pm; ℡03/6391 2230, ⓦwww.woolmers.com.au) in 1819. It was his reports of vast land grants and excellent sheep-farming on terrain similar to their home county of Herefordshire that encouraged William and two other Archers to try their luck in the colony. All prospered and Woolmers passed through six generations of Archers until Thomas the sixth bequeathed it as a historical estate in 1994. Commanding excellent views from a low hill a few kilometres further along the hawthorn-hedged Woolmers Lane, the original Archer bungalow with its dark warren of rooms still stands, albeit enveloped by an impressive Italianate villa adjoined in 1843. A guided **tour** of the house, where the grand dining room is laid as it was for a royal visit in 1868, is fascinating as much for the interiors as for the family story (daily 11am, 12.30pm, 2pm & 3.30pm, plus 10am Oct–Apr; $18 including outbuildings and Rose Garden). You can also take a self-guided tour ($12) of the grounds, whose estate outbuildings include a marvellous wool shed (*c.*1819), believed to be the oldest in use in Australia. Admiral Nelson's pre-Trafalgar peptalk "England expects every man to do his duty" is stencilled on a beam by the entrance. The orchards were dug up to create the **National Rose Garden**, with over four thousand plants and five hundred rose types. It's a scenic spot too, perched above the Macquarie River with views across the Great Western Tiers. A good **café** in the servants' quarters prepares country fillers such as home-made soup with doorsteps of damper bread.

Practicalities

Tassielink schedules weekday **buses** from Launceston to Longford via Perth. It also runs half-day trips from Launceston to the estates (Tues & Thurs except July–Aug to Brickendon; $12; entry fees extra). In the town behind the green, *Longford Riverside Caravan Park* (℡03/6391 1470, ⓔlongfordcaravanpark @bigpond.com; campsite $16, units and cabin ➋, van for four people ➌) is a lovely tranquil spot beside the river and is well maintained. For **accommodation**, the *Racecourse Inn*, at 114 Marlbrough St (☎03/6391 2352, ⓦwww .racecourseinn.com; ⑤), is the premier address in town, especially in the antique-furnished rooms downstairs; wood-panelled accommodation in the attic is snug but not as elegant. Outside central Longford, you can stay at both historic estates. ⚑ Brickendon (same contacts as above; ⑤–⑥) has a trio of lovely modern-rustic cottages created from recycled timber, with chickens pecking outside the front door and views to the mountains of Ben Lomond at the back. More idyllic are its Georgian cottages for the homestead's gardener and coachman; full of character and period charm, they rank among the most memorable places to stay in Tasmania. At Woolmers (same contacts; ⑤) the conjoined free-settlers' cottages have been refurbished to create self-contained units that bring contemporary style to cottage scale.

The **restaurant** of the *Racecourse Inn* (dinner only; open to non-guests; booking required) prepares excellent, moderate to expensive international cuisine that leans towards Asia. More casual eating options in Longford are chirpy café *Sticky Beaks* at 1 Marlbrough St (closed Mon), just south of the church, whose pizzas earn the respect of locals, and central *JJ's Bakery* at 52 Wellington St (daily 8am–5pm), which is a good option for a snack and coffee break. A wall of leaflets inside passes for the town's **information** centre. One of the most appealing options in the area is ⚑ *River's Edge Café* at 1 Tannery Rd (9am–4pm Wed–Sun), within the brick walls of a former tannery. Laidback and with an eclectic eye for decor, the café-restaurant prepares a daily menu of contemporary bistro-style dishes from whatever's fresh. Moderate prices and nice garden too. It's located 3km northwest of the town: take the B52 west of Longford towards Devonport and turn right after 1km at an unsigned crossroads.

The Central Plateau

Edged to the north and east by the long crest of the Great Western Tiers, the Central Plateau ("Lake Country") is the heartland of Tasmania. Most of the area is over a thousand metres above sea level. Frost is a possibility for much of the year, and sleet and snowstorms lash in winter; a rarity in Tasmania's generally temperate climate and a quirk that permitted a 65-kilometre wide ice cap to gouge out a collage of shallow **lakes** that are renowned for their superb trout fishing.

Unsurprisingly, the unforgiving environment deterred settlement. Aborigines of the Big River Tribe only made hunting forays onto the plateau between October and March, establishing temporary settlements and firing the bush to encourage regrowth and lure prey. During the colony's formative decades the high country was left to outlaw bushrangers and stockmen, usually ex-convicts, and it was left to Scottish settlers to create **Bothwell**, the only town which is hunkered down in the foothills. The absence of year-round inhabitation changed in the last century. Fibro-shack villages were knocked up alongside hydroelectric projects and now eke out a living as getaways for trout-obsessed anglers. On a fine weekend in summer, the population on the Central Plateau can swell to 25,000 and every car seems to tow a tinnie (an aluminium dinghy). Out of season, the plateau is practically deserted – only about eight hundred people live here year-round.

Trout fishing aside, much of the appeal of this remote, even bleak, upland lies in the broad landscapes and huge skies around **Great Lake** and **Arthurs Lake**, dotted with quirky shacks. Just south, you can look around a 1930s hydro-power station, while gateway town **Bothwell** has modest colonial architecture and the oldest golf course in Australia. Metro bus #140 runs from Hobart to Bothwell on weekdays; otherwise there is no public transport.

Bothwell

Turning west off the Midlands Highway, the Highland Lakes Road (A5) ascends into the high country of Tasmania's heartland. Remote and free of tourist glitz, the small town of **BOTHWELL** is nevertheless a rather handsome place. Georgian coaching inns conspire with a wide thoroughfare to make you feel that you've arrived somewhere, albeit somewhere in rural northern Britain rather than Australia. Its name (Bothwell is a small town in Lanarkshire) is the legacy of a boatload of free-settler Scots who put down roots in 1821, encouraged by a favourable survey that reported fertile plains that were well-watered by the Clyde River, then known by hunters as the "Fat Doe River". The settlers also brought **golf** with them to bequeath Bothwell the oldest course in Australia. A round on the Ratho links (green fees $15; club hire from museum in town $10; ☎0409 595702, ⓦwww.rathogolf.com), 1km north on the Launceston road, is an experience faithful to the game's cross-country roots – the home green is just below the shearing shed and sheep nibble the fairways to acceptable levels. Currently nine holes with a par of 34, the course is due to be upgraded to fifteen holes soon.

Back in the centre on the pretty town green, Market Place, a small **golf museum** (daily 9am–4pm; $4; ☎03/6259 4033, ⓦwww.ausgolfmuseum.com) traces the history of the sport. It doubles as the **information centre** (same times and contacts) and stocks a handy leaflet that lists the historic architecture in Bothwell. Just along from the museum, **St Luke's Church** was a joint effort by John Lee Archer and Daniel Herbert; the convict sculptor of Ross Bridge fame chiselled the busts for its portal. Follow Alexander Street to its end and you can cross the Clyde River and ascend Barrack Hill to a stocky former **garrison building** (now a private residence), which commands a view over the grid of streets. Outside the town, 2km off the continuation of Market Place, boutique whisky producer **Nant Distillery** (☎03/6259 5790, ⓦwww.nant .com.au; by appointment) runs tours of its stills in a National Trust-listed settler's farm, washed down with a dram of single malt.

Accommodation

Bothwell's most glamorous address is country retreat and fishing lodge *The Priory* (☎03/6220 2123; ⓦwww.theprioycountrylodge.com.au; ⑨) in a Tudor-style heritage building overlooking the town on Barrack Hill. A sister property to Hobart's sumptuous boutique hotel *The Islington*, the refined four-room lodge with a gourmet restaurant for guests opened in April 2008 and seems destined to become one of Tassie's premier country retreats. On Alexander Street, *Bothwell Grange* (☎03/6259 5556; ⑤) is a nineteenth-century coaching inn-turned heritage B&B. Bar a couple of self-catering cottages (⑥) sourced through the visitor centre, Bothwell's other beds are in the *Castle Hotel* (☎03/6259 5502; ④), no hardship as the pub has revamped its accommodation to provide small but upmarket rooms. Another reason to stay is that the pub guarantees dinner for guests; it serves non-guests on Friday and Saturday only (pizzas are occasionally rustled up on Wed). Either way, there's little on offer for vegetarians. A municipal caravan park (☎03/6259 5503; camping $15) is in fact a car park behind the visitor centre, with a scrap of grass for tents; water and powered sites are available, and check-in is at the council offices on Alexander Street.

Up the Highland Lakes Highway

North of Bothwell, you drive through empty hills before the terrain becomes more rugged as you climb into high country; fill up with petrol in Bothwell if you're below a quarter-tank. After 34km, signs direct you to the **Steppes Sculptures** in a bush clearing. The circle of twelve dolerite monoliths is the work of sculptor Stephen Walker, the most prolific public artist in Tasmania (he also created the Tank Stream fountain at Sydney's Circular Quay), to commemorate Aboriginal and pioneer life in the unforgiving environment of the Central Plateau. It's an atmospheric spot, all the more enigmatic because you're likely to have it to yourself.

A turning west at 20km bounces along an unsealed loop road (C178) to arrive after 27km at **Waddamana Power Station**. Though plans to harness the Great Lake for hydroelectricity were implemented as early as 1910, bitter winters bankrupted the private company and it was only through nationalization to create the Hydro-Electric Department – forerunner of today's Hydro Tasmania – that the first hydro station in the state was completed by 1916. Isolation remained a problem, however. Aspirant construction workers were told at interview that the site was a "comfortable" two-day walk from Deloraine and successful applicants were given a tent and straw mattress. A **museum** in the Waddamana A power station (daily 10am–4pm; free; ☏03/6259 6158) documents the pioneering years of hydropower; hydroelectricity now meets the

Trout fishing in central Tasmania

Trout bred at Salmon Ponds near New Norfolk were introduced to the Central Plateau in 1860 and rapidly penetrated the network of streams. Writing in 1862, explorer F J Cockburn reminisced about "very good fishing, very good beer and capital whisky". With or without whisky, the **fishing** here is world-class. Wild brown trout are the prize quarry, followed by rainbow trout. The season generally runs from late August to April, although fishing – fly, lure and loch-style from boats – is most rewarding from late October to March. The Mecca for brown trout is **Arthurs Lake**, whose average catch-rate of two fish per day accounts for a third of all brown trout landed in Tasmania. **Great Lake** also has browns, but is better for rainbow trout. **Bronte Lagoon** is a good hunting ground for both species, as is the nearby Bradys system, where early-season bait fishing pays dividends.

In terms of equipment, an all-purpose rod of around 6ft and lines with a 2-3kg breaking strain should suffice. If using waders, pack thermal longjohns for the cold waters, advisable in any case in this fickle climate. The choice of fly – woolly buggers, scruffy jassids, possum emergers or royal wulffs to name a few – fills books of its own, and the best advice is to seek local knowledge; baits are sold at stores and hotels throughout the lakes area (see p.45 for details of **licences**). The most convenient options for visitors are organized **fishing trips** which include the day's licence, gear, transport, lunch and tuition. Daily prices average $500–600 for one person or $250–375 per person for two people, and some outfits offer accommodation. Many operators are based at Miena and Cressy, a trout-obsessed gateway to Arthurs Lake and venue for the Tasmanian Trout Expo fish-fest that starts the season (usually a weekend in Aug/early Sept). Cressy-based operators include Venture Fly Fishing Tours (☏03/ 6397 8349; ⓦwww.ventureflyfishing.com.au), which also provides B&B beneath the Western Tiers, and Trout Territory (☏03/6397 5001, ⓦwww.troutterritory .com.au), a specialist in all styles of fishing. Otherwise, the best source of accredited professionals is the website of sport regulator Trout Guides and Lodges Tasmania (ⓦwww.troutguidestasmania.com.au), a useful site which also has general advice on the choice of equipment.

majority of Tasmania's energy needs. What impresses most is the sheer scale of the retro-futurist machinery, much of it installed in the late 1920s when the station was beefed up to accommodate the generating potential of a new dam at Miena.

Going north from the crossroads where the C178 rejoins the highway is **Arthurs Lake**, a rather brooding presence amid these bleak hills. On the west shore, there are **campgrounds** at Pumphouse Bay ($3.30 per person; pit toilets; hot showers Oct–Apr; water; firewood in theory) and 4km further at Jonah Bay ($2.20 per person; pit toilets) and precious little else. Both sites can get busy in summer when anglers set up camp to enjoy the best **trout fishing** in the state (see box, p.157). For considerably more comfort, *Blue Lake Lodge* (closed May–Aug; ☎03/6259 8030, ⓦwww.bluelakelodge.com.au; ❽) is a luxury fishing retreat on the lake shore that throws a three-course dinner into the price and has professional fishing guides in-house. The sealed road continues north to traverse the desolate Great Lake Conservation Area before descending downs the Tiers towards Longford.

West of the crossroads, the **Great Lake** is the largest natural freshwater lake in Australia; Lake Pedder southwest trumps its 158 square-kilometre area, but is man-made. Scooped out by a glacier, it is also the nation's highest lake at an elevation of 1036m, and is notorious for changeable climate. **Trout** lures most of its vistors. The only settlement of note in the area is **MIENA**, a fishing village on the south shore that was established for hydro-damming projects in the 1920s. You can **stay** in comfy en-suite rooms at the *Central Highlands Lodge* (☎03/6259 8179, ⓦwww.centralhighlandslodge.com.au; ❺), a fishing retreat with a good restaurant and organized fishing trips, or in the shoreside *Great Lake Hotel* (☎03/6259 8163, ⓦwww.greatlakehotel.com.au; campsites $20; angler cabins with shared facilities ❸; motel units ❹), 2km west at the Marlborough Highway (B11) junction. Its pub prepares no-nonsense tucker at reasonable prices. The hotel also has the only public payphone in Miena; forget about mobile reception up here. You can also bushcamp at *Little Pine Lagoon* (free; pit toilets; fuel stove only), 5km southwest on the Marlborough Highway. A general store near the hotel sells basic supplies, takeaway fish and chips, and fuel.

From Miena you can either switch south on the Marlborough Highway for a bone-shattering 35-kilometre drive to the Lyell Highway, or continue up the west shore of Great Lake towards Deloraine and the Liffey Falls. En route at **Liawenee**, a Parks & Wildlife field centre (☎03/6259 8148; times vary) has information about **walks** in the area. One of the best is to Pine Lake just north of the Great Lake. A flat gravel trail (30min return) heads to a stand of pencil pines, an ancient species unique to the Tasmanian Highlands.

The Derwent Valley

There's a real sense of transition as you travel west along the **Lyell Highway** (A10). The route is one of the great drives in Tasmania, which for much of the journey follows the **Derwent River** as it flows from its source at Lake King William, south of Lake St Clair. The mature river is surrounded by broad bucolic landscapes that morph into rolling parched hills around colonial **Hamilton**, the result of a rain shadow from mountains southwest and cloud-seeding by Hydro Tasmania to maintain reservoir levels. Further west are steep valleys where hydroelectric schemes have created a string of **lakes** beloved by trout anglers, and finally you ascend to the **highlands** of the river's source, at the fringe of the World Heritage Area wilderness. Part of the appeal is the lack of development – west of Hamilton, only **Tarraleah**, a former Hydro base turned upmarket adventure resort, has infrastructure for tourism. Tassielink's West Coast **coach** service to Strahan plies the highway daily except Monday and Wednesday.

Hamilton

More oversized village than rural town, **HAMILTON** is the only urban centre on the run west. It's a drowsy one-street sort of place whose low-key atmosphere seems out of kilter with its Georgian streetscape. That is the legacy of a heyday in the mid-1840s, by when an original hamlet of Norfolk Island refugees had blossomed into an eight hundred-strong settlement with a couple of breweries, seven inns, eleven constables and a free labour force of over three hundred convicts. So bright seemed the future that surveyors drew up plans to create a major country town of English squares and esplanades. Mechanization put paid to that, reducing the labour required for the surrounding sheep farms, and also destroyed much of the architecture, as building stone was recycled. Hamilton is at least free from the tourist razzmatazz you'll find in historic towns such as Richmond or Ross, something which accounts for much of its charm.

Worth a look among the remaining Georgian edifices are **St Peter's Church** (1834) on the main road to the east – its narrow single portal was intended to thwart convicts from stampeding to freedom during services – and former coaching inn **Glen Clyde House** (daily 9.30am–5pm; ☎03/6298 3276, Ⓦwww.glenclyde.com) on the corner beyond. Now a renowned crafts gallery, it sells a walking tour leaflet ($2) and has a good café-restaurant that prepares honest home-style cooking. There's also a lovely garden terrace, weather permitting. Behind oak trees at the other end of town, the **Hamilton Heritage Centre** (daily 9am–5pm; keys from adjacent council chambers Mon–Fri, Glen Clyde House Sat–Sun; free) displays a few colonial knick-knacks in the gaol warden's cottage. The *Hamilton Inn* a little further on retains the facade of a handsome Georgian coaching inn, even if its bar is blighted by 1970s tat. Uphill just before the main road crosses the Clyde River, you can idle in two gardens of **Prospect Villa** (in theory daily 9am–4pm; $5 donation), residence of the colonial town's district surgeon: there's rambling English-cottage style at the rear, formal Italian fashion at the side.

Hamilton's sheep-farming heritage is showcased at *Curringa Farm*, 3km east. Its sixth-generation owners provide the only tours of a merino sheep farm in Tassie (1.5hr; daily 10am–4pm, Sept–April; $47, includes lunch or BBQ provisions; booking essential, see "Accommodation"). Tours generally include a demonstration of dog work and shearing, and a spin out to see crops such as opium poppies – Tasmania accounts for nearly half of global production for the pharmaceutical opium market.

Hamilton is on Tassielink's year-round West Coast **coach** route and its Lake St Clair & Cradle Mountain summer service.

Accommodation

As well as free riverside camping on the village park, there's plenty of historic accommodation should you decide to stay.

🏃 **Curringa Farm** Three kilometres west of town ☎03/6286 3332, Ⓦwww.curringafarm .com. Amid the grazing hills of a sheep farm, this is the remote getaway par excellence, a four-star self-contained spa cottage (sleeps six) beside a

lake – great views from the lounge or large deck beside the water, and a canoe to paddle. ⑥ **Hamilton Cottage Collection** 33 Franklin Place ☎03/6286 3270. Manages four quaint Georgian cottages that sleep up to four, each faithful to the

period and set in a pretty English-style garden. ❺
Hamilton Inn Tarleton St ☎03/6286 3204. Comfy
en-suite rooms in the historic pub. ❹
Jackson's Emporium 13 Franklin Place
☎03/6286 3232. Three cottages– two vintage,
one modern – in two acres of garden feature

their own vegetable and fruit gardens for
guests. ❻
The Old School House Main Rd ☎03/6286 3292,
ⓦwww.hamiltonschoolhouse.com. An old-
fashioned English-style B&B in one of the town's
showpiece houses. ❺

West to Derwent Bridge

Northwest of Hamilton, you roll into – and rapidly out of – **OUSE** ("ooze").
This small village represented the western frontier of civilization when it
emerged on a river crossing in the 1820s, and still feels further than its 88km
from Hobart. The *Lachlan Hotel* (☎03/6287 1215; rooms ❸) provides pub grub
and beds should you decide to stop. Hydro-dams created the slender lakes – or
"lagoons" as Tasmanians know them – that characterize this reach of the
Derwent, most deserted save for trout fishermen on their banks. There's a basic
bushcamp (free) at a picnic area at Repulse Lake, 2km southwest of Ouse.
Alternatively *Wayatinah Campground* (☎03/6289 3317; campsite $9), beside a
hydro-lake 23km from Ouse, provides the full range of amenities plus a heated
swimming pool at summer weekends ($3; open to non-guests).

   TARRALEAH, 12km northwest of the *Wayatinah Campground*, owes its
origins to hydroelectricity. A town in miniature, with a police station, a
church, a pub, a community hall and meticulously spaced cottages, the village
was intended to house officers and management staff of the Hydro Electric
Commission during power projects in the 1930s. Their massive pipes power
down either side of the valley; impressive or a scar depending on your point
of view. A multi-million dollar overhaul has reinvented the village as a resort
that's a curious hybrid of elite retreat and activities base. If you can overlook
the somewhat soulless institutional architecture, the resort (☎03/6289 0111,
ⓦwww.tarraleah.com) has excellent facilities as an activities base: there's
camping (pitches $15) at the *Highland Caravan Park* and contemporary
mezzanine studios in the old school (❺), while the Art Deco cottages
(❼; minimum 2 nights) at the lip of the valley have been renovated into
spacious and rather elegant **accommodation**. *The Lodge* (☎03/6289 1199;
ⓦwww.tarraleahlodge.com; ❽) represents the exclusive arm of the resort – a
contemporary take on the country retreat with a vibe (and decor) inspired
by its Art Deco building. Effortlessly stylish and drooled over by the travel
press, it was lauded as the best lodge accommodation in the country in the
Australian national tourism awards of 2007. A café at the resort, *Teez* (daily
8am–4pm; licensed), prepares good bistro dishes plus huge sandwiches,
served with views of the Nive Valley from a veranda. In the evenings, there's
pub food at the *Highlander Arms*. For guests and non-guests alike, the resort
runs **activities** (same contacts) in the area, though none are particularly
cheap. Among the range are: guided mountain-bike trips ($50; 3hr; $220 per
day, includes kayak trip); birdwatching tours by kayak ($150; 5hr; includes
lunch); fly-fishing lessons ($220; 3.5hr – rod hire available, $75 per day); and
one-day 4WD excursions ($180).

   The highway north of Tarraleah hairpins across the Nive River by two hydroelectric power stations: Art Deco-infused Tarraleah power station and adjacent
Tungatinda power station, one of the world's largest iron-and-glass structures
when it was built in 1953. Information boards at a picnic site detail the stations'
history. You then climb into the high-altitude lakes which are used as water
storage for the generation of electricity. **Brady's Lake** and **Lake Big Jim** east
of the highway are popular trout-fishing spots. Highland Lakes Boat Hire

(☎03/6289 1143 or 0438 725562, ⒲www.boathiretasmania.com) at Bradys Lake rents a range of dinghies and fishing gear.

BRONTE PARK west is another hydro-turned-angling village. As well as offering accommodation, Bronte Park Highland Village (☎03/6289 1126, ⒲www.bronteparkvillage.com.au; three-bed cottages & motel-style chalets; ❹) retains three huts in the centre as a testament to the primitive conditions endured by dam construction workers in the 1950s. Incidentally, the village's cabins are named after the national teams who stayed here for the world fly-fishing championship in 1988; nearby Ausprey Tours ($330 per day for one person, $240 for two people; ☎03/6330 2612, ⒲www.gotroutfishtasmania .com.au) offers good-value **fly-fishing** tours. A general store has the last food supplies before Lake St Clair (fresh produce a few times a week) and fuel. It also has EFTPOS facilities.

Along the Great Western Tiers

Where the Central Plateau drops abruptly to surrounding plains north and east is known as the **Great Western Tiers**. Its northern wall forms a boundary to the rich pasture of the **Meander Valley**, whose undulating terrain provided a natural avenue for colonial settlement from Launceston. Gorgeous bucolic scenery broken by dolerite slabs such as Quamby Bluff and a couple of sleepy Georgian villages, notably Westbury, with a quaint village green, make for a pleasant journey west to **Deloraine**, the valley hub with a mellow vibe and an arty bent. You could drive it in thirty minutes on the Bass Highway, but it's best savoured over a day or so on its forerunner, the B54. West of Deloraine, the landscape becomes wilder as you approach Cradle Country: there are extensive **cave systems** around **Mole Creek**, a good base for bike rides and walks, and remote hiking in the **Walls of Jerusalem National Park**, a lake-pocked corner of the Central Plateau that is accessed southwest of Mole Creek. Regional tourism website ⒲www.greatwesterntiers.org.au is a useful reference for planning. Redline operates a weekday **bus** schedule to all destinations between Launceston and Mole Creek; bookings are required for all stops.

Hadspen and Carrick

HADSPEN has been bounced into modernity by the Bass Highway that swoops to its south. The village is effectively a dormitory suburb for Launceston, with only a handful of sandstone buildings on Main Street to bear witness to the original colonial village. A more complete picture of past glory is **Entally House** (daily 10am–4pm; $8; ☎03/6393 6201; ⒲www.entally.com.au), off the main road one kilometre west. The National Trust-listed country homestead (controversially leased to forestry giant Gunns) was built in 1819 by Thomas Haydcock Reibey, the eldest son of a shipping magnate, and Mary Reibey, a plucky convict-made-good who co-founded the Bank of New South Wales and is depicted on the $20 note. Though a little bare, rooms contain Regency furniture and silverware plus a few oil paintings by colonial landscape master John Glover. Equally appealing are the gardens (true to the original designs), plus agricultural outbuildings, a chapel and what is reputed to be Australia's oldest cricket pitch. **Food and accommodation** hereabouts is in *Rutherglen Holiday Village* (☎03/6393 6307, ⒲www.rutherglen.biz; ❹), a dated motel complex with a swimming pool, on the main road opposite Entally House, or *Cosy Cabins Launceston* (☎1800 281 885, ⒲www.cosycabins.com.au; camping

$25; cabins ⑤) beside the main road in Hadspen. Near the holiday park there's a general store with fuel, while at the other end of the street there's a pretty picnic ground beside the Liffey River. Metro **bus** #78 from Launceston terminates at Rutherglen (via Hadspen), and Redline's weekday Mole Creek service will stop if you pre-book.

Five kilometres west of Hadspen but more rural British in feel, colonial **CARRICK** is a sleepy village whose Georgian structures date from the 1830s. Just uphill from the centre, the **Tasmanian Copper and Metal Art Gallery** displays metal crafts made on site (Mon–Fri 9.30am–5pm; free; ☎03/6393 6440, Ⓦwww.tascoppermetalart.com) and beside it are the ruins of Heritage-listed **Archer's Folly**; apparently, the mid-1800s mansion never progressed beyond a shell after the ship carrying its building stone foundered in the Bass Strait. You can just make out the tunnel-like carriageway intended by the luckless (and uninsured) English settler. Arguably the biggest attraction is the old millhouse at the western end of the village that has been reinvented as an English-style pub, *Mill Inn*; a waterwheel spins in the dining room. There's also a pleasant beer garden. In the centre, *The Stables at Hawthorn Villa* (☎03/6393 6150, Ⓦwwwhawthornvilla.com; ⑤) is a great place to stay with split-level modern-rustic apartments.

Westbury

Only Ross comes as close to recreating village England in Australia as **WESTBURY**. The quaint village green, Georgian architecture, hawthorn hedgerows and English-style churches represent a yearning for England that is so homesick its realization verges on cliché. Westbury was planned in 1828 as a gateway to the northwest frontier, and it was initially populated by an Irish regiment, many of whose soldiers were persuaded to settle as civilians by the grant of a small cottage and a five-shilling weekly pension. Today the town's big jamboree is **St Patrick's Festival** (mid-March), a three-day event with a parade and, rather schizophrenically, English maypole dancing.

As you enter from the east, **Westbury Maze** (daily 10am-5pm; closed Aug; $6) is a neatly clipped traditional hedge maze whose paths wind for over a kilometre. There's also a pleasant on-site café. There are over two hundred vintage tractors and agricultural machinery, with one or two usually in action, at **Pearn's Steam World** (daily 9am–4pm; $5; ☎03/6393 1414, Ⓦwww.pearnssteamworld.org.au). **John Temple Gallery** (daily 10am–5pm; free; Ⓦwww.johntemplegallery.com.au) further along sells spectacular photographs of Tasmanian landscapes.

Quaint William Street heads south of a central crossroads and leads to the **village green** one block across on the right. Planted with native British trees and ringed by Georgian buildings such as **St Andrew's Church**, whose foundation stone was placed by Lieutenant-governor Arthur himself, it seems far too quaint to have been a military parade ground with a stocks and gallows. To compound the suspicion that you've been beamed to the Cotswolds there's the corner store (1841) of shopkeeper Thomas White at the south end. Managed by the National Trust, **White House** (Tues–Sun 10am–4pm, closed July & Aug; $8; ☎03/6393 1171) houses an enjoyable miscellany of period odds and ends. Rooms of English oak furniture and Staffordshire china are fairly missable, but a handmade Victorian doll's house abounds in period detail such as handpainted wallpaper in a chinoiserie boudoir. Outbuildings house collections of vintage bicycles, toys and vehicles, the latter including a jaunty horsedrawn carriage that dispensed sodas to beach-goers in Adelaide.

Practicalities

The post office (Mon–Fri 9am–6pm; ☎03/6393 1233) on William Street doubles as a **visitor information centre** at which to pick up a map of historic buildings. Unsurprisingly, there's lots of heritage **accommodation**. On the green, elegant *Elm Wood*, at 10 Lonsdale Promenade (☎03/6393 1893, ⓦwww.elmwoodclassicbedandbreakfast.com.au; ⑥) is a luxury B&B with a contemporary take on Victorian decor, or *Winchmore*, at no. 12 (☎03/6392 1282, ⓔjohnshebeale@bigpond.com; ④) is a historic self-catering cottage with modern facilities. *Westbury Gingerbread Cottages* (☎03/6393 1140, ⓦwww.westburycottages.com.au; ⑤–⑥), up from White House on the corner of William Street, manages a clutch of colonial properties furnished in various grades of bygone style; farm labourer's cottage Gingerbread House is the most traditional, the Bungalow is the most modern. You can **camp** behind *Andy's Bakery* ($5 per person; ☎03/6393 1846; laundry) between the maze and steam museum. Open 24 hours a day, the bakery is a good bet for the usual pies and sandwiches, and serves award-winning Italian-style ice cream. Otherwise, there's refined dining at *Hobnobs*, at 47 William St (dinner Thurs–Sat, lunch Sun; ☎03/6393 2007), with a menu of Asian-inspired dishes plus excellent King Island steak, and modern European cuisine in a light-flooded dining room at *Fitzpatrick's Inn* at 107 Meander Valley Rd (lunch & dinner Wed–Sun; motel rooms ④). For a cheap feed, you could do worse than the solid fillers at the *Westbury Hotel* at 107 Bass Highway (☎03 6393 1151; rooms ③). A picnic ground with a barbecue is on Westbury Common behind the village green.

Deloraine

DELORAINE, an ideal base from which to explore the Tiers area, is a mellow hilly town among farmsteads, often shrouded in mist even on summer mornings, and divided into two parts by the burbling **Meander River**. Although the area was settled by Europeans in the 1830s, it didn't really begin to develop until after 1847, when the removal of a probation station on the west bank wiped clean the convict stain. Even then, settlement was sluggish until the government sold off land at the knockdown rate of £1 per acre. Deloraine is a National Trust–classified town, yet historic architecture plays second fiddle to its much-vaunted "Creative Community"; appropriate considering the town was probably christened after Sir William Deloraine, a character in Sir Walter Scott's epic poem *The Lay of the Minstrel*. Wooed by cheap real estate and superb scenery, artists congregated from the late 1970s to give Deloraine an alternative, even cosmopolitan bent that is out of keeping with a rural town of just two thousand people. Café culture is strong, and sculptures and galleries are dotted throughout the town. In addition, the town hosts Australia's largest working crafts fair, the **Tasmanian Craft Fair**. It concludes on the first Monday in November, and hosts around thirty thousand visitors, meaning accommodation is sparse throughout the area then. At other times, the arts-and-crafts scene can be witnessed at a **market** on the first Saturday of every month across the river, opposite the *Apex Caravan Park*.

Any walking tour of the town begins at **West Parade**, which follows the river; at no. 17 near the roundabout, **Bonney's Inn** dates from 1830 and is the town's oldest remaining building (now a B&B; see p.165). A block south, East Westbury Place rises steeply towards the high spire of **St Mark's Church**, built in 1860. Beyond it a scenic **lookout** gives a panoramic view over the town and the Western Tiers to the south. Emu Bay Road, west of the roundabout, is lined with quirky **sculptures** – a leaflet from the information centre (see p.165) puts names to the bronzes that were installed in 2002 – and a few bric-a-brac shops. There are also a handful of **galleries** (shop hours unless where stated): Artifakt (40 Emu

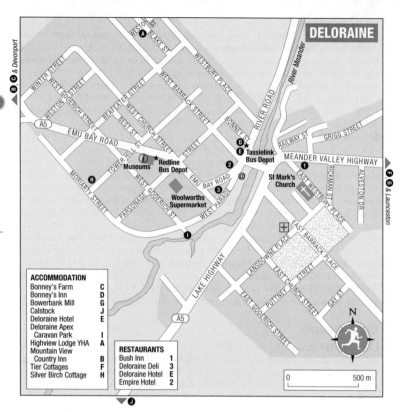

ACCOMMODATION
Bonney's Farm   C
Bonney's Inn   D
Bowerbank Mill   G
Calstock   J
Deloraine Hotel   E
Deloraine Apex
  Caravan Park   I
Highview Lodge YHA   A
Mountain View
  Country Inn   B
Tier Cottages   F
Silver Birch Cottage   H

RESTAURANTS
Bush Inn   1
Deloraine Deli   3
Deloraine Hotel   E
Empire Hotel   2

Bay Rd) and adjacent Bondfields sell contemporary fine crafts and traditional leather and merino wool wear respectively; Gallery B opposite specializes in glass; and by the third roundabout, the Artists' Garrett workshop (29 West Church St; daily 9.30am–5.30pm) displays crafts by artists from throughout the state. The **information** centre nearby holds flyers for out-of-town galleries – Weetah Art (Tues–Sun 10am–4pm; ☏03/6382 2688, ⊛www.weetah-art.com) 5km north has contemporary wares; *Bowerbank Mill* (see "Accommodation") 2km east has more traditional crafts and painting – and Deloraine's two **museums**. The first, **Yarns Artwork in Silk** (daily 9am–5pm, except Sat–Sun June–Sept 10am–4pm; $7), is a 16m by 13.6m historical silk tapestry of the Deloraine area. It's a superb artistic work which impresses not from the ten thousand hours, three hundred people and three years of its making, but the local colour depicted in its four panels. Viewings held every half-hour in a dedicated theatre are prefaced by an audiovisual presentation about the tapestry's creation in the 1990s; proving the area's artistic roots run deep, it was the brainchild of a local farmer. **Deloraine Museum** (same ticket) is small beer by comparison: the usual colonial dioramas displayed in rooms of a nineteenth-century pub.

Accommodation

Reservations are essential when the Tasmanian Craft Fair rolls into town for the four days before the first Monday in November. You can **camp** at the riverside *Deloraine Apex Caravan Park*, at 51 West Parade (☏03/6362 2345; campsites $19).

Bonney's Farm 76 Archer St, 4km northwest off C710 to Weetah ☎03/6362 2122. Three self-contained units on a farm are fairly dated but clean and the location among pasture is peaceful. Good value and ideal for young families. ❹

Bonney's Inn 19 West Parade ☎03/6362 2974, ⓦwww.bonneys-inn.com. Period-style en suites in Deloraine's oldest building are comfy rather than luxurious and a little pricey for their size. Good breakfast and garden, though. Business was for sale at time of research. ❻

🏃 Bowerbank Mill 2km east on main road ☎03/6362 2628, ⓦwww.bowerbankmill .com.au. In a Georgian flour mill, this has rustic charm by the bucketload: there are two cottages furnished with English antiques and three early colonial-styled rooms (shared kitchenette) upstairs in the mill, including the marvellous, antique-filled suite of its former owner, leather artist Garry Greenwood. ❺–❼

🏃 Calstock off Lake Highway, 2km south of centre ☎03/6362 2642, ⓦwww.peppers .com.au/calstock. Calm and luxury reign supreme in this elegant boutique hotel in a Georgian country manor, now part of the Peppers chain. Decor is in *belle époque* style, service is immaculate, and there's gourmet French cuisine in the restaurant (guests only). One of Tasmania's premier stays. ❽

Deloraine Hotel Corner of Emu Bay Rd and Barrack St ☎03/6362 2022. A dated but decent cheapie in the centre; rooms at the rear are quietest. Shared amenities and en suites, large roof terrace. ❸

Highview Lodge YHA 8 Blake St ☎03/6362 2996, ⓔdeloraineyha@yahoo.com.au. On a hill 15min walk from the centre and commanding unrivalled views of Quamby Bluff, this is a hostel of the old school; simple but comfy enough. Dorms $21, rooms ❷

Mountain View Country Inn 144 Emu Bay Rd ☎03/6362 2633, ⓦwww.mountainviewcountryinn .com.au. An old motel whose decor is stuck in the Seventies, but has great Tiers views; the best are from rooms 11–24. Has film library. ❹

Silver Birch Cottage 42 Tower Hill St ☎0416 161183, ⓦwww.silverbirchcottage.com.au. One of the most appealing self-catering options in town, this quietly stylish three-bed house has all mod cons and a lovely garden. ❺

Tier Cottages 54 Bass Rd, 1km east of centre ☎03/6352 4500, ⓦwww.tierscottages.com. Pleasant modern holiday chalets above a lake by the main road; good value though a little soulless. ❹

Practicalities

The two major **bus** companies make regular stops in Deloraine. Redline stops on its once-daily Launceston–Devonport service and its Launceston–Deloraine service, which continues to Mole Creek once daily on weekdays; Tassielink stops on the erratic Launceston–Queenstown service (Tues, Thurs and Sat). Tassielink is based at *Sullivans Restaurant*, at 17 West Parade. The depot for Redline is the **Great Western Tiers Visitor Information Centre**, at 98 Emu Bay Rd (daily 9am–5pm; ☎03/6362 3471, ⓦwww.greatwesterntiers.org.au). As the name suggests, the centre covers the Great Western Tiers region, including walking trails and an excellent reference section, as well as making the usual free accommodation bookings. The **Online Access Centre** (Mon–Fri 10am–4pm, Sun 1–4pm; $3 per half-hour, $5 per hour) is behind the library at 21 West Parade.

Among the **activities** operators in the area are Jahadi Indigenous Experiences (☎03/6363 6172, ⓦwww.jahadi.com.au; two-hour or one-day 4WD tours; prices vary on group size), a niche operator that showcases the rich ecology and Aboriginal culture – expect wilderness walks, indigenous sites and a bush-tucker barbecue. The Tasmanian Fly Fishing School (☎03/6362 3441, ⓦwww .tasmanianflyfishing.com.au; one person $450 per day, two people $300 per person per day) offers dry-fly fishing guiding and tuition in pursuit of trout during "gentlemen's hours".

Eating and drinking

The pick of the informal **places to eat** on Emu Bay Road is the *Deloraine Deli* at no. 36 (Mon–Fri 9.30am–5.30pm, Sat 9.30am–2.30pm), a popular deli-counter and café serving fresh healthy meals, many of them vegetarian, for around $15 a plate. The revamped *Empire Hotel* just downhill specializes in

Walking around Deloraine

Deloraine is an ideal base for walks under the Great Western Tiers that sawtooth the southern horizon. It's a great drive there too, following the Lake Highway as it plunges towards the rock escarpments that jut above temperate rainforest. Just past Golden Valley, there's a difficult walk (and occasional scramble) up **Quamby Bluff** (6.5km; 6hr), renowned for its myrtle rainforest. The track begins at Brodies Road, poorly signposted off the Lake Highway about 1km before Golden Valley, and passes through pasture, mixed forest and then high-altitude scrub, before you reach a stupendous 360-degree panorama from the summit (1226m). Twenty three looping kilometres south of Deloraine, beneath the spectacular ridge of Drys Bluff, **Liffey Forest Reserve** is a popular area of rainforest just within the boundaries of the World Heritage Area. From an upper car park at Liffey Falls Picnic Area, a good gravel path descends through mixed myrtle and sassafras forest to **Liffey Falls** (45min return) via several river lookouts. A less busy route to the falls goes from a second car park further south (Liffey Falls Lower Car Park) on the **Gulf Road Walk** (2–3hr return), burrowing north through dense rainforest where the Liffey is slower beneath the falls. Be warned: it's frequently muddy.

Meander Falls in Meander Forest Reserve, in the shadow of the Tiers about 25km southwest of Deloraine (via Meander and Meander Falls Road), is a remote day-hike circuit (6–7hr return) through the World Heritage Area. Begin at the picnic ground and sign in at a walker registration at the Meander Falls car park; there's also an information booth here. Other walks from the car park are **Split Rock Track** (2–3hr return) past waterfalls and sandstone features; and the **Stone Hut/Bastion Cascade Circuit** (5–6hr return) to an area of standstone cliffs and overhangs. A free leaflet issued by Forestry Tasmania has a **map** of the Meander Forest Reserve and tracks; you can pick it up from the Deloraine information centre (see p.165) or basic notes are published on the website ⓦ www.forestrytas.com.au/visiting.

A basic **bushcamp** (free; pit toilet) is in Meander Forest Reserve at the head of the walking tracks, 3km past the picnic area. Camping elsewhere is forbidden. *Mountainside Nature Retreat* (ⓣ 03/6369 5226; ⓔ mountainside@activ8.net.au; dorms $25; all units ❹), 1km south of Golden Valley, has simple self-contained units on the slopes of Quamby Bluff. Larger hostel-style units sleep up to six; Quoll Cottage for two offers most in the way of creature comforts. All units have kitchens. There's a large outdoor fireplace and wildlife everywhere.

Thai dishes, but retains the inevitable Scotch fillet. Pub meals are rustled up daily at the *Deloraine Hotel*, which has a large menu, and at the *Bush Inn* (ⓣ 03 6362 2655; also has basic rooms ❷) on the other side of the river.

West to Mole Creek

Bucolic hills and the great slab of the Tiers make for a gorgeous **drive** through the Upper Meander Valley west of Deloraine. The natural drama may explain why this was sacred ground for Tasmanian Aborigines known as *Kooparoona Niara* ("Mountains of the Spirits"). A location where tribal territories overlapped may also have had something to do with it; certainly, the valley plains hosted *corroborees* (meeting ceremonies) of the Leterre Mairerer, Pallitorre and Lee-now-wenne tribes. If you're in no hurry, a scenic backroute on the C167 (south of Deloraine towards Meander), C166 (to Western Creek), C168 (to Caveside) and C169 (to Mole Creek) meanders through the rich sheep-pasture that rolls south to the Tiers, an ever-present wall on the journey.

The direct route to Mole Creek on the B12 swings lazily through farming villages, with a handful of diversions to break up the 23-kilometre trip. First is **41° South** (daily Nov–Mar 10am–5pm, Apr–Oct until 4pm; ☎03/6362 4130, ⓦwww.41south-aquaculture.com), 3km south of the B12 on the C164 to Meander. This small eco-inspired fish farm produces delectable smoked salmon – herb-marinated fillets are available in a café or to take away from a shop. Back on the B54, **CHUDLEIGH** is an unremarkable village save for its **honey farm** (daily except Sat 9am–5pm; ☎03/6363 6160, ⓦwww .thehoneyfarm.com.au), a chirpy place on the high street with an obsessive

▲ Rolling farmland beneath West Tiers

range of bee byproducts – tastings of fifty honey varieties, sales of medicinal products such as Manuka honey, skin-care ranges, bee pollen – and excellent ice cream. Carved out of the bush a kilometre or so out of the village, the **Trowunna Wildlife Park** (daily 9am–5pm; $16; ☏03/6363 6162, Ⓦwww .trowunna.com.au) rehabilitates injured and orphaned species prior to release. The park's fame is for a Tasmanian Devil breeding programme – sanctuary owner Andrew Kelly is a world authority on Devil husbandry – and the beleaguered native icon features on tours (1hr 15min; 11am, 1pm & 3pm), during which you'll get to pat or hold more docile species such as wombats. *Mole Creek Holiday Village* (☏03/6364 6124, Ⓦwww.molecreekholidayvillage .com.au; ❹) near the park turn-off operates self-contained country chalets, a little old-fashioned but spotless and with outstanding views to the Tiers.

Alum Cliffs is a surprise among this gentle bucolic scenery. From an unsealed loop road north off the B12, a good path (30min return) threads from the car park through forest to a lookout, where the Mersey River elbows through 800m cliffs. As well as having a stupendous view, the cliffs were important as a dreaming site for Aboriginal Pallitorre – it was known as *Tulampanga* ("red ochre hill"). Only women were permitted to hack ochre from ruddy southern cliffs for its use as body paint during *corroborees*. The site remains significant for contemporary indigenous Tasmanians, and interpretative boards on Aboriginal culture provide information along the track. A short way west of the car park, ⚘ *Blackwood Park Cottages*, at 445 Mersey Hill Rd (☏03/6368 1208, Ⓦwww .blackwoodcottages.com.au; ❺) is a magical place with two superb cottages: Hobbit Cottage is a cute rustic nook with rough walls and stone floors; Georgian-built Heritage Cottage is larger and a mite grander, with a wood stove in a main room. Both look onto the pasture of a dairy and alpaca farm.

Mole Creek and around

Having retired as a rail terminus for logging in 1985, **MOLE CREEK** is now a sleepy place that serves as an activities base. The plains beneath the Tiers south make cycling a joy, while not far away is, arguably, the most inspiring remote walking destination in Tassie, the Walls of Jerusalem National Park. A new **Parks & Wildlife Visitor Centre** (☏03/6363 1487; Tues–Fri 9am–5pm) can advise on walking and cycling in the area, and sells national park maps and tickets for cave trips (see below). The **Online Access Centre** (Mon 9am–5pm, Tues–Thurs 10am–4pm, Sat–Sun 10am–2pm) is in the same building. There's also a good general store with an ATM, fuel and delicious local honey from **Stephens Honey** (factory tour and outlet Mon–Fri 9am–4pm). Places to **stay** range from a lovely small campsite (☏03/6363 1150; $12 per person), beside a stream 1km west of the town, to the congenial *Mole Creek Guesthouse* (☏03/6363 1399, Ⓦwww.molecreekgh.com.au; ❺), which has original pressed-tin ceilings, a lounge with a log fire and a DVD "cinema" room. Its restaurant, *Laurel Berry*, is the best choice in the area for food, with a small, varied menu of global dishes and outstanding steaks. The coffee is the best you'll sip in this end of the valley. For cheap feeds there's the usual pub grub in the *Mole Creek Hotel* (☏03/6363 1102; rooms ❸).

Most visitors pass through the town en route to the **Mole Creek Karst National Park** – Tasmania's only underground national park – and its network of over two hundred caves. About 14km west of Mole Creek are two spectacular ones: **Marakoopa Cave**, the aboriginal word for "handsome", has huge caverns, streams, pools and more glow-worms than you'll see in any other cavern in Australia (daily hourly 10am–4pm; 50–80min; $15); 6km further west is the smaller but more richly decorative **King Solomons Cave**, where caverns are encrusted with stalactites and stalagmites (daily 10.30am, 11.30am, 12.30pm, 2.30pm, 3.30pm & 4.30pm; 45min; $15). The principal ticket office for both is at Marakoopa – ticket sales at King Solomons are by credit card or EFTPOS only. Bear in mind, too, that the underground temperature never gets above nine degrees. For something less packaged, Wild Cave Tours (☎03/6367 8142, ⓦwww.wildcavetours.com) runs excellent half-day ($85) and full-day ($170) caving trips into the Mole Creek caves, underground streams and subterranean systems. Tours are tailored to be as challenging as you want and include lunch and all equipment. Aardvark Adventures runs combined abseil and caving expeditions in the area ($150; see p.44).

The road from the caves twists south towards the access point for the Walls of Jerusalem National Park. A turn-off after 6km ascends steadily on an unsealed road (often closed by snow in winter) towards the **Devil's Gullet** lookout and a great view over the Fisher River into the World Heritage Area and the distant bluffs of the Cradle Mountain–Lake St Clair National Park. Though impressive, the view is probably not worth the thirty-kilometre round trip, so it's worth continuing on the rough track to reach **Lake Mackenzie**; nothing special, but a unique opportunity to ascend by car onto the remote sub-albine plateau. If you can persuade someone to drop you off, you can hike from here back down to Mole Creek on the **South Mole Creek Track**, though it's a tough day-long hike. Seek advice and maps from the Parks & Wildlife visitor centre in Mole Creek.

Walls of Jerusalem National Park

A series of five dolerite peaks that enclose a basin, the **WALLS OF JERUSALEM NATIONAL PARK** represents the northwestern corner of

▲ Pencil pines by lake, Walls of Jerusalem National Park

the Central Plateau. It's an isolated area characterised by collages of lakes – its nickname is the "Land of Three Thousand Lakes" – and pencil pines, set in this richly textured landscape of tiny footbridges and stunted alpine flora. The biblical nomenclature of the Walls region adds to its mystique: Mount Jerusalem, Herods Hall, The Temple, Damascus Vale, Solomons Throne or King Davids Peak were coined in the early 1900s by a solicitor and keen hiker from Launceston. In many ways, its pristine wilderness represents a remote alternative to the Cradle Mountain area just west, though hiking it requires experience and a high level of fitness. The best time to visit is November through to April, but the weather up here is notoriously unpredictable; people have died of exposure, so make sure you're well-prepared. You'll also need Tasmap's *Walls of Jerusalem National Park Map and Notes* ($10.90), sold at the Park & Wildlife Service visitor centre at Mole Creek, and a compass.

Because the Walls of Jerusalem is the only national park in Tasmania you can't drive into, the **walk** in begins outside the park boundaries. From King Solomons Cave (see p.168), head south, following the Mersey River and the unsealed road east of Lake Rowallan; the car park is at Howells Bluff. From here you walk through uninspiring wilderness to reach the park area, which has no facilities, not even a ranger (although rangers do patrol). However, the track is well-kept, with boardwalks over boggy areas, and there's plenty of clean water to drink from the streams and lakes. There are also a few small leaky huts – *Trappers Hut* and *Dixons Kingdom Hut* have interpretive boards on the area's cultural heritage – but these are for emergencies only. So fragile is the wilderness that wardens ask hikers to forgo soaps or detergents, and like all national parks it is fuel stove-only.

On a long day going at steady pace (approx 10hr return; 14km), there's sufficient time to make the stiff climb onto the plateau, then walk to the *Wild Dog Creek Campsite* (pit toilet). However, it's best to camp here for the night, then proceed through **Herods Gate** to views of Barn Bluff and Cradle Mountain to the northwest. A great onward track beneath the sheer face of Wailing Wall descends through **Damascus Gate** – where you get stunning views of Cradle Mountain–Lake St Clair National Park immediately west – to the emergency shelter of *Dixons Kingdom Hut*. There are numerous side routes to the peaks and lakes en route and an experienced, well-equipped walker could easily spend three days or more exploring the park.

Among the **tour operators** who specialize in getting to the park, Maxwell's (T03/6492 1431) runs bushwalker transport on demand from Devonport ($180 for one to four people; $45 per person for five or more people) and Launceston ($240/$60). Alternatively, you can reach the park car park with Launceston-based Outdoors Recreational Transport (two people $125 each, three people $94 each, four people $77 each; T03/6391 8249, Wwww .outdoortasmania.com). **Organized walks** include transport and equipment in the price of the expedition: Tasmanian Wilderness Experiences runs a five-day walk from its base near Hobart ($982; Nov–April; see p.45); Launceston-based Tasmanian Expeditions schedules a six-day circuit ($1390; Oct–May; see p.45); and Craclair runs four-day expeditions from Launceston ($960; Oct–May; see p.44).

By January 2010, the area should have its first accommodation buried in the bush a few kilometres south of Lake Rowellan. If all goes to plan, wilderness retreat *Walls of Jerusalem Lodge* will have a luxury bushwalkers' lodge and camping platforms. Seek advice on its progress at the visitor centre at Mole Creek.

Travel details

Buses

Campbell Town to: Bicheno (Mon–Fri 1 daily; 1hr 40min); Evandale (Thurs 1 daily; 50min); Hobart (Mon–Thurs & Sun 3 daily, Fri 4 daily, Sat 2 daily; 1hr–1hr 35min); Launceston (same times as Hobart; 1hr 15min); Oatlands (same times as Hobart; 25min); Ross (Mon–Thurs 3 daily, Fri 4 daily, Sat & Sun 2 daily; 5min); Swansea (Mon–Fri 1 daily; 1hr).

Deloraine to: Burnie (Mon–Fri 3 daily, Sat & Sun 1 daily; 1hr 45min); Devonport (same times Mon–Fri 3 daily, Sat & Sun 1 daily; 40min); Launceston (Mon–Thurs 5 daily, Fri 6 daily, Sat & Sun 1 daily; 45min–1hr); Mole Creek (Mon–Fri 2 daily; 40min); Westbury (Mon–Thurs 5 daily, Fri 6 daily, Sat & Sun 1 daily; 15min).

Evandale to: Campbell Town (Thurs 1 daily; 35min); Launceston (Thurs 1 daily; 20min).

Hamilton to: Hobart (Tues & Thurs–Sun 1 daily; 55min); Lake St Clair (Tues & Thurs–Sun 1 daily; 1hr 30min); Strahan (Tues & Thurs–Sun 1 daily; 4hr 45min).

Hobart to: Bothwell (Mon–Fri 1 daily; 1hr 30min); Campbell Town (Mon–Thurs 3 daily, Fri & Sun 4 daily, Sat 2 daily; 1hr 45min); Hamilton (Tues & Thurs–Sun 1 daily; 55min); Oatlands (Mon–Thurs 3 daily, Fri & Sun 4 daily, Sat 2 daily; 1hr); Ross (Mon–Fri 3 daily, Sat & Sun 2 daily; 1hr 30min).

Launceston to: Campbell Town (Mon–Thurs & Sun 3 daily, Fri 4 daily, Sat 2 daily; 50min–1hr 35min); Deloraine (Mon–Fri 5 daily; 45min); Evandale (Thurs 1 daily; 20min); Hadspen (Mon–Fri 11 daily; 1hr); Mole Creek (Mon–Fri 2 daily; 1hr 20min); Ross (Mon–Thurs 3 daily, Fri 4 daily, Sat & Sun 2 daily; 55min).

Longford to: Launceston (Mon–Fri 4 daily, 30min); Perth (Mon–Fri 4 daily; 10min).

Mole Creek to: Deloraine (Mon–Fri 2 daily; 30min); Westbury (Mon–Fri 2 daily; 45min); Launceston (Mon–Fri 2 daily; 1hr 30min).

Oatlands to: Campbell Town (Mon–Thurs 3 daily, Fri & Sun 4 daily, Sat 2 daily; 45min); Hobart (Mon–Thurs 3 daily, Fri & Sun 4 daily, Sat 2 daily; 1hr); Launceston (Mon–Thurs 3 daily, Fri & Sun 4 daily, Sat 2 daily; 1hr 30min); Ross (Mon–Fri 3 daily, Sat & Sun 1 daily; 30min).

Ross to: Campbell Town (Mon–Fri 3 daily, Sat & Sun 2 daily; 15min); Hobart (Mon–Fri 3 daily, Sat & Sun 2 daily; 1hr 35min); Launceston (Mon–Fri 3 daily, Sat & Sun 2 daily; 1hr); Oatlands (Mon–Fri 3 daily, Sat & Sun 2 daily; 20min).

Westbury to: Burnie (Mon–Fri 3 daily, Sat–Sun 2 daily; 2hr); Deloraine (Mon–Fri 5 daily, Sat–Sun 2 daily; 15min); Launceston (Mon–Thurs 5 daily, Fri 6 daily, Sat & Sun 1 daily; 50min); Devonport (Mon–Fri 3 daily, Sat–Sun 2 daily; 1hr).

The east coast

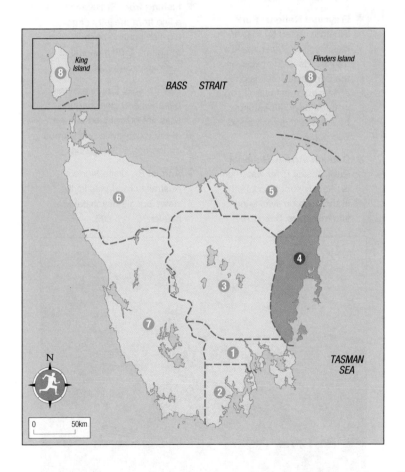

CHAPTER 4

Highlights

✳ **Maria Island** From easy trails to abundant fauna and an intriguing history, this national park has everything except development. See p.179

✳ **Freycinet National Park** Whether visited by foot or kayak, iconic Wineglass Bay transcends all the hype, and the Peninsula Track is one of Tassie's great walks; two or three days of beautiful beaches and granite peaks. See p.186

✳ **Douglas-Apsley National Park** Apsley River waterhole is a lovely spot to cool off in the bush on sweltering summer days. See p.197

✳ **St Marys** A mellow hill town with an arty vibe and fantastic accommodation at *Seaview Farm*. See p.198

✳ **Fishing from St Helens** Cast a line from the jetty or go big-fish hunting offshore from the game-fishing capital of Tasmania. See p.201

✳ **Bay of Fires** Empty powder beaches and clear turquoise seas are guaranteed in front of the most idyllic bushcamps on the coast. See p.204

✳ **Angasi** Exquisite Modern Australian food plus idyllic views equals beach café heaven. See p.206

▲ View of Wineglass Bay from the Hazards

The east coast

The eastern seaboard is Tasmania's holiday playground. Pristine **beaches** stretch empty by the kilometre and there's an easygoing vibe to the fishing towns, many of which also function as small resorts. In summer, luminescent light gives an astonishing intensity to the powder-white sand, the orange lichen splashed onto smooth granite boulders or the aquamarine sea that stretches into a cloudless sky. And a backdrop of hills shelters the coast from the prevailing westerly winds, combining with warm offshore currents to provide one of the most benign temperate climates in Australia. Throw in generally safe swimming beaches, good fishing and some decent surf breaks, and it is no surprise that the renown of this coast has spread rapidly in mainland Australia.

If fame has brought investment – an increasingly sophisticated tourist infrastructure that has ditched the heritage clichés and added a clutch of gourmet restaurants – it has also increased visitor numbers, especially in the school holidays. Prices go up, and accommodation is scarce from Christmas to the middle of February. Yet the east coast remains relatively undeveloped. No concrete hotel towers blight the beaches, the towns are small – **St Helens**, the largest settlement, is less than 2,000-strong – and spread far apart, and the three national parks include an uninhabited island, **Maria Island**, and an entire peninsula, the glorious **Freycinet National Park**. There's also an abundance of idyllic (and free) bushcamping.

Paradoxically considering today's lack of development, the east coast was at the forefront of British settlement. Explorers such as Captain Tobias Furneaux and especially the French commander Nicolas Baudin followed in the wake of Dutchman Abel Tasmen to make it one of the most well-chartered areas of Van Diemen's Land by the turn of the nineteenth century. Even before its official abrogation by the British in 1803, whalers and sealers had established small coastal settlements, and almost every town retains buildings that were erected using the **penal labour** that opened up the coast. Convicts carved out the infrastructure that founded most east coast towns, cut the steep pass that descends north of St Marys, and built a coastal road whose route is more or less followed by the Tasman Highway. Maria Island served as a penal settlement like those at Sarah Island and Port Arthur, albeit not entirely successfully.

With only one road on the run north, this is a classic touring route. **Orford** and **Triabunna** are gateways for Maria Island National Park, as intriguing for its history as its current incarnation as a haven for endangered wildlife. The coast's oldest town, **Swansea**, lies sheltered in **Great Oyster Bay** across from the Freycinet Peninsula, while to the north, the small fishing town of **Bicheno** offers fantastic diving, and is a convenient launchpad from which to visit both

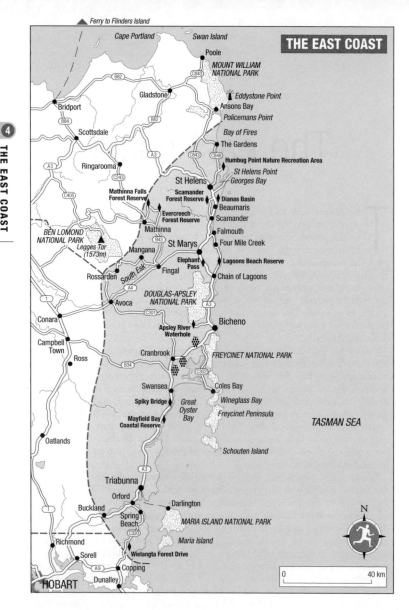

 Ferry to Flinders Island

THE EAST COAST

Cape Portland
Swan Island
Poole
*MOUNT WILLIAM
NATIONAL PARK*
Gladstone
Eddystone Point
Bridport
Ansons Bay
Policemans Point
Scottsdale
Bay of Fires
The Gardens
Ringarooma
Humbug Point Nature Recreation Area
St Helens Point
St Helens
Georges Bay
**Mathinna Falls
Forest Reserve**
**Scamander
Forest Reserve**
Dianas Basin
Beaumaris
**Evercreech
Forest Reserve**
Scamander
*BEN LOMOND
NATIONAL PARK*
Mathinna
Falmouth
St Marys
Four Mile Creek
*Legges Tor
(1573m)*
Mangana
**Elephant
Pass**
Lagoons Beach Reserve
Rossarden
Fingal
Chain of Lagoons
Avoca
*DOUGLAS-APSLEY
NATIONAL PARK*
Conara
**Apsley River
Waterhole**
Bicheno
Campbell
Town
Ross
Cranbrook
FREYCINET NATIONAL PARK
Swansea
Coles Bay
Spiky Bridge
*Great
Oyster
Bay*
Wineglass Bay
**Mayfield Bay
Coastal Reserve**
Freycinet Peninsula
TASMAN SEA
Oatlands
Schouten Island
Triabunna
Orford
Darlington
Buckland
Spring
Beach
MARIA ISLAND NATIONAL PARK
Richmond
Maria Island
Sorell
Wielangta Forest Drive
Copping
HOBART
Dunalley

N

0   40 km

the Freycinet National Park, home to the state's most iconic beach, **Wineglass Bay**, and the **Douglas–Apsley National Park**. Further inland, the hill town of **St Marys** is worth a detour, if only for its arty alternative bent. The last stop before the Tasman Highway switches west is **St Helens**, nothing special in itself, but a base for the best game fishing in Tasmania, and also for the astounding **Bay of Fires**, whose beaches are fast becoming lauded as the best in Tasmania.

North to Orford

From Sorrell, the Tasman Highway (A3) climbs steadily through parched fields to **Bust-Me-Gall Hill** – an oath of settler bullock-drivers who hauled carts over its summit – then **Break-Me-Neck Hill** – the curse as they rattled back down. After 37km is the isolated crossroads village of **BUCKLAND**, whose pride is its diminutive church, built by convicts in the 1840s. A surprise in the otherwise unremarkable neo-Gothic interior is the late-medieval English stained glass in the chancel window, a gift to the dean from his friend Lord Robert Cecil, then serving as Secretary of State for the Colonies. Hearsay has it the glass was salvaged from Battle Abbey in Hastings, during the dissolution of the monasteries by Henry VIII.

Another 17km further on via a narrow river gorge, the village of **ORFORD** is set on the estuary of the Prosser River. Once a whaling settlement, then a port to serve the convict settlement on Maria Island, it is a mellow, somnambulant place and a more pleasant spot to wait for the ferry to Maria Island than Triabunna. There's a "Convict Walk" along Old Convict Road – hand-built in the 1840s for no discernable reason other than to work convicts at a local probation station, the road on the north side of the bridge peters out 7km upriver in the bush. **Shelly Beach** arcs around the bay 2km south of the bridge, or better still is the strand that fronts **Spring Beach** village a further 2km south, although the rips here are too strong for swimming offshore. A shore path links the two beaches via a bluff whose sandstone provided the stone for Melbourne's general post office and old Law Courts building.

You can also reach Orford via the scenic **Wielangta Forest Drive**, a good unsealed route from Copping that passes through managed forest and a pocket

Getting around the east coast by coach and bike

East coast **coach services** are characterized by weekend transport gaps and bus changes, often involving several hours' wait or a switch to local operators – both are good reasons to cycle or drive if possible. If you don't fancy getting stuck for a couple of days, check timetables carefully; Tassielink (see p.30) has timetable downloads on its website, while Redline (see p.30) offers a search facility on its site.

From Hobart, Redline goes to Bicheno on weekdays – although you have to change at Campbell Town – and to St Helens via the A4 (Mon–Fri & Sun), though again you have to change just north of Campbell Town. Tassielink stops all the way up the Tasman Highway to Bicheno (Wed, Fri & Sun), continuing on Friday and Sunday to St Helens. It also operates a confusing schedule to all destinations from Hobart to Swansea (Mon–Fri, term-time; Tues, Thurs & Sat during holidays).

From Launceston, Redline has services to St Helens via Fingal and St Marys (Mon–Fri & Sun) and to Bicheno, the Coles Bay turn-off and Swansea via towns along the Midlands Highway (Mon–Fri). Two local coach companies also operate: Calow's (☏03/6372 5166 or 0400 570 036) between St Helens and Launceston via the A4; and the Bicheno Coach Service (☏03/6257 0293), whose schedules connect with major coach services to go to Coles Bay and the Freycinet National Park.

On a happier note, the east coast is Tasmania's best **cycling route**: bar the occasional hill the terrain is flat and the winter climate is mild enough to tackle it in colder months. Distances between towns are reasonable, and there's a string of youth hostels, so you don't need to camp, although there are also some appealing bushcamps en route. Between Tasmania Expeditions and Island Cycle Tours (see p.46), there are year-round trips from five to seven days, costing $735–2200, that go from Launceston to Hobart, skimming south alongside the coast from Freycinet National Park.

of rainforest. The preservation of the forest in December 2006 represented a high-profile triumph for Greens senator Bob Brown; he convinced Federal Court judges that wide-scale logging of the state-owned area would endanger the wedge-tailed eagle, broad-toothed stag beetle and swift parrot. A year later, the decision was overturned on appeal by Forestry Tasmania. Brown hit back with a counter-appeal that is currently before the High Court. In the hiatus between writs, the 29-kilometre route is something of a PR exercise by Forestry Tasmania and timber giant Gunns, scattered with information boards about the sustainability of logging practices. There are also boardwalks through man ferns (a rarity on the east coast) and stands of giant blue gum, as well as intermittent ocean views and a pleasant picnic ground at the **Thumbs Lookout** just south of Orford.

Accommodation

Blue Waters Tasman Highway ℡03/6257 1102, Ⓦ www.islandcabins.com.au. Just over the bridge, this motel is a useful fallback so long as you can bear garish colour schemes. ❸–❹

Orford Riverside Cottages Old Convict Rd ℡03/6257 1655, Ⓦ www.riversidecottages.com.au. Luxury self-contained cottages on the north side of the Prosser River, with modern(ish) furnishings, DVD players and large decks over the river. A pleasant spot to kick back for a day or so. ❺–❻

Prosser Holiday Units beside bridge ℡03/6257 1427, Ⓕ03/6225 4884. Good-value chalet-style units for up to five people are self-contained and bright. Well-located at the village centre. ❹

Sanda House 33 Walpole St, 500m south of bridge ℡03/6257 1527, Ⓦ www.orfordsandahouse .com.au. This hospitable B&B in Orford's oldest house, built of local stone in 1840 and set in a pleasant garden, has three upmarket heritage rooms. ❺

Eating and drinking

Orford has two good eateries at its centre: *Sorchers* (daily 10am–9pm, closed Wed & Aug; BYO) prepares excellent wood-fired pizzas and pasta with a Tassie twist – fresh wild scallops, smoked salmon, mussels – and has a good wine list; adjacent *Café Orford* (daily 7am–6pm) is a bright, city-style place with a menu of salads, fresh toasties and wraps.

Triabunna

Named after a native hen hunted by the Aborigines, **TRIABUNNA**, north of Orford, served in the mid-1800s as a barrack town for the Maria Island prison settlement. A small fishing fleet aside, it remains a service town for the island, its workaday grid of streets worth seeing only in passing to Maria Island itself. Even the Georgian sandstone barrack buildings near the jetty are semi-derelict. On the plus side, Triabunna has a good supermarket to buy provisions – the one in Orford also has an excellent choice – and a well-stocked **visitor information centre** (℡03/6257 4772; daily 9am–4pm; Internet access; hot showers $2) by the wharf has contacts for current fishing charters as well as information on ferries to Maria Island and details of walks, activities and bike rental. For Triabunna-based tour operators and bike hire for Maria Island, see p.183. The **Online Access Centre** (Mon 1–6pm, Tues–Thurs noon–5pm) is on the corner of Vicary and Melbourne streets.

Accommodation, eating and drinking

The *Tandara Motel* serves surprisingly good meals alongside pub favourites, even though the dining room is rather soulless. More earthy is the rough-and-ready *Spring Bay Hotel* (℡03/6257 3115; rooms ❸) beside the jetty.

Tandara Motel Tasman Highway ℡03/6257 3333,
ⓌWww.tandaramotorinn.com.au. Motel with
pleasant refurbished rooms and older backpacker-
friendly digs that sleep four. You can also camp on
a patch of grass for $8. Has a small swimming
pool. Old rooms ❸, otherwise ❺
Triabunna Cabin and Caravan Park Vicary St
℡03/6257 3575, ⓌWww.mariagateway.com.
Camping and cabins in a small site with laundry
facilities by the Liberty garage. Camping $15,
vans ❷, cabins ❸–❹

Udda Backpackers YHA Spencer St,
east Triabunna (700m across bridge)
℡03/6257 3439. On a peaceful farm, this is
everything a backpackers' should be: well-run
without being regimented, clean and hospitable.
Has a laundry, barbecues, alcohol licence and
sells fresh eggs and produce. Ask about bike
rental for Maria Island. Dorms $20, rooms &
van ❷, cabin ❸

Maria Island

Here may the invalid laze the hours away and, book in hand, become intoxicated
with the splendour of the scenery and the sounds of the unceasing sea... Here may
the sportsman roam, here may the angler bait his hooks with great results, here
may the tourist contemplate the history of the centuries.

Maria Island brochure, 1890s

"No cars, no shops, no worries," states a Parks & Wildlife Service leaflet about
Tasmania's most idyllic island. Save for its resident ranger, the 25km by 12km
national park of **MARIA ISLAND** (pronounced "Ma-*rye*-a") is now uninhabited (it once had a population of six hundred in the late 1800s). Today it has a
haunting, almost mythic quality; an intriguing Treasure Island of sheer dolerite
bluffs, patterned cliffs, historic ruins steeped in tales of imprisonment and folly,
and beautiful sweeping bays drenched in brilliant light. Endangered native
species such as Forester kangaroo, Bennetts wallabies and the Tasmanian Devil
have been introduced, so Maria Island serves as a reserve for threatened species;
Errol Flynn's father, Professor Thomas Flynn, nominated it as a Tasmanian tiger
sanctuary as far back as 1914. **Birdlife** is especially prolific – over 130 species
thrive on the island (most notably the rare Cape Barren goose) and Maria Island
contains eleven of the state's twelve endemic bird species, including the reclusive
forty-spotted paradolte. A lack of tourist infrastructure and infrequent ferry
service ensure visitor numbers are kept to a minimum, and instead the park's
few visitors come to bushwalk or cycle, to snorkel in the marine national park
or simply idle on deserted quartzite beaches.

A short history

Maria Island's history is part of its allure. The Aboriginal Tyraddemmaa tribe
made seasonal crossings on reed-canoes to forage for seafood on the shore of
"Toarra-marra-monah". The first European hereabouts was Dutch navigator
Abel Tasmen. He spotted the island while en route north in 1642 and
christened it in honour of Maria Van Diemen, wife of the Batavia governor
after whom he had already named Van Diemen's Land. Englishman **Captain
Cox** aboard the *Mercury* became the first European ashore in 1773, enjoying
amicable contacts with the Aborigines, and in 1802 the scientific expedition
of French commander **Nicolas Baudin** spent eight days on the island. Their
accounts of meetings with the indigenous peoples provide most knowledge
of the contemporary culture of Tasmanian Aborigines. The Aborigines were
as fascinated by the French – they pulled so hard at zoologist François Péron's
gold ear-ring it came out and clean-shaven crewmembers had their genitals
groped to ascertain their sex. The French presence lingers in the names of

island landmarks: Ile du Nord, Cape Boullanger (named after marine surveyor Charles Boullanger), Cape Maurouard (a midshipman), Cape des Tombeaux, Point Lesueur (the expedition artist) and Cape Peron, named for the one-eyed, accident-prone zoologist.

With Van Diemen's Land in British hands and the West Coast prison settlement of Sarah Island nearing capacity, Lieutenant-governor Arthur in 1825 directed that Maria Island become a **penal settlement** for convicts whose crimes were "not so fragrant a nature". Up to 150 prisoners were stationed at **Darlington** and put to work in timber, tanning, cloth- and brick-making and quarrying. But within a decade the centre was closed, derided by Arthur as "a place of ease and leisure" whose surroundings were like "agreeable pleasure grounds". A second convict era began in 1842, with around four hundred prisoners assigned to probation stations at Darlington and Point Lesueur under the command of assistant superintendent Horatio Tennyson, brother of the English poet. Again, Maria Island's benign climate and beauty proved unconducive to a penal settlement. An inspection in 1845 discovered prisoners helping a magistrate's wife brew beer and rife homosexuality in the barracks. So intense was the embarrassment in Hobart Town and London – Secretary of State for the Colonies, William Gladstone, thundered in Parliament about "this great moral evil" – that the Colonial Office quietly wound down the penal settlement until it closed in 1850.

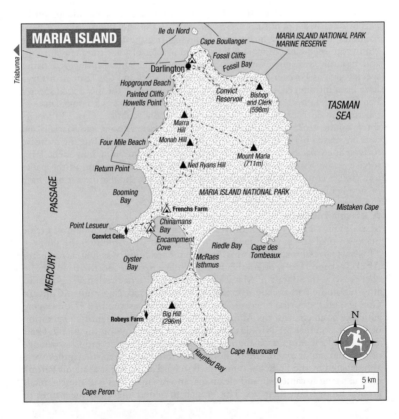

The island was leased intermittently to sheep farmers until it caught the eye of **Diego Bernacchi** in 1884. A flamboyant entrepreneur, the Italian negotiated an annual lease of 10¢ and established a silk industry and a French Riviera-styled holiday resort at Darlington, which he retitled San Diego. The former convict buildings became a health resort and coffee palace, mulberry trees and vineyards were planted on surrounding hills, and a small township emerged. Yet even though investors dined while fireworks popped in the sky above – Bernacchi is even said to have tied bunches of grapes to his vines to open wallets – the resort failed and the Maria Island Company went into liquidation in 1896. Bernacchi left for Melbourne; his 20-year-old son Louis sailed to London and into history with Captain's Scott's first Antarctic Expedition (see p.74). In 1920 the irrepressible "King Diego", as he was parodied in the Hobart press, returned with plans for a cement works at Darlington. It proved another damp squib. Inferior lime from the island's cliffs sank the National Portland Cement with debts of $165,000 within a decade. Jinxed for industry, the island's population dwindled. Industrial buildings were dismantled by sheep-farmers to create family dwellings and after a half-hearted attempt to revive limestone mining collapsed, the island was declared a national park in 1972.

Getting there and around

The **ferry** to Maria Island leaves from Triabunna. At the time of writing, the contract was out to tender and a stop-gap service was being provided by Sea Wings (9am & 3.15pm from Triabunna, 9.30am & 4pm from Darlington; $40 return; bikes $20; backpacks $10; daysacks free; ☎0419 746 668, ⓦwww .seawingsecotours.com.au). Times were similar under the former contractor, though prices were $25 – consult the visitor information centre at Triabunna (daily 9am–4pm; ☎03/6257 4772) or the Parks & Wildlife website (ⓦwww .parks.tas.gov.au) for up-to-date information. National park entry fees and camping/bunkroom fees are payable at the Parks & Wildlife office in the commissariat store (Mon–Fri 9.30am–5pm, plus to coincide with ferry arrivals; ☎03/6257 1420, ⓔmaria.island @parks.tas.gov.au) – bring a receipt if you have a car pass. It also stocks free information leaflets and, in theory, sells a hiking map by Tasmap ($9.90). You can also get this at the Triabunna centre.

Getting around is by foot or bike – the latter can be rented in Triabunna from Sea Wings ($20 per day), although Go Dive (see "Tours and activities", p.183) plans to stock bikes, possibly at Darlington. There are no shops on the island, so buy supplies in the well-stocked supermarkets at Orford or Triabunna, both open daily. Because Maria Island is a national park, all rubbish must be carried out.

Accommodation

You'll need **to stay** overnight to do more than take in the convict ruins at Darlington and the Fossil Cliffs. Basic rooms and six-bed dorms are in the historic penitentiary (dorms $15; rooms ❷; reservations essential). The basic units have wood fireplaces (wood supplied), table and chairs, and bunks with mattresses, but you'll need your own cooking equipment and bedding. Hot-water showers are available ($1). A popular **campsite** at Darlington ($12 per person) is the island's best-equipped, with a public phone, toilets, fireplaces (wood provided), cold-water taps and tank-water for drinking. Free gas barbecues are located behind the dunes of Darlington Beach. The **bushcamps** at Frenchs Farm and Encampment Cove are free; both have pit toilets and untreated rainwater; Frenchs Farm is fuel-stove only, Encampment Cove has fireplaces. Visitors are requested to wash boots, bike tyres, tent pegs, etc before arriving, to prevent the spread of diseases such as the phytophthtora root fungus. **Check-in** for all accommodation is at the commissariat store near the jetty.

Darlington

The ferry lands at main settlement **DARLINGTON**, dotted with squat structures from the island's penal, tourist and industrial phases, many labelled with information boards. Behind the cement works silos at the jetty, a convict-built barn of the penitentiary farm contains relics of its secondary use as a cement factory workshop (and in spring nesting Cape Barren geese), and there's the island cemetery. The chimney stack in the bush south is all that remains of Diego Bernacchi's *Grand Hotel*, the heart of his San Diego resort where up to thirty guests could indulge in health cures when not loafing in the drawing room.

On the path that runs behind the beach from the jetty, you pass the squat commissariat store, the oldest building on the island (1828). Uphill, the former penitentiary buildings are fronted by the late nineteenth-century **San Diego Coffee Palace**. Restored in late-Victorian style, its reading and dining rooms contain a museum (times vary; free) of island history, told through the diary entries of early settlers, photographs and reports from Hobart's *Mercury* newspaper. The long penitentiary building behind, where 280 convicts were bunked down "like bottles of gin" in sixty-centimetre wide compartments separated by wooden battens, is now an atmospheric **bunkhouse**. It is bookended by the former convict mess hall and three cottages, the central of which is where Irish political prisoner **William Smith O'Brien** wrote his autobiography. Though the founder of the Irish labour movement described the island as "one of the loveliest spots formed by the hand of nature", he made several escape attempts until he was shifted to the more secure penal settlement at Port Arthur, amid rumours of a relationship with the commandant's daughter.

Even if you don't like hiking, there is some great – and easy – **walking** around Darlington. The visitor centre at Triabunna and the ranger station in the commissariat store (see p.181) stock information leaflets about all walks. A

▲ Cape Barren Goose, Maria Island

In addition to the operators below, Tasmanian Wilderness Experiences ($1675; see p.45) runs five-day hiking tours to Maria Island in summer. There's also excellent snorkelling in a marine national park that wraps around the north and northwest coasts: Go Dive rent equipment (mask and snorkel $6 per day, wetsuits $20 per day, full scuba set $60 per day).

East Coast Eco Tours Triabunna wharf ☏03/6257 3453, ⓦspringbay.net/ecotours. Gentle custom-designed trips that can take in fur seal colonies and, with luck, dolphins and white-bellied sea eagles along the way; prices vary by tour and group size. Owner Brian Hawkins also provides fishing trips, from $85 per person per day.

Go Dive Liberty garage, Vicary St, Triabunna ☏03/6257 3555, ⓦwww.godivetassie .com. Two-dive boat trips in the marine park from $110 (not including equipment rental), plus dives to the wreck of the Troy Dee, a 65m freighter scuttled in 27m just south of Painted Cliffs.

The Maria Island Walk ☏03/6227 8800, ⓦwww.mariaislandwalk.com.au. An award-winning, signature experience of Tasmania, this four-day guided walk heads up the coastline and spends two nights in luxury wilderness camps, one in the restored home of entrepreneur Diego Bernacchi, with three-course gourmet meals each night. Walks average 10km a day, backpacks and rainwear provided. Mon, Wed & Fri, Oct–Apr; $1799; max eight people.

Sea Wings Triabunna wharf ☏03/6257 1226, ⓦwww.seawingsecotours.com.au. Exhilarating ecology cruises in a speedboat-style cruiser, taking in caves and skimming close to the cliffs on three-hour circuits of the island, also visiting a fur seal colony on Isles de Phoque, north of Maria Island. $90 per person.

grassy path from the commissariat store goes along the shore to shell-studded Fossil Cliffs (1.5hr return), then circles slowly back to Darlington. From the penitentiary, a gravel track south goes via Hopground Beach to Painted Cliffs (2hr return), a sandstone bluff sculpted by the elements and daubed with swirls of iron oxide. A more rigorous walk in the area is to Bishop and Clerk (4hr return), from whose dolerite tabletop you get outstanding views of the Freycinet Peninsula north and of blue ocean everywhere. You can either go inland east of Darlington or hook up with the track on the Fossil Cliffs Circuit. Either way, prepare to cross scree- and boulder-fields.

The rest of Maria Island

The absence of people in the bush and beach south make Darlington seem positively crowded. The main route south skirts the eastern flanks of the hills through forests of blue gum and man ferns to reach Frenchs Farm (3.5–4hr walk one way from Darlington; 11km), where you can bushcamp among the ruins of a farmholding. A sidetrack en route cuts east to **Mount Maria** (6–7hr return to Darlington), the island's highest peak (711m) with superb views over the island from the summit. You can also reach Frenchs Farm on a slightly longer trail that tracks the shore south of Painted Rocks. Another bushcamp, Encampment Cove (4.5hr walk one way from Darlington; 12.5km), pleasantly sited by the sea, lies 30min further southwest. From here you can follow a path back into the bush (20min) to a row of sixteen convict cells, all that remains of the Point Lesueur probation station. Freshwater lagoons on either side mean this a good spot to see mobs of Forester kangaroo at dusk.

Going east of the campgrounds, you round **Chinamans Bay** – named after a few enterprising Chinese fishermen who harvested abalone here in the late

1800s – and reach a narrow isthmus. **Reidle Beach** on its east side is world-class, a gorgeous four-kilometre crescent of white powder-sand lapped by turquoise sea; the best beach no one knows about in Tassie. Across the isthmus, the track runs west, arriving eventually at the remains of smallholding Robeys Farm (6hr; 17km). More appealing as a destination is **Haunted Bay** (6.5hr; 18km), a lonely port at the far south of the island framed by granite cliffs; keep an eye out for fairy penguin burrows on the track down to the sea.

Swansea

On a sunny day, the drive north from Triabunna is one of the best in Tasmania; a spectacularly beautiful run that hugs the coast past brilliant-white, empty beaches and looks across the intense aquamarine of **Great Oyster Bay**. En route, 30km north of Triabunna, **Mayfield Bay Coastal Reserve** ($2 donation) has shady campsites in the bush with pit toilets and 5km of beach that's usually deserted save for weekend fishermen; a good spot to bushcamp for the night. Seven kilometres further, **Spiky Bridge** was built by convicts on the old coach road in 1841, and named after the rock shards embedded in its rail; no one is sure if they were to prevent cattle from pausing while being driven or just for decoration. Nearby Spiky Beach is a tiny piece of paradise, rarely visited.

Ten minutes further on is the holiday town of **SWANSEA**. Once a rather old-fashioned resort, it is enjoying a quiet renaissance thanks to the proximity of the Freycinet National Park. A couple of elegant restaurants and B&Bs show a town leaving behind the sort of ugly older motels that blight one end of the waterfront, and there is talk about a ferry to Coles Bay in summer. That said, it remains a laid-back place that sells itself on nothing more complicated than good fishing and sparkling beaches. You can also take the well-signed **Loon.tite.ter.mair.re.le.hoin.er path** from Waterloo Beach (first on the seafront when you enter from the south) around Waterloo Point to a short-tailed shearwater rookery. From mid-September to April, the birds return to nest at dusk after feeding at sea – the track's name refers to Aborigines who harvested "muttonbird" chicks in spring. Year-round there are good coastal views on the route (50min return), which concludes around the headland at Schouten Beach.

Before it became a beach resort, Swansea was a minor whaling and farming settlement, then a barracks town served by the Campbell Town road. Some well-preserved colonial architecture from the mid-1800s remains – Morris's General Store, on Franklin Street, has been run by seven generations of the family since 1868. The town's past can also be revisited at the **Glamorgan War Memorial Museum and Community Centre** (Mon–Sat 9am–5pm; $3), further along Franklin Street – the usual municipal odds and sods are less enthralling than the chance to rack up in a historic billiards room ($2 a game). Swansea's most impressive heritage item is the restored **Swansea Bark Mill** (daily summer 9am–6pm, until 5pm winter; $10; ☎03 6257 8382) on the Tasman Highway at the north fringe of town. The mill was cobbled together in situ from salvaged timber and junked metal, finally clattering into operation in 1880 to pulp blackwattle bark for leather-tanning acids. The current operating speed is a tenth of what it was when the tanning business closed in 1960. An adjoining **heritage museum** (same ticket) has so-so dioramas of Swansea's early agricultural history, prefaced by a room on indigenous Aboriginal culture and early French exploration before British settlement.

Practicalities

Swansea is served by daily **coaches** on the east coast routes of Tassielink and Redline. The visitor information centre (☏03/6257 8382; daily 9am–5pm summer, 10am–3pm winter) is at the bark mill, north just outside the centre. An **Online Access Centre** (☏03/6257 8806; Mon, Tues & Fri 10am–3pm, Wed 10am–5pm, Thurs 10am–4pm) is in the library at the north end of Franklin Street. Be aware that Swansea occasionally suffers poor **water** quality due to a small reservoir and old pipes; locals have boiled theirs for years, so seek advice when you arrive. Bikes ($20 per day) and kayaks ($20 per hour) can be rented from Swansea Backpackers (see below).

Accommodation

As one of the east coast's largest resorts, the Swansea area has the best choice of accommodation on the east coast, and some of its most stylish options. Not much of it is cheap, however. Most self-contained accommodation is outside the centre.

Avalon Rocky Hills, Tasman Highway, 15km south of Swansea ☏1300 361 136, ⓦwww .avaloncoastalretreat.com.au. Lauded by architects, fêted in the style press, this glass-walled temple to interior design sleeps six in an ultramodern minimalist unit that juts over the ocean. Modern art, state-of-the-art appliances and aspirational glamour throughout. As exclusive as it gets in Tasmania and priced accordingly. ❽

Kabuki-by-the-Sea Tasman Highway, 12km south ☏03/6257 8588, ⓦwww.kabukibythesea.com. Sea views are sensational in these clifftop cottages, furnished in a comfy, westernized Japanese style. A fine Japanese restaurant has the same views (daily for morning and afternoon tea and lunch; dinner: Dec–April Tues–Sat, May–Nov Fri & Sat). ❻

Meredith House 5 Noyes St ☏03/6257 8119, ⓦwww.meredith-house.com.au. A National Trust-listed B&B with friendly owners in a convict-built manor just off Franklin Road. Georgian grandeur and country house charm in en suites. Also has self-contained heritage-styled rooms in the mews. ❻–❼

🏃 **Piermont Retreat** Tasman Highway 3km south ☏03/6257 8131, ⓦwww.piermont .com.au. Classy beachshack chic in a boutique resort on a private beach – Mediterranean-styled cottages combine rough earth or stone walls with streamlined furnishings and white cotton sheets. Three cottages open directly onto the beach. ❼–❽

🏃 **Swansea Backpackers** Tasman Highway, 600km north of centre ☏03/6257 8560, ⓦwww.swanseabackpackers.com.au. Opened in late 2007, this bright backpackers' by the *Barkmill Tavern* is more appealing than many budget hotels. Has four-bed dorms, an airy communal hall with a pool table and plasma TV, a great kitchen, laundry and free Internet access. Linen and doonas (duvets) provided; disabled-friendly. Dorms $34, rooms ❸

Swansea Holiday Park at Jubilee Beach Shaw St ☏03/6257 8177, ⓦwww.swansea -holiday.com.au. The more appealing of the company's two sites is on the beach opposite the bark mill – the one south at Schouten Beach (☏03/6257 8148) is a little barren. Camping $24, two-bedroom cabins ❹–❻

Swansea Motor Inn 1 Franklin St ☏03/6257 8102, ⓦwww.swanseamotorinn.com. The better of the two 1970s motels on the seafront is dated but acceptable, all of its rooms fitted with fridge, TV and DVD player. Sea views are worth the extra $10. ❹

Tubby & Padman 20 Franklin St ☏03/6257 8901, ⓦwww.tubbyandpadman.com.au. In the centre of Swansea, this smart B&B in an 1840s house provides three heritage suites – book the Pepper Suite for a splurge – and two contemporary modern apartments. ❻

Wagner's Cottages Tasman Highway 2km south ☏03/6257 8494, ⓦwww.wagnerscottages.com. Five self-contained stone cottages in a comfy modern-heritage hybrid style, plus there's one contemporary open-plan studio. Each is secluded within a cottage garden. ❻–❽

Eating and drinking

The Banc Corner of Franklin and Maria streets ☏03/6257 8896. Gourmet dishes based on modern European and Asian cuisine from one of Tasmania's most respected chefs, John Bailey.

Great east coast tasting plate entrée, superb steaks and daily fresh fish. Mains around $28. Lunch Sun–Mon, dinner Wed–Mon.

Barkmill Tavern Tasman Highway, 600m north of centre. More sophisticated fare than the average pub – wild scallops in a Thai sauce or chargrilled lamb are on offer – plus wood-fired pizzas and ten beers on tap. Good value and good bottleshop too.

Ebb 11 Franklin St. Seafood, especially oysters, feature in the Asian-flavoured modern Australian dishes prepared in this bright place on the seafront. Fairly expensive but relaxed and friendly. Lunch & dinner, closed Mon.

 Kate's Berry Farm Tasman Highway, 3km south. One of Tassie's gems, *Kate's* provides superb cakes, fruit tarts, Devonshire teas, home-made jams and sauces, and sensational ice cream, all in a cute cabin with superb views to the Hazards, and hosted by the irrepressible Kate. Daily 10am–5pm.

The Ugly Duck Out 2 Franklin St. A licensed café and takeaway with a wide-ranging menu of fish, grills, burgers and salads, some made from organic ingredients. Great value. Daily Dec–April 8.30am–9pm, May–Nov 11.30am–9pm

View Point 3 Maria St. This rather old-fashioned place near *The Banc* serves the usual chicken and fish, plus better North African and Middle Eastern specialities. The same owners also manage small rooms (⑤) and spacious apartments (⑦).

North of Swansea

The drive from Swansea onwards is winding, with fantastic views of rural countryside contrasted with dramatic mountain- and sea-scapes. After 4km, a right turn-off from the highway goes to **Nine Mile Beach**, a ribbon of pristine sand that sweeps towards the Hazards' granite humps. It's free of all development save for a few houses at Dolphin Sands. Local fisherman say the bream fishing at the Swan River at the beach's far end is excellent. If you're **cycling** to Coles Bay from Swansea, you can cut 40km off the journey by riding along Nine Mile Beach Road and taking a ferry across the Swan River to **Swanwick**, about 6km northwest of Coles Bay. Past the turn-off to the beach, the Tasman Highway cuts inland then rolls into wine country at Cranbrook.

Tasting tours

Going from south to north, the following tours are all recommended. New family estate **Spring Vale Wines** (daily 10am–4pm; ☎03/6257 8208, ⓦwww .springvalewines.com) provides a cellar of award-winning gewürztraminers, pinot gris and opulent pinot noirs in a convict-built barn. **Craigie Knowe Vineyard** (daily 10am–4pm; ☎03/6257 8298) crafts Bordeaux-style wines, notably an acclaimed Cabernet blend; and sun-soaked **Freycinet Vineyard** (daily: Oct–Apr 9.30am–5pm, May–Sept 10am–4.30pm; ☎03/6257 8574, ⓦwww.freycinetvineyard.com.au) is consistently in the Tassie wine gongs for hand-crafted pinot noirs and chardonnays, plus it produces well-structured fizz. Without your own transport, you can join tasting tours from Coles Bay.

Freycinet National Park

Freycinet ("*Frey*-zin-ay") National Park is one of Tasmania's iconic destinations. Idyllic images of the beach at **Wineglass Bay** or the **Hazards mountains** glowing at dusk appear state-wide, two highlights of a park characterized by its azure bays and knuckles of shell-pink rock that punch through the bush. The price of popularity is crowds, especially in January when reservations are essential. The park receives around twenty thousand visitors a year, and experi-enced Tassie bushwalkers make snide jokes about it being a "pensioners' playground". However, few visitors stray far from the park's service town, **Coles Bay**, except to make the pilgrimage to Wineglass Bay. There are isolated

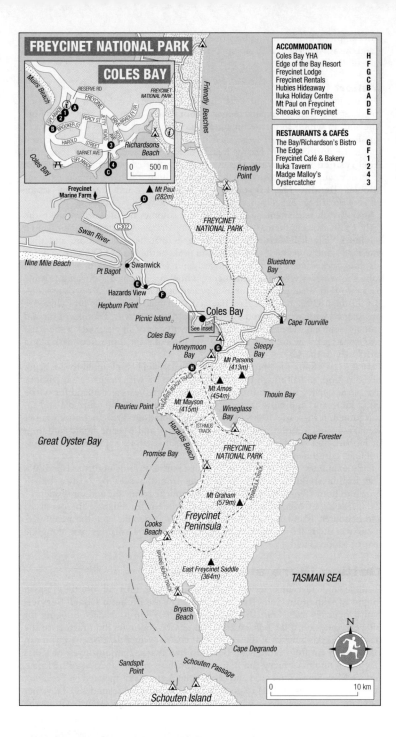

FREYCINET NATIONAL PARK

COLES BAY

ACCOMMODATION

Coles Bay YHA	H
Edge of the Bay Resort	F
Freycinet Lodge	G
Freycinet Rentals	C
Hubies Hideaway	B
Iluka Holiday Centre	A
Mt Paul on Freycinet	D
Sheoaks on Freycinet	E

RESTAURANTS & CAFÉS

The Bay/Richardson's Bistro	G
The Edge	F
Freycinet Café & Bakery	1
Iluka Tavern	2
Madge Malloy's	4
Oystercatcher	3

Reserve Rd

RESERVE RD

FREYCINET NATIONAL PARK

Muirs Beach

ESPLANADE

FREYCINET

PERCY ST

DRIVE

BRADLEY DR

BROOKER ST

JETTY ROAD

PINE

HAROLD STREET

Coles Bay

GARNET AVE

ESPLANADE

Richardsons Beach

0   500 m

Friendly Beaches

Friendly Point

Freycinet Marine Farm

Mt Paul (282m)

D

FREYCINET NATIONAL PARK

Swan River

C302

Nine Mile Beach

Pt Bagot

Swanwick

Hazards View

Hepburn Point

E

F

Bluestone Bay

Cape Tourville

Coles Bay

See Inset

Picnic Island

Coles Bay

Honeymoon Bay

G

Sleepy Bay

H

Mt Parsons (413m)

Mt Amos (454m)

Thouin Bay

HAZARDS BEACH TRACK

Fleurieu Point

Mt Mayson (415m)

Wineglass Bay

ISTHMUS TRACK

Cape Forester

Great Oyster Bay

Hazards Beach

Promise Bay

FREYCINET NATIONAL PARK

PENINSULA TRACK

Mt Graham (579m)

Freycinet Peninsula

Cooks Beach

East Freycinet Saddle (364m)

TASMAN SEA

BRYANS BEACH TRACK

Bryans Beach

Cape Degrando

N

Sandspit Point

Schouten Passage

0   10 km

Schouten Island

bushcamps for those who are prepared to hike to them – or pay for a water taxi – and this is wilderness with amenities: accommodation, restaurants and an array of activities operators.

A short history

During the thirty thousand years before Freycinet was lauded as a coastal paradise, the Toorernomairremener **Aborigines** migrated east from the Midlands in winter to forage for mud oysters and hunt seals on the peninsula's foreshore. The remains of large shell middens are behind Richardsons Beach and at the north end of Hazards Beach. European history began in 1642 with **Abel Tasmen**. Fooled by the Hazards peaks, he charted the peninsula as a chain of islands, and the mistake was not rectified until 1802, by French explorer **Nicolas Baudin**. The **Freycinet brothers**, Henri and Louis, were senior officers aboard his expedition ships, *Le Géographe* and *Le Naturaliste*.

After British settlement, sealers plundered colonies on offshore rocks in the early 1800s. Among them, apparently, was an African-American captain named **Richard "Black" Hazard**. The story goes that he swam ashore and then traversed – and so named – the mountain peaks at the head of Oyster Bay, while his shipwrecked crew clung to Refuge Island. More damaging than the sealers were the seasonal **whaling** settlements, whose operations transformed pristine bays into putrid cesspools. A camp appeared at "The Fisheries" opposite Coles Bay in the 1820s, and Wineglass Bay was so named because its bowl-like bay was stained with whale blood. A visitor in 1840 recorded: "Chunks of fat and entrails swam on the surface and ringed it with greasy ripples, and on the stage two carcasses lay steaming. . . from the vast mass of meat, a stream of dark blood ran slowly to the sea".

By the late 1840s, the Southern Right Whales had been hunted to the brink of extinction, and although the industry limped on with deep-sea expeditions for sperm whales, it had sputtered out within forty years as demand for whale oil (a lubricant) and bone (a corset-stiffener) waned. Mining for coal and tin was joined in the early 1900s by quarrying operations: Freycinet pink granite went into the Commonwealth Bank head office and Marine Board buildings in Hobart, and the New Parliament House in Canberra. Farming in small-holdings continued into the 1960s.

Early explorers extolled the area's beauty, but it was not until the late 1800s that **holidaymakers** arrived. Most came from Swansea by boat; a tourist brochure from 1895 names the park as "a favourite picnic ground for residents". Concerns about over-hunting led the government to designate the peninsula and Schouten Island as game reserves in 1906. A decade later, the peninsula's status was upgraded to full national park, making it Tasmania's first alongside that of Mount Field.

Getting there and around

Redline and Tassielink services drop you at the turn-off on the Tasman Highway, 31km from Coles Bay. Both are met by the **Bicheno Coach Service**, which operates daily from Bicheno to Coles Bay (up to 3 daily; booking for off-peak times on ☏03/6257 0293). The service continues 4km further to the start of the hiking tracks at the car park. If you're cycling the east coast, you can take a short cut from Nine Mile Beach to Swanwick, 7km northwest of Coles Bay on an unofficial **ferry** (book the night before on ☏03/6257 0239; $15; no service May–Sept). You could also charter the **Aqua Taxi** operated by Freycinet Adventures (see box, p.191) to go direct to Coles Bay, for around $80. Freycinet Adventures also operates a scheduled bushwalkers' shuttle service within the park area, going from the public jetty at Coles Bay via Richardsons Beach to: Hazards Beach (three daily; $40 one-way, $70 return); Cooks Beach (one daily; $50 one way, $90 return); and Schouten Island (two daily; $70 one-way, $140 return). Reservations are essential and note that services are reduced in winter. **Mountain bikes** can be rented from Coles Bay Boat Hire (see box, p.191).

Practicalities

The **national park visitor centre** (daily 8am–5pm summer, 9am–4pm winter; ℡03/6256 7000, @freycinet@parks.tas.gov.au) is 1km east of Coles Bay behind Richardsons Beach. As well as interpretive displays about the park, it provides free sketch maps and sheets on day-walks, and sells national park passes, Tasmap's hiking map ($9.95), basic hiking and camping equipment, first aid items, and a surprisingly wide selection of books on Tasmania.

A passable range of **supplies** is available at the two supermarkets: the Iluka on the Esplanade and general store Coles Bay Trading Co on Garnet Avenue. Both operate daily (8am–6pm, until 7pm Jan–Feb) and have an ATM, payphone and fuel. The former has visitor information for the Coles Bay area (℡03/6257 0383), while the latter has the town post office and a coffee shop with great views of the Hazards. Water is in short supply in Coles Bay, which is officially the driest town in Tasmania – try to use it sparingly. Tents and sleeping bags can be rented through Freycinet Adventures (see box, p.191; $15 per day); *Freycinet Lodge* (see "Accommodation" below) hires small day-hike kits (rucksack, binoculars and fieldguides; $10 per day).

Accommodation

Local tourism website ⓦwww.freycinetcolesbay.com is an excellent source for self-contained accommodation. At the time of research, Tasmanian hotel giant Federal Resorts (ⓦwww.federalresorts.com.au) had finalized plans for *The Hazards*, a five-star-plus luxury hotel near the Edge of the Bay resort, which was scheduled to open in 2009 or 2010.

Coles Bay YHA 2km west of Freycinet Lodge ℡03/6234 9617. One of two hostels in the area (see *Iluka Holiday Centre*), this one is seriously basic – fridge and stove, cold shower, pit toilet – but with a serene beachside location in the park. Pre-booking essential and available by ballot only 15 Dec–15 Feb. Dorm $15, rooms ❸

Edge of the Bay Resort 2038 Main Rd, 7km northwest of Coles Bay ℡03/6257 0102, ⓦwww.edgeofthebay.com. Suites and cottages in (currently) the most sophisticated address in Coles Bay. Rooms have tasteful metropolitan styling but are on the small side – instead, you're paying for the spectacular view of the Hazards from each. ❼–❽

Freycinet Lodge 2km southwest of national park office ℡1800 420 155, ⓦwww.puretasmania .com.au. The only hotel accommodation in the national park is in these luxury cabins that make up in location for what they lack in cutting-edge style. The focus on nature also means no TVs. ❽

Freycinet Rentals 5 Garnet Ave, Coles Bay ℡03/6257 0320, ⓦwww.freycinetrentals.com. The

hub of self-contained accommodation in town, this agency has fifteen holiday homes on its books, from cottages to open-plan shacks. Most have views and there's a DVD library for guests. ❺–❼

Hubies Hideaway 35 Esplanade, Coles Bay ℡0419 255 604. An informal, largely open-plan beachshack that sleeps up to five; well-equipped and just 100m from the *Iluka Tavern*. ❺

Iluka Holiday Centre Esplanade, Coles Bay ℡03/6234 0115 or 1800 786 512, ⓦwww .ilukaholidaycentre.com.au. Offers the full range of budget accommodation, well-placed for the pub and supermarket. Also has large self-contained units by Muirs beach and hosts the YHA hostel *Iluka Backpackers*, with four-bed dorms. Camping $20, dorms $25.50, rooms ❸, vans ❸, cabins ❹–❺

Mt Paul on Freycinet off Main Rd, 10km northwest of Coles Bay ℡03/6257 0300, ⓦwww .mtpaul.com. Deep in the bush, this is one of the more interesting options in the area. Two luxury timber lodges built in 2004 offer wilderness with style, plus panoramas of bush and coast from the

balcony. Nearby, *Saltwater Shack* is simple, sweet and secluded. Shack ⑤, lodges ⑧
Sheoaks on Freycinet 47 Oyster Bay Court, Swanwick, 7km northwest of Coles Bay ☎ 03/6257 0049, ⓦ www.sheoaks.com. Smart

contemporary style softened with antique furnishings in a luxury B&B by the beach. Sea views from rooms, all en suites. Picnic lunches and dinner for guests on request. ⑥

Camping in the national park

The **main park campsite** is sheltered among bush and dunes behind Richardsons Beach ($12 per person). It has nineteen powered sites ($15), a car-free backpackers' area, flushing toilets, non-treated water, electric barbecues and plans for a shower block. It's also packed in summer. Bookings are taken from December 18 to the March bank holiday weekend, but for the peak Christmas/New Year holiday period sites are allocated by ballot only. Ballot entries can be made to the park visitor centre by phone, fax or email (see p.189) and are drawn on October 1 – rangers advise submissions should be made ideally by early August. A sign at the visitor centre flags up any late availability due to cancellations. From late summer to Easter, there's a second site nearby behind idyllic Honeymoon Bay.

Free campsites on the peninsula are at: the southern ends of Wineglass Bay and Hazards Beach; Cookes Beach; Bryans Beach; and on Schouten Island at Moreys Bay and Crocketts Bay. All have composting pit toilets, and some have unreliable water tanks – Cookes has the most reliable water supply on the peninsula, but check with the ranger for the current state of supplies. Elsewhere in the park, there's camping at Isaacs Point behind Friendly Beaches (busy over Christmas/ New Year holidays), at Freshwater Lagoon at the beach's southern end and at Bluestone Bay northeast of Coles Bay. The latter two sites are accessible by 4WD. Standard park entry fees apply for all sites and all are fuel-stove only.

From the Tasman Highway to Coles Bay

From the turn-off on the Tasman Highway 33km north of Swansea, Coles Bay Road (C302) follows the shore of **Moulting Bay Lagoon**, an important wetland for breeding migratory waterfowl that holds the largest number of black swans in Tasmania (around nine thousand). After 8km, a left turn takes you 3km to **Friendly Beaches**, a later addition to the national park area whose name derives from an amicable meeting between early explorers and indigenous Aborigines. Such is the hype that surrounds Wineglass Bay, this exhilarating stretch of sugary beach and aqua seas is often deserted; even when it has visitors, overcrowding is hardly a problem on a beach that's 12km long. A campsite north of the car park at Isaacs Point is a great spot to bushcamp if you don't mind roughing it a bit.

Coles Bay, on the north edge of the Freycinet National Park, has arguably the most striking setting in Tasmania: a sheltered inlet where fishing boats are moored in the deep-blue water, a fringe of pristine beach, and rising straight from the sea, the craggy **Hazards**. These shell-pink granite peaks – Amos, Dove and Mayson – have defined the area for Europeans since the first exploration in 1642. The bay is named after Silas Cole, a settler pioneer who made lime from shells in the Aboriginal middens on Richardsons Beach, and the township has served as the base for the park (as well as for fishing and recreation) since the 1930s. In more recent history it achieved fame by becoming the first place in Australia to ban plastic shopping bags in 2003. Some decent **beaches** lie in its vicinity: Muirs Beach just to the west, and Richardsons Beach east at the head of Coles Bay, in front of the Parks & Wildlife office and a busy park campsite. Further around the bay past *Freycinet Lodge* hotel, around 2.5km from the village centre, Honeymoon Bay is a gorgeous little cove tucked into the granite foreshore; shallow waters make it a warm spot for a dip by late afternoon.

Activities and tours around Coles Bay

As Tasmania's favourite coastal playground, the Freycinet National Park is one wilderness in which you're not short of ways to spend your money. Unless stated, all outfits are in Coles Bay. The award-winning, three-day "lamping" (luxury camping) tour by Freycinet Escape (☎03/6257 0018, ⓦwww.freycinetescape.com.au) was suspended in late 2007 due to the discovery of an eagle nest at its campsite. A new site was promised: check the website to see if the tour has restarted.

Freycinet is also on the itineraries of most Tassie tour operators. **Day-trips from Hobart** are run by Bottom Bits Bus ($105; daily except Sat) and Tassielink ($85; Fri & Sun; also from Launceston). Under Down Under ($275 or $495; Sun, Tues & Thurs, plus Mon & Fri in summer) and Island Cycle Tours ($295; Fri) visit on their two-day east coast trips; see p.45 for contact details.

Access Freycinet 6 Garnet Ave (in *Oystercatcher* café) ☎03/6257 0033. Tailored fishing charters on Great Oyster Bay and Schouten Passage for up to five people. Prices vary.

All4Adventure cabin by Iluka Supermarket, Esplanade ☎03/6257 0018, ⓦwww .all4adventure.com.au. The first carbon-neutral business in Coles Bay runs small-group off-road tours to destinations north and east of Coles Bay by quadbike and mini-jeep (drivers require standard licences for both): 2.5hr, $105; half-day, $195.

Coles Bay Boat Hire Coles Bay jetty ☎0419 255 604. Equipment rental for most self-guided activities: 3m dinghies with outboards $45 per hour; two-seater Canadian canoes $55 per hour; fishing gear $35 per day; snorkelling gear $25 per day; bikes $35 per half-day.

Freycinet Adventures Corner of Esplanade and Freycinet Drive ☎03/6257 0500, ⓦwww.freycinetadventures.com.au. Morning and twilight sea-kayaking tours on Great Oyster Bay (3hr; $90) and half-day abseiling trips down coastal cliffs ($125; summer only). It also leads four-day all-inclusive hiking and kayaking trips ($990; start Sat) around the peninsula via Schouten Island for groups of four to ten people, bushcamping on the beach, and rents single and double sea kayaks ($55 per day) and camping equipment (tents, sleeping bag and mat $15 per day).

Freycinet Air Friendly Beaches Airfield, 18km northwest of Coles Bay ☎03/6375 1694, ⓦwww.freycinetair.com.au. Scenic flights over the peninsula take in Wineglass Bay; longer flights also take in Maria Island or Bicheno: 30min, $95 per person; 45min, $142; 1hr, $190.

Freycinet Experience PO Box 43, Battery Point, Hobart ☎1800 506 003, ⓦwww .freycinet.com.au. Wilderness with luxury on four-day walking tours based in sophisticated eco-lodges at Friendly Beaches. The price includes all boat and fishing trips, superb cuisine, wet-weather gear and backpacks, and Hobart transfers; Nov–Apr; $1975.

Freycinet Lodge see "Accommodation". Activities geared towards the hotel's older clientele that are also open to non-guests: 4WD tour to Bluestone Bay (3hr, $55); Tasmanian food and wine tasting ($35); Wineglass to Wineglass guided walk and cruise to the bay for a gourmet lunch (1 day, $245).

Freycinet Sea Cruises Coles Bay jetty ☎03/6257 0355, ⓦwww.freycinetseacruises .com. A trio of scenic eco-tours (daily Sept–May) on a boat with an underwater camera: Wineglass Bay and peninsula circuit, with lunch (3.5hr; $110); Beach to Bush cruise and walk on the Hazards (4.5hr; $150); cruise to seal colony at Schouten Island (2.5hr; $75). Also runs game-fishing charters on request.

The Grape Escape ☎03/6257 0344 or 0417 570 344, ⓦwww.thegrapeescapetours .com.au. Full-day tasting tours of the Freycinet wine estates ($110), dinner tours of a wine estate (4hr, $125; alcohol not included), and sunset wine and cheese trips (3hr, $65).

The national park

All walking trails in the park begin at the **Walking Track Car Park**, on the south side of Coles Bay, 4km from the park office, where you can get notes on all trails. Note that **water** is scarce, so you must carry all you'll need – including to the Wineglass Bay lookout – although the ranger can advise about streams where the water is safe to drink. The most popular walk is to the lookout over **Wineglass Bay**, the park's – and one of Tasmania's – iconic destinations, which is often named as one of the world's top beaches. Wear footwear suitable for a steep ascent up six hundred steps and expect crowds in January, when over five hundred people a day walk the route. From the lookout, you can continue down to the perfect curve of sand whose pristine quality belies a past as a whaling camp (2–3hr return from lookout; 4–5hr return from beach). Rangers request that you do not feed the wildlife, however friendly. To save you retracing your steps, you could loop back to the car park on Isthmus Track to **Hazards Beach** – a lookout at the north end offers great views south – then follow the foreshore on the Hazards Beach Track (2hr from Wineglass Bay). **Boat trips** to Hazards Beach (see box, p.188) provide an easy thirty-minute stroll to Wineglass Bay for anyone unable (or unwilling) to climb. You can also visit the bay by canoe – a spectacular way to arrive (see box, p.191). Another route from the car park ascends **Mount Amos** (454m; 3hr return) for good views and a summit you're likely to have to yourself.

The great bushwalk of the park is the thirty-kilometre **Peninsula Track**, an excellent circuit (10–11hr) that is undertaken in an anticlockwise direction. From the Hazards Beach Track, you head south of Hazards Beach to **Cooks Beach**, where there's a campsite, then ascend via a heathland plateau with great views between mounts Freycinet and Graham to descend to Wineglass Bay. The route is best done over two days and makes a good dry-run (literally) for the bigger hikes in Tasmania's southwest. A sidetrack (1hr) from Cooks Beach goes to a second campsite at **Bryans Beach**. Both sites are also accessible by boat – perfect for really secluded camping.

A sideroad left off the carpark route goes to the rugged east coast. After 1.5km there's a car park at **Sleepy Bay**: you can either scramble down to its pretty foreshore or follow a track 5min south to **Little Gravelly Beach**, a pretty

▲ Kayaking in Coles Bay

notch in the ruddy granite that rarely gets busy. From the beach, a path marked by cairns and arrows scrambles up **Mount Parsons** (2hr return). Four steep kilometres further from the car park – a fairly brutal ride if you're cycling – is **Cape Tourville**, marked by a lighthouse. Although busy, a boardwalk (20min; disabled access) that circles around the headland provides a stupendous panorama of empty ocean and the sugarloaf knobble of Mount Freycinet rising behind the southern corner of Wineglass Bay.

Schouten Island, off the tip of the peninsula, is the ideal camping getaway, if only because you're likely to have it to yourself; it only gets busy as an anchorage for yachties in summer. There are campsites at **Moreys Bay**, which has a hut to sleep in and unreliable water tanks (consult the ranger rather than trust either), and **Crocketts Bay**, where a stream is a fairly reliable source of water, though again, check before leaving. Although there are no proper tracks on the island, walking is easy. Access is by boat from Coles Bay, either with Freycinet Adventures' Aqua Taxi (see p.188; $70 one-way) or through a tour run by Freycinet Sea Cruises (see box, p.191; $75). For the full outdoors experience, get there by a kayak rented from Freycinet Adventures (see box, p.191).

Eating

Out of season, many operators close and the only options for dinner are the hotels and the pub. Locals' choice for seafood supplies is Freycinet Marine Farm off Main Road, 8km northwest of Coles Bay (☏03/6257 0140; daily 9am–5pm; 2hr tours 9am Mon, Wed & Fri, $40), which sells the freshest, fattest mussels and oysters you'll buy.

The Bay/Richardson's Bistro Both in *Freycinet Lodge* hotel ☏03/6257 0101. The former offers fine dining using the best of state produce, such as platters of local seafood or Flinders Island lamb. The latter provides cheap and cheerful fillers: veggie wraps, pasta, grilled fish. Both have the best sunset view in Coles Bay. Bistro lunch & dinner Oct–Apr, *The Bay* dinner daily.

The Edge 2038 Main Rd, 7km northwest of Coles Bay ☏03/6257 0102. Sophisticated and stylish dining at the Edge of the Bay Resort, where creative modern Australian cuisine rules and views of the Hazards astound. Dinner only.

Freycinet Café & Bakery Esplanade. Beside the Iluka supermarket, serving breakfasts, freshly squeezed juices, pies and thin-crust pizzas (after 6pm). Daily 8am–9pm in summer, until 4pm in winter.

Iluka Tavern Esplanade. Above-average prices for above-average pub grup. The menu has a daily roast and fish special plus a few veggie options. Lunch & dinner daily.

Madge Malloy's Garnet Ave ☏03/6257 0399. Small chirpy fish restaurant where the ingredients are caught by the owners; the house special is seafood chowder. Mains around $27. Dinner Tues–Sat.

Oystercatcher 6 Garnet Ave. Sandwiches and fish 'n' chips to eat in or take away to the jetty just downhill. Daily 9am–8.30pm.

Bicheno

The midway point on the coastal run north, **BICHENO** ("*bish*-eno") styles itself the "warm heart of the east coast". The sheltered sites of **Waubs Bay** and **The Gulch**, which make the amiable resort ideal for fishing and diving, also maintain a sizeable crayfishing and abalone fleet. As well as being attractive in the bay, this brings a refreshingly prosaic edge to what could be just another resort town. Admittedly the town centre on the Tasman Highway offers little to encourage you to stop, but surrounding it are golden beaches enclosed by smooth granite outcrops, and great diving in a marine reserve. Add in the amenities of a medium-sized resort, and you have a pleasant spot to kick back for a few days.

A short history

Despite its modern appearance, the town has deep roots – for around a decade before the British arrogation in 1803, whalers and sealers had sailed from a settlement here known as **Waubs Boat Harbour** in honour of an Aboriginal woman, Waubedebar. Enslaved as a 15-year-old by sealers – a common tactic to exploit the superb hunting skills of indigenous women – she swam to the rescue of two sealers whose boat had smashed on rocks. She died in 1832 and is commemorated by a grave erected belatedly by "a few of her white friends" south of Waubs Beach. Snowdrops are said to flower on it each winter. The town was renamed in the 1840s after James Ebenezer Bicheno, a genial colonial secretary who was famous for his girth; allegedly he could fit three full bags of wheat into his trousers. At the same time, it acquired its few historic buildings, the best being the National Trust-listed Old Court House and Gaol on James Street, near the visitor information centre. Bar flurries of excitement in the late 1800s during a coal boom and later a mass exodus to the Victorian goldfields, Bicheno settled into fishing, only disturbed by the rise of tourism in recent decades.

Arrival and information

Bicheno is on Tassielink and Redline's daily east coast **coach** services from Hobart and Launceston, the former via Fingal and St Marys, the latter via

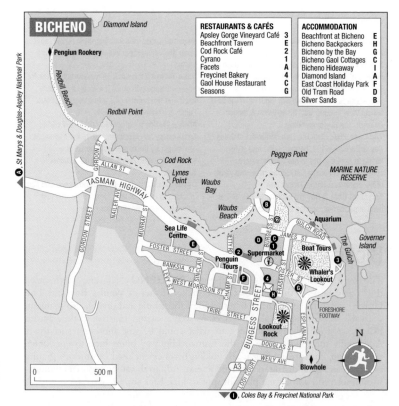

Campbell Town. In addition, Bicheno Coach Service operates two or three services daily (booking for off-peak times on ☎03/6257 0293) to Coles Bay and the Freycinet National Park; services leave from the *Bicheno Takeaway* on Burgess Street. The **visitor information centre** (☎03/6375 1500; summer daily 9am–5pm, winter Mon–Sat 10am–4pm) is 50m north of the town centre on Burgess Street. The **Online Access Centre** is further along in The Oval community centre opposite the library (Mon, Tues & Thurs mornings and Wed & Fri afternoons), although more convenient and central is *Swell Café* (Tues–Sat 10am–10pm, Sun 10am–8pm; $2.50 per 15min).

Accommodation

The closest free bushcamping is 11km west of Bicheno at the Apsley River Waterhole of the Douglas-Apsley National Park (p.197).

Beachfront at Bicheno Tasman Highway, 400m west of centre ☎03/6375 1111, ⓦwww .beachfrontbicheno.com.au. Though nothing to quicken the pulse, this is a central affordable motel with a pool and beach views. ❺

Bicheno Backpackers 11 Morrison St ☎03/6375 1651, ⓦwww.bichenobackpackers.com. A small friendly hostel, well-equipped, with cabin-like dorms in one block and sea views in some rooms of the second block. Dorms $22, rooms ❷

Bicheno by the Bay The Esplanade ☎03/6375 1171, ⓦwww.bichenobythebay.com.au. A family-orientated resort in a shady area between The Gulch and the "green", with twenty modern(ish) chalets for two to eight people. All are self-contained and have a washing machine. ❻

Bicheno Gaol Cottages Corner of James and Burgess streets ☎03/6375 1430, ⓦwww .bichenogaolcottages.com. Self-contained accommodation in the old prison (1860s), with pit-sawn floorboards and a bathroom in the cells. More modern accommodation is in a converted stable and the old school house (with disabled access). All ❻

Bicheno Hideaway Harvey's Farm Rd, 3km south of Bicheno ☎03/6375 1312, ⓦwww .bichenohideaway.com. Accommodation in quirky and self-contained cylindrical chalets. The location is gloriously peaceful, in six acres of bush by an empty foreshore. Laid-back and friendly vibe; good value too. ❺

Diamond Island Tasman Highway, 2km west of Bicheno ☎03 6375 0100 or 1800 030 299, ⓦwww.diamondisland.com.au. Spruced up in 2005, this resort is now the smartest in town, offering one and two-bed executive villas with four-star mod cons. A little bland, perhaps, but bright, modern and with sea views guaranteed. ❻

East Coast Holiday Park 4 Champ St ☎03/6375 1999, ⓦwww.bichenoholidaypark.com.au. This well-equipped and central park occupies the block behind the elbow of the main road. Camping $20, units ❸, studio apartments ❸, cabins ❹

Old Tram Road 3 Old Tram Rd (off Burgess Rd) ☎03/6375 1298, ⓦwww.oldtramroad.com.au. Old-fashioned charm and private entrances in a smart B&B with en-suite rooms in a small heritage house. ❺

Silver Sands Peggy's Point ☎03 6375 1266, ⓦwww.silversandsbicheno.com.au. Overlook the tired, rundown motel and garish decor, focus instead on a great location beside Waubs Bay. Also has bunk rooms for backpackers. ❸–❺

The Town

The **Bicheno Foreshore Footway** (3.5km one way) runs all the way along the shore from Redbill Point, north of the centre (reached via Gordon Street off the Tasman Highway), to Rice Beach as you enter from the south, via several points, bays and beaches. Arguably the most picturesque section is **The Gulch**, a natural harbour created by a low islet just east of the town centre. At its north end is an aquarium (daily 10am–4pm early Sept–April; $3) with a few small tanks of local sealife: giant crabs, abalone, tiny seastars and tubby pot-bellied seahorses. The clear waters at the northern end of the Gulch are protected as the **Governor Island Marine Nature Reserve**, which has a rich variety of marine life, spectacular large caves and extraordinary vertical rock faces with swim-throughs and drop-offs. Bicheno Dive Centre (see p.197) organizes trips or you can see the reserve on forty-minute, **glass-bottom-boat tours** by Bicheno Glass Bottom Boats (☎03/6375 1294; 10am & 2pm Sept–June, plus noon in peak season; $15) from The Gulch jetty. Continuing south, the track reaches the **Blowhole** (also signposted off Tasman Highway), which spurts when large swells crump onto the coast, and an adjacent eighty-tonne boulder balanced to rock in the tide. Another walk ascends up the smooth granite outcrop of **Whalers Lookout** in the centre of town, from which you get a good view over The Gulch. The route is scattered with rock orchids in early summer.

Bicheno's only tourist sight, such as it is, is the **Sea Life Centre** (daily 9am–5pm; $6.50; ☎03/6375 0221, ⊛www.sealifecentre.com.au) off the Tasman Highway behind Waubs Beach, though its tanks of native marine species are no great shakes for anyone without children to entertain. More engaging are the trips by Bicheno Penguin Tours ($20; ☎03/6375 1333, ⊛www.bichenopenguintours.com.au; pre-booking essential). Visits at dusk are to a **penguin rookery** near Redbill Beach, whose noisy birds are blasé about the spectators who greet them as they return to their nests. Bird numbers are greatest in September to November, and bookings are made at East Coast Surf in central Bicheno. There's another smaller rookery by the Blowhole, although bird numbers are not as impressive: visit at dusk and do not use torches or a camera flash.

Swimming is best in the shelter of Waubs Bay, where there's good snorkelling by the breakwater. One bay north, Redbill Beach has the best **surf** in Bicheno, either a beachbreak or a point depending on the swell direction and size; it works best at mid- to high tides. At low tide a sandbar links the beach to Diamond Island; a goal for a stroll more than anything especially intriguing. Both Redbill and Waubs beaches provide good flathead and salmon **fishing**, while The Gulch is the spot for mackerel, mullet and squid.

For a change of beach, Denison's is a long stretch of sand that runs alongside the Tasman Highway just north of Bicheno. A few kilometres further on, **East Coast Natureworld** (daily 9am–5pm; $15; ☎03/6375 1311, ⊛www.natureworld.com.au) has the usual native fauna, including Tasmanian Devils in a dedicated interpretive centre, in a small rather underwhelming park (feeding times 10am & 4pm). That said, it has Australia's largest display of tiger snakes (feeding 12.15pm).

Eating

Eat-in *Freycinet Bakery* (daily 8am–4pm) next to the post office is a good café option, while on the other side of the central grass traffic island, the *Cod Rock Café* cooks up fresh fish (daily 10am–8pm) as well as surprises such as home-made venison burgers.

Apsley Gorge Vineyard Café The Gulch ☎03 6375 1221. Just a few tables by the retail outlet of a wine estate (itself an old fish-packing factory), but superb simple dining on the freshest crayfish and oysters or baguettes, all washed down with good wines. Great value. In theory, 10am–5pm Nov–Mar, but call first.

Beachfront Tavern Tasman Highway, 400m north of centre. This motel pub serves up the best counter meals in town: big servings at moderate prices, with a great salad bar.

Cyrano 77 Burgess St ☎03/6375 1137. Classic French cooking and cottagey decor in a Bicheno institution whose owners boast "Bien sur on parle francais" – and they do. BYO. Dinner daily. Moderate.

Facets Diamond Island, 2km north of Bicheno ☎03 6375 0100. Seafood here is consistently excellent, and sea views are superb whether on the deck or in the slick dining room. Good value, with mains starting at $22. Lunch & dinner daily.

Activities and tours around Bicheno

Bicheno Backpackers (see p.195) Rents bikes ($10/$20/$30 per hour/half-day/day) and kayaks ($15/$20/$35).

Bicheno Dive Centre 2 Scuba Court ℡03/6375 1138, ⓦwww.bichenodive.com.au. Awarded the title of best Australian resort dive centre in 2005, this operator, just north of the town centre, runs boat- and shore-dives to a large number of colourful sites, most at depths of 20–30m; a single boat dive with full gear costs $112, two dives costs $152. The centre also rents out gear, including snorkelling gear (mask and snorkel $10 per day, wetsuit $20 per day).

Le Frog Trike Rides ℡03/6375 1777. This French-owned company has a range of fun motortrike tours, from fifteen-minute blasts ($12) along the coast to two-hour rides to Freycinet National Park ($120) or up the hairpin bends over Elephant Pass ($170). Book in the shop beside the central newsagent.

Gaol House Restaurant Bicheno Gaol Cottages, Burgess St ℡03/6375 1430. Chef's special is seafood bisque, and there are scallops and a fish of the day in this quietly smart place in a garden. Mains around $26. Mon–Thurs & Sat dinner.

Seasons Foster St. A locals' favourite for eating out, the lodge-style eaterie of the *Bicheno by the Bay* resort has a large, reasonably priced menu of modern European dishes, plus pizzas. Lunch Thurs–Sun (summer only), dinner daily.

The Douglas-Apsley National Park

Just 4km north of Bicheno on the Tasman Highway there's a turn-off to the **Douglas–Apsley National Park**. It was declared a national park in 1989 in the rush of conservation campaigns that followed successes in the Franklin and Gordon rivers. Unlike those landscapes, Douglas-Apsley was never true wilderness; its rugged terrain had been crisscrossed by trappers, loggers, coal miners and farmers for over a century. But it does hold Tasmania's only remaining large dry sclerophyll forest; flora similar but far more diverse than that on the mainland's southeast. Botany aside, the park's attraction is its contrasts: rock-hopping in river gorges, lonely waterfalls and remote hikes through crackling eucalyptus forest, or just a picnic and a dip in a clear greeny-blue waterhole – a rarity in a state characterized by its tannin-stained streams, and a great way to cool off on airless summer days. This is an untouristy park, so be prepared for basic bushcamping and for longer walks don't set off without Tasmap's **hiking map** *Douglas–Apsley – Map and Notes* ($10), on sale in the visitor centre at Bicheno.

The unsealed route north of Bicheno goes 7km to the park's southern access point, **Apsley Waterhole**. From the car park, the Lookout Track (10min return) leads through open forest to a platform above the waterhole. There's also a basic **campsite** here (free; pit toilet; river water only; fuel stove only Oct–Apr). To continue, you can forge the Apsley River and take the **Apsley Gorge Circuit** (3-4hr return), an occasionally rough tagged route to a gorge of sheer dolerite cliffs. Because the route then rock-hops down the gorge back to the waterhole, the walk should only be tackled in dry weather, when river levels are low.

The more remote northern section of the park is reached via a forestry road, poorly marked by a yellow sign off the Tasman Highway midway between Seymour and Chain of Lagoons. Be warned, the last 2km are pretty rough. A car park at Thompsons Marshes is the launchpad for the **Heritage & Leeaberra Falls Trail** (6–7hr return), a difficult tagged route that traverses marshland and open forest to reach waterfalls that plume into deep gorges: orange triangles indicate the main track, yellow ones the side-routes. A minimal campsite is nearby (no facilities). The falls route also represents the first section of the **Leeaberra Track** (2–3 days; north-south only) that concludes at the Apsley Waterhole. A medium-to-difficult walk with steep sections, it is for experienced bushwalkers only.

St Marys

Thirty kilometres north of Bicheno, just past Chain of Lagoons, the A4 cuts inland off the coastal Tasman Highway and slaloms around hairpins to the **Elephant Pass**. It's a spectacular (if slow) climb through forest, with the occasional clearing allowing views of the surrounding coastline, although the narrow road makes the route inadvisable for cyclists. You can stop at the top for pancakes, views and atmosphere at the *Mount Elephant Pancake Barn* (daily 9am–3pm): pricey but tasty.

Beyond the pass, the route descends to the fertile expanse of Break O'Day Plains, a name bequeathed by Irishmen who settled the area in 1857. Nearby are Irish Town and German Town. The principal settlement of **ST MARYS** is a mellow Fingal Valley town surrounded by state forest and waterfalls. Once a stolid farming community, the isolated location has lured a growing tribe of artistic and eco-aware residents since the late 1990s, introducing an alternative bent (not to mention a sprinkling of galleries) to what would otherwise be a rather old-fashioned town. Yet it remains a mellow, self-reliant sort of place that seems unimpressed by tourism – rather refreshing after the resorts on the east coast.

The Town

Heading west of the centre, there's a small **local history room** in the old train station, a Heritage-listed timber building from 1886 which holds a café (daily 9am–5pm). But apart from soaking up the backwoods atmosphere, the activity here is **walking**: there are a couple of subalpine peaks to bag and walks through wet and dry sclerophyll forest, long-threatened with logging; details of a vocal conservation campaign are at ⓦwww.southsister.org. Six kilometres from the centre, via unsealed German Town Road (from Franks Road, opposite the pub), a rough sidetrack that is just about manageable in a 2WD splits off to ascend to a lay-by just beneath the summit of **South Sister** (832m). The panorama from the lookout is superb: east to the coast, west to the bluffs of Ben Lomond, north to the Bass Strait on clear days, and south to the wide Break O'Day Plains. Shame about the telecoms masts though. The rocks beneath the summit also provide great free climbing. Further north along German Town Road (which becomes Dublin Town Road) is twin peak **North Sister**. Though lower, the track up is tougher, involving a steep ascent up a gulley then a scramble over rocks to a summit that provides a view to South Sister. Pyengana-based Break O'Day Adventure Tours (☏03/6373 6195, ⒺJnicklason@hotmail.com), run by a leading eco-campaigner in the region, provides bespoke guided bushwalks and 4WD tours. Prices are by negotiation, but since the aim is partly to raise awareness of threatened forests, you may be able to tag along for free if she's off on a bushwalk.

Practicalities

The hub of St Marys' "greenie" scene is the licensed *e.ScApe Tasmanian Wilderness Café* at 21 Main St (☏03/6372 2444; 9am–5pm Mon–Sat, 9am–3pm Sun), which doubles as the local **visitor information centre**. It prepares simple **food** well and has great coffee, a pool table and the odd art exhibition. Around the corner on Storey Street, *Purple Possum Wholefoods Café* is a fantastic little place in a health-food store (closed Sun), renowned for its fruit scones and cakes. Cheap bar meals are prepared in *St Marys Hotel* (☏03/6372 2182; rooms ❸), a friendly, knockabout pub which hosts occasional live music.

To **stay**, *Seaview Farm* (☎03/6372 2341 or 0417 382 876, ⓦwww
.seaviewfarm.com.au), 8km uphill on German Town Road, is magical. Run by
conservationist farmers, it offers hostel accommodation in a small house with
a big eat-in kitchen and a snug lounge heated by a wood stove – "dorms" are
cottagey rooms with beds not bunks ($24, with linen and towel $27). There's
also a row of en-suite rooms (❸) that open onto a veranda with astounding
views east. Everywhere panoramas and peace rule. You can arrange a pick-up
in advance if you don't have your own transport and there's good walking in
the area. Alternatively, 2km east of St Marys, *Rainbow Retreat* (☎03/6372 2168,
ⓦwww.rainbowretreat.com.au; ❻) has four solar-powered cabins among the
bush, each heated by a wood stove and with great views north from the
balconies. Its owners can prepare dinners on request. You can **camp** for free
on St Marys' recreation ground, about 500m south of the town centre.

St Marys is on Redline's east coast **bus** route and Tassielink's Launceston–
Bicheno service. It is also served by St Helens coach company Calow's (p.202).
There's an **Online Access Centre** at 23B Main St. The post office at no. 36
offers **bank services**, and there's an ATM in the supermarket (8am–6pm
Mon–Fri, 8am–12pm Sat) on Main Street.

Fingal and around

The somnambulant country town of **FINGAL**, west of St Marys, only really
comes to life for the Fingal Valley Festival. Held on the first or second Saturday
in March, this country fair showcases rural pursuits – sheaf-tossing, shearing,
tree-felling, plus the world coal-shovelling and roof-bolting championships
– and concludes in the *Fingal Hotel*, probably with a few drams from the 348
bottles of whisky for which the pub is acclaimed. The *Fingal Hotel* (☎03/6374
2121; ❷) – your best bet for a **room and food** in town – is one of a number
of mid-1800s **colonial buildings** that characterize Fingal; others include
St Peters Anglican Church (1886) with good stained glass, Holders General
Store (1859), and small brick huts off the main road near the town hall
– actually holding cells (1827) from Fingal's foundation as a convict probation
station. West on the B42, beneath the sheer bluffs of Ben Lomond, *Craggy
Peaks* (☎03/6385 2032, ⓦwww.craggypeaks.com.au; ❼) has self-contained
luxury accommodation to service a smart resort geared around a nine-hole
golf course (green fees $35, club hire $25). All **coaches** for St Marys also pass
through Fingal.

Going north of Fingal, the B43 tracks the South Esk River through dense forest.
Hard to believe today, but in the 1860s the area around **Mathinna** was gripped by
gold-fever as its Golden Gate mine became the second-most productive in the
state. About 5km before Mathinna, a right turn off the B43 goes to the **Evercreech
Forest Reserve**. From a pretty picnic ground, a twenty-minute circuit leads to the
White Knights, the tallest white gums in the world, then up a hillside for a
bird's-eye view of their trunks that soar over 90m high. A short drive further
southwest via Claytons Road leads to **Mathinna Falls** (30min return), a four-tier,
eighty-metre cascade that you hear long before you see. You can bushcamp by the
river for free a couple of kilometres west of Mathinna at Griffin Camping Area
(toilets; fireplaces) – it gets busy on summer weekends, so arrive early.

North to St Helens

Good surf breaks and brilliant white beaches characterize the run north of
Chain of Lagoons. Bar one exception, this is a section of scalloped coastline
with little development, so it's largely overlooked by visitors on the rush to

St Helens. A few kilometres after the St Marys turn, **Lagoons Beach Reserve** has an abundance of bushcamping sites (free; pit toilet; fireplaces, BYO firewood), either behind the lagoon or on the long beach that's empty except for a few fishermen. Ten minutes beyond is **FOUR MILE CREEK**, a pleasingly ramshackle village that's home to around fifty people and a fickle right-hand point-break. Accommodation in the area is either 2km south in bright bayside chalets at *White Sands* (T 03/6372 2228, W www.white-sands .com.au; ❺–❻), an old-fashioned resort, slowly being rejuvenated and which has a highly regarded restaurant (lunch daily, dinner Mon–Sat), or at *Ivory Fields* (T 03/6372 2759, W www.ivoryfieldsretreat.com.au; ❻) just south of the village, which has elegant modern rooms and spa treatments.

Bypassed by the main road, the oversized village of **FALMOUTH**, 5km from Four Mile Creek, is a popular spot for fishing for bream (in a creek) and flathead (off the beach). Facing the sea at its back on Frank Street, *Saltwater* (T 0428 999756, W www.saltwaterbnb.com; ❻) provides a grown-up getaway in three cube-like villas flooded with light and exuding stylish serenity.

The only resort of any size in the area is **Scamander**. Signs trumpet its uncomplicated charms of "sea, surf, sand", all of which are faultless. The resort itself, however, is as dated as its 1970s hotel blocks. Sister resort **Beaumaris** just beyond is equally bland. Should you strike a good swell in an area with a wealth of surf breaks, or get hooked on fishing for flathead and bream, *Scamander Beach Resort* (T 03/6372 5255; ❹) and the nearby *Kookaburra Caravan Park* (T & F 03/6372 5121; camping $16; cabins ❸) are both central options in Scamander. The nearest bushcamping is 8km west of Beaumaris at Scamander Forest Reserve (free; pit toilets; water; electric barbecues; picnic tables), a pretty picnic site by a river renowned for its good bream and trout fishing, or 4km north at Diana's Basin (free; no facilities), reached via a right-turn off the Tasman Highway. South of Scamander, 1km along Upper Scamander Road, is ⚚ *Eureka Fruit & Berry Farm* (T 03 6372 5500; daily 8am–5pm), which serves light lunches, delicious gateaux, great coffee and the most fruity ice creams in the state. A treat.

St Helens and around

Sheltered at the head of Georges Bay, **ST HELENS** has a setting it fails to live up to. Officially, it is the largest town on Tasmania's east coast. In reality, it is little more than a few streets laid across the Tasman Highway, and suburbs that nibble a little deeper into the surrounding bush every year. A settlement of sealers and whalers since the 1830s, the town flourished briefly through the export of tin from the Blue Tier Mountains. But since the boom fizzled out in the 1890s, St Helens has ticked over through fishing and, increasingly, tourism, a second wind that has hiked real estate prices to new highs. It has done almost nothing for its looks, however, and the predominant architecture of utilitarian 1970s boxes (in places fairly tatty to boot) certainly won't quicken the pulse. The attraction lies instead in the environs: good **walks** in the nearby coastal reserves, the best **game fishing** in Tasmania and the postcard-perfect beaches in the **Bay of Fires**. Another point in St Helens' favour is the most benign climate in Tasmania – thanks to warm ocean currents and a microclimate sheltered by hills, its winters are milder than those in Melbourne.

The town's cultural sight is the **St Helens History Room** (free; 9am–5pm daily) in the **visitor information centre**. Among the musty hoard of pioneer

▲ Bay of Fires

bric-a-brac and farming tools organized by theme are sections on the port and boatbuilding industries, and tin mining on the Blue Tier plateau northwest of St Helens during the late 1800s. If you're going hiking in the Blue Tier area, it provides a useful context to the mining relics you'll see around Lottah and Poimena (see p.201). The centre also provides **maps** and walk information on the Blue Tier. By 2009 there should also be a holographic animation of one of the thousand or so Chinese miners who worked the area.

St Helens has any number of places to cast a **fishing** line. From the jetty you stand a chance of catching mackerel, bream, flathead, trout and salmon – for local knowledge consult tackle and bait shop East Lines, at 28 Cecilia St, or pick up fishing maps from the visitor centre. It's the lure of big pelagic fish that brings many visitors to the self-styled game-fishing capital of Tasmania. To get to the bountiful deep waters offshore you'll need to hook up with one of the many professional operators in town (see p.204) – none come cheap, but then it's not often you get to catch tuna, shark or marlin.

Although St Helens lacks a decent beach in its centre, strands are scattered along the 50km of coastline of **Georges Bay**. The best are in the **St Helens Conservation Area**, which runs along the south of the bay. Several safe swimming beaches line the estuary north of a road that runs to the bay's tip. The southern ocean side has kilometres of gloriously empty beach and startling aquamarine sea backed by the **Peron sand dunes**, a minor Sahara of tussocked dunes which heave up to 20m high. Several tracks amble among the dunes, all of which are accessible from points off the road. St Helens Point at the end of the peninsula road (also the most easterly point in Tasmania) is the start point for a great **coastal walk** (1hr return) from Burns Bay on the northern side around the headland to Beer Barrel Beach. The former allows safe swimming, the latter good surfing when there's a hint of southerly swell. You can also reach Beer Barrel Beach on a turn-off before St Helens Point to go via St Helens Light lighthouse, from which there are impressive coastal views.

On the north side of George's Bay, Binalong Bay Road heads northeast of St Helens 10km to the turn north for The Gardens (see p.205). South of the road, **Humbug Point Nature Recreation Area** is characterized by heathland and its variety of birdlife: honeyeaters, wattlebirds, raucous yellow-tailed black cockatoos, or by the coast wedge-tailed eagles, gannets and petrels. A day-walk (6–7hr return) circles around Humbug Point from a campsite at Dora Point (free; toilets and cold-water showers) beside the coast of Georges Bay, or a shorter walk (1hr return) traces the rocky shore of Skeleton Bay to a picnic ground at Skeleton Point.

Practicalities

Two out of three Tassielink east coast **coach** services from Hobart terminate at St Helens. Redline has scheduled routes daily except Saturday from Launceston via St Marys and Fingal; note that "Redline" is in fact local company Calow's Coaches (☎03/6372 5166 or 0400 570 036). The depot is by a BP garage on Circassian Street, behind the *Bayside Inn*, and opens an hour before departures. The **visitor information centre** at 61 Cecilia St (daily 9am–5pm; ☎03/6376 1744) provides the usual leaflets and stocks walking information for the surrounding area and the northeast. The **Online Access Centre** (Mon–Fri 9am–5pm, Sat–Sun 10am–noon; ☎03/6376 1116) is in the library by the visitor information centre. For money, there's a Westpac

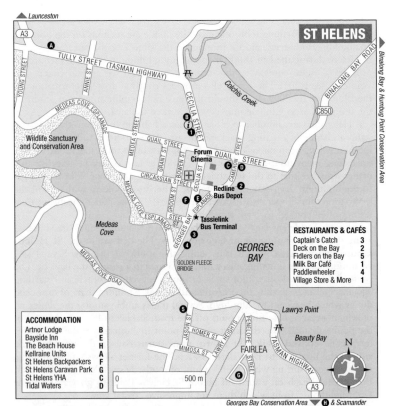

▲ *Launceston*

ST HELENS

Binalong Bay & Humbug Point Conservation Area

Wildlife Sanctuary and Conservation Area

TULLY STREET (TASMAN HIGHWAY)

Colchis Creek

C850

Forum Cinema

QUAIL STREET

CIRCASSIAN STREET

Redline Bus Depot

Medeas Cove

★ Tassielink Bus Terminal

GEORGES BAY

GOLDEN FLEECE BRIDGE

RESTAURANTS & CAFÉS	
Captain's Catch	3
Deck on the Bay	2
Fidlers on the Bay	5
Milk Bar Café	1
Paddlewheeler	4
Village Store & More	1

Lawrys Point

Beauty Bay

FAIRLEA

N

ACCOMMODATION	
Artnor Lodge	B
Bayside Inn	E
The Beach House	H
Kellraine Units	A
St Helens Backpackers	F
St Helens Caravan Park	G
St Helens YHA	C
Tidal Waters	D

0   500 m

Georges Bay Conservation Area ▼ **H** & *Scamander*

ATM and Commercial Bank in the town centre on Cecilia Street, and an ANZ with an ATM just around the corner on Quail Street. The **Forum Cinema** (☎03/6376 1000; ⓦwww.forumcinema.com.au) on Pendrigh Place screens three films a week and has a funky café-bar with couches, art exhibitions and an eclectic affordable menu. Considering the size of St Helens, **bars** – or even pubs – are thin on the ground. The *Bay Bar* (bar meals daily) of the *Bayside Inn* motel is fairly uninspiring, its functionality mitigated only by the bay views through a large window. *Crossroads* bar, on Quail Street, 20m from the Cecilia St junction, has a retro lounge vibe and occasional live music. St Helens hosts Tasmania's largest jazz event, the **Suncoast Jazz Festival**, over three days on the last weekend in June.

Accommodation

St Helens has plenty of places to stay, few particularly exciting in decor, although most reasonably priced. See p.206 for camping and rooms east of St Helens in the Bay of Fires area.

Artnor Lodge 71 Cecilia St ☎03/6376 1234. A small motel by the visitor information centre, modern(ish) and tidy, with good-value simple rooms. Shared facilties ❸, en suites ❹

Bayside Inn 2 Cecilia St, ☎03/6376 1466, ⓦwww.baysideinn.com.au. St Helens' old-fashioned central motel is crying out for a refurb: large upper rooms with bay views are dated but decent, those in an annexe are little better than a backpackers' – haggling often pays dividends. Also has a small pool. ❸–❺

The Beach House 97 St Helens Point Rd, 2km southeast ☎0418/996 080, ⓦwww.top.com.au /beachhouse. Wood floors, painted panelled walls and log fires lend a laid-back beach vibe to this two-bed house overlooking Georges Bay. Also has games, CDs and DVDs for guests. ❻

Kellraine Units 72 Tully St, 700m north of the centre on Tasman Highway ☎ & ⓕ03/6376 1168. Dated one-bed motel units with a kitchen and laundry. Bit of an early 80s timewarp, but a great price. ❸

St Helens Backpackers 9 Cecilia St ☎03/6376 2017. Well located in the centre of St Helens, opposite the *Bayside* pub, this clean backpackers' has four-bed dorms and a wood stove in the communal lounge. Secure luggage storage. Dorms $22, rooms ❸

St Helens Caravan Park 2 Penelope St, ☎03/6376 1290, ⓦwww.sthelenscp.com.au. An immaculate, family-friendly resort south of the centre, this has cheerful budget cabins plus smarter modern villas. Camping $27, cabins ❹, villas ❺

St Helens YHA 5 Cameron St ☎03/6376 1661, ⓔthehumphreys@gmail.com. Homely and clean, this small place is one block back from the main street. Wi-Fi access and cheap calls via Skype. Dorms $27, rooms ❷

Tidal Waters 1 Quail St ☎1800 833 980, ⓦwww.tidalwaters.com.au. In theory, St Helens' most sophisticated address, where each two-bed room has its own balcony. In practice, four-and-a-half star standards but a rather bland large resort for an older clientele. Good restaurants though. ❻

Eating

Salty Seas (Medea Cove Esplanade; Mon–Sat 9am–5pm), supplier of fish and seafood to some of Sydney's finest restaurants, has a wholesale outlet one block west of the jetty: produce varies by season, but expect local fish plus crayfish, mussels and oysters, all straight-from-the-holding-tank fresh.

Captain's Catch Marine Parade. Takeaway fish and chips from fish straight off the boat – as fresh and tasty as it gets. Also does fish sales. Lunch Mon–Sat.

Deck on the Bay 1 Quail St. Thanks to that deck, the bistro of the Tidal Waters resort is an idyllic spot for lunch or a casual dinner. Gourmet pizza, steamed mussels or fresh oysters are on the moderately priced menu. Lunch & dinner daily, fine

dining is in adjacent *Ocean View Restaurant* (dinner only; expensive).

Fidlers on the Bay Tasman Highway, 100m south of bridge ☎03/6376 2444. Reasonably priced fish and seafood feature alongside feted specials like roast wild hare in this small, highly regarded old-hand in the local dining scene. Dinner daily Sept–April, Thurs–Sat May–Aug.

Activities and tours in the St Helens area

Smaller activity operators are contactable by phone only rather than through a dedicated office. The visitor centre stocks the usual flyers for other operators.

Ahoy! St Helens YHA, 5 Cameron St ☏0418 164 089. Available to rent for non-guests and at cheaper rates for guests are: bikes ($15 per half-day, $50 per day); double and single kayaks ($15 per hour, $90 per day); fishing boats with outboard engine ($80 per hour, $190 per day; tackle available on request). Enquire about rental of camping equipment.

Bay of Fires Dive 291 Gardens Rd, Binalong Bay ☏03/6376 8335, ⓦwww .bayoffiresdive.com.au. A friendly local operator that runs a wide variety of beach and boat trips around the Bay of Fires: swimthroughs, dropoffs, reef systems, plus dolphins and even whales in Oct–Nov. Four-hour novice dives $175.

Gone Fishing Charters ☏0419 353 041, ⓦwww.breamfishing.com.au. Small-group estuarine tours run by bream fishing specialist Mike Haley; one trip aims solely to snag big bream. Half-day tours from $150 per person ($200 for two people).

Johno's "Quicky" 4WD Tours ☏03/6376 3604, ⓦwww.johnos4wdtours.com.au. Johno runs half-day off-road trips up the Bay of Fires to Eddystone Point Lighthouse, or into the Blue Tiers (both $70); day-tours to Bay of Fires ($140) include Mount William National Park. Also has wildlife-spotting "Night Critter" trips (1.5hr; $30).

Keen Angler ☏0409 964 847. Big game or reef-fishing trips for up to four people on a small boat with a video to record your catch. Prices from $160 per half-day.

Privateer Marine Parade ☏0489 830 776, ⓦwww.privateer.com.au. Cruises and wildlife tours on Georges Bay (approx $160 per person half-day, $260 full day), and private charter for up to six people to destinations such as Bay of Fires ($650 per half-day, $1000 per day). Marine taxi rates approx $35 per hour.

Rocky Carosi Marine Parade ☏0419 383 362, ⓦwww.gamefish.net.au. Reef and deep-sea fishing trips from a knowledgeable pro skipper; charters from $280 per person for a day's game fishing, or $100 per person for half-day of estuary fishing.

Milk Bar Café 57B Cecilia St. Trendy little place doing good coffee and organic snacks. BYO. Mon–Sat 9am–5pm.

Paddlewheeler Marine Parade. Fish and seafood with modern European flavours, served aboard a wood-panelled ship. BYO. No credit cards. Dinner Tues–Sun.

Village Store & More 55 Cecilia St. A store, Internet café, delicatessen and café in one, with a mellow, friendly vibe and a small menu of excellent homecooking: pies plus tasty daily specials such as aromatic curries or roasted vegetables at low prices. Mon–Sat 7am–5pm, Sun 7am–3pm.

The Bay of Fires

A bronze of a bikini-clad beach babe nicknamed "Serena" marks the entrance to **Binalong Bay** village at the south end of the mesmerizingly beautiful **BAY OF FIRES**. Tobias Furneaux christened the thirty-kilometre bay after seeing a shoreline glittering with Aboriginal fires when he sailed past on board HMS *Adventure* in 1773. The British explorer erroneously concluded that the area must be densely populated – in fact, the blazes were probably seasonal cooking fires – but shell middens testify to around five thousand years of seasonal inhabitance by the Panpekanner tribe. **Skeleton Point** to the southeast was an important indigenous meeting site, while **Eddystone Point** was leased back to indigenous Tasmanians in 2006. The Bay of Fires is considered by some to be one of the best beaches in the world. For the moment, at least, it is the real deal: a scalloped coastline of almost luminescent aquamarine sea and sugary white sand, its sculptural granite boulders like sunken Henry Moores splashed by orange lichen, all free of crowds and development.

Of the three sections of the bay, the most accessible is the southern stretch that runs from **Binalong Bay** to the shackies' village of **The Gardens**. From Binalong Bay, you can walk along the beach via several idyllic coves to **Cosy Corner** in around two hours, from where it's another thirty minutes or so to the wilder sweep of **Taylors Beach**. Always stay alert for rips if swimming – the safest place to swim is in **Grants Lagoon**, behind Jeanneret Beach at the south end. Fishing is acclaimed at the next beach north, **Swimcart Beach**, while the best surfing is at **Taylors Beach**. All beaches are accessible off the road which runs 13km north to The Gardens if you're driving, and there's a campsite at each (see "Practicalities", p.206).

▲ Interior of Angasi restaurant, Binalong Bay

The bay's mid-section is uninhabited, reached only on foot north of The Gardens or south from Policemans Point. It's a forty-kilometre drive north of St Helens on the unsurfaced C843, then on South Ansons Road to reach Policemans Point, where there's a remote campsite (no facilities) beside a creek. You can also short-cut onto the C843 just south of The Gardens via a rough road that's manageable in a 2WD if you take it easy. The beaches in the north Bay of Fires – arguably the most spectacular of them all – are covered in the Mount William National Park (see p.246).

Practicalities

Although there is no **public transport** to the Bay of Fires, it is an easy flat cycle ride from St Helens. A **taxi** from St Helens with East Coast Taxis (℡03/6376 5166 or 0417 513 599) will cost around $15 each way, or you can join a day-tour from St Helens; see box on p.204 for bike rental and tours. St Helens boat charter Privateer (see box) also runs water taxis to the area on request, although it's far more expensive than by taxi. However, if you can gather a group, a day's private boat charter is an unforgettable way to explore the area.

There's free **camping** for up to four weeks behind the beaches in the south section. The first three sites (Grants Lagoon, Jeanneret Beach, Swimcart Beach) are the most accessible to motorhomes, so the busiest; Cosy Corner and Seatton Cove have smaller pretty sites; Taylors Beach site at the north end is snuggled among the bush overlooking its arcing strand. All campsites have a pit toilet but no water or firewood and you must remove all rubbish. There's a tap with non-potable water at the toilet block in Binalong Bay.

The **visitor information centre** at St Helens is your best source of up-to-date info on the burgeoning self-catering market at Binalong Bay. **Accommodation** options include *Bay of Fires Character Cottages* (℡03/6376 8222, Ⓦwww.bayoffirescottages.com.au; ❻–❼), which are pleasant and fairly modern, sleeping up to six people in comfort, and the view north from their balconies is unbeatable. Three kilometres west, hillside hideaway *Bed in the Treetops* (701 Binalong Bay Rd, ℡03/6376 1318, Ⓦwww.bedinthetreetops .com.au; ❽) has two luxury suites, one mellow and rustic, the other a smarter contemporary-style unit, both with views over Georges Bay from a private balcony.

For **food**, ⚐ *Angasi*, at Binalong Bay (℡03/6376 8220; breakfast, lunch, dinner daily; dinner reservation recommended; also apartment for three people; Ⓦwww.angasi.com.au; ❽), ticks every box: an unfussy menu perfectly prepared to showcase the freshest local ingredients; a stylish yet laid-back vibe; friendly service; and a view that's worth the price alone.

Most **activities** in the area are provided by operators in St Helens (see box on p.204). The **Bay of Fires Walk** (℡03/6331 2006, Ⓦwww.bayoffires .com.au; Oct–April; $1850) is a four-day guided luxury walk into the astounding upper reaches of the park; packs and gourmet cuisine are provided, accommodation is in luxury "ecotents" and an architectural glass-and-timber lodge suspended 40m above the sea, with unrivalled views of the pristine empty coast. Arguably, this is the signature experience of contemporary coastal Tasmania.

Travel details

Coaches

Bicheno to: Campbell Town (Mon–Fri 1 daily; 1hr 5min); Coles Bay (Mon–Thurs 3 daily, Fri–Sat 2 daily, Sun 1 daily; 30–40min); Hobart (Wed, Fri & Sun 1 daily; 3hr 5min); Launceston (Mon–Thurs & Sun 1 daily, Fri 2 daily; 2hr 30min–2hr 45min); St Helens (Wed & Fri 1 daily; 1hr 5min); St Marys (Fri & Sun 1 daily; 40min); Orford (Wed, Fri & Sun 1 daily; 1hr 35min); Scamander (Wed & Sun 1 daily; 40min); Swansea (Mon, Tues, Thurs & Sun 1 daily, Wed & Fri 2 daily; 35–40min); Triabunna (Wed, Fri & Sun 1 daily; 1hr 30min).

Coles Bay to: Bicheno (Mon–Thurs 3 daily, Fri–Sat 2 daily, Sun 1 daily; 30min–40min).

Hobart to: Bicheno (Wed, Fri & Sun 1 daily; 3hr 5min); Coles Bay turn-off: (Mon, Wed & Sun 1 daily; 2hr 50min); Orford (term time: Mon, Tues & Thurs 1 daily, Wed & Fri 2 daily, Sun 1 daily; school holidays: Tues–Sun 1 daily; 1hr 20min–1hr 35min); St Helens (Fri & Sun 1 daily; 4hr 10min); Scamander (Fri & Sun 1 daily; 3hr 45min); Swansea (term time: Mon, Tues & Thurs 1 daily, Wed & Fri 2 daily, Sun 1 daily; school holidays: Tues–Sun 1 daily; 2hr 15min–2hr 25min); Triabunna (term time: Mon, Tues & Thurs 1 daily, Wed & Fri 2 daily, Sun 1 daily; school holidays: Tues–Sun 1 daily; 1hr 30min–1hr 35min).

Launceston to: Bicheno (Mon–Thurs & Sun 1 daily, Fri 2 daily; 2hr 30min–2hr 40min); Coles Bay turn-off (Mon–Thurs & Sun 1 daily, Fri 2 daily; 2hr 30min–2hr 45min); St Helens (Mon–Fri & Sun 2 daily; 2hr 30min); St Marys (Mon–Thurs 2 daily, Fri & Sun 3 daily; 1hr 40min–1hr 50min); Swansea (Mon–Fri 1 daily; 2hr).

Orford: to: Bicheno (Mon, Wed & Fri 1 daily; 1hr 45min); Coles Bay turn-off (Mon, Wed & Fri 1 daily; 1hr 30min); Hobart (term time: Mon, Tues & Thurs 1 daily, Wed & Fri 2 daily, Sun 1 daily; school holidays Tues–Sun 1 daily; 1hr 20min–1hr 25min); Richmond (term time: Mon–Fri 1 daily; school holidays Tues, Thurs & Sat; 50min); St Helens (Fri & Sun 1 daily; 2hr 50min); Scamander (Fri & Sun 1 daily; 2hr 25min); Swansea (term time: Mon, Tues & Thurs 1 daily, Wed & Fri 2 daily, Sun 1 daily; school holidays Tues–Sun 1 daily; 50min); Triabunna (term time: Mon, Tues & Thurs 1 daily, Wed & Fri 2 daily, Sun 1 daily; school holidays Tues–Sun 1 daily; 10min).

St Helens to: Bicheno (Fri & Sun 1 daily; 1hr 10min); Coles Bay turn-off (Fri & Sun 1 daily; 1hr 25min); Hobart (Fri & Sun 1 daily; 4hr 30min); Launceston (Mon–Fri & Sun 2 daily; 2hr 30min); Orford (Fri & Sun 1 daily; 2hr 40min); Perth (Mon–Fri & Sun 1 daily; 2hr 15min); St Marys (Mon–Fri & Sun 2 daily; 40min); Scamander (Mon–Thurs 2 daily, Fri & Sun 3 daily; 15min); Swansea (Fri & Sun 1 daily; 1hr 50min); Triabunna (Fri & Sun 1 daily; 2hr 35min).

St Marys to: Bicheno (Fri & Sun 1 daily; 40min); Coles Bay turn-off (Fri & Sun 1 daily; 55min); Launceston (Mon–Thurs 2 daily, Fri & Sun 3 daily; 1hr 40min–1hr 50min); Perth (Mon–Fri & Sun 1 daily; 2hr 10min); St Helens (Mon–Fri & Sun 2 daily; 45min); Scamander (Mon–Fri & Sun 2 daily; 25min).

Swansea to: Bicheno (Mon, Tues, Thurs & Sun 1 daily, Wed & Fri 2 daily; 40–50min); Campbell Town (Mon–Fri 1 daily; 50min); Coles Bay turn-off (Mon, Tues, Thurs & Sun 1 daily, Wed & Fri 2 daily; 35–40min); Hobart (term time: Mon, Tues & Thurs 1 daily, Wed & Fri 2 daily, Sun 1 daily; school holidays Tues–Sun 1 daily; 2hr 15min–2hr 20min); Launceston (Mon–Fri; 1hr 55min); Orford (term time: Mon, Tues & Thurs 1 daily, Wed & Fri 2 daily, Sun 1 daily; school holidays Tues–Sun 1 daily; 50min); Richmond (term time: Mon–Fri 1 daily; 1hr 40min; school holidays Tues, Thurs & Sat 1 daily; 1hr 40min); St Helens (Fri & Sun 1 daily; 1hr 30min); Triabunna (term time: Mon, Tues & Thurs 1 daily, Wed & Fri 2 daily, Sun 1 daily; school holidays Tues–Sun 1 daily; 40min).

Triabunna to: Bicheno (Mon, Wed & Fri 1 daily; 1hr 40min); Coles Bay turn-off (Mon, Wed & Fri 1 daily; 1hr 25min); Hobart (term time: Mon, Tues & Thurs 1 daily, Wed & Fri 2 daily, Sun 1 daily; school holidays Tues–Sun 1 daily; 1hr 35min); Richmond (term time: Mon–Fri 1 daily; school holidays Tues, Thurs & Sat; 1hr); St Helens (Fri & Sun 1 daily; 2hr 40min); Swansea (term time: Mon, Tues & Thurs 1 daily, Wed & Fri 2 daily, Sun 1 daily; school holidays Tues–Sun 1 daily; 40–45min).

Ferries

Triabunna to: Darlington, Maria Island (summer 2 daily, winter 1 daily; 25min).

5

The northeast

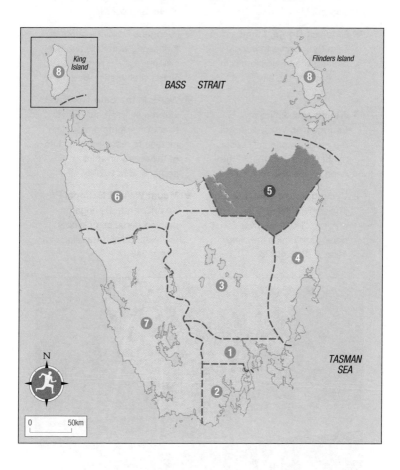

CHAPTER 5 # Highlights

* **Queen Victoria Museum and Art Gallery, Launceston** Industrial heritage and superb artwork combine to make this the top museum in Tasmania. See p.221

* **Cataract Gorge, Launceston** Take the chairlift to dangle over a slice of wilderness in the heart of the city. See p.222

* **Wining and dining in Launceston** Whisper it, but the foodie scene in "Lonnie" might well trump that in the capital. See p.225

* **Cycling up the Tamar Valley** The perfect way to eat, drink and be idle on the river's west bank. Don't miss the wine estates. See p.228

* **Ben Lomond National Park** Subalpine walks and skiing on a magnificent mountain plateau – nerve-wracking to drive up, thrilling to cycle down. See p.238

* **Pyengana** Delicious cheeses, thundering waterfalls and beer-swilling pigs – quirky country Tassie in a nutshell. See p.243

* **Walks in the Blue Tier** Head into magnificent old-growth forest on a remote mountain plateau to discover remnants of the area's tin-mining heritage. See p.243

* **Mount William National Park** An under-rated, kangaroo-nibbled paradise of empty white sands and dazzling sea. See p.246

▲ Alexandra Suspension Bridge at Cataract Gorge, Launceston

The northeast

he northeast sees itself as a land apart from the south. Distance has something to do with it, as does Launceston's traditional rivalry with Hobart. But as important is that the landscapes are just as appealing as any in the east and south but have few of the tourists. North of Launceston, the bucolic Tamar Valley is a sort of gentle Tasmanian Tuscany where wine estates and fields of pasture, orchards and walnuts roll down to a broad river. Travel an hour east and you're alone among steep forested valleys or on a coast lined with bleached sand. If one part of the northeast's appeal is the diversity of landscapes, another is the lack of visitors.

It wasn't always that way. Mapped by English pioneers George Bass and Matthew Flinders in 1798 and named "Port Dalrymple", the **Tamar River** provided an artery for some of the earliest colonial settlement in Australia. Only Sydney and Hobart are older than **George Town**, founded at the river mouth in 1804. Launceston's rapid rise as a port city nurtured early development of the agricultural land along the riverbanks and served as a gateway for exploration of the valleys east nearly a half-century later. By the late 1800s, the northeast was gripped by a tin-mining boom that fizzled out almost as rapidly as it had flared. Today, forestry has replaced mining as the primary industry in the area, much to the alarm of conservationists who fear its old-growth forest will be quietly stripped while attention is fixed on the southwest. Look behind the strips of trees that fringe major roads and you're likely to see swathes of clear-felling. Pro-forestry lobbies argue that without it, the area would have become dilapidated for want of its mines.

Thanks to cheap flights from Melbourne and brave redevelopment projects, **Launceston** has rediscovered its stride in the last decade to emerge as a small city with buzzy arts and restaurant scenes alongside its existing attractions of Victorian pomp and the **Cataract Gorge**. Beyond the eastern suburbs, bush-covered hills fold back to **Ben Lomond**, a skiing and hiking destination just an hour's drive away, while the **Tamar Valley** north is a place to idle: in prestige wineries around Pipers Brook or genteel riverside villages along the east bank. Only gold-mining town Beaconsfield or the mellow coastal resorts of **Low Head** and **Greens Beach** are at odds with the rural atmosphere.

Heading east beyond the agricentre of **Scottsdale**, the Tasman Highway (A3) zips towards the east coast through ghost towns of the Blue Tier mining plateau. **Derby** sums up the area's flash-in-the-pan history in looks as well as its museum, while old pack-trails around **Lottah** provide opportunities for remote walking. Then there is the northeast coast, overlooked and underdeveloped – two good reasons to go. Beyond the amiable resort of **Bridport**

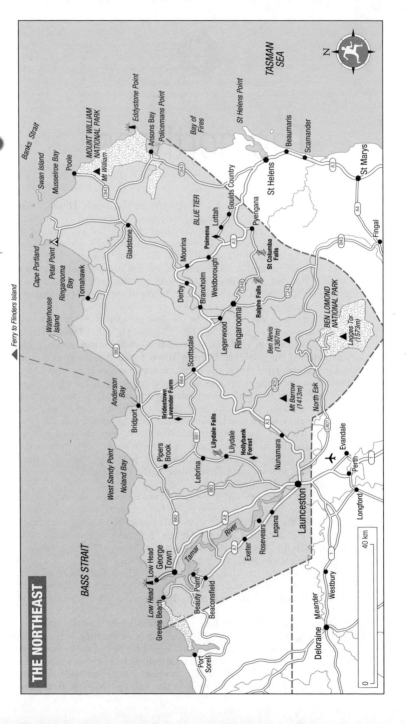

THE NORTHEAST

stretch kilometres of deserted sand, and the beaches in **Mount William National Park** are as dazzling as any of the famous bays further south, but the only mobs you'll encounter are kangaroos. Bushcamps at the tip are as remote as it gets.

Public transport is minimal and centred on Launceston. Weekday services operate along both banks of the Tamar Valley and to Derby, while from Scottsdale you can connect to Bridport.

Launceston

For much of its existence, **LAUNCESTON** has stood in opposition to its great rival, Hobart. Whereas Hobart became the centre of the agricultural and forestry industries, Launceston flourished as an industrial mining hub. Its streets feature some outstanding Victorian architecture to counter the grand Georgian edifices south. The **Tamar River** dominates Launceston's centre just as the Derwent flows through Hobart. Its *Examiner* newspaper espouses the conservative politics prevalent in the north, compared to the more measured tone of the southern *Mercury*. Even its beer, Boag's, stands against that brewed in Hobart, Cascade.

The rivalry stems largely from Launceston's status as Tasmania's second-largest city and the "northern capital", with a population of around 98,000. Yet for most of its recent history, especially since the demise of its industrial base in the 1930s, Launceston struggled to live up to its past. It was a worthy but dull provincial town that traded on its natural assets – it is sited at the confluence of the narrow North Esk and South Esk rivers, with the **Cataract Gorge** only fifteen minutes' walk from the centre. In truth, the gorge remains the principal sight for visitors, but "Lonnie", whose handsome parks have earned it the nickname "City of Gardens", has benefited from a revitalized arts scene centred on the Inveresk Precinct. It also has one of the best regional museums in Australia, the **Queen Victoria Museum and Art Gallery**, as well as a restaurant and café scene that can hold its own against anything in Hobart.

The infamous "Launceston haze" of woodsmoke that hangs over the valley in winter remains a problem, and suburbs south of the centre are hugely under-whelming. In addition, it's never going to feel like a major city, and can seem distinctly provincial outside weekends. Instead, Launceston allows a slice of city lifestyle on a pocket-size scale. Factor in some good-value accommodation and excellent transport links, and it makes an admirable base from which to explore the region.

A short history

Launceston's early history is very much the story of white colonization. Indigenous Tasmanians, who knew the area as *Ponrabbel*, were forced from the Tamar River by the arrival of Lieutenant-colonel William Paterson in 1805. With cattle at George Town suffering for want of fresh water, he ordered a move downriver to establish the military camp of Patersonia on flat well-watered pasture at the head of the Tamar; the name was changed to Launceston soon afterwards to honour the Cornish birthplace of Governor Philip King, commander of New South Wales. The settlement nearly starved to death in the first few years, but as conditions normalized Launceston capitalized on its assets – a sheltered port and a location close to the mother colony of New South Wales – to emerge as the centre of the island's northern administrative dependency.

The capital that never was

By the time the north and south administrative dependencies in Van Diemen's Land were united in 1812, Launceston was shaping up nicely as a potential capital of the new colony. For a start, it was closer to the mother colony than Hobart Town. And it had the natural assets of a deep-water port and fertile pasture. Then high farce intervened. In February, a semaphore from George Town alerted Governor-major George Gordon that the merchant brig *Active* from Calcutta would dock with a passenger of some importance. **Jonathan Burke McHugo** stepped ashore dressed as a maharaja and before the assembled townsfolk declared himself the descendant of Mary Stuart, Queen of Scotland; the rightful heir to the British throne who was on an incognito tour as court vice-regal of the southern lands. Gordon surrendered command to his higher authority and was promptly sentenced to hang by McHugo, who set about wooing public favour with easy credit and a cargo of liquor and food. At this point second-in-command Lieutenant Lyttelton returned from business in Longford. He found the settlement in near anarchy and arrested McHugo. The mysterious maharaja was dispatched on the next ship to Sydney where he was unveiled as an Irish snuff-seller's son who was in a state of "outrageous insanity". Gordon, for his part, was swiftly recalled to Sydney. Meanwhile, Launceston was placed under the jurisdiction of Hobart and any capital ambitions it might have harboured were nipped in the bud.

By the early 1830s, Launceston had a population of two thousand in what was still officially a military town. The army presence permitted a small penal work force; five hundred or so convicts lie in unmarked graves in southern suburb Glen Dhu. But if Hobart is founded on penal labour, Launceston is a product of settlers' graft, either ticket-of-leave men or free settlers who were mostly engaged in agriculture. Launceston has hung on to little of the Georgian buildings from its time as an agricultural and whaling port. Instead, the street-scape is Victorian, a reflection of a golden age in the 1870s and 1880s when Launceston boomed as the hub of mineral exploration in the northeast. By 1881 it had its own stock exchange, and the city council was blazing ahead with an urban overhaul that introduced massive public edifices to Civic Square and laid out several Victorian parks. In many ways, Launceston has been trying to recapure that heroic mood ever since.

Arrival, information and city transport

Launceston Airport is 20km south of the city, near the town of Evandale. The **Airporter** shuttle bus (☎03/6343 6677 or 0500 512 009) meets all flights and drops off at accommodation for $12; a **taxi** costs about $30. Serenity Shuttles (daily 7am–8pm; ☎03/6424 9251, @www.serenitytas.com) links the airport to destinations northwest; as an idea of prices, two adults to Devonport costs $45, to Ulverstone $55. All the main car rental companies have desks at the airport. Long-distance **coaches** arrive in the city centre at the Cornwall Square Transit Centre, on the corner of Cimitiere and St Johns streets. Both Redline (☎1300 360 000) and Tassielink (☎1300 300 520) have ticket offices here – Redline also has left-luggage (☎/03 6336 1446; $1.50 per bag, though no access after terminal closes around 8pm) – and there is a café plus the tourist information centre at the back (see opposite). The terminal for Brendan Manion's coaches to Beauty Point is at 168 Brisbane St. If you're driving, note that most streets operate on a **one-way system** and that Cameron Street is interrupted by Civic Square, and Brisbane Street by the Mall.

Information

Your first stop for tourist information should be the **Tasmanian Travel and Information Centre** behind the transit centre on the corner of St John and Cimitiere streets (Mon–Fri 9am–5pm, Sat 9am–3pm, Sun 9am–noon; ☎03/6336 3133 or 1800 651 827, ⓦwww.discoverlaunceston.com), which can also arrange car rental and book accommodation and travel tickets. A touchscreen terminus provides information outside of office hours.

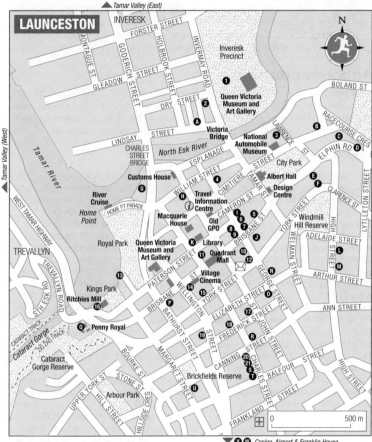

▼ ⓥ, ⓦ, Casino, Airport & Franklin House

ACCOMMODATION			
Airlie on the Square	K	Mercure	J
Arthouse	A	Penny Royal	Q
Ashton Gate	M	Peppers Seaport Hotel	G
Batman Fawkner Inn	I	Sandors on the Park	E
Colonial on Elizabeth	O	The Sebel	H
Country Club Tasmania	V	Sportsman's Hall Hotel	T
The Edwardian	R	Strathesk House	F
Elphin Villas	C	Treasure Island	
Fiona's of Launceston	N	Caravan Park	W
Glebe Cottages	B	TwoFourTwo	S
Hatherley House	L		
Irish Murphy's Backpackers	P		
Launceston Backpackers	U		
The Lido	D		

RESTAURANTS & CAFÉS		Konditorei Manfredi	10
Blue	1	Luck's	8
Calabrisella	19	Me Wah	2
Cube	G	Morty's	14
Dockside Cafe	G	Mud Bar	G
Elaia Cafe	21	Novaro's	5
Fee & Me	18	O'Keefe's Hotel	12
Fish 'n' Chips	G	Pasta Pasta	7
Flip	4	Pierre's Coffee House	
La Fournil du Yorktown	6	and Restaurant	9
Fresh	17	Smokey Joe's	3
Hallams Waterfront	13	Star of Siam	11
Hari's Curry	15	Stillwater	16
Izakaya Japanese		Swiss Chocolatier	8
Restaurant & Sushi Bar	6	Tant Pour Tant	20

City transport

Launceston is compact – locals make jokes about it being a "five-minute city" – and most accommodation is within walking distance of the city centre. Nevertheless, **public transport** by Metro bus is useful for a couple of scattered attractions and some outlying accommodation (buses run until 6.15pm Mon–Thurs, 10pm Fri & Sat; restricted services Sun). The **bus interchange** (information ☎13 22 01, ⓦwww.metrotas.com.au), where all buses arrive and depart, is on St John Street, on either side of the Brisbane Street Mall. Single fares are inexpensive ($2 in the city centre), but it may be worth buying a Day Rover ($5) for unlimited off-peak travel (buy on board) or a ten-trip ticket (from $16; buy at any one of twenty or so Metrofare ticket agents, including Teagues Newsagency, opposite the post office).

Accommodation

Compared to Hobart, accommodation in Launceston is good value, though rates often rise in the busy December-to-February period when **hostel** beds can be scarce. In broad terms, **motels** are concentrated along Brisbane Street. There's also an abundance of **B&Bs** and self-catering accommodation.

Hotels, motels and B&Bs

Airlie on the Square Civic Sq ☎03/6334 0577, ⓦwww.airlielodge.com.au. A chintz-free heritage B&B in a Victorian house with six rooms and friendly management. Relaxed and as central as it gets. ❺

Ashton Gate 32 High St ☎03/6331 6180, ⓦwww.ashtongate.com.au. Classified by the National Trust, this pleasant weatherboard B&B has been taking guests for over forty years. Bedrooms are large and light; all are en suite, with TV and hot drinks. ❺–❻

Batman Fawkner Inn 35–39 Cameron St ☎03/6331 7222. This pleasant pub, established in 1822, offers bargain, single en-suite rooms with TV and phone ($45); larger, more attractive rooms have similar facilities. Light breakfast included. A nightclub operates on Fri & Sat nights, so it can get a bit noisy – better to stay here midweek. ❹

Colonial on Elizabeth 31 Elizabeth St ☎03/6331 6888, ⓦwww.colonialinn.com.au. Behind the heritage building is a large rather old-fashioned block; its pseudo-heritage style is a little dated, though the plus points are that it's central, four stars and quiet. Its upmarket pub, *3 Steps on George*, serves high-quality bar meals. ❺–❻

Country Club Tasmania Prospect, 9km south of Launceston ☎1800 030 211, ⓦwww.countryclubtasmania.com.au. In the city suburbs, Federal Resorts' hotel attached to the casino and golf course has a relaxed, rural air to assuage a generally older clientele, not to mention five-star amenities and an award-winning restaurant, *Terrace*. ❽

Fiona's of Launceston 141a George St ☎03/6334 5965, ⓦwww.fionas.com.au. In a quiet precinct near the centre, a small friendly place with compact and colourful en suites. ❺–❻

Hatherley House 43 High St ☎03/6334 7727, ⓦwww.hatherleyhouse.com.au. Lauded by the style press and voted the nation's best B&B in 2005, this gorgeous 1830s colonial mansion set in English-style gardens (views stretch to Ben Lomond) combines period features with jackdaw pickings from around the globe – tapestries, carvings and sculptures from India, Africa and the Orient – all overlaid with a gloss of contemporary five-star luxury. Effortlessly glamorous without ever showing off. ❽

Mercure 3 Earl St ☎1300 656565, ⓦwww.mercure.com.au. Following a roof-to-floor revamp in 2006, this is an above-average outpost of the Accor chain, with smart modern looks and a central location. ❺–❻

Penny Royal 145–147 Paterson St ☎03/6331 6699, ⓦwww.leisureinnhotels.com. Built in 1840 as a corn mill, this hotel was renovated in 2007 to add contemporary zip to its old-world charm. More modern self-contained apartments are spacious and reasonably priced. Close to the city centre and a short walk to the gorge and Cliff Grounds. Rooms ❻, apartments ❻–❽

Peppers Seaport Hotel 28 Seaport Boulevard ☎03/6345 3333, ⓦwww.peppers.com.au. The modern resort that finally gave Launceston the waterfront lifestyle it craved. Rooms are a stylish blend of natural wood furnishings and luxury fabrics. Spacious suites feature fully equipped kitchen and laundry. Most rooms have river views; "city view" rooms provide an uninspiring vista of dual carriageway. ⑦–⑧

Sandors on the Park 3 Brisbane St ☎03/6331 2055 or 1800 030 140, ⓦwww.sandors.com.au. The best of a bunch of motels on this strip overlooking City Park – but not the most expensive – and just a short walk from the centre. Friendly professional service; guest laundry. Discounts for Internet bookings. ④

The Sebel Corner of St John and William streets ☎1800 990 970, ⓦwww.mirvachotels.com. Boutique style in a slick central hotel with stream-lined minimalist suites, all with balcony. One or two bedrooms. ⑥

Sportsman's Hall Hotel 252 Charles St ☎03/6331 3968. Pleasant pub with well-furnished, comfortable rooms (shared bathrooms). Breakfast included. Excellent, café-style bistro downstairs serving up very reasonably priced meals. ③–④

Self-catering

The Edwardian 229 Charles St ☎03/6334 7771, ⓦwww.theedwardian.com.au. Lovely, two-storey red-brick Edwardian house near Princes Square, with self-contained suites in heritage style. Handy for the supermarket and good value. No children. ④–⑤

Elphin Villas 29A Elphin Rd ☎03/6334 2233, ⓦwww.elphinvillas.com.au. Pleasant modern apartments close to the centre, plus large two-floor villas that sleep six in comfort. Not the "touch of Tuscany" claimed, mind. ⑤–⑥

Glebe Cottages 14 Cimitiere St ☎03/6334 3688, ⓦwww.glebecottages.com. Good-value, spacious one- and two-bedroom apartments with office areas in a convenient location near City Park, though they prefer stays of at least a week. Wi-Fi in both. ⑤

The Lido 47–49 Elphin Rd ☎03/6337 3000, ⓦwww.thelido.com.au. Luxury serviced apartments in a 1930s block whose streamlined period decor is pepped up with touches of modern glamour. All mod cons and spacious lounge and dining areas. ⑥–⑧

Strathesk House 18 York St ☎03 6334 6335, ⓦwww.strathesk.com.au. The cottage and coachman's house of beer magnate James Boag's residence have been converted into two mini-houses bursting with character. A quirky blend of Victorian style, bygone knick-knacks and the odd sprinkling of kitsch. ⑥

TwoFourTwo 242 Charles St ☎03 6331 9242, ⓦwww.twofourtwo.com.au. Three retro modernist apartments full of designer toys on Launceston's gentrified strip: think Gaggia coffee machines and Arco lamps meets bespoke kitchens crafted from Tasmanian timbers. Relaxed chic rather than clinically stylish. ⑥–⑦

Hostels and caravan parks

Arthouse 20 Lindsay St, ☎03 6333 0222 or 1800 04 11 35, ⓦwww.arthouselaunceston.com. Good reports about this new backpackers' near the Inveresk Precinct, which unites period features of its historic building with modern furnishings. Spacious four-, six- and eight-bed dorms, single rooms $55, garden with cooking herbs free for guests' use. Also claims to be the world's first carbon-neutral hostel. Dorms $23–27; rooms ③

Irish Murphy's Backpackers 211 Brisbane St ☎03/6331 4440, ⓦwww.irishmurphys.com.au. Hostel accommodation above a lively and central pub. Facilities include TV lounge and a fully equipped kitchen, but no laundry. Bedding $3 extra for dorms. Dorms $17, rooms ②

Launceston Backpackers 103 Canning St ☎03/6334 2327, ⓦwww.launcestonbackpackers .com.au. Long Launceston's best hostel and still cheerful, clean and well-run without ever being regimental. Communal facilities and kitchen are good, and there's Internet access. Dorms come in three-, four- and six-bed varieties (sheet hire $2, blanket 50¢), single rooms are available ($40), and there are some en suites. Dorms $18–20, rooms ②–③

Treasure Island Caravan Park 94 Glen Dhu St, South Launceston, 2km south of the centre ☎03/6344 2600. A small park wedged beside a noisy freeway. Hard, uneven ground and crowded in summer – probably for diehard campers only. Camp kitchen with TV. Bus #21 or #24 to Wellington Street (stop 8). Camping $22; vans ②, en-suite cabins ③

The City

The Brisbane Street Mall is the hub of the city, which is arranged in a grid. Pastel-tinted **Brisbane Street** is the main shopping precinct and Civic

Square a block north is home to the town hall. Both are a short walk from most things to see and do: west to the bars and restaurants of Old Launceston Seaport or the art collection of the Queen Victorian Museum, then Cataract Gorge a ten-minute walk beyond; east to City Park; north across the river to Inveresk Precinct, the railway-turned-arts hub. Valley-side suburbs east and west of the centre feature some grand Victorian architecture, though the area south of the centre is less inspiring. A gentrified strip of **Charles Street**,

▲ Design Centre of Tasmania

south of Princes Square, is where you'll find the city's style-conscious latte-and-sunglasses set. A historic **walking tour** of the centre departs from the visitor centre on the corner of St John and Cimitiere streets (Mon–Sat times vary; $15; ☎03/6331 2213).

Civic Square and the Central Business District

Shady **Civic Square**, closed to traffic, conveys the spirit of Victorian civic-mindedness espoused by the town motto "Prosperity with prudence". Here, the impressive **Town Hall** originates from the start of the area's boom in the late 1860s. **Macquarie House** to the west was built as a warehouse in 1830; apparently, it stored supplies for John Batman's pioneering trip to what became Melbourne (see p.230). Its cellar houses an atmospheric little café, *Flavas* (Mon–Fri 8am–4pm). **Cameron Street** was one of the first streets laid out after the city's settlement in 1806, and the stretch from Civic Square to Wellington Street is an almost perfectly preserved nineteenth-century streetscape, including the imposing **Supreme Court** building and, opposite, a row of fine Victorian red-brick terraced houses adorned with wrought-iron work.

South of Civic Square is the main shopping destination, the pedestrianized **Brisbane Street Mall**, a modest precinct taking up one small city block. Just off here is the arc of the **Quadrant Mall**, bounded by Brisbane and St John streets, with several lanes and an arcade leading from it. **Gourlay's Sweet Shop** here is a Launceston institution – for something really local, try the leatherwood honey drops.

East of Quadrant Mall and one block north along George Street, **The Old Umbrella Shop** at no. 60 is a **National Trust information centre** (Mon–Fri 9am–5pm, Sat 9am–noon; ☎03/6331 9248), housed in an 1860s blackwood-lined shop, the last genuine example of its period in Tasmania. Going the other way up George Street then west one block, **Princes Square** is a splendid slice of Victoriana with flowerbeds planted in ballgown colours. Its fountain was bought at the Paris Exhibition in 1858. However, the town's moral guardians spluttered at its semi-nude nymph, which is why it was lopped off and replaced with a pineapple. While you're here, take a look behind on St John Street for an elegant terrace of Georgian houses; a rarity in the city's predominantly Victorian streetscape.

City Park and the old wharf area

City Park (daily 8am–5pm), east of the centre, is a treasure. Its disparate elements – impressive wrought-iron gates, manicured lawns and Victorian architecture – combine perfectly to create the impression of a formal, English park, a feeling reinforced by the preponderance of native British trees. They were imported from the Royal Society, London, in 1838 as the finishing touch to an area that was initially a government farm for grazing and wheat. To add to the bygone English atmosphere there's the **John Hart Conservatory** (Mon–Fri 8.30am–4.30pm, Sat–Sun 9am–5.30pm; free), full of ferns and hothouse blooms, and a gloriously fiddly wrought-iron drinking fountain erected for Queen Victoria's Diamond Jubilee in 1897. Six years earlier the city had added **Albert Hall**, which boxes in the park to the west. Built to host the Tasmanian International Exhibition trade fair in 1891, when a quarter of a million people came to a city of just seventeen thousand, its park-side café (daily 9am–5pm) is a pleasant spot to spend an hour. Abutting its northern end is an earlier Victorian residence that houses community radio station City Park Radio FM (station and museum tours Oct–Apr Mon–Sat 10am–2pm; donation) and contains what is alleged to be Australia's oldest wisteria in its back garden; 170 years and counting. In fact the only shock of modernity in the park area is a new enclosure for the twenty or so Japanese macaques near the main gate – locals know City Park as "Monkey Park".

On the corner of Tamar and Brisbane streets is the **Design Centre of Tasmania** (Mon–Sat 9.30am–5.30pm, Sun 10.30am–3.30pm; ☏03/6331 5505, ⓦwww.designcentre.com.au), established in 1976 to promote Tasmanian designers and home to the **Tasmanian Wood Design Collection** ($2.20). Australia's only museum collection of modern wood design showcases superb pieces all crafted by Tasmanian designers from native woods; understandably, prices are steep. But the centre is also an excellent source of more portable craft items such as woodwork, leatherwork and jewellery.

Cimitiere Street runs along the park's north flank. Here, the **National Automobile Museum of Tasmania** (daily summer 9am–5pm, winter 10am–4pm; $9.50; ☏03/6334 8888, ⓦwww.namt.com.au) displays a century's worth of motors in an eighty-exhibit collection of cars and motorbikes and hosts occassional themed auto-exhibitions. On the Esplanade is the massive Neoclassical **Customs House**, just east of the Charles Street bridge, and the **wharf area** around William Street, which has several interesting industrial buildings, including the still-operational **J. Boag & Son brewery**, first built in 1881. Though ownership by a series of multinational corporates has reduced its potency as a symbol of north Tasmanian identity, Boag's beers retain a definite sense of regional association. The subject of beer wars with the Cascade Brewery in Hobart – a topic of friendly rivalry between Tasmania's north and south – crops up on brewery tours (Mon–Fri 8.45am–4pm; 1hr $18, 1.5hr with cheese platter $25; bookings essential in summer; ☏03/6332 6300, ⓦwww.boags.com.au), during which you'll get to sample a few brews. Visitors must wear enclosed footwear. Booking and departure is from the **Boag's Centre For Beer Lovers** opposite at 39 William St, where there are a few displays about the brewery's history and a gift shop.

Inveresk Precinct

The north bank of the river was the hub of Tasmania's rail and mining boom during the early 1900s. Once an urban wasteland, its complex of old railway infrastructure has been revamped into a multimillion-dollar arts-and-museum complex. Nowhere encapsulates Launceston's revitalization like the **Inveresk Precinct**. Glass-walled former engine sheds house the University of Tasmania's Academy of the Arts and School of Architecture and Design, injecting an arty vibrancy into what was derelict ground.

Much of the railway heritage has been incorporated into the Queen Victoria Museum and Art Gallery (see opposite). One wing contains the former **Railway Workshops** – a history of Tasmania's defunct railways is hardly compelling stuff for non-enthusiasts, though you can peer into steam engines and there's a great playzone for kids. The old **Blacksmith Shop** behind is a fascinating cathedral of industrial design, however; you follow a walkway through blackened beams and rusting machinery that dates back to the 1930s, while an occasional soundscape of machinery and voices adds to the atmosphere. Ask for an explanatory leaflet when you buy your ticket. There's also a museum café (licensed) in the workshops, with some seating in an old train carriage.

The **Launceston Tramway Museum** (Sat 9am–5pm, Sun 10am–4pm; $2) contains more rail memorabilia organized around the last tram to run in Launceston; managers hope that the restored No. 29 soon will be operational. You'll find it behind the excellent *Blue* café (see p.225) – Powerhouse Gallery (Mon–Fri 10am–3pm; free) above has occasional exhibitions of student work.

The former railway site spans a large expanse of riverfront land optimistically called the **Northbank Experience** by the council. It includes the Aurora Stadium (formerly York Park), which finally brought live Australian Rules football to Launceston. Sheds a short walk behind it host the all-purpose **Eskmarket** on Sunday (9am–2pm). Alternatively, you can take to a boardwalk along the North Esk River to reach the **Heritage Forest** parkland (45mins–1hr one way; 2.5km). The small pocket of forest behind a meander of the North Esk River is crisscrossed by several walking, bike-riding and horse-riding trails; nothing special but a pleasant destination for a stroll.

The Queen Victoria Museum and Art Gallery

Collections of the excellent **Queen Victoria Museum and Art Gallery** are divided between two centres: a nineteenth-century museum at Royal Park and renovated railsheds at Inveresk (both daily 10am–5pm; free but charges for touring exhibitions; ⓦwww.qvmag.tas.gov.au). The former, purpose-built in 1891 to mark fifty years of Queen Victoria's reign and showing its age, was due to close for restoration and reopen in 2009 purely as an art gallery. All previous permanent exhibitions will shift to the Inveresk site except a **Planetarium** (Tues–Sat 3pm; $5). Once restored, the museum should prove a grand space for arguably the best **art collection** in Tasmania: over a hundred paintings, prints and sculptures, from colonial to contemporary, compiled under the banner "Aspects of Tasmanian Art". Among historical paintings are landscapes by the nineteenth-century French painter W.C. Piguenit and Englishman John Glover, the first great visionary of Tasmanian landscapes. Look too for an image of Launceston wedged into the valley before its late-1800s boom. The collection is particularly strong on Aboriginal images. There's Glover's famous canvas of an indigenous settlement at Risdon Cove near Hobart, site of an infamous massacre in 1803, and dignified plaster busts of tribal leader Woureddy and Truganini, two icons of Tasmanian Aboriginal communities, sculpted in their lifetimes in 1836. Less successful is Robert Dowling's vast canvas of Tasmanian Aborigines (1859); the value behind its Rousseau-esque hogwash of noble savages is as contemporary portraiture based on earlier sketches.

Until renovation is complete, the art collection will remain at Inveresk. Its industrial heritage renders an incredible sense of space to the interior – half of the appeal of a visit – and provides an ideal forum to show off the collections. There's a richly poylchromed Chinese temple from the *Weldborough Hotel* (see p.242) that was constructed by native tin miners during the 1870s. Look too for a section on traditional and contemporary **Aboriginal works** that includes decorative arts, especially the *Strings Across Time* display of shell-necklaces that includes recent examples from the Cape Barren Islanders. Elsewhere, there are so-so exhibits from the Royal Park site: a history of mining in Tasmania; accounts of local geology; and displays of state fauna, with big sections on the Tasmanian tiger and the Tasmanian Devil. The highlight for many visitors is actually the former railway Blacksmith Shop behind (see opposite).

Royal Park to Ritchies Mill Arts Centre

The extensive parkland that backs the museum on the other side of Bathurst Street is **Royal Park**, whose slopes run down to the Tamar River; there's even a croquet lawn just to nail any doubts about its English lineage. A boardwalk heads north to Home Point and the quay for the excellent **Tamar River Cruises** (see box, p.224) which head along the Tamar and into the mouth of Cataract Gorge, allowing a close-up view of Victorian mansions in the wealthy suburb of **Trevallyn**. The boardwalk winds up at the lively metropolitan hub of bars and restaurants clustered in the former docks area at **Old Launceston Seaport** – if you want to feel the pulse of contemporary Launceston, this is your spot. It's also a great place to hang out, with views over the yachts in the marina to the Trevallyn hillside.

Another popular lunchspot is reached by going west of the museum to **Ritchies Mill Arts Centre**. Its nineteenth-century flour mill and millers' cottage have been converted into galleries and an excellent restaurant, *Stillwater*. It's a pretty spot on a bend of the South Esk River overlooking moored yachts – the Tamar Yacht Club held its inaugural regatta on the river in 1837 and so become the first yacht club in Australia.

Cataract Gorge and beyond

Few cities have such a magnificent natural feature so close to their centres as Launceston. So powerful an icon is **CATARACT GORGE** that it features on labels of Boag's beer, no small symbol of the city itself. In 1804 explorer William Collins saw its clear river and cliffs and burbled about "a scene of natural beauty probably not surpassed in the world". At the end of the century, in industrious Victorian style, the area was developed as a resort. A beautiful view of Cataract Gorge is provided from wrought-iron **Kings Bridge**; the current decorative bridge is a replica (1904) of the original shipped from Manchester, England, in 1863. Seen from its span, the cliffs rise almost vertically from the South Esk River as it empties into the Tamar. It looks even more dramatic when floodlit after dusk.

Though it's worth picking up a Cataract Gorge Reserve leaflet from the visitor information centre before you set off, the main walking trails are easy to follow. The **Zig Zag track** (25min one way) is the more strenuous of the two routes along the gorge; a rocky path shrouded by bush that is satisfyingly secluded. The track runs along the southern side of the gorge, from Kings Bridge to **First Basin**, a deep lake in a river canyon. You can also get here on the easier but busier **Cataract Walk** (40min one way), which begins on the other side of Kings Bridge by a small tollhouse of the original resort; the stroll is suitable for wheelchairs and offers spectacular views of the gorge. From the trail, you may see people canoeing and abseiling; Tasmania Expeditions leads abseiling trips (see box, p.224).

Cataract Walk leads to **Cliff Grounds**, the original Victorian resort. Much of it was paid for with money donated by Launceston ladies' clubs, which may account for the genteel, English-style gardens, parading peacocks and a splendid 1896 bandstand – a bizarre slice of prim Victoriana in such a wild setting. An interpretive centre here (daily 9am–4pm) records the story of the gorge's development. *Gorge Restaurant* (☏03/6331 3330; closed Mon) has superb views over the First Basin, as does an adjacent glass-walled café, *The Basin* (daily 8am–6pm summer, until 5pm winter). A rough track heads uphill from the bandstand to **Eagle Eyrie Lookout** (15min one way) from where you get a good view of the ensemble. However, if you reach First Basin on the Zig Zag track or by car or bus (parking available at First Basin; bus #51B, #52B, #58B or #62B), you'll find an enormous, unattractive **swimming pool** (daily Nov–Mar 9am–5pm; free), built mainly to stop people drowning in the basin's deep cold waters.

The focus of activity in the gorge is the **Launceston Basin Chairlift** (daily 9am–4.30pm weather permitting; $8.50; ☏03/6331 5915), which spans the river from First Basin to Cataract Gorge. It takes an exhilarating six minutes to cover 457m – it's supposed to have the longest single span (308m) of any chairlift in the world – and the views are wonderful. If you suffer from vertigo then you might want to cross on foot via the **Basin Walk** underneath, although

▲ Old Launceston Seaport

this route is impassable when the river is in flood. The other alternative, the narrow **Alexandra Suspension Bridge** upstream, is even shakier when pounded by joggers – locals nickname it "Swinging Bridge". On its north bank there's a rough, steep track to Alexandra Lookout, or a more gentle ascent to Cataract Lookout beyond.

Staying on the south bank, **Duck Reach Track** (45min one way) follows the bush upstream to the narrower **Second Basin** and then the disused **Duck Reach Power Station** (90min return). The hydroelectricity plant was built in 1895 – the first in Tasmania – but proved incapable of satisfying later energy needs, a story told in a museum (daily dawn to dusk; free).

Trevallyn State Recreation Area

From the station you could continue further north along the river to the **Trevallyn State Recreation Area** parkland north of the gorge (daily 8am–dusk; no camping). At Aquatic Point, there's an **information point**, summer canoe and windsurf boards rental, a playground, toilets and barbecues. The rest of the area consists of open eucalyptus forest and reed beds, with marked bushwalks and nature trails shared with horse riders. It's also a favourite spot for mountain-biking – Mountain Bike Tasmania leads trips (see below). For other thrills, there's Cable Hang Gliding at **Trevallyn Dam** on the west side of the park (daily Dec–April 10am–5pm, May–Nov Sat–Sun 10am–4pm; $20; ℡0418 311 198, ⓦwww.cablehanggliding.com.au). Harnessed beneath a wing, you

Tours in and around Launceston

Coach Tram Tour Company ℡03/6336 3133. Offers city-sights tours (Jan–April daily 10am & 2pm; May–Dec 10am; 3hr; $26) leaving from the Gateway centre.

Launceston City Ghost Tours 14 Brisbane St ℡03/6331 2213, ⓦwww.launceston cityghosttours.com. Tales of skulduggery in old Launceston at dusk (1hr 30min; $25). Also has Yesteryear Tours from main gate of City Park (daily 1.30pm; same price). Bookings essential for both.

Mountain Bike Tasmania 120 Charles St ℡03/6334 0988, ⓦwww.mountainbike tasmania.com.au. Guided excursions including bike rental, snacks/lunch and transfers: easy cycle along the North Esk River (Mon & Thurs; 2–3hr; $75); trails through Cataract Gorge and Trevallyn Reserve (Tues & Fri; 3–4hr; $90); and a thrilling Ben Lomond Descent down hairpin bends then forest trails (Wed & Sat; 6–7hr; $150).

Pepper Bush Adventures ℡03 6352 2263, ⓦwww.pepperbush.com.au. Excellent high-end 4WD tours provided by a knowledgeable (and characterful) guide, Craig Williams: bushwalk daytrips ($275 approx) explore remote locations in the region, while nocturnal wildlife tours ($115) are highly recommended. All include fine food and wine.

Tamar River Cruises Home Point ℡03/6334 9900, ⓦwww.tamarrivercruises.com.au. Short cruise into the mouth of Cataract Gorge and then a short way downstream (daily: Sept–May hourly 9.30am–3.30pm & Jan–Mar until 4.30pm; June & Aug hourly 11.30am–1.30pm; 50min; $19); or down the Tamar to the vineyards at Rosevears (daily Oct–Apr 3pm; 2.5hr; $58 including afternoon tea); or a lunch cruise downriver to Batman Bridge (daily Sept–May 10am; 4hr; $98 including tea, lunch and glass of wine/beer). Longer cruises also enter Cataract Gorge.

Tasmanian Expeditions ℡03/6339 3999 or 1300 666 856, ⓦwww.tas-ex.com. Abseiling and rock-climbing in Cataract Gorge ($100 per half-day, $180 per day) plus a two-day cycle tour along the Tamar River (Sat–Sun Oct–May; $600; includes bikes, accommodation and food). Also has guided day-walks in Ben Lomond and Narawntapu national parks, and Meander Reserve on request (Oct–Apr; $110 per half-day, $220 per day), plus longer guided walks throughout the state.

Tassielink ℡1300 300 520, ⓦwww.tassielink.com.au. Big commercial coach tours: Launceston city sights and Cataract Gorge (Mon, Wed & Fri 9.30am; 3hr; $55); and Cradle Mountain tour (Tues, Thurs & Sat; full day; $134), which gives 3hr 30min at the park and calls at Sheffield.

Tiger Wilderness Tours ℡03/6394 3212, ⓦwww.tigerwilderness.com.au. Offers various minibus day-trips, including Tamar Valley Eco Tour, with an afternoon of four short walks (half-day; $60); Cradle Mountain including Mole Creek caves and Sheffield, and a walk around Dove Lake (full day $125); and Meander Falls Remote Walk, including a six-hour return walk and lunch (full day $120).

Wine tasting tours in the Tamar Valley See box on p.237.

sprint off a runway, soar over an eighteen-metre cliff and land 200m away. Great fun. To reach the area by road, go via the suburb of Trevallyn, following Reatta Road. Buses #80, #86, #90 and #95 go to Trevallyn.

Franklin House

A rare complete picture of Launceston's Georgian heritage is provided by **Franklin House** (Mon–Sat 9am–4pm, Sun noon–4pm; $8; ☎03/6344 7828), 8km south of the centre. The country mansion was built by convicts in 1838 for one of their own – a ticket-of-leave man who made his fortune as a brewer and innkeeper – and stands on a hillside beside the Midland Highway, then the premier coaching road of the colony. Its downstairs rooms reflect a later incarnation as a Victorian boys' school and features outstanding red-cedar woodwork. A formal reception room upstairs is more traditional Georgian in design, with silk curtains and European antique furnishings, including a seventeenth-century oak trunk said to have been owned by Prince Charles, later King Charles II of England. A café at the site serves teas and light meals. Metro bus #21 to Franklin village stops outside the house.

Eating

Possibly due to its proximity to Melbourne, possibly to its recent revival, Launceston has a thriving restaurant and café scene. Several of the finest eateries in the state are here and all are central – a point where it scores over rival Hobart. If you're undecided, head to the Old Launceston Seaport to browse from waterfront outlets to suit all budgets. Telephone numbers are included where reservations are advisable. As ever, pubs offer good solid meals.

Restaurants

Blue Invcresk Railyards, off Invermay Rd. Funky and arty by turns, this café/bar in a former powerhouse is a laid-back art-college hangout during the week and a popular brunch venue at weekends. Foodwise it ticks all the boxes: tasty bistro-style mains for around $20, snacks for under $10, gourmet pizzas and a tapas menu. DJs spin chilled grooves as it morphs into a late-night bar Wed–Sat. Daily breakfast & lunch, dinner Wed–Sat.

Calabrisella 56 Wellington St ☎03/6331 1958. A crowded, noisy, atmospheric and affordable Italian restaurant. BYO. Dinner nightly except Tues.

Fee & Me Corner of Charles and Frederick streets ☎03/6331 3195. One of Tasmania's finest, this award-winning restaurant in a historic house serves entrée-sized plates of Modern Australian cuisine featuring seasonal produce; expect to pay around $70 per head (excluding wine). Reservations essential. Dinner Tues–Sat.

Fish 'n' Chips Old Launceston Seaport. Bright, buzzing place that rustles up cheap meals and has a veranda that hangs over the river. Lunch & dinner daily.

Hallams Waterfront 12 Park St. A local favourite for fish and seafood, this semi-smart restaurant looks over the river. Also does good-value fish and chips to take away.

Hari's Curry 152 York St. Very cheap, recommended Indian eatery – average mains are $10 and there's nothing over $20. BYO. Dinner daily.

Izakaya Japanese Restaurant and Sushi Bar Yorktown Square ☎03/6334 2620. This excellent, long-established place serves all the favourite Japanese dishes: *ramen*, sushi, tempura and *bento*, though noodles are available lunchtime only. Mains average $15. Licensed (sake) and BYO. Lunch Wed–Fri, dinner Tues–Sun.

Luck's Corner of George and Paterson streets ☎03/6534 8596. Stripped decor that nods to French bistro lets the superb cuisine do the talking: unfussy modern European flavours and a small menu that features the best Tasmanian ingredients. One of Launceston's finest, and fairly priced, with mains averaging $28. Lunch Tues–Fri, dinner daily.

Me Wah 39–41 Invernay Rd ☎03/6331 1308. The best Cantonese cuisine you'll eat in Tasmania served in an upmarket restaurant. You'll pay around $25–28 for a main, or dim sum is delicious for a cheap lunch. Lunch & dinner Tues–Sun.

Mud Bar and Restaurant Old Launceston Seaport. Renowned for Modern Australian cuisine and a sensational risotto, this is a hip restaurant-cum-bar with retro modernist decor; ideal for lazy meals (mains around $28–30) on the riverside deck and also evening drinks. Lunch & dinner daily.

Novaro's 28 Brisbane St ☎03/6334 5589. Classic Italian haute cuisine that many aficionados say is the best in the state. The dining room is snug, the atmosphere smart without being snooty. Reservations essential. Dinner Mon–Sat. Expensive.

O'Keefe's Hotel 124 George St. Tasty pub meals, including huge steaks and a big range of international dishes such as curries and seafood are on offer, and there are cheap $12 lunch specials. Lunch Mon–Sat, dinner daily.

Pasta Pasta 75 George St. A local institution for inexpensive freshly made pasta ($9–14) with inventive as well as traditional sauces, all delicious. Plenty of vegetarian choices, too, such as roasted vegetables in a Napoli sauce, or pesto with pumpkin and pine nuts. Also has takeaway. Mon–Sat 10.30am–7.30pm, Thurs–Sat until 8.30pm.

Smokey Joe's 20 Lawrence St. Cheap and friendly little place north of City Park that rustles up spicy Creole cooking; great barbecue ribs and prawn gumbos. Lunch & dinner Tues–Sat.

Star of Siam Corner of Charles and Paterson streets ☎03/6331 2786. Launceston's favourite Thai restaurant, worth booking on weekends. Mains average around $16. Licensed and BYO. Lunch Tues–Fri, dinner nightly.

Stillwater Ritchies Mill Arts Centre, Paterson St ☎03/6331 4153. A hugely popular riverside café/restaurant and wine bar (featuring Tasmanian wines) with a great laid-back atmosphere. By day, it's an al fresco café, with generous breakfasts and moderately priced board specials. By night it's a serious temple to gourmet cuisine that features the Asian-inspired creations of one of Tasmania's star chefs, Don Cameron. Breakfast & lunch daily, dinner (reservations essential) Mon–Sat.

Cafés and takeaways

Cube Old Launceston Seaport. The hip little café-cum-bar of the waterside *Peppers Seaport* hotel; a top spot for breakfasts on sunny days. Daily 8am–11pm.

Dockside Cafe Winebar Old Launceston Seaport. More refined than neighbouring bars and oriented towards an older clientele who laze in wicker chairs. The wine list is as good as you'd hope and the menu's not bad, with decent wood-fired pizzas and steaks. Mon–Sat 11am–11pm.

Elaia Café 240 Charles St. A retro café-bar at the centre of gentrified Charles St. Serves contemporary bistro-style cuisine with Mediterranean flavours; it's buzzing for breakfast at weekends. Great coffee too. Mon, Tues & Sun 9am–5pm, Wed–Sat 9am–9pm.

Flip 23 George St. The best burgers in town, from straight gourmet to Mediterranean to Thai fish burgers. Tues–Sat 10am–midnight, until later Fri & Sat.

Fresh 178 George St. Retro rules in this funky café, a well-spring of the city's alternative and green cultures. Great fresh juices and a small menu of healthy veggie food. Mon–Thurs 9am–3am, Fri & Sat 9am–9pm.

Konditorei Manfredi 106 George St. German cakes and pastries accompanied by delicious coffee; also a full menu of contemporary meals

served on the smart upper level, licensed bar and outside courtyard. There's a sandwich bar for takeaways. Mon–Sat 8.30am–5.30pm.

La Fournil du Yorktown Yorktown Sq. Superb croissant and pain au chocolat plus baguette sandwiches in a heritage-styled precinct; look for the sign for "French Bakery Café". Mon–Fri 8am–3pm, Sat 8am–1pm.

Morty's Corner of Brisbane and Wellington streets. Popular foodcourt near the cinema, with lots of Asian kitchens including Thai and Chinese. Also fish and chips, pancakes and a juice bar. Licensed. Daily 10am–9.30pm.

Pierre's Coffee House and Restaurant 88 George St ☎03/6331 6835. Established in the 1950s by a French immigrant, *Pierre's* feels like a classic Gallic café-bistro. There's great coffee, fabulous hot chocolate, cakes and posh sandwiches, and Tasmanian wines by the glass. Mon–Thurs 10am–9pm, Fri 10am–10pm, Sat 10am–2pm & 6pm–10pm.

Swiss Chocolatier 83 George St. Not a café, admittedly, but some connoisseurs consider these soul-melting chocolates the finest in Australia.

Tant Pour Tant 226 Charles St. Tiny and full of understated elegance, this French-styled patisserie serves exquisite gateaux and pastries. Mon–Fri 8am–6pm, Sat–Sun 9am–4pm.

Entertainment and nightlife

The entertainment section in the Thursday edition of the *Examiner* newspaper, based in Launceston, details weekly events. The **Princess Theatre**, at 57 Brisbane St (☎03/6323 3666), stages regular drama, opera, ballet and concerts.

It also takes bookings for the Annexe, a student theatre group of the School of Visual & Performing Arts that performs modern classics. Behind the theatre, the **Earl Arts Centre**, at 10 Earl St (☎03/6334 5579), has fringe theatre productions. Hugely popular Australian Rules football matches and occasional large music festivals are held in the Aurora Stadium (ex-York Park) just north of the Inveresk development (details at Ⓦwww.aurorastadium.com). The **Silverdome**, out of town on the Bass Highway at Prospect (☎03/6344 9988, Ⓦwww.silverdome.com.au), is the venue for major exhibitions as well as entertainment and sports events. You can gamble at the **Country Club Casino**, 9km out of town, off the Bass Highway at Prospect Vale (daily noon–1am, Fri & Sat until 4am; buses #61, #64, #65; ☎03/6335 5777). The only **cinema**, the four-screen Village 4, at 163 Brisbane St (☎03/6331 5066, Ⓦwww.villagecinemas.com.au), shows mainstream films. Friday is the big **clubbing** night in Launceston. As well as the pubs listed here, restaurants and cafés at the Old Launceston Seaport morph into hip bars as the evening progresses – perfect bar-hopping territory.

Pubs, bars and clubs

Irish Murphy's 211 Brisbane St. Spirited Irish pub that's more authentic than its Hobart counterpart. Guinness on tap, live music (Wed–Sun) and pub meals.

Launceston Saloon 191 Charles St ☎03/6331 7355. Always packed out on event nights with a young student crowd. The huge main *Saloon Bar* has plasma screens, local bands (Wed nights) and irregular interstate band events, and commercial club nights on Wed, Fri & Sat (9.30pm–5/6am; some $6) when the mezzanine level becomes a karaoke bar. Big-screen TV and pub food served in the *Sports Bar*.

James Hotel 122 York St ☎03/6334 7231. A port of call for touring Aussie alternative-rock bands two or three times a month, plus it hosts the *Reality* nightclub on Thurs–Sat nights.

Royal Oak Hotel 14 Brisbane St ☎03/6331 5346. Popular, genial watering hole with live blues and jazz Thurs to Sat nights. Crowded bistro serves Greek dishes as well as counter meals (mains $12–18). Mon–Sat until midnight, Sun until 10pm.

Royal on George 90 George St ☎03/6331 2526. Renovated glass-fronted, light and colourful pub with an emphasis on food (from 8.30am for breakfast). A modern café-style menu – gourmet sandwiches and salads, pasta and risotto, plus classic but meaty mains. Live rock, jazz or acoustic music Fri and Sat. Mon–Thurs & Sun until midnight, Fri & Sat to 3am.

Star Bar 113 Charles St ☎03/6331 6111. Hip pub with slick decor and pavement tables that attract a young clubby crowd at weekends, when DJs play. Brasserie-style Mediterranean food available. Daily 11am until late.

Festivals

The highlight of the year is **Festivale** (Ⓦwww.festivale.com.au), held in City Park over the second weekend in February. One of Tassie's big bashes, this family-friendly event celebrates gourmet produce against a backdrop of the arts and entertainment. Around seventy food and wine producers set up stalls in the park, and there's dance and funk, rock and world music in a couple of stages that run until 11pm on Friday and Saturday. There's also a varied programme of street theatre. **MS Fest** at Inveresk is an annual rock concert of big-name Australian bands in mid-February, while the month rounds off with the **Launceston Cup**, the premier event in the state's racing calendar. In October there's the **Royal Launceston Show** over a mid-month weekend, an agricultural show with entertainment and the usual wood-chopping and shearing competitions, and the **Launceston Blues Festival**, which has become a fixture on the last weekend of the month and hosts a few international acts. The city is also worth visiting when the **Melbourne to Launceston Yacht Race** over the last weekend in December fills the Tamar with sails.

Listings

Banks and foreign exchange Commonwealth Bank, 97 Brisbane St, plus many on St John Street beside Civic Square; Travelex, 98 St John St (Mon–Fri 9am–5.30pm, Sat 10am–1pm).

Bike rental Mountain Designs (120 Charles St; ☏03/6336 3113) rents mountain bikes for $30 per day. Rent-A-Cycle Tas (4 Penquite Rd; ☏03/6334 9779, ⊛www.tasequiphire.com.au) in east suburb Newstead has bikes for $20 per day, plus weekly rental of touring bikes with panniers ($160 first week, $96 second week).

Books Fullers Bookshop, 93 St John St. Second-hand bookshops are on Elizabeth Street, west of Princes Square: Nicholsons at no. 106 has a good selection of vintage Tasmania books.

Camping equipment A good option for renting and buying traditional bushwalking and camp gear is Allgoods (☏03/6331 3644; ⊛www.allgoods .com.au), with stores at 71–79 York St and 60 Elizabeth St. Paddy Pallin (☏03/6331 4240, ⊜launceston@paddypallin.com.au) 110 George St, focuses on the top end of the market; though more expensive, it allows return of equipment in Hobart – a huge benefit if you're doing the Overland Track. Both sell freeze-dried foods, guidebooks and maps. Rent-A-Cycle Tas also has a large stock of backpacking gear for rental at good rates.

Car rental Avis, airport and *Hotel Grand Chancellor*, 29 Cameron St (☏03/6334 7722 or 13 6333); Europcar, airport and 112 George St (☏03/6331 8200 or 1800 030 118), also has 4WDs; Autorent-Hertz, airport and 58 Paterson St (☏03/6335 1111), also has campervans. For cheaper rates try Economy Car Rentals, 27 William St (☏03/6334 3299), or Lo-Cost Auto Rent, 80 Tamar St (☏03/6334 6202, ⊛www.locostautorent.com).

Golf The par 71 course of Country Club Tasmania (☏03/6335 5740), 9km south of the city centre (buses #61, #64, #65 to Casino), is open to non-members; nine holes costs $20, 18 holes $30, club rental $25.

Hospital Launceston General, Charles St (☏03/6332 7111).

Internet access Launceston's Online Access Centre (Mon–Thurs 9.30am–6pm, Fri 9.30am–7pm, Sat 9.30am–2pm) is on the ground floor of the State Library, Civic Square. Cyber King (Mon–Fri 8.30am–7.30pm, Sat–Sun until 6.30pm) is at 113 George St.

Markets Esk Market every Sunday (9am–2pm) has everything from second-hand goods and antiques to discount lines and crafts. Launceston Farmers Market sells fresh local produce on the first and third Sunday of the month (same times). Both are held on the Inveresk area on the north bank, the former in a pavilion behind the Aurora Stadium.

Motorbike rental Tasmanian Motorcycle Hire, 17 Coachmans Rd, Evandale (☏03/6391 9139, ⊛www.tasmotorcyclehire.com.au; from $110 per day, helmets and gloves included).

Pharmacy Amcal Centre Pharmacy, 84 Brisbane St (daily 9am–10pm; ☏03/6331 7777).

Post office 111 St John St, Launceston, TAS 7250. ☏13 13 18.

Swimming and spas The Launceston Swimming Centre (Mon–Fri 6am–7pm, Sat & Sun 9am–7pm except April to Oct daily from 11am; $3.20) on the corner of York and High streets has three heated pools, one 50m long. Aquarius Roman Baths, at 127–133 George St, is a self-indulgent complex of hot and cold baths, sauna, steam rooms, gym, massage and solarium (Mon–Fri 9am–9pm, Sat & Sun 9am–6pm; admission to baths and saunas $26 or $44 per couple; ☏03/6331 2255, ⊛www .romanbath.com.au).

Taxis Taxi ranks are on George Street between Brisbane and Paterson streets, on St John Street outside Princes Square. Central Cabs ☏13 10 08; Taxis Combined ☏13 22 27.

Volunteering International green group Conservation Volunteers (☏03/6334 9985, ⊛www.conservationvolunteers.com.au) has an office at 49 Elizabeth St and recruits for eco-work throughout the region; unpaid but with free accommodation and transport.

The Tamar Valley

To the north of Launceston is the beautiful **Tamar Valley**. For 64km, its broad tidal waters wind through orchards, strawberry farms, lavender plantations, forested hills and grazing land. Scattered along the east bank are dozy villages such as **Rosevears**, and boats moored in numerous bays. The area was settled early – **George Town** and **Low Head** on the east bank predate Launceston and have a smattering of Georgian architecture. History is not

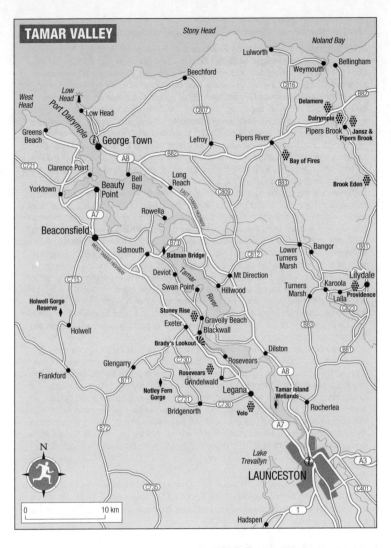

TAMAR VALLEY

Stony Head

Noland Bay

Lulworth
Weymouth
Bellingham

Beechford

C816

Delamere

West
Head

Low
Head

Low Head

C807

Dalrymple

B82

Greens
Beach

George Town

Lefroy

Pipers River

Pipers Brook

Jansz &
Pipers Brook

C721

Clarence Point

A8

B82

Bay of Fires

B83

Brook Eden

Yorktown

Beauty
Point

Bell
Bay

Long
Reach

C809

Rowella

A7

Beaconsfield

Sidmouth

B73

Batman Bridge

C812

Lower
Turners
Marsh

Bangor

B81

Lilydale

C715

Deviot

Mt Direction

Turners
Marsh

Karoola

Providence

Swan Point

Hillwood

Lalla

C823

Holwell Gorge
Reserve

Stoney Rise

Gravelly Beach

B83

Holwell

Exeter

Blackwall

Brady's Lookout

Dilston

B81

Glengarry

C730

Rosevears

A8

Frankford

B71

Rosevears

Grindelwald

Legana

Tamar Island
Wetlands

Rocherlea

Notley Fern
Gorge

C731

C730

Bridgenorth

Velo

A7

B72

N

C735

Lake
Trevallyn

LAUNCESTON

A3

C401

1

0   10 km

Hadspen

really the point, however. The tourist board's catchphrase of a "Valley of the Senses" comes closer to the mark, specifically its excellent restaurants and cool-climate **wine estates**, and with few sights to tick off, simply drifting around is the greatest pleasure. Development is minimal even in the tourist centre, **Beauty Point,** which hosts the valley's big-ticket draws of a platypus centre and seahorse aquarium. Even **Beaconsfield**, a working gold-mining town with an excellent mining museum, is a far cry from Queenstown on the west coast. The only blots on the idyllic horizons are the Batman Bridge, near Deviot, the Bell Bay industrial complex and the possibility of a pulp mill at Long Reach – probably the most divisive project in Tasmania since the Franklin Dam (see box, p.234).

John Batman and **John Pascoe Fawkner** are forever associated with Melbourne, the city they co-pioneered in 1835, but both are Tasmanian sons in spirit if not birth. Born in 1801 to a convict father, Batman sailed to Hobart Town aged 20. He secured a government grant of six hundred acres near Ben Lomond with a contract to supply beef to the military camp at George Town. By all accounts a dynamic, measured man, he won official favour by capturing bushranger Matthew Brady and for involvement in the state war against Aborigines. Accounts of his role vary: some sources condemn him as a key player in the "Black Line" that attempted to herd indigenous tribes onto the Tasman Peninsula, others claim he was in favour of conciliation; Lieutenant-governor George Arthur is said to have written that he was one of the few settlers who advocated kindness. By the age of 33, he was a self-made man with a 7,000-acre cattle farm and contacts to the highest officials in the colony. The infertile terrain was always going to limit his horizons, however. Arthur had already rejected Batman's proposal for a land grant at Westernport (west of today's Melbourne), and with the colony desperate for meat and other explorers nosing around the area, Batman and a coalition of free settlers formed the **Port Phillip Association**. In May 1835, the chartered schooner *Rebecca* set sail from George Town for Melbourne with a complement of four settlers and seven Sydney Aborigines to smooth the negotiations of land rights with the area's Aboriginal ancestral owners – the fall-out from the treaty continues today. Batman died within four years of the expedition; his ghost is said to appear in the former *Steam Packet Inn* in George Town.

The trip prompted a frenzy. The *Launceston Examiner* newspaper reported that "there was nothing in Launceston but the New Country – lots of people will go". One was Launceston publican John Pascoe Fawkner, who built the Cornwall Inn (now the Batman Fawkner Inn) on Launceston's Cameron Street. One story goes that he overheard Batman's party discussing their plans in his pub, but it's more likely that his interest was pricked by the reports of sealers and whalers. He might have beaten Batman to it, too, had he not become embroiled in a fist-fight shortly before his 55-tonne schooner, the *Enterprise*, was due to depart. Fawkner was bound over for breaching the peace and was in court the day the *Rebecca* sailed. Even though the assault charge prevented Fawkner from taking line-honours in the race, he proved the long-term winner. A small man with an aggressive energy and keen sense of moral purpose who despised officialdom, Fawkner staked his claim in August 1835 and outlived his rival to become a prominent figure in Melbourne's early history.

Local **coach** companies Sainty's (℡03/6334 6456, ⓦwww.saintyscoaches .com.au) and Brendan Manion (℡03/6383 1221) run regular weekday services from Launceston up the river's east and west banks respectively. The west bank is a joy for cycling.

Launceston to Exeter

You're only just free of the north suburbs that sprawl 8km along the West Tamar Highway (A7) before you arrive at **Tamar Island Wetlands**. The only reserve of its kind in Tasmania, the reed-choked environment of lakes, woods and fields is a minor safari park of fauna, especially birdlife – from its hide, rangers say you can spot the occasional white-bellied sea eagle as well as the usual waterbirds. You can pick up information sheets about the wildlife and colonial heritage in a **visitor centre** (daily Oct–Mar 9am–5pm, Apr–Sept 10am–4pm). It marks the start of a two-kilometre **boardwalk** ($3 donation; disabled access) which hops across the lakes on islets to reach paths on wooded Tamar Island itself; en route is evidence of an agricultural past, most enjoyably an abandoned plough now lodged in the boughs of an oak tree. Be warned that there are a lot of snakes in the area: keep your eyes peeled from early to mid-morning, when they often bask on the boardwalk.

From Legana, an unremarkable satellite town best forgotten, a diversion west through Bridgenorth then north on the C730 winds up eventually at **Notley Fern Gorge**. The valley reserve is a pocket of the beautiful temperate rainforest that coated the area before it was cleared for agriculture. A signed circuit walk (1hr return) descends through forest to reach a stream canopied by mossy man ferns up to 20m high, then hauls back up the hillside to a large burned-out gum known as Brady's Tree. The story goes that bushranger Matthew Brady sheltered inside it when on the run in the area in the 1820s, a tale given credence by the flintlock muskets that were found nearby. You can also reach the reserve from Exeter, by taking the second left (Loop Road) off the B71.

A second diversion from just north of Legana goes to **GRINDELWALD**. The Swiss-styled village-resort (☎1800 817 595, ⊛www.tamarvalleyresort.com.au; rooms and chalets ❻) is the whim of a local supermarket magnate, Roelf Vos, who was enthused by a holiday in Switzerland. His woodcarvings lie among the flat-gabled Alpine chalets. It's not particularly authentic whatever the PR puff, but there's a Swiss-styled shopping village to wander, a restaurant and a golf course. And if Vos's resort is bizarre, the Alpine styling in a neighbouring private housing development is baffling.

Back on the highway around 5km from Legana, **Brady's Lookout State Reserve** provides magnificent views of the Tamar Valley as it processes north to Low Head, 34km away, and of Ben Lomond southeast. Bushranger Matthew Brady is said to have spied on shipping from its natural castle in the mid-1820s. After a murderous flight through central Tasmania, the desperate outlaw decided a ship was his only hope of escape from the law. He boarded the *Glory* off Rosevears, but an unfavourable wind forced him to double-back into the bush south of Launceston, where he was captured by stockman John Batman (see box, opposite). A display at the site tells Brady's story, though his account is rather at odds with the blood-spattered facts. At **Exeter** you'll find the useful **Tamar Visitor Centre** (daily 8.30am–5pm; ☎1800 637 989, ⊛www.tamarvalley.com.au), friendly and a fount of wisdom on walks in the area. Pies and family-sized tarts from the *Exeter Bakery* (daily 7am–5pm) opposite are the stuff of local legend.

Rosevears to Robigana

Rather than blast north on the highway, it's worth detouring just north of Legana onto a picturesque road (C733) that meanders beside the river; a great cycle route. A procession of rather smart villages and river walks break up the journey. First is **ROSEVEARS**, location for Brady's attempted snatch of the brig *Glory* and home of the 1831-vintage *Rosevears Tavern*. A little way north of the pub, the **Treeform Gallery** (Mon–Fri 10am–5pm, Sat–Sun 10am–4pm; ☎03/6330 3646) produces contemporary furniture from native timbers. If you are unable to drag yourself away – and the pub's terrace is idyllic for a sundowner – *Pastimes B&B*, at 149 Rosevears Drive (☎03/6330 2333, Ⓔpastimes@bigpond.com.au; ❺) has two lovely modern self-contained units that look onto the river. On the other side of the highway, *Rosevears Vineyard* (☎03/6333 3599, ⊛www.rosevears.com.au; ❼–❽) manages ultra-stylish modern lodges whose glass walls and deck afford astounding valley views. It also has a slick restaurant, *Estelle*, serving modern cuisine (☎03/6330 1911; breakfast & lunch daily). Elsewhere, there's above-average pub grub daily by the riverside at *Rosevears Tavern*. Just south, at 95 Rosevears Drive, the restaurant of Ninth

Island Vineyard, ✗ *Daniel Alps at Strathlynn* (lunch daily, closed Aug; reservations essential; ☎03/6330 2388), is one of Tasmania's top restaurants. Classy without ever trying hard, it has dishes that lean towards modern European and gorgeous river views beyond the vineyards – all in all a memorable experience. Brendan Manion's **Coaches** operates weekday services to Rosevears only – ask the driver (☎0419 548 948) if you need collection from Rosevears.

GRAVELLY BEACH, north of Rosevears, is a small village with a gentrified feel. *Koukla's* (lunch Wed–Sun, dinner Fri–Sat; BYO; ☎03/6394 4013) is a pleasant spot for good-value Mediterranean dishes. To walk it off there's a riverside footpath that tracks through a remnant of the area's indigenous paperbark forest; start from a parking area at the north end of the village. The path winds round the bay (6km) to **Swan Point**, where there's a sliver of beach and another walk beside the river to Paper Beach (1.5km), just north of Robigana. The information centre in Exeter stocks notes for all trails. Campervans can park overnight at a riverside picnic area at Swan Point.

Robigana itself passes in the blink of an eye, though keep one open for the **Artisan Gallery** (daily 10am–5pm; ☎03/6394 4595, Ⓦwww.artisangallery .com.au). It showcases the resident artists' ceramics plus their pick of modern woodwork, jewellery, fine art and glass, most keenly priced. North of it is the Supply River – it was, explorer William Collins noted in his log in 1804, an excellent spot to resupply ships. A ten-minute walk leads to the ruins of a flour mill (1825); worth a visit for a pretty waterfall. If the water's low, you can rock-hop across its upper platform to find "AH 1804" carved by Collins's mineralogist, Adolarius Humphreys. Under the Batman Bridge beyond is the Gothic revival church of Auld Kirk, built by Scottish free settlers (with a lot of help from convict labour) using rubble in 1845. The real attraction is the riverbank location and view up the Tamar.

Beaconsfield

BEACONSFIELD is as urban as it gets in the sleepy western Tamar. With the possible exception of Legana it is the largest town on this side of the river, with a touch of the frontier about its workaday main street. It developed as a **gold** town after a strike in 1877, prompting a prospecting stampede that only stalled when the uneconomic small leases were amalgamated to create Tasmania Gold Mining a decade later. Today, Beaconsfield represents something of a modern Australian folk tale. In April 2006, a shaft of the reopened mine collapsed, trapping two miners. During the thirteen days and fourteen nights they were stuck 1km underground, the duo became national heroes who epitomized all the traditional Aussie virtues: they endured the hardship without complaint and dryly asked their rescuers to send down a newspaper with a jobs section. Gold mining operations continue behind the excellent **Grubb Shaft Gold & Heritage Museum** (daily 9.30am–4.30pm; $9), which is housed in brick buildings of the original mine. Interactive displays cover social history and early mine operations, including a noisy ore-crushing stamp battery powered by a waterwheel, and a visit pass through the original shaft whose collapse in 1914 closed the first mine. A section on the 2006 rescue is promised.

Beaconsfield Backpackers at the *Exchange Hotel* (☎03/6383 1113, Ⓔfelisia_w @hotmail.com; dorms $22; rooms ➋), on the main road just north of the mine, is a good option for cheap accommodation in the area, with spacious rooms in a characterful late-nineteenth-century boozer. **Holwell Gorge Reserve**, a couple of kilometres west of Beaconsfield, is one of the more atmospheric spots for a walk in the area, with a track that goes through a fern-filled river gorge (3hr return) and a couple of waterfalls ten minutes' walk from the carpark.

Beauty Point

Named for a settler's prize bullock rather than its looks, the overgrown village of **BEAUTY POINT** is an attractive spot nonetheless, with a wide spread of river frontage and only the industrial chimneys at Bell Bay opposite to spoil things. It is the principal resort on the Tamar's west bank with its biggest attractions. **Seahorse World** at Inspection Head Wharf (tours 9.30am–3.30pm, every 30min; $18; 45min–1hr; Ⓦwww.seahorseworld.com.au) is the world's only commercial seahorse farm. By successfully breeding the creatures for aquariums and Chinese traditional medicine – dried seahorse is a tonic and aphrodisiac, apparently – the farm helps to reduce their depletion in the oceans. Several species drift about the tanks, none more engaging than the Weedy Sea Dragon and related Leafy Sea Dragon, which resemble Chinese shadow puppets. The centre itself is housed in a hangar on a wharf of the **Australian Maritime College (AMC)**, established in 1978. The college developed the interpretive material at the farm – a display about its activities is on the top floor, beside a café with wonderful water views. In an adjacent hangar is the **Platypus House** (daily 9.30am–4.30pm Dec–Mar, until 3.30pm Oct–Nov; Ⓦwww.platypushouse.com.au; film and guided tour 50min; $18). Platypus are elusive in the wild, but here you're guaranteed a glimpse of one of four resident animals, and also echidnas. From a jetty just south, the **Shuttlefish Ferry** (Ⓣ0412 485 611 or 03/6383 4479, Ⓦwww.shuttlefishferry.com.au; Nov–Apr daily except Tues; bookings essential) embarks on a programme of river cruises (30min–2hr 15min), one of which crosses the Tamar to George Town (10.30am, 1pm & 3pm; $11 one way, $20 return; bikes $1).

You can **eat** at the pub just above the jetty or at Tamar Cove (see below) further south. For lunch it's hard to beat waterfront *Carbone's Café* (closed Mon), north of the jetty near the service station. It serves breakfasts and delicious Italian and Australian lunches such as fishcakes with lemon and sweet chilli sauce; good value too at around $17 a main. For a chilled Boag's beer, try the garden of the *Riviera Hotel* that rolls down to the river. The pub itself is fairly drab, mind.

Accommodation

Beauty Point packs in more accommodation than any village in the Tamar Valley, most of it strung along the main road south of the jetty. Little of it is budget, however, so consider Beaconsfield if money is tight.

Beauty Point Cottages 14 Flinders St Ⓣ03/6388 4556, Ⓦwww.beautypointcottages .com.au. Open-plan units with a contemporary beach-house vibe and elegant touches such as silk pillows and crisp white sheets; nice view over a garden to the river too. ⑥

Beauty Point Tourist Park 36 West Arm Rd Ⓣ03/6383 4536, Ⓦwww.beautypointtouristpark .com.au. A small riverside site 1km north of the jetty, with twelve cabins and a couple of vans – if you're camping, bag an unpowered pitch on the shore. Camping $25; vans ③; cabins ④.

Beauty Point Waterfront 116 Flinders St, above the jetty Ⓣ03/6383 4363, Ⓦwww .beautypointhotel.com.au. Faded motel units with fantastic river views in a pub annexe. The pub itself is rather upmarket, with tables on a large deck above the water and a menu that features a wide range of seafood. ④

Pomona 77 Flinders St Ⓣ03/6383 4073, Ⓦwww. pomonaspacottages.com.au. B&B accommodation (⑤) in a period-style house with great views from the veranda, or four luxury timber self-catering cottages finished in heritage style (⑦–⑧).

Riviera Hotel Lenborough St Ⓣ03/6383 4153. Decent pub rooms that are more modern than the building suggests. ③

Tamar Cove 4421 Main Rd, 1km south of jetty Ⓣ03/6383 4375, Ⓦwww.tamarcove.com. This friendly small motel has nine modern(ish) rooms and a small pool. Its restaurant (lunch & dinner daily) serves the finest food in Beauty Point, with plenty of fresh seafood (around $24 per main). ④

York Town to Greens Beach

YORK TOWN north of Beauty Point has only a couple of farmsteads and an interpretive trail to bear witness to what was the fourth settlement in Australia. A battalion of woes – poor soil, pilfering of supplies, bushrangers, piracy, stock losses and simple incompetence – stalled development beyond what Colonel William Paterson called "an acceptable looking village". You're better off heading to **GREENS BEACH** at the end of the main road. This mellow little resort beloved by Tasmanians for summer holidays has a general store and picnic area. You can camp behind the dunes at a small caravan park (☎03/6383 9222; camping $15) or at *Kelso Sands Holiday Park* (☎03/6383 9130, ⓦwww .kelsoholidaypark.com.au; camping $24, two-bed cabins ❹) two kilometres south, an expansive resort on the riverbank favoured by families and wombats. Beach houses rule up here: *Beaches 'N Greens*, at 2 Tamar Crescent (☎0438 344 436, ⓦwww.greensbeach.com.au; ❺) has four spacious two-bedroom houses; *Greens Beach Luxury Escape*, at 19 Pars Rd (☎03/0408 376 211, ⓦwww .luxuryescapestas.com.au; ❼) is an aspirational lifestyle pad for four, full of light and designer detailing. For more activity than paddling in the shallows of the safe beach, there's the **West Point walking track**, which circuits a headland of the Narawntapu National Park (see p.261; standard fees apply) a two-kilometre drive west of the village or a four-hour return walk. Also accessible from the car park is **Badger Beach**, an effortlessly spectacular crescent of wild empty sand,

The Tamar Valley Pulp Mill

Tasmania stands at a crossroads over its future. One path continues along the road of primary industry. Another blazes a trail of all that is clean and green. If you want to sum up the debate in a nutshell – and unleash a torrent of opinions while you're at it – ask anyone about the pulp mill that forestry giant **Gunns** plans for Long Reach, on the west bank just north of the Batman Bridge. No single issue since the Franklin River dam in the early 1980s has so polarized opinion in Tasmania, nor has any development been as potent a symbol of the increasingly fractious internal arguments about environmental policy.

Gunns first mooted a mill in the late 1990s, claiming that only by exporting paper-pulp (as opposed to woodchips) to Japan could it compete with rival companies in China and South America. The $2 billion project was unveiled with the blessing of the state government in November 2003. Reaction was instant. Wine-growers in the valley were horrified. **Environmental campaigners** were aghast at possible chlorine contamination of the river. The Wilderness Society launched a Federal Court challenge to halt the project. As experts of the Resource Planning and Development Commission (RPDC) investigated the potential impact in 2006, the debate soured when campaigning became more strident on both sides. The projected emissions of acid rain gas nitrogen oxide were questioned, and Gunns was forced to admit it had under-estimated emissions figures for poisonous dioxins by 45 times. On its behalf, it argued that the mill would create over 3,000 jobs during construction, 1,600 more during operation and would safeguard the state forestry industry. Campaigners hit back that more jobs would be lost in tourism and that more forestry just meant more ancient forests clear-felled in the northeast.

Against swelling dissent, Gunns turned to strong-arm tactics. It had already threatened to take the mill to Asia during a torrid state election campaign for the minority government in February 2006. Now, in 2007, it withdrew from the RPDC approval process, citing its over-long time frame and forcing the issue to fast-track approval by parliament. Like the Franklin Dam in the early 1980s, Tasmania's pulp mill became

5

especially when the tide drops to reveal its scale. A lookout a few hundred metres from the car park is also a good spot to hunt a wave – Badgers picks up good surf in northeast swells.

Launceston to George Town

Leaving Launceston and heading north along the East Tamar Highway, it's only a few minutes before you're zooming through scenic countryside, passing through **Dilston**, where cows graze in paddocks at the base of bush-covered hills. At **Hillwood**, after 20km, you can divert to a berry farm (daily 8am–5pm) – a local institution for strawberries and cream, or huge ice cream sundaes – then take a sixteen-kilometre scenic route beside the river (part unsealed) that emerges just below **Batman Bridge**. The 206-metre, cable-stayed suspension bridge was Australia's first (1968), though a distinctive single-tower design was compromised due to soft clay on the east bank rather than any brave modernist design. On the other side of the highway from Hillwood, **Mount Direction** is topped by ruins of a colonial semaphore station that relayed messages between Launceston and George Town. A path from a lay-by (2hr return) ascends through ash- and peppermint-gum forest to the summit, where you'll find remnants of the signalkeeper's cottage and well, plus walls of the garden in which he managed to grow a few vegetables: be warned, it's stiff going near the top.

a **federal election issue**. In June, an anti-mill protest attracted ten thousand campaigners to the largest rally ever held in Launceston. A month later, forestry unions claimed eleven thousand pro-mill protestors at their own rally (the police put the number at five thousand). Both sides took out adverts on state TV. On the mainland, politicians in rich districts of east Sydney found their seats under threat due to the anti-mill feeling in the cities. Meanwhile, Liberal and Labor party leaders were careful not to rock the boat, fearful of losing Tasmanian seats during the tightest election Australia had witnessed for over a decade.

When the government's chief scientist gave the mill a green light with 48 stringent conditions attached in October 2007, the matter should have been laid to rest. Instead, the dispute rumbled on. Gunns said the Tamar Valley mill would be the greenest in the world. Campaigners countered that the modelling used in the parliamentary approval was faulty and the remit too narrow; it did not take into account the source of the four million tonnes of woodchips. Gunns said no old-growth would be felled to feed the mill. Flinders Island council threatened legal action if a single fish was killed from the 64,000 litres of effluent that would be pumped daily into its pristine fishing grounds in the Bass Strait. And the Wilderness Society hoped the issue had become so toxic that no bank would dare to lend Gunns the capital. As ever in Tasmania, the debate had become personal and the facts were often obscured as a result; views on either side are aired at Ⓦwww.gunnspulpmill.com.au (pro); and Ⓦwww.tamarpulpmill.info and Ⓦwww.wilderness.org.au (anti).

The pulp mill is no longer simply a project. It is a symbol of the environmental storm clouds gathering over Australia. "The lucky country" is wracked by drought, and for metropolitan Australians (and many Tasmanians) the mill is symptomatic of why. It encompasses the balance of business against the environment, profits against probity, and the wider issue of Tasmania's forestry policy and continued plunder of limited natural resources. Construction was scheduled to begin in January 2008. Then it was pushed back to June. With Greens declaring the mill the next Franklin dam, whether it begins at all remains to be seen.

You're headed for the port of **GEORGE TOWN**, where Colonel William Paterson landed in 1804 to begin settlement of northern Tasmania, making it the third-oldest town in Australia. Despite its history, George Town isn't particularly compelling. The **visitor information centre** on Main Road on the way into town (daily summer 9am–5pm, winter until 4pm; ☎03/6382 1700) has self-guided heritage trail leaflets that point out what remains of historical interest. The **Watch House** (Mon–Fri 10am–4pm, Sat–Sun 10am–2pm, shorter hours winter; donation; ☎03/6382 4466) on the corner of Macquarie and Sorrell streets is as good an introduction as any to the town's history, if only for its model of the town in the early 1800s. Beside the roundabout further down Macquarie Street, the **Bass & Flinders Centre** (daily 10am–4pm summer, until 3pm winter; $8) houses a life-size Huon-pine replica of the *Norfolk*, the tubby brig that George Bass and Matthew Flinders anchored just offshore while on their voyage of discovery in 1798. There's also a replica of the pilot boat *Elizabeth* in which swashbuckling whaler and adventurer Captain James Kelly circumnavigated Tasmania in 1816. The white Georgian building further along the same road, Elizabeth Street, was the *Steam Packet Inn* where John Batman bunked down before he embarked to found Melbourne; his ghost is said to materialize in the upper central window. The only colonial building you can look inside, **The Grove** (☎03/6382 1336, ⓦwww.thegrovetas.com) is an elegant stone Georgian mansion at 25 Cimitiere St. However, opening times are erratic (currently Thurs 10.30am–3pm; $7.50), so confirm before you visit.

Practicalities

Sainty's **Coaches** (☎03/6334 6456) runs to all destinations en route to George Town on weekdays, and continues to Low Head once a day if pre-booked. The **Shuttlefish Ferry** (☎0412 485 611 or 03/6383 4479, ⓦwww .shuttlefishferry.com.au; Nov–Apr daily except Tues; bookings essential) crosses the Tamar to Beauty Point three times a day (10.40am, 2.10pm & 3.50pm; $11 one way, $20 return; bikes $1); see p.233 for times from Beauty Point. The most comfortable **accommodation** in George Town is at the waterfront *Pier Hotel*, at 5 Elizabeth St (☎03/6382 1300; rooms & apartments ❻), either in modern motel-style rooms or self-catering units. The restaurant there serves the best **food** in the locale, ranging from pasta to Asian curries and a daily fresh fish special. *Nana's Cottage* in the grounds of Georgian manor The Grove (see above; ❹) is in fact two self-contained units with old-fashioned cottagey charm.

Low Head

LOW HEAD, 5km north of George Town, is a more appealing proposition, with a village atmosphere and 24 National Trust–listed buildings, whitewashed cottages and rambling houses set amid extensive parkland. A trail of red-roofed information posts provides historical context as the "Low Head Experience", beginning opposite the caravan park at She Oak Point. Beside it is the original convict-built **Pilot Station**, the earliest of its type in Australia (1805) that is still providing a base from which pilots guide ships into the river. The earliest of its brick buildings, gathered like a village around a green, is a long pilots' building (1835) designed by ubiquitous colonial architect John Lee Archer. It houses a **museum** (daily 9am–5pm; $5) of maritime memorabilia whose so-so themed displays are perked up by exhibits of shipwreck and convict finds. The road terminates at a **lighthouse**, from where coastal panoramas are superb. There's a small **beach** just south of the lighthouse at Dotterell Point; you can also reach it on the Low Head Coastal Trail, which begins by the pilot station. The beach

Closer to Melbourne than Hobart in terms of climate as well as location, the Tamar Valley is the premier wine-growing region in Tasmania. The valley's wines are distinctly flavoured, crisp, cool-climate wines: riesling, pinot gris, sauvignon blanc and chardonnay among whites, as well as pinot noir and sparkling varieties. The **Tamar Valley Wine Route** (available from information centres in Launceston and Exeter; also as a download from Ⓦwww.tasmanianwineroute.com.au) lists 24 vineyards in the area, from small family concerns to large corporate estates, and the tasting experience (virtually all daily 10am–5pm) varies accordingly. Most wine gongs go to the estates in the **Pipers Brook** area east of George Town, and you could lose a pleasant day exploring its rolling hills. A minibus **tour** from Launceston lets you swallow as well as taste: two good operators are Tiger Wilderness Tours (Tues, Thurs & Sun; $120 including lunch; ℡03/6364 3212, Ⓦwww.tigerwilderness .com.au); and Valleybrook Wine Tours ($70 per half-day, $110 per full day with lunch; ℡0400 037 250, Ⓦwww.valleybrook.com.au).

Vineyards

Bay of Fires Wines off B83, 1km south of Pipers River ℡03/6382 7622, Ⓦwww .bayoffireswines.com.au. The sparkling Arras label created by one of Australia's finest young winemakers, Fran Austin, receives national acclaim. Tastings, also of table wines, are in a stylish gallery-like space. Daily 10am–5pm.

Brook Eden 167 Adams Rd, Lebrina (off B81) ℡03/6395 6244, Ⓦwww.brookeden .com.au. A family producer whose pinot noir picked up trophies in 2005 and took best red at the Tasmanian Wine Show in 2007. Also produces chardonnay and rosé. Daily 11am–5pm, closed July.

Dalrymple Vineyard Pipers Brook (junction of B82 and C818) ℡03/6382 7222, Ⓦwww.dalrymplevineyards.com.au. Fruit-driven wines produced by a small estate: pinot noir and sauvignon blanc win wine gongs by the wall-load. Daily 10am–5pm.

Delamere Vineyard Pipers Brook (B82 1km west of C818 junction) ℡03/6382 7190, Ⓦwww.delamerevineyards.com.au. A small 27-acre outfit that specializes in pinot noir and chardonnay. Daily 10am–5pm.

Jansz Pipers Brook (C818, 2km off B82) ℡03/6382 7066, Ⓦwww.jansz.com. Part of the Yalumba group, this is a premier-league producer of Australian bubbly; expect finely structured wines based on chardonnay. There's information on the wine-making process in a modern-rustic interpretive centre. Daily 10am–5pm.

Pipers Brook Vineyard Pipers Brook (C818, 2km off B82) ℡03/6382 7527, Ⓦwww .kreglingerwineestates.com. Established in 1974 and now part of the large Kreglinger Estate, the winery is housed in a sleek architectural complex with self-guided tours that include tasting of Ninth Island wines. Café and vine-covered courtyard. Daily 10am–5pm.

Providence Vineyards 236 Lalla Rd, Lalla (near Lilydale) ℡1800 992 967, Ⓦwww .providence.com.au. The oldest vineyard in Tasmania, established by the Frenchman who revived wine-growing in the state in 1956, Jean Miguet. Pinot noir, sémillon and chardonnay crafted by itinerant wine star Andrew Hood, plus dessert wines. Daily 10am–5pm, by appointment July–Aug.

Stoney Rise Vineyard Hendersons Lane, Gravelly Beach ℡03/6394 3678, Ⓔstoneyrise@yahoo.com. A boutique vineyard that's twenty years young. European-styled wines represent a new breed of Tassie wines, especially the chardonnay and pinot noir of the exclusive Holyman label. Thurs–Mon 11am–5pm, closed Sept.

Velo 755 West Tamar Highway, Legana ℡03/6330 3677, Ⓦwww.velowines.com.au. Hand-crafted wines from the small estate of Michael Wilson, Tasmania's only Tour de France cyclist. Star wines produced from the oldest cabernet sauvignon vines in Tasmania. Daily 10am–5pm, by appointment June–Aug.

is also a rookery for **Little Penguins**. Guided tours (daily; 1hr; $15; bookings on ⓣ0418 361 860, ⓦwww.penguintours.lowhead.com) run at sunset to a wooden viewing platform above the birds' burrows – wrap up, as it gets chilly.

Other wildlife tours go to a **fur seal colony** on Tenth Island with Seal and Sea Adventure Tours (3hr; $120; bookings ⓣ0419 357 028, ⓦwww.sealandsea.com). It also runs fishing and diving charters on request – the diving just offshore from the pilot station is outstanding, notable for kelp forests, drop-offs into the sixty-metre deep shipping channel and a colourful cold-water sponge garden just off the breakwater. Go Dive in Launceston, at 69A Caning St (ⓣ03/6331 6608, ⓦwww.godivetassie.com) also organizes trips. East Beach ("Easties"), east of the main road to the lighthouse, is a good **surf** beach with mellow waves, though the best break in the area is a reef at Tom O'Shanter Bay east of George Town, near Lulworth.

For **accommodation**, you can stay in rather spartan heritage cottages at the Pilot Station (three- and four-bed; ⓣ03/6382 1143 or 1800 008 343; ❺) and in the former lighthouse keepers' two-bed residences, *Belfont Cottages* (ⓣ03/6382 1399, via ⓦwww.cottagesofthecolony.com.au; ❺). They're pretty basic, too, but the location and views are unbeatable. To **camp** there's *Low Head Tourist Park*, at 136 Low Head Rd (ⓣ03/6382 1573, ⓔlowheadtp@lgh.com.au; camping $22, cabins ❸, cottages ❹).

Ben Lomond National Park

The dolerite plateau of the **Ben Lomond Range**, over 1300m high and 84 square kilometres in area, lies entirely within **BEN LOMOND NATIONAL PARK**, 50km southeast of Launceston. Precipitous cliff faces such as Stacks Bluff are a dramatic presence on the route north through central Tasmania, making this hallowed ground for the state's rock climbers. However, it is better known for its **skiing**. A small ski "village" – actually just a few huts and a pub – nestles among the boulderfields beneath **Legges Tor** (1572m), the second-highest point in Tasmania, and can be reached in an hour from Launceston. The ski season runs from mid-July to the end of September, and **accommodation** is limited to six simple units that sleep two to four at the *Ben Lomond Creek Inn* (ⓣ03/6390 6199, ⓔcolemear@hotmail.com; ski season ❻, otherwise ❹). This is open year-round and booked out at weekends in season, when reservations are essential. The region's accessibility means there's no real need to stay, however. **Meals** are available at the inn, or there's fast food from a ski-resort kiosk.

An all-day pass on the six **ski lifts** costs around $40 (details and snow conditions from ⓣ03/6390 6116 and ⓦwww.ski.com.au/reports/benlomond). Some rental of ski and snowboard equipment plus toboggans is available from a ski school on the mountain, or there's a better range at Launceston Sports Centre, at 88A George St (ⓣ03/6331 4777). The **Travel and Information Centre** in Launceston (see p.215) can advise on ski packages and also a **bus service** from Launceston that operates during the season. If you're driving, be warned that the final 20km to the ski village and the last leg, **Jacobs Ladder**, is an exhilarating – or terrifying – journey up hairpin bends that plummet as sheer cliffs behind the wire barriers. Though the route has finally been upgraded to a sealed road, a 30kmph speed limit is in force and you must give way to descending traffic when driving up. In winter, you must also carry wheel-chains, which can be rented from Launceston. Otherwise, you can park just before the Ladder and take a **shuttle bus** ($15).

Outside the ski season, services cease and all businesses except the inn close, but the scenery and the alpine vegetation are magnificent enough to lure **bushwalkers**. There's a 12.5-kilometre track from *Carr Villa*, on the slopes of Ben Lomond, to Legges Tor. Alternatively, from the Alpine Village you can walk over alpine boulderfields to Little Hell, a name handed down by pioneer climbers that does no justice to the view to the dolerite columns of Stacks Bluff. Pick up Tasmap's walking and skiing map of the plateau ($4) from outdoors shops in Launceston. Bear in mind that the temperature on the mountain is around 15°C lower than that at ground level, and can hit minus 10°C in winter. Bush **camping** is permitted anywhere in the national park, but *Carr Villa* is an informal camping area with a pit toilet. For more information, contact the ranger (℡03/6230 8233).

Tasmanian Expeditions (see p.224; $110 per half-day, $220 per day) leads day-walks that include transfers from Launceston. An exhilarating way to experience the mountain and also surrounding forests is on a (mostly) downhill ride with Mountain Bike Tasmania (see p.224; $150; 5–6hr; includes transfers from Launceston and lunch). From the summit, you hairpin down Jacobs Ladder – a test of nerves when your backwheel skids – then take to forest trails. Highly recommended. It's a considerably easier ride than the King of the Mountains uphill race that closes the summit road on the first weekend in April (or last in March). The record is an impressive 1hr 15min, averaging 28kmph.

East of Launceston

You're in rugged dairy and forestry country east of Launceston. There's also the odd patch of lush green rainforest and a coastline of dazzling white beaches and turquoise sea. What unites the richly textured region, though, is a lack of tourism, as this is one of the most overlooked corners of Tasmania. You could idle in beachside bushcamps for a week without seeing another visitor. Even amiable Bridport is a small fry resort compared to those on the east coast. The interior, meanwhile, is almost deserted. For around fifty years from the late 1800s, hills north of the Tasman Highway around the Blue Tier mountain plateau witnessed frenzied activity as roadside villages boomed into tin-mining centres for a transient population of thousands. Around 1200 Chinese miners, most hailing from Guangdong province, were exploited as cheap labour; the tourist board promotes their legacy as The Trail of the Tin Dragon (ⓦwww.trailofthetindragon .com). With the Great Depression, the large mines that fed the local economy closed, miners drifted away, and the roaring mine settlements became **ghost towns** left to a few die-hard tin-scratchers. Now even they have gone.

The Tasman Highway is the quick road to the sights, though arty **Lilydale** and a tree-top ride in Hollybank Forest are good reasons to slow down. From area hub **Scottsdale**, there's mining heritage in **Derby** and on forest walks around ghost town **Lottah**. Nearby dairy village **Pyengana**, with its beer-swilling pigs, has its own forest trails to waterfalls. A second road from Scottsdale loops up to **Bridport**, home to Australia's premier public golf course, then to **Mount William National Park**, with some of the most astounding beaches in Tasmania and mobs of Forester kangaroo loping in the bush at dusk.

Public transport throughout is minimal: Redline runs services along the B81 to Winnaleah, via Scottsdale and Derby on weekdays and Sunday; Stan's Coaches links from Scottsdale to Bridport.

East to Scottsdale

The only excitement you'll have on the Tasman Highway (A3) from Launceston to Scottsdale is when dodging logging trucks loaded up from the state forests. You're far better off taking the B81 instead. South of the road after 13km, the **Hollybank Forest** (daily summer 7am–9pm, until 7pm winter) is a popular picnicking area in managed plantation forest; colonial settlers planted its stands of ash as a ready supply of wood for their cricket bats. Forestry Tasmania has mapped out a few walks to push its sustainable forestry message. More thrilling is the latest realization of its forest playgrounds concept, the **Hollybank Treetops Adventure** (daily summer 9am–6pm, winter 10am–5pm, last tour three hours before closing; $99; ☎03/6395 1390, ⓦwww.treetopsadventure.com.au; bookings essential). Opened in 2008 and said to be unique in Australia, it whizzes visitors through the forest canopy on a series of cable-runs that are 30m above ground and up to 370m long – the world's longest unbroken treetop ride.

Further along the B81, **LILYDALE** just about warrants its title of "town" in a settlement with understated charm. Despite some late-Victorian buildings on the sleepy high street – barn-like Bardenhagen's General Store (1888) is listed by the National Trust and bakes good bread – Lilydale sells itself through the **murals** painted on its telegraph poles, a reflection of a sizeable artistic community whose work is showcased in a few galleries on the main street. This aside, there's little to keep you from heading a few kilometres north to pretty **Lilydale Falls** (20min return walk) reached from a picnic ground. This is also a tranquil spot to camp ($6; ☎03/6395 1156); pay and collect the key for the shower and laundry block ($50 deposit) from the newsagent on the main street opposite the garage. For rooms, there are basic motel-style units at *Lilydale Tavern* (☎03/6395 1230; ❸) or, for considerably more comfort, *Plovers Ridge Country Retreat* (☎03/6395 1102, ⓕ03/6395 1107; ❺), west of the centre on Lalla Road (towards Providence Vineyard), has two tranquil lodges with valley views. Each sleeps up to four and the owners provide organic dinners if warned in advance.

▲ Beer-drinking pig, Pyengana

Past Lebrina, where the north-going B81 finally swings east, you can divert north to the acclaimed vineyards of **Pipers Brook** (see p.237), arguably the finest in Tasmania, or press on towards Scottsdale. Halfway along the twenty-kilometre leg is **Bridestowe Lavender Farm** (daily Oct–Apr 9am–5pm, Mon–Fri Sept & May–Aug 10am–4pm; free except Dec–Jan $5, includes tour every half-hour). Established in 1922, the hillside estate is crossed with contour lines of lavender bush, smudged with purple by late November and then bursting into colour in December through to harvest in late January; a tranquil spot whatever time of year. The accompanying shop sells all things lavender – the isolated location means Bridestowe lavender is world-renowned for its purity – while a café produces light lunches and (what else?) lavender ice cream.

Scottsdale

It's hard to get worked up about **SCOTTSDALE**. If its name is nothing more exciting than a dedication to a government surveyor, James Scott, who mapped the area in the 1850s, its raison d'etre is to service the forestry and farming industries that surround it. These may explain why Scottsdale has a no-nonsense, utilitarian air, and the best that can be said of main drag King Street is that it has all the banks and supermarkets you'd expect of the northeast's administrative capital. There's also the **Scottsdale Forest EcoCentre** on the outskirts of town at 88 King St (daily summer 9am–5pm, winter Mon–Fri 9.30am–4.30pm, Sat–Sun 10am–3pm; free), yet another PR exercise by Forestry Tasmania. This self-regulating, energy-smart building is nicknamed "The Stump" for the tree stump it is supposed to resemble. An eco-walk inside the circular building provides historical and ecological context to the local forestry industry, and there's a pleasant café and a **visitor information centre** (same times; ☎03/6352 6518) stuffed with print-outs for walks in the region. The **Online Access Centre** is in the library at 51 King St (Mon–Tues 2–5pm, Wed–Fri 10am–5pm).

Not the most appealing place **to stay**, Scottsdale is nevertheless handy for both coast and country. Pick of the bunch is the graceful Victorian-era B&B *Beulah of Scottsdale*, at 9 King St (☎03/ 6352 3723, ⓦwww.beulaheritage.com; ❺). Its attic bedrooms have mountain views and goose-down duvets, and there's a guest lounge and dining room. *Lords Hotel* opposite (☎03/6352 2319, ⓕ03/6352 2190; ❷) is a good cheapie, though can be noisy at the front, while there are flowery one- and two-bed motel-style units at *Anabel's*, at 46 King St (☎03/6352 3277, ⓔseandreablake@hotmail.com; ❺), a colonial property set in mature rhododendron gardens. You can **camp** for free (water; toilets; cold showers) on a small site at North East Park beside the Tasman Highway, 1km west of the high street. Non-guests can book into the à la carte **restaurant** at *Anabel's* (dinner Tues–Sat), the smartest in town. Otherwise, *Steak Out* in the town centre has a wide-ranging menu of unpretentious fillers, and award-winning pies and bread are on offer in *Cottage Bakery* (Mon–Fri 9am–5pm, Sat until 2pm), a local institution on Victoria Street off the far end of the high street.

Derby to Weldborough

DERBY (pronounced as in the American "*Dur*-by") is pinning its hopes on tourism to arrest the slow decline since its tin mine closed in 1952. There's still a hint of the rough-and-ready mining town about it, even if the weatherboard houses strung along the Ringarooma River no longer cover the hillside. The discovery of tin in 1876 transformed the town into a thriving frontier settlement of three thousand people, but the mine was temporarily closed in 1929 after heavy rain caused a dam to collapse. Fourteen people died as a 33-metre wall of water surged into the valley; contemporary accounts report houses being lifted from their foundations and swirled downstream while smoke billowed from their chimneys. The second hit was the economic slump of the 1930s that effectively killed the mine as soon as it had reopened in 1934. The population today is around 170. In an attempt to arrest the decline, the **Derby Tin Mine Centre** (daily 10am–5pm; $4.50; ☏/03 6354 2262) is scheduled to shift to new premises full of whizz-bang gadgetry. The future of the current centre adjacent is uncertain, though it is expected to retain a **local history museum** that contains an interesting display of Chinese artefacts, and, hopefully, an enjoyable recreation of the frontier shanty town lined by cottages and shops. Worth a look beside the museum is the restored **National Bank of Tasmania**, dating from 1888. At the east end of town by the bridge, a track cuts up to the site of the fateful **Cascade Dam**, where there's a view over the town but little else.

Accommodation is thin on the ground in Derby: the best option is self-contained cottage *Adelines* (☏03/6354 1066; ❺) on the corner of Main and Christopher streets near the *Painted Door* café. There's better accommodation at Branxholm 5km west, either in the good-value rooms of the characterful old *Imperial Hotel* (☏03/6354 6121; ❷) in the village centre, which also serves good meals daily, or cottagey *Cloverlea B&B* at its west edge (Legerwood Lane; ☏03/6354 6370; ❹). You can **camp** for free at the riverside picnic ground in Derby (toilets; barbecue) or pay for the luxury of a hot shower ($4.30) at Branxholm's Centenary Park (☏03/6354 6168; campsites $11); the site keys are held at the supermarket, which also has the nearest ATM. No surprise that the Michelin gourmet have bypassed Derby again: *Painted Door Art Café* (daily 9am–5pm) is your best bet for daily **lunches** and fresh quiche.

Derby's day on the airwaves comes on the last weekend in October for the **Derby River Derby** town fete. As well as woodchopping and gumboot-hurling competitions, there's the Duck Race on Saturday that brings good-natured mayhem onto the river on anything that floats.

If you're driving, it's worth a side-trip to the little logging village of **LEGERWOOD**, 7km west of Branxholm. A line of trees in the centre have been chainsaw-carved into memorials for seven villagers who fell in World War I; the trees were planted in 1918. It's a very Tasmanian tribute – slightly naïve, dignified and awkwardly moving. You could continue southeast from here to Ringarooma then on to Ralphs Falls and St Columba Falls. Otherwise, going east of Derby on the A3, you zip quickly through **MOORINA**, once the distribution centre for the Blue Tier region, now a ghost town. Its cemetery contains a few Chinese headstones plus a cone-shaped oven in which Chinese miners burned paper to honour their dead. The centre of the former Chinese mining community, **WELDBOROUGH**, is now little more than the *Weldborough Hotel* (☏03/6354 2223; ❷). During the glory years of the late 1800s, the pub held the first casino in the state – its gamblers playing mahjong rather than roulette – and a Chinese temple that is now in the Queen Victoria Museum in Launceston. You can get a cheap **meal** (Mon–Sat) and a basic **room** (with shared bath) for the night, thankfully no longer three to a bunk as was routine for Chinese miners. There's also free camping if you buy dinner. It's worth taking the twenty-minute **Weldborough Pass Rainforest Walk** east of the pub; a boardwalked path goes through predominantly myrtle forest, interspersed with man ferns and occasional tall blackwoods. A little further out of town, the **Weldborough Pass** (595m) is probably the most beautiful part of the drive east, with views across the valleys to the sea. A short way on, Roadside Little Plains Lookout provides another vantage point before the road descends; the adjacent rough track winds up eventually in Lottah (see below), though it's a teeth-jarring drive that should be taken slowly in a 2WD.

Pyengana and St Columba Falls

The road from the pass winds down into the dairy valleys of the George rivers. The first turn south is the C428 for **PYENGANA** (1km) and **St Columba Falls** (a further 4km). Its rich pasture – the aboriginal word *pyengana* means "earth" – is behind the award-winning Cheddar-style produce of the **Pyengana Cheese Factory** (daily 9am–5pm; free), where you can watch cheese being made (except Fri & Sat) and buy all the ingredients for a picnic at the falls. The site's *Holy Cow Café* (same times) rustles up hearty country dishes. Further along, the one-storey *St Columba Falls Hotel* (☎03/6373 6121, @pubinthepaddock @bigpond.com) – aka the "Pub in the Paddock" – is a real country local with old photos on the wall and a handful of characters propping up the bar. It dates from 1880 and in years past hosted Saturday night dances and cinema in its barn, once the pigs had been chased out from beneath the floorboards. Nowadays it serves huge steaks (from $18.50), and has cute tidy rooms with rural views (❸), though it's as famous for the resident beer-drinking pigs. You can buy "special pig beer" from the bar and then go out and give the swine their swill – a classic Tassie photo opportunity if ever there was one.

The rolling pasture beyond ends at the cool, temperate rainforest of the **Columba Falls State Reserve**. From a lay-by there's an easy walk (20min return) to a viewing platform at the base of **St Columba Falls**, passing through a mossy forest of man ferns canopied by sassafras and myrtle. At 90m, the falls are among the highest in Tasmania and pour with tremendous force over the cliffs – truly thunderous in winter. You could continue west of the falls on a winding, unsealed road through **Mount Victoria Forest Reserve**, where the longest single-drop waterfall in Australia, **Ralphs Falls**, plumes down fluted cliffs. It's another easy walk (20min return) from the car park to a lookout at the top of the falls, this time through a stand of myrtle forest. **Cash's Gorge Walk** (1hr return) continues from the falls through teatree bush and tall melaluca before it circuits back to the car park.

The volume of tourist traffic to the area may increase with the completion of a wilderness retreat, *Thylacine Lodge*, in the forest northeast of St Columba Falls. Stage one should see self-contained luxury units in place by early 2009; ask tourist information in St Helens or Launceston for details. Incidentally, most sightings of the (probably) extinct thylacine (Tasmanian tiger) are reported in the northeast forests. Keep your eyes peeled.

The Blue Tier

East of the Pyengana turning on the Tasman Highway, a road ascends northwest to **Goulds Country**, where a line of dilapidated wooden buildings pass for what was once a pioneer mining town in the foothills of the Blue Tier. The unsealed road continues uphill to another ghost town, **LOTTAH**, lost among beautiful old-growth forest at the heart of the Blue Tier. "Hands Off The Blue Tier" notices highlight the fierce campaign that is being waged by locals to prevent logging of one of the few old-growth forests left in the northeast. Information on the campaign (Ⓦwww.bluetier.org) and walks in the area are posted in a small caravan at the centre – ask at the adjacent house if it's locked. You can **camp** in the centre of Lottah on a picnic ground (no facilities), actually the old mining town's cricket pitch. From Lottah, you could return to the Tasman Highway by turning left onto two routes. Anchor Road passes remains of the

Anchor Stamp Battery that crushed tin ore, powered by the largest waterwheel in the southern hemisphere, before it emerges west of the Pyengana turning. Or you can take Lottah Road on a bone-shattering drive towards Weldborough Pass (see p.242); turn left at a quarry to locate a short trail into an ancient stand of sassafras and man ferns.

Continue northwest from Lottah, however, and you ascend on a steep, unsealed road to **Poimena**, formerly the principal settlement on the Blue Tier. Although the buildings have long since collapsed into the bush, there's some superb walking on the old pack-trails. From a base camp at the car park (pit toilet; fireplaces), you could spend at least two days on little-trod routes marked by coloured posts. The easiest is boardwalked **Goblin Forest Walk** (20min; wheelchair accessible), lined by interpretive boards that help you to imagine the mining town here. Another short walk (30min return) heads to the 810-metre summit of the Blue Tier, **Mount Poimena**, for views right across the northeast to the coast, or you can loop around Australia Hill (2hr), in places still littered with rusting mine machinery. It's worth driving to a second car park further along from Poimena, to take the **Mount Michael Track** into a magical stand of old-growth myrtle trees. St Helens History Room (see p.200) has details on all Blue Tier walks. Better still are the trips run by Leslie Nicklason as Pyengana-based Break O'Day Adventure Tours (T03/6373 6195, Ejnicklason@hotmail.com) – a passionate eco-campaigner in the region, she provides excellent, not-for-profit bushwalks lasting from one hour to seven days.

Bridport

Twenty-one kilometres northwest of Scottsdale, you hit the coast at the fishing town and holiday spot of **BRIDPORT**. It's an amiable small resort on Anderson Bay, which only emerged in the 1920s after the Scottsdale Progress & Tourist Association wooed Launceston city-dwellers with sports days and sandcastle competitions. What keeps them coming today are the **beaches**: from pretty notches of sand between smooth granite boulders to long empty strands, with good swimming and fishing on most. You can take your pick of beach on a two-kilometre foreshore path that begins where the Bird River flows into the sea east of the centre. None is more idyllic than **Mermaid's Pool** at the path's west end. A coast road goes a further 2km west to a **wildflower reserve**, from where you can take trails through scrub and sheoak forest to the main road (50min) – wild orchids flower in spring. Alternatively, a scramble along the granite foreshore west of the car park leads to long Adams Beach.

Strung behind a crescent of beach 2km east of Bridport, **Barnbougle Dunes golf course** (T03/6356 0094, Wwww.barnbougledunes.com; 18 holes $98, 9 holes $60; club rental $30) is a true bump-and-run, links course where fairways meander between the sand dunes. Aficionados rank it the best public-access course in Australia. A smart clubhouse restaurant (lunch & dinner daily; reservations recommended at weekends) prepares classy seasonal cuisine such as wallaby in red wine sauce.

Practicalities

Stan's **Coaches** (T03/6356 1662) runs twice a day between Bridport and Scottsdale. A volunteer-run **visitor information centre** (daily 10am–4pm; T03/6356 1881) is in a central pavilion in front of the **Online Access Centre** (Mon & Fri 10am–noon & 1–4pm, Tues & Sat 10am–noon, Wed 1–4pm). **Camping** is beachside, at *Bridport Caravan Park* (T03/6356 1227, Ebridportcaravan @bigpond.com; sites $16), which stretches for about a kilometre along Anderson Bay. For **food**, *Bridport Bay's* bar rustles up fish, beef 'n' reef and Italian cuisine in rib-sticking portions. The town's best restaurant is *Joseph's*, at *Bridport Resort* (dinner Tues–Sat; open to non-guests): fish and sea views from a veranda are the reasons to visit. Going 3km south on Bridport Road (B84) brings you to the chirpy *Flying Teapot Garden Café* (summer Wed–Sun 9am–4pm; ℡03/6356 1918) on Manalanga cattle farm. Its garden café beside the owner's private airfield is a pleasant spot for lunch.

Accommodation

The most central accommodation is at *Bridport Bay Inn* (℡03/6358 1238, ⓦwww.bridportbayinn.com.au), either in motel-style rooms or units (both ❹) – the latter are worth the extra $10 – and more modern "cottages" fronted by a deck (❺). Heading east along Main Street, at no. 47 there's the modern *Bridport Seaside Lodge YHA Backpackers* (℡03/6356 1585, Ⓔbridportseasidelodge @hotmail.com; dorms $24, rooms ❷–❸), whose sunny lounge looks over the river estuary, and the smart *Bridport Resort* at 35 Main St (℡03/6356 1789, ⓦwww.bridport-resort.com.au; ❺), with spacious open-plan chalets and four-star facilities. The most tranquil address in Bridport is the eco-friendly *Platypus Park Country Retreat* (℡03/6356 1873, ⓦwww.platypuspark.com.au; ❹–❻), a kilometre out of town near the George Town road T-junction; bright, homely cottages and units sleep up to six and have verandas that look out over forty-odd acres of bush teeming with wildlife.

East to Gladstone

By Tassie standards, the drive east of Bridport is one of monumental boredom. The road runs ruler-straight east, with only the ghost village of **Waterhouse** after 20km to break up the flat sandy pasture. It's not much more than a couple of farmsteads and shows no sign of a goldrush in 1869 that introduced four hotels and a police station. A dirt road, Homestead Road, heads north to reach a series of remote bushcamps behind empty beach. *Waterhouse Point Camping Area* (free; no facilities) on the point's east face is the pick of the bunch. Forty kilometres from Bridport, **TOMAHAWK** straggles behind another stretch of sandy nothingness that curves away into the far distance. The low-key resort – a supply port for Waterhouse during the goldrush, now "Tasmania's Best-Kept Secret", apparently – has a caravan park (℡03/6355 2268; camping $18; cabins & vans ❸) with fuel and a general store, and that's about it.

After the Tomahawk turn-off, a good dirt road allows a quick blast to **GLADSTONE**, a town that's been in terminal decline since its tin mine closed. A combined service station and general store with EFTPOS facilities sells the last supplies before the Mount William National Park (see p.246) as well as park passes. Ask here about a bed at the *Mount William Holiday Park* opposite (℡03/6357 2182; campsites $10; dorms $20; rooms ❷–❸; self-contained unit ❹) or you can find a room at the *Gladstone Hotel* (℡03/6357 2143, Ⓔgladstone.hotel@bigpond.com; ❸), also your only option for a meal (daily except Sun). Across the Ringarooma River, east, the road forks. A left will take you on a lonely unsealed road north via Rushy Lagoon. Just under 19km north, an iffy track left goes to a superb bushcamp at Petal Point (free; pit toilet) sheltered behind a sparkling white beach, or you can keep going north to a second, wombat-infested campsite on the headland. Go right just beyond the Petal Point turn and end up at **Cape Portland**. It's another gloriously remote spot: just a cemetery of long-forgotten settlers lost somewhere in the bush behind a lagoon and the white powder sands of Little Musselroe Bay. If you visit, be aware that the ecology of the area is extremely fragile.

Mount William National Park

With its epic sweeps of dazzling beach, pretty bushcamps, Aboriginal heritage and diverse wildlife, **MOUNT WILLIAM NATIONAL PARK** is not nearly as well-known as it deserves to be. Its white quartzite sands lapped by shimmering turquoise waters represent the northern extremity of the acclaimed Bay of Fires (see p.204), and its heath supports mobs of Forester kangaroo. It was the decline in animal numbers as habitats were cleared for farming that provided the impetus for the establishment of the park in 1973. In the last couple of decades, however, it has been acknowledged for its value to Aboriginal communities. Essentially a single huge midden, Eddystone Point, or *Larapuna* as it is known to the Palawa pukana people, has been subject to an aboriginal land rights campaign since 1999 – campaigners are dug in for the long haul to reclaim its sixty acres from the state – and the point also hosts a community gathering in late January or early February.

Entry to the park is from Gladstone, where you can buy national park passes and pick up last-minute basic supplies. The road forks after 10km, with the left-hand branch, unsealed Musselroe Road, tracking into the park via a rangers' office where there's an information board. Your best chance of spotting **kangaroo** is on the Forester Kangaroo Drive, a couple of kilometres beyond the ranger station. This loops off Musselroe Road and into the open pasture where the animals graze at dawn and dusk. After 5km a side-track heads south for the walk up **Mount William** (1–1.5hr return; 216m), an easy climb to the park's highest point that provides a sweeping coastal panorama that extends from Ben Lomond in the south to Flinders Island, north. A second turn on the drive leads east to **campsites** at Stumpys Bay (see opposite) and also a track (1.5–2hr return) to Cobler Rocks; a good spot to see coastal birdlife such as

▲ Kangaroos at Mount William National Park

gannets and terns plus the occasional white-bellied sea eagle or albatross. Musselroe Road finally rolls to a halt at **Musselroe Bay**, a remote shackies' village with a few camp-pitches beside a lagoon. The scrub just north has been proposed for an ultra-modern eco-retreat development, *Mussel Roe* (ⓦwww .musselroe.com); completion is scheduled for mid-2009. Other plans for the area include a wind farm submitted by Roaring 40s, the company behind the plant at Cape Grim on the northwest tip.

Take the right-hand fork east of Gladstone and you arrive, eventually, at **Ansons Bay**. Tracking around its southern side takes you to the remote bushcamp (free; no facilities) of Policemans Point in the middle section of the Bay of Fires. A left-turn before Ansons Bay takes you to **Eddystone Lighthouse** – built in 1889 from pink granite quarried from the foreshore – and three stone cottages from which the light-keepers maintained their 24-hour vigil on the point. Superb beaches lie on either side. Off the road before the car park, a track leads south through the dunes to an exhilarating sweep of powdery quartzite sand that can pick up good surf.

North of the point is one staggeringly beautiful bay after another. Harbour-like Gulch, north of the lighthouse, or sheltered Larc Beach by the bay offer safe swimming, while off the road to the Deep Creek campsite is **Picnic Rock Beach**, a picture-postcard vision of white sand and turquoise sea between sculptural granite boulders. If water levels are low, you could ford the stream at the Deep Creek site to reach yet another empty crescent of beach on Purdon Bay.

Free **camping** is available beside the lagoon at Musselroe Bay or at Policemans Point, south of Ansons Bay, both of which are outside the park area. Neither have facilities. Sites within the national park (standard fees apply) are located behind a beach just south of Musselroe Bay at Top Camp and Stumpys Bay, where there are four sites, and at Deep Creek north of Eddystone Point. Each site has pit toilets. Non-potable bore water for washing is at Deep Creek and Stumpys campgrounds 1 and 3, and Stumpys 4 has a picnic area with free gas barbecues. As ever, take out any rubbish you bring in. Stumpys 2 is fuel-stove only, but most sites permit small campfires in designated fireplaces (firewood available at Gladstone), conditions permitting.

Travel details

Flights

Launceston to: Melbourne (10 daily; 1hr); Sydney (4 daily; 1hr 35min).

Coaches

Beaconsfield to: Beauty Point (Mon–Fri 5 daily; 10min); Launceston (Mon–Fri 5 daily; 45min); Rosevears (Mon–Fri 1 daily or 4 daily with booking; 25min).
Beauty Point to: Beaconsfield (Mon–Fri 5 daily; 5min); Launceston (Mon–Fri 5 daily; 1hr); Rosevears (Mon–Fri 1 daily or 4 daily with booking; 30min).
Bridport to: Scottsdale (2 daily; 45min).

Derby to: Launceston (Mon–Fri 5 daily; 2hr 35min); Scottsdale (Mon–Fri 5 daily, Sun 1 daily; 1hr 5min).
George Town to: Launceston (Mon–Fri 3 daily; 50min).
Launceston to: Beaconsfield (Mon–Fri 5 daily; 50min); Beauty Point (Mon–Fri 5 daily; 1hr); Bicheno (Mon–Fri & Sun 1 daily; 2hr 40min); Burnie (Mon–Thurs 3 daily, Fri 4 daily, Sat–Sun 2 daily; 2hr–2hr 30min); Coles Bay turn off (Mon–Fri & Sun 1 daily; 2hr 30min); Cradle Mountain (Tues, Thurs & Sat 1 daily; 3hr); Deloraine (Mon–Fri 5 daily, 40–50min); Devonport (Mon–Fri 4 daily, Sat–Sun 2 daily; 1hr–1hr 30min); Derby (Mon–Fri 5 daily, Sun 1 daily; 2hr 35min); Evandale (Thurs 1 daily; 15min); George Town

(Mon–Fri 3 daily; 50min); Hobart (Mon–Thurs 4 daily, Fri 5 daily, Sat–Sun 3 daily; 2hr 30min); Longford (Mon–Fri 4 daily; 30min); Mole Creek (Mon–Fri 2 daily; 1hr 25min); St Marys (Mon–Fri & Sun, 1 daily; 1hr 45min); Rosevears (Mon–Fri 3 daily or 5 with booking; 25min); St Helens (Mon–Fri & Sun, 1 daily; 2hr 30min); Scottsdale (Mon–Fri 2 daily, Sun 1 daily; 1hr 10min); Sheffield (Tues, Thurs & Sat 1 daily; 2hr); Queenstown (Tues, Thurs & Sat 1 daily; 6hr 50min); Strahan (Tues, Thurs & Sat 1 daily; 8hr; 45min).

Scottsdale to: Bridport (2 daily; 45min); Launceston (Mon–Fri 2 daily, Sun 1 daily; 1hr 10min); Derby (Mon–Fri 5 daily, Sun 1 daily; 1hr 5min).

Ferries

Beauty Point to: George Town (Nov–Apr, Wed–Mon 3 daily; 30min).
Bridport to: Cape Barren Island (Mon 1 daily; 7hr); Lady Barron (Mon 1 daily; 8hr).
George Town to: Beauty Point (Nov–Apr, Wed–Mon 3 daily; 30min).

THE NORTHEAST | Travel details

The Northwest

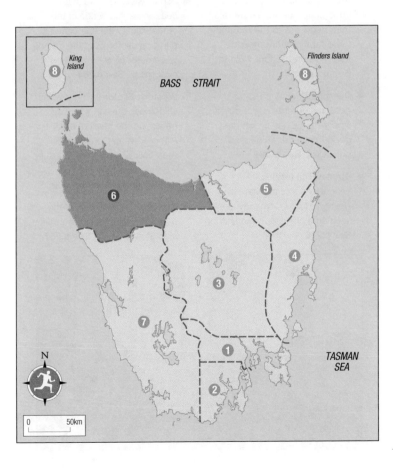

CHAPTER 6

Highlights

✳ **Narawntapu National Park** This coastal wildlife wonderland, described as the "Serengeti of Tasmania", also has great camping and beach walks. See p.261

✳ **Sheffield** Wander around a streetscape of scenic murals then head out to the real thing – the fabulous countryside south around Mount Roland. See p.262

✳ **Penguin** Pristine beaches, good restaurants and a quirky vibe – Penguin is proof that good things come in small packages. See p.268

✳ **Stanley** The historic headquarters of the Van Diemen's Land Company, best seen on a chairlift up the Nut. See p.276

✳ **Devil-watching in Marrawah** Hunker down in a hut at dusk to wait for the banshee wail of a Tasmanian Devil outside – an unforgettable Tasmanian experience. See p.284

✳ **Arthur River** The untamed coastline at the "Edge of the World" meets the untouched primeval rainforest of the Tarkine wilderness, all accessible via a river cruise. See p.284

✳ **Western Explorer** The greatest wilderness drive in the state, traversing the heart of the Arthur Pieman Conservation Area, following rugged coastline – dotted with remnants of Aboriginal heritage. See p.286

✳ **Corinna** The antithesis of the packaged wilderness resort with a great river cruise. See p.287

▲ Mural, Sheffield

6

The northwest

The Bass Strait coastline is densely populated by local standards, with the three largest urban centres outside Hobart and Launceston, and a profusion of villages in their hinterland. This stands in marked contrast to the **far northwest**: flailed by heaving Southern Ocean swells that have rolled unopposed from South America, its tortured west coast is strewn with huge washed-up tree trunks. Inland are rainforests that indicate a direct link to the primeval forest that once covered the Earth, providing beleaguered native species such as the Tasmanian Devil with a refuge. Some conservationists even speculate that the extinct Tasmanian tiger may rove deep within the wilderness. Just in case you were in any doubt as to the area's remoteness, there's a sign at Arthur River to confirm where you are – "End of the World".

The isolation suited the Aborigines and the northwest's boundaries include some of the most visible remnants of **indigenous culture** in Tasmania, not least the valuable art sites at Devonport and near Marrawah. British penetration into the bush from the 1820s led to settlements founded on cattle and sheep, or on timber exports; all solid, traditional industries that have helped to foster the northwest's reputation as a bastion of conservative attitudes. **Forestry** is part of the area's psyche, whether as woodchopping, a sport born as a pub bet in Ulverstone, or the logging that horrifies conservationists. Cattle-farming is the other mainstay. Some of the best beef in Tasmania, fed on pasture soused by the purest rain in the world, comes from the northwest. Steak lovers take note.

Tasmania's third-largest city, **Devonport**, serves as little more than a gateway for the Bass Strait ferry, with only its indigenous rock art or passable beaches to delay you. But it's a good launchpad to see wildlife in the **Narawntapu National Park** or **Latrobe**, or to visit the small town of **Sheffield**, which is enjoying a second wind through a streetscape of murals. And the colour-saturated scenery south is so stupendous that pioneer settlers were impelled to give their villages names such as Promised Land and Paradise. The **Bass Highway** which skirts the northwest coast from Devonport bypasses the characterful little beach town of **Penguin**, reached by a back road from Ulverstone, but carves instead through industrial **Burnie**, which is pinning its hope on crafts to revive a waning manufacturing base. It is the last major town on the route west: afterwards there's Wynyard and idyllic Boat Harbour Beach, and then the tiny **Rocky Cape National Park** and pretty **Stanley**, former base of the Van Diemen's Land Company that opened up the area by order of King George IV. From **Smithton** you can dive into the much-disputed logging heartland which nibbles into the Tarkine wilderness, or head southwest towards surfers' paradise **Marrawah**. Beyond is sleepy **Arthur River**, gateway to the

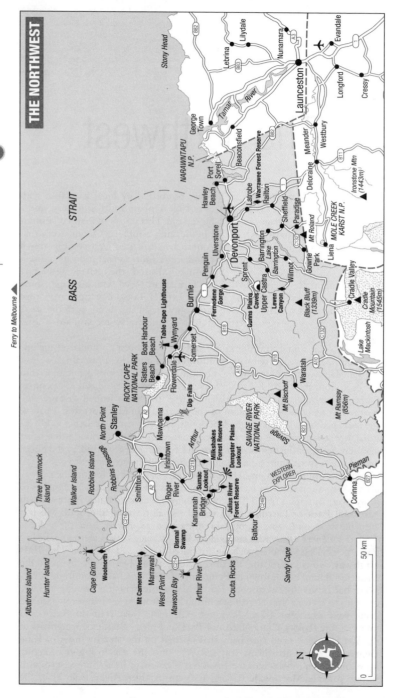

Ferry to Melbourne ▲

BASS STRAIT

50 km

0

N

Tarkine rainforest on a river cruise. The area to the south remains wild: only a couple of vehicles a day take the lonely **Western Explorer** road, but it's a superb trip through the Arthur Pieman Conservation Area, with diversions en route to some dramatic coastline. Civilization of sorts returns at tiny **Corinna**, a historic gold-mining outpost revived as a remote wilderness base.

Travellers never fail to underestimate the distances involved in the northwest. Regular coaches ply the Bass Highway and swing south to Sheffield en route to Cradle Mountain and Queenstown, but to get to the most interesting places your own vehicle is essential, preferably one that's reliable if you want to explore the far west. Remember, too, that the area's temperate rainforest or pasture is lush for a reason – rainfall is heavier in the northwest than in the east.

Devonport

Since the industrial port of **DEVONPORT** replaced Launceston as the terminal of the **Bass Strait ferry** in 1959, it has styled itself as "The Gateway to Tasmania". It's not the most thrilling welcome. As the ship eases up the Mersey River, you could almost be arriving at a 1950s English seaport, were it not for the tin-roofed weatherboard bungalows on the west bank, the brittle quality of the light and the bush-covered hills which peal south. Though the third-largest city in Tasmania, with a scattering of sights such as the only dedicated **Aboriginal museum** in the state, Devonport is hardly a destination in itself. The centre is so small, the residential grid so sprawling, that it's tempting to see it less as a city than a suburb attached to a port. Yet because it is a jumping-off point for Cradle Mountain, the Overland Track and the rugged west coast, Devonport has developed a significant tourism infrastructure, and it makes a good base for trips into the countryside around Sheffield or the Narawntapu National Park. Another trump card is its two excellent **beaches**, just five minutes' walk from the centre.

Arrival, information and transport

The *Spirit of Tasmania* **ferries** from Melbourne (see p.24) dock at the terminal in East Devonport, just across the Mersey River from the city centre. Company representatives and car-rental desks are in the terminal, and you can buy bus passes and tickets here for waiting Redline and Tassielink **express coaches** to Launceston and Hobart. Other coach routes leave from depots in town (see "Coaches", p.258). The *Torquay* ferry shuttles across the river between the port and city centre from a quay 400m north of the ferry terminal by Murray Street (on demand Mon–Sat 7.30am–6pm; $2.50, bikes 50¢). **Devonport Airport** is 10km east of the city. A shuttle bus runs into the city via the ferry terminal ($10; ☎0400 035 995 or 1300 659 878; booking recommended) or you can catch a taxi into Devonport for about $20; again, it's a good idea to pre-book (Taxis Combined ☎03/6424 1431).

The **Tasmanian Travel and Information Centre** (daily 7.30am–5pm and until 9pm when day-sailings arrive; ☎03/6424 4466, ✉ttic@dcc.tas.gov.au) fronts the business district on the west bank at 92 Formby Rd. A one-stop shop for all things Tasmania, it books accommodation, tours and travel (including car rental), sells bus and national park passes, YHA membership, See Tasmania cards, fishing licences, and has a small stock of maps and guides. A better range of maps, bushwalking tips and local knowledge is available at the excellent

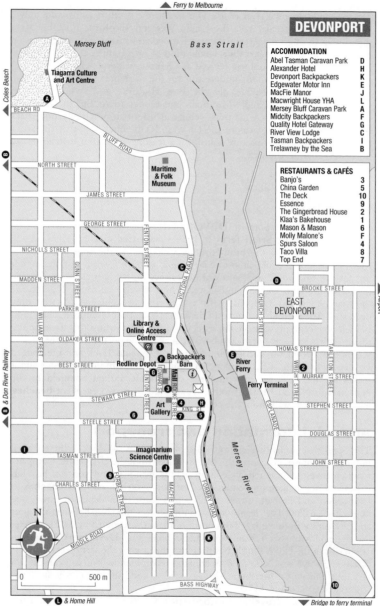

DEVONPORT

ACCOMMODATION

Abel Tasman Caravan Park	D
Alexander Hotel	H
Devonport Backpackers	K
Edgewater Motor Inn	E
MacFie Manor	J
Macwright House YHA	L
Mersey Bluff Caravan Park	A
Midcity Backpackers	F
Quality Hotel Gateway	G
River View Lodge	C
Tasman Backpackers	I
Trelawney by the Sea	B

RESTAURANTS & CAFÉS

Banjo's	3
China Garden	5
The Deck	10
Essence	9
The Gingerbread House	2
Klaa's Bakehouse	1
Mason & Mason	6
Molly Malone's	F
Spurs Saloon	4
Taco Villa	8
Top End	7

Backpackers Barn, at 10–12 Edward St (Mon–Sat 9am–6pm; ☎03/6424 3628, 🕸www.backpackersbarn.com.au), which specializes in planning itineraries, renting and selling equipment for bushwalkers, and booking bushwalking transport charters and tours. The tours, run with the in-house Tasmanian Tour Company (☎1300 659878, 🕸www.tasmaniantourcompany.com.au), visit

Cradle Mountain among other destinations. Backpackers Barn also offers travellers a day-room, showers ($2) and huge lockers ($1 per day, $5 per week) and there's a great organic café, *Rosehip*. A warehouse-sized Allgoods at 6 Formby Rd (☎03/6424 7099; closed Sun) also sells outdoors gear.

The Redline **coach** depot is opposite Backpackers Barn and Tassielink leaves from the tourist information centre. The depot for Merseylink (☎1300 367 590, ⓦwww.merseylink.com.au) local **bus** services is on Rooke Street, just south of the Oldaker Street roundabout. Devonport's **Online Access Centre** (Mon–Fri 9.30am–5.30pm, Sat 9.30am–1.30pm) is at the library nearby at 21 Oldaker St.

Accommodation

Devonport has plenty of accommodation, most of it intended for transient ferry passengers. Hotels, motels and B&Bs take advantage of the summer trade to raise their prices. For self-contained heritage accommodation, *Devonport Historic Cottages* (☎1800 240 031, ⓔ66wenvoe@pocketmail.com.au; ⑤) has three fairly central historic properties on its books.

Abel Tasman Caravan Park 6 Wright St, East Devonport ☎03/6427 8794. Just 800m north of the ferry terminal and 400m from the river ferry, with campsites behind East Devonport Beach. A spacious site, it has indoor and outdoor camp kitchens, a BBQ area, a laundry and a playground. Camping $20, vans ❸, cabins ❹

Alexander Hotel 78 Formby Rd ☎03/6424 2252, ⓦwww.goodstone.com.au. Neat, well-furnished rooms, some with port views, all with shared bathrooms, in a historic pub, though noisy at weekends. TV room, plus tea and coffee room; meals available in a decent bistro. ❸

Devonport Backpackers 16 Formby St ☎0400 656 345, ⓔdevonportbackpackers@ozemail.com. Spacious rooms in a historic late-1800s house that's far better than its drab exterior suggests. Two eight-bed dorms, doubles, and a smart communal lounge. Dorms $18, rooms ❷

Edgewater Motor Inn 4 Thomas St, East Devonport ☎03/6427 8441, ⓦwww.edgewater-devonport .com.au. Modern rooms in a new motel with a decent bistro, plus small older rooms in a courtyard. Both are as convenient as it gets for the ferry terminal. ❹–❻

MacFie Manor 44 MacFie St ☎03/6424 1719 ⓦwww.view.com.au/macfiemanor. Five en-suite rooms in a rambling, two-storey B&B full of early twentieth-century character and with distant views of the water from its wrought-iron balcony. ❹–❺

Macwright House YHA 115 Middle Rd, 3km south ☎03/6424 5696 ⓔinfo@devonfield.com.au. A hostel of the old school: well-maintained though with only one bathroom, and the psychedelic carpets could induce a migraine. Laundry by donation. Roughly 40min walk from the centre,

closest shop 1km; Mersey link Bus stops outside on weekdays. Dorms $18.50, rooms ❶

Mersey Bluff Caravan Park Mersey Bluff ☎03/6424 8655, ⓔmbcp1@bigpond.net.au. The most appealing campsite in Devonport, a little cramped perhaps, and a fifteen-minute walk from the centre, but well-sited for the beaches on either side of Mersey Bluff. Camping $15, vans ❷, two-bed units ❸

Midcity Backpackers Above *Molly Malone's Irish Pub*, 34 Best St ☎03/6424 1898, ⓔmollymalones@vantagegroup.com.au. Convenient backpackers' accommodation, with four-bed dorms and comfortable rooms – some en suite – well away from the noise of the Irish theme-pub downstairs. Good facilities and security. Dorms $16, rooms ❷

Quality Hotel Gateway 16 Fenton St ☎03/6424 4922, ⓦwww.gatewayhoteltazmania.com. Quiet and centrally located, Devonport's best hotel offers views over the port and river mouth. Rooms are spacious and tastefully decorated. Bar, restaurant and room service. Discounts for online reservation. ❺

River View Lodge 18 Victoria Parade ☎03/6424 7357. A reassuringly old-fashioned guesthouse on the waterfront with a convivial atmosphere. Serves generous cooked breakfasts. Some en-suite rooms but most share bathroom; TV in all. ❹

Tasman Backpackers 114 Tasman St ☎03/6423 2335, ⓦwww.tasmanbackpackers.com.au. A well-established large hostel in a former nurse's quarters. Dorms come in five-, seven- and eight-bed varieties, plus there are well-furnished twins and a couple of en-suite doubles. Nightly movies on big-screen TV. Affordable tours available plus work contacts. Fifteen minutes' walk from the city centre, but free pick-ups on request. Dorms $16, rooms ②–③

Trelawney by the Sea 6 Chalmers Lane (off north end of Percy St) ☎03/6424 3263,

ⓔ dickinson.services@bigpond.com. In one of the smartest districts in Devonport, a self-contained two-bed unit that's a bit dated in style but has great sea views plus a deck and spa. ⑤

The City

Central Devonport is bounded by the Mersey to the east and Formby Road, which tracks the wharf. The compact centre is a fairly uninspiring grid centred on Stewart Street, where the only mild thrill is seeing ferries or occasional freighters docked at the end of the street. The **Devonport Art Gallery**, in a converted church at 45 Stewart St (Mon–Sat 10am–5pm, Sun 2–5pm; free; ☎03/6424 8298), has a small permanent collection, predominantly twentieth-century ceramics and woodcraft, and hosts touring exhibitions by largely Tasmanian names.

Devonport is more appealing north of its malls in the neat parkland that fringes the river. There's a picnic spot at the river mouth and just around the corner the **Devonport Maritime and Folk Museum**, at 47 Victoria Parade (Tues–Sun summer 10am–4.30pm, winter until 4pm; $4). It plays up to the maritime heritage with an extensive display of model ships, ranging from sailing vessels to modern passenger ferries. **Mersey Bluff** further west has pretty beaches on either side of the headland. The discovery here of ancient Aboriginal rock carvings (petroglyphs) by a local teacher in 1929 prompted its protection in statute, and, belatedly, the opening of the **Tiagarra Tasmanian Aboriginal Culture and Art Centre** (☎03/6424 8250; daily 9am–5pm; $3.80), in truth the only really compelling place to visit in town. Named after the Aboriginal word for "keep" or "keeping place", the centre has preserved around 270 of the Aboriginal rock engravings which are estimated to be ten thousand years old. Simple circles with small spirals and slashes scored into the rock, they are accessed behind the display centre. The centre itself has a series of dioramas that provide a generalized (and rather rushed) taped background information on the lifestyles of the northwest's original inhabitants. There are good displays of indigenous crafts though.

Continuing west 1km, **Coles Beach** is another pretty crescent of fine sand that's safe for swimming and picks up the occasional wave for surfing. The beach is also an embarkation point for the Don River Railway (20min past the hour 10am–4pm; see opposite). A walking and cycling trail which begins at the rail crossing wanders through teatree forest beside the tracks to reach the museum and terminus 3km south.

Just south of the centre, at 19–23 MacFie St, the **Imaginarium Science Centre** is Tasmania's kiddie-friendly, hands-on science discovery centre (Mon–Thurs 10am–4pm, Sat & Sun noon–5pm; $8; ☎03/6423 1466). Alongside fifty or so modest science displays created in partnership with the National Science and Technology Centre in Canberra, it hosts changing themed exhibitions; nothing special for the PlayStation generation and with a whiff of the school display about it, but enough to amuse younger children. A couple of kilometres south on Middle Road, just over the Bass Highway flyover, whitewashed-timber **Home Hill** (Sept–June Tues–Thurs & Sat–Sun 1.30–4pm; $8; ☎03/6242 8055) was the residence of Joseph Lyons. It was built by the future Australian prime minister (1932–39) a year after his marriage to Enid, the first woman member of the House of Representatives, it remained his residence for all but five years of his life. The political significance of its personal mementos will probably wash over most non-Australians, but the couple's untouched rooms are a fun time-warp back to the 1950s.

The Don River Railway

Beloved by rail enthusiasts for having Tasmania's largest steam engine collection, the **Don River Railway** (hourly 10am–4pm; 30min; $10 return; ☏03/6424 6335, Ⓦwww.donriverrailway.com.au) in the suburb of Don, 4km west of the centre, maintains a working collection of steam and diesel locomotives along a former limestone railway to Coles Beach. Trips run every day (though atmospheric steam journeys are only on "Steam Sundays") and there's a small museum of rail memorabilia to entertain you while you wait to depart. You can also embark at Coles Beach, so long as you buy a ticket at the other end. The adjacent Don Recreation Ground is a pleasant spot for a picnic. If you're driving, either go west on Steele Street and then follow Don Road, or follow signs off the Bass Highway. Continue beyond the junction for a couple of kilometres and the highway hits the coast at **Lillico Beach**, where there's a viewing platform above a Little Penguin rookery; the birds waddle back to their burrows just after dusk between October and April.

Eating, drinking and nightlife

Banjo's Rooke Street Mall. All the usual benefits of the ubiquitous Tassie bakery chain: early opening, cheap fresh-baked products and unlimited tea and coffee. Daily 6am–6pm.

China Garden 33 King St ☏03/6424 4148. Popular Cantonese restaurant with $9 lunch specials and all-you-can-eat buffets. Licensed & BYO. Lunch & dinner daily.

The Deck Café Restaurant 188–190 Tarleton St, East Devonport ☏03/6427 7188. Devonport's city-style waterfront hangout: you can relax on sofas with a coffee and cake or have a beer outside – shame about the Bass Highway adjacent, mind. By day, there's sushi, pasta and risotto ($12.50–18.50), pizzas and gourmet sandwiches ($8.50). Lunch until 5pm, after which there's a pricier dinner menu; from a Tasmanian seafood plate ($32) to prime sirloin steaks. Fully licensed bar. Lunch & dinner daily.

🏃 **Essence** 28 Forbes St ☏03/6424 6431. This old charming house offers the best of Tasmanian produce – traditional European stand-bys of venison, lamb, beef, trout, turkey and duck – with a contemporary edge. The crisp-skinned confit of duck is always popular. Mains around $24. If you prefer you can just come in for a drink in the *Lounge Bar*, where several Tasmanian wines are available by the glass. Lunch Tues–Fri, dinner Tues–Sat.

The Gingerbread House Corner of Wright and Murray streets, East Devonport. A characteristically quirky first (or last) stop in Tasmania, this serves tasty international tucker (mains average $20) just above the ferry terminal. Lunch & dinner Wed–Sun.

Klaa's Bakehouse 11 Oldaker St. The best pies and sausage rolls in town, plus French and German bakery specialities. Mon–Fri 9am–5pm.

Mason & Mason 38 Steele St. Located in a modern interiors shop, this popular place has rich coffee, healthy light lunches and filling gateaux. Mon–Sat 9am–5pm, Sat 9am–2pm.

Molly Malone's Irish Pub 34 Best St. Characterful and extensive Irish theme-pub with a great bistro. Lots of meaty pub favourites – including a roast of the day for $10 – and fish as well as vegetarian choices.

Spurs Saloon 18 King St ☏03/6424 7851. A popular Western-themed bar that gets rowdy at weekends. Commercial dance music is pumped out in the attached *Warehouse Niteclub*, also a venue for touring bands. Wed–Sun 5pm–late.

Taco Villa Kempling St. Enchiladas and tortillas are on the menu in this modest Mexican place. BYO. Dinner Wed–Sun.

Top End 12 Rooke St. This light contemporary café has comfy sofas, magazines, a big spread of healthy food and a fresh juice bar. Good coffee, pots of tea including chai, and yummy cakes. Vegetarian choices include curry samosas served with salad for $7.50. Licensed. Mon–Sat 7am–6pm.

Listings

Bookshop Angus & Robertson, 43 Rooke St ☏03/6424 2022.

Bike rental Derrico (☏03/6424 3121), behind the Mobil service station at the corner of William and Oldaker streets.

The Tasmanian Trail

The **Tasmanian Trail** is a 480-kilometre multipurpose recreational trail extending from Devonport on the north coast to Dover on the south coast. Created by connecting forestry roads, fire trails and country roads (often going through small historic towns) and at times traversing private land, it's primarily used for mountain-biking and horse-riding. For more details, visit Ⓦwww.tasmaniantrail.com.au or Ⓦwww.parks.tas.gov.au/recreation/tastrail.html. Alternatively, the *Tasmanian Trail Guidebook* is available from tourist offices and bookshops for $25.

Coaches Redline and Tassielink both have ticket desks at the ferry terminal. Redline's depot is at 9 Edward St (Ⓣ1300 360 000; left luggage $1 per item); Tassielink (Ⓣ1300 300 520) services leave from the tourist office at 92 Formby Rd. Backpackers Barn (see p.254) is the booking office and collection point for Tasmanian Tour Companies' on-demand bushwalking charter service to Cradle Mountain, Frenchmans Cap and Walls of Jerusalem. The similar Maxwells charter service is based in nearby Wilmot (Ⓣ03/6492 1431).

Car rental Firms located at the airport and ferry terminal include Autorent-Hertz (Ⓣ03/6424 1013), Avis Tasmania (Ⓣ03/6427 9797) and Budget (Ⓣ03/6427 0650). Cheaper alternatives are Lo-Cost Auto Rent (Ⓣ03/6424 9922, Ⓦwww.locostautorent.com) and VW beetle specialist Rent-A-Bug (Ⓣ03/6427 9304,

Ⓦwww.rentabug.com.au), both on Murray St by the ferry terminal, East Devonport.

Cinema CMAX Cinemas, 5–7 Best St (Ⓣ03/6240 2111, Ⓦwww.cmax.net.au), is a four-screen cinema complex showing blockbusters. Discounts on Tues.

Diving, canoeing and kite-surfing Canoe 'n' Surf (141 William St; Ⓣ03/6424 4314) leads diving and canoeing courses in summer, plus occasional kite-surfing lessons.

Post office Corner of Stewart St and Formby Rd, TAS 7310.

Swimming The shallow beaches at Mersey Bluff offer safe swimming. The outdoor multi-pool Devonport Aquatic Centre (daily Nov–March times vary, generally 8am until dusk; $4; Ⓣ03/6424 9029) is in the Don Reserve at the west end of Steele St.

Taxi Taxis Combined Ⓣ03/6424 1431.

Around Devonport

You don't have to travel far to leave the city behind. Within the environs of Devonport are a scattering of minor tourist destinations beloved by Tasmanians for weekend day-trips. Only **Narawntapu National Park** rewards a special effort to get to, due to its abundant wildlife and effortlessly wild beaches. But if you want to spot a platypus in the wild, **Latrobe** is one of the best bets in Tasmania.

Latrobe

No other town in Tasmania trades on platypus like **LATROBE**, 5km south of Devonport. Thanks to a large local platypus population, there are images of platypus on hoardings and sculptures dotted at intervals along a historic main street. There's also a tacky **Big Platypus** in front of the **Platypus Experience**, a pretty dire adjunct to the Axeman's Hall of Fame (see opposite). You're better off trying to spot real platypus at dusk or dawn in the streams of adjacent park Bells Parade or, ideally, in the **Warrawee Forest Reserve** 4km south of town (access is via Hamilton Street, off Gilbert Street). The 565 acres of bushland has 5km of walking trails and a couple of picnic areas, plus the ponds that are home to the platypus themselves. You may spot the shy animals on your own if you dress in dark colours and use bushes and trees as natural cover, but your chances are far greater on a platypus-watching tour with Latrobe Platypus Encounters (dawn and dusk; 1.5–2hr; $10). Not only do local guides know the current whereabouts of the animals, all proceeds go towards preserving their habitat. You can book through the visitor centre or by calling ☎03/6246 1774 or 03/6246 1095. All tours depart from the visitor centre.

Latrobe's stronger claim to fame is as the home of **woodchopping**, a centre-piece of any rural show in Tasmania. It hosted the nation's first woodchopping contest in 1891 – folklore has it the sport originated as a £25 pub bet to settle whether a bushman from nearby Ulverstone or a visiting Victorian could fell a tree fastest – and the funeral of local hero and former world champion George Foster inspired the **Australian Axeman's Hall of Fame** (daily 9am–5pm; $10), signposted off the main road as you enter from the east. The Foster dynasty – especially David "Big Dave" Foster, a woodchopping giant in every sense who won the world championship for 21 consecutive years and was Australia Axeman of the Year nine times in a row – star in trophy cabinets that form the core of the display. Elsewhere there's a cursory exhibit on woodchopping competition disciplines, notably the demanding tree-felling event that requires lumberjacks to chop from narrow boards inserted into the trunk. Just behind the centre is restored colonial cottage **Sherwood Hall** (Tues & Thurs 10am–2pm, Sat & Sun 1–4pm; $2; ☎03/6246 2888). Relocated from Frogmore, 1.5km south of Latrobe, to its current location where Latrobe grew up as a river port in the 1840s, the contemporary three-room house is the oldest in the area, and retains the original furnishings and floors of its former owners, ex-convict Thomas Johnson and his half-Aboriginal wife Dolly. The live-in managers swear "dinky di" that they and visitors sometimes see the ghosts. Bells Parade opposite is a pleasant spot for a picnic.

Latrobe itself is a characterful jumble of Victorian architecture with 75 listed buildings along its main street, Gilbert Street, many containing antiques and crafts galleries. Most date from the late 1800s, when a port on the Mersey River transformed Latrobe into the largest town on the north coast, and the third-largest in Tasmania. **Reliquaire** at no. 139 is a kooky toy-shop–museum hybrid stuffed full of bizarre curios. Behind a war memorial in the centre, the dusty-pink **Courthouse Museum** (Tues–Fri 1–4pm; $2) has displays of local history with plenty of photos, though it's nothing to get excited about. Arguably more fulfilling is the tasting centre and shop of Belgian chocolate manufacturer **House of Anvers** (daily 7am–5pm; factory tours, numbers permitting, Mon–Fri $2; ☎03/6426 2703), which does some excellent fudge, truffles and orange chocolate. Nice gardens too. It's on the north-bound Bass Highway, 1km north of the Latrobe roundabout.

Practicalities

Merseylink bus #40 from Devonport goes to Latrobe hourly on weekdays from 8am to 5.30pm. In addition, Merseylink's Shearwater Shuttle (☎03/6243 3231 or 0409 006 013) from Devonport to Port Sorell stops at least once a day from Monday to Saturday, and twice (three times on Mon & Thurs) if the driver has advance warning; if you want picking up from Latrobe on the second service you'll have to call first. The large **tourist information centre** (Mon–Sat 9am–4pm, Sun 9.30am–3pm; ☎03/6421 4599, ✉tourism@latrobe.tas.gov.au) beside the *Lucas Hotel* on Gilbert Street hands out free maps and books platypus tours. The town also hosts an excellent rural **market** on Sunday (7am–3pm), with stalls of fresh produce, crafts and bric-a-brac.

To **stay** in the centre, *Latrobe Mersey River Caravan Park* (☎03/6426 1944; camping $18, vans ❸, en-suite cabins ❹) is a small site near the Platypus

Experience, or the *Lucas Hotel* at 46 Gilbert St (☎03/6426 1101, ⓦwww
.lucashotellatrobe.com.au; ❹) has above-average spacious accommodation in
cheap shared facilities or more expensive en suites. Its restaurant serves posh
pub grub daily. On a hillside near the Bass Highway roundabout, *Lucinda*, at
17 Fort St (☎03/6426 2285, ⓔlucindabnb@ozemail.com.au; ❺) is a classic
old-fashioned B&B with four rooms in a Victorian mansion, while on the
roundabout itself, 2km from the centre, the *Latrobe Motel* (☎03/6426,
ⓦwww.budgetmotelchain.com.au; ❹) is a dated fallback managed by the
Budget chain.

Small but popular, Latrobe offers surprisingly good **eating**. *Glo Glo's* at 78
Gilbert St (dinner Mon–Sat) serves complex modern Australian dishes in a
former bank. Its garden bistro (from 5.30pm) is more relaxed in style and
cuisine, preparing gourmet pizzas or a two-course $36 menu. Further along
Gilbert Street, there are pastas and stir-fries in colourful café-bistro *Blasé*, at no.
145 (lunch & dinner daily), and true café culture in adjacent *Bicci Blue* (daily
9am–5pm), a home to good coffee and home-cooked pies filled with the likes
of slow-cooked beef or roasted vegetables.

Port Sorell, Shearwater and Hawley Beach

The flat, fertile soils around Devonport nurture forty percent of the vegetables in
Tasmania, and the drive east is coloured with ruddy iron-rich fields and roadside
hoardings for potatoes. There are also vines at **Ghost Rock Vineyard** (Wed–Sun
11am–5pm except daily Jan–Feb; ☎03/6428 4005, ⓦwww.ghostrock
.com.au), 5km west of Port Sorell on the B74. Tastings ($3, redeemable on
purchase) of its cold-climate wines – pinot noir, a Chablis-styled chardonnay, zesty
sauvignon blanc and a few sparklings – are held in a bright modern building that
looks to the Bass Strait. Roughly 20km from Devonport, the road ends up at the
three merged resorts of the **Rubicon River estuary**. Uncomplicated and easy-
going, **Port Sorell** to the south is an odd blend of pensioners' playground and
beach-and-fishing resort. **Shearwater** is an uninspiring bungalows-ville worth a
visit only for a large supermarket, takeaways, a couple of pubs, a watersports shop
or a seasonal visitor centre (by the newsagent; daily Nov–April 9am–3pm;
☎03/6428 7920). **Hawley Beach**, a few kilometres north, is a more exclusive
place, its road a catwalk of swish beachhouses. The attraction is the shiny sands,
which are broadest around Port Sorell, though reduce to a sliver at high tide, or
the excellent fishing off Port Sorell jetty. You can wade out to estuarine islets at
low tide, but be careful of rips when swimming, especially on a falling tide. A
ten-kilometre return walk links Point Sorell and Hawley Beach.

Practicalities

You can **camp** just behind the beach at *Port Sorell Lions Caravan Park*
(☎03/6428 7267, ⓔptsrlcaravanpark@bigpond.com; campsites $18, vans ❷,
cabins ❸), at 42 Meredith St, though most pitches are in a site that gets busy
at weekends. *Sails on Port Sorell* at 54 Rice St (☎03/6428 7580, ⓦwww
.sailsonportSorell.com.au; ❺), a few hundred metres north, provides bright and
breezy modern studios and two-bed villas, or *Heron on Earth Organic Farm* (off
Edward St; ☎03/6428 6144, ⓦwww.herononearth.com; ❹) has a self-catering
solar-heated house with three bedrooms. It also rents bikes and canoes for you
to paddle across to the Narawntapu National Park. More luxurious heritage
accommodation is provided near the end of the road in Hawley Beach at the
Victorian-era *Hawley House* (☎03/6428 6221, ⓦwww.hawleyhousetas.com;
❻–❽). It has a fine restaurant and its own vineyard producing chardonnay and
pinot noir.

Merseylink's Shearwater Shuttle (☎03/6243 3231), from Devonport to Shearwater and Port Sorell via Latrobe, operates at least twice daily from Monday to Saturday.

Narawntapu National Park

It's a meandering forty-kilometre drive from Devonport southeast then north up the Rubicon River estuary to the **NARAWNTAPU NATIONAL PARK**. What makes the trip worthwhile is the variety and visibility of its fauna. At dusk, Bennett's wallabies and pademelon graze the plains behind Bakers Beach, and wombats and Tasmanian Devils emerge from the bush, the latter pair in some of the highest densities in Tasmania. You are, proclaims the Parks & Wildlife Service, in the "Serengeti of Tasmania". The park also hosts a reintroduced population of Forester kangaroo and rich birdlife, especially waterbirds in a lagoon behind Bakers Beach – there's a hide on the north bank.

Having read the information displays and bought national park passes if necessary in a combined ranger office and visitor centre (summer 10am–5pm, until 4pm winter; ☎03/6428 6277), you can embark on the **Springlawn Nature Walk** (1hr return), which heads off through a coastal thicket to the kangaroo-trimmed grassplains and bird hide, then returns via the dunes. Rangers also lead guided nature walks during summer holidays; times are posted at the visitor centre. A sidetrack halfway round the nature walk circuit ascends behind the beach up **Archers Knob** (1hr 30min–2hr return) for a superb panorama over **Bakers Beach** – all in all the most spectacular walk in the park. You can also hook up with the track from Bakers Beach. A longer trail (10km return; 6–8hr) zig-zags up the bluff at the east end of Bakers Beach and then follows the coastline around Badger Head to reach **Badger Beach**. An effortlessly glorious sweep of sands, it is named after the convict Charlotte Badger, who escaped from a ship anchored offshore in 1806 and is believed to have taken refuge among the area's indigenous Punnaalaapunnaa people, who knew the Badger Head area as *Narawntapu*. You could continue walking all the way along Badger Beach to reach Greens Beach (8–9hr one-way; see p.234) in the Tamar Valley; a spectacular if tiring coastal route. **Swimming** is safe on Bakers and Badgers beaches, though take care of rips at the west end of Badgers and in the Port Sorrel estuary, especially when the tide is falling. Fishing is good from both beaches and oyster hunting on the rocks at low tide pays dividends.

Self-registering **campsites** ($12 per pitch) are at the west end of Bakers Beach: *Horse Yards* is camping only; principal campground *Springlawn* has powered sites, a shower block (tokens from visitor centre), a payphone and an electric barbecue; and Bakers Point/Springlawn Beach on the estuary shore is big enough for caravans but has no power. Toilets and bore- and tank-water are at all campgrounds. Campfires are permitted at *Horse Yards* and Bakers Point (some firewood provided), although fire bans are frequent in summer, so fuel stoves are recommended. Be warned that the park is renowned for the occasional spectacular storm that whips up from nowhere and sends strong winds roaring along the beach.

Buses to Greens Beach provide access to Badger Beach, but since the visitor infrastructure and most wildlife is at the other end of the park, you'll really need your own transport. The only other option except a taxi from Devonport is to join a guided day-walk with Tasmanian Expeditions (see box, p.224; Oct–April Tues, Thurs & Sat; $110 half-day, $220 full day).

The rural hinterland

Within a half-hour's drive from the coast you're among fantastic scenery: lush farming country dominated by saturated colours and the mighty slab of **Mount Roland**. A bucolic vision of Paradise, in fact – which is a village just south of Sheffield. Many visitors skip the area en route to the more dramatic scenery of Cradle Mountain, but you could lose a happy day or so on the C-roads that criss-cross the area. Outside of area hub **Sheffield**, a charmingly old-fashioned place known for its murals, you're between villages all the way, dotted here and there with whimsical attractions – places such as maze-mad **Tasmazia**, south of Sheffield, or **Wilmot** with its novelty postboxes. There's rugged scenery here, too: Mount Roland for a day-hike or the river gorge of Leven Canyon.

Sheffield

SHEFFIELD, 30km south of Devonport, is a popular stop en route to Cradle Mountain. Sited among red volcanic farmland beneath the heaving crags of Mount Roland, it's a gentle, old-fashioned place with an uncomplicated charm. An ailing rural economy prompted the community to reinvent itself through the unlikely medium of **murals** – artist John Lendis was commissioned to paint the first in 1986, since when it has been joined by over thirty works painted on every spare wall, most depicting the history of Sheffield and the Kentish region. The "Town of Murals" adds a new work to its streetscape-gallery every year through the International Mural Fest (ⓦwww.muralfest.com.au) on the last full week of March. Nine hopefuls have a week and an inspirational poem provided by judges to come up with a design, and non-selected works remain on display until the next event as an open-air gallery in **Mural Park**. This is adjacent to a highly efficient **visitor information centre** (daily 9am–5pm; ☎03/6491 1036), where you can also buy a book of the murals, pick up a free map that locates every work, and reserve accommodation. A walking tour should take about an hour, and Lendis arguably provides the highlights: his original work,

▲ Mount Roland

Stillness and Warmth, beside a car park behind Main Street, is a serene image of Cradle Mountain enthusiast Gustav Weindorfer and native fauna in winter; a little further along Main Street opposite a motel is a detailed mural of pioneer settlers at Cradle Mountain. Both are small beer compared with a ninety-metre work he created in Gowrie Park (see below).

The "murals effect" has also encouraged a sprinkling of **art galleries** onto Main Street. Most are west of the tourist office; Art Etude at the far end has modern art and old-fashioned tin toys. Going the other way from the visitor centre, the **Kentish Museum** (in theory Mon–Fri 10am–4pm, but times vary; donation; ☏03/6491 1180) houses an assortment of bygones trawled from homesteads in the area, including, bizarrely, the world's first automatic petrol pump, and displays on the hydroelecytric projects south. Further east still, the **Red Water Creek Railway** (11am–4pm; $4; Ⓦ www.redwater.org.au) operates on the first weekend of the month. Built for a mining railway at Zeehan, the 1907-vintage steam locomotive hauls a couple of carriages – one a miners' passenger wagon, the other a late-1800s passenger carriage – along 4km of track from the original Sheffield railway station. It forms the centrepiece of steam machinery extravaganza **SteamFest** on the second weekend in March.

Around Sheffield

Christened after a pioneer's daughter rather than a former railhead, **RAILTON**, 12km northeast, has attempted its own themed revival since 1999. Let's just say a "Town of Topiary" is less gripping than one of murals. A leaflet and map from the Sheffield visitor centre pinpoints its 35 hedge sculptures, many rather leaf-bare. The small town is also the home of Cement Australia – Sydney can thank Railton's cement for the Sydney Harbour Bridge.

The countryside south of Sheffield is spectacular. Just fifteen minutes down the road and you're among red volcanic soils and livid green pasture, a hyperreal vision of farmland drenched in luminous light. Ahead Mount Roland thrusts a sudden slab of dolerite over a kilometre into an intensely blue sky. It's especially inspiring when the mountain glows pink at sunset like a Tasmanian version of Ayers Rock. Many of the Scottish pioneers who opened up the area for settlement in the 1850s had been forced to emigrate as a result of the Clearances. Their euphoria at what they found on the other side of the world, remembered as village names, still thrills today: Promised Land, Garden of Eden (today named Sprent), or simply, Paradise. Promised Land is en route to Tasmazia, Paradise on the C137 off the road to Gowrie Park.

Heading southwest of Sheffield on the C136, you reach **GOWRIE PARK** itself, a former hydroelectricity base in the bosom of the mountains; John Lendis's mural on a corrugated shed in the centre provides a hundred-metre summary of the decade-long construction project that created the Mersey Forth HEP plant from 1963. The village also represents the start of the ascent up **Mount Roland** (1223m; 4–6hr return), which is neither as tough nor as steep a walk as it looks from a distance. The track begins from a car park in O'Neills Creek Picnic Reserve, a few hundred metres from the mural, and hauls uphill to a plateau path to conjoined southern mountains Mount Van Dyke (1084m) and Mount Claude (1034m). Needless to say, the views from the summit are sensational, stretching to Cradle Mountain southwest and the Bass Strait north. Route notes are available from the visitor centre at Sheffield, and there's free camping at the picnic ground; alternatively you're permitted to camp on the plateau itself.

Going southwest of Sheffield on the C140, you pass through the rolling pasture around Promised Land to reach whimsical maze and museum complex **Tasmazia** (daily Nov–April 10am–5pm, May–Oct until 4pm; $16; ☎03/6341 1934, ⓦwww.tasmazia.com.au) set in the model village of "Lower Crackpot" – it has its own postbox should you want the name franked on your postcards home. Once past a giftshop and pancake parlour, there are eight mazes to get bamboozled by – including what is alleged to be the largest maze in the world – and a replica of the kilometre-long hedge maze at Hampton Court, just outside London. A place for children – big and little. A side road beyond slaloms downhill to **Lake Barrington** (road often gated 8pm–6am); halfway down, the Billet Creek Nature Way (2hr return) leads through the eucalyptus forest to a small rainforest. The slender lake provides a venue for international rowing competitions and is studded with jetties for a dip, plus there's good fishing for black fish and rainbow and brown trout. The C140 continues southwest via **Staverton**, base of horse-riding operator Highland Trails (☎03/6491 1553 or 0417 145 497, ⓦwww.highlandtrails.com.au), before it hits a T-junction with possibilities: left to Gowrie Park or Mole Creek; right to the Cradle Mountain-Lake St Clair National Park.

Practicalities

Tassielink's West Coast scheduled **coach** service from Launceston (via Devonport) stops in Sheffield and Gowrie Park on Tuesday, Thursday and Saturday. (The service continues to Cradle Mountain.) You will need your own transport for other destinations. The visitor information centre in Sheffield offers Internet access; the **Online Access Centre** (Mon–Sat, times vary) itself is in the high school on Henry Street.

Accommodation

There's a fair spread of accommodation in the area, much of it trading on mountain views and serving as an alternative to the more expensive options at Cradle Mountain 30km southwest. Some also have restaurants open to non-guests. In Sheffield, you can camp in motorhomes for free (no facilities) at a recreation ground north of the Red Water Creek Railway at the east end of Main Street. The nearest free bushcamp (toilets; picnic shelter) is the picnic ground at Gowrie Park.

AAA Granary 1km south of Promised Land ☎03/6491 1689, ⓦwww.granary.com.au. Large self-contained two- to four-bed cottages, all with a laundry, and most with mountain views, on a family-friendly rural resort. Has a games centre, bicycles, go-carts to amuse the kids, plus free Internet, gardens and DVD library. Also has one van (③) if you're on a budget. ⑥

Eagles Nest Retreat Careys Rd, off C141 5km southwest of Sheffield ☎03/6941 1151, ⓦwww .eaglesnestretreat.com.au. Two exclusive spa retreats which bring quirky individualism to their modern opulence; guests are also pampered with an in-house chef and masseurs. Far from cheap, but the selling point is an astounding 360-degree panorama of the countryside which features an unsurpassed view of Mount Roland. ⑧

Glencoe Barrington, on B14 8km northwest of Sheffield ☎03/6492 3267,

ⓦwww.glencoeruralretreat.com. The French couple behind the prestigious *Calstock* manor-hotel near Deloraine have concocted the same blend of modern-country elegance in this stylish B&B, created in a small heritage house with four bedrooms plus a lovely lounge. Guests are treated to the gourmet French cuisine of master chef Remi Bancal nightly in the restaurant (see opposite). ⑥

Gowrie Park Wilderness Cabins & Backpackers Gowrie Park, ☎03/6491 1385, ⓦwww.weindorfers.com. Spectacularly located beneath Mount Roland, this former hydro-base has the only backpacker accommodation in the area. Bunkhouse or warmer dorms in an outside block, basic self-contained units, camping, free Internet, TV room and a great rustic hall with a large fireplace. At the time of writing the business was for sale as a going concern, so confirm before a visit. Camping $5 per person; dorms $10; units ❸

Sheffield Motor Inn 49–53 Main St, Sheffield ☎03/6491 1800, ⓦwww.sheffieldmotorinn.com.au. Comfy if rather old-fashioned motel rooms, but still good value because of the central location. Also has self-contained studios and one- and two-bed apartments. ❹–❺

Silver Ridge Retreat Gowrie Park ☎03/6491 1727, ⓦwww.silverridgeretreat.com.au. Spacious two-bed lodges on a farmholding beneath Mount Roland, all with wood-burning heaters and views (spa cottages are probably not worth the extra), plus one backpacker chalet (no facilities; ❸). Heated pool, plus wildlife tours and horse-riding led by friendly owners. ❻–❽

Tanglewood 25 High St, Sheffield ☎03/6491 1854, ⓦwww.tanglewoodtasmania.com. B&B in an art-filled 1906 house amid a mature garden, with three pastel-tinted en suites and a communal lounge.

Eating

🏃 **Coffee on Main** 43 Main St, Sheffield. The best eating in town: fair-trade organic coffee served by trained baristas, gourmet sandwiches and salads by day, and dinners ($14–28) from fresh local produce by the European-trained chef-owner; expect the likes of creamy prawn pasta and sirloin steaks in mustard sauce. BYO. Lunch Wed–Sun, dinner Fri–Sat.

🏃 **Glencoe** Barrington, on B14 8km northwest of Sheffield. The Provençal cuisine of owner Remi Bancal (ex-Paris Ritz, Melbourne's Mietta and Banc in Sydney) was the stuff of legend at former boutique hotel *Calstock* near Deloraine. Now he prepares light lunches of prawn gratin, crêpes or tarts at bargain prices (mains $15–25), all served on the deck. Lunch and tea Wed–Sun.

Highlander Restaurant 60 Main St, Sheffield. An old-fashioned tea room that rustles up solid home-cooking at low prices once you get past the tartan decor. Also has a small gluten-free menu. May change as the business was for sale at the time of research. Lunch daily, dinner daily Dec–Feb.

Sheffield Hotel 38 Main St, Sheffield. The locals' choice for roasts. There's a reliable choice on a no-nonsense pub menu. Lunch & dinner daily.

Weindorfers Gowrie Park ☎03/6491 1385. A great rustic place in a shingle-roofed hall, this serves hearty country fare at moderate prices every day in summer; there's a platter of Tasmanian produce. The business was for sale during our last visit, so call for times.

Wilmot and Leven Canyon

Though just the other side of Lake Barrington, the area west of Sheffield is reached on a tortuous route via backroads. Far quicker is the B16, which zips southwest of Forth near Devonport en route to Cradle Mountain. After 22km, you emerge on the brow of a hill with a staggering view to Mount Roland, then roll down to the rural village of **WILMOT**, which a century ago was little more than a few houses scratched out of a clearing in the bush. Sepia photos of the pioneer village are displayed alongside odds and ends rescued from local barns in a tiny **museum** in the old church and school room (Sat–Sun 9am–3pm or by appointment, ☎03/6492 1479 or 1165; free). Hard to believe, then, that sleepy Wilmot is the cradle of Australian supermarket chain Coles. The original store (Mon–Fri 7am–7pm, Sat 8am–6pm, Sun 9am–5pm), opened by the father of George Coles (who subsequently founded the supermarket chain in the early 1900s), is an authentic barn of a building, with a make-do feel to its box shelving and old tins and bottles displayed alongside general produce. Wilmot's other claim to fame is novelty **letterboxes**, knocked together from whatever junk was lying around the barn. There's a skeleton on a bike, a cow and calf, Ned Kelly extending a welcoming hand – a holiday snap if ever there was one. Not as highbrow as Sheffield and its murals, but more fun than Railton's topiary. Should you want **to stay**, there's B&B in the old-fashioned *Old Wilmot Bakehouse* (☎03/6492 1117; ❹) or the more modern *Robin's Nest* on Back Road (☎03/6492 7310, ⓔthreeangels@bigpond.com.au; ❹), 4km northwest of Wilmot overlooking a valley en route to Upper Castra. For **eating**, *Lake Barrington Garden Café* (daily 10am–4pm; ☎03/6492 1394) has a menu of

▲ Original Coles store, Wilmot

healthy modern food (mains around \$17) and idyllic gardens above the lake. It's 2km east of the village – take side roads north or south of Wilmot – and serves as the launchpad for a stroll to Forth Falls (1hr–1hr 30min return).

Southwest of Wilmot, the C128 rolls through remote farmsteads to conclude 42km from Ulverstone at **Leven Canyon**; if you're coming from Wilmot, take the first left turning north of the village, grind up a steep valley to Upper Castra, then turn south. From the car park, a short gravelled path (500m) climbs gently to a vertiginous lookout nearly 300m above the Leven River canyon. It's also a great spot to see geography in the raw: an ancient landslip produced the sheer tilted ridge around which the river doglegs. To **walk** a circuit back to the car park, take a side path that descends steeply through forest via seven hundred steps, then switches uphill to return through a pretty glade of tree ferns. The picnic place at the car park itself is a splendid spot carved out of the bush, with toilets, water, fireplaces (firewood provided) and a shelter with a wood-burning stove. For all its wilderness appearance, however, this is forestry territory; behind a modest strip that rings the car park are regulation rows of plantation forest. The **canyon floor** is accessed from a path 1km downhill from the lookout car park. A ten-minute walk leads to a footbridge strung across the rock walls of the gorge – magnificent when the river is in flood. You can follow the river on the Canyon Floor Walk (10hr), or a second trail climbs steadily through farmland to subalpine plateau Black Bluff (1339m; 6–7hr return).

Gunns Plains

Head west of the C128 via the C126 and you reach Preston, where the Preston Falls tumbles into a valley by the roadside, to emerge suddenly at **Gunns Plains**, an open bowl whose patchwork of pasture is vividly lush against the dark forest that cloaks the hillsides. You can also get there on the B17 that loops 25km inland between Ulverston and Penguin (no public transport). Now supporting sheep and dairy farming, the river valley was once a hop-growing region, which accounts for the lines of poplar trees that are planted as windbreaks. **Wing's Wildlife Park** (daily 10am–4pm; $17; ☎03/6429 1151, ⓦwww.wingswildlife .com.au), a short way north of the few houses that pass for a centre, is a gentle wildlife park-cum-rehabilitation centre for orphaned and injured wildlife. Alongside the standard Tasmanian species – Devils, wombats, possums, pademelons and Bennetts wallabies – there's a large aquatic display including young freshwater crocodiles. The park also provides simple **accommodation** (camping $5, backpacker units ❶, self-contained chalets ❹) and sells basic supplies and farm eggs in a café-shop. Another option for camping is the superb community-run *Pioneer Park Campground* (☎03/6437 6137; $4 per person) near Rianna, 17km north of Gunns Plains on the B17 or 15km south of Penguin. Amenities include hot showers (20¢), fireplaces and electric barbecues, water and a nature trail. **Gunns Plains Caves** (tours hourly 10am–noon & 1.30–3.30pm; 50min; $10; ☎03/6429 1388), signposted off the B17 southwest of the wildlife park and part of the **Gunns Plains State Reserve**, are worth visiting for their remarkable limestone formations which, when lit from behind, glow red.

Ulverstone

Redline buses follow the unmemorable coast west of Devonport, stopping after 20km at **ULVERSTONE**, where the **Leven River** flows into the sea. It's a popular family resort famed for its fishing – cod, couta and wrasse are caught off the river breakwall on an incoming tide – and clean **beaches.** A population of **Little Penguins** comes to breed on the beach here between September and March, and Penguin Point Twilight Tours takes small groups from the *Ulverstone Waterfront Inn* out at dusk (daily except Sat; 2–3hr; $15; bookings ☎03/6425 1599 or 0439 693377). For more remarkable wildlife, Todd Walsh takes groups on a day-long bush-bash to see the **giant freshwater crayfish**, a threatened species that lives only in the northern flowing rivers of Tasmania and can grow up to several kilograms. The tours – actually, a chance to join Walsh's scientific population survey – are by arrangement and must be booked in advance (☎03/6425 5302 or 0439 693377; prices vary by group size). The Ulverstone **visitor information centre** (daily 9am–5pm; ☎03/6428 2839) at 13–15 Alexander St, near the clock tower (see below) can provide more information, not to mention free maps of the town.

The main occupation away from the shore is to stroll and picnic in parks that ring the beach and river, and lend an amiable air to the town. Reibey Street has a couple of second-division historic buildings from the late 1800s, some mounted with storyboards of local yarns. However, the dominant landmark is an awkward **clock tower war memorial** at the centre. It's not clear whether local pride or weariness at questions prompted the tourist board to publish a leaflet about the bizarre modernist monument, in which its uncompromising looks are explained away by the fact that its designer was a Slovenian émigré from communist Yugoslavia. Around the corner on Main Street, **Ulverstone History Museum** (Tues, Thurs, Sat & Sun, 1.30–4.30pm; ☎03/6425 3835; $4) prides itself on the mock-ups of early shops and the town high street. It also has a sizeable collection of early photographs.

Accommodation and eating

The town's **accommodation** possibilities include the *Ocean View Heritage B&B* at 1 Victoria St (☎03/6425 5401; ❻), which has sea views from most rooms, and the splendid 1903 red-brick *Furners Hotel* at 42 Reibey St (℡03/6425 1488; ❹), the latter with a bistro that specializes in chargrilled steaks. Alternatively you can **camp** at the waterfront *Ulverstone Caravan Park*, 1km east of the centre (℡03/6425 2624; vans ❷, cabins and units ❸). The best place **to eat** is *Pedro's* on Wharf Road (lunch & dinner daily; ℡03/6425 6663) at the bottom of Reibey Street, the perfect spot for a seafood dinner beside the river. Attached is one of Tassie's most acclaimed fish-and-chips shops. For café culture head to King Edward Street, off Reibey Street, where you can choose between *Red Olive Café* (Mon–Fri 9am–5pm), in an belle époque-styled giftshop, or *Retro Mania Café* (Mon–Sat 9am–5pm), which rustles up triple-decker club sandwiches and artery-clogging desserts.

Penguin

The best route west from Ulverstone follows the old Bass Highway (Penguin Road) along the coastline, passing the bird sanctuaries of Three Sisters Island and Goat Island. You can walk to the latter at low tide from West Ulverstone Beach and spend a few hours exploring shallow caves among the rocky shoreline – keep an eye on the tide though. Beyond is Penguin Point, where Little Penguins roost, then a beautiful array of flowers line the road as you roll into **PENGUIN** itself, 12km along the highway from Ulverstone. Immaculately scrubbed and with a breezy uncommercial innocence, the little beach town competes with Stanley for the title of prettiest on the north coast. Penguin's multicoloured main street is jumbled with small historic buildings and a strong café culture, but it also makes much fun of its namesake: cute plastic penguins cluster along the shopfronts, while in the foreshore park a tubby two-metre-high **Big Penguin** is acclaimed tongue-in-cheek as the largest in the world.

The town's quirky character explains the polemic over plans for a swish tower of boutique shops and apartments, whose seven glass-skinned storeys are due to rise over the beach by early 2009. The green light for the project in 2007 split the community along lines of character versus jobs. The other notable edifices in town are the timber **Uniting Church** on Main Street (1909), characterized by a flutter of gables; and a replica **Dutch windmill** in Hiscutt Park one block behind – the third-scale model was a bicentennial gift from the town's Dutch community in 1988. Penguin's three small beaches – lovely stretches of bleached sands backed by flowers to the east or Norfolk Island pines in the centre – are all safe for swimming. The excellent Sunday **market** (9am–3pm; Ⓦ www.penguinmarket.com) is an attraction in its own right, with three hundred stalls of antiques, collectables, crafts and food. It is held in a hall behind Main Street just east of the *Neptune Hotel*.

Five kilometres south of Penguin, there are a number of walking and cycling trails through eucalyptus forest reserve **Dial Range State Forest.** Though there are no designated camping areas and certainly no facilities except a picnic table, you can camp at the stream-side picnic areas. To get to the reserve, drive south on Dial Road (maps are available from the visitor centre). You could also walk there on the first section of the Penguin Cradle Trail (5–7 days). This occasionally tough but rewarding eighty-kilometre bushwalk traverses a diverse range of landscapes – rich pasture in Gunns Plains, Leven Canyon and its river gorge and the subalpine Black Bluff are the highlights – before it arrives at Cradle Mountain. Ulverstone-based North West Walking Club (Ⓦ www.nwwc.org.au) publishes an eighteen-page trail guide with notes and maps on its website, and announces planned logging activity in the area. For an easier walk, drive to enchanting **Ferndene Gorge** 5km south (via Ironcliffe Rd, off Crescent Rd behind Main St). A stream path (30min return) burrows through a corridor of greenery roofed by man ferns to two abandoned silver-lead mine shafts; bring a torch and keep quiet and you may see glow-worms in the evening.

Practicalities

Penguin is a stop on Redline's daily Devonport–Burnie service and is also connected to Burnie and Ulverstone by Metro bus #76. The **visitor information centre** on Main Street (Mon–Fri 9am–4pm, Sat & Sun 9am–12.30pm; ℡03/6437 1421) can provide more details about activities in the area including twilight penguin trips (Sept–March Sun–Fri; 1hr 30min; ℡03/6437 2590; $10). An excellent **Online Access Centre** (Mon & Wed 9am–9pm, Tues, Thurs & Fri 9am–5pm, Sat 10am–noon; ℡03 6437 0771) is in the high school, 1km south of the centre at 125 Ironcliffe Rd. It's worth calling to confirm its volunteer workforce are there before you attempt the tiring walk up a steep hill.

Beachfront boutique **hotel** *The Madsen* (℡03/6437 2588, Ⓦwww.themadsen .com; ❺) offers refined bed and breakfast and sea views in the spacious quarters of a former bank, while there are eye-poppingly bright budget rooms above *Neptune Grand Hotel* on Main Street, opposite *Wild* restaurant (℡03/6437 2406; ❷). Two-bedroom self-contained *Kunnie's Beach House*, at 117 Main St (℡03/6224 6749, Ⓦwww.kunniesbeachhouse.com; ❺) makes up in location above the beach what it lacks in contemporary style. To **camp**, go 500m west of the centre to small *Penguin Beachside Holiday Resort* (℡03/6437 2785; camping $20, cabins ❸) above Johnsons Beach.

For **food**, the 🍴 *Groovy Penguin* (Tues–Fri 10am–4pm, Sat–Sun 10am–3pm) by the visitor centre is a fantastically colourful, retro café with an alternative feel and young and friendly owners – filling fare includes superb lentil burgers and lasagne. More sophisticated dining is at slick beach café-restaurant *Wild* at 87 Main St (lunch & dinner Wed–Sun; licensed); expect classic modern Australian fare such as teriyaki quail wrapped in prosciutto or scallops in hazelnut and coriander butter. Prices average around $28 per main course.

Burnie

No place in Tasmania attracts bad press like **BURNIE**. In a state that prides itself on heritage and wilderness, the industrial and paper-manufacturing industries of Tasmania's fourth-largest city is anathema. Even its football club mascot, a snarling pug-nosed bruiser in a docker's beanie, jars with Tassie's open-armed image. Burnie is never going to win prizes for its looks; the centre is a lumpen conglomeration of modern boxes and the Bass Highway slices through its heart. Yet it has a dynamism that is lacking even in larger Devonport, and its urban grit is a refreshing jolt from sleepy heritage towns. In recent decades, the tourist board has strived to develop attractions: a couple of museums, a gallery and, increasingly, crafts manufacturers as a new take on the manufacturing heritage. Bizarrely, Burnie now attracts a growing quota of cruise ships.

The rethink was necessitated by changing circumstances. In the 1980s, Burnie was a byword for environmental vandalism. Its shore was stained a dirty orange from the industrial waste pumped into the sea and sulphurous fumes from factory chimneys fell as acid rain to etch the paint of local cars. So infamous was

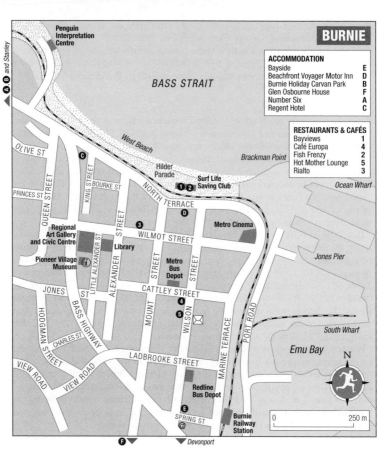

BURNIE

ACCOMMODATION
Bayside	E
Beachfront Voyager Motor Inn	D
Burnie Holiday Carvan Park	B
Glen Osbourne House	F
Number Six	A
Regent Hotel	C

RESTAURANTS & CAFÉS
Bayviews	1
Café Europa	4
Fish Frenzy	2
Hot Mother Lounge	5
Rialto	3

the industrial pollution that iconic environmental rockers Midnight Oil released *Burnie* in 1981, a bleak song about humanity sacrificed to industry. But when the industrial base scaled back production in the mid-1990s, Burnie was forced to diversify – the largest employer in the city is now plant machinery manufacturer Caterpillar. And as it has cleaned up its act, so it has rediscovered its waterfront and added a couple of restaurants. The container port, with its controversial pile of export woodchips, and the nearby Australian Paper mill are still not pretty, of course. And Burnie is unlikely to be anyone's favourite town. But it has some interesting sights and an energy which suggests the transition from industrial to cultural need not be too painful.

The city and outskirts

The main sight for cruise-ship visitors is the **Pioneer Village Museum** (Mon–Fri 9am–5pm; $6), which reconstructs an early twentieth-century street in the visitor centre on Little Alexander Street. Though rather contrived, it's an engaging enough attraction, largely thanks to the clutter of tools in the street's tiny shops; apparently over thirty thousand period items were collated to create the exhibit. Visitors to the museum receive free parking for two hours in the municipal car park – pick up a ticket from the visitor centre where you buy your ticket. The **Burnie Regional Art Gallery** (Tues–Fri 10.30am–5pm, Sat & Sun 1.30–4.30pm; free; ☏03/6430 5875), in the Civic Centre north of the museum on Wilmot Street, houses art and crafts exhibitions and a permanent collection of B-list Australian art that can be viewed by arrangement. A gallery shop sells cards and handmade crafts.

Just outside the centre, Burnie's **penguin interpretive centre** on Parsonage Point is reached via a boardwalk that runs along central West Beach. You can watch through spyholes as Little penguins return to their burrows after dusk between November and April. Free interpretation tours (☏0437 436 803) are held in season one hour before dusk. Should you fancy a stroll, **Burnie Park**, on the other side of the highway from Parsonage Point, contains the town's oldest building, the *Burnie Inn* pub, while the best beach is 3km further west at Cooee (buses #60 and #65).

The ructions caused by strike action during the wane of the **Australian Paper mill** (free tours Mon–Fri 2pm; ☏03/6430 7777), 1km east of the centre, prompted much soul-searching about Burnie's future. One upshot was the community-based, non-profit **Creative Paper Mill** (Mon–Fri 9am–5pm, Sat 9am–4pm & Oct–April Sun 9am–4pm; tours every 30min, 9.30–11.30am & 1–3.30pm; $15; ☏03/6430 7717, ⓦwww.creativepapertas.com.au), created as a government Work For Dole scheme. Its ethos of organic papers crafted from recycled materials is taken to a logical conclusion in Roo Poo paper. There's also beer paper in a showroom, plus an art gallery whose showstopper attraction is a lifesize ensemble of paper jazz musicians. You can also muck in and create your own sheets. The mill is scheduled to relocate to a multi-million dollar new home at the western end of West Beach in mid-2009. It is currently sited behind the industrial paper mill at Old Surrey Road (C112), 100m off the Bass Highway on the eastern side of Burnie.

Three kilometres further along Old Surrey Road, Lactos is a prize-winning speciality **cheese factory** (tastings Mon–Fri 9am–5pm, Sat & Sun 10am–4pm; free) and nearby, at 153 Old Surrey Rd, **Hellyers Road Distillery** (daily 9.30am–5.30pm; free tours; ☏03/6433 1092, ⓦwww.hellyersroaddistillery .com.au) offers tastings and sales of its light single malt whiskies and a premium vodka in a swish restaurant-bar. Fork off Old Surrey Road just after the old Creative Paper Mill, however, and you reach platypus reserve **Fernglade** on a peaceful stretch of the Emu River. Several spots on an eight-hundred-metre rainforest walk offer vantage points from which to look for platypus at dawn and after dusk – the road bridge before the site is also a reliable viewing spot. Conservationist William Walker (☏03/6435 7205, ✉wagwalker@bigpond .com) runs nature tours, visiting Fernglade and the penguins and other local points of interest, and specializes in day-walks with local gourmet food.

Practicalities

Burnie airport is actually at Wynyard (see p.273). Redlines depot is at 117 Wilson St and Tassielink departs from outside the **Tasmanian Travel and Information Centre** at the Civic Square precinct, off Little Alexander Street (Mon–Fri 8am–5pm, Sat & Sun 10am–4pm; ☏03/6434 6111). Local Metro **buses** depart from the central block of Cattley Street (Mon–Sat 7am–6pm). Buses #76 and #77 run to Ulverstone via Penguin, and #60 and #65 go to Wynyard. Burnie's busy **Online Access Centre** (Mon–Fri 9am–5pm, Sat 9.30am–12.30pm) is in the library at 2 Spring St.

Burnie **Farmers' Market** has around fifty stalls of regional farm produce and crafts. It is held at the Wivenhoe Show Grounds 1.5km east of the centre on the first and third Sunday of the month. Thylacine Expeditions (☎03/6436 2302) conducts small-group **tours** to destinations such as Dismal Swamp and Cradle Mountain, plus evening wildlife-watching tours in the Burnie area.

Accommodation

The visitor centre offers free bookings of accommodation and displays more options on its window for out-of-hours help.

Bayside 139 Wilson St ☎03/6431 4455, ⓔres@baysideburne.com. Renovation in late 2007 transformed this dated hotel block into pleasant, though fairly anonymous, modern business accommodation. ❻

Beachfront Voyager Motor Inn 9 North Terrace ☎03/6431 4866, ⓦwww.beachfrontvoyager.com.au. On the beachfront and not nearly as old-fashioned as its 1970s building suggests, following refurbishment to bring the rooms up to four-star standard and contemporary style. Those at the front have sea views but are noisier. ❺

Burnie Holiday Caravan Park 253 Bass Highway, Cooee, 3km west ☎03/6431 1925. Opposite the beach on the non-industrial side of town, this small holiday park incorporates two YHA dorms and the *Ocean View Motel* to provide something for everyone. Small swimming pool too. Buses #60 and #65. Camping $15, dorms $18, vans ❷, cabins ❹, motel ❹.

Glen Osborne House 9 Aileen Crescent ☎03/6431 9866. A charmingly old-fashioned Victorian-era B&B, with en-suite rooms and a lovely garden of lawns, roses and fruit trees. ❻

Number Six 6 Mollison St, 600m west of Burnie Park ☎0439 353 491, ⓦwww.seabreezecottages.com.au. A Fifties-style jukebox and shaggy carpets give character to this self-contained two-bed house with great views of the Bass Strait. Its managers also have two beachside properties at Cooee: contemporary *The Beach House* and smart heritage-styled *Somersby*. All ❻

Regent Hotel 26 North Terrace ☎03/6431 1933. The only backpackers' accommodation in town is above a pub. The usual shabby rooms are a cocoon of pastel orange but perfectly acceptable, and all have basins. There's a kitchenette (microwave, no oven) with free tea and coffee, and a large lounge that looks over West Beach. ❷

Eating

Bayviews West Beach. A slick restaurant-lounge bar that would have been unthinkable in Burnie even ten years ago. Above *Fish Frenzy*, it has similar seafront dining but offers more upmarket dishes – mains average $28 – plus cheaper gourmet pizzas. Breakfast, lunch & dinner daily.

Café Europa Corner of Cattley and Wilson streets. A cosmopolitan hangout with some Greek Cypriot offerings on the Mediterranean menu, plus good-value toasted Turkish sandwiches, snacks and lots of different kinds of coffee. Licensed. Tues–Thurs 8.30am–9pm, Fri until midnight, Sat 10am–midnight, Sun 10am–6pm.

Fish Frenzy West Beach. Modern, bright and busy, this new outpost of the acclaimed Hobart fish-and-chip restaurant provides similar quality and great beach views. Lunch & dinner daily.

Hot Mother Lounge 70 Wilson St. Always busy, this fun little place is reliable for fresh healthy lunches such as Thai pumpkin soup and roast Mediterranean vegetable wraps. Mon–Fri 7.30am–3pm.

Rialto Gallery 46 Wilmot St. Italian food from a veteran of the Burnie dining scene. Moderately priced daily pasta specials are prepared with seasonal ingredients and there are good wood-fired pizzas, all served in a snug dining room with art on its walls. Lunch Mon–Fri & dinner Mon–Sat.

Entertainment

Metro **Cinema**, at the corner of Marine Terrace and Wilmot streets (☎03/6431 5000, ⓦwww.metrocinemas.com.au) is the entertainment focus, while *Sirocco's*, in a converted cinema at 64 Wilmot St, is the nightlife hub, with a lounge bar and pool room on its upper levels. Irish-styled *Magintey's* on the corner of Spring and Wilson streets is a popular spot that hosts rock and blues bands at weekends.

Along the coast to Stanley

West of Burnie you can either cut south towards Strahan via the A10 (see p.289) or continue along the coast. With the area's major settlements behind, you kick back into small-town pace all the way – only minor agri-centre **Wynyard** warrants the name of town (and even then only just). Along the coast-hugging run west is a string of superb beaches, from idyllic nooks like **Boat Harbour Beach** to the wild coast of the **Rocky Cape National Park**, until you reach pocket-sized, historical **Stanley**, the northwest's premier resort.

Wynyard

WYNYARD, 19km west on the old Bass Highway from Burnie, snuggles into lush English-style pasturelands between the **Inglis River** and the sea. Though surrounding scenery impresses, **central Wynyard** hardly quickens the pulse. A late-starter that emerged in the 1850s as a port, then enjoyed rapid growth on the back of the Victorian gold rush, the town serves as a low-key agricentre for the surrounding dairy, onion and potato farms, and there's little to excite on main drag Goldie Street. The town is at its most picturesque at the river mouth wharf, where a few fishing boats are moored and a fresh fish shop rustles up good fish and chips; keep an eye out for the resident seal, Winnie. The wharf is also a good spot to cast a line for trout. The only dedicated tourist attraction is **Wonders of Wynyard** (9am–5pm; $6) at the visitor information centre (see p.274). Stars of the glossy vintage motors collection – the largest group of restored Fords in Australia – are a buggy-like Model A Ford, the world's joint-oldest Ford (1903), which covered 28,000 miles, and a rare luxury Model K (1907) saloon. There are also some immaculate Cadillacs and a couple of vintage motorbikes.

For anyone other than petrol-heads, the interest is elsewhere. There are over 12km of riverside walking tracks to amble, starting from the riverfront park on the corner of Goldie and Hogg streets; pick up a *Scenic Walks of Wynyard* leaflet from the visitor centre. It's an easy three-kilometre walk (or drive) upriver then across a bridge to reach **Fossil Bluff**, where layers of sedimentary rock containing fossilized seashells can be examined at low tide. Whelk razor shells are common, though previous finds include Australia's largest fossilized marsupial and a huge prehistoric whale skeleton. A suburb behind rather dampens the natural splendour, mind. The beach also provides a good view of the 170-metre seaface of **Table Cape**, a solidified lava lake that plugged an ancient volcano. A five-kilometre drive up to the **lookout** on Table Cape will reward you with magnificent views of the coast and hinterland, and is particularly pretty when the cape's **tulip fields** lay a multicoloured patchwork over the flat cape in October.

If you fancy seeing Wynyard and surrounds from the air, Western Aviation (☎03/6442 1111, ⓦwww.westernaviation.com.au) operates **scenic flights** from the airport lasting thirty minutes to two hours (prices vary by group size and flight time), covering inaccessible destinations such as the Tarkine and northwest coast.

Practicalities

Wynyard may be the first place you see in Tasmania because "Burnie" **airport** (☎03/6442 1133) is just a five-minute stroll from the town centre, off Dodgin Street. All the major names have **car rental** at the airport: Autorent-Hertz

(☎03/6442 4444), Avis (☎03/6442 2512) or Budget (☎03/6442 1777). The Burnie Air-Bus connects the airport with town ($30; ☎0439 322 466 or 0419 581 800). Metro **buses** connect Wynyard with Burnie, departing from 38 Jackson St. Redline calls at Gale's Auto Service, 28 Saunders St (☎03/6442 2205), en route from Burnie to Smithton via the turn-offs to Table Cape, Boat Harbour Beach and Rocky Cape. Wynyard **tourist information** (9am–5pm; ☎03/6443 8330, ⊛www.wowtas.com) is at 8 Exhibition Link off Dodgin Street, and signposted from the Bass Highway as you enter from the east. Wynyard's **Online Access Centre** (Mon–Fri 10am–5pm) is in the library at 21 Saunders St, near the visitor centre.

For budget **accommodation**, *Beach Retreat Tourist Park* (☎03/6442 1998; camping $22, budget rooms ➋, motel-style units ➌, self-contained cabins ➍) is a friendly place 1km from the centre on the Old Bass Highway back towards Burnie. No prizes for guessing it is beside the beach. However, the best place to stay is riverfront *The Waterfront Wynyard*, at 1 Goldie St (☎03/6442 2351; ➍). Small but quietly stylish motel rooms open onto the wharf and are equipped with mod cons such as satellite TV and DVD players. The on-site café-**restaurant** is the best in town: couches, a river-view terrace, great coffee and cake served daily from 8am, and a restaurant at night; mains, such as roast of the day or seafood curry, start at $17. A takeaway fish-and-chip shop on the wharf is good (daily 11am–7pm), or on the Smithton road, at 4 Inglis St, *Buckaneers* (daily 9am–8pm; ☎03/6442 4104) is one of Tasmania's best fish-and-chip shops. Its idiosyncratic nautical-themed restaurant offers an à la carte menu on Friday and Saturday nights and is always busy; reservations are recommended.

Boat Harbour Beach

Eleven kilometres west of Wynyard, a turn-off winds down to idyllic **Boat Harbour Beach**. Like Wineglass Bay on the East Coast, this is the iconic beach of the northwest and has similarly starred in Australia's Top Ten Beaches list. The hype has introduced a couple of holiday resorts that jar against the ramshackle charm of the original village, but commercialization is relatively restrained – for now. The steep hill the village tumbles down permits a microclimate for semi-tropical plants, while below is a perfect bay of bleached quartzite sand and shallow turquoise sea. The bay picks up decent surf when swells pump from the northeast and offers clear **diving**; equipment can be rented from the Scuba Centre at 62 Bass Highway in Wynyard (☎03/6442 2247, ⊜shop@scubacentre.net.au; $90 per dive), which also organizes excursions. Licensed café-restaurant ⚲ *Jolly Rogers on the Beach* (☎03/6445 1710; reservations recommended for dinner) has a beach-shack feel and tables right on the sands; a perfect place to while away an afternoon. *Harbour Houses* (☎0407 805 305, ⊛www.harbourhouse.com.au; ➏) has the pick of the aspirational **accommodation**, with three bright beachpads right on the beach. Cheaper one- and two-bed cottages are at *Boat Harbour Garden Cottages* (☎03/6445 1233; ➎) by the Bass Highway turn-off.

Rocky Cape National Park and Sisters Beach

Stretching for a mere 12km along the coast, from **Sisters Beach** – seven kilometres west of Boat Harbour Beach, less developed and markedly cheaper – to Rocky Cape, are the rugged hills and cliffs of **ROCKY CAPE (TANGDIMMAA) NATIONAL PARK**. Tasmania's smallest national park was created in 1967 to preserve its remarkable **Aboriginal archaeological**

finds. The mainly quartzite hills are pocked with **caves**, of which the two major ones, North Cave and South Cave, contain huge shell middens, bones and stone tools dating back as far as eight thousand years. The Aboriginal Rar.rer.loi. he.ner people occupied the area during the British arrogation of the island in the early 1800s, and Rocky Cape is now managed in consultation with the Tasmanian Aboriginal Land Council. To protect the caves' heritage, you cannot enter, although it's okay to look in from the entrances. North Cave is at the western end of the park, a fifteen-minute return walk from the road, reached by driving 5km into the park and taking the left fork at the lighthouse. Two more caves, Wet Cave and Lee-Archer Cave, where there's a platform to help you look inside, are located on a headland in the centre of the park. Access is by a coast road west from Sisters Beach or the Inland Track (3–4hr one way), which goes to the west end of Sisters Beach. A **circuit walk** that returns by the coast will take around seven hours – be aware that snakes are common, so wear sturdy shoes and thick socks. In spring and summer, a profusion of wild flowers bloom on the heathland scrub, including endemic orchids. The park also holds Tasmania's only stands of saw-tooth Banksia, a shrubby tree with dark green serrated leaves. At dusk you may see wallabies and echidnas. Tasmap publishes a national park **hiking map** with notes ($9.10) but it's hard to find; Service Tasmania in Burnie (48 Cattley St; ☎1300 13 55 13) or Backpackers Barn in Devonport (see p.254) are your best hopes.

Elsewhere, the park is characterized by beaches in a scalloped rocky shore that offers superb **snorkelling and diving** – the coastline is known for its wonderful rockpools brimming with multicoloured seaweeds and delicately patterned starfish. As conditions can be treacherous for the inexperienced, it's worth taking a trip to Scuba Centre at 62 Bass Highway in Wynyard (☎03/6442 2247, ✉shop@scubacentre.net.au; $90 per dive). Safe **swimming** is at Sisters Beach, Forwards Beach and Anniversary Bay.

There's no drinking water in the park, through toilets are at Mary Ann Cove and Burgess Cove near North Cave. Camping is not permitted in the park area, but you can **camp** at *Rocky Cape Tavern* (☎03/6443 4110; $12) by the Bass Highway turn-off, with a petrol station nearby. A more attractive option is the bush clearings of eco-friendly *Crayfish Creek Van & Cabin Park* (☎03/6443 4228, ✉caradale@ow.net.au; camping $12, vans ❷, cabins ❸–❺), a few kilometres further west. It also has a three-bed treehouse (❻), a little dated in decor but appealing for the branches that sway through its deck.

The nearest non-camping **accommodation** is at Sisters Beach, 7km west of Boat Harbour Beach. You can stay in small bungalows in the bush at *Birdland Holiday Cottages*, at 7 Banksia Ave (☎03/6445 1471; ❸); in larger split-level cottages behind the beach at *Beach Houses*, on Kenelm Ave (☎03/6445 1147; ❺); or in a modern open-plan apartment at *Sea Change B&B* at 6 Elfrida Ave as you enter the village (☎03/6445 1456, ✉kbradmor @bigpond.net.au; ❹). The village has a general store (daily 7.30am–7.30pm) with fuel – ask here for other accommodation options. There's precious little else except the long beach in front of it.

West of Rocky Cape

The scenic coast-hugging drive west of Rocky Cape National Park is marred only by the industrial scene at Port Latta. About 5km beyond here, a turn-off leads 27km south on the C225. At **MAWBANNA** after 13km, **Water Wheel Creek Timber Heritage Experience** (daily mid-Sept–mid-June; tours 10am, 11.30am, 1pm, 2.30pm & 4pm; $10; ☎03/6458 8144, ⊛www.waterwheelcreek .com.au) provides an insight into the bush timber operations that fed the

Victorian goldrush of the late 1800s. Guided interpretative tours feature displays of bush skills and the state's only timber tramway in action. Mawbanna's place in the history books is for the last sighting of a thylacine (Tasmanian tiger) in the wild. It was spotted in 1930 and shot pretty soon afterwards by bushman Wilf Batty – its crime, that it had attacked his chickens. The road concludes at the **Dip Falls Forest Reserve** and its must-see **Big Tree**, a gigantic eucalyptus measuring 17m at its base and thought to be over 400 years old. Botanists rank it the third-largest tree in Tasmania. The base of Dip Falls is reached on a short, steep walk, and from a platform by the picnic ground at the top you get a good view of its unusual hexagonal basalt columns.

Back on the highway, a few kilometres beyond the C225 turn, are a string of great bushcamps: *Peggs Beach* (pit toilets; picnic tables; fireplaces; non-potable water), sandwiched between the beach and highway; and 2km further west off the main road, *Black River Camping Area* (pit toilets; fireplaces) where you can pitch in grassy clearings among the bush. Both are managed by Parks & Wildlife and have an honesty box for the $6-per-night fee.

Stanley

Few small towns in Tasmania are as fastidious about their streetscape as **STANLEY**. The most northerly settlement in Tasmania and premier resort of the northwest coast, the tiny coastal town is awash with history and charm, its weatherboard houses strung along a cat's-cradle of lanes. Long before you arrive at Stanley, 7km north of the Bass Highway, you'll see **Circular Head** – a volcanic plug that withstood the erosion that removed soft surrounding sediments. Locals call its table-like headland "the Nut". Navigator Matthew Flinders, in an uncharacteristic touch of whimsy in 1798, described it as "a Christmas cake".

Stanley itself shelters on a small peninsula beneath. Its early story is that of its instigator, the **Van Diemen's Land Company** (see box, p.279). When company officials pitched tents on October 21, 1826, Stanley became not just the first settlement in northwest Tasmania, but the headquarters from which the company developed the surrounding area. Livestock and agricultural equipment were landed within a year, as were weapons, with dire consequences for the

▲ View of Stanley and the Nut

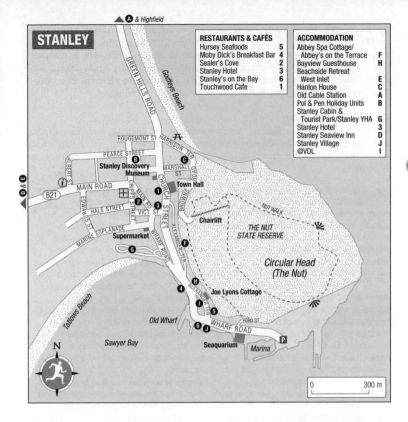

region's Aboriginal population. But the stuttering success of sheep-farming, exacerbated by negligible communications with London, made development slow, and the fledgling town atrophied as the wool enterprise stalled. The wane of the Van Diemen's Land Company forced Stanley to diversify into fishing, and one of the largest fleets on the north coast still sails for lobster, abalone, oysters and pelagic fish species. However, tourism now fills the town's coffers.

Information and tours

For tourist **information**, accommodation bookings and Internet access, visit the Stanley Visitor Centre on the way into Stanley at 45 Main Rd (Mon–Fri 9.30am–5.30pm, Sat & Sun 10am–4pm; ℡03/6458 1330, ⓦwww.stanley.com .au) – it also covers the Circular Head region, south to Arthur River and west to Cape Grim. The centre serves as the Redline **bus** depot and sells bus tickets; Stanley is reached on the route between Burnie and Smithton (Mon–Fri daily either way). The town supermarket, on the corner of Wharf Road and Marine Esplanade, has an ATM, while a newsagent towards the end of Church Street also has supplies and is an ANZ bank agent; there are more banking facilities a few doors up at the post office.

Stanley-based Wilderness to West Coast Tours (℡03/6458 2038, ⓦwww .wildernesstasmania.com) runs a dusk platypus-viewing tour (2hr; $35) and a penguin tour (1hr; $15; both tours combined $45). The "Tarkine Discovery Tour" explores the northwest tip by 4WD, through farm country, temperate rainforest, gum forests and buttongrass plains (6hr; $198); a longer version also visits the west coast (8.5hr, $249; two- or three-day excursions $399 per day). Day-trips include morning tea and gourmet lunch; multi-day excursions include all food and accommodation. Stanley Seal Cruises (daily 10am; also April–June 3pm; 1hr 30min; $44; ℡0419 550 134), in a booth at the port, visits a populous colony of **Australian fur seals**, weather permitting.

Accommodation

Stanley is awash with holiday accommodation. In keeping with its historic ambience, "colonial" B&Bs rule, actually self-contained cottages. Nevertheless, reservations are recommended in January and February. Budget accommodation is limited.

Bay View Guesthouse 16–20 Alexander House ℡03/6458 1445, ⓦwww .bayviewguesthouse.com. One of the best-value options in town, this former sailors' pub provides en-suite accommodation in three spacious suites with kitchenettes. Contemporary decor is stylish without showing off. ❹

Beachside Retreat West Inlet Main Road, 2.5km south of centre ℡03/6458 1350, ⓦwww.beachsideretreat.com. All luxury cabins in this eco-retreat on a private nature reserve have fantastic views, framed by huge porthole windows or a single glass wall, and there's access to a private beach. ❻–❽

Hanlon House 6 Marshall St ℡03/6458 1149, ⓦwww.hanlonhouse.com.au. This upmarket B&B, in a 1904 house, provides formal heritage accommodation in five en-suite rooms. Superb views over Godfrey Beach from the breakfast room. ❻

Old Cable Station West Beach Rd, 3km north of town, beyond Highfield House ℡03/6458 1312, ⓔcablestation@westnet.com.au. Once the communications link between Tasmania and the mainland via King Island, this peaceful retreat is surrounded by a pretty flower-filled garden and has views stretching across fields to water. Choose from a spacious three-bedroom cottage, or two stylish en-suite rooms. Rooms ❺, cottage ❻

Pol & Pen Holiday Units Corner of Cripps and Pearse streets ℡1800 222 397, ⓦwww .abbeyscottages.com.au. These two good-value timber cottages (❹) from accommodation agency Abbey's Cottages are snug and homely for short stays. Other properties on their books include *Abbey's on the Terrace* and *Abbey's Spa Cottage*, both on Alexander Terrace with gorgeous bay views

from the veranda (both ❻), or the heritage charm of *Estowen House* on Main Road. (❹).

Stanley Cabin and Tourist Park and Stanley YHA Wharf Road ℡03/6458 1266, ⓦwww .stanleycabinpark.com.au. In a great seafront location behind Tatlow Beach with the general store nearby, just a short stroll away from the wharf and centre. Tidy and well-maintained facilities. The youth hostel is perennially popular. There's also the option to camp. Camping $22, dorms $24, hostel rooms ❷, motel-style rooms ❹, self-contained cabins ❸–❹

Stanley Hotel Church Street ℡03/6458 1161. Brightly painted and semi-smart accommodation in the old pub; good-value singles for $35. Rooms ❸, en suite ❹

Stanley Seaview Inn 1km along Dovecote Road ℡03/6458 1300, ⓦwww.stanleyseaviewinn.com .au. Some of the best views of the Nut across green fields are from the spacious, well-appointed accommodation here. Motel-style rooms are dated but spotless and perfectly comfy, and there's a good restaurant on-site. The hotel also manages two deluxe apartments, *Horizon* (❻), with spectacular views of the Nut. Motel rooms ❹–❺

Stanley Village 15-17 Wharf Rd ℡03/6458 1404, ⓦwww.stanleyvillage.com.au. A rather old-fashioned motel complex, but you're paying for the location: nestled under the Nut and overlooking Tatlows Beach. ❺

@VDL 16 Wharf Rd ℡03/6458 2032, ⓦwww .atvdlstanley.com.au. A tranquil boutique hotel in the renovated waterfront warehouse of the Van Diemen's Land Company. Rooms feature serene contemporary decor in shades of chocolate and taupe, while airy public areas retain historic character. ❼

The Town

Stanley's high street, **Church Street**, runs below the foot of the Nut and holds most of the town's immaculately maintained cottages, many converted into cafés or galleries – check out the contemporary wood designs in Stanley Artworks Studio Gallery near the post office – and the occasional fine-food providore. Most herald from the 1850s and 1860s, the only exception being a boxy town hall (1911) and the two-storey *Stanley Hotel*. Halfway along, in a former church hall, the **Stanley Discovery Museum** (Sept–June daily 10am–4pm, July–Aug Tues–Sun 10am–4pm; $3; ℗03/6458 1309) houses a so-so hoard of memorabilia to narrate town history, largely from the pre-World War I glory years when Stanley flourished as a timber exporter and shipping terminal. Among the clutter are historical shipwreck finds.

Historic Alexander Terrace at the base of the Nut has a string of quaint weather-board cottages. The boxy shingle-roofed building at no. 14 was the **birthplace of Joe Lyons** (daily Sept–May 10am–4pm, June–Aug 11am–3pm; donation; ℗03/6458 1145), the only Tasmanian prime minister of Australia. Memorabilia of the pre-war leader who died in 1939 while in office may leave non-Australians cold, but the simply furnished rooms have a cottage charm. The house looks out over the curve of **Tatlows Beach**, which stretches for kilometres southeast, and Marine Park, where Stanley made its debut as a tented settlement in 1826. If you're by the water's edge at dead low tide, look for the remains of a 1923 **shipwreck**, a victim of the "furies" of the Bass Strait. The original wharf has made way for Fisherman's Dock, with a large fleet and **Stanley Seaquarium** (daily 10am–4pm; $8), full of various creatures hauled up by fishermen. Port Jackson and Gummy sharks get so excitable at feeding times (posted at door) that they wriggle. There's

The Van Diemen's Land Company

...how is it that an absentee owner across the world got this magnificent and empty country without having paid one glass bead?

Cassandra Pybus

The Van Diemen's Land Company (VDL) was the brainchild of a group of prominent and well-connected individuals, who in 1824 managed to obtain by Royal Charter 250,000 acres of the mainly thickly forested, unexplored northwest corner of Tasmania – to go "beyond the ramparts of the unknown" as the charter put it. The plan was to create their own source of fine wool in the colonies, which could be relied upon even if Europe was subject to political upheaval. The *Tranmere* arrived at Circular Head in 1826, with the personnel, livestock, supplies and equipment to create the township of Stanley.

The first flocks were grazed at Woolnorth on Cape Grim, a plateau of tussock grass and trees that might have been made for the purpose but, in fact, was prime Aboriginal hunting land. When hunting parties began to take the precious sheep, whites killed Aborigines in retaliation and thus began a vindictive murderous cycle. The most tragic incident (a version of events denied by Woolnorth) was supposed to have occurred around 1826 or 1827: a group of Aboriginal men, seeking revenge for the rape of the tribe's women, speared a shepherd and herded one hundred sheep over the cliff edge. These deaths were ruthlessly avenged when a group of thirty unarmed Aborigines, hunting for muttonbirds near the same spot, were killed by shepherds and their bodies thrown over the cliff (now euphemistically called "Suicide Bay"). Ultimately, the Aboriginal people of the northwest were systematically hunted down: the last group, middle-aged parents and their five sons, were captured by sealers near Arthur River in 1842 after the VDL's chief agent offered a £50 reward.

Though the hills resembled the dales of England in appearance, their extreme cold and rain were not conducive to sheep-farming. Struggling in the 1840s, the company changed its emphasis from wool to the sale and lease of its land, whereupon it finally prospered. It now holds just a fifth of its original land. Still registered on the London Stock Exchange, it is the only remaining company in the world operating under a Royal Charter.

also an excellent hands-on rockpool for the kids, with sea stars, sea cucumbers and a giant hermit crab called "Roy".

You can make the strenuous twenty-minute walk up the steep grassy slopes of **the Nut**, but it's more exhilarating and far more comfortable to ascend on a **chairlift** reached via the ramp opposite the post office (Sept–June daily 9.30am–5.30pm, earlier shoulder months; weather permitting; call ☎03/6458 1286 to double-check; cash/cheque only, $10 return, return only). There's a car park at the base if you're driving and a seasonal café which provides great views. Better still are those at the top while you make a blustery two-kilometre circuit walk around the **Nut State Reserve**; you gaze over the town and port, the two beaches and can see southeast as far as Table Cape.

North of the centre, **Godfreys Beach** is an exquisite stretch of sand and blue water, backed by the Nut. Rips can be strong, so be careful if you swim. The headland at its west end hosts a rookery of Little Penguins which return to their burrows just after dusk from November to early April. Green Hills Road runs north alongside the beach and then winds uphill to **Highfield** (daily Dec–March 9am–5pm, April–Nov 10am–4pm; $9; ☎03/6458 1100, ⓦwww .historic-highfield.com.au), the original headquarters of the Van Diemen's Land Company, 2km north of Stanley. Considering that it was created in the 1830s, when the wool enterprise already teetered on the brink of bankruptcy, and was planned with a deer park beneath its perch – you pass its gates as you ascend Green Hills Road – the homestead's grandiose Regency style is something of a monument to vainglorious colonial folly. The rooms themselves are fairly spartan in furnishings, though some original fittings remain such as the timber shutters, marble fireplaces and then-innovative tongue-and-groove floorboards. However, the interpretive boards on self-guided tours provide an honest history of the VDL Company and the northwest, with lots from the Aboriginal perspective. Also appealing are a pretty cottage garden and the spectacular view over Godfrey's Beach to the Nut. If you have your own transport, it's worth returning to Stanley on a seven-kilometre scenic drive that continues beyond Highfield and passes a lookout.

Eating

Hurseys Seafoods Wharf Rd, next to Marine Park. One of the best fish-and-chip shops in Tasmania, all straight-from-the-tank fresh – you can select live fish (around twenty kinds) and crayfish from its huge holding tanks inside. Daily 9am–6pm.

Moby Dick's Breakfast Bar 5 Church St. Bargain-priced, tasty breakfasts – from light starts such as cereals and waffles to the full fry-up – plus fresh fruit juices. Daily 7.30–11am.

Old Cable Station West Beach Rd, north of town, beyond Highfield House ☎03/6458 1312. By popular consensus, this serves the finest cuisine in town. Lobster and fresh fish star on a menu that leans towards Mediterranean in its choice of flavours, most dishes slow-cooked in a wood-fired oven. Reservations recommended; moderate to expensive. Dinner summer only.

Sealer's Cove 2 Main Rd. Cosy and always friendly, this small restaurant serves up good-value Italian dishes, and has pizzas to take away. Dinner, closed Tues.

Stanley Hotel Corner of Church and Victoria streets. A credit to Stanley, this serves fresh seafood, tasty steaks from local beef and other above-average, moderately priced pub grub in a lounge bar bistro with terrace dining and views. Lunch & dinner daily.

Stanleys on the Bay 15 Wharf Rd ☎03/6458 1404. A well-regarded seafood and steak restaurant inside the old stone bond store on the wharf. Crayfish is consistently excellent. Mains average around $26. Dinner Mon–Sat; closed July & Aug.

Touchwood Coffee Shop 31 Church St. Expansive views inside and out, the best coffee in Stanley and light contemporary food with lots of seafood; from lemon-and-chilli chargrilled squid ($15) to crayfish rolls ($15.50) via toasted sandwiches and delicious biscuits. Daily except Fri 10am–4pm.

The remote northwest

Lieutenant-governor George Arthur declared the island's northwest tip "beyond the ramparts of the unknown" in the mid-1820s. The epithet still has a ring of truth about it, as this is one of Australia' great wilderness secrets. If you stand on the west coast to watch the sun drag the sky sizzling into the sea, it'll be rising simultaneously over Patagonia. Between you and South America there's nothing except the Southern Ocean, flailed by the Roaring Forties into heaving swells that explode on a tortured coastline. Inland are the magisterial rainforests of the ancient **Tarkine**, much of it undisturbed by so much as a footprint. The air is offcially the cleanest in the world. It is not an area for tourist sights – though Forestry Tasmania's **Dismal Swamp** site en route to Marrawah bucks the trend – so much as for raw nature: the superb coastline around **Marrawah**, the dusty wilderness drive along the **Western Explorer** or **boat trips** from Arthur River and Corinna.

West to Cape Grim and Smithton

Seven Mile Beach (known as Anthonys Beach) is another of the effortless wild beaches at which Tasmania excels; just kilometres of deserted bleached sand that stretch west towards the private dairy pasture of Robbins Island. You reach it by turning right just over 4km west of the Stanley turn-off on the Bass Highway. At the car park you'll find good interpretive boards on the northwestern Aboriginal tribes, the last to maintain their traditional lifestyles as British colonialization encroached, and also the birdlife that flourishes in the wetland of Robbins Passage.

Tasmania's rugged northwest tip remains under the control of the Van Diemen's Land Company (see box, p.279). Cattle and sheep grazing remains the focus of operations at **Woolnorth**, the original VDL beef and wool property. It's sited on **Cape Grim**, where the air, carried thousands of kilometres across nothing except Southern Ocean, is officially the cleanest in the world. The Roaring Forties winds that helter-skelter across the ocean have also led to the largest **wind farm** in the southern hemisphere. The only way to access the area is on **tours**: half-day tours (9.45am, departure from property gate 40km west of Smithton; $65; bookings essential; ☎03/6452 1493, ⊚www.woolnorthtours .com.au) take in the homestead, wind farm, morning tea at the 1970s directors' lodge and a quick romp around the headland. The full-day tour (9am, depart from Smithton; $125, includes morning tea and lunch; bookings essential; same contacts) adds in either the remote Robbins Passage Wetlands (Sept–June) or northern tip Woolnorth Point (July–Aug), the old cottages and a lunch around VDL's eighteenth-century boardroom table. You'll also go a couple of kilometres east of Cape Grim, to stand where the Bass Strait meets the Southern Ocean and walk along the spectacular, rugged coastline. Alternatively you can just tour the wind farm (45min; 9.45am; $16.50; same contacts).

SMITHTON itself, 22km west of Stanley at the mouth of the Duck River, is a missable medium-sized town. Its only tourist sight is a volunteer-run **heritage centre** (Mon–Thurs 10am–3pm; $4) on the corner of King and Nelson streets, one block across from the high street. There's minor interest here – farming and forestry memorabilia documenting pioneers of the early 1900s, a diverting board on the ill-fated thylacine (Tasmanian tiger), plus a plastercast of the fossilized giant wombat dredged from a nearby swamp in 1908 – but nothing to quicken the pulse. What Smithton lacks in aesthetics it makes up for by its efficacy as a launchpad for the remote northwest coast: it has the last good supermarkets and banking facilities before Rosebery and Zeehan, plus fuel. There's an **Online Access Centre** on Nelson Street (Mon–Thurs 10am–7pm, Fri 10am–5pm) and the Redline **coach** depot is at 27 Victoria St. The resort-like *Tall Timbers Hotel Motel* on Scotchtown Road (☏03/6452 2755, ⊛www .talltimbershotel.com.au; ➏–➐), built from local timber, has a vast and popular bistro and motel or self-catering accommodation. It also runs day-tours of the Tarkine and northwest coast either by 4WD ($179) or helicopter (prices vary by tour and group size; per person, in a group of five, you'll pay $435 for a flight over Cape Grim, including a BBQ lunch, and $295 to fly over the west coast at sunset).

The Tarkine forestry reserves

South of Smithton, ten **forestry reserves**, ranging from rainforests to blackwood swamps and giant eucalyptus forests, are accessible on the South Arthur Forest Drive. This sixty-kilometre loop-road off the C218 between Rodger River and Kanunnah Bridge cuts into the edge of the remote Tarkine rainforest – an easily accessible taster of its much-debated wilderness (see box, p.285). Site managers Forestry Tasmania have helpfully positioned information points at either end of the loop, and signs throughout direct off the unsealed road to boardwalks and lookouts. Heading clockwise (north to south), once over the Tayatea Bridge you can divert to **Milkshakes Hills Forest Reserve**, with a beautiful picnic area and an easy boardwalk (10min) into the rainforest or up a "Milkshake" hill (1hr return) for a view over undulating grass plains. Two-thirds of the way around, **Dempster Plains Lookout** gazes over the buttongrass at the heart of the Tarkine, while a little further on, **Lake Chisholm** is a gem, a flooded sinkhole whose brown waters reflect thick myrtle forest. At the southern end of the loop, 208-acre **Julius River Forest Reserve** has two easy walks (30min return) through the cool temperate forest, the best heading into a stand of moss-clad myrtle in another sinkhole. The river also provides a refuge for endangered giant freshwater lobster. **Sumac Lookout** beyond offers a spectacular view of the rainforested gullies and eucalyptus ridges in the Tarkine before you rejoin the road at Kanunnah Bridge, no mean spot on the river itself. Both the visitor centre in Stanley and Forestry Tasmania, at the corner of Nelson and Smith streets in Smithton (☏03/6452 1317), stock **maps** and route information. It's also worth double-checking the state of the route here – Tayatea Bridge was washed away by floods in mid-2007 and the rebuild was expected to take a year. There are basic sites for campervans at the picnic areas, both of which have toilets.

If you prefer your flora more manicured, **Allendale Gardens** (daily Oct–April 9am–5pm; $7.50), signposted off the C218 seven kilometres after Irishtown, has six acres of landscaped gardens carved out of a 65-acre plot of rainforest.

Southwest to Marrawah and around

From Smithton, the Bass Highway cuts inland having traversed the length of the northwest coast. Thirty kilometres along the way, Forestry Tasmania has come up with a novel stunt in the form of **Dismal Swamp** (daily Nov–March 9am–5pm, April–Sept 10am–4pm; $20; ☏03/6456 7199) – the dour name derives from the sodden experience of a survey party in 1828. Its latest installation in a PR-friendly policy of "forests as playgrounds" is this 110-metre slide (children must be over eight years old and over 90cm high), which swooshes you down at up to 35kmph to a sinkhole of swampy blackwood forest. From the bottom, you can access a maze of short boardwalked trails dotted with art installations – don't explore all at once because your ticket is good for three rides. The visitor centre itself, an award-winning structure like a squashed tube, makes a good break in its own right, if only for a smart café and a small gallery of woodcraft.

Stockmen opened up the pasture southwest in the 1880s. The first land grant was taken as recently as 1889, and yet the low hills were stripped bare within fifty years, and now contain a few scattered farmsteads which continue to nurture some of the finest beef in Australia. The dispersed community helps explain why **MARRAWAH** turns out to be little more than a general store with an attached café (Mon–Thurs 7.30am–6.30pm & until 7pm Fri, Sat 8am–7pm & until 6pm Sun) and the *Marrawah Tavern*, the "Best in the West", which serves the only lunches and dinners on the northwest coast – no-nonsense fillers all. As well as basic supplies – better than those available at Arthur River, but fresh produce is still minimal – the store has a post office plus the last **fuel** before Zeehan or Rosebery.

Visitors come for **Green Point Beach**, 2km west from Marrawah, one of the three best **surfing** beaches in Australia. Competitors of Tasmania's biggest surf contest, the West Coast Classic, swagger into the region in March to ride raw Southern Ocean swells which can jack up to seven metres high. The left-hand reef break works from mid- to high-tide in front of the car park, often with good tubes, and, depending on conditions, another left breaks off a cluster of rocks 200m offshore. **Ann Bay** also provides superb windsurfing, though you'll need your own gear. For everyone else, the beach is simply a gloriously wild spot, with views of the windmills on Cape Grim whirling in the distance. More good surf in the area is at **Nettley's Bay**, 1km south of Green Point, which receives some shelter from northwest winds behind a point, and at **Lighthouse Point**, reached via a side-road 3km south of Marrawah – it faces due west, so southwesterly swells here pack a punch.

Accommodation at Green Point Beach consists of a small camping area (toilets at nearby picnic ground) and two-bed self-contained *Marrawah Beach House* (℡03/6457 1285; ➍) with uninterrupted views over the empty sands.

▲ Tasmanian Devil road sign

Ann Bay Cabins (☏03/6457 1361, ⊛www.annbaycabins.com.au; ❺) has rather smart open-plan spa units on the road down to the coast, though it was for sale at the time of research. Excellent-value spacious rooms are at ⚑ *Glendonald Cottage* on the Arthur River Road, 3km south of Marrawah (☏03/6457 1191, ⊛www.kingsrun.com.au; ❹). The owner, Geoff King, a passionate conservationist and expert on the Aboriginal history of the area, has set aside his 830-acre farmholding to conduct Kings Run Wildlife Tours. His nocturnal **viewings of Tasmanian Devils** in the wild ($75; one hour before sunset until midnight; same contacts) must rank as one of the signature experiences of Tasmania. You hunker down in a lonely fisherman's hut at dusk and wait for Devils to scavenge on road-kill placed outside the window. So the animals are not habituated to feeding, tours only run on five nights a fortnight, meaning pre-booking is essential. Hugely atmospheric, highly recommended.

The curve of Ann Bay here is shrouded by the hump of **Mount Cameron West** to the north. Three kilometres north of this bluff, at the end of a long exposed beach, is the most complex Aboriginal art site in Tasmania, the **Preminghana Indigenous Protected Area**. Rock carvings of geometric or nonfigurative forms cover slabs of rock at the base of a cliff, whose 524 acres were handed back to the Aboriginal Land Council of Tasmania in 1999. Following damage by fishermen in 4WDs, the art has been buried in the sand and access is restricted to a lookout.

Arthur River

A new sealed route zips over 20km south of Marrawah to a scattering of holiday homes at **ARTHUR RIVER**. Named after the river, the tiny settlement is home to 25 permanent residents at the boundary of one of the great coastal wildernesses of Tasmania. It's superb rugged country: salt-bleached tree trunks that have been washed downriver litter the foreshore, heaved ashore like twigs by the Southern Ocean swells that pound the rocks. The next land mass west is South America, and one can almost sense that at Gardiners Point, "**The Edge of the World**", on the south side of the river mouth. A lookout and picnic area at the point are a great vantage point to gaze over the tortuous coastline. It's too dangerous to swim here due to the wild conditions, but there's good fishing in the estuary and a southwesterly aspect means pumping surf – a lefthander breaks just off the point at mid- to high-tide (entry is from a small beach beside the lookout). Even walking along adjacent **Arthurs Beach** can be an obstacle course, but it's possible to go 10km south to Sundown Point (see p.287); arrange a pick-up vehicle or allow a full day to do the return walk. A slightly shorter route tracks north (7km one way) to **Bluff Hill**. Keep an eye open for compacted mussel and scallop shells where the paths cut into the shore, its humps the remnants of Aboriginal campsite middens. Note that the sites posesses the same cultural weight for indigenous communities that Westerners attach to museums, so don't touch anything.

As you come into the settlement on the sealed Arthur River Road, a Parks & Wildlife office (daily 9am–5pm; ☏03/6457 1225) has the latest information on road conditions south, camping and off-road 4WD permits. There's also a public phonebox – the last chance to make a call before Corinna – and the Arthur River Store (daily 7.30am–8pm; ☏03/6457 1207), which has basic preserved foodstuffs and takeaway snacks. It also rents fishing rods, sells tickets for the Arthur River Cruise (see p.286) and books **accommodation**: options on either side of the river mouth include the spacious *Ocean View Holiday Cottage* (☏03/6457 1100; ❹–❺), with stunning views, and the

excellent but smaller two-bed units of *Sunset Holiday Villas* opposite
(T03/6457 1197, Wwww.sunsetholidayvillas.com; ❹–❺). **Camping** at
Arthur River is a truly pleasurable experience, with facilities that range from
the fully serviced *Peppermint Campground* (cold-water showers) near the Parks
& Wildlife office to secluded sites equipped merely with a pit toilet and
water tap, such as *Manuka Campground* north or *Prickly Wattle Campground*
past the Gardiners Point turning. Campsites cost $6 per night (or $30
weekly), payable in an honour box at the Parks & Wildlife office. Be warned
that possums and Devils swipe any food left outdoors. If facilities are more

The Tarkine

"This ancient, unbroken tract of rainforest shows a world beyond human
memory and is a living link with the ancient super-continent Gondwana."

World Wildlife Fund report, July 2004

The Tarkine, covering 930,000 acres in northwest Tasmania, was named after the
Tarkiner band of Aboriginal people who once roved here. It's Tasmania's largest
unprotected wilderness area – stretching from the west coast to Murchison Highway
in the east and from the Arthur River in the north to the Pieman River in the south.
Conservationists have been pushing for a Tarkine National Park since the 1960s and
the area was recommended for UNESCO's World Heritage list in the 1990s. Of its
593,000 acres of forest, seventy percent constitutes Australia's largest tract of
temperate rainforest, second only in global significance to tracts in British Columbia.
This "forgotten wilderness" of giant myrtle forests, wild rivers and bare granite
mountains – a living link to Gondwana forests that has changed little over 65 million
years – is the sort of place where the Tasmanian tiger, long thought extinct, might still
be roaming.

After a twenty-year moratorium on **logging** was lifted in October 2003 and deputy
Paul Lennon gave the green light to logging of old-growth red myrtle in the Savage
River corridor, deep in the heart of the Tarkine, Tasmania's forests became a political
football in the 2004 federal election. The area was nominated for national park status
and in 2005, 182,000 acres (mostly rainforest) of the Tarkine received protection from
forestry, an outcome the Wilderness Society described as "outstanding". More good
news for campaigners came in September 2007 when the Australian Senate bowed
to environmental pressure and unanimously agreed to nominate the area for World
Heritage protection. However the battle is far from won. That November, a proposal
to carve a 132-kilometre tourist road through the forest was unveiled by area
stewards Forestry Tasmania. It argued that the $20 million project would allow around
fifty thousand tourists a year to experience a region currently seen only by a handful
of bushwalkers. At the time of writing, the plan has not been implemented – nor has
it received national park status. As awareness of the Tarkine grows – in 2007 Channel
Nine named it Australia's best-kept wilderness secret – the area seems destined to
assume an iconic status similar to that of the Gordon River and Southwest National
Park in the early 1980s. As such it may become another frontline in the bitter war
between conservationists and forestry, and another emblem of the debate about
Tasmania's future direction.

Tarkine National Coalition, based in Burnie (T03/6431 2373, Wwww.tarkine.org)
produces guides to three self-drive Tarkine routes that don't involve the Western
Explorer; these can be downloaded from their website. Ecotourism operator Tarkine
Trails (T03/6223 5320, Wwww.tarkinetrails,com.au) specializes in Tarkine tours; it
has a six-day walking expedition through giant myrtle forests and waterfalls ($1399),
six days walking on the battered west coast (from Launceston or Burnie; $1649) and
a six-day vehicle-supported trip that covers both areas ($1849). All operate from
November to April.

critical than setting, the minimal *Arthur River Cabin Park* (☎03/6457 1212, ⓦ www.arthurrivercabinpark.com; camping $20; budget cabins ❷–❸; standard cabins ❹) is a couple of kilometres north.

To get out on the river, take a **cruise** or visit Arthur River Canoe & Boat Hire on the north side of the bridge (☎03/6457 1312; canoes $12 per hour, $50 per day; dinghies with outboard motor $25 per hour, $120 per day).

Arthur River cruises

Arguably the biggest attraction of the northwest coast is a cruise up the Arthur River. It's one of Tasmania's last true wilderness rivers, where dense rainforest – myrtle, sassafras, celery-top pines, laurel and giant tree ferns – crowds the banks to create an infinity of greens reflected in tannin-rich water. The birdlife is spectacular, too: black cockatoos, Tasmanian rosellas, black jays, wedge-tail eagles, white sea eagles, pied heron and azure kingfishers are just some of the species, though you'll hear more than you see. At one time the entire west coast looked like this. But the progressive damming of rivers has left the **Arthur Pieman Conservation Area**, east and south of Arthur River, part of the Tarkine wilderness area (see p.285), as a unique reminder.

A canoe will take you some way upriver, but the only way to see remote forest is a river cruise. The original tour is on the charmingly old-fashioned MV *George Robinson* (daily mid-Sept–May; 10am, returning 3pm, enquire about summer evening cruises; $74; bookings ☎03/6457 1158, ⓦ www .arthurrivercruises.com). It sails 14km upriver to the confluence of the Arthur and Frankland rivers at Turks Landing, travelling at a stately pace so you can take in the tranquillity of the river and experience the transition from coastal scrub woodland to the edge of **the Tarkine** – the second-largest tract of temperate rainforest in the world. Morning tea on the boat includes rum-spiked hot chocolate if you're up to it. Before a two-hour barbecue lunch (with wine) in a clearing, there's an informative half-hour guided bushwalk, where you'll learn about the rainforest species. The friendly crew even entertain with rollicking bush poetry on the return trip. A similar trip is aboard more modern cruiser MV *Reflections* (daily 10.15am, returning 4.15pm; 6hr; $77; ☎03/6457 1288, ⓦ www.arreflections.com), which heads upriver past the Arthur–Frankland confluence to Warra Landing for lunch and a guided rainforest walk. It lacks the charm of the *George Robinson*, but then again it does have an upper flybridge with 360-degree views. Whichever cruise you take, temperatures are cooler on the river, so bring a coat.

The Western Explorer

There's only one way south of Arthur River, and that's the **WESTERN EXPLORER**. Dubbed "The Road to Nowhere" when it was hastily planned and finished in 1996, the lonely road through the heart of the sensitive Arthur Pieman Conservation Area infuriated conservationists when it was unveiled. The campaigners' polemic that the route is a subterfuge for a logging road has some justification – forestry operations of area steward Forestry Tasmania bite chunks out of the old-growth in the north. Yet the dust-choked drive to Corinna is also, arguably, the greatest in Tasmania; a gloriously remote route that leaves behind the rainforest of Arthur River to snake along the boundary where windswept coastal heathland meets inland forest. The 110-kilometre route is unsealed for all but the steepest sections, is frequently rough and is often severely corrugated, limiting your speed to an average of 50kmph. Be aware too that there is no fuel en route – fill up either in Marrawah north or Zeehan south – nor mobile phone reception. In case of breakdown wait for help to pass by; this could be a day or more's wait, so water is a good idea. The track can also become degraded after heavy rainfall – advice on current road conditions is available from Parks & Wildlife in Arthur River, Stanley visitor centre, or if coming from the south, in Corinna. However, the Western Explorer is perfectly manageable in a 2WD if taken slowly, which in any case is the only way to absorb the views and silence.

Several rough side roads off the Western Explorer directly south of Arthur River bump down to a wild coastline pounded by massive swells. From **Sundown Point** – 10km south of Arthur River, then right at a T-junction – you can walk along the remote coast north to Sundown Creek (1.5km return). Shell middens, hut depressions and 2000-year-old circular engravings around Sundowner Point reveal the former presence of Tarkinner Aborigines; some ethnologists suggest the group occupied the area for around thirty thousand years. As well as being of major ethnographic importance, the area has continuing cultural value to indigenous communities – tread lightly and do not disturb any sites, nor remove anything from the area except the rubbish you introduce. Going left at the T-junction leads to a cluster of fishermen's huts at Nelson Shacks, from where you can walk south to **Couta Rocks** (10km return). You'll ford a small river and creek to reach the heath-cloaked foreshore around Sarah Anne Rocks, its black-sheened rocks carved by the surf into gulleys, then follow the remote coast for 2km to reach Couta Rocks; a bay with the islet of its name. If a member of your group doesn't want to walk, they can drive here on a side-route off the Western Explorer to pick you up again. The draw is less a specific sight than the raw coastline. The road south of Couta Rocks continues to **Temma**, a former sea port for the tin mine at Balfour, now reduced to a few fishermen's shacks. You can camp discreetly here, though there are no facilities. A very rough 4WD track continues south to Sandy Cape, but should not be taken lightly – quicksand is not unknown.

The West Explorer, meanwhile, turns east at Couta Rocks to reach a cross-roads after 16km. The C214 continues ahead then swings northeast towards the circuit-drive in the South Arthur Forests and back to Smithton. The onward route is right, on the C249, to begin the slow grind south. After 11km you can sidetrack east to **Balfour**, a ghost village after its tin mine was abandoned, while 67km south (11km north of Corinna), a lay-by at the brow of a hill provides the start for boardwalked walk **"the Longback"**, which ascends a ridge for a great view into the Tarkine.

The *Western Explorer Travel Guide* pamphlet issued by the Department of Infrastructure, Energy and Resources is available in the visitor centre at Stanley and, in theory, from the Parks & Wildlife Service office at Arthur River, though don't bank on it. Stanley-based Wilderness to West Coast Tours (see p.277) runs two- and three-day tours to Sandy Cape. With more time, a rewarding way to experience the wild coast between Corinna and Arthur River is on a six-day cultural and ecology excursion organized by Tarkine Trails (Nov–March; $1649; ☏ 03/6223 5320, Ⓦ www.tarkinetrails.com.au).

Corinna and the Pieman River

Though only a handful of huts, **CORINNA** feels like civilization after the Western Explorer. (It can also be reached on the unsealed 26-kilometre C247 south of Savage River, west of Waratah, or on the C249 north of Zeehan.) It's hard to believe that 2500 people once occupied what is now just a few shacks among dense bush. Yet the discovery of gold in the 1850s sparked a rush that led to a wild mining settlement infamous for its booze and brawling. It was "the very roughest place it had ever been my experience to strike… I spent two of the happiest years of my life there", prospector and mine manager Mark Ireland wrote in the 1890s. By then, the town was at its roaring peak following the 1883 discovery of a 7.5kg nugget in the Rocky River, a few kilometres upstream. That nothing even close to the largest gold strike in Tasmania was ever found again has led to speculation that it was imported from Ballarat, Victoria, to stake a mining claim. Corinna even had its own port, despite the dangers of navigating the narrow river mouth from the ocean – James Kelly, the swashbuckling whaling captain who circumnavigated Tasmania in a whaling boat in 1816, was almost swamped while attempting the entrance, which explains its name, "the Retreat".

New owners have pumped $2 million into Corinna to restore it as the last example of a remote west-coast mining township. Signs explain the origination of its historic timber and aluminium buildings, most of which double as **accommodation** for the ⚓ *Corinna Wilderness Experience* (☏03/6446 1170, ⓦwww.corinna.com.au). Options include four original miners' cottages (one- and two-bedroom ⑤–⑥), the old weatherboard pub, with atmospheric snug singles for $50 and doubles (⑥), and more modern, solar-powered, one- and two-bedroom cottages with comfy queen beds and log fires (⑤–⑥). A rebuild of one of Corinna's three hotels is promised. There's also free parking for motorhomes and a couple of **camping** pitches (no showers; $10), plus a general store that sells basic groceries. Though the few boardwalked nature trails that vanish into the rainforest won't detain you all day, the resort is the antithesis of the more packaged wilderness of Strahan. That the area is a habitat of ultra-rare orange-bellied parrots or that the last credible sighting of a thylacine, the extinct Tasmanian tiger, was made in surrounding forest only add to the appeal. All in all, well worth an overnight stop.

As much of a reason to visit as the stillness of the forest is the beautiful Pieman River. The story goes that the river was named after a convict escapee from the penal colony at Sarah Island, who was recaptured on the riverbank having battled through the thick bush north of Macquarie Harbour for a week, sustained by prime cuts of his fellow escape gang. In truth, the yarn probably confuses the grisly tale of cannibal convict Alexander Pearce (see p.306) with that of the escapee, a baker named Thomas Kent. In later decades, the reserve was a logging area and still holds one of the biggest stands of remaining Huon pine – saved because the water here was too deep to allow a dam to be built. The river is too dangerous for swimming, with an average drop of nearly 2m from the banks. However, you can go on a **river cruise** aboard MV *Arcadia II*, a 1923 cruiser (daily 10am; 4hr; $70 including morning tea, $7.50 extra with picnic lunch; bookings advisable; ☏03/6446 1170). From its deck you can see Huon pine, leatherwood and pandanus ferns among the temperate rainforest that crowds the river's north bank; the drier southern bank has mainly brown stringybark eucalyptus. The trip goes all the way to the foaming river mouth at Pieman Heads, and allows you an hour to wander on your own along a beach littered with logs that have been washed down by river floods. It's an invigorating spot, with nothing except empty Southern Ocean west to Argentina. Alternatively you can link up with Pieman Head Adventure Tours (book through ☏03/6446 1170) for a 4WD excursion to Granville Harbour near Zeehan (see p.307) (6hr; $150, $170 with BBQ lunch).

The "Fatman" barge – the only cable-driven **vehicle barge** in Tasmania – ferries across the Pieman River (daylight saving 9am–7pm, otherwise 9am–5pm; $20 car, $10 bike) to continue on the C249 to Zeehan, and then on the B27 to Strahan.

The A10 to the west coast

The fast-track route from the north to west coasts is the Murchison Highway (A10), which cuts off the Bass Highway at Somerset, 6km west of Burnie. Scenic **Hellyer Gorge State Reserve** after 50km is a perfect midway break on the drive to Waratah, with a pretty picnic ground near the Hellyer River and a couple of walking trails. There's a pretty riverside walk (10min return) or a path into myrtle and sassafras forest (30min return) from the west side of the road, by the bridge. A lay-by 3km south of the picnic ground provides a viewpoint over the lush upper Hellyer Gorge.

Tiny, windswept **WARATAH**, set in mountain heathland 8km off the A10, peaked in the early twentieth century after thirty years of tin mining at **Mount Bischoff**. For a while it was known as the richest mining town in Australia that had paid shareholders a $2 million return on their original $58,000 investment, and was linked to Burnie by the Emu Bay Railway to Zeehan and Rosebery; a road link did not appear until 1963. Waratah's scattered collection of scruffy weatherboard cottages shows little sign that it pulled Tasmania from the brink of bankruptcy. Nor is there much evidence of a population that once stood at three thousand people. There's a small local **history museum** in the old courthouse (daily 9am–5pm; free; keys from council office opposite weekdays or Waratah Roadhouse at weekends) and next to it a replica of a late nineteenth-century miner's hut known as Philosopher Smith Hut. Mine manager James "Philosopher" Smith stumbled upon the Mount Bischoff tin deposit in 1871, though the pioneer failed to grasp the value of his discovery and put his money into property instead. The tale is told in **Kenworthy's Stamper Museum** opposite the history museum (same hours), whose informative displays of local history are gathered around an old tin-ore stamper. It's worth going a little further west for a view of a **waterfall** that plumes over the valley head; engineers harnessed the water sluice to generate hydroelectricity in 1883. Opposite the falls, *Bischoff Hotel* (T03/6439 1188; rooms ❸, en suites ❹) has rooms and prepares **meals**, or you can stay in nearby *Waratah Lodge B&B* (rooms ❹, en suites ❺). A municipal caravan park (T03/6439 7100; $15) is nothing more than a car park behind the council office, where you pick up the toilet block key, though it has good sites beside Waratah Lake.

It's worth filling up if you are heading southwest of Waratah; the last fuel stop on the road is the former mining town of **Savage River**, 45km along the B23. Just over 9km along the route a wooden sign for "W'fall" directs you onto an overgrown vehicle track for a kilometre to begin the walk to the **Philosopher's Falls** (4–5hr return), arguably the finest day-walk in the Tarkine forest, though not one to be taken lightly. The forty-metre waterfall lies deep within the majestic myrtle forest of the Tarkine, though the tagged track is difficult and requires good bushwalking skills. The reward is the sense of isolation and the intrinsic beauty of old-growth forest that usually requires several days' hike to see. Follow the tags and on no account blunder ahead unless you can see the next one. Ideally inform someone that you are going.

Travel details

Coaches

Burnie to: Boat Harbour Beach turn-off (Mon–Fri 1 daily; 30min); Devonport (Mon–Thurs 4 daily, Fri 6 daily, Sat & Sun 2 daily; 50min–1hr); Launceston (Mon–Thurs 3 daily, Fri 5 daily, Sat & Sun 2 daily; 1hr 30min–2hr); Penguin (Mon–Fri 7 daily, Sat & Sun 1 daily; 25min); Rocky Cape National Park turn-off (Mon–Fri 1 daily; 30min); Smithton (Mon–Fri 1 daily; 1hr 30min); Stanley (Mon–Fri 1 daily; 1hr 5min); Ulverstone (Mon–Fri 7 daily, Sat & Sun 1 daily; 50min); Wynyard (Mon–Fri 13 daily, Sat 4 daily; 30min).

Devonport to: Burnie (Mon–Thurs 3 daily, Fri 5 daily, Sat & Sun 2 daily; 50min–1hr); Cradle Mountain (Nov–March 1 daily, April–Oct Tues, Thurs & Sat 1 daily; 1hr 30min); Deloraine (Mon–Thurs 3 daily, Fri 4 daily, Sat & Sun 2 daily; 1hr 30min); Gowrie Park (Tues, Thurs & Sat 1 daily; 40min); Hobart (Mon–Fri 4 daily; Sat & Sun 3 daily; 4hr–4hr 30min); Latrobe (Mon–Fri 12 daily, Sat 1 daily; 15min); Launceston (Mon–Fri 4 daily; Sat & Sun 3 daily; 1hr 15–30min); Port Sorell/Shearwater (Mon–Sat 3 daily; 30min); Queenstown (Tues, Thurs & Sat 1 daily; 5hr 20min); Sheffield (Nov–March 1 daily, April–Oct Tues, Thurs & Sat 1 daily; 30min); Strahan (Tues, Thurs & Sat 1 daily; 7hr 15min); Zeehan (Tues, Thurs & Sat 1 daily; 4hr).

Latrobe to: Devonport (Mon–Fri 12 daily, Sat 1 daily; 15min); Penguin (Mon–Thurs 3 daily, Fri 5 daily, Sat & Sun 2 daily; 30min); Port Sorell/Shearwater (Mon–Sat 1 daily; 20min).

Gowrie Park to: Cradle Mountain (Tues, Thurs & Sat 1 daily; 50min); Devonport (Tues, Thurs & Sat 1 daily; 50min); Launceston (Tues, Thurs & Sat 1 daily; 2hr); Queenstown (Tues, Thurs & Sat 1 daily; 4hr 50min); Strahan (Tues, Thurs & Sat 1 daily; 6hr 45min); Zeehan (Tues, Thurs & Sat 1 daily; 3hr 20min).

Penguin to: Burnie (Mon–Fri 7 daily, Sat & Sun 1 daily; 25min); Devonport (Mon–Thurs 3 daily, Fri 5 daily, Sat & Sun 2 daily; 30min); Ulverstone (Mon–Fri 7 daily, Sat & Sun 1 daily; 15–35min).

Smithton to: Boat Harbour Beach turn-off (Mon–Fri 1 daily; 1hr); Burnie (Mon–Fri 1 daily; 1hr 40min); Rocky Cape National Park turn-off (Mon–Fri 1 daily; 45min); Stanley (Mon–Fri 1 daily; 15min); Wynyard (Mon–Fri 1 daily; 1hr 10min)

Port Sorell and Shearwater to: Devonport (Mon–Sat 3 daily; 30min); Latrobe (Mon–Sat 1 daily; 20min).

Sheffield to: Cradle Mountain (Nov–March 1 daily, April–Oct Tues, Thurs & Sat 1 daily; 1hr); Devonport (Nov–March 1 daily, April–Oct Tues, Thurs & Sat 1 daily; 30min); Gowrie Park (Tues, Thurs & Sat 1 daily; 10min); Launceston (Nov–March 1 daily, April–Oct Tues, Thurs & Sat 1 daily; 2hr); Queenstown (Tues, Thurs & Sat 1 daily; 4hr 50min); Strahan (Tues, Thurs & Sat 1 daily; 6hr 45min); Zeehan (Tues, Thurs & Sat 1 daily; 3hr 20min).

Stanley to: Boat Harbour Beach turn-off (Mon–Fri 1 daily; 45min); Burnie (Mon–Fri 1 daily; 1hr 25min); Smithton (Mon–Fri 1 daily; 25min); Wynyard (Mon–Fri 1 daily; 1hr); Rocky Cape National Park turn-off (Mon–Fri 1 daily; 30min).

Ulverstone to: Burnie (Mon–Fri 7 daily, Sat & Sun 1 daily; 50min); Devonport (Mon–Thurs 4 daily, Fri 6 daily, Sat & Sun 1 daily; 30min); Penguin (Mon–Fri 7 daily, Sat & Sun 1 daily; 15–35min).

Wynyard to: Boat Harbour Beach turn-off (Mon–Fri 1 daily; 10min); Burnie (Mon–Fri 13 daily, Sat 4 daily; 30min); Rocky Cape National Park turn-off (Mon–Fri 1 daily; 20min); Smithton (Mon–Fri 1 daily; 1hr 10min); Stanley (Mon–Fri 1 daily; 45min).

Flights

Devonport to: King Island (Mon & Wed 2 daily, Tues, Thurs & Fri–Sun 1 daily; 1hr 20min); Melbourne (4 daily; 1hr 15min).

Wynyard (Burnie) to: King Island (Tues–Fri 2 daily, Mon, Sat & Sun 1 daily; 50min); Melbourne (4 daily; 1hr 10min).

Ferries

Devonport to: Melbourne (late Dec–mid-April 2 daily, otherwise 1 daily; 9–11hr).

The west and southwest

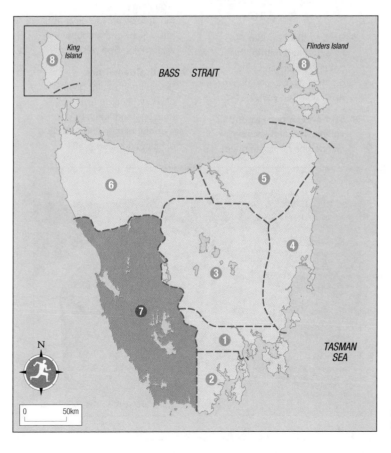

CHAPTER 7

Highlights

* **Gordon River cruises** A touristy but essential trip on the mirror-like river that snakes deep into the heart of the World Heritage Area. See p.303

* **Cradle Mountain** Never mind the tour groups, the Overland Track emphatically transcends any hype. See p.312

* **Rafting the Franklin** Wild by name and nature, the untamed Franklin is the greatest river expedition in Australia. See p.321

* **Styx and Upper Florentine valleys** The anti-logging campaigns hit home once you're immersed in a green cocoon of old-growth forest. See p.326

* **Gordon River dam** The highest commercial abseil in the world – enough said. See p.329

* **South to Scotts Peak** Mountain peaks sawtooth the horizon as you drive into the bosom of the southwest wilderness. See p.329

* **South Coast Track** Seven spectacular days of mountains, mud, beaches and leeches – utterly exhausting, utterly exhilarating. See p.331

▲ Sign on the Overland Track

The west and southwest

t's the lure of pure **wilderness** that attracts a certain type of traveller to Tasmania, and few places on earth are as untamed as the glaciated scenery of the west and southwest. Everything about the dramatic landscape is on an epic scale. It has one of the world's greatest cool temperate rainforests, in places more impenetrable than the Amazon and probably never visited by man. It has some of the tallest hardwood trees on earth – giant swamp gums nearly 90m high. Huon pines that were already saplings two millennia ago grow on the banks of the last wild river in Australia, the Franklin, and one stand near Rosebery is estimated at ten thousand years old. Southern Ocean swells that have travelled from South America explode onto the coast as waves up to forty metres high. Three metres of rain a year is not uncommon.

It's hard to be neutral in the face of such grandeur. The reactions of pioneers George Bass and Matthew Flinders in 1798 sum up what European visitors have felt ever since. The southwest coast "ranks among the foremost of the grand and wildly magnificent scenes of nature. It abounds with peaks and ridges, gaps and fissures", Bass enthused. Navigator Flinders saw instead "as dreary and as inhospitable a shore as has yet been discovered...The eye ranges over these peaks with astonishment and horror". In later decades, the wilderness was both the "Gates to Hell" for convicts bound for Sarah Island and a paradise for pioneers such as Cradle Mountain's Gustav Weindorfer. The dichotomy is realized today in the views of wilderness as a resource (forestry) or a reserve (environmentalists), an increasingly fractious debate that goes to the heart of the battle over Tasmania's future.

In the early 1980s, a proposal to dam the Gordon River below the confluence with the **Franklin River** prompted a battle between environmentalists and the state government, fought under the spotlight of a rapt media. The federal government stepped in, and, following a landmark High Court ruling in 1983, nearly all of the west and southwest was protected as a UNESCO World Heritage Area. Its richly textured wilderness occupies twenty percent of Tasmania's land area in three national parks: popular **Cradle Mountain–Lake St Clair National Park**, whose spectacular glaciated scenery, easily accessible from the north near Sheffield and the south via Derwent Bridge, can be traversed on the outstanding Overland Track; adjoining whitewater rafters' paradise **Franklin–Gordon Wild Rivers National Park**, which can be

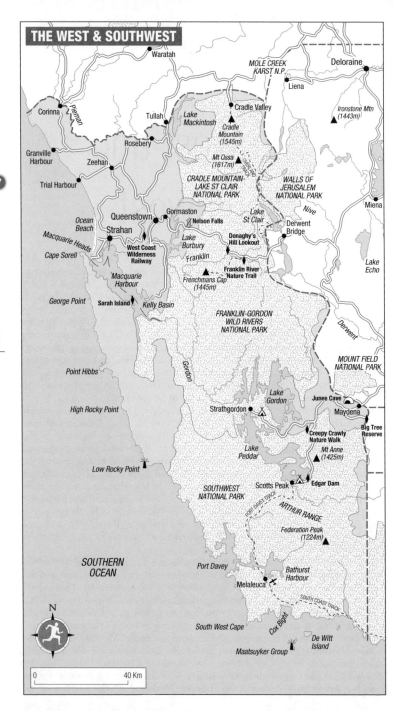

reached via the Lyell Highway; and the **Southwest National Park**, a keenly abandoned area of rugged coastlines, wild rivers, open buttongrass plains and tangled rainforests, spectacular peaks and more rain than any part of Australia except tropical Queensland.

Though much of the area is off-limits to all but experienced bushwalkers, **Strahan** serves as a wilderness gateway, notably for **cruises up the Gordon River**. The resort is one of only four towns in the entire region: the others are nearby **Queenstown**, the last operational relic of a mining boom that swept the west in the late 1800s, and now synonymous with ecological disaster; **Zeehan**, whose boom-and-bust history sums up the area as neatly as its pioneer museum; and mining backwater **Rosebery**. South of this cluster, the B61 spears west from Maydena, past the contested forests of the **Styx and Upper Florentine valleys**. In concludes at the Gordon River dam and the highest commerical abseil on earth, while off a sideroad south are some of the greatest wilderness walks in Tasmania.

Towns in the west

Go west for the wilderness. Notwithstanding Strahan, towns in the west are the sort of solid, plaid-shirt practical settlements that have some interest but are not worth making a trip to in themselves. The reason, as ever, is historical. The small towns emerged as mining frontiers that have long eked out an existence cut off from the rest of civilization. It wasn't until 1932 that the Lyell Highway linked the area to the rest of Tasmania by road. It would be another thirty years until the Murchison Highway went north. Small wonder Tasmanians crack jokes about the west and rednecks. The exception is **Strahan**, a beautifully sited resort village on Macquarie Harbour that serves as a gateway to the wilderness. **Queenstown** and **Zeehan** provide a taste of the mining era as well as passable array of facilities.

Queenstown

The biggest town in the west, **QUEENSTOWN** is worth a visit, but not for the usual reasons. Having passed Lake St Clair and World Heritage-listed forests on the Lyell Highway, you emerge with a jolt into barren hills. If ever you wanted evidence of the devastation that single-minded commercial exploitation can wreak in such a sensitive environment, "Queenie" is it. It is also a definitive break from the usual heritage aspic. Though turning to tourism, Queenstown is Tasmania's classic mining town, with a utilitarian streetscape of tin-roofed houses and a reputation for rednecks. That great Australian institution, "the character", is in his element here and pubs can get rowdy at weekends.

A short history

Queenstown has been a mining centre since 1883, when three prospectors discovered gold on a rocky outcrop of Mount Lyell known as the **Iron Blow** (see p.299). A decade later the mountains had been ravaged by rapacious exploitation as the Mount Lyell Mining and Railway Company began to extract copper.

While two thousand tonnes of timber a week went into the smelters in the early 1900s, sulphurous fumes stripped the vegetation and heavy rainfall leached away topsoils. Water also filtered through the sulphide-rich mine tailings to brew a toxic cocktail of sulphuric acid laced with metals. Since the smelters closed in 1969, patches of teatree scrub have appeared to bring a green fuzz back to the slopes – indeed, they are almost verdant compared to a decade ago – but it's estimated the worst damage will take another four hundred years to repair. That any regrowth has occurred at all is due to a multi-million dollar clean-up operation begun in the 1990s. The lease for the Mount Lyell mine was taken up in 1995 by **Copper Mines of Tasmania**, now part of Indian mining corporation Vedanta and the major employer in west Tasmania. Stipulated into its contract was that mine tailings were dumped into a dam instead of the **Queen River**, which runs through the town and is slowly regaining some aquatic life. The **King River** into which it flows has some way to go. Though no longer the toxic grey sludge of the 1980s, its banks, stained orange down to the delta near Strahan, attest to the damage caused by dumping 1.5 million tonnes of mine tailings and five million gallons of raw sewage annually.

The Town

There was some debate about the merits of reforestation – the bare hills were Queenstown's premier tourist attraction, some argued. Stand on the town's

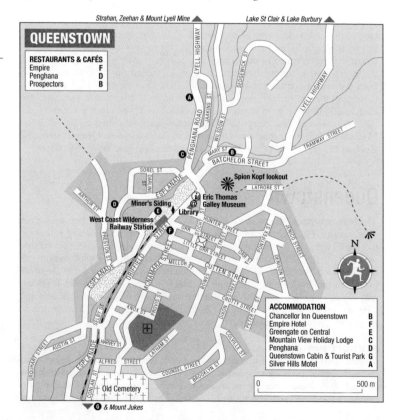

shabby high street and you can see their point. The best view of the copper-stained slopes is from **Spion Kopf lookout**, uphill off Hunter Street; an old mine train and smelters are by the car park. From its summit, you can gaze across at the slopes being carved into great slabs by current open-cut mining. To see the **Mount Lyell mine** up close, you can go seven kilometres down a working mine shaft with underground **tours** run by Douggies Mine Tours, based at the mining operation 1km north of the centre on Penghana Road (daily 10am & 1pm; 2.5hr; $58; bookings essential; minimum age 12; ☎0407 049 612, ✆romanabt@tassie.net.au). On its underground **tours**, you don hard hats, overalls and gum boots, and then descend by 4WD to a depth of 250m to see the workface where drills hammer out eight thousand tonnes of copper, gold and silver ore a day. It also runs surface tours of the open-cut mine on request. Alternatively, Mount Lyell Environmental Tours focuses on the environmental devastation of the copper mine on its own surface trips (10am & 2pm; 1hr; $20; ☎0419 104 148).

There's little else to detain you in the centre: Stephen Walker's **Miner's Siding** sculpture-cum-water feature in a small central park which commemorates a century of mining perhaps, or the **Galley Museum** (summer Mon–Fri 9.30am–6pm, Sat & Sun 12.30–6pm; winter until 5pm; $4; ☎03/6471 1483), opposite in the old *Imperial Hotel* pub. Its couple of rooms plastered with photographs of west coast pioneer life, focusing on local mining activity, are more appealing than the musty themed displays upstairs. The nearby *Empire Hotel*, finest of the thirty original mining pubs, is worth a look for a National Trust-listed blackwood staircase that was hewn from the local bush, carved in England and then returned when the pub was erected in 1904. The **West Coast Wilderness Railway Station** opposite has a room of photographs to commemorate the rack-and-pinion Abt steam locomotive (see box, p.298) – it's best to time a visit to coincide with the real thing (departure 10am & 3pm, arrival 2.30pm & 7pm).

Practicalities

Queenstown is accessed from the east and north on Tassielink's west coast **coach** services from Hobart and Launceston; connections link to Strahan. **Tourist information** is in the Galley Museum (same times) and a **Parks & Wildlife Service office** (☎03/6471 2511) is the base for the Franklin–Gordon Wild Rivers National Park. It stocks the department's rafting and bushwalking guidelines, but is not always manned, so call before making the trip 1km north on Penghana Road. Queenstown's **Online Access Centre** (Mon–Fri, times vary) is in the library on Driffield Street, near the museum.

Accommodation and eating

Though not as appealing a place to bunk down as Strahan, Queenstown is a bargain in comparison. A couple of hostels were scheduled for 2008 pending approval from the local council. A cheaper, more scenic alternative for camping is the east shore of Lake Burbury, 11km east.

Chancellor Inn Queenstown Batchelor St ☎03/6471 1033, ✆www.ghihotels.com. Bland but comfortable four-star hotel for visiting mine executives. Menus change daily in its *Prospectors Restaurant* (open to non-guests). ❺

Empire Hotel 2 Orr St ☎03/6471 1699, ✆www.empirehotel.net.au. The best value in the centre, this historic pub has a good range of rooms and budget singles ($30), a little shabby but all spotless, plus good-value bar meals in the heritage dining-room. Rooms ❷, en suites ❸

Greengates on Central 7 Railway Reserve ☎03/6471 1144. Four modern self-catering cabins that sleep up to four, one designed for disabled access, with a quiet central location. All have laundry plus limited cooking facilities. ❹

Mountain View Holiday Lodge 1 Penghana Rd ☏ 03/6471 1163, ✉ mtview@bigpond.net.au. Across the river from the centre, this has budget accommodation in what were the mine's single-men's lodgings – note that it can be block-booked by mine contractors at times. Dorms $20, budget rooms ❷, motel units ❸

Penghana 32 The Esplanade ☏ 03/6471 2560, ⓦ www.penghana.com.au. Spacious B&B-style accommodation in a National Trust-listed mansion owned by the manager of the original Mount Lyell mine. Most rooms are en suite, though those with shared facilities are larger, and there's a kitchen for guests. Its owners also provide the finest dining in Queenstown (open to non-guests, bookings essential): two-course modern menus $35, three dishes for $40. ❺

Queenstown Cabin & Caravan Park 17 Grafton St ☏ 03/6471 1332, ✉ queenscabins @southernphone.com.au. The only camping in Queenstown itself is 1.5km south of the centre, via Driffield Street. The site is small and fairly barren. Camping $20, vans ❷, cabins ❸

Silver Hills Motel Penghana Rd ☏ 03/6471 1755, ⓦ www.innkeeper.com.au. North of the Mountain View and a touch more modern, this motel has DVD players in its rooms, all of which are en suite. A restaurant serves up a reliable if unexciting menu of fillers (open to non-guests). ❸–❹

The West Coast Wilderness Railway

In 2002 the opening of the 35-kilometre **West Coast Wilderness Railway** between Queenstown and Strahan completed the $30-million redevelopment of the old **Abt Railway**, which included restoring or replacing forty bridges and recreating various stations and associated buildings. Two of the four surviving locomotives from 1963 were restored and each carriage – built as replicas of the timber and brass originals – was designed using different Tasmanian woods. The original railway was completed in 1896 to connect the Mount Lyell Mining Company in Queenstown with the port of Teepookana for the transport of copper ore, and in 1899 the line was extended to Regatta Point in Strahan. The railway closed in 1963, when it became more economical to transport by road, but years of lobbying finally led to the federal government financing its redevelopment. **Reconstruction** took three years; the original workers took two-and-a-half to hand-cut through the rugged rainforest terrain, struggling in the harsh, wet conditions. In fact, mining heritage is the main thrust of this trip and the informative commentary concentrates on it. The "wilderness" is something of a misnomer – at least for half of the journey the line follows slowly alongside the ravaged King River, its banks rusty from mine tailings and lined with tree stumps. Most people take the trip from Strahan: from Dubbil Barril, as the train climbs over 200m up a 1:16 rack gradient using the restored rack-and-pinion track (a system invented by a Swiss engineer, Dr Roman Abt), there are stunning gorge views and the train is immersed in rainforest scenery. Queenstown is some contrast – a shanty town of tin shacks and wooden houses.

Trains leave from Queenstown at the reconstructed station on Driffield Street, opposite the *Empire Hotel*, and at Strahan from the original station at Regatta Point (see p.305). There's a daily service in both directions, both of which provide a one-hour lunchstop at Dubbil Barril (packed lunch included). The train from Queenstown stops at the reconstructed historic settlement of Lynchford for half an hour for morning tea and a try at gold panning; the Lower Landing morning-tea stop from Strahan is on the unscenic polluted King River and includes a lame honey-tasting exercise. Trains are hauled by steam between Queenstown and Dubbil Barril and diesel between here and Strahan. You can travel one-way from either Strahan or Queenstown with a coach return (with a 30min break in Queenstown or 1hr 30min in Strahan). Either way, try to secure a seat on the river-side: when facing forward, the right-hand side from Strahan or left from Queenstown. Note that services only run from October to March (departs Queenstown 10am & 3pm, departs Strahan 10.15am & 3.15pm; one way 4hr, return 5hr; $99 one way, $185 premier class, includes light lunch and unlimited drinks; extra $15 for 45min return coach; bookings necessary, ☏ 1800 628 288, ⓦ www.puretasmania.com.au).

Around Queenstown

After a slalom east up the naked flanks of Mount Lyell, you surmount a hill to arrive after 3km at the **Iron Blow** outcrop, where mining began in the area. A path descends to a small lake pooled where the first open-cut mine hollowed out the hillside. The forerunner to Queenstown, **Gormanston**, lies beneath the Iron Blow, and lived and died with its mine in the 1880s. There's no evidence today that it was a home to nearly two thousand prospectors, and it has little of interest except a couple of contemporary buildings. From here it's a straight downhill run to **Lake Burbury** for a spot of trout fishing. There's a campsite on the east bank (camping $5; toilets; water; gas barbecues) beside a pretty picnic ground.

For a better view of the lake, created as a hydroelectricity project in the 1990s, take a scenic drive south of Queenstown towards **Mount Jukes**; stay on the east bank of the Queen River via Conlan Street to reach Mount Jukes Road. You emerge from a wooded valley, ease up the mountain slopes and are rewarded with a panorama of the lake cupped in the mountains while further peaks peel away into the distance; the far bluff is Frenchmans Cap. The unsealed road beyond degrades as you go south, and the last 3km along Narrow Road (right turn at the junction) are 4WD-only. If you are prepared to park earlier and walk to the car-park start, the **Bird River Walk** (3–4hr return; 7.5km) is an outstanding ramble. The flat path follows an old rail cutting through moss-clad rainforest to emerge on the southeast shore of Macquarie Habour, at Kelly Basin. The North Mount Lyell Railway terminated here at the port of Pillinger, a thousand-strong company town of an early Queenstown mining corporation; interpretive boards at the site relate its history. The last resident left in 1945 and now only haunting ruins remain; a massive boiler, brick kilns and a chimney, or a section of rail track by the old jetty all slowly disappearing into the bush. Consult Mount Lyell Environmental Tours (see p.297) about organized walking tours along the track.

Strahan and around

Many visitors are surprised that **STRAHAN** (pronounced "Strawn") is a top resort and not a lonely fishing village on the shore of Macquarie Harbour. When the Franklin River campaign set up its headquarters here in 1982, it catapulted a town that was dying for want of a port into the big league of state resorts. By the early 1990s it was already a beacon of ecotourism that was receiving ninety thousand tourists a year. Today it is the hub around which all tourism in the west revolves; an obligatory stopover for a cruise on Macquarie Harbour, a magnificent body of water six times the size of Sydney's; a departure point for the West Coast Wilderness Railway (see box opposite); or any number of wilderness attractions that are Strahan's stock in trade. A small fishing fleet sails for abalone, crayfish and shark, and there's commercial fish-farming of rainbow trout and Atlantic salmon in the harbour, but for visitors all this is a sideshow.

At times Strahan can feel a little too polished, a little too popular, for its own good. And yet despite all the grouching about coach tours and a frenetic pace in peak season, it retains an uncomplicated appeal. Having buffed up some of the existing port architecture, the tourism development is far from the eyesore it could have been considering the aggressive marketing campaign. The bayside setting is magnificent, too, and there are plenty of activities to enjoy. And the natural attractions nearby are as compelling as ever.

Practicalities

The place to make enquiries and bookings for Tassielink **coach** services is Strahan Activity Booking Centre on Esplanade (summer daily 7.30am–7pm, until 9pm Dec–Feb, winter daily 9am–5pm; ☎03/6471 4300). There's a scheduled service from Launceston and Devonport via Cradle Mountain (Tues, Thurs & Sat), connecting with the service from Hobart to Strahan (5 weekly) via Lake St Clair. The centre also pre-books many activities in the area. The best source of local knowledge and accommodation, however, is **West Coast visitor information and booking centre** (daily: Oct–March 10am–6pm, until 9pm Jan; April–Sept 11am–6pm; ☎03/6472 6800, ✉wcvibcs@westcoast.tas.gov.au).

Strahan Supermarket (daily 7am–7pm), 1km uphill on the Queenstown road, Reid Street, has EFTPOS facilities, a small pharmacy and is a Westpac bank agent; otherwise, there's an ANZ **ATM** outside *Banjo's* bakery on Esplanade. At Esplanade's far end, the old Customs House contains the **post office** (also a Commonwealth Bank agent) and a **Parks & Wildlife office** (Mon–Fri 9am–5pm; ☎03/6471 7122), where park passes are available. An **Online Access Centre** (Tues 12.30–4.30pm, Wed 10am–2pm & Thurs 1–5pm) is in the library nearby. Note that if you're driving, Strahan is one of the few small towns that charges for all-day parking: $2 in the main car park west of the visitor information centre, $4 in the car park of Strahan Village. Short-term parking is free at the visitor information centre (1hr) and in limited spaces in

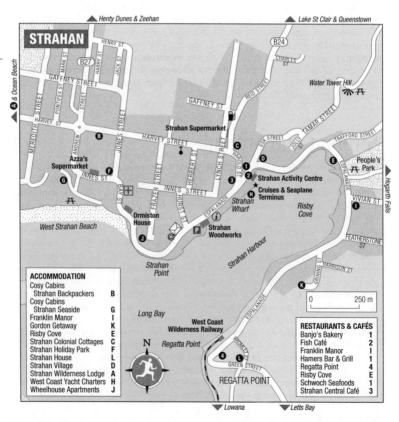

ACCOMMODATION	
Cosy Cabins Strahan Backpackers	B
Cosy Cabins Strahan Seaside	G
Franklin Manor	I
Gordon Getaway	K
Risby Cove	E
Strahan Colonial Cottages	C
Strahan Holiday Park	F
Strahan House	L
Strahan Village	D
Strahan Wilderness Lodge	A
West Coast Yacht Charters	H
Wheelhouse Apartments	J

RESTAURANTS & CAFÉS	
Banjo's Bakery	1
Fish Café	2
Franklin Manor	I
Hamers Bar & Grill	1
Regatta Point	4
Risby Cove	E
Schwoch Seafoods	1
Strahan Central Café	3

the centre (30min). **Taxis** are available through Strahan & West Coast Taxi (℡0417 516 071). **Bike rental** is covered in the "Activities" box on p.304.

Accommodation

If you have your own transport, you can **bushcamp** for free at Ocean Beach and Henty Dunes (see p.306); although there are no facilities, free hot showers are available in the toilet block opposite Strahan post office. Accommodation in Strahan is expensive and gets booked up in summer; to be safe, book ahead or bring a tent – otherwise you might have to head back to Zeehan or Queenstown. The west coast visitor information and booking centre has a free accommodation-booking service. For something different, you could also bunk aboard West Coast Yacht Charters' ketch *Stormbreaker* (single $50, cabin ❹; see p.304); also enquire about their comfortable self-contained holiday units, *The Crays* (❻).

Cosy Cabins Strahan Backpackers 43 Harvey St ℡03/6472 6211, ⓦwww.bestonparks.com.au. A modern hostel with spacious rooms and common kitchens, eating areas and a lounge. Well-maintained timber cabins (double or twin) share the same bathrooms and kitchens as the hostel. New owners Beston Parks propose to open the hostel Dec–April only. Camping $30, dorms $35, rooms ❷–❸, cabins ❸

Cosy Cabins Strahan Seaside Corner of Andrew and Innes streets ℡03/6472 6200, ⓦwww .bestonparks.com.au. Bought in late 2007 by national chain Beston Parks (though it may retain the Cosy Cabins branding), this holiday park has well-positioned camping and cabins near the harbour beach. Camping $30, cabins ❹, cottages ❻

Franklin Manor Esplanade ℡03/6471 7311, ⓦwww.franklinmanor.com.au. Serene and elegant boutique accommodation in a heritage property set in mature gardens. The lovingly maintained historic interior is pepped up with contemporary furnishings and modern art; classical music plays in the guest lounge filled with fresh flowers. Also has a couple of rustic cottages in the gardens. ❻–❼

Gordon Gateway Grining St, Regatta Point ℡03/6471 7165, ⓦwww.gordongateway.com.au. A small complex whose peaceful hillside spot guarantees a view of the town and harbour. Among the accommodation options are spacious studios with kitchenettes; elegant spa units; and homely A-frame timber cabins for up to six. Guests get free use of a gas BBQ in two acres of gardens. The managers also look after *Piners Loft* (❽), a lovely lodge built of recycled timbers and raised on poles. ❻–❽

Risby Cove Esplanade ℡03/6471 7572, ⓦwww.risby.com.au. An old wharfside sawmill, fully renovated using corrugated iron and salvaged Huon pine, this has upmarket one- and

two-bedroom suites with kitchenette areas. All are bright and modern and face the harbour – the location in a quiet corner of Strahan appeals, too. Digital film theatre (nightly 7pm; $9.50) and a good on-site restaurant. ❻–❼

Strahan Colonial Cottages 7 Reid St ℡03/6471 7019, ⓦwww.strahancolonialcottages.com. Three beautifully renovated and well-equipped colonial cottages, one the police superintendent's cottage, another a renovated church. ❻

Strahan Holiday Park Corner of Jones and Innes streets ℡03/6471 7442, ⓦwww.islandcabins .com.au. Powered sites for motorhomes and self-contained units, some for up to ten people, on an attractive well-maintainted site carved out of a sliver of rainforest. Sites $30, vans ❸, cabins and cottages ❺

Strahan House 5 Bromley St ℡0417 017 566, ⓦwww.strahanhouse.com. The finest view to Strahan from the living area and deck of a spacious upmarket three-bed spa house above Regatta Point. Style is comfortable rather than opulent. Also has a large garden. ❽

Strahan Village Esplanade ℡03/6471 7160 or 1800 628 286, ⓦwww.strahanvillage.com.au. Federal Resort's upmarket accommodation (all en suite) is along and above the Esplanade. The best-positioned options are the spacious "Terrace" rooms above the *Hamers Hotel*, with balcony access looking over the boats (❻); be prepared for some noise in summer. A variety of "village" units (❻) line the Esplanade, some of which look like cute colonial cottages but are really motel rooms. Whether "Waterfront" or "Hilltop", all smart "Executive" rooms have private balconies and great views at the head of the harbour (❼–❽). The cheapest rooms, "Hilltop Garden View", are tucked behind (❺).

Strahan Wilderness Lodge Ocean Beach Rd, 2km west ℡03/6471 7142, ⓔstrahanlodge@keypoint .com.au. An escape from the peak-season crowds, this B&B in a 1903 mine manager's residence has basic, spacious rooms, plus simple self-contained units in a peaceful location above Smugglers Cove. Rooms ❸, units ❹

🏃 **Wheelhouse Apartments** 4 Frazer St ☎03/6471 7777, ⓦwww.wheelhouse apartments.com.au. Two striking apartments made with local timbers and a stylish maritime theme, perched on a cliff above the harbour. Cantilevered wall-to-ceiling windows in the living room give a nautical feel and awesome views. Upstairs is a master bedroom with a spa and second bedroom. Full kitchen and laundry in both apartments. Understated and luxurious. ❻

The Town

Strahan exists less for its history than as a service centre for tourism in the area. Nevertheless, your first stop should be the wood-and-iron **west coast visitor information and booking centre** on Esplanade (daily: Oct–March 10am–6pm, until 9pm Jan; April–Sept 11am–6pm), whose innovative exterior design echoes the area's boat-building and timber industries. An interior exhibition ($2; same hours) features a huge glass wall providing views of the harbour. Displays are organized by theme: the Aborigines that occupied the area for at least ten thousand years; convicts on Sarah Island; the logging for Huon pine; ecology; local economy; wilderness; and conflict, notably the clash over the Franklin River. An outdoor **amphitheatre** behind hosts an entertaining two-man show, *The Ship That Never Was* (daily 5.30pm plus 8.30pm performance in Jan; $15), which retells in slapstick-style the true story of a convict escape from Sarah Island in 1834; if you don't want to know the twist to one of the strangest yarns of colonial Tasmania, be careful how you read the box on p.306.

In a corrugated-iron shed adjacent to the visitor centre, **Strahan Woodworks** (daily 8am–5pm) sells well-designed woodwork; you're also welcome to roam around Morrison's Saw Mill next door and watch native timbers being processed. Also worth a visit is the **Forestry Tasmania** office next to *Hamers* pub (Mon–Fri 9am–5pm; ☎03/6472 6000), with a window display of a Huon pine log morphing into the bow of a boat. Inside are leaflets on native trees, plus

▲ Tourists on cruise boat entering Hells Gates

The Gordon River is deep, its waters dark from the tannin that leaches out of button-grass plains – even the tap water in Strahan has a hint of colour though it's fine to drink. Cruise boats used to travel 30km upriver, but the speed at which they had to go was eroding the riverbanks. They now travel 14km upriver to **Heritage Landing**, where there's a chance to see a section of unadulterated **rainforest**: a boardwalk above the rainforest floor allows you to get close without disturbing anything. The swampy conditions are ideal for Huon pines, a threatened species unique to Tasmania. The massive pines, which can reach a height of 40m, occasionally grow from seed but more often regenerate vegetatively, putting down roots when fallen branches touch the soil. The slow-growing trees are estimated to be the second-oldest living things on earth after the bristlecone pines of western North America, and are noted for the resin-rich methyl eugenol oil in the trunks that slows fungal growth. You see one fallen tree on the walk that is reckoned to be around two thousand years old; another trunk found in the area was carbon-dated to thirty thousand years by Forestry Tasmania and was still workable. The wood's oil content also helps explain why Huon pine was so highly sought by foresters: not only was it rot-resistant and tough, it was one of the few green timbers that floated in Tasmania. Huon pine logs were floated down to a boom camp and fashioned into huge rafts to be rowed across Macquarie Harbour. Incidentally, the river is named for James Gordon, the mate who loaned sealer, whaler and explorer Captain James Kelly the 25-foot whale boat in which he became the first European to explore the area during his swashbuckling circumnavigation in 1816 (see p.78).

Two operators offer **river cruises**; both visit Macquarie Heads ("Hells Gates"), the fish farms, have guided tours of Sarah Island and make a thirty-minute stop at Heritage Landing. Booking in Strahan is at the waterfront Strahan Activity Booking Centre. Federal Resorts' **Gordon River Cruises** operates the high-tech *Jane Franklin II* (daily: departs 8.30am, returns 2pm, Nov–April extra cruise departs 2.45pm, returns 8pm; atrium seats $85, window seats $110, buffet lunch included; upper-deck seats including smorgasbord lunch, snacks and drinks $180; ☎03/6471 4300 or 1800 420 555, ⊛www.puretasmania.com.au). Though it has pre-designated seats, there are floor-to-ceiling windows and you can move freely on deck. **World Heritage Cruises**, with two boats operated and owned by a local family, offers a slightly cheaper cruise (daily: departs 9am, returns 2.45pm; $65 standard seat, $85 premium seat; snacks and $15 buffet meal available; licensed; ☎03/6471 7174, ⊛www.worldheritage cruises.com.au), plus a similar afternoon summer cruise (Jan–March 3–8.30pm; same prices) – to make the most of the experience, turn up early to bag a good seat. For both cruise operators, bring water- and wind-proof gear, so you can brave the prow of the boat – by far the most exhilarating spot when you whizz through Macquarie Heads and down the broad harbour.

Overnight cruises are available aboard World Heritage Cruises's *Discovery*, a luxury 33-metre cruiser launched at the end of 2004 that takes 24 passengers for three-day, two-night cruises on the Gordon River, mooring overnight at Heritage Landing and Sarah Island ($1995). There are inclusive shore and kayaking excursions, and cuisine prepared by a former chef of the Sultan of Brunei. Charter outfit West Coast Yacht Charter (see box, p.304) runs substantially cheaper overnight river cruises ($320 and $250) and has the only government licence to travel 30km upriver to Sir John Falls.

sights information. Over the road, **Strahan Activity Booking Centre** has a photographic display of Strahan's history and interpretive material relating to a unique Tasmanian tiger rug, which is exhibited in Strahan over summer; the rug is displayed at 3.30pm with an accompanying talk (free).

Going the other way from the visitor centre, you pass the former **Customs House**, a handsome edifice from the early mining boom, then **Ormiston**

House (now a B&B) on a kink in Bay Street. One of the most flamboyant examples of Australian "Federation" architecture from the early 1900s, it was created by self-made retail magnate Frederick Ormiston Henry. Within ten years of his arrival on the west coast in 1887 with £100, the "Father of Strahan" was one of the richest men in Tasmania, thanks to his chain of pioneer stores

Activities and tours in Strahan

You're not short of things to do around Strahan, and most activities take advantage of the area's natural splendour. You can rent **mountain bikes** from *Risby Cove* (half-day $10, full day $25) and Strahan Holiday Park (two hours $8, full day $22; see p.301 for contact information). The latter has tandems ($15 two hours, $50 per day). It also rents sand toboggans for the Henty Dunes (half-day $10). The Shack (℡03/6471 7396), on the junction of Esplanade and Harold Street, rents sandboards ($30 per half-day), windsurfers ($30 per half-day) and canoes ($35 per hour, $45 per half-day). For other operators below, make bookings in person at the Strahan Activity Centre unless stated otherwise.

4 Wheeler Bikes ℡03/6471 7622 or 0419 508 175. Popular four-wheel-motorbike guided tours of Henty Sand Dunes (40min; $40; driver's licence required) and longer tours to Teepookana on request.

Gordon River cruises See p.303.

Piners and Miners ℡1800 084 620, ⓦwww.puretasmania.com.au. The latest signature experience from Federal Resorts is this small-group one-day excursion ($354) in a 4WD converted to run on the tracks of the West Coast Wilderness Railway to Lynchford. From here, you drive on roads south for the excellent Bird River Walk to the ghost town of Pillinger, then pick up a cruiseboat for the return to Strahan. Gourmet food and wine throughout. Reservations essential.

Strahan Four Wheel Drive Tours Ormiston House, Bay Street ℡03 6471 7077 or 0419 763 119. Tours to Ocean Beach by day or sunset (1hr, $25, or 1hr 30min, $45), wildlife-spotting bush trips at night (2hr; $55) and Strahan heritage tours that include a look inside historic marvel Ormiston House (1hr; $25).

Strahan Marine Charters ℡0418 135 983. Private fishing or sightseeing tours; prices vary according to duration and party size, but include all tackle.

Strahan Seaplane & Helicopters Esplanade ℡03/6471 7718, ⓦwww.adventureflights .com.au. Helicopter flights (prices per person based on two people) to: Hells Gates and Macquarie Harbour (15min; $120); and the Teepookana Forest, which includes a landing and walk to see the old-growth Huon pine (1hr; $195). Scenic seaplane flights provide the unforgettable image of the dark ribbon of the Franklin River rippling through rainforest before you land at Sir John Falls landing, 30km upstream (1hr 20min; $290). Also has aeroplane flights to Cradle Mountain (1hr 5min; $240).

West Coast Wilderness Railway See p.298.

West Coast Yacht Charters Esplanade ℡03/6471 7422, ⓦwww.tasadventures .com/wcyc. Morning sails on Macquarie Harbour on a sixty-metre ketch, *Stormbreaker*, with kayaking or fishing and a fresh-fish lunch (daily 10am–1pm except May–Aug; $70 or $80 with crayfish in season; $50 without lunch). The skipper also runs overnight Gordon River cruises: upriver to Heritage Landing via Sarah Island (depart 2pm, return 1pm; $320); and a Franklin rafters' pick-up that travels 15km beyond the other cruisers to Sir John Falls (departs 2pm, returns 1pm; $250). Both overnighters include meals and bedding.

Wild Rivers Jet Esplanade and Harold St junction ℡03/6471 7396. You can blast up the ravaged King River just south of Strahan (50min; $65), but a better option is probably a combined jet boat–4WD trip to the Teepookana Plateau (11am daily; 1hr 40min; $85).

The great outdoors

Tasmania is defined by its scenery and Tasmanians love the outdoor life. With an adventure playground full of wild tannin-stained rivers, rainforest, glaciated mountain ridges and surf-fringed powder beaches in their backyard, not to mention the bucolic river valleys, fern-filled gorges or fishing lakes, it's no wonder they've invented endless ways to enjoy it.

The coast

You're never more than two hours' drive from the sea in Tasmania, and **coastal culture** – whether on the beach or afloat – is a central part of life. The 3000km coastline is longer than that of New South Wales and Victoria combined, yet has been largely spared similar development. That means there's a lot of coast to discover, much of it completely wild. Anywhere else, you'd expect hotels or restaurants. Crowds at least. Tasmania has a habit of throwing out one effortlessly epic empty beach after another with barely a shrug.

The **east coast** is fringed by white-powder sands and impossibly blue turquoise seas: places like Reidle Beach on Maria Island, the improbable geometric arc of Wineglass Bay in Freycinet National Park, the Bay of Fires or Picnic Rock Beach in Mount William National Park are some of the most pristine beaches you'll find. The rugged **west coast** couldn't be more different. Pounded by waves and unsettled except for singularly Tasmanian shack villages, it is only accessible – by car at least – at Marrawah and Arthur River, or around Strahan.

Other areas of the coast have a different, more **active** appeal. Whether casting a line from game-fishing hub St Helens; climbing up, diving beneath, boating around or hiking over Australia's highest sea-cliffs on the Tasman Peninsula; or simply strolling kilometre after kilometre of empty sands pretty much everywhere, Tasmania lives on its coastline. Just watch out for rips if you swim and remember to do as the locals do and "slip, slop, slap" – slip on a T-shirt, slop on the sun cream and slap on a hat.

Bay of Fires ▲

Coastline, Tarkine wilderness ▼

Pirates Bay, Eaglehawk Neck ▼

The highland lakes

The **central highland** is another world compared with the coast. Mostly over a thousand metres above sea level and notorious for its fickle weather, it is a remote upland of broad grass landscapes that merge into huge skies. More than anything, it is characterized by a collage of shallow glacial lakes. Arthurs Lake provides the best **fishing** for wild brown trout in the Southern Hemisphere; try Great Lake for rainbow trout. Only eight hundred people live up here, but on a summer weekend the population can swell to 25,000 – most of them clutching a rod.

▲ Lake Oberon, Western Arthur Range

▼ Pencil pine

Forests

If you only do one thing in Tasmania, experience the magisterial old-growth forest in the west. Like cathedrals of greenery, the state's temperate **rainforests** are among the most ancient on Earth. The Tarkine, the second-largest temperate rainforest in the world, is a genuine living link to the global super-continent of Gondwana. The only place with species similar to its endemic myrtle, sassafras, laurel, celery-top pine and leatherwood is Tasmania's erstwhile neighbour, Chile. From Strahan, Arthur River and Corinna you can see **Huon pine trees** that were saplings two thousand years ago. The Tahune Air Walk, near Geeveston, provides an opportunity to explore the upper canopy, while the Styx Valley's swamp gums are among the tallest hardwoods on Earth.

▼ Myrtle tree and pandani

Forests on the other side of the state are of the drier smaller **eucalyptus** variety. The Douglas-Apsley National Park has trails beneath eucalyptus to its river canyons, and Evercreech Forest Reserve shelters the world's tallest **white gums**.

Bushcamping in the Franklin-Gordon Wild Rivers National Park ▲

Hiker on summit of Cradle Mountain ▼

Cradle Mountain ▼

World Heritage Area

The World Heritage Area – almost everything stretching from Cradle Mountain down to the southwest tip – is the essence of Tasmania. It is the quintessential great outdoors from which the state derives its identity of pristine wilderness. Comprised of five national parks, the World Heritage Area has a lot to explore. The most accessible point to sample its unique blend of razor-edged **glaciated mountains**, **rainforest** and **buttongrass plains** is the ever-popular Cradle Mountain–Lake St Clair National Park, traversed by the superb 65km Overland Track. Strahan is the gateway to the Gordon River, noted for its mirror-like reflections of rainforest.

With more time, you can spend up to a week **rafting** down rapids of the Franklin River, **hike** into remote scenery such as the remote Walls of Jerusalem National Park or spend a week on the exhausting, exhilarating mudfest of the South Coast Track.

Top 5 World Heritage Area activities

▶▶ **Cruising the Gordon River** Wilderness without the wild on cruises by catamaran or yacht. See p.303.

▶▶ **Walking at Cradle Mountain** Unmissable glacial landscape whose day-walks hint at the drama south on the Overland Track. See p.315.

▶▶ **Rafting the Franklin River** Spend several days on the last great, untamed river in Australia. See p.321.

▶▶ **Abseiling the Gordon Dam** The world's highest commercial abseil. See p.329.

▶▶ **South Coast Track** Self-reliance required on a week-long coastal trek that's as remote as it gets. See p.331.

and speculation in mining shares. **West Strahan Beach** a little further along the shore is a surprisingly good strip of fine sand that's safe for swimming.

The **Strahan Historic Foreshore Walkway** is a pleasant 7-kilometre gravel track around the harbour – self-guided-walk maps are available from the tourist office. Halfway around you pass the **People's Park**, a botanic garden-cum-rainforest from where you can take the rainforest walk to **Hogarth Falls** (40min; 2km return): nothing special but a pleasant amble accompanied by interpretive boards about the surrounding forest. *Risby Cove* opposite, a hotel and restaurant incarnated from an old sawmill, has interesting wood carvings in a crafts gallery. The route concludes on the opposite bank to Strahan centre at **Regatta Point**, site of the train station built in 1899 for the mining railway – the best time to be here is when the **West Coast Wilderness Railway** arrives or departs (see p.298). From here, you could go 1km south via Green Street to **Letts Bay** – a throwback to Australia of the 1960s realized in a collection of ramshackle tin shacks with jaunty paint-jobs.

Eating and drinking

Banjo's Esplanade. Outside water-facing tables are a pleasant spot for (pricey) cooked breakfast and pastries. It also serves pizzas after 6pm. Daily 6am–8/9pm.

Fish Café Esplanade. Fish and chips raised up a notch with fresh seafood and Asian flavours alongside the usuals in a city-style café on the wharf. Lunch from 2pm & dinner daily.

Franklin Manor Esplanade ☏ 03/6471 7311. Classy eating in a relaxed dining room provided by Strahan's gourmet restaurant. An award-winning chef creates changing menus of fine modern Australian cuisine with an emphasis on fresh local produce; expect the likes of local seafood with Hokien noodles, roast duckling with a fig and port glaze or grilled Macquarie Harbour trout with a tomato and thyme salsa. Top-notch wine cellar, too. Reservations essential. Dinner daily.

Hamers Esplanade. The restored 1930s pub that is the focus of the town's social life, in the public bar at least, is always a lively place for a drink. Next door, *Hamers Bar & Grill* is a fine bistro which serves up a varied selection of moderately priced

contemporary seafood, pasta, grills and curries (mains around $20). Lunch & dinner daily.

Regatta Point Esplanade. The locals' choice for a meal on the other side of the bay serves high-quality pub food such as fresh Macquarie Harbour trout and good steaks alongside a menu of daily specials; prices are around $20 per main. Lunch & dinner daily.

Risby Cove Esplanade ☏ 03/6471 7572. Stylish and bright, this relaxed waterfront restaurant has a good reputation for a large menu of contemporary Australian food – trevalla in a Tuscan crust, venison and mushroom pie in a brioche case – that isn't too pricey; mains cost around $26. Reservations recommended. Dinner daily.

Schwoch Seafoods Esplanade. Good pizzas to take away plus an adjacent fish-and-chip outlet selling the catch of local fishermen.

Strahan Central Café 1 Harold St. An airy metropolitan-styled café with art on the walls and leather sofas. Good coffee and toasted sandwiches, but not as close to the water as *Banjo's*. Daily 11am–4pm.

Around Strahan

Six kilometres east of town, **Ocean Beach** is the longest in Tasmania, an untamed 30km of sand. The Southern Ocean waves that break upon its shore have travelled unopposed from South America, whipped up by the Roaring Forties as they helter-skelter around the world. The largest swell recorded was 23 metres, which would have bombed the sand with a 46-metre wave. It was also the last swell recorded before the wave buoy off Cape Sorrell was ripped from the sea-bed. Unsurprisingly, the tannin-stained waters are not safe to swim in or even surf. The central section of the beach is accessed from Ocean Beach Road west of Strahan; come at dusk to observe marvellous sunsets and watch migratory **muttonbirds** roost (Oct to Feb) – they're easiest to spot from the beach. Hay's Adventure Tours runs trips from Strahan in season ($12; ☏ 03 6473

Sarah Island: the ultimate prison

"The name of Macquarie Harbour is associated exclusively with remembrance of inexpressible depravity, degradation and woe. Sacred to the genius of torture, Nature concurred with the objects of its separation to exhibit some notion of a perfect misery. There, man lost the aspect and the heart of man."

Reverend John West, 1853

Though the convict penitentiary of Port Arthur is synonymous with brutality, it is **Sarah Island** in Macquarie Harbour that deserves the reputation as a hell on earth. A trial run for Port Arthur, it was reserved for the worst convicts of the young colony who committed crimes after transportation, and only existed for eleven years. Yet within a few years of the brig *Sophia* sailing into the harbour with 74 prisoners and a detachment of guards in 1822, the island was feared as "Devils Island" among convicts. Marcus Clarke's 1870 novel *For The Term Of His Natural Life* only reinforced its reputation as the sink of the colonies.

"You must find work and labour, if it only consists of opening cavities and filling them again," Lieutenant-governor Sorrell ordered first commandant Lieutenant Cuthbertson. But the inmate population, which averaged 250, didn't have time to dig holes. Organized by the seriousness of their crimes, convicts were allocated to tanning, cobbling, brick-making or shipbuilding in a yard that produced over a hundred vessels during the island's lifetime, including a 226-tonne 33-metre barque. The lowest class of prisoners suffered hard labour in the lumber yards or, worse, worked chest-deep in the cold river and in irons to log stands of Huon pine. A lack of fresh produce meant scurvy was rife, later combatted with thrice-weekly cocktails of water, lime juice and sugar with a splash of grog. Officers, meanwhile, supplemented their diets with delicacies such as wombat stew, swan, eel pies or echidna roasted with sage and onion.

What distinguishes Sarah Island from Port Arthur is the relentless use of **punishment**. The island surgeon reported to an 1838 parliamentary select committee that Cuthbertson ordered 6560 lashes per year on his two hundred prisoners. Convict Scrummy Williams holds the dubious record of having received a total of five hundred lashes from the "Macquaire cat", a heavier and larger instrument than the standard-issue army and navy model with a double rather than single whipcord. One convict related that an offender "was immediately sent to work, his back like bullock's liver and most likely his shoes full of blood, and not permitted to go to the hospital until next morning, when his back would be washed by the doctor's mate and a little hog's lard spread". Fourteen days in grave-like solitary confinement cells was common,

1247, ⓦ www.haystour.com), though the business was for sale at the time of research; consult the visitor centre in Strahan for current information.

Alternatively, you can take a bumpy unsealed road 11km south to Macquarie Heads, known as **Hells Gates** ever since convicts bound for Sarah Island labelled it as such. Despite an islet lighthouse, the eighty-metre river mouth is a treacherous channel for shipping, where waves contest with river currents that run at eight knots in full flood and ebb. You can park at a campsite at the end, then walk to the river mouth and north along the beach, except at high tides. In theory, you could loop back further up the beach on 4WD tracks, but they are tricky to find. Swan Basin picnic ground on the way down to Hells Gates is a pretty sheltered spot on the banks of Macquarie Harbour.

Fourteen kilometres north of Strahan on the Zeehan Road (B27), the extensive **Henty Dunes**, which roll in waves up to 30m high, are also worth seeing. Scatterings of shells among the sands are evidence of at least three thousand years of occupation by Tasmanian Aborigines, and the area remains valuable to the though many prisoners welcomed this as a break from work. Escape was near impossible. The surgeon before the House of Commons reported that of 116 prisoners who absconded during the camp's lifetime, only fifteen got clean away; others were shot, recaught or simply vanished into surrounding rainforest that was thicker than the Amazon. With the odds stacked against them, some prisoners murdered fellow convicts to be sent to Hobart Town for execution. A public hanging on Sarah Island to set an example backfired when the condemned, thrilled to be so close to "escape", cracked jokes and kicked off their shoes into the crowd.

Yet some nearly made it. **Matthew Brady** escaped in 1824 and terrorized central Van Diemen's Land for two years until he was seized near Launceston. And in 1834, the final ship of Sarah Island, the *Frederick*, was snatched and sailed to Chile by ten convicts. The gang spent two years in South America until a new governor handed over four to the British – the other six had by then already bolted. The convicts were returned by prison hulk to Hobart Town in 1837, but escaped the gallows on the legal technicality that because the *Frederick* had not been registered, not only were they not guilty of the charge of piracy but they could not have stolen a non-existent ship. The judge handed down life sentences, which is what they were serving anyway.

No escapee is more infamous than **Alexander Pearce**. In 1822, the Irish thief bolted into the bush at Kelly Basin with Matthew Travers and Robert Greenhill among a gang of desperados. Soon starving in the rainforest, a cabal conspired to murder and eat one of their fellow escapees. So horrified were two gang members that they weighed up their odds and quietly returned to Sarah Island. A couple of days later, another convict was dispatched with an axe while asleep then bled by former butcher Travers. Then another was eaten after he drew the shortest straw. The group continued east, now in open country abounding with game. Yet when Travers's foot became infected, Greenhill still wielded the axe. Now only Greenhill and Pearce were left; both wary of their companion, both fighting to stay alert. Before a dying fire, Greenhill's head drooped. Pearce leapt, snatched up the axe and swung. He was captured soon after, confessed, was disbelieved and returned to Sarah Island a hero. He escaped again, but when he was recaptured with smoked cuts of co-escapee Thomas Cox in his pocket, he was sent to the gallows in Hobart Town in 1824.

Although the farce of the *Frederick* damaged Sarah Island, it was the difficulties of administration from Hobart Town that closed it in 1833. And by then, Port Arthur had opened.

indigenous community. Go far enough north towards the Henty River and you may also come across bleached whale bones. Two fun ways to experience the dunes are on a quadbike excursion or by hiring sandboards from The Shack (see box, p.304). You can **camp** for free at the picnic area or in other clearings, and campfires are allowed. **Teepookana Plateau** has an awe-inspiring stand of ancient Huon pines (some nearly two thousand years old), accessible via an elevated walkway and a viewing tower that provides a 360-degree panorama of forest, mountain and harbour; the only way to reach it, though, is by tour with Wild Rivers Jet and 4 Wheeler Bikes (see box, p.304).

Zeehan

ZEEHAN, 46km north of Strahan off the A10, is the boom-and-bust mining town of the west coast. Its modern outskirts are not particularly inspiring and at weekends it practically lapses into the ghost town it nearly became. For thirty years, however, Zeehan was a frenzy of activity. Once just a few tin-scratchers' huts in the bush, the town was pegged out in 1890 to accommodate over 150 mining companies clamouring for a lease of recently discovered silver-lead. In its pomp during that decade, "Silver City" boasted a population of ten thousand and was the third-largest town in Tasmania after Hobart and Launceston. Sixty dealers traded in a Zeehan Stock Exchange, thousands of miners swilled in 27 pubs and – move over Sydney – Zeehan built itself the largest opera house in Australia, the **Gaiety Theatre** (1898), which remains the most elaborate facade in town. Stars such as Dame Nellie Melba and Lola Montez, the infamous Irish erotic dancer who bewitched European high society and scandalized a Melbourne audience by hitching her skirts to flaunt a lack of underwear, trod the boards of the thousand-seater venue.

By 1908 the mines had begun to fail, and the town did not see any sort of revival until the 1970s, when it became a dormitory for miners at the Renison Bell tin mine 17km northeast near Rosebery. At present, Zeehan is a hostage to the fortune of mining contractor Metals X. World economics slowed operations at Renison Bell to tick-over in 2005, and Zeehan is now keen to woo tourism.

Fortunately, the **West Coast Pioneer Memorial Museum** (daily 9am–5pm; $10; ☏03/6471 6225), in the former Zeehan School of Mines and Metallurgy on Main Street, is outstanding. The themed photographic displays upstairs provide as comprehensive an introduction to the opening of the west coast in the late 1800s as you'll find anywhere in Tasmania, with contemporary images of everything from large-scale mining operations at Zeehan and Queenstown, to Strahan as a booming port or debutante balls. Below, the school's mineral exhibits include a lump of crocite, mineral emblem of Tasmania, and in a section on Aboriginal history you'll find a cast of the circular carvings at Mount Cameron, near Marrawah (see p.283). Steam locomotives of the mine railway catch the eye among outdoors exhibits. The ticket also permits you into the Gaiety, a boxy auditorium that is slowly being restored to its Victorian splendour.

With your own transport, you can access more mining relics in the area. Zeehan's pioneers lie in a **memorial cemetery** by the junction of the road to Strahan. From here, the Strahan Highway carves 4km south between former slag heaps to reach the remains of the smelters and the start of a gravel track up **Mount Zeehan** (702m; 3hr return). North of the museum, there's the **Spray Tunnel scenic drive**, a circuit that traverses a short abandoned rail tunnel (maximum height 3m, width 2.2m) and passes the mouth of the Spray Mine shaft. The route starts near the golf course, 7km north from the museum in Zeehan – pick up circuit guides from there. It may also have a few photocopied walking guides knocking about.

Practicalities

Accommodation is expensive as Zeehan catches Strahan's overflow. Options include functional rooms in the *Heemskirk Motor Inn* (☏1800 639 876 or 03/6471 6107, ✉heemskirk@tasparkside.com.au; ●) near the Strahan turn-off, and basic pub rooms and self-contained cottages at the *Hotel Cecil* on Main Street (☏03/6471 6221; rooms ●, cottages ●), where you can get lunchtime snacks and decent counter meals in the evenings. *Mount Zeehan Retreat Bed and Breakfast* at 12 Runcorne St provides evening meals on request as well as cabin-like rooms (☏03/6471 6424; no en suites; ●). The cheapest option is the friendly *Treasure Island Caravan Park* (☏03/6471 6633; camping $20, vans ●, cabins ●), nicely situated 1km from the centre on Hurst Street. The ANZ **bank** has restricted opening hours (Mon & Tues 2–4pm, Wed 9.30am–noon, Thurs

9.30am–4pm & Fri 2–4pm), but there's an ATM at Vickers General Store on the main street. The **Online Access Centre** (Mon–Sat, times vary) is in the library opposite the medical centre on Main Street.

Around Zeehan

A couple of remote shack settlements on the wild coastline northwest of Zeehan epitomize the dogged self-sufficiency typical of west Tasmania. Neither have mains electricity or water, nor shops or accommodation. Around 23km west, Zeehan's former port, **TRIAL HARBOUR**, is populated by itinerant fishermen and surfers who pit themselves against a chunky reef break; the surf is best at mid-tide on swells over two metres. There's a small **local history museum** (knock on the house next door if it's closed; free) and a camping area (pit toilet). Climb the sand dunes just past the shacks and you are rewarded with a spectacular view down Ocean Beach at its most rugged; tracks lead down to the beach, though swimming here is dangerous. Sunsets, on the other hand, are stupendous. Another good option to get off-track is **GRANVILLE HARBOUR**, 38km northwest of Zeehan en route to Corinna (see p.287), on an inlet thick with bull kelp. The fishermen's shack settlement also marks the start of a remote 4WD track up the coastline to Pieman Heads at Corinna; consult Parks & Wildlife rangers at Queenstown or Arthur River for information.

Rosebery and Tullah

Sited in a remote valley beneath the knuckles of Mount Black, **ROSEBERY**, 22km north of Zeehan, is a working zinc-mining town that belongs to the Tasmanian Minerals Extraction Company. With a population just over a thousand, it's one of the larger settlements of the west coast. But outside the few black-and-white photos in a **Mining Heritage Centre** (call for times, ☎03/6473 2222; free) at the Zinifex Rosebery Mine, there's little to make you stop except a good supermarket, an ANZ bank, an ATM outside the newsagents and fuel.

The highest waterfall in Tasmania, the 103-metre **Montezuma Falls** (3hr return on foot), is at the end of an abandoned tramline 8km south of town. The miniature cablecar that spans the A10 south transported ore from a mine for processing until 1968. Hay's Adventure Tours at 10-12 Esplanade (☎03/6473 1247, ⓦwww.haystour.com) runs 4WD tours to the falls (4hr; prices vary by group size) and **Lake Johnston Nature Reserve** (3hr; $70 per person), whose stand of Huon pine is thought to have self-seeded for ten thousand years. However, the company was for sale during research, so call before you visit. There's motel-style B&B **accommodation** at *Mount Black Lodge* just north of the main drag on Hospital Road (☎03/6473 1039, ⓦwww.mountblacklodge .com; also licensed restaurant; ❺), which attracts bushwalkers and can organize photographic tours.

Originally a silver-lead mining town in the late 1890s and briefly a hydro-electricity base eighty years later, tiny **TULLAH** has turned to tourism for survival. Activities are based around **Lake Rosebery** and **Lake Mackintosh**, west and east respectively; Tullah Horseback & Boat Tours at Mackintosh Track (☎03/6473 4289, ⓦwww.tullahhorseback.com.au) runs short and extended riding excursions, plus fishing trips and cruises on Lake Rosebery. The former pub serves as the *Gateway Café* (9am–5pm; licensed) and **Tullah Museum** (free), with topographical models and displays on the Hydro

Electricity Commission project that flooded two river valleys in the 1970s – the Aboriginal word *tullah* refers to a meeting of two rivers. **Radford Woodcrafts** (daily 9am–5pm; ☎03 6473 4344) opposite produces woodcrafts from native timbers. The town's other sight is the **Wee Georgie Wood locomotive** that runs on a narrow-gauge tramline of the former Mount Farrell Mine. Passenger trips in carriages pulled by the 1924 steam engine operate most Sundays from September to early April, and on the occasional Saturday (10am–4pm; 25min; $12; ☎03/6473 1229; ⓦtullah.org); the timetable is published on the website.

On the former Hydro base, *Tullah Lakeside Resort* (☎03/6473 4121, ⓦwww .tullahchalet.com.au; dorms $25, rooms ❹–❺) peps up fairly plain **accommodation** with quirky details such as timber slivers for bed heads and colourful linen; apparently there will soon be new chalets and a holiday park. As much of a reason to visit is the lodge-style **restaurant** (lunch Mon–Fri, dinner daily) which serves pub meals in a rather glamorous modern-rustic setting above the lake – a marvellous spot for lunch.

The World Heritage Area

> If we can revise our attitudes towards the land under our feet; if we can accept a role of steward, and depart from the role of conqueror; if we can accept the view that man and nature are inseparable parts of the unified whole – then Tasmania can be a shining beacon in a dull, uniform, and largely artificial world.
>
> Olegas Truchanas, conservationist, 1971

Many visitors come to Tasmania only for the national parks of its wild west. At a combined total of 3.4 million acres, the **Cradle Mountain–Lake St Clair National Park**, **Franklin–Gordon Wild Rivers National Park** and **South West National Park** represent around twenty percent of Tasmania's total land area and comprise the **WORLD HERITAGE AREA**. When the application landed on UNESCO's doorstep in 1982, it ticked more boxes for world heritage status than any other the organization had received. The value of the parks is not simply the spectacular beauty of their glaciated scenery or their natural purity, nor the evidence of Aborigines who inhabited the region for around thirty thousand years. It is also as a missing link to the primeval forests of global super-continent Gondwana. The infinity of green within the cool temperate rainforests – and some of the fauna within – have a lineage that can be traced to when Australia split off from South America fifty million years ago. It's a thrilling idea.

With the exception of Cradle Mountain–Lake St Clair National Park, access by **public transport** is limited. Tassielink runs frequent services to Cradle Mountain and Lake St Clair, and a bushwalkers' service in summer to Scotts Peak in the Southwest National Park. Private bushwalkers' coach charters fill in the gaps (see p.31). Even with your own transport you have to hike a bit to immerse yourself in the drama of the World Heritage Area – wilderness rather loses its impact with crowds and roads. There are several stop-offs along the Lyell Highway to Queenstown to sample the Franklin–Gordon Wild

Rivers National Park, and a couple of roads that nip around the fringes of the Southwest National Park.

Some history

The future of the parks could have been very different had it not been for a bitterly fought battle waged by environmentalists in the 1980s. In 1972 the flooding of **Lake Pedder** (see p.328) led to the formation, in 1976, of the **Wilderness Society**. The society began a campaign against the next plan for the southwest put forward by the Hydro Electricity Commission (HEC), to build a huge dam on the Lower Gordon River that would destroy Tasmania's last wild river, the Franklin. Pro-HEC forces included the then Tasmanian Premier, Robin Gray. Years of protests and campaigns ensued, and in 1981 the southwest area was proposed for the World Heritage list. The **Franklin Blockade**, organized by the Wilderness Society and led by Dr Bob Brown, began on December 14, 1982, the day the southwest officially joined the list – a fact the Tasmanian government chooses to ignore.

For two months, blockaders from all over Australia travelled upriver from Strahan to put themselves in front of the bulldozers in non-violent protest. The protest attracted international attention, notably when British botanist David Bellamy joined in and managed to get himself arrested for trespassing alongside 1200 other campaigners. During the course of the battle, Bob Hawke's Labor government was voted in, and in March 1983, following a trailblazing High Court ruling, the federal government forbade further work by the HEC. It ordered an Australian Air Force jet to reconnaissance the site just to confirm the Tasmanian government had complied. Though the blockade had failed to stop the preparatory work on the dam, it had changed, or at least challenged, the opinion of many Australians forever.

Cradle Mountain–Lake St Clair National Park

This must be a national park for the people for all time. It is magnificent, and people must know about it and enjoy it.

Gustav Weindorfer, botanist and mountaineer, 1910

Of all the World Heritage parks, **CRADLE MOUNTAIN–LAKE ST CLAIR NATIONAL PARK** is the most loved and most accessible; its northern **Cradle Mountain** end is easily reached from Devonport, Sheffield or Launceston, its southern **Lake St Clair** end from Derwent Bridge on the Lyell Highway. One of the most glaciated areas in Australia, studded with lakes and tarns, the park covers some of Tasmania's highest land and includes craggy mountain peaks such as **Mount Ossa** (1617m), the state's highest point. At its ends are two lakes: **Dove Lake**, backed by the ice-carved outline of Cradle Mountain, is a breathtaking sight, and Lake St Clair at the park's south end is the country's deepest freshwater lake at over 167m, occupying a basin gouged out by two glaciers. Between them winds the **Overland Track**, the most acclaimed bushwalk in Australia, which any self-respecting trail-junkie should try. Its eighty-kilometre route attracts walkers worldwide for five or more mud-filled days of exhilaration, exhaustion and stunning scenery. However, you can do the start and ends of the walk or make any number of day-walks around Cradle Mountain or Lake St Clair. Remember that the weather can change rapidly for the worse at all times of the year, and rain is frequent.

Cradle Mountain

The most thrilling glacial scenery is in the northern end of the park around **Cradle Mountain**. Its iconic silhouette, said to resemble a miner's cradle, and the variety of landscapes in the area – mountain ranges that peel away to hazy outlines, buttongrass plains and temperate rainforest, still pools stained by tannin – inspired Gustav Weindorfer (see p.316) to dedicate his life to promoting the area. Today it is one of the busiest bits of wilderness in Australia, and can verge on hectic in January and February; at that time the car park at Dove Lake is often full by 9am and you'll find some walkways thronged with day-trippers. Popularity also means that accommodation, though more abundant than at Lake St Clair, is expensive. Even during peak season, however, it is not hard to escape the crowds with a bit of effort.

Arrival and getting around

Tassielink runs a scheduled **coach** service from Launceston and Devonport to Queenstown via Cradle Mountain (Dove Lake) three times a week, connecting with a Queenstown to Strahan service. A daily Launceston to Cradle Mountain summer service runs via Deloraine, Sheffield and Devonport. Private charter operators include: Maxwell's Coaches (☎03/6492 1431), which connects Devonport and Launceston to Lake St Clair ($70 one way), and Launceston and Devonport to Cradle Mountain ($40 one way); McDermott's Coaches, which will take passengers one way as part of its day-tour from Launceston (see p.314); or bushwalkers' transport providers such as Outdoor Recreational Transport (prices vary by group size and distance; ☎03/6391 8249, ⓦwww.outdoortasmania.com.au) and Tiger Wilderness Tours (see p.31). That said, it's worth asking around for a lift at hostels because the park is on most people's must-see list.

▲ Dove Lake, Cradle Mountain–Lake St Clair National Park

A **shuttle bus** (daily mid-Sept–April; national park day-pass holders $7.50, other pass holders free) links Cradle information centre, 2km north of the main visitor centre, to Dove Lake. Other stops are the Cradle Mountain visitor centre, Snake Hill and Ronny Creek (near Waldheim). Buses operate every 15min between 8am and 5pm and from 8am and 8pm in summer, and you can get off at any stop; just don't bet on the next bus having free seats in peak season. To walk into the showstopping scenery around Dove Lake – a more rewarding way to arrive – you can take the **Cradle Valley Boardwalk** from the main visitor centre. Distances are 3km to Snake Hill (1hr), 2km to Ronny Creek (45min) and 3km to Dove Lake (1hr) – you can always hop on (or off) a shuttle if you change your mind.

If you're **driving**, the Cradle information centre has the most parking, though there are some spaces at the main visitor centre, where an electronic readout records the number of spaces left at Dove Lake and at Ronny Creek. **Fuel** is (usually) available at the Cradle Wilderness Café (daily 9am–5pm, until 8pm summer) at the Cradle information centre. For information on **bike rental**, see the "Activities" box on p.314.

Practicalities

Parks & Wildlife operates two **information centres** in the area: Cradle information centre, tacked onto a café as you enter the park area, and the principal Cradle Mountain visitor centre 2km south, just within the World Heritage boundary, the registration point of the Overland Track (both daily 8am–5pm, until 6pm Jan–Feb; ☎03/6492 1110, ✉cradle@parks.tas.gov.au). Both sell **national park passes**, hand out basic **maps** and sell walking guides and Tasmap's *Cradle Mountain Day Walks – Map & Notes* ($4). The latter centre also stocks a decent range of bushwalking kit, including brand-name waterproofs, and has interesting historical and nature displays plus a good library on local flora and fauna. Both have public **payphones** – the only mobile phone reception in the park is at the *Cradle Mountain Chateau*, which has its own antenna. The main visitor centre also provides EFTPOS facilities for up to $50. The nearest supermarkets are at Sheffield and Rosebery. The only **supplies** in the area are at *Cosy Cabins Cradle Mountain* (frozen meals, basic foodstuffs and alcohol for guests), though Cradle Mountain Shop near the main visitor centre sells snacks, ice creams and drinks.

Accommodation and eating

Accommodation is in short supply in the vicinity of Cradle Mountain, and budget accommodation almost non-existent. Whether you go high- or low-end, reservations are essential throughout summer. If you have your own transport, consider cheaper options around Sheffield, a forty-minute drive away. Unless stated, all options are signposted off park entry road Cradle Mountain Road, between the two visitor centres.

Cosy Cabins Cradle Mountain 2km from park entrance ☎1800 068 574 or 03/6492 1395, ⓦwww.cosycabins.com.au. The only privately owned budget accommodation and campsite, located in a pleasant setting. Private pitches in the bush for camping, impressive stone-built camp kitchens with open fireplaces, a YHA-affiliated hostel with heated dorms that sleep up to four, basic huts and well-set-up cabins that sleep up to six. Also has a small shop and Internet access. Rates fall outside peak season. Camping $30, dorms $40, cabins ❺–❻

Cradle Mountain Chateau ☎03/6492 1404 or 1800 130 002, ⓦwww.puretasmania.com.au. Smart hotel-style accommodation is in ground-floor rooms of two adjoining wings. Only Deluxe and King rooms have bush views – Standards look onto the car park. Casual and upmarket à la carte restaurants (both open to non-guests), a bar serving snacks, a billiard room and spa with the full range of massages, facials and wraps (open to non-guests $95–140 per hour), plus a good tour desk. ❻–❽

Organized activities and guided tours

Given the park's iconic status, several tour companies run **day-trips from Launceston**, including backpacker-friendly small-group operator Bottom Bits Bus (daily: departs 8am, returns 7pm; $105; see p.44); McDermott's (Mon, Wed, Fri & Sun: departs 8.15am, returns 5.15pm; $13; ⓣ03/6394 3535, ⓦwww.mcdermotts.com.au), which stops at Sheffield and a cheese producer; and Tassielink, which also pauses in Sheffield (Tues, Thurs & Sat: departs 8.30am, returns 5.30pm; $134; see p.45).

Parks & Wildlfe rangers run short guided walks from the main visitor centre at Cradle Mountain in summer. The tours below all run from Cradle Mountain itself.

Cradle Country Adventures ⓣ1300 656 069, ⓦwww.cradleadventures.com.au. Half-day quadbike or horse-riding trips in the Vale of Belvoir conservation area, on the fringes of the national park. Both $89, including transfers from accommodation.

Cradle Mountain Helicopters office at Cradle information centre ⓣ03/6492 1132, ⓦwww.adventureflights.com.au. These spectacular thirty-minute flights buzz the big sights in the northern end of the park and land at Australia's deepest gorge, Fury Gorge. Operates Sept–May (weather permitting), prices vary by group size, from $190 per person (four people).

Cradle Park Explorer Tour ⓣ03/6394 3535, ⓦwww.mcdermotts.com.au. The company behind the park shuttle bus also runs short tours from the visitor centre, stopping at Waldheim and Dove Lake (10.30am & 1pm; $15), plus 4WD wildlife tours at dusk ($25, or $40 with entry to Devils@Cradle).

Tasmanian Mountain Adventure Tours office at Cradle Mountain Chateau ⓣ0428 138 593, ⓦwww.tasmanianmountainadventuretours.com. A small friendly operator that ticks most boxes: three- to five-hour guided walks from easy strolls to tougher hikes up Hansons Peak or Mount Campbell ($27–35); canoeing trips on Dove Lake (3hr; $55); night-time wildlife-spotting (1hr; $25); and fly- and spin-fishing for trout (3–4hr; $85). Also rents mountain bikes for $15 per half-day or $30 per day.

Waldheim Alpine Spa Cradle Mountain Lodge ⓣ1300 134 044. The perfect place to get pampered after a bushwalk. The Sanctuary ($25 per hour) facility lets you gaze at

---

Cradle Mountain Highlanders 1.5km from the park entrance, ⓣ03/6492 1116, ⓦwww.cradlehighlander.com.au. Not as chic as other hotels but the most characterful accommodation in the park area, these charming timber cabins secluded in the bush have bags of rustic charm. Built for up to four guests, all have cooking facilities – from basic kitchenettes to full kitchen – and heating, many by wood fires. ⑥–⑧

Cradle Mountain Lodge ⓣ03/6492 1303, ⓦwww.cradlemountainlodge.com.au. Near the visitor centre on the edge of the national park, this large resort has contemporary cabins of varying degrees of streamlined luxury, all with log- or gas-fires and bathrooms, none with TVs or cooking facilities. At the lodge itself are country lounges, the superb Waldheim Alpine Spa and a booking centre for guest activities. Non-guests can book in to eat seriously good food at the classy *Highland Restaurant* (the buffet breakfast is well worth $25) or drop in to eat and drink at the *Tavern Bar* – worth it for a great terrace overlooking the park alone. ⑧

Cradle Mountain Wilderness Village 1.5km from the park entrance ⓣ03/6492 1500, ⓦwww.cradlevillage.com.au. A new resort (built in 2005) that's adjacent to *Highlanders* but rather antiseptic in feel. Self-catering cabins with verandas are comfy though fairly bland. Its licensed *Cradle Wilderness Café* (daily 8am–5pm, until 8pm in summer) on the main road sells fast food and bistro-style dishes plus fuel. ⑥–⑧

Lemon Thyme Lodge Dolcoath Rd, Moina, 31km northeast, then 8km south on gravel road ⓣ03 6491 1112, ⓦwww.lemonthyme.com.au. Cabins in the treetops are the choice of accommodation options in this rainforest retreat, rustic rather than luxury despite a few spa cabins. Also has a few rooms in the largest log cabin in the Southern Hemisphere and a restaurant that prepares contemporary Australian cooking. Rooms ⑤, cabins ⑧

Waldheim near Ronny Creek, 5km inside park ⓣ03/6492 1110, ⓔcradle@parks.tas.gov.au. The only acccommodation inside the park (except hikers'

the wilderness through glass walls while luxuriating in a sauna, steam room, Jacuzzi and cold plunge pool (swimwear required; for sale at spa).

Multi-day bushwalking tours

All tour prices include park fees, bushwalking gear, food and transfers. CraClair and Tasmanian Expeditions also run combined Cradle Mountain–Walls of Jerusalem National Park expeditions.

Craclair Tours see p.44. The most experienced touring operator in the area runs guided trips on the Overland Track (Oct–May, 7 days; $1950), camping trips around Cradle Mountain (Oct–April, 4 days; $950), plus cabin-based day-walking trips around Cradle Mountain (year-round, 3 days; $750) and Lake St Clair (Oct–June, 4 days; $1150). Transfers from Launceston.

Cradle Mountain Huts ☏03/6331 2006, ⒲www.cradlehuts.com.au. Wilderness without the wild on a small-group tour from the company behind the exclusive Bay of Fires Walk – you stay in private huts, have hot showers, real beds and three-course meals. As close to luxury as it gets on the Overland Track (Oct–May, 6 days; $2450). Transfers from Launceston.

Tasmanian Expeditions see p.45. Eight days on the Overland Track (Oct–May; $1850) and three days of walking in the Cradle Mountain from cabins (year-round; $750). Transfers from Launceston.

Tasmanian Wilderness Experiences see p.45. The Overland Track over eight days with a Hobart-based operator – it runs some south–north routes from Lake St Clair outside of peak season (Nov–April, $1880; Oct & May, $1775). Transfers from Hobart and pre- and post-walk acommodation at base camp near New Norfolk.

Wilderness Expeditions Tasmania ☏03/6423 6244, ⒲www.wildernessexpeditions .net.au. Based in Devonport, this operator is one of the few outfits to trek the Overland year-round (Nov–early May, 6 days; $1475; mid May–Oct, 6 days; $1750). Transfers from Devonport or Launceston.

---

huts) is in these eight basic self-catering huts (linen extra $7.50 per person) managed by Parks & Wildlife Service near the former home of park pioneer Gustav Weindorfer. Dorms sleep four to eight, have generator electricity, pot-bellied stoves and a shared amenities block. Dorms $25.

Walks and sights in the park

Walks in the Cradle Mountain area divide neatly into those around the Cradle Mountain visitor centre and those at Dove Lake. Either way, it's worth stopping at the visitor centre to peruse displays about the park's Aboriginal and pioneer heritage and its fauna, or to pick up notes on the day-walks in this area of the park, or to buy a **map** if you intend to go for longer day-walks around Dove Lake. A display in the centre categorizes the twenty **park walks**, ranging from twenty minutes to six hours. Rangers also lead free guided short walks from the centre in summer – where and when is posted on the main door. You can warm up with a gentle twenty-minute circuit from the centre through rainforest to the **Pencil Pine Falls**, whose boardwalks make it ideal for wheelchairs or strollers. The **Enchanted Walk** nearby (1km one way; 20min) is a pretty child-friendly route that follows either side of a creek via rainforest to *Cradle Mountain Lodge* hotel. The excellent **Cradle Mountain Boardwalk** south to Dove Lake (2hr 45min one way; 8.5km) gives a sense of transition from buttongrass plains to the dramatic alpine peaks around Cradle Mountain. Five kilometres into the park from the visitor centre, **Waldheim** is the (rebuilt) pine chalet of Austrian-Australian **Gustav Weindorfer**, the enthusiast who inspired the push to national park status. Now a museum (open 24hr; free), its displays are an enlightening look at initial tourism in the area. There's also a twenty-minute forest walk from the hut that shows off ancient King Billy pine and myrtle, and a heated day-shelter – a cosy spot for a winter picnic.

Despite the image being ubiquitous state-wide, the jagged dolerite towers of Cradle Mountain above **Dove Lake** is still a thrilling sight. The start of the Overland Track (see box, p.318) is also the hub of activity for day-trippers. The popular **Dove Lake circuit** (2–3hr) is an easy all-weather walk around the shore of the lake. A tougher, at times steep, hike tracks steadily up to **Marion's Lookout** (2–3hr return) for a close-up of the mountain from a natural rock chair. You could continue from the lookout on a steep and strenuous day-walk to the summit of **Cradle Mountain** (1545m; 6hr return; seek weather and track advice from the ranger first). Sign in and out at the registration hut for all but short walks.

Though not as exhilarating perhaps, there are a couple of sights as you enter the park. At *Cradle Mountain Chateau* (see "Accommodation", p.313), the excellent nine-room **Wilderness Gallery** (daily 10am–5pm; $5, free for

Gustav Weindorfer (1874–1932)

If anyone deserves the title Father of Cradle Mountain, it is **Gustav Weindorfer**. The Austrian-born wine-maker emigrated to Melbourne in 1900 and served as honorary chancellor at the Austro-Hungarian consulate. Here, Weindorfer, a sprightly enthusiastic man, pursued his passion for botany and mountaineering, and met his wife Kate Julia Cowle through a nature club. In 1906 the pair honeymooned with a botanical expedition on the flanks of Mount Roland, near Sheffield, and it was from its summit that Weindorfer first spied the craggy outline of Cradle Mountain. Having settled on a hundred-acre farmstead at Kindred, near Devonport, in 1910, the couple were able to pursue a dream of promoting the natural splendour of the region.

What impresses most is their vision. Not only did they pioneer ecotourism in an area populated only by itinerant trappers, they pressured bureacrats to grant it national park status. Weindorfer wrote enthusiastic articles about Cradle Mountain for the *Victorian Naturalist* magazine and urged the government to build a road into the region. In 1912, the couple purchased two hundred acres of bush and began to build **Waldheim** (literally, "Forest home") as a resort chalet for bushwalkers, lugging in a stove and bath for 14km after the cart-track petered out in the bush. It opened for Christmas and quickly won popular acclaim. Weindorfer was a gregarious host with an impish sense of humour who treated guests to wombat stew laced with garlic and songs from his homeland. Carved on the cabin's lintel was his legend: "This is Waldheim, where there is no time and nothing matters."

After Kate died from a protracted illness in 1916, Weindorfer sold the farm – he became the victim of ugly anti-German prejudice despite volunteering for the Australian Air Force – and moved into Waldheim full time as a ranger. Yet the gregarious "Dorfer" found himself increasingly isolated once his summer guests had departed. In his diary he confesses: "It is not only awful to be quite alone, but the tiger cats [Tasmanian tigers] are getting so bold I am afraid they are going to eat me". Later, he revealed he found solace by building a fire and leaving his front door ajar, so that animals would "come in, one by one, without their usual fear of man or of one another and share with me, in the stillness, the grateful warmth". The "hermit of Cradle Mountain" died at Waldheim in 1932 and was buried just outside. Although Weindorfer never lived to see the national park he strived for, his efforts led to almost 160,000 acres from Cradle Mountain to Lake St Clair being gazetted as a Scenic Reserve in 1922. And Waldheim continued to be used for accommodation until 1974, when it was faithfully rebuilt out of King Billy pine using bush carpentry techniques.

guests) features inspiring landscape photography of Tasmania, Antarctica and the Pacific from well-known and emerging local and international nature photographers. The star of the show is the late, great Tasmanian **Peter Dombrovskis**. His haunting images of the late 1970s and 1980s brought the state's then-unknown wilderness into the public realm; his Franklin River scene *Morning Mist, Rock Island Bend* probably did more than the thousands of words to touch a nerve in the Australian psyche and halt the Franklin Dam. Further south, between the two Parks & Wildlife centres, **Devils@Cradle** (daily: tours 10am–4pm, feeding tours 5.30pm, plus 8.30pm Oct–May; $25; ☏03/6492 1491, ⓦwww.devilsatcradle.com) is an interpretation and conservation facility for the beleaguered Tasmanian Devil, with sixteen animals held captive for breeding. Much of its work involves mapping the spread of devil facial tumour disease (DFTD), which has halved the endemic Devil population in a decade – you can join rangers on their monitoring and spotting programme every Friday night in summer (2.5hr; $55).

Lake St Clair

The less-visited south end of the park at Lake St Clair, 5km off the Lyell Highway, is gentler but no less spectacular for that. The lake, Australia's deepest at 167m, was known by the indigenous Lamairremener Aborigines as *Leeawuleena* ("sleeping water"): an appropriate name for a large brooding body of water surrounded by thickly wooded slopes and overlooked by mountain bluffs. Some British explorers viewed its placid waters through the lens of Romanticism and saw a brooding presence cupped in the mountains; touring with Governor and Lady Franklin in 1842, journalist David Burn enthused about mountains "like a gigantic castle with battlement and curtain wall". Franklin declared it the most beautiful lake he had ever seen. The lake is the focus of tourist activity, concentrated at the south end around **Cynthia Bay**, christened rather mawkishly after the Greek goddess of the moon. There's a good **ranger station** (daily 8am–5pm; ☏03/6289 1115) with an interpretive centre on fauna and early explorers, and an attractive lodge bar and bistro (daily: spring and summer 7am–6pm plus dinner daily Dec–March and Fri–Sat shoulder months; winter 9am–5pm), with views over the lake and a hearty menu of walkers' fillers.

Arrival

Tassielink calls at Lake St Clair year-round on its scheduled Hobart–Queenstown service (five weekly). This is supplemented from November until the end of April with a daily Hobart–Lake St Clair service via Mount Field National Park. Both go via Derwent Bridge. Maxwell's Coaches (☏03/6289 1125) runs a $10 shuttle service on demand between Lake St Clair and Derwent Bridge.

Accommodation and eating

Lakeside St Clair Wilderness Resort (☏03/6289 1137, ⓦwww.lakestclairresort.com .au) has a range of **accommodation** in a patch of open eucalyptus forest. There are several two-bed lodges for up to six (⑥) and also a backpackers' lodge (dorms $28; rooms ❸). Compared to Cradle Mountain, the campsite (pitches $10) is poor – there's no kitchen and there's a small fee to use the hot showers. For all options, it's worth booking ahead in summer – Derwent Bridge, 5km south, is the only fallback in the area (see p.319), otherwise you're looking at Bronte Park 30km east (see p.161). The resort's reception is in the airy bar-bistro (daily: spring and summer 7am–6pm plus dinner daily Dec–March and Fri–Sat shoulder months; winter 9am–5pm) at the visitor centre, a pleasant spot for a **meal** in summer with a hearty menu of healthy walkers' fillers – out of these times a sign directs you

The Overland Track

There are longer bushwalks in Tasmania. There are also more difficult and more remote ones. But there is only one **Overland Track**. In summer and autumn, around fifty people a day depart from Cradle Mountain to hike what is probably Australia's greatest extended bushwalk; 80km, unbroken by roads and passing through button-grass plains, fields of wild flowers, and forests of deciduous beech, Tasmanian myrtle, pandanus and King Billy pine, with side-walks leading to views of waterfalls and lakes and starting points for climbs of the various mountain peaks. It's an exhausting but thrilling hike; at times the scenery is so pure you can imagine yourself walking through a pocket of Eden. The **best time to walk** it is during February and March, when the weather has stabilized, though it's bound to rain, and may even snow. The track is at its most crowded from Christmas to the end of January. Much of the track is boardwalked but you'll still end up ankle-deep in mud at times. Along the route are six basic coal-stove- or gas-heated huts (not for cooking – bring your own stove), with composting toilets outside. There's no guarantee there'll be space, so you must carry a good tent; a warm sleeping bag is also essential even in the heated huts in summer.

The direct walk generally takes six days – five, if you catch a boat from Narcissus Hut across Lake St Clair. If you want to go on some of the side-walks – up Tasmania's highest peak, **Mount Ossa** (1617m), to waterfalls or into the mazey lake-and-hill scenery of **The Labyrinth** at the south end – allow eight to ten days. Most walkers average it out at six to eight days. You should take enough food and fuel for the duration, plus extra supplies in case of an accident or if bad weather sets in; there's always plenty of unpolluted fresh water to drink from streams. You should also bring good waterproofs because it is almost certain to rain at some point – on the plus side swirling mists introduce an ethereal quality to the landscapes and moisture intensifies floral colours. Be aware, too, that the fauna en route has become adept at filching food from hikers' rucksacks – possums chew through rucksacks and currawongs have learned how to open zips and Velcro. Don't leave foodstuffs in external pockets and ideally store them in screw-top jars and Tupperware-style plastic boxes.

Because the track was being eroded at peak periods, an **Internet booking system** (Ⓦ www.overlandtrack.com.au) limits numbers for departure dates between November and the end of April, and a fee of $150 per person in addition to the park entry fee is applicable. During this period, it is obligatory to walk from north to south, though since this is more downhill than up it's a good idea in any case. The rest of the year you can register at either end in the **national park offices**, where you receive an obligatory briefing and have your gear checked to make sure it's sufficient. The office sells last-minute camping gear and supplies: fuel stoves, meths, water bottles, trowels, warm hats and gloves. The *Cradle Mountain–Lake St Clair Map and Notes 1:100,000* ($9.90) is an essential purchase, and *The Overland Track: A Walker's Notebook* ($12) produced by the Parks & Wildlife is a handy reference. John and Monica Chapman's *Overland Track* ($13) is a good longer guidebook. The Parks & Wildlife Service Overland Track website (see above) is excellent for pre-planning. Once you end up at Derwent Bridge, exhausted and often mud-spattered, there are hot showers at the campsite, for which there's a small charge.

The logistics of doing a one-way walk are smoothed by a couple of operators: Maxwell's Coaches (see p.31) and the Tasmanian Tour Company (☎ 1300 659 878) do **transfers** to get you back to your car, while Tassielink has special Overland Track fares that include transfers from Launceston, Devonport or Hobart to Cradle Mountain, then back from Lake St Clair to one of the three ($75–119). It provides baggage transfer for an extra charge. If you intend to rent hiking gear and go one way, it's worth knowing that Paddy Pallin (see p.228) allows you to rent in Launceston and return in Hobart. Organized **overland tours** run from Launceston and Hobart from October to May and offer varying levels of comfort (see "Activites" box, p.315).

towards the site manager's house. Off-season you'll either need food supplies or a trip to the pub at Derwent Bridge. There's also a free bushcamp (pit toilet) beside the lake, a ten-minute hike north up the Overland Track.

Walks and cruises in the park

Walks around Lake St Clair, detailed on a board outside the centre, come in a broad range of difficulties – meaning that they are as tough as you want them. The best short walk near the centre unites the Larmairremener tabelti Aboriginal heritage walk with the Watersmeet track to Platypus Bay as a figure-of-eight loop (1hr 30min return). Rangers also lead short guided nature walks by the centre in summer. For a more challenging day-hike, the **Shadow Lake Circuit** (4–5hr return) ascends to the subalpine plains by its eponymous lake and provides views of Mounts Byron and Olympus. Pick up area sketch **maps** and Tasmap's hiking map *Lake St Clair – Day Walk Map & Notes* ($4) at the ranger centre. You could also hop aboard the MV *Idaclair* for a **cruise** to Narcissus Hut at the north end of the lake, start of the the Overland Track from the south. From here you can walk back to the centre (5–6hr) or explore the scenery beneath the Acropolis at the end of the Overland Track. Alternatively, you can get off at Echo Point halfway up the lake and return on a three-hour bushwalk (summer: Cynthia Bay 9am, 12.30pm & 3pm; Narcissus Hut 10.30am, 1.20pm & 4.20pm; round-trip on first and last ferries in day, 1hr 30min; to Echo Point $18; to Narcissus Hut $25 one way, $35 return). Tickets (bookings essential) are sold at the bistro, where you can enquire about renting canoes, kayaks and dinghies with outboard motors.

Derwent Bridge

The gateway to the lake is **Derwent Bridge** on the Lyell Highway. As good a reason to visit is the phenomenal **The Wall** (daily 9am–5pm, until 4pm winter; $7.50; ☏03/6289 1134, ⓦwww.thewalltasmania.com), 2km east of Derwent Bridge, a work-in-progress by self-taught Adelaide sculptor Greg Duncan. The frieze depicts pioneer life in the Central Highlands through bas relief panels, carved from rot-resistant Huon pine and standing three metres high. They are

▲ Carved Panels on The Wall, Derwent Bridge

superb inspirational works, powerful and confident, with the sort of muscle typical of 1930s Communist sculpture. Duncan started his legacy project in 2005 and expects to complete all hundred metres of it after ten years. South of the highway, **Lake King William** is equivalent in size to Lake St Clair and popular with trout anglers.

You can **stay** in Derwent Bridge at the well-appointed *Derwent Bridge Chalets & Studios* (℡ 03/6289 1000, ⓦ www.derwent-bridge.com; B&B ❺–❼), which was completely upgraded in 2007 into rather swish self-catering units. The focus of the small community, the *Derwent Bridge Wilderness Hotel* (℡ 03/6289 1144) is a barn of a building with a brick fireplace and high-ceilinged interior. It serves generous pub meals and has accommodation in old-fashioned, lodge-style rooms (❹, some en suite) or basic hostel rooms (dorms $25; no kitchen) out the back.

Franklin–Gordon Wild Rivers National Park

The **FRANKLIN–GORDON WILD RIVERS NATIONAL PARK** was declared in June 1980 and in 1982 was included with the adjoining parks on the World Heritage List. As most of its peaks and wild river gorges are virtually inaccessible, the park exists for its own sake more than as a visitor attraction. The watershed victory of the Franklin Dam project in 1983 transformed the Franklin River from being just a river into a powerful idea of pure wilderness. It also ensured that the **Franklin**, one of the great rivers of Australia, was the only major wild-river system in Tasmania not dammed. It flows for 120km from the Cheyne Range to the majestic **Gordon River**, from an altitude of 1400m down to almost sea level. Swollen by the storms of the Roaring Forties and fed by many other rivers, it can at times become a raging torrent as it passes through ancient heaths, deep gorges and rainforests. The discovery in 1981 of stone tools in the **Kuta Kina Cave** on the Lower Franklin proved that during the last Ice Age southwest Tasmania was the most southerly point of human occupation on earth. The cave was returned to the Aboriginal community in 1995. You can cruise up the stately Gordon or fly over it from Strahan, and the adventurous can explore by **rafting the Franklin** (see box opposite) or walking the **Frenchmans Cap Track**, both accessible from the **Lyell Highway**, which extends from Strahan to Hobart and runs through the park between Queenstown and Derwent Bridge. Plenty of short **walks** also lead from the highway to rainforest, rivers and lookouts.

Along the Lyell Highway (A10)

Heading towards Queenstown from Derwent Bridge, the Lyell Highway (A10) enters open buttongrass plains fringed with trees that reach back to mountains of the King William range. This is **Wombat Glen**, which looks as though it's been cleared into grazing country until you step out into it and discover its bog-like nature. After around 12km, there's a lookout at **King William Saddle** for a view south towards the King William range peaks and west to Frenchmans Cap in the distance. The highway hugs the southern flank of Mount Arrow-smith for 6km to **Surprise Lookout** and a view of a U-shaped valley whose interlocking spurs were bulldozed away during the last Ice Age, eighteen thousand years ago. Continuing on the Lyell, you finally reach the upper reaches of the mighty Franklin River. From a roadside picnic area, a ten-minute **nature**

One of the most rugged and inaccessible areas left on earth, the surrounds of the **Franklin River** can't really be seen on foot – few tracks lead through this tangled and seriously wet rainforest. **Rafting** is the only way to explore the river and even this is possible only between October and early April. The Franklin is reached by rafting down the Collingwood River from the Lyell Highway, 49km west of Derwent Bridge. The full trip takes eight to fourteen days, ending at the Gordon River, where rafters head to Strahan by West Coast Yacht Charter (see p.304) or seaplane with Strahan Seaplane & Helicopters (see p.304) from Sir John Falls Camp.

One of the most dangerous Australian rivers to raft, with average **rapids** of grades 3 to 4 – and up to grade 6 in places – the Franklin requires an expedition leader with great skill and experience (though even guides have died in the rapids). It's also very remote, and in the event of an accident help can be days away. The weather, too, can be harsh – and the water is cold. Consequently, the only way for most visitors to experience the river is on a **tour**. Operators don't require you to be experienced – just fit, with lots of stamina and courage. Prices are high, but this is an experience of a lifetime, with the seaplane flight back to Strahan usually included in the price. Franklin specialist Water By Nature (☎0408 242 941 or 1800 111 142, ⊛www .franklinrivertasmania.com) offers a five-day trip on the Lower Franklin ($1640), a seven-day trip on the Upper Franklin ($1940), or ten days rafting the full navigable length of the river ($2560). The seven- and ten-day trips include a day-walk to Frenchmans Cap, while the five- and ten-day trips include a seaplane flight return to Strahan. Trips are also offered by Rafting Tasmania (see p.45; Nov–March; 5 days $1550; 7 days $1850; 10 days $2400) and Tasmanian Expeditions (see p.45; Nov–April, 9 days $2290; Jan–March, 11 days $2490).

The route

From the **Collingwood River**, it takes about three days to raft to the **Frenchmans Cap Track**. This is the **Upper Franklin**, alpine country with vegetation adapted to survive snow and icy winds. Watch out for two endemic pines, the Huon pine and celery-top pine. There are lots of intermediate rapids along this stretch and a deep quartzite ravine and large, still pool at Irenabyss. The **Middle Franklin** is a mixture of pools, deep ravines and wild rapids, as the river makes a fifty-kilometre detour around Frenchmans Cap. Dramatic limestone cliffs overhang the **Lower Franklin**, which involves a tranquil paddle through dense myrtle beech forests with flowering leatherwoods overhead. The best raftable white-water is here at Newlands Cascades. It's a short distance to **Kuta Kina Caves** and **Deena-reena**; only rafters can gain access to these Aboriginal caves.

---

trail heads down to the river, here an oversized fairly tranquil stream that flows around large boulders. A longer 25-minute circuit loops through the cool temperate rainforest via the Surprise River. An interpretive board by the picnic area provides blurb about the river and local fauna.

Further along the highway, the **walking track to Frenchmans Cap** (see p.322) begins with a fifteen-minute stroll to a suspension bridge over the river. You could continue to Mount Mullens (2hr 30min return) for a unimpeded view of the Cap. In fine weather the dome of silvery Precambrian quartzite can be seen from the highway, framed by hills and glinting in the sun as if permanently snow-topped. For a more spectacular viewpoint that takes in the Franklin River Valley, **Donaghy's Hill Wilderness Lookout Walk** begins further along the highway on the left. Walk from the parking area along the old road to the top of the hill, where a sign marks the beginning of the forty-minute return track. A short way west, **Collingwood River** is the starting point for raft or canoe trips down the Franklin (see box, p.321), with some basic camping facilities. From here it's a straight slalom west through the rainforest to reach Nelson River bridge, from where **Nelson Falls** is an easy twenty-minute return walk through temperate rainforest – a pleasant spot to break the journey west, with falls tumbling into a wooded glade.

The Frenchmans Cap Track

The most prominent mountain peak in the Franklin–Gordon Wild Rivers National Park – and one of the most dramatic in Tasmania – is the white-quartzite dome of **Frenchmans Cap** (1443m). Its distinctive outline – a domed summit with an astounding bluff – reminded early Europeans of the headgear of a French revolutionary. Its southeast face is a sheer 500-metre cliff and from its summit are uninterrupted views of Mount Ossa in the Cradle Mountain–Lake St Clair National Park, Federation Peak and Macquarie Harbour. On a fine day, the whole of the southwest wilderness lies at your feet. It takes three to five days to do the 54-kilometre return trip to the summit, best tackled between December and March, though around a hundred of the seven hundred bushwalkers who walk the track each year do so outside of these months. Frenchmans Cap is much more demanding than the relatively straight-forward Overland Track; it has some very steep extended climbs, is often exposed and frequently rough and muddy, especially on the swampy Lodden Plains – the "Sodden Loddens". Factor in that the weather is temperamental – it rains frequently, and it can snow even in summer – and Frenchmans should only be attempted by skilled bushwalkers, preferably with experience of other Tasmanian walks. Beyond Barron Pass, you are above 900m and can expect high winds, mist, rain, hail and snowfalls at any time of year.

The track begins at the Lyell Highway, 55km from Queenstown, served by Tassielink's scheduled Hobart–Queenstown service (five weekly), or you can charter Maxwell's Coaches (T03/6492 1431) for around $70 from Lake St Clair. A fifteen-minute walk from the road brings you to the suspension bridge across the river for the start of the walk. Record your plans in the registration book here and again in the logbook at the two huts at Lake Vera and Lake Tahune that provide basic **accommodation**, though you must bring tents and stoves with you; like all World Heritage areas, the vicinity of Frenchmans Cap is fuel-stove only. There are composting toilets at both huts and plenty of camping spots along the way; water along the track is safe to drink. From the Franklin River to Lake Vera the well-defined track crosses plains and foothills, then becomes steep and rough as it climbs to Barron Pass – where there are magnificent views – becoming easier again on the way to Lake Tahune, close to the cliffs of Frenchmans Cap. From here it's a steep one-kilometre walk to the summit, before returning the same way. Approximate walking times are: six hours to Lake Vera Hut; four hours to Lake Tahune Hut; and two hours to the summit.

Further **information** is available in the free *Frenchmans Cap Track Bushwalker Notes* or in hiking map *Frenchmans Cap – Map and Notes* ($9.95) available from the visitor centre at Lake St Clair, among other places; or contact the Queens-town Ranger Station (T03/6471 2511). As ever, the Parks & Wildlife website (Wwww.parks.tas.gov.au) is handy for planning. For **organized tours**, it's easiest to go from Launceston with Craclair Tours (5 days, Oct–March; $1200; see p.44) or Tasmanian Expeditions (5 days, Oct–March; $1210; see p.45). However, Tasmanian Wilderness Expeditions (5 days, $1229; see p.45) makes infrequent trips from Hobart in autumn.

The Southwest National Park

Nowhere else in the state comes close to the isolation of the **SOUTHWEST NATIONAL PARK**. To walk the **South Coast Track** is to feel utterly at the limit; a sense of complete self-reliance that is simultaneously sobering and exhilarating. Its six thousand square kilometres are not just some of the most inaccessible in Australia, but one of the greatest temperate wilderness areas on Earth. Everything about it is epic; whether the arrow-sharp quartzite ranges that slice through the buttongrass plains, the sodden marsh between pristine deserted beaches, or the climate that swings between brilliant sunshine and rain-lashed whiteout when a southwesterly front rolls in. The isolation, rough terrain and unpredictable weather – the southwest experiences more than two hundred days of rain a year – means that most of the area is for experienced bushwalkers only. Being able to use a compass and read a map are critical, but so is a tolerance for trudging through deep mud and swampy buttongrass while laden with supplies and plagued by leeches.

The first Europeans took one look at the tangled rainforests and mountains that bucked and reared along the coast, and wrote off the area as uninhabitable. However, indigenous communities survived here for thirty thousand years. They burned off the bush to hunt game during the last Ice Age and were squeezed towards the coast by the inexorable march of the forests as temperatures rose in the post-glacial era. Campsite middens containing abalone and warrener shells, stone tools and wallaby bones remain on the shore, and archeologists speculate that Aboriginal caves may have been submerged when sea levels rose. Aside from a few convict bolters from Sarah Island (see box, p.306), the first Europeans in the area were the surveyors who hacked through the bush in the mid-1800s. By and large, they were also the last for a century.

Only in recent decades has the southwest opened up. The controversial Gordon Dam of the late 1960s and early 1970s introduced the Gordon River Road, which spears west to allow easy access to the north of the park, and unsealed Scotts Peak Road that tracks to the south shore of Lake Peddar as a gateway to the wilderness. In 2007, the granting of an exploration licence for the Cox Bight–Melaleuca area to Mineral Resources Tasmania renewed the prospect of mining in the area.

Your choice of destinations accessible by four wheels, at least, is limited. The only township worth the name, **Maydena** is a gateway to the west that is linked by a bitumen road to **Strathgordon**, wedged between lakes Peddar and Gordon. The heartland of the park south is accessed via an unsealed road to Scotts Peak on the bank of Lake Peddar. To skip direct to the far wilderness you can fly into **Melaleuca** at the southwest tip.

Arrival and information

From late November to March, Tassielink operates scheduled services for bushwalkers from Hobart to Scotts Peak (Tues, Thurs & Sat), passing the start of the Mount Anne track, and to Cockle Creek (Mon, Wed & Fri) for the South Coast Track. Track package fares (such as Hobart to Cockle Creek then Scotts Peak to Hobart or vice versa) are slightly cheaper. Two airlines operate **flights** into the national park from Cambridge aerodrome, 15km from Hobart. As well as its tourist flights (see box, p.324), Par Avion (℡03/6248 5390 or 1800 144 460, ⓦwww.paravion.com.au) offers a charter service to Melaleuca, weather permitting (45min; $160 one way, $300 return); you can register your walk at the airstrip. TasAir (℡03/6248 5088, ⓦwww.tasair.com.au) flies to Melaleuca or Cox Bight (both $176 one way, $330 return, min 2 passengers),

Tours in the Southwest National Park

CraClair Tours see p.44. Regular trips along the South Coast Track (Nov–March, 9 days; $2160), plus occasional longer Central Plateau Explorer expeditions that unite the Port Davey and South Coast tracks (prices & dates on application) and Western Arthurs Traverse (prices & dates on application). Incudes transfers from Hobart or Launceston.

Par Avion Cambridge Airfield ⊤03/6248 5390 or 1800 144 460, ⓦwww.paravion .com.au. Spectacular scenic flights from Hobart over the World Heritage Area, with boat trips from Melaleuca: half-day ($180; includes refreshments) tours include a boat trip on Bathurst Harbour, full-day tours ($290; includes lunch) explore the waterways of Port Davey.

Roaring 40s Ocean Kayaking ⊤03/6267 5000, ⓦwww.roaring40skayaking.com.au. Tassie's premier kayaking outfit offers amazing expeditions in the area (Nov–April). You're flown in to Melaleuca, then spend six days camping and kayaking on Port Davey and Bathurst Harbour ($2250; 3-day trip on Bathurst Harbour only, $1550). It also runs 3-day walking tours ($1550) and wilderness weekends of walks, kayaking and good food (Dec–March; $995).

TasAir Cambridge Airport ⊤03/6248 5088, ⓦwww.tasair.com.au. Standard scenic flights over the park allow you 30min at Cox Bight of Melaleuca ($243; 2hr 30min), Deluxe versions throw in a gourmet lunch hamper ($316; 3hr 30min).

Tasmanian Expeditions see p.45. Organized trekking expeditions from one of the state's most experienced operators. Frequent tours of South Coast Track (Nov–March, 9 days; $1990), plus less frequent expeditions on Mount Anne Circuit (Jan–March, 4 days; $890), Western Arthurs Traverse (Jan & March, 12 days; $3100) and a combined Port Davey and South Coast Track (Jan & March, 16 days; $3200). Transfers from Launceston or Hobart depending on expedition.

Tasmanian Wilderness Experiences see p.45. Trekking throughout the South West National Park, including accommodation before and after hikes at a base camp near New Norfolk: Mount Anne Circuit (4 days; $1031), South Coast Track (8 days; $2370), Western Arthurs Traverse (11 days; $2320), Southwest Cape (10 days; $2257); Mount Anne Circuit (6 days; $1031); Federation Peak (11days; $2320); Port Davey Track (8 days; $1547).

which can cut out the trudge from Melaleuca; it also offers scenic flights. If you're planning an extended walk, you can arrange for either airline to drop food supplies for you ($5 per kilo). If you are **driving**, fuel is available at Maydena, a handy base for the region, and in theory at *Lake Peddar Chalet* at Strathgordon, though the reservoir can run dry; fill up earlier or call ahead rather than leave it to chance in peak season.

The **ranger station** at Mount Field National Park (see p.99) covers the northern end of the Southwest National Park and is a helpful source of bushwalking information; it sells maps and also **walking guides**. You can also glean basic information about the Strathgordon area at *Lake Peddar Chalet*. The map *South Coast Walks* ($9.90) covers the southern gateways to the World Heritage Area: Cockle Creek through Port Davey to Scotts Peak, as well as Moonlight Ridge and Southwest Cape, including notes on track conditions, weather and campsites. For the rest of the area you'll need to purchase Tasmap topographic **maps**, available at scales of 1:100,000 and 1:25,000. John Chapman's hiking guide *South West Tasmania* ($35) is excellent. You should register at logbooks provided for the Port Davey, Timbs, Mount Anne/Eliza tracks, but remember to sign out afterwards. However, note that a search will only be mounted if you are reported overdue – informing others of your plans is always a good idea.

Maydena and around

Unless you're flying in, or beginning a walk at **Cockle Creek**, south of Hobart, access to the Southwest National Park is via the **Gordon River Road**, which passes Mount Field National Park. It's worth dropping in at the visitor centre to ask about road conditions and check you're adequately prepared if hiking. Eight kilometres west, **MAYDENA** is the last township worth the name before you enter the World Heritage Area. Created in the 1940s as a logging base for Australian Newsprint Mills near New Norfolk, it is little more than a modest

▲ Southwest National Park

scattering of houses, but the village makes a good base for day-trips west. But two general stores with basic provisions, snacks and fuel (generally Mon–Sat 8am–6.30pm, Sun 9am–6am) are encouraging local tourism chiefs to capitalize on the settlement's proximity just an hour from deep forest. A **Maydena Heritage Room** in the school (Tues–Fri 10am–4.30pm; free) has balanced displays on the controversial forestry industry in surrounding valleys, and an **Online Access Centre**. Plans are also underway to create a rail-bike attraction so visitors can pedal through the bush on a 2.7-kilometre section of former lumber railway. The **Rail Track Rider** is expected to be unveiled in summer 2008 and will cost around $10 a ride. A Forestry Tasmania project for a tourism railcar was shelved in December 2007 in favour of a nonspecific "eagle's nest" plan for Abbotts Lookout – you'll be able to get a superb view of the Florentine Valley and, doubtless, read about sustainably managed forests while the chainsaws trill at the fringes of the World Heritage Area nearby.

Accommodation and eating

Giant's Table (℡03/6288 2293, Ⓦwww.giantstable.com.au; ❺–❻) has tasteful contemporary accommodation in renovated cottages plus a good restaurant (dinner only; licensed; open to non-guests) whose good-value meals are all home-made and fresh. Nearby *Roydon Alpaca Stud* (℡03/6288 2212, Ⓦwww .roydonalpacastud.com; ❹) has a snug modern cabin that opens onto an alpaca farm, plus B&B in the farmhouse. By mid-2008, backpacker-friendly *Southwest Adventure Base* (℡03/6288 2210, or 0400 786 327; Ⓔswadventure @wildmail.com; dorms $25, rooms ❸), in a small house as you enter Maydena from the east, should be open.

The Styx and Florentine valleys

Junee Road at the west end of the village leads to the short rainforest track for **Junee Cave** (20min return), the slab-sided mouth of a thirty-kilometre subterranean system comprised of nearly three hundred caves. Take an empty water bottle – the stream at its mouth is so pure that the water is bottled and sold by Hartz Mineral Water. West of Maydena are the bitterly contested **Styx and Upper Florentine valleys** (see box opposite). The Styx is reached on a righthand turn 2km west of Maydena that loops back underneath the bridge – be aware that logging trucks use the gravel roads and might is always right. It's a fourteen-kilometre drive from the turn-off to the **Big Tree Reserve**, where a short track opposite the lay-by leads to two giant swamp gums 86m and 87m high. It's also worth taking the track near the lay-by to enter a lovely stand of mossy old-growth myrtle beside the Styx River.

The most enchanting walk in the area is the dreamlike **Tolkein Track**: go 800m up Waterfall Creek Road, 600m beyond the lay-by, park at a grassy track and then walk back a little to find the start of the trail. Marked by pink ribbons, the tagged route explores Logging Coupe SX13C that was at the epicentre of the successful conservation campaign in 2004. Though the coupe is not large, paths are only approximate, so walk from one tag to the next rather than blunder ahead in hope. From a twin-trunked swamp gum nicknamed Fangorn 100m or so from the entrance, ribbons lead downhill to **Gandalf's Staff**, a knobbly 84-metre giant in which Greenpeace and Wilderness Society protesters mounted their campaign from a "Global Rescue Station" 65m up. You can continue from here for twenty minutes to a small waterfall. Or double back and go uphill from Fangorn to reach an ancient hollowed tree, before you emerge with a jolt into the open where clear-felling finally halted. It's a sobering sight. To return to your car on the road beyond, turn left.

December 1999: to promote a proposal for a 150 kilometre-square **Valley of the Giants National Park**, the Wilderness Society festoons an 80m-high swamp gum with lights to create the world's largest Christmas tree. The stunt prompts a series of savage media articles condemning forestry practices in the Styx Valley and catapults a local spat to national level.

The confrontation had been simmering for a while. Industrial logging of the Maydena area had begun in the 1940s to feed an Australian Newsprint Mills plant near New Norfolk. But its acceleration in recent decades had made the Styx and nearby Upper Florentine valleys a frontline in the bitter war between conservationists and the timber industry. The prize for both sides are stands of giant **Eucalyptus regnans** (also known as mountain ash or giant swamp gum) that grow up to 90m high and 19m in girth, making them some of the largest and oldest hardwoods in the world.

After the Wilderness Society's success in 1999 the mood soured incrementally. The "greenies" upped the ante. In 2002 they bought a $20,000 advert space in Sydney airport, and emblazoned an image of a clear-felled coupe in the Styx with the slogan: "Discover Tasmania before 2003". Forestry and tourism officials were incensed. After a five-month sit-in protest in 2004 drew around two thousand people to the Styx Valley – itself sparked by the accidental destruction of a 79-metre giant called El Grande during a botched regeneration burn in the Upper Derwent Valley – the Styx became a federal election issue. The opposition challenger, Labor's Mark Latham, visited the protestors and vowed to halt clear-felling by 2010 – and the gamble arguably cost him the election. The victorious prime minister, John Howard, struck a protection deal for 296,500 acres of old-growth forest in 2005, with a target of 46,000 acres to be saved in the Styx and Upper Florentine valleys. In the end, only 11,000 acres won protection. Timber corporation Gunns had already reopened wounds by lodging a $6.3 million writ against seventeen individuals and three green groups that had protested in the Styx Valley in 2004. The action claimed $465,000 damages from thirteen of the defendants for actions which were carried out "wilfully, maliciously, recklessly and contumaciously". The corporation said the protests harmed its reputation and business. Greens countered that such was democracy – as its bumper stickers read, "So Sue Me". The case continues, chronicled for the defendants (the "**Gunns 20**") at ⑩www.gunns20.org.

Forestry Tasmania and Gunns argue that logging provides jobs, that nearly a quarter of the valley has World Heritage protection, and also claims that only one per cent of the available Styx Valley forest is cleared a year. Conservationists counter that logging has already ripped out 85 percent of the area's old-growth trees and are incensed at the permanent destruction of forest and natural habitat comparable to that in the World Heritage Area for short-term profit. The emotive issue is stoked by the fact that many of these massive trees are destined for the wood-chipper for paper manufacture. Sensing a changing mood, Forestry Tasmania has pledged not to remove trees over 85m tall. The contentious **Tamar Valley pulp mill** (see box, p.234) has diverted attention in recent years, but while clear-felling continues to replace old-growth with plantations of non-native species such as Douglas Fir, protests are likely to continue. What Forestry Tasmania calls "harvesting", greens dub "looting", and the battle becomes increasingly entrenched. As ever, both sides see their argument as fundamental to what the state represents, and the polemic obscures many of the hard facts.

To raise public awareness, the Wilderness Society (☎03/6224 1550, ⑩www .wilderness.org.au) publishes self-guide leaflets to the valleys on its website; sites in the Styx Valley are indicated with a blue post marked "W". Forestry Tasmania counters by promoting the Styx Valley as the Big Tree Reserve and putting the case for sustainable logging in its own leaflet, *Giants of the Styx Forest*. Both are available from the ranger station at Mount Field National Park.

Going 35km north from the roadbridge on logging routes Florentine River Road, then Tiger Road and Range Road, you eventually reach a car park for the start of the two-day return hike to **Lake Rhona**. It's a remote trek that requires considerable bushwalking experience, plus you'll need to ford the Gordon River. The reward is the cirque's location in the bosom of the jagged Denison range and bushcamping among quartzite sand dunes on the north shore – a more initimate version of iconic Lake Peddar before it was drowned. Contact rangers at Mount Field National Park for more details.

West of the Styx Valley, you enter the World Heritage Area and cross the **Humboldt Divide**, from which you get a vista of raw peaks looming above the contested forests in the Upper Florentine Valley; the best view is from a path to Thumbs Lookout just downhill from the divide, 18km west of Maydena. Three kilometres further west (18km west of the Styx turning), a lay-by car park permits access to the tagged **Timbs Track** (4hr return) that buries into beautiful forest to reach the Florentine River. The **Tiger Lookout** thirty minutes along the track offers a goal for a shorter walk, not to mention a view of the Tiger Range peaks, or Twisted Sister track (15min return) heads off from the start of the route to the eopymous giant tree; pink tags indicate the route. **Snakes** are common on the Timbs Track – most slither into the bush as you approach but solid boots and thick socks are advisable. Avoid them and they'll avoid you.

West to Strathgordon

Distant mountains and brooding primeval rainforest make for an epic drive west, only marred by electricity pylons that march inland from the Gordon River dam. For much of the way, the sealed B61 heads through state forest and the Southwest Conservation Area, where the amazing craggy landforms of the **Frankland Range** loom above and signposts helpfully point out the names of the features. Two kilometres along the usealed road for Mount Anne and Scotts Peak, 22km from Maydena, the **Creepy Crawly Nature Trail** (20min return) is a short child-friendly loop through some lovely

---

The flooding of Lake Pedder

To Senator Bob Brown, Tasmania's foremost Green activist, **Lake Pedder** "was one of the most gently beautiful places on the planet". The glacial lake, in the Frankland Range in Tasmania's southwest, had an area of 9.7 square kilometres until 1972, when it and the surrounding valleys were flooded as part of a huge hydroelectric scheme, creating a reservoir covering a massive 240 square kilometres and reached by the Lake Gordon Road via Maydena. Before then, the lake was so inaccessible that it could only be visited by foot or by light aircraft, which used to land on the perfect sand of the lake beach. The battle for its protection presaged the fight over the Franklin Dam – indeed, conservationist and photographer Olegas Truchanas, then working as a clerk for Hydro Electricity Commission, turned his attention to the Franklin River as soon as he realised the lake was doomed.

In late 1994, a scientist revealed that, beneath the water, the sandy beach remained in place at the centre of the new body of water. In 1995, divers filmed the impressions of light-aircraft tyre tracks still visible on the drowned quartzite sand. Certain scientists and conservationists, backed by the Wilderness Society, believe that if Lake Pedder were drained it would revert to its former state, though it might take up to thirty years. Half-hearted campaigns are still mounted for the lake to be restored. But in truth the debate has moved on. For most conservationists, Lake Peddar is iconic less as a body of water than as an emblem of the destruction of wilderness.

temperate rainforest. It's more impressive than the overgrown Wedge Nature Trail, 6km west on the B61. Its car park is the start of the track for Mount Wedge (5hr return).

You finally swing alongside the iconic **Lake Pedder** (see box opposite) to reach **STRATHGORDON**, a former construction base for the **Gordon Dam power station** that spectacularly fails to live up to its setting. The power plant lies at the end of the road 12km west, beyond haunting reservoirs whose drowned trees poke above the water when water levels are low. If the statistics for the dam are impressive – 140m high, nearly 8m thick and holding back 12.5 billion tonnes of water, or around twenty-seven times that in Sydney Harbour – the walk along its crest, peering down into the narrow Gordon River gorge, is breathtaking. If you're after a thrill you can **abseil** down it – the world's highest commerical abseil – with Aardvark Adventures (℡03/6273 7722, @www.aardvarkadventures.com.au; 4–5hr; $180). The double-concave design may be admirable at holding back water, but it also means that within ten metres of cresting the edge – equivalent to climbing out of a mid-storey window of the Empire State Building – you are dangling in space at the end of a rope. Not for the faint-hearted. The power station, buried into surrounding cliffs, is small beer by comparison – consult *Lake Peddar Chalet* for details of tours.

You can **stay** at Lake Pedder at the refurbished *Lake Pedder Chalet* (℡03/6280 1166, @www.lakepedderchalet.com.au; shared-bathroom or en-suite rooms ❸–❹; self-contained units ❺), a former staff house for the Hydro Electric Commission that has superb lake views from some rooms and in its bar and bistro. It doubles as the **information centre** (daily 7am–7pm; same contacts) for details of walks in the area and the rental of fishing dinghies ($60 half-day, $100 full-day) and fishing rods ($6 per day) – the drowned vegetation of Lake Pedder nurtured a good stock of trout. Alternatively, there are a number of free **campsites** in the area: just down the road on the shore of Lake Pedder, *Teds Beach* has a shelter shed, electric barbecues, water and toilets.

Mount Anne Circuit and Scotts Peak

Unsealed Scotts Peak Road tracks south off the B61 29km west of Maydena and towards the heart of the wilderness. It's a great drive, grander than the main route because it is unsullied by pylons. Looming on the left is the highest peak in the southwest, **Mount Anne** (1423m), a part of a small range capped with red dolerite that is in stark contrast to the surrounding white quartzite. Views from the summit are spectacular in fine weather, but even in summer the route to the summit is very exposed and prone to bad weather. It's suitable only for experienced walkers carrying a safety rope. The three- to four-day walk begins 21km along Scotts Peak Road at Condominium Creek (where there are basic camping facilities) and ends 9km south at Red Tape Creek; a car shuttle might be advisable, or you can be picked up and dropped off from Hobart with Tassielink's "Wilderness Link" service (Nov–April). For a shorter walk from the Mount Anne car park, you can grunt up a steep, exposed ridge to **Eliza Plateau** (5–6hr return), in the shadow of the peak, which offers great views from its ridge. There's a shelter and toilet just before the plateau – come prepared for mud.

The road continues along the east shore then south shore of Lake Pedder to reach *Edgar Campground* (toilets; water; fireplaces and firewood) and, beneath Scotts Peak beyond, *Huon Campground* (toilets; water; fireplaces and firewood; picnic shelter), the start of the tracks into the great southwest

Western Arthurs Traverse and Federation Peak

Arguably the most spectacular bushwalk in Tasmania, only 20km in length and 5km in width, **Western Arthurs Traverse** takes in 25 major peaks and thirty lakes. The last glacial period gouged into this range, leaving sharp quartzite ridges, craggy towers and impressive cliffs, and carving circular valleys that are now filled by dark, tannin-stained lakes and buttongrass plains. Violent storms, mists and continuous rain can plague the route in summer, since it's in the direct path of the Roaring Forties. Despite the conditions, the range was commonly scaled by local Aborigines – they guided George Augustus Robinson across in 1830 during his negotiation tour to pursuade indigenous tribes to resettle elsewhere, making the tubby 43-year-old the first European to hike the traverse. Crossing these ranges makes for a superb but difficult walk, taking between nine and twelve days, and camping areas are limited. Though there's no man-made track, the route, starting at Scotts Peak Road, is not difficult to follow; it involves scrambling over roots and branches and making short descents and ascents into gullies and cliff lines, and you'll need to use a rope at some points.

The **Eastern Arthur Range** is the location of the major goal for intrepid southwest walkers. An almost perfectly triangular outline rising starkly above the surrounding rugged peaks and ridges, **Federation Peak** is the most prestigious one to bag for hardened hikers, and is often considered the most challenging in Australia. It was named by a surveyor in 1901, the year of federation, when most of the major landmarks in the southwest were still unvisited. In fact, the peak was not successfully scaled until 1949, and its thick scrub, forests and cliffs have kept most walkers at bay. Although the walk is now easier since the terrain has been "broken in", each year around half of the walkers who tackle the route are turned back by the worst weather in Tasmania, and one person has died in the attempt. All the ascents are extremely difficult – some say the final push is dangerous – and most parties take between seven and ten days to reach the peak and return. Plan for at least ten to twelve days in the bush to allow for poor weather, and come prepared for minor rock-climbing to get to the summit. The walk begins at the same point as the Port Davey Track below.

For **organized expeditions** to both ranges see the box on p.324.

Port Davey Track

Going straight through the heart of the World Heritage Area, from Scotts Peak Dam south to Melaleuca (where you fly out; see p.323), is the little-used seventy-kilometre **Port Davey Track**, a wet, muddy four- to five-day trek over buttongrass plains, with views of rugged mountain ranges along the way. It's less interesting than some of the other walks in the area and most groups combine it with the South Coast Track for a ten- to sixteen-day wilderness experience, which requires a drop-off of food supplies. This combined walk is often called the **Southwest Track**. Tassielink offers a "Wilderness Link" (Nov–April) service to Scotts Peak. Tasmap's South Coast Track hiking map extends up from the south coast to cover the route.

South Coast Track

The **South Coast Track** is known for magnificent **beaches** and spectacular coastal scenery of Aboriginal middens, rainforest and buttongrass ridges. Less appealing is its reputation for mud albeit reduced by recent boardwalks. You will need to plough through sections of mud and may sink thigh-high in places. Buy the best gaiters you can afford and treat them with love. At 85km, the walk is one of the longest tracks in the South West National Park – a six- to eight-day moderate-to-difficult walk, usually done from Melaleuca east to Cockle Creek. Since the route is mostly along the coast, the climate is milder than in many parts of the World Heritage Area, but there is exposure to cold southerly winds and frequent rain. Even in summer, it can sleet or snow on the Ironbound Range (900m) that forms a natural barrier midway along the route; you can go from snow to sunburn in a day. There are no huts along the way, except at the Melaleuca airstrip. Around a thousand people do the walk each year, 75 percent of them between December and March, when the weather is at its most stable. Nevertheless, you should take excess food in case you have to wait for conditions to calm before you can row across New River Lagoon and Bathurst Narrows in boats provided – both are tough going alone.

The best **approach** is to fly direct to Cox Bight with TasAir, cutting out the boring buttongrass-plains walk from Melaleuca, then head for Cockle Creek, where Tassielink provides a "Wilderness Link" (Nov–April) service to Hobart, or Geeveston-based Evans Coaches (☏03/6297 1335, Ⓦwww.evanscoaches .com.au) provides charter services. Alternatively, you can begin at Cockle Creek and fly out at Melaleuca with TasAir or Par Avion, or arrange for extra food supplies to be flown in at Melaleuca and continue along the Port Davey Track across the water, using the rowboats provided. Several companies provide organized walks of the track (see p.324) – you need to be very fit for the nine-day trip, as each party member humps a share of the food and tents, a weight of 18–20kg.

Information about the route is printed on the rear of Tasmap's excellent *South Coast Walks – Map & Notes* ($9.95) available in outdoors centres in Hobart. Its 1:100,000 scale is adequate so long as you stick to the track – if you want more detail, its 1:25,000 maps of Recherche, Prion, Cox and Melaleuca cover all of the route except for the Ironbounds. John Chapman's *South West Tasmania* guidebook also covers the route.

Southwest Cape

The granite **Southwest** Cape juts out for 3km into the wild Southern Ocean. Walking is fairly easy here, though the rough unmarked tracks across open countryside require sound navigation, and some high, windy ridges have to be crossed. As such, it is a sort of wilderness in miniature; a destination that demands respect and excellent navigation skills on tracks that are rough in places, but whose shorter circuits do not entail the week-long periods of isolation and self-reliance you get on the South Coast Track. All routes start and end at Melaleuca or Cox Bight, but there are a variety of ways to the cape and beyond, taking in different beaches and bays. Depending on which you choose, a simple route will take from three to seven days, and the full circuit between six and nine. Because of the growing popularity of the walks, they may be overcrowded in the summer months.

Travel details

Buses

Cradle Mountain to: Devonport (late Nov–late March 1 daily; 1hr 30min–1hr 50min; other times Tues, Thurs & Sat 1 daily; 1hr 30min); Launceston (late Nov–late March 1 daily; 2hr 45min–3hr; other times Tues, Thurs & Sat 1 daily; 3hr); Sheffield (late Nov–late March 1 daily; 1hr; other times Tues, Thurs & Sat 1 daily; 1hr); Strahan (Tues, Thurs & Sat 1 daily; 3hr); Zeehan (Tues, Thurs & Sat 1 daily; 2hr 20min).

Lake St Clair to: Frenchmans Cap Track (Tues, Thurs & Sat 1 daily; 35–55min); Hobart (late Nov–late March 1 daily, 2hr 45min–3hr 15min; other times Tues, Thurs & Sat 1 daily; 2hr 30min–2hr 50min); Queenstown (Tues, Thurs & Sat 1 daily; 1hr 45min–2hr); Strahan (Tues, Thurs & Sat 1 daily; 2hr 30min–3hr 35min).

Maydena to (late Nov–late March only): Hobart (Tues, Thurs & Sat 1 daily; 1hr 45min); Mount Anne (Tues, Thurs & Sat 1 daily; 55min); Mount Field (Tues, Thurs & Sat 1 daily; 20min); Scotts Peak (Tues, Thurs & Sat 1 daily; 1hr 30min); Timbs Track (Tues, Thurs & Sat 1 daily; 10min).

Queenstown to: Cradle Mountain (Tues, Thurs & Sat 1 daily; 2hr 45min); Devonport (Tues, Thurs & Sat 1 daily; 4hr); Frenchmans Cap Track (Tues & Thurs–Sun 1 daily; 1hr); Hobart (Tues & Thurs–Sun 1 daily; 4hr 30min–4hr 50min); Lake St Clair (Tues & Thurs–Sun 1 daily; 1hr 30min–1hr 45min); Launceston (Tues, Thurs & Sat 1 daily; 5hr 30min); New Norfolk (Tues & Thurs–Sun 1 daily; 4hr–4hr 20min); Sheffield (Tues, Thurs & Sat 1 daily; 3hr 30min); Strahan (Tues & Thurs–Sun 1 daily; 45min); Tullah (Tues, Thurs & Sat 1 daily; 1hr 45min); Zeehan (Tues, Thurs & Sat 1 daily; 55min).

Scotts Peak to (late Nov–late March only): Hobart (Tues, Thurs & Sat 1 daily; 2hr 45min); Maydena (Tues, Thurs & Sat 1 daily; 25min); Mount Anne (Tues, Thurs & Sat 1 daily; 25min); Mount Field (Tues, Thurs & Sat 1 daily; 1hr 20min); Timbs Track (Tues, Thurs & Sat 1 daily; 50min).

Strahan to: Cradle Mountain (Tues, Thurs & Sat 1 daily; 3hr 30min); Devonport (Tues, Thurs & Sat 1 daily; 5hr); Hobart (Tues & Thurs–Sun 1 daily; 5hr 10min–7hr 30min); Lake St Clair (Tues & Thurs–Sun 1 daily; 2hr 20min–4hr 30min); Launceston (Tues, Thurs & Sat 1 daily; 6hr 30min); New Norfolk (Tues & Thurs–Sun 1 daily; 4hr 40min–6hr 30min); Queenstown (Tues & Thurs–Sun 1 daily; 45min); Sheffield (Tues, Thurs & Sat 1 daily; 4hr 30min); Tullah (Tues, Thurs & Sat 1 daily; 2hr 45min); Zeehan (Tues, Thurs & Sat 1 daily; 2hr).

Flights

Cox Bight/Melaleuca to: Cambridge (on demand; 45min).

Bass Strait Islands

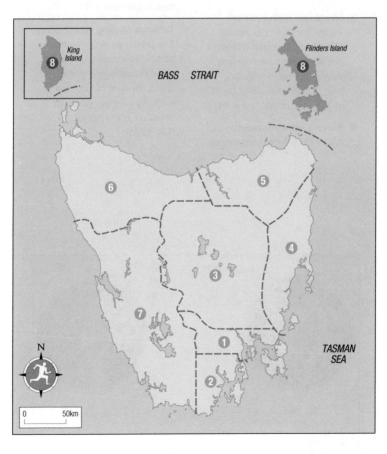

CHAPTER 8

Highlights

✱ **Diving** Whether exploring the wrecks off King Island or soaring down sponge-covered drop-offs at Flinders Island, the diving in the Bass Strait islands is first-class. See p.338 and 347

✱ **Strzelecki National Park** Tackle the four-hour return climb to the summit of Mount Strzelecki for a tremendous view over Franklin Sound, then laze in captivating bays at Trousers Point. See p.341

✱ **Surfing on King Island** Always breaking somewhere, always offshore, King Island offers plenty of scope for great surfing – British Admiral Beach is consistent, but don't miss one of Australia's best beachbreaks at Martha Lavinia Beach. See p.345 and 347

✱ **Tastings at King Island Dairy** The purest air in the world plus rich pasture plus dairy cows equals some of the finest cheeses in Australia – it's the simplest gourmet equation in the book. See p.345

King Billy   Trucanini

▲ William "King Billy" Lanne and Truganini

Bass Strait Islands

What Tasmania is to Australia, the Bass Strait Islands are to Tasmania. The remote islands of a remote offshore island, **King Island** and **Flinders Island** are the largest of the Hunter and Furneaux groups respectively, located in the tumultuous Bass Strait 80km northwest and 50km northeast of the state's corners. They are a sort of Tasmania concentrate: battered by the Roaring Forties winds, the rugged landscapes and beaches are more deserted, the solitude more intense. Islanders have a laid-back fatalism and the resilience of a people who live almost cut off from the mainland. Should Tasmania ever feel too hurried or too touristy, this is your place.

Notwithstanding that Flinders Island is a remnant of a drowned landbridge to the mainland, the islands – and their occupants – have always been lands apart. Shipwrecked mariners, such as those of the Sydney Cove, beached on Preservation Island in 1797, reported abundant fur seals and muttonbirds (short-tailed shearwaters). Sealers roamed the Bass Strait and formed encampments on the islands before Tasmania was officially settled. A piratical bunch, **"Straitsmen"** were a colourful band of renegades who traded with indigenous communities; the more ruthless among them also enslaved Aboriginal women for their seal-hunting skills. To Hobart officialdom they were outcasts who were beyond the pale. That Straitsmen also dabbled in wrecking and sheltered escaped convicts forced the authorities into strong-arm tactics, but isolation rendered official pressure largely ineffectual. Indeed, the government only became involved to manage a shameful Aboriginal camp on Flinders Island in the 1830s, and subsequently to resettle World War veterans in an attempt to populate the islands.

Today the islands consist of low-key rural communities: dairy, beef and kelp are the main economies on King Island; fishing plus sheep and dairy on Flinders Island. However, aided by reasonable aviation links, **tourism** is growing as the islands' reputation for ultimate escapism increases year on year. For visitors, solitude and a slower pace of life where locals are keen to chat is much of the appeal – but there are also attractive landscapes and activities. On Flinders Island, white sands and granite boulders are similar to the East Coast and there are bushwalks in a national park, plus excellent fishing. Famed for its cheeses and beef, lush King Island has several good surf beaches that are littered with shipwrecks and tousled by bull-kelp. There is no public transport on the islands, so you'll need to rent a car or organize a tour.

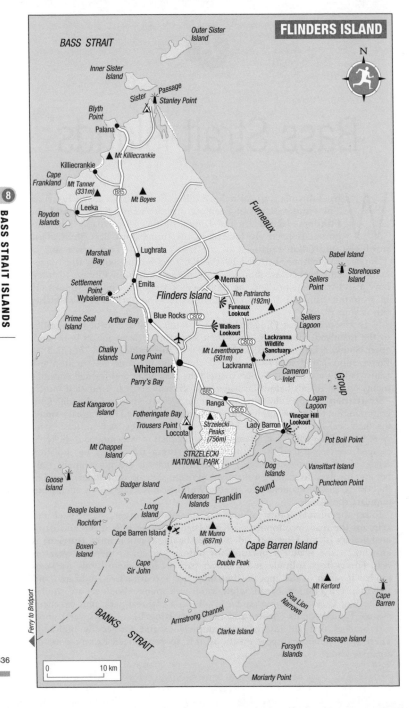

FLINDERS ISLAND

N

BASS STRAIT

Outer Sister Island

Inner Sister Island

Sister Passage
Stanley Point

Blyth Point

Palana

Mt Killiecrankie

Killiecrankie

Cape Frankland

Mt Tanner (331m)

B85

Mt Boyes

Leeka

Roydon Islands

Marshall Bay

Lughrata

Furneaux

Babel Island

Storehouse Island

Sellers Point

Settlement Point
Wybalenna

Emita

Memana

Flinders Island

The Patriarchs (192m)

Funeaux Lookout

Sellers Lagoon

Prime Seal Island

Arthur Bay

Blue Rocks

C802

Walkers Lookout

Lackranna Wildlife Sanctuary

C803

Chalky Islands

Long Point

Mt Leventhorpe (501m)

Lackranna

Cameron Inlet

Whitemark

Group

Parry's Bay

B85

East Kangaroo Island

Ranga

C805

Logan Lagoon

Fotheringate Bay

Vinegar Hill Lookout

Trousers Point
Loccota

Strzelecki Peaks (756m)

Lady Barron

Pot Boil Point

Mt Chappel Island

STRZELECKI NATIONAL PARK

Dog Islands

Vansittart Island

Goose Island

Badger Island

Franklin Sound

Puncheon Point

Beagle Island

Long Island

Anderson Islands

Rochfort

Cape Barren Island

Mt Munro (687m)

Cape Barren Island

Boxen Island

Cape Sir John

Double Peak

Mt Kerford

Cape Barren

BANKS STRAIT

Armstrong Channel

Sea Lion Narrows

Clarke Island

Forsyth Islands

Passage Island

Ferry to Bridport

Moriarty Point

0   10 km

Flinders Island

"Where mountains meet the sea" is a much-repeated sobriquet on **FLINDERS ISLAND**. It is the largest of 52 named islands that make up the Furneaux group, though the population is only eight hundred and nearly half of these are absentee landowners. The islands are the peaks of a drowned isthmus that arcs 240km to meet southeast Victoria.

Geographically, Flinders Island has a spine of low western mountains that tails off into farmland to the east. Settlement is on the western shore, focused on **Whitemark**, the administrative centre. **Emita** and **Wybalenna** concentrate key moments of European and Aboriginal heritage at one location, while on the south coast, the fishing town and deep-water port **Lady Barron** is the island's second settlement – more picturesque than Whitemark and with more accommodation, but fewer facilities. However, Flinders Island is less about settlements than scenery; best appreciated via activities such as bushwalking, snorkelling and scuba diving, fishing or simply idling on silver beaches that you'll usually have to yourself. As locals say, if there's someone on the beach, go to another. (And they're only half-joking.) **Strzelecki National Park** is arguably the most inspiring spot on the island; there's good hiking in its mountains draped in thick bush, and good loafing in the bays at Trousers Point. Nature-lovers are well served everywhere on the island – you'll see the endemic protected **Cape Barren goose** and also plentiful wombats.

Some history

Around thirty thousand years ago, Tasmania's Aborigines fled across the landbridge under threat from more technologically developed tribes. Higher sea levels after the last Ice Age raised the drawbridge behind them twenty thousand years later. The first Europeans to sight the Bass Strait Islands were on board the vessel *HMS Adventure*, under the command of Captain Tobias Furneaux, in 1773. The captain who lent his name to the Furneaux group stumbled across Flinders Island on March 19, having become separated from Captain James Cook's *Endeavour* in fog. Pioneer navigator **Matthew Flinders** explored the coastlines of what are now Clarke and Cape Barren Islands and found the reefs and rocky shores teeming with seals. This heralded an era of exploitation by hunters, who slaughtered seals in their tens of thousands and, so legend goes, lured many ships to their demise for a spot of piracy.

Ironically, these rough men provided a vital link in the survival of the Tasmanian Aboriginal people by abducting women to work for them on the islands. Mixed-race sealers' descendants remain on the Furneaux group, especially Cape Barren Island. When sealing ended, communities survived by muttonbird harvesting (see box, p.340), a seasonal industry that continued after land-rights claims in 1995 gave the Aborigines title to several outlying, unoccupied islands. In 2005, there was a further breakthrough when Tasmania's Legislative Council approved the handover of Aborigine-occupied Cape Barren Island (population 75) and Clarke Island (population six), with the land managed by the Cape Barren Island Aboriginal Association. Paradoxically, then, although a government camp on Flinders Island in the 1830s and 1840s effectively completed the British genocide of full-blooded Tasmanian Aborigines, the Furneaux Group is now a wellspring of indigenous culture.

Arrival and getting around

Airlines of Tasmania (☎1800 144 460, ⓦwww.airtasmania.com.au) schedules **flights** to Flinders Island from Launceston ($155 one way, $310 return) at least three times a week and daily from December to April, and from Melbourne Essendon ($210 one way, $420 return) three or four times a week. All land 5km north of Whitemark at an airstrip that brings new meaning to the term minimal. You can also go by **ship** to Lady Barron from Bridport on the northeast coast of Tasmania. Southern Shipping Co (Mon departures, times depend on tides; ☎03/6356 3333, ⓦwww.southernshipping.com.au) operates a car and passenger ferry. Because the capacity is limited to twelve vehicles, car costs are prohibitive ($515 return), only mitigated by rebates of $168 through the government's Bass Strait Passenger Vehicle Equalization Scheme; for details search at government websites ⓦwww.infrastructure.gov.au or ⓦwww .centrelink.gov.au. The return passenger fare of $96.10 is good value if you can put up with a possibly rough, eight-hour trip. Book at least four weeks in advance – two months over Christmas for vehicles – and be aware that no meals are available onboard.

Rental cars and vans are available at the airport through Flinders Island Hire & Drive (☎03/6359 2188, ⓔwhitemarkcars@hotmail.com) and Flinders Island Car Rentals (☎03/6359 2168, ⓔflindersislandcarrentals@hotmail.com). Prices start from around $70 per day. Fuel is available in Whitemark and Lady Barron. For a **taxi** call ☎03/6359 2112. *Flinders Island Cabin Park* (☎03/6359 2188) has mountain bikes for rent. Otherwise, you could hook up with Flinders Island Adventures for package tours, including speciality activities or nature deals (see below; 3 days, $486 or $798 with accommodation; flights extra).

Practicalities and tours

Whitemark-based marketing board Flinders Island Tourism (☎1800 994 477 or 03/6359 2380, ⓦwww.flinders.tas.gov.au) can help with pre-planning and deal with general inquiries and **information** on activities such as cruises, scuba diving, fishing, birdwatching, scenic flights, and walking and climbing guides. Head for the Area Marketing and Development Office as you come into Whitemark on Lagoon Road (Mon–Fri 8.15am–5pm). A gem shop on the veranda of the *Interstate Hotel* in Whitemark doubles as an information hub (☎03/6359 2160, ⓔflindersisinfo@bigpond.com).

In Whitemark there's a **supermarket**, known locally as Walkers (Mon–Fri 9am–5.30pm, Sat 9am–noon, Sun 1–5pm; fresh produce arrives Mon & Tues), a pub and the main post office on Patrick Street, and an **Online Access Centre** (Mon 4–7pm, Wed–Fri 10am–1pm & 2–5pm) in the library on Davies Street. The post office (☎03/6359 2020) in Whitemark houses the island's only **bank** – Westpac (Mon–Thurs 10am–2.30pm, Fri 10am–4/5pm) – with EFTPOS, but no ATM facilities. In Lady Barron, the Lady Barron Multistore, tucked away on Henwood Street, is hard to find: head uphill from the pub. It has EFTPOS and a post office plus petrol and is open daily. **Mobile phone reception** is non-existent on the island – public phone boxes are in Whitemark, Lady Barron and Killiecrankie as well as the airport.

The main **tour operator** is **Flinders Island Adventures** (☎03/6359 4507, ⓦwww.flindersisland.com.au). As well as offering Flinders Island package holidays, the knowledgeable Luddington family tick most boxes when it comes to island tours. Among several other half- or full-day trips, including cruises to the outer islands, fishing and diving trips, are: bespoke full-day 4WD tours ($166, includes lunch) and a good-value boat trip to observe the muttonbirds return to their nests at dusk (Oct–March; 2hr 30min–3hr). Whitemark-based Chris Rhodes (©chris_rhodes@bigpond.com; ☎03/6359 6506 or 0427 596506) runs bespoke half-day and full-day birdwatching tours.

Accommodation

There's a **campsite** with water and showers (☎03/6359 8560) at Killiecrankie Bay in the northwest of the island, or you can camp for free at the coastal reserves; there are two points either side of Lady Barron. There are designated sites at Allports Beach, Lillies Beach, North East River and Trousers Point, all with toilets and fireplaces, though only the last has water and a gas barbecue. Most accommodation is in self-contained holiday homes (❹–❺), the greatest number in Lady Barron: it's best to book through visitor information centres before you go.

Elvstan Cottage 7 Esplanade, Whitemark ☎03/6359 2008. A recently renovated self-contained holiday cottage, a short walk north of the centre and just across the road from the beach. Has wood floors and a breezy yellow-and-blue colour scheme. Great views of sunsets from here. ❹

Flinders Island Cabin Park 1 Bluff Rd, Whitemark ☎03/6359 2188, ⊛www.flindersislandcp.com.au. The place to camp in comfort, a few kilometres out of Whitemark near the airport, located in pleasant sheltered grounds. Also has tasteful, spacious and mostly en-suite cabins, all with kitchens and wood-burning stoves. Provides car rental. Camping $7, cabins ❷–❹

Furneaux Tavern Franklin Parade, Lady Barron ☎03/6359 3521. The village pub has ten decent units in an acre of gardens, all en suite, with queen-size double beds and tea- and coffee-making facilities. ❹

Healing Dreams Retreat Trousers Point ☎03/6359 4588, ⊛www.healingdreams.com.au. Serenity with spa treatments in a small eco-retreat that only has room for 14 guests, secluded in the most idyllic corner of the island. Opulence and fresh organic food, plus a gym, spa and massage centre and outdoor hot-tub. A sign of the direction Flinders is heading. ❻

Interstate Hotel Patrick St, Whitemark ☎03/6359 2114, ©interstatehotel@trump.net.au. B&B in the pub in Whitemark, one of the island's oldest buildings. Recently refurbished, all rooms have TVs – some are en suite – and there's a shared lounge for guests. ❸–❹

Lady Barron Holiday Home 31 Franklin Parade, Lady Barron ☎ & ℱ03/6359 3555. Just along from the pub, a pleasant three-bed place, homely, bright and with good views of Franklin Sound. Guests get access to the veggie garden. ❹

Partridge Farm Badger Corner, 5km west of Lady Barron ☎03/6359 3554. Two four-star lodges nestled in the eucalyptus forest – a one-bed and a three-bed, both with wood heaters in open-plan lounges and large windows – plus a modern bungalow spa unit with views over Franklin Sound. Gas barbecues available. ❺

Silas Beach Cottage Pot Boil Rd, Lady Barron ☎03/6359 3521, ©potboil@bigpond.com. Located on a point in a coastal reserve, a 15min stroll east of the pub, this three-bed cottage is airy and bright thanks to an open-plan living area and a wall of windows in front of its deck. ❺

Whitemark and north Flinders Island

WHITEMARK, strung behind a beach of crunchy golden-brown sand, is the island capital, with a population of two hundred. Aside from its good amenities, there's only a modest history room in **Bowmans General Store** to detain you. Situated on the main corner of the village, the old-fashioned store has been a hub of the community for eighty years; you can pick up everything from local interest books to clothes and kitchen equipment. Birdwatchers could walk along the beach a couple of kilometres south of Whitemark to The Bluff. A habitat of Chestnut teal and other waterbirds, the tidal marsh also offers a great view of Mount Strzelecki.

Heading north of Whitemark, you can turn right after a kilometre onto Memana Road to head up to **Walkers Lookout** in the Darling Range. From its viewpoint you get the best panorama of Flinders and the surrounding islands, with signs pointing out the landmarks – it's a good introduction to the island. For an overview of island culture, however, head around 20km north of Whitemark to **EMITA** for the **Furneaux Museum** (Jan daily 1–5pm, summer Sat & Sun 1–5pm, winter until 4pm; other times by appointment; $4; ☎/03 6359 2010). Housed in a group of huts is an engaging clutter of island odds and ends, much of it related to sealing and the shipwrecks that litter the coastline. The star exhibit is the anchor of the *Sydney Cove*, which sprang a leak in heavy seas while heading for *Sydney* with a cargo of rum in 1797. She was beached on Preservation Island, near Cape Barren Island, and while the passengers set up camp in a nearby bay – accidentally establishing the first European settlement south of Sydney – a rescue party rowed to the south Victorian coast in a longboat for help. Only three of the seventeen-strong party made it into Sydney 76 days later – the rest were picked off by disease and attacks by Aboriginal tribes. The castaways, meanwhile, had to wait a year until rescue. Small wonder that they salvaged sixty percent of the rum. Elsewhere are a passable range of Aboriginal exhibits – traditional shell necklaces crafted by Cape Barren Islanders and a mock-up of a muttonbird-processing shed from the mid-twentieth century, its three rooms furnished with artefacts for plucking, scalding and salting a traditional food source (see box below).

A darker role of Flinders Island in the tragedy of the Tasmanian Aboriginal people was played out a few kilometres west of Emita. Between 1831 and 1834, colonial conciliator George Augustus Robertson persuaded beleaguered Tasmanian tribes of mainland Tasmania to accept temporary relocation here. If they swallowed the line that they could practise traditional lifestyles without

Muttonbirding

Muttonbirds, or short-tailed shearwaters as they are properly known, are deeply rooted into the culture of Flinders Island. One of the world's great migratory travellers, the birds fly 15,000km south from Siberia to breed in south-east Australia from the end of September. Pairs mate for life, and maintain a single burrow where they nurture a single chick, born in January. Fattened on a diet of krill by both parents, it plumps up into a tubby bundle of grey down that weighs around 1kg, around twice as much as an adult bird. When the chick is ready to fly around late March the parents desert it, and the muttonbird harvest begins.

Both Aboriginal and European cultures practised **harvesting** of sea-birds, so its continuation on Flinders Island represented a cross-fertilization of two traditions. The stranded crew of the *Sydney Cove* survived on the birds until rescue, and they were a key source of food and income for sealers in the nineteenth century. By the early 1900s, birding was a family cottage industry based at Lady Barron. Every part of the bird was used: the down and feathers were packaged for bedding, the fat sold as machine grease and cattle food supplement, and the birds' fishy stomach oil retailed as a pharmaceutical cure-all reputed to maintain good skin and long life. Once salt-cured, the meat was sold to the mainland. Cans of muttonbird meat ended up in American solders' rations during World War II, and until the 1950s, it was sold in Britain as "squab in aspic".

Today commercial muttonbirding is only practised by a couple of families on Great Dog Island. However, non-commercial activity continues and is strictly controlled through a quota of government licences. Holders are limited to around 25 birds a bag, though this notoriously messy practice is less about quantity than Aboriginal culture. Birders are descendants of the indigenous peoples who see the exercise not just as a way of continuing island traditions, but as a metaphor for the survival of Aboriginal culture.

being impinged on by colonial conquest, they must have been dismayed by windswept **WYBALENNA** on the west coast of the island. Left without adequate food in convict-built homes – *Wybalenna* translates as "black man's houses" – amid a military barracks, they were forcibly Christianized. Numbers dwindled as their culture was expunged and the climate bit – of the three hundred tribespeople relocated here, only 45 were alive when the settlement was abandoned in 1847. Following a successful land-rights claim in early 1999, Wybalenna was handed to the Aboriginal people of Flinders Island and it is now up to them to decide how they'll run it. Academic arguments continue about whether the camp was created with good intentions to protect them from rape and murder by settlers or whether it was simply a British gulag established through the lie of temporary resettlement. Bar humps of broken bricks, little remains of the settlement except Robertson's **chapel** veiled by casuarina trees. Built in 1838, it was used as a shearing shed until it was restored by the National Trust in 1973. A nearby fenced cemetery holds British graves – the only Aboriginal headstone belongs to Manalargena, last chief of the Ben Lomond Tribe, who was considered "friendly" by Robertson. Many of the unmarked native graves outside the fence are said to be empty – medical and scientific bodies in Europe paid handsomely for Aboriginal skeletons. Perhaps it's no surprise that it's an eerie, haunted spot.

There's a walk to **Settlement Point** from Wybalenna, where a viewing platform looks over an extensive **muttonbird** rookery – the sight and sound of hundreds of thousands of birds flying to the nesting islands each evening at dusk during the breeding season (Oct to late March) is extraordinary. Another walk goes to **Castle Rock** (1.5hr return), a massive granite boulder on Marshall Beach north of Emita – turn left to Allports Beach and look for the signposts to the track.

North of Emita, you're on gravel roads. You can drive up **Mount Tanner** for a good view south down Marshall Beach – take a turning left after nine kilometres – or continue up to **Killiecrankie**. Head down to the bay, overlooked by the granite hunk of "The Old Man", and you may find "Killie-crankie Diamonds", actually semi-precious clear, pale-blue or pink topaz stones. General store Killiecrankie Enterprises, at 527 Killiecrankie Rd (⊕03/6359 8560) runs occasional fossicking tours or can point you in the right direction after renting you shovels and sieves (or you could just buy them in Whitemark at the gem store by the pub). The main road continues north towards **Palana**, where there's a pretty beach. Cut off east on a rough track beforehand and you'll wind up at the island tip at the North East River estuary, an important fish nursery and seabird habitat. You can explore rockpools on the granite bluffs of Holloway Point or pitch a tent at a free campground (pit toilet) by a lighthouse.

The rest of Flinders Island

History aside, Flinders Island is a great location for **bushwalkers** and **rock-climbers**. Only about half of the island is cultivated, and you can walk its entire length in roughly six days on the partially signposted north–south **Flinders Trail**, a route that samples the various terrains. (You can arrange with Flinders Island Adventures to have food and water delivered en route.) However, the focus of activity is the **Strzelecki National Park** in the southwest corner (ranger ⊕03/6359 2217). Here you'll find the island's best-known walk, the Strzelecki Peaks Walking Track that ascends to the summit of **Mount Strzelecki**; the distinctive mountain is named after Polish count, explorer and scientist Paul Edmund Strzelecki who climbed it in 1842. The climb to the top starts on Trousers Point Road, about 6km from the B85 – look out for a brown national park sign. Though navigation is easy, it's a strenuous walk – about 6km return (4–5hr) – and the wind can be fierce at the summit, where mists roll in, so take warm clothing at all times of year and something wind- and waterproof.

Trousers Point itself, also in the park, is a great introduction to the island's deserted beaches. With its fine, white sand and rust-coloured rock formations, the site is spectacular, with Mount Strzelecki adding to the drama behind the granite headland. The jury's out over whether the name commemorates a shipwrecked sailor who crawled ashore without his trousers after the wreck of sixteen-ton schooner *Sarah Anne Blanche* in 1872, or the discovery of a box of trousers washed up from the wreck of the *Cambridgeshire* a few years later. From a free camping area (pit toilet; water tank; free gas barbecue), a short circuit track (1.5hr return) passes through casuarina woods and coastal heath before it hits the coast. Another trail goes a kilometre along the coast to **Fotheringate Bay**, a popular picnic site that's more sheltered on windy days.

The only settlement of note in the south is the island's commercial port, **LADY BARRON**, which makes Whitemark seem like a metropolis. Once you've taken in the best view from any pub in Tassie from the *Furneaux Tavern* on the seafront road, Franklin Parade, go to the east end of Barr Street, one block behind, and head up to Vinegar Hill Lookout for a splendid view over the tiny village to the islands on the other side of Franklin Sound. Follow Franklin Road to its east end and you arrive at Silas Beach. Its sliver of sand is passable for a dip in Lady Barron, though be aware that Franklin Sound is renowned for severe currents. Tracks lead off to small bays enclosed by knobbly rock formations.

A sealed road a few kilometres before Lady Barron cuts north through rich farmland towards Memana and then loops back to Whitemark. At Lackrana, you can divert to Cameron Inlet, a breeding ground for black swan and ducks. Back on the main road north, a kilometre or so south of Memana, Lookout Road ascends up **Tobias Furneaux Lookout**, named for the commander of Captain James Cook's support ship who stumbled across the archipelago in 1773; a plaque at the lookout tells the story and there are pleasant views over the island's prime farmland. From Memana itself, you could switch 2km east on a dirt road to Patriarch Inlet, a wetland braided by streams where migratory waders feed. Nearby community-owned conservation reserve **Patriarchs Wildlife Sanctuary** (no hours; donations) is home to assorted friendly wallabies and the occasional wombat.

Eating and drinking

If you don't like pub meals, get used to self-catering on Flinders Island. The *Interstate Hotel* in Whitemark serves meals (lunch Mon–Fri & dinner Mon–Sat) in the heritage rooms of its 1911 building, with fresh seafood featuring on the menu. For more upmarket dining head to the *Furneaux Tavern* in Lady Barron: you can either go for no-nonsense bar food in *Tavern Bar* (lunch & dinner daily) or enjoy fine dining in spacious *Shearwater Restaurant* (lunch & dinner Wed–Sun, small menu for guests Mon & Tues; ✆03/6359 3521), which has a decent wine list and open fireplaces, and is blessed with great views over Franklin Sound and its islets. Crayfish is highly recommended in season. For cheap eats, *Flinders Island Bakery* (Mon–Fri 9am–5pm, Sat 9am–1pm) in Whitemark serves up great home-baked pies and pastries.

King Island

Smaller but more heavily populated than Flinders Island, **KING ISLAND** is known for its rich dairy produce, with crayfish, kelp and wind farming as secondary industries. Green, low and windswept, it can't offer anything like Flinders Island's dramatic landscape, nor its history, though it did witness around sixty **shipwrecks** between 1801 and 1995, many of which can be dived, and there are several working lighthouses – **Cape Wickham Lighthouse** in the north is the tallest in the southern hemisphere.

European history here began early. The island was first sighted in 1797, then Captain John Black anchored the *Harbinger* offshore a few years later and named the island for Governor King. At present-day Naracoopa in 1802, the British formally claimed King Island (and by association Van Diemen's Land). A few hardy **pioneer settlers** followed, to eat out a living hunting kangaroo and seals, and also farm dairy, cattle and sheep, still the island mainstays thanks to land grants given to World War II veterans. But throughout the 1800s, King Island was known more as a graveyard of shipping; a combination of massive Bass Strait seas between the island and the Victorian coast (captains knew the area as "the eye of the needle"), a jagged coastline, uncharted reefs and the Roaring Forties. More **shipwrecks** litter this coastline than any other in Australia. Indeed, one theory goes that King Island pasture is so lush because European grass seeds were washed ashore from sailors' straw mattresses in shipwrecks, though the metre or so of rainfall each year may have something to do with it. The most infamous wreck came in 1845, when the emigrant ship *Cataraqui*, bound from Liverpool to Melbourne, smashed into uncharted rocks in Fitzmaurice Bay, a kilometre north of the point that bears her name. She broke up in massive seas just 150m offshore, and the deaths of four hundred passengers and crew represent the worst civilian maritime disaster suffered in Australia. Many wreck sites are marked by cairns on the shore.

Aside from wreck-diving, **fishing** is good on King Island and the **surfing** is excellent – pounded by Southern Ocean swells, the island has some of the best surf beaches no one knows in Australia, and you're guaranteed a break to yourself. However, arguably the best thing about it is **food**. Gourmets rhapsodize about local beef, as well as seafood – especially crayfish – and delicious cheeses and creamy milk, which you can drink unpasteurized while on the island – a rare treat.

Arrival and getting around

Several commercial airlines operate daily **flights** to King Island airport, located 7km north of Currie. Most convenient is Tasmania's regional airline, Tasair (℡03/6248 5088 or 1800 062 900, ⓦwww.tasair.com.au), which flies daily to King Island from Burnie (Wynyard) and Devonport (both $198 one way) with connecting Tasair flights from Hobart. Otherwise, Regional Express (℡13 17 13, ⓦwww.rex.com.au) flies daily from Melbourne Tullamarine (from $118 one way) and King Island Airways (℡03/9580 3777, ⓦwww.kingislandair.com.au) flies a couple of times a day from Melbourne, Moorabbin. The latter also has good-value package deals that include two nights accommodation. At the time of writing, there was no **shipping** service to King Island, although Southern Shipping Co (℡03/6356 3333, ⓦwww.southernshipping.com.au) was considering the logistics of a car-and-passenger service from Bridport.

Transport on King Island is by car only. Cheapa Island Car Rental, at 1 Netherby Rd, Currie (℡03/ 6462 1603, ⓕ03/6462 1257) and King Island

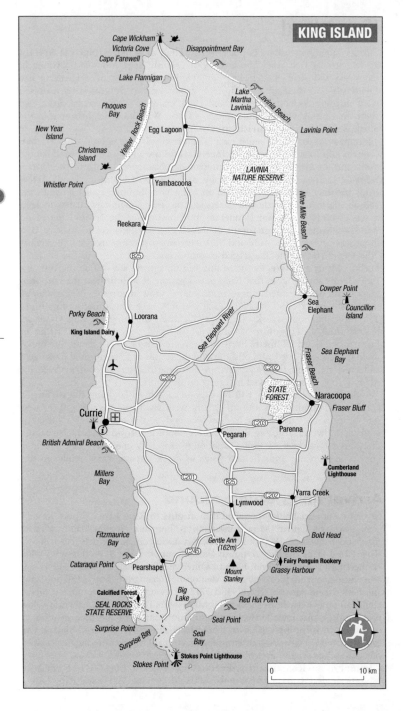

Cape Wickham
Victoria Cove
Cape Farewell
Disappointment Bay
Lake Flannigan
Phoques Bay
Lake Martha Lavinia
Lavinia Beach
New Year Island
Lavinia Point
Christmas Island
Egg Lagoon
LAVINIA NATURE RESERVE
Whistler Point
Yambacoona
Reekara
B25
Nine Mile Beach
Cowper Point
Porky Beach
Loorana
Sea Elephant River
Sea Elephant
Councillor Island
King Island Dairy
C202
Sea Elephant Bay
Fraser Beach
C202
STATE FOREST
Naracoopa
Currie
Fraser Bluff
British Admiral Beach
C203
Parenna
Pegarah
Millers Bay
C201
Cumberland Lighthouse
B25
C202
Yarra Creek
Lymwood
Fitzmaurice Bay
Gentle Ann (162m)
Bold Head
Cataraqui Point
C245
Grassy
Pearshape
Mount Stanley
Fairy Penguin Rookery
Grassy Harbour
Calcified Forest
Big Lake
Red Hut Point
SEAL ROCKS STATE RESERVE
Surprise Point
Seal Point
Surprise Bay
Seal Bay
Stokes Point Lighthouse
Stokes Point

N

0   10 km

Car Rental, at 2 Meech St, Currie (☎1800 777 282 or 03/6462 1282, Ⓔkicars@bigpond.com) allow pick-ups and drop-offs at the airport. Prices start at around $65 per day for a basic runaround. King Island Coach Tours (see box, p.347) does pre-booked **airport transfers** to Currie ($20 for 1–4 passengers) and Grassy. Unless you're happy to stay in one place, those without a driving licence can see the island on a tour (see box, p.347).

Practicalities

In main town Currie, **tourist information** – as well as fuel, fishing bait and souvenirs – is available at multi-purpose outlet The Trend at 26 Edward St (daily 8.30am–6.30pm; ☎03/6462 1360) or you can contact **King Island Tourism Inc** (☎1800 645 014, Ⓦwww.kingisland.org.au). There are supermarkets in Currie and Grassy, while Currie has a post office (on Main St) and a Westpac bank with an ATM on the corner of Main and Edward streets. The **Online Access Centre** in Currie is at the regional development centre at 5 George St (Mon & Wed 10am–5pm, Thurs 1–5pm, Fri 10am–9pm, Sat 10am–noon). **Mobile phone coverage** on the island is with Telstra "Next G" networks only – GSM and 3G do not work. You can rent a phone at the airport shop (☎03/6462 1526 or 0427 621 526).

The island

The leisurely main town is **CURRIE** on the west coast, based above a small fishing harbour – Fox Fishing (☎03/6462 1715) on the wharf sells crayfish and giant crab direct from the boats. On the south side of the harbour, a striking **steel lighthouse** dates from 1880; a 312-piece pre-fabricated package, it was shipped from England after two shipwrecks in quick succession. The former lighthouse keeper's house holds a **Historical Museum** (daily 2–4pm, closed July & Aug; $4), where, for obvious reasons, the sixty-plus wrecks feature strongly among displays of local history. The only shipwreck visible above the waves is that of the *Shannon*, a Murray River paddle-steamer bound for Melbourne with a payload of coal in 1906. Twisted in heavy seas and her planks sprung, she was beached at the south end of Yellow Rock Beach 27km north of Currie, where you'll see remains of her boiler, engine and drive shafts. Visit at low tide to inspect them properly.

Further south of Currie, the eighteen-hole golf course (green fees $20, club rental $10; ☎03/6462 1126) is a true coastal links – hole three is played from a cliff top. Beyond, on Netherby Road, is the town's **kelp factory** (Mon–Fri 8am–4pm; ☎03/6462 1340, Ⓦwww.kelpind.com.au). Bull kelp is gathered from the surrounding shores and left to dry outside the factory on racks – you'll see it as you pass by – then milled into granules and shipped to Scotland to be processed into alginates. This is used as a gelling agent in literally thousands of products, from toothpaste to ice cream. Kelp-sculpture souvenirs are sold in KI Kelp Craft at 6 Currie Rd, Grassy. At the end of the road, **British Admiral Beach** is a glorious curve of sand backed by dunes. Named for the iron full-rigger that sank here in 1874, it is one of the island's premier surf beaches and is rarely flat. The best waves are at the southern end of the beach.

Surfing apart, near the top of the list of things to do on the island is a visit to the **King Island Dairy** (Sun–Fri noon–4.30pm, closed Wed May–Sept), 8km north of Currie, for free tastings of the rich local dairy produce; the brie and the thick cream in particular have legendary gourmet status around Australia. Shame you can only see the cheese-making on a video, though. **Porky Beach** just west has white sands and decent surf; it breaks with a hint of swell and maxes out at 2m. Other **surf breaks** further north include west-facing Phoques

▲ Cape Wickham lighthouse, King Island

Bay (Yellow Rock Beach) on the northwest coast, which works best at low to mid-tide, and, best of all, Martha Lavinia Beach on the northeast coast, caused by southwesterly swells wrapping around Cape Wickham. Voted the best beach-break in Australia, it is reached by following a dirt track off Haines Road, just north of Egg Lagoon, around 30km north of Currie.

Going south of Currie on South Road, you go through marvellously named Pearshape to reach Seal Rocks Reserve, home to the **Calcified Forest**, a fifteen-minute walk away from the car park. Interpretive boards beside a raised platform explain the geological process that petrified a forest in the lime-rich sand dunes to leave its haunted dusty-white stumps and branches. You can also walk beyond the site to gaze over the Southern Ocean from the bluff of Seal Rocks itself, or follow a track south of the car park to see the sawtoothed coastline around Surprise Bay, a sheltered cove where ships sought refuge. The track concludes a kilometre beyond at southern tip Stokes Point.

The only other village on King Island, **GRASSY**, on a plateau on the southeast corner, is a moribund place that is decaying for want of the tungsten mine that sustained its economy for 73 years from 1917. It pins hopes of revival on its **Kelp Craft shop** and a **Fairy Penguin rookery** at the end of a breakwater. The birds return to their burrows at dusk from November to April – you are requested neither to use flash photography nor torches unless covered with a red film.

Accommodation

Community site ⓦwww.kingisland.net.au and area tourism website ⓦwww.kingisland.org.au serve as shop windows for accommodation on the island; the latter allows online booking. The most obvious **places to stay** are around Currie. Most outfits provide airport transfers.

Bass Cabins King Island 5 Fraser Rd, Currie ⓣ03/6462 1168, ⓔd.stansfield@bigpond.com. One of the cheaper options in Currie, this place 1km north of the centre has two two-bed cabins, both en suite and with laundry facilities. Also has a tiny campsite for a few tents. ❹

Boomerang By the Sea Golf Club Rd ⓣ03/6462 1288 or 1800 221 288. A fully serviced motel ten minutes' walk south of the centre, whose comfy if unremarkable suites command good sea views. They're better still from its glass-walled restaurant. ❺

Activities on King Island

Ayton Aviation ⓣ03/6462 1112 or 0408 500 012, ⓔgeoff.ayton@kingisland.net.au. Scenic flights depart from the airport (weather permitting) then soar to wherever takes your fancy – the rugged coastline and surf beaches or over shipwrecks. Prices by group size.

King Island Coaches 95 Main St, Currie ⓣ1800 647 702 or 03/6462 1138, ⓔdinojohn@bigpond.com. Handily based in the main town, with a range of island tours (subject to numbers): half-day Currie Tour and dusk trips to see the Little Penguin rookery at Grassy (both 3hr; $40) plus day-trips to explore the attractions in the south of the island or beaches and shipwrecks (both $95, includes lunch and tea). Can also provide bushwalking and wildlife tours.

King Island Discovery Tours Nugara ⓣ03/6462 1118. Personalized small-group tours by mini-bus, with airport transfers available on request. Priced $65 per person.

King Island Dive Charter Currie ⓣ03/6461 1133, ⓦwww.kingislanddivecharter.com.au. Managed by a local couple with over thirty years' experience of diving in the area, this operator specializes in wreck dives. Single boat dives (Nov–Apr; $75) and good-value three- to five-day dive holiday packages ($400–$700, seven-day on request) that include accommodation, lunches and car rental. Also runs five-hour fishing charters ($75, includes rods, bait).

8

BASS STRAIT ISLANDS | King Island

347

Devils Gap Retreat Charles St, Currie ℡/03 6462 1180, ℯdevilsgap@kingisland.net.au. Two delightful cottages in a bracing seafront location, where rustic stone walls, open fireplaces and wood-cladding are pepped up with art works by exuberant potter/manager Caroline Kininmonth. She also has a good-value two-bed fisherman's cottage on Lighthouse Street (❹) – think 1950s with a splash of bright colours. ❺

Green Ponds Guest House 38 Edward St, Currie ℡03/6462 1543, ℯkigreenponds@bigpond.com. An old-fashioned B&B in the centre of Currie, with pastel-tinted flowery rooms and hospitable hosts. ❹–❺

King Island Gem Motel & A Frame Cottages 95 Main St, Currie ℡03/6462 1260 or 1800 647 702, ℯdinojohn@bigpond.com. Incorporates several styles and standards of accommodation on a site 1.5km from town: modest motel rooms or, better, three self-contained A-frame cottages: two-storey, three-bed and with sea views. Rooms ❹, cottages ❺

King Island Hotel 7 Main St, Currie ℡03/6462 1633, ℘www.kingislandhotel.com.au. The town's pub has ten en-suite motel rooms in a separate annexe; nothing particularly exciting yet comfy and some with two bedrooms. ❺

Portside Grassy Harbour Rd, Grassy ℡03/6461 1134, ℘www.portsidelinks.com.au. A new addition to the island, this small resort to serve Grassy golf course has a handful of smart open-plan units just behind a beach. Styling is contemporary, views are excellent. ❻

Eating and drinking

Famed King Island beef and seafood are the picks here. No surprise that most options are in Currie. Despite a rather soulless dining room, *King Island Hotel* at 7 Main St rustles up good bistro fare that highlights the island's seasonal produce (lunch & dinner daily). For a splurge it's hard to beat the restaurant of cliff-side *Boomerang by the Sea* (dinner daily except Sun in winter) – steak is excellent, seafood always fresh off the boat, and the rugged coastline is just the other side of large windows. For a cheap eat, *King Island Bakery* at 5 Main St (7am–4pm) makes delicious, gourmet-status pies – including crayfish and local beef – and handmade breads, while *Nautilus Coffee Lounge* on Edward Street (daily 8am–5pm) is a locals' choice for lunch, serving rich coffee and tasty light meals such as pasta – and good breakfasts too.

Travel details

Flights

Currie to: Devonport (1 or 2 daily; 1hr 15min); Burnie (Wynyard) (Mon–Fri 2 daily, Sat & Sun 1 daily; 1hr 20min); Melbourne (Mon–Fri 3 daily, Sat–Sun 2 daily; 1hr).

Whitemark to: Launceston (Mon–Fri 3 or 5 daily, Sat–Sun 1 daily; 40min); Melbourne (3 or 4 weekly; 1hr 15min).

Ferries

Bridport to: Lady Barron (Mon 1 daily; 8hr).

Contexts

Contexts

History..351

Flora and fauna..364

Books 369

Australian English 372

History

More than any other Australian state, Tasmania is steeped in its past. Whereas the mainland has ridden a post-war boom into the future, there is a tangible sense of history just beneath the everyday in Tasmania. The reason – and the principal influence that shaped the state – is isolation. Just as being cut off from the mainland meant Tasmania missed out on modernization in the 1950s and 1960s, perpetuating a British influence that permeates almost every aspect of contemporary life, so it permitted the survival of endemic species. Isolation also added a Tasmanian twist to the familiar tale of Australia's penal past. As they had on the mainland, Europeans ignored the rights of the Aborigines and saw Tasmania as an empty *terra nullius*. Unlike on the mainland, they implemented policies to fulfill that preconception. It's a paradox that much of the contemporary knowledge of the island's unique Aboriginal culture derives from the very acts that ended it. It hasn't helped that successive generations have quietly airbrushed out the island's first inhabitants. It's a legacy that Tasmania is only just starting to grapple with – another example of history lived in the present.

From Gondwana to culture

After the break-up of global super-continent **Gondwana** around 45 million years ago, Tasmania drifted away from Antarctica to reach its current location approximately fifteen million years ago. There's plenty of evidence of the former links. Tasmania shares the same Jurassic dolerite as Antarctica in features such as the Organ Pipes on Hobart's Mount Wellington, the Walls of Jerusalem, the Western Tiers and Cradle Mountain. Endemic Tasmanian myrtle (*Nothofagus gunnii*) and Dicksonia tree ferns are found only in Antarctic fossils and former neighbour South America. Fossilized platypus are unearthed in South America, while the only living relatives of the Tasmanian cave spider – one of the most primitive spiders in the world – or the Port Davey skate are in Chile and Patagonia respectively. At the time, Tasmania was still linked to the mainland by a 260-kilometre land bridge that arced from its northeastern tip to Victoria. Tasmania's **first human inhabitants** crossed from the mainland around thirty thousand years ago. Why is a subject of debate. There's no direct evidence for continuous migration to Australia, but since the earliest estimate of migration to Australia from Indonesia and New Guinea is put at 45,000 years, it seems plausible that Tasmanian Aborigines were pushed southward as island-hopping increased. Certainly, their stone tools match those of early mainland inhabitants from the Pleistocene period – later mainland tribes ditched stone in favour of more advanced tools such as the boomerang.

The earliest finds come from the southwest, making the Tasmanian Aborigines the most southerly people in the world during the last Ice Age. A post-glacial rise in sea levels approximately twelve- to eighteen thousand years ago flooded the land bridge, effectively raising the drawbridge behind the Aboriginal tribes to inculcate a unique island culture. Information is sketchy, though archeological finds show that technological advances of the mainland passed by Tasmanian Aborigines. They produced simple stone tools, spears and hunting waddies (cudgels whose tips were hardened by fire). Non-figurative rock-carvings of concentric and interlocking circles at Mount Cameron West (near Marrawah) and Devonport suggest strong spiritual belief.

At the time of first contact, in the 1770s, it is estimated around six thousand **Tasmanian Aborigines** lived in "bands" throughout the state. These were subsets of nine larger tribes, each with its own land rights and mutually incomprehensible language. Bands lived a nomadic hunter-gatherer existence dictated by seasonal food sources, and set up camp in caves or bark huts that ranged from primitive windbreaks to beehive-shaped structures capable of holding thirty-strong family groups. Food sources included game – Aborigines practised controlled burns to increase pasture and attract game – and seabirds, seafood such as abalone, fish and birds' eggs. Seals were also hunted by Aboriginal women, who were superb swimmers. Some communities also made reed boats or dug-out canoes. Both sexes wore kangaroo furs. Women wore shell necklaces, while men matted their hair with red ochre and animal grease, causing more than one French explorer to make comparisons with fashionable seventeenth-century ladies' wigs.

The first Europeans

"November 24: Good weather and clear sky. Course kept E by N, wind from the SW. Afternoon, about 4 o'clock, saw land. It was very high land – towards evening saw in the ESE three high mountains and in the NE also two mountains." With that entry written in the ship's log by **Abel Jansz Tasman** in 1642, Europe discovered Tasmania. The Dutch navigator named his find "Anthoonij van Diemenslandt" in honour of the Dutch East Indies governor who had funded his expedition. After sighting the west coast – mounts Zeehan and Heemskirk were named after the expedition ships – Tasman scooted east before a gale to drop anchor near Dunalley. The pilot was sent ashore and returned with a few herbs and strange cuboid animal poo (a wombat's). He reported hearing trumpets (probably a currawong, a native bird) and seeing tiger-like footprints (a thylacine, or Tasmanian tiger) and steps carved 1.5m apart up a tree. Tasman deduced that the natives might be giants and after sending the carpenter ashore to plant a flag, he sailed on to discover New Zealand.

The first explorers to Van Diemen's Land followed the eastbound route and charts of Tasman. On March 4, 1772, **Marion du Fresne** made the first contact between Europeans and Aborigines near where Tasman's shore party had landed. It ended badly. The Frenchman was forced to beat a retreat under a shower of stones, and after a midshipman was speared, du Fresne ordered a musket volley that killed one Aborigine. A year later, English explorer **Tobias Furneaux** arrived in Adventure Bay, Bruny Island aboard the *Adventure*, after he became separated from Captain **James Cook**'s *Resolution*. His reports of water and abundant timber encouraged Cook himself to pause in 1777 and later Captain **William Bligh**. The master of the *Bounty* planted Tasmania's first apple tree before embarking on his ill-fated journey to Tahiti. Meanwhile, interest about the Great Southern Land grew in Europe. The question of who would claim it first was resolved when the First Fleet, under Captain Arthur Phillip, sailed into Sydney Cove in 1788. Australia was a godsend for the British. With the loss of the American colonies, jails in the mother country were full to bursting. It was ideal to offload convicts and at the same time secure a foothold in the Pacific.

Captain Cook had tacked Tasman's research onto his detailed 1770 chart of Australia. Consequently contemporary opinion ran that Van Diemen's Land was actually the tip of the mainland. That most expeditions arrived from the west then sailed on east to the Pacific meant there was no way to dispel the notion. The French arrived in southeast Tasmania in 1792 and 1793 to effect repairs while hunting the overdue *La Pérouse*; she eventually washed up in California. They enjoyed several friendly encounters with the local tribes – the crew even held a beach-sports competition – and Admiral **Bruni D'Entrecasteaux** lent his name to the area's channel and its island, while his ships, *L'Espérance* and *La Recherche*, gave their names to two bays. Lieutenant **John Hayes** was also westbound when he became the first European to sail up the Derwent River in 1793, probably as far as today's New Norfolk. He named Cornelian Bay (in Hobart) after the semi-precious stones he found on the beach. Confirmation that Van Diemen's Land was an island came in 1798 thanks to **Matthew Flinders**. In the company of George Bass, the ship's surgeon when he first sailed to Australia, the 24-year-old navigator circumnavigated the state in just under two months aboard a tubby sloop named the *Norfolk*. He went on to repeat the feat around the mainland in 1804.

British settlement

Britain had encouraged sealers to establish footholds south of Sydney throughout the 1790s, establishing piratical settlements on the Bass Strait islands that seized or traded Aboriginal women for their hunting skills. By 1800, war had broken out between Britain and France. Nevertheless, a French scientific expedition under **Nicolas Baudin** charted the east coast in 1802 and 1803 without harassment. Fired by Rousseau-esque ideals of noble savages, the French were entranced by the Aborigines. By all accounts, the feeling was mutual. The Aborigines pulled so hard at zoologist François Péron's gold earring it came out, and every clean-shaven crewmember had his genitals groped to ascertain his sex. "We were so novel to each other," Baudin wrote. Yet spooked by rumours that the expedition was a masquerade for French settlement, New South Wales Governor Philip Gidley King decided to act. In 1802, the British dropped anchor at King Island and hurried ashore at present-day Naracoopa where the French were working to claim the island for the Crown. Lieutenant Robbins hoisted the Union Jack upside down in his hurry, causing Baudin to observe caustically that the flag looked like a rag hung to dry. The following year, King dispatched a fleet to establish a toe-hold on Van Diemen's Land proper.

On September 12, 1803, 18-year-old naval officer **Lieutenant John Bowen** sailed into Risdon Cove on the east bank of today's Bowen Bridge, Hobart. Aboard his 360-tonne whaler *Albion* and its guardship escort *Lady Nelson* were a party of 49 settlers, among them 24 convicts and a small detachment of troops of the New South Wales Corps. Within a fortnight of the nascent settlement of Hobart Town, named after the Secretary of State for the Colonies, both convicts and soldiers had probed the limits of young Bowen's authority, and within two months the groups were in collusion to plunder government stores. When the first convicts inevitably escaped, Bowen returned to Governor Macquarie in Sydney to appeal for aid.

During his absence, **Lieutenant-colonel David Collins** sailed into the Derwent in 1804 with a party of around 240 convicts, a small platoon of marine guards and thirty or so free settlers who had been bound for Port Phillip (today's Melbourne) until Collins found it "unsuitable for settlement". He took command of the chaotic encampment at Risdon Cove. On May 3, 1804, it saw the first clash between settlers and Aborigines at the "Battle of Risdon", a misnomer for an unprovoked, one-sided action by nervous (or simply bored) soldiers who massacred an indigenous group herding kangaroo. Eyewitness reports varied from three to fifty dead. It was the last straw for Collins. Five days later he shifted the camp 10km downriver to Sullivan's Cove. Bowen returned to find **Hobart Town** in a new location with a larger population, while he, taunted as the "Governor of Risdon Creek" by Collins, commanded a handful of Irish convicts and soldiers. Within a few months, Bowen and his charges packed up and returned to Sydney. Collins, however, went on to serve for six years as Lieutenant-governor of Australia's second town, the most southerly in the world.

While Hobart Town was finding its feet, Governor King received orders from London to take command of the Bass Strait with a naval base. On October 15, 1804, **Lieutenant-colonel William Paterson** set sail from Sydney to found George Town, Australia's third town. Within a couple of years, they shifted site to found **Launceston** at the head of the river.

Life for both settlements was tough. The military encampments gradually developed into wattle-and-daub villages, and had small convict workforces for manual labour. But for the first two years, food was scarce and scurvy rife as settlers spurned the abundant seafood as inedible. Several times, both camps nearly starved. In 1806, Lieutenant-governor Collins had six whalers flogged for refusing to hand over their ship's casks of biscuits and flour. So dire was the situation in Launceston in 1807 that **Lieutenant Thomas Laycock** was dispatched to Hobart Town. Collins refused aid – Hobart Town was just as wracked – but Laycock became the first European to traverse the island by foot, taking just over a fortnight to make the return journey. He was rewarded with a cow – quite a prize during famine. To alleviate hunger, officers and convicts alike received guns to hunt local game. A desperate measure for desperate times. Gauge their suffering against that of the Aborigines: their hunting grasslands were stolen, and their game – and frequently they themselves – were shot at.

The convict colony

The British had settled Van Diemen's Land by accident, but they soon found a use for it. When the prison islet of Norfolk Island reached capacity, the transportation ships docked in Hobart Town. Until the colony was established in its own right in 1825, Van Diemen's Land was a dumping ground for the worst convicts from Sydney. Much of the period coincided with the administration of Lieutenant-governor **Colonel Thomas Davey** (1813–17), an eccentric ex-commander at the Battle of Trafalgar whose sailor's manners earned him the nickname "Mad Tom". It's said his first request on disembarking was a barrel of rum. During his chaotic rule, the state was beset by bushrangers (escaped convicts) who ganged up to terrorize the farmsteads north and west from Hobart Town. Davey declared martial law in 1815 and hanged three men before Sydney told him he had exceeded his authority. When his successor, **William Sorell**, assumed command of Van Diemen's Land in 1817 he inherited a volatile community of unruly frontiersmen, whalers, brutalized convicts and bushrangers who were in open revolt against authority. Yet within eighteen months of his rule, bushranger leader Michael Howe had swung from the gallows and all bushranger sympathizers had been arrested. Sorell believed honest free settlers could tame the lawlessness. He handed out land grants to promote sheep-farming in the centre and upgraded the area's barracks – Oatlands, Ross, Campbell Town and Perth – into towns. Merino wool became a key industry alongside whaling and timber.

As a deterrent to convicts committing crimes after transportation – and a sop to settlers uneasy about the penal workforce – Sorell established a distant prison for secondary offenders in Macquarie Harbour. The most brutal penal institute the colony would see, Sarah Island, was so far from civilization it might as well have been on the other side of the world. Stern but fair, tactful but firm, "Old Man Sorell" also refused to indulge those **free-settler merchants** who had arrived to coin a quick buck. A garrulous and egotistical breed of chancers and racketeers, many in cahoots with corrupt officials, they had swaggered through Hobart Town under Davey secure that profits always came before the law. Sorell refused to pander to such prima donna excesses and was duly unseated. To add insult to the coup, the merchants ousted Sorell by persuading London that he lacked morals.

They probably regretted it when **Lieutenant-governor George Arthur** disembarked at Hobart Town in 1824. They had hoped for a return to Davey's boozy luncheons. Instead they got Evangelical prayer meetings with a teetotal disciplinarian. Arthur was a borderline autocrat of steely character and determined purpose. He was also a reformer. It was Arthur who demanded the autonomy of Van Diemen's Land from New South Wales. And it was Arthur who took in hand the convict issue. Transportation was on the up as Victorian Britain shipped over felons for such petty crimes as stealing a loaf of bread. Most were refugees washed up by the Industrial Revolution. So dire were the slums in English cities, so poor some Irish villages, that many convicts fared better after transportation than they had as free men – at least they now had three meals a day and clothes for the duration of their sentence, typically seven years.

Life for convicts was no picnic, mind. A scholar of contemporary penal policy, Arthur believed in reform through a strict system of rules, reward and punishment. While "trusted" convicts were employed as servants on free-settlers' farm estates, many offenders were assigned to construction chain-gangs, sparking a building boom that introduced roads and bridges throughout the island. The worst offenders and secondary-offenders were dispatched to new **prison camps**: Maria Island for minor criminals, Port Arthur for hardened felons. Opened on the Tasman Peninsula in 1830 as a replacement for Sarah Island, Port Arthur was the very model of its governor: ultimately well-meaning, but tough and uncompromising, prepared to break men on principle rather than invite a suggestion of leniency. That said, Lieutenant-governor Arthur pushed through ticket-of-leave regulation by which transportees could earn their freedom by working out a sentence without misdemeanour. Initially a ruse to save money, the system soon became a central tenet of the penal system.

The Black Wars

Relations with the Aborigines, meanwhile, had gone from bad to worse. By the time Lieutenant-governor Arthur arrived, the indigenous population probably numbered one or two thousand. The rest had either succumbed to

European disease or perpetual harassment in an increasingly bitter tit-for-tat war fought as colonists went deeper into the bush. Seeing their hunting grounds occupied by farmers, their women raped or stolen by convicts and bushrangers, and their men maltreated or murdered by shepherds and stockmen who had no rights to ancestral homelands, the Aborigines retaliated. Livestock and white settlers were speared alike. Arthur's pictorial posters to explain white law that would punish offenders on both sides came to naught, as did an absurd law in 1828 that forbade Aborigines from entering settled land. The capture of indigenous "ringleaders" only made matters worse.

In 1830, Arthur devised a military strategy. He planned a line of soldiers and civilians that would march across the island like beaters on a game hunt and sweep the Aborigines onto the Tasman Peninsula, capturing whoever was found

The "last" Tasmanian Aborigines

The last full-blooded Aboriginal male to survive Wybalenna, **William Lanne** spent his final years on a whaling ship until he died aged 34 in March 1869. What happened next is the stuff of horror movies. As he lay in the morgue of Hobart Town hospital, a dispute broke out between the Royal College of Surgeons in London and the Royal Society in Tasmania over who should possess the cadaver. On behalf of the former, a surgeon decapitated the corpse to secure the skull, removed the skin from the head then rolled it over a skull from a white body. He replaced this on the body. Tasmanian society doctors retaliated by lopping off Lanne's hands and feet to make the cadaver "worthless". "King Billy" was buried in bits – neither the skull nor scrotum, said to have been made into a tobacco pouch, were recovered.

Another Wybalenna survivor, **Truganini**, was distraught. The most famous of the Tasmanian Aborigines, daughter of the chief of the Nuenone people of Bruny Island, Truganini (also spelled "Trucanini") had accompanied George Augustus Robinson (see opposite) from the start. She saved him from hostile tribes more than once and his diary hints at a physical relationship – unlikely considering she was, by all accounts, young and pretty with mesmeric eyes while he was a portly 41-year-old with a wig. She died in Hobart Town in 1876, and immediately became an icon. The government declared her the last of the Tasmanian Aborigines at a public funeral. Much though the authorities would have liked to have closed a dark chapter of Tasmanian history, indigenous Tasmanians remained, including Fanny Cochrane, born at Wybalenna in 1834 and who recorded several songs to wax cylinder for the Tasmanian Museum and Art Gallery before she died in 1905. Later, Truganini featured in a stamp series of Australian women – again, used as an icon and conveniently overlooking the fact that she rejected being considered Australian.

In modern times Truganini has also proved potent. A century after her skeleton went into a display case in the Tasmanian Museum and Art Gallery in 1876 – the public burial had been a charade while her bones were cleaned – it was ritually cremated by the Aboriginal community. In 1978 her life was fictionalized in a film, *The Last Tasmanian*, to pedal the myth that the Aborigines had died out with her. Today her image is resurrected as a modern-day symbol of indigenous rights – a little too conveniently, since the power of Truganini is as the "last Tasmanian Aborigine", the very issue activists refute. The indigenous community, generically known as the **Palawa**, numbers around 150,000. Most are descended from a small number of women who were stolen by (or traded to) white sealers in the early 1800s. The matter of Aboriginal identity is far from settled, however. While historians engage in an academic bunfight over the extent of oppression and the suitability of the term genocide, the Aboriginal community fights among itself over who has the right to claim ancestry. If anything, the issue of the Tasmanian Aborigines becomes more clouded by the decade.

along the way. Historians debate whether the intent was genocide or an Aboriginal "reservation" to end the bloodshed on both sides. Either way, the "**Black Line**" that November was a farce. The Aborigines could as easily avoid detection as they could slip through a dragnet of 2200 men who could not hope to span the island in one day let alone seven weeks. The bush was so thick in places that soldiers had to march in single file. It's a surprise that an old man and a 15-year-old boy were caught at all. But as a gesture of omnipotence to the remaining tribes it was a powerful piece of theatre, albeit an expensive one at £30,000 (a hefty £23 million in today's money). Far more than Arthur's posters, it showed that the colonists intended to stay and to rule. When **George Augustus Robertson** was dispatched "to conciliate" with "hostile tribes" in the 1830s, he came across a depleted and often demoralized band.

Robertson, a portly 41-year-old who had emigrated as a builder, was a most unlikely peacemaker. Nevertheless, he won the confidence of Aborigines from Bruny Island by persuading them that by resettling elsewhere they could pursue their traditional lifestyles unharassed. Among their number was Truganini (see box opposite), today an icon of what is often interpreted as colonial double-crossing that cheated the Aborigines of their lands. With the Bruny islanders in tow, the "conciliator" travelled anticlockwise around the island to Launceston, cut through the centre to the once-feared Big River and Oyster Bay tribes of the centre, now severely depleted due to relentless settlement, then returned to Hobart Town.

In 1834 all but a dozen Aborigines later discovered in the northwest were resettled on Flinders Island. The chosen site was **Wybalenna**, literally "Black Man's Houses". Managed by soldiers who acted as jailers, housed in barracks and subject to exposed conditions, the Aborigines succumbed rapidly to pneumonia and despair. By the time Robinson took direct command in 1835, only 147 of the original three hundred or so survived. He thrust European civilization upon them. A devout Wesleyan, he forced them to adopt Christianity, found menial work for them, and provided schooling and British clothing. Children were removed into foster care. Robinson's missionary zeal smacks of arrogance rather than conciliation, though is perhaps best seen in the light of contemporary opinions about European society and Christianity as forces for good. Certainly, Robinson's diary suggests he saw himself as the saviour of the Aborigines – a vain and seriously flawed insight as it turned out. Nor did he see the bitter irony in the colonizers of a remote offshore island incarcerating its first inhabitants on a remote offshore island.

Even less defensible was Robinson's apparent willingness to let the Aborigines believe their resettlement was temporary. Contemporary accounts reported that most were glad to go to Flinders Island as a stop-gap while conditions stabilized in their ancestral lands. By 1846 they were still waiting to return and down to 47 in number. That February they sent a petition to Queen Victoria – the first to a reigning monarch from an Australian Aboriginal group – and were resettled again to Oyster Cove, Bruny Island. Conditions were not much better, but by then it was too late. By 1857, there were ten Aborigines from Wybalenna. And in 1876, Truganini, the last member of Robinson's original group, died in Hobart.

The birth of Tasmania

With the "Aboriginal problem" settled, Van Diemen's Land stabilized in the late 1830s. It was still a violent frontier; public executions were so frequent that they were seen as public entertainment, drunkenness rife, and a contemporary newspaper commentator, Dr James Ross, described Hobart Town in the 1830s as "the very gorge of sin... the general receptacle for the worst characters in the world". But at last the colony began to prosper on the back of free convict labour – an 1835 census recorded seventeen thousand convicts in a total population of thirty-nine thousand. Hobart Town started to assume the appearance of a small town in Georgian England. It hugely impressed the 26-year-old naturalist of the survey ship *Beagle* in 1836. "If I was obliged to emigrate, I should prefer this place... All on board like [it] better than Sydney", wrote **Charles Darwin** during the eleven days he spent sketching new insect species on Mount Wellington. Meanwhile, penetration into the bush gathered pace. In the 1820s, Lieutenant-governor Arthur had written of northwest Tasmania as "beyond the limits of the unknown". Now teams of government surveyors beat paths through the bush in all directions to prepare the way for settlement. With bushrangers almost a memory, central towns on the new stagecoach route between Hobart Town and Launceston flourished in the 1830s, boosting the export of merino wool, wheat, cattle hides, sealskins, timber and whale oil. That imports in the 1840s included fine silks, pianos, handcrafted English furniture and rich glassware speaks volumes about the boom.

In 1846, when the convict population in Van Diemen's Land stood at 28,459, just over 38 percent of the island's population, Victorian moralists forced London into a two-year moratorium on transportation to the colonies. When that ended, Van Diemen's Land became the only place in the empire open for transportation. The island's society began to voice its doubts about this dubious honour. Among the most vocal members of the anti-transportation lobby were prosperous merchants who had arrived as free settlers and had grown fat on the back of early government land grants. Effectively the state's landed gentry, they spoke of the "**convict stain**" on the island, and rallied under the banner of the Anti-Transportation League funded by rich settlers such as William Pritchard Weston, a deeply religious sheepfarmer from Longford, and led by eloquent moralists like Launceston's Reverend John West. The duo represented the colony at a national meeting in Melbourne in 1851 that resolved to reject convict labour and use legislative power to end transportation. The campaign triumphed the next year. On May 26, 1853, the last transport ship of the British Empire, the 630-tonne *St Vincent*, tied up alongside Hobart Town's New Wharf. The total convict population sent to Van Diemen's Land in fifty years was around 74,000, just under half the total number sent to Australia. The prisons still operated, of course. Prisoners worked out their sentences, and Port Arthur continued to receive colonially sentenced secondary offenders. In fact, it would be twenty years more before the last convict left the site.

Campaigners had argued that end of transportation would encourage more settlers and boost a stagnating economy. But a few years after the last convicts disembarked, nothing had changed – without convict labour the economy had sunk deeper into the doldrums. Worse, many settlers had emigrated across the Bass Strait to seek a fortune in the 1850s Victorian gold-rush. Van Diemen's Land needed a new image to escape its past – as author Anthony Trollope noted a couple of decades later, the name "Van Diemen's Land" was "harsh with the crack of the jailor's whip". In 1855 the British Constitution Act granted "Responsible government" to Van Diemen's Land and the nascent parliament voted to start from scratch. That New Year's Day, in a neutral rebranding that celebrated a largely forgotten Dutch navigator, Van Diemen's Land became Tasmania.

Initial tourism and exploration

Whether because it was peripheral to the mainland or because it was the last Australian state to cut off ties, Tasmania retained strong links to Britain. Perhaps the landscape and climate engendered a more British mentality. The first tourists who began to arrive with the end of transportation were astounded. Darwin had already noted in 1836 how "from the climate being damper, the gardens, full of luxuriant vegetables and fine corn fields, delightfully resemble England". Now the French Marquis de Beauvoir in 1870 gawped, "Would you believe that in this country, the nearest to the South Pole after Patagonia, a classical English mail coach with four horses runs daily?", while the ever-opinionated Anthony Trollope remarked in 1873: "Everything in Tasmania is more English than in England herself".

Most visitors came to Hobart Town, though the action was in the north and west. While southern Tasmania busied itself with orchards – the first shipment of Tasmanian apples to Britain was in 1881 – Launceston and the north coast emerged from the shadow of the capital as they exported timber – and fortune-hunters – to Victorian gold-fields. A couple of decades later, prospectors hurried back across the Bass Strait for what the *Launceston Examiner* newspaper reported as "the wildest, maddest and most reckless outbreak of **gold fever** ever experienced in Tasmania". The first rush near Bridport fizzled out almost as soon as it began in 1869, whereas that in Beaconsfield on the Tamar River has lasted to this day, albeit at a much reduced level.

The influx of prospectors in 1870 led to the discovery of **tin** on the Blue Tier plateau east of Launceston, and on Mount Bischoff in west Tasmania. In the northeast and west alike, shanty towns scratched out from the bush boomed into mining towns for a transient population of thousands. The finds also brought a spirit of optimism to the close of the nineteenth century. Mount Bischoff was hailed as the richest mine in Australia, one that had pulled Tasmania from the brink of bankruptcy. On the back of the success, prospectors pushed into the bush south – the first pioneers in the area since loggers followed the military detachment to Sarah Island. As mineral-rich mountains were plundered, so a series of mining towns spread south in succession: Corinna, home to the largest gold strike in Tasmania; then silver town Zeehan, known as "Silver City", which became the third-largest town in Tasmania after Hobart and Launceston; and in the late 1890s gold-turned-copper town Queenstown, still mining today, and still living with the legacy of sulphurous fumes that scarred surrounding slopes.

1900–1960

Not all was well, however. The first signal of hard times to come was the collapse of the Van Diemen's Land Bank on August 3, 1891. It probably contributed to the sense that a small island would do best to throw in its lot with Australia, which led Tasmanians to vote in favour of joining the Australian federation by a ratio of four to one in June 1898. The direct upshot was that on January 1, 1901, Tasmania became a state. Local loyalties remained with the British Empire nevertheless. In 1898, Tasmanians had fought in the Boer War.

Just over a decade later they heeded the old country's call when World War I was declared. Within two weeks of the outbreak of hostilities, over two thousand Tasmanians had signed up, and in total around thirteen thousand men left home to fight on a front on the other side of the world.

While they battled in Europe, Tasmania edged towards modernity. In 1916 its first national parks were declared, Mount Field and Freycinet, and the **Great Lake Power Scheme** was implemented, a project to harness the lake in the central highlands for hydroelectricity that created the Waddamana Power Station. By 1927 a line had been laid from the Great Lake to supply power to Sheffield, Devonport, Ulverstone and Penguin in the northwest. But then the Great Depression bit, and the mines in the northwest and west were sealed up to leave just a few die-hard tin-scratchers. By 1930 the Unemployed Workers Movement had branches in both of Tasmania's cities. The only positive upshot was a work-for-dole scheme that built roads up Mount Wellington and the Lyell Highway that linked Hobart to the west for the first time.

Though mainland Australia was also suffering, Tasmania again felt exiled. The swearing-in of a local son as federal prime minister in January 1932 at least meant it would not be overlooked. Having resigned from the Labor cabinet over its "dishonest" policy of inflation and debt repudiation as a way out of the financial crisis, state premier **Joseph Lyons** came into office on the ticket of a conservative coalition. Tasmania's first (and so far only) prime minister, "Honest Joe" was a plump, straightforward man, caricatured as a koala by political cartoonists. Under his cautious economic stewardship, Australia eased out of the Great Depression. When he died suddenly in office of a heart attack in 1939, Britophile Robert Menzies succeeded just in time to lead Australia into war. Again Tasmanians raced to the recruiting station, and over thirty thousand men and women served the Allies abroad. Those Tasmanians left would have been forgiven for wishing their soldiers had remained at home. First Tasmania was isolated when the Bass Strait closed to shipping after a British steamer was sunk by a mine in 1940. Then in February 1942 Singapore fell to the Japanese. The shockwaves were felt south, reviving memories of a Japanese declaration in 1927 that Australia was a target for expansion. When a Japanese submarine surfaced in Oyster Bay the next month and launched a seaplane on a reconnaissance mission over Hobart, Tasmania got the jitters. Air-raid trenches were dug in Franklin Square.

The end of World War II – which passed without incident – introduced change. The War Service Land Settlement Act 1945 provided land grants for returned soldiers, increasing the development of remote farming regions such as King Island. It also introduced migrants from Britain and south and eastern Europe, many still in their army uniforms. Their labour for the Hydro Electric Commission (HEC) in the late 1940s and 1950s brought a string of power plants to the Derwent Valley and Central Highlands. The influx also introduced the first cosmopolitan stock to Tasmania for a century. A census in 1966 found that of the 371,410 people in the state, nearly a tenth (31,415) were from Europe, albeit just over half from the UK – the "ten-pound poms" who were given assisted passage to emigrate under the Aussie slogan "Populate or perish!"

The Franklin dam

Post-war soul-searching about national identity led mainland Australia to forge an identity independent from Britain and, ultimately, create today's country.

The mood was watered down across the Bass Strait as rural Tasmania once more missed out on the good times that modernized cities on the mainland. Notwithstanding the temporary influx of foreigners, depopulation was a problem as a lack of jobs forced young people across the Bass Strait – unemployment hit ten percent in the early 1980s. Tasmania seemed a forgotten rural backwater. And then the HEC expanded its power programme.

In the late 1960s, few people outside Tasmania knew or cared about the state's wilderness. Within the state it was a different story. When the HEC proposed to flood **Lake Peddar**, the only body of water in the pristine southwest wilderness, environmental campaigners mobilized, fuelled by anger that this was less an imperative than part of the commission's expansion agenda. Business steamrolled on regardless and the lake was flooded in 1972. But the sense of injustice about wilderness being sacrificed to industry led to the creation of environmental coalition the **Tasmanian Wilderness Society** (TWS), the first Green party in the world, led by Doctor Bob Brown. So when the HEC turned its attention to dams for the **Gordon and Franklin rivers** in 1978 the opposition was well-organized.

While both Labor and Liberal parties scrapped over the dam site in 1981, the TWS appealed to federal politicians for protection under the auspices of UNESCO's World Heritage list, a case boosted by the discovery of an Aboriginal cave whose finds dated back 24,000 years. A state referendum did little to resolve the issue. For a start, the ballot paper only gave voters a choice between two dam sites rather than a "no dams" check-box the TWS had demanded – thus 44 percent of voters scrawled "No dam" across their papers. It also sparked a constitutional crisis after the government's preferred scheme won just nine percent approval and led to a vote of no confidence motion. The subsequent election campaign ousted the Labor government and introduced the Liberal Party led by **Robin Gray**. A staunch proponent of the dam, he declared the Franklin River as "nothing but a brown ditch, leech-ridden and unattractive to the majority of people", revoked a parks deal of his Labor predecessor to get around UNESCO's new World Heritage listing, and ordered in the bulldozers in December 1982.

By now the mainland had taken an interest. In the Franklin River, the last wild river in Australia, mainlanders saw a powerful symbol of wilderness in an increasingly suburbanized nation. On the same day that the Senate passed the World Heritage Protection Bill, the **Franklin River blockade** began near Strahan, manned by protestors from throughout Australia. The largest mass civil disobedience campaign the nation had seen, it lasted until March 1983, during which time 1400 environmental campaigners – including celebrities such as Professor David Bellamy, state and federal politicians, Dr Brown, who was imprisoned for three weeks and even Moorilla wine-estate founder and millionaire Claudio Alcorso – were arrested. The dam also became a federal election issue that easily swept Labor's Bob Hawke to power on the back of a promise to halt construction. Gray was unimpressed. He mounted a challenge to the federal order in the High Court – and lost.

It was a landmark ruling. Not only did it establish the principle of a state's subservience to a sovereign federal constitution, it enshrined the doctrine of environmental protection on issues of international importance. Moreover, it established the value of Tasmanian wilderness in the national psyche. In many respects, the Franklin was the first skirmish in the ongoing war between those who see Tasmania in terms of primary industries and those who see it in terms of preservation. Cynical environmentalists also say that it established the idea of government and business in cahoots at the expense of the environment.

Current trends

While Hawke and Gray quietly agreed a $270 million compensation deal and Dr Brown resigned as director of the TWS (which became the Wilderness Society) to found the Tasmanian Greens (now the Australian Greens), a raft of similar campaigns was floated. In 1986 confrontations between "greenies" and forestry workers in the Southern Forests at Farmhouse Creek provoked another High Court ruling that safeguarded forests and led to the nomination of new areas for World Heritage listing. The next year the **Douglas-Apsley National Park** was declared.

It's tempting to suppose that the Franklin campaign also awoke a liberal conscience. Flushed with eulogies in the media and public demonstrations of support from the mainland, islanders realised that Tasmania could become synonymous with quality. Having been one of the most conservative states in Australia, condemned in the press as a "bigot's island" in the Eighties, Tasmania unveiled some of the nation's most progressive policies in the 1990s. Descendants of Tasmanian Aborigines, led by activists such as Michael Mansfield, had followed the lead of the mainland during the 1970s and early 1980s to demand **Aboriginal rights**; a surprise for some Australians who didn't know Tasmania even had an indigenous population. Early successes had achieved recognition of the Aboriginality of Tasmanians and seen the return of skeletons and cultural material from museums. Land rights proved a more thorny issue. In 1992, in a gesture loaded with significance, Aborigines occupied Risdon Cove, site of the first indigenous massacre by the British in 1804. It, along with Oyster Cove, Cape Barren Island and several smaller islets, was handed freehold to custodians the Aboriginal Land Council through the Aboriginal Lands Act 1995. If that was a surprise for many people, it was a shock when in 1997 Tasmania became the first state to formally apologize to the Aboriginal people for past actions. Two years later the government confronted one of the darkest chapters in Tasmanian history by handing Wybalenna, on Flinders Island, to the Aboriginal community. That more than twenty thousand Tasmanians took part in an Aboriginal reconciliation walk across Hobart's Tasman Bridge the following year, one of the largest public rallies held in the state, suggested public approval. Tasmania notched up another first in November 2006 when it became the first Australian state to offer financial compensation to the tune of $5 million for the "stolen generation" – Aborigines forcibly removed from their families between 1900 and 1972.

Tasmania's tarnished image continued to improve under Labor premier **Jim Bacon**. A one-time Melbourne Maoist student leader and unionist who assumed power in 1998, he carved a swath through outdated laws from Tasmania's tightly buttoned past. Laws on blasphemy or bizarre strictures that prohibited men from wearing drag during daytime were repealed. Tasmania had dragged its heels as the last state in Australia to decriminalize homosexuality in 1997 but in 2004 it became the first to permit same-sex couples to register their relationships. Bacon retired prematurely that March due to lung cancer and was buried three months later beneath a Tasmanian flag. He is often credited with turning around a depressed Tasmania – he wiped out a $1.6 million debt in six years and laid the foundations for the modern tourism industry.

However, critics argue that this progress came at the expense of the environment. Under Bacon, Tasmanian forestry corporation Gunns rose into abillion-dollar monopoly that is now the largest hardwood-woodchip exporter in the world. Its controversial forestry policies have reopened the debate about industry versus environment, and led to accusations of corporate greed with government connivance. The Tasmanian environment has become a political football kicked about during every federal election. Both Liberal Prime Minister John Howard and Labor Opposition leader Mark Latham were forced into the open over clear-felling of old-growth forest during the 2004 campaign – many political pundits suggest Latham's ad hoc conservation policies alienated conservative voters and contributed to a Labor loss. Fast-forward to 2007 and the issue was a pulp mill proposed by Gunns for the Tamar Valley (see box, p.234), a contentious project already dogged by accusations of political mismanagement. Like the Franklin before it, the mill became a key issue for metropolitan political seats on the mainland. With the outcome on a knife-edge, neither Howard nor Labor challenger and eventual winner Kevin Rudd dared rock the boat, and both hid behind a claim that the decision was out of their hands; not strictly true as the Franklin had proved.

The issue puts in a nutshell Tasmania's ability to seduce and appall outsiders in equal measure. In that respect nothing has changed since it was founded; Mark Twain summed up Tasmania as "a bringing of heaven and hell together". The state is more optimistic than it has been in generations. Exports are at a record high and economic growth is double that of the mainland. For the first time in decades Tasmanians are choosing to work in their homeland. The "convict stain" is worn as a badge of honour and recognition of the Aboriginal community grows even as revisionist historians continue to squabble. Yet the state is frequently wracked internally over its future. On one side are conservatives who advocate continuation of traditional primary industries to safeguard jobs. On the other are liberal progressives and conservationists who see Tasmania's potential as a beacon of all that is clean and green. The key to long-term success will be to reconcile the two.

Flora and fauna

The Tasmanian ecosystem evolved first from Australia's isolation, then through twenty thousand years cut off from the mainland. As a consequence, Tasmania's ecology consists of Australian species that are adapted to the colder climate alongside several endemic one-offs. The nearest relatives of some animals and plants are in South America. Another influential factor is the variety of habitats, which range from warm dry forest to cool rainforest, from beach to alpine mountain.

The two centuries since colonization have put huge pressure on the Tasmanian ecology, something that has increased in recent decades as industrial practice is applied to traditional industries such as forestry. Clear-felling of old-growth forest rips out native forest, including the vital understorey that maintains the ecosystem, and replaces it with fast-growing foreign trees in plantations. Housing developments eat into virgin bush. Greenpeace and the Wilderness Society estimate that three-quarters of Tasmania's old-growth forest has already been lost. So as well as having some of the most distinctive species on earth, Tasmania also has some of the most vulnerable – over six hundred species are on the endangered list. In some respects, the island is a Noah's Ark whose varied habitats are a final refuge – a last chance – for many species that have become extinct on the mainland. Perhaps the greatest threat yet is the **fox**. The first fox was discovered in the Longford area in 2001, then more were found in Burnie in 2003. Rangers warn it will smash the state's delicate balanced ecosystems if it ever becomes established. If you spot (or hear) any sign of one, inform Parks & Wildlife Service immediately on its freephone fox hotline, ☏1300 FOX OUT – 1300 369 688. It also publishes information on threatened species as well as images and video of all native animals on its website, ⓦwww.parks.tas.gov.au.

Mammals

After the demise of the dinosaurs, Australia split away from the rest of the world and its animal species evolved along different lines. While placental mammal species ascended elsewhere, marsupials – mammals that give birth to semi-developed embryos which develop in a pouch – and egg-laying monotremes (creatures with a single duct for reproduction, defecation and urination) became established in Australia. Both are nocturnal, so your best chance of seeing wildlife is at dusk or dawn. Thanks to Warner Bros' Looney Tunes character, the **Tasmanian Devil** is known worldwide. Black with an occasional white stripe across its chest, the squat, terrier-sized scavenger became extinct on the mainland around six centuries ago, probably ousted by dingos, and is the world's largest carnivorous marsupial. It is an omnivore with a voracious appetite – carrion, reptiles and amphibians, insects, even sea squirts are fair game – and a call that varies from a snorting groan to an unearthly wail like a bad-tempered banshee; the Aborigines knew it as *Taraba*, "the nasty one". Despite the historical bad press, Devils are subject to considerable concern due to Devil Facial Tumour Disease (DFTD). This contagious cancer causes grotesque, bulbous lesions that are fatal within three to eight months. Since it was detected in northeast Tasmania in 1996, DFTD has advanced steadily west at around 15km a

Once or twice a year, someone somewhere will spot a **Tasmanian tiger**. The problem is that they are supposed to be extinct. The official line is that the tiger, or thylacine, was hunted to extinction by European settlers in the early twentieth century, thereby eradicating the world's largest carnivorous marsupial from its final refuge after dingos had wiped it out on the mainland.

A slender, wolfish marsupial the size of an average dog, with chocolate-coloured stripes on its hind quarters, a long snout that opened to a wide bite and a fused backbone that tapered to a stiff kangaroo-like tail and produced an awkward gait, the thylacine was done for as soon as sheep-farming became established. By the late 1800s bounty hunters had reduced their numbers to a handful – Professor Thomas Flynn, father of 1950s Hollywood heart-throb Errol, proposed Maria Island as a refuge in 1914 – but the "last" animal died in Hobart Zoo in 1936. No hard evidence has been produced of its survival, despite several official searches, and in 1986 the species was declared "presumed extinct".

That has not deterred the stubborn conviction that tigers skulk somewhere in the rugged remote forests: the northeast, the Tarkine and the Southwest National Park are cited as prime candidates. Every year, Parks & Wildlife Service receives sightings, and conspiracy theorists whisper about a government cover-up to save the bureaucracy of reopening the file. A cloning project was mooted by the Australia Museum in Sydney but then shelved in 2005 due to the poor quality of the source DNA from a pickled cub. Today the Tasmanian tiger is extinct but everywhere: sneaking across Cascade beer bottles or propping up Tasmania's heraldic crest, for example. It's probably no surprise. Mysterious, wild, ancient, the thylacine seems a very Tasmanian enigma.

C

CONTEXTS | Flora and fauna

---

year, reaching Cradle Mountain in 2006. Studies suggest it is spread by saliva but its cause is a mystery and some estimates put the current wild population as low as 25,000 animals. Though a number of breeding programmes have been established, scientists are already talking about mapping the genome to prevent devils following the Tasmanian tiger into extinction. Spotted-tailed quolls and eastern quolls are related as marsupial carnivores, but after that the similarity ends. Slender and more agile, they are more like cat-size stoats.

Kangaroos and **wallaby** species in Tasmania are smaller than those on the mainland. The state's largest marsupial is the Forester kangaroo, known on mainland Australia as the grey kangaroo. Conservation programmes have pulled it back from the brink in Tasmania, though introduced mobs are largely confined to Mount William, Maria Island and Narawntapu national parks. You're sure to see Bennetts wallabies and **pademelons** bouncing off into the bush or loping around campsites at dusk. The latter are slightly smaller and plumper, with darker brown or grey-brown fur; Bennetts wallabies, recognizable by their black noses, have a russet tinge to the neck and shoulders, though a snow-white sub-species is at Adventure Bay, Bruny Island. **Wombats** are chunky marsupials with sandy brown or grey fur: reclusive and nocturnal, they dig burrows in heathland, coastal scrub and open forest, and mark out territory with cuboid dung that stacks on elevated surfaces like faecal bricks. **Possums** are an adaptable, tree-dwelling marsupial with a pointed face and thick silver-grey or silver-gold fur. Of the state's five species, the brushtail possum is the most likely culprit for the overnight raid on your food supplies at a campsite. They're often hard to avoid.

Platypus and **echidnas** are the only species of monotreme. Because they lay eggs then suckle their young through specialized pores, and have lower body temperatures than other mammals, they were once seen as a missing link between reptiles and mammals. In fact, they are a distinctive family that emerged around 150 million years ago. Platypus are aquatic animals that look like a hybrid of duck and beaver, having rubbery bills, webbed feet, thick brown fur and broad flat tails. Males have a poisonous spur on their hind feet. Tasmanian platypus can weigh up to 3kg, making them giants compared to those on the mainland. They are just as elusive, however. They dive repeatedly for food and keep a low body profile when swimming on the surface, typically in slow-flowing streams and in lakes of the Central Highlands. Due to their acute hearing and sight, your chances of seeing one are limited – be quiet and use natural cover. Worryingly, the emergence of an aquatic fungal disease that causes ulcers then death by infection is threatening population levels. Another unique concept creature, echidnas lie somewhere between a flattened porcupine, a hedgehog and an anteater, with short spines and a long snout that is used to root out ants and termites. The Tasmanian version is thicker-set than its mainland relative, with hair among its spines, but has similarly appalling eyesight. You may see one ambling along with its rolling gait through dry scrub, oblivious to your presence.

Reptiles, amphibians, birds and marine life

There are three **snakes** in Tasmania: the olive-green white-lipped snake (or "whip snake") is the smallest, and most often spotted as it likes to bask in patches of sunshine in heath or open forest; the lowland copperhead, named for an orangey-brown streak above its belly; and the pale-yellow to grey-brown tiger snake. All are highly poisonous but timid – bites are very rare and treatable by a standard anti-venom. You're more likely to see skinks skitter away across rocks – there are sixteen species – or the sluggish **blue-tongue lizard**, which grows to around 30cm. **Frogs**, of which there are many, are generally heard rather than seen: the rhythmic cricket-like creak of brown tree frogs or rougher common froglets drift across still evenings throughout the state. If it sounds less rhythmic, it's probably a smooth froglet or southern toadlet. The **giant freshwater crayfish**, the world's largest freshwater invertebrate, is only found in the rivers of the northwest. Known for its longevity, the species has been known to grow to 80cm long and 5kg in weight.

With a climate that extends from temperate to subalpine, from wet to dry, Tasmania has a rich birdlife. The most widespread endemic species is the **black currawong**. A fearless opportunist that resembles a crow, it is common at picnic grounds in highlands and has a coarse clattering call. The three endemic species of **honeyeater** are more spectacular – you're most likely to hear the high-pitched "psssip" of the black-headed honeyeater. Two unique species of **parrot** are the orange-bellied parrot, down to a few hundred birds near Melaleuca in the southwest, and the forty-spotted paradolte, an elusive tiny bird that is close to extinction. Colonies are restricted to Maria Island and around Bruny Island. Non-native species include perennial Aussie favourite the **kookaburra**, and a vast array of teals, ducks, egrets and grebes; black swans are common throughout the state.

Among birds of prey, **wedge-tailed eagles** have evolved into a distinctive subspecies of those on the mainland, and there are spectacular **white-bellied sea eagles** on the coasts around Freycinet Peninsula, Maria Island and

Macquarie Harbour. The world's smallest penguin, the **Little Penguin** (formerly known as "Fairy Penguins"), make an endearing sight when they waddle from the sea to sand-dune burrows at dusk; rookeries are at Bruny Island, Bicheno, Low Head, **Devonport** Penguin and Stanley. **Short-tailed shearwaters** migrate in their millions from the Bering Strait to breed in October. Nicknamed "muttonbirds" thanks to a Royal Marine officer who called them "flying sheep", they play a central role in the continuation of Tasmanian Aboriginal culture on Flinders Island (see p.340).

Southern Right whales were taken to the brink of extinction in the first half of the 1800s, when whale oil propped up the Tasmanian economy – because they floated when harpooned, they were deemed the "right" species to hunt. Today an estimated seven hundred animals migrate from Antarctica via Tasmania's east coast between June and September, returning between October and November. **Humpback whales** follow a similar pattern en route to Queensland. **Fur seals** are slowly recovering from the destruction of colonies by hunters – wildlife boat trips to the Tasman Peninsula or Bruny or Maria islands are your best hope of seeing them – while **dolphins** are common around the east coast.

Flora

Rainforest is central to Tasmania's appeal. The west contains 95 percent of the cool temperate rainforest in Australia due to annual rainfall that exceeds 1.2m. It's magisterial stuff – cool, damp, open forest whose silent cathedral-like quality is enhanced by a thick carpet of sphagnum moss. If you do only one thing in Tasmania, it should be to experience this ancient forest. It's here, too, that you'll find most of the endemic Tasmanian trees, many of them "living fossils" that evolved on the supercontinent of Gondwana: myrtle-beech, sassafras with lance-like serrated leaves, laurel and leatherwood. The latter produces delicate nectar-rich white and pale-pink flowers that produce a unique honey. **Horizontal** is an understorey shrub that's the bane of bushwalkers due to the tangled thickets created by its growth patterns – like arboreal spiderplants, branches grow horizontally and bend to the ground to sprout new vertical shoots. Cool temperate rainforests also contains endemic **pandani**, a palm-like heath plant also found in subalpine habitats, and **tree ferns**, another Gondwana relic found in fertile rainforest and gullies of wet eucalyptus forest.

No species is so prized as **Huon pine**, an endemic slow-growing species found in the wet southwest and west. Despite widespread early logging – its resin-rich, rot-resistant wood was irresistible to boat-builders and architects – trees survive on the area's riverbanks. They are recognizable by a rather shabby look and feathery foliage and are slow-growers – the oldest trees exceed 3,000 years old. Other native pines in western Tasmania are **celery-top pine**, with sprunts of celery-like leaves, and **King Billy pine**, a long-lasting, medium-sized redwood lookalike named after Tasmanian Aborigine William Lanne (see p.356) and found in high rainforest. Its relative, **pencil pine**, grows around highland lakes and tarns, though it's been severely affected by fire in the last two centuries.

Going higher still, you're into the alpine and subalpine conditions of the west and Ben Lomond. Notwithstanding pencil pine and a few hardy snow gums up to 1300m, these areas are above the treeline, so are bare except for mosaics of heath or herbfields interspersed with moorland; not particularly dramatic, but species whose links to Antarctic Gondwana – today realized as New Zealand and South America – make this a tremendously valuable habitat. It's also a fragile one, which is something of a surprise considering it can cope with ice-laden storms and subzero temperatures. **Buttongrass moorland** lies in the broad valleys beneath the peaks of the southwest and central wilderness. Another prehistoric throwback that has roots in the late Cretaceous period, it is formed of clumps of sedge that grow in the soggy nutrient-poor plains. Again, it is a highly sensitive environment – a plant can take forty years to recover from a misplaced boot, which explains the use of boardwalks through the plains. As well as poor nutrients, fire kills off invading forest species. The Aborigines practised controlled regenerative burn-offs to lure wallabies and wombats.

Tasmanian **eucalyptus forest**, also known as sclerophyll forest, provides the greatest biodiversity. Wet eucalyptus forest contains the tallest flowering plants in the world, the **swamp gum** (*Eucalyptus regnans*). These massive trees grow as high as 90m, allowing a dense understorey of broad-leaf shrubs to develop beneath; the most accessible large stands are in Mount Field National Park and the Styx Valley. Dry eucalyptus forest relies on fire for propagation – trees such as blue gum, the floral emblem of Tasmania, black peppermint and silver peppermint shed bark and leaves to deposit a thick layer of tinder on the forest floor. The extreme heat once this catches fire bursts the trees' seedpods to begin the germination process. **Blackwood**, a Tasmanian species of wattle, thrives in the swamp forests of the northwest but exists in wet and dry eucalyptus forests. In fact the definitions are too convenient, as most eucalyptus forest lies somewhere between the two ends of the scale according to the rainfall it receives. Wet forest is further west and dry forest is nearer the east coast, such as that in the Douglas-Apsley National Park. Coastal areas are harsh habitats for plants, so are characterized by scrubby heath. One plant that has made this hostile environment its own is **pigface**, which spreads thick carpets of succulent leaves over the foreshore.

Finally a word on longevity. Many Tasmanian species adapt to the cold-climate through slow growth. Alongside the Huon pine, King Billy and pencil pines can reach 1200 years. **King's lomatia** is a shrub of the Proteaceae family that is only found in two locations in the southwest. What makes the scraggy plant unusual is that all plants are genetically identical. All five hundred or so plants derive from a single plant that has been cloning itself for at least 43,600 years and possibly 135,000 years, based on carbon-dating analysis of fossilized leaf fragments found 8km away.

Books

For a geographically isolated, sparsely populated island with a tiny home market, Tasmania has left a distinctive mark on Australian literature. Most works are a product of the unique culture rooted in a convict past and landscape. Take a history of penal brutality in Van Diemen's Land, add in pinches of parochialism, hardship and an uncompromising wilderness and you have a rich stew for fiction. The term "Tasmanian gothic" is often bandied about, but modern Tasmanian fiction is a step on from historical novels that wallowed, often rather gratuitously, in the convict era and seriously tarnished Tasmania's image abroad. Novelist Richard Flanagan, the multi award-winning doyen of state fiction and one of the leading names in Australian literature, leads the charge when not penning withering critiques of Tasmanian conservation policy in the international press. Non-fiction has burgeoned in recent decades; a slew of tomes on the minutiae of island history fill the shelves alongside outdoors guides and coffee-table books whose large-format photographs show off the island's remote places. For a taster of contemporary literary life, pick up quarterly journal *Island* (⑩www.islandmag.com) from independent bookshop Fullers in Hobart or Launceston.

What follows is a collection of books about Tasmania either currently in print, or out of print (o/p). Titles marked 🏃 are particularly recommended.

Travel and biography

Martin Flanagan *In Sunshine or in Shadow*. Subtitled "A Memoir About Going Home", this confronts what the author calls the absences in his life – Irish convict ancestors, Aborigines and the Tasmanian tiger – in a search for the nature of home and belonging.

Christobel Mattingley *King of the Wilderness: the Life of Deny King*. Gushing biography of a bushman and miner whose encyclopedic knowledge of the flora and fauna of his home in the southwest wilderness was tapped by scientists.

🏃 **Nicholas Shakespeare** *In Tasmania*. Part-time English émigré Shakespeare went to Tasmania after writing a biography of Bruce Chatwin and accidentally uncovered Anthony Fenn Kemp, a renegade ancestor who played a pivotal role in the young colony. Packed with anecdotal gems and character, this is a compelling blend of biography, island history, cultural dissection and travel writing.

Fiction

Marcus Clarke *For the Term of His Natural Life*. A romantic tragedy from 1870 whose tales of transportation and penal brutality titillated the British Empire. Though overblown by modern tastes, many of the yarns are based on real events and characters.

Bruce Courtenay *The Potato Factory*. Imagined family conflict in fledgling Van Diemen's Land, founded on real-life transportee Ikey Solomon, the East End fence said to have inspired Dickens' Fagin.

🏃 **Richard Flanagan** *Death of a River Guide*. The labyrinthine debut of the state's best-known author, in which environmentalist narrator Aljaz Cosini skips over his life as he drowns in the Franklin River. It established Flanagan's hallmarks of thoughtful writing about Tasmanian landscape, place, migration and the significance of history.

Richard Flanagan *The Sound of One Hand Clapping*. A fractured tale of reconciliation for Sonja Buloh and her Slovenian father, a post-war dam worker whose wife disappeared into a blizzard.

Chloe Hooper *A Child's Book of True Crime*. Claustrophobic and tightly coiled, Hooper's debut concerns the paranoia of a small-town primary teacher who is having an affair with her brightest pupil's father. A sophisticated and original "goodbye-to-childhood" book.

Matthew Kneale *English Passengers*. An epic historical swashbuckler set on the high seas during colonialization and played out with a cast of twenty voices. Vivid, humorous and quietly intellectual.

Julia Leigh *The Hunter*. A taciturn mercenary goes in search of the Tasmanian tiger, with his biotech corporation cast as the bad guy. In truth the thylacine is a bit-player in a novella that explores the relationship between psyche and landscape, profit and nature.

Danielle Wood *The Alphabet of Light and Dark*. A rich award-winning novel in the gothic Tasmania vein. Essie returns from western Australia to Bruny Island lighthouse (where Wood's great-great-grandfather was keeper) to write a family history and becomes immersed in the stories of her ancestors.

History, politics and culture

James Boyce *Van Diemen's Land*. A gripping revisionist history that mixes passion and consummate storytelling with scholarly research. Boyce argues that Van Diemen's Land was less a hell-hole than an Eden in which prisoners found hope; he weaves in environmental insights and a sure grasp of frontier politics to support his case.

Pete Hay *Vandiemonian Essays*. Passionately Tasmanian yet internationally resonant essays about politics, economics and culture by one of Tasmania's leading environmentalists and thinkers. Erudite and beautifully written.

Robert Hughes *The Fatal Shore*. Tasmania put in the bigger picture of convict transportation to Australia. A thorough and enjoyable history that presents the traditional view of convict servitude in paradise.

Robert Manne (editor) *Whitewash: On Keith Windschuttle's Fabrication of Aboriginal History*. The rebuke to Windschuttle's book (see below), provided in the form of essays by an impressive line-up of authors.

Michael Nash *Bay Whalers*. Nash's account of the dangerous and dirty shore-based industry that propped up the economy of the young colony.

Lloyd Robson *A History of Tasmania, Volumes I and II*. A reliable and surprisingly readable history of the island that concludes in the early 1990s.

Keith Windschuttle *The Fabrication of Aboriginal History, Vol 1: Van Diemen's Land, 1803–47* (o/p). The scourge of the left, Windschuttle resurrects the colonial notion of Australia as a *terra nullius*, unoccupied by its first inhabitants. Probably the most controversial modern study of Australian history.

Ecology and environment

Greg Buckman *A Visitor's Guide to Tasmania's National Parks.* A comprehensive guidebook written for all visitors. There is practical information alongside details of walks, history and fauna. Maps and colour images throughout.

Peter Dombrovskis *On the Mountain.* A tribute to Hobart's Mount Wellington by the late great Dombrovskis, the photographer who did more than any other to alert the word to Tasmania's landscapes. His out-of-print *Wild Rivers* has romantic and documentary photographs captured during the Franklin Rivers campaign, with text by then-unknown campaigner Bob Brown.

Sven Klinge *Cycling the Bush.* An excellent primer on the top hundred cycles in the state: city and trail day-rides as well as overnighters in the wilderness.

David Leaman *Step into History in Tasmanian Reserves.* This provides a catalogue of – and guide to – all protected areas in the state: why to go, what to see and do, when to go.

Matthew Newton *Shack Life: Tasmanian shacks and shack culture.* Accompanied by colour photographs, Newton celebrates an enduring Tassie icon: ingenious, colourful, eccentric, peripheral, often funny, occasionally brilliant.

David Owen *Thylacine: The Tragic Tale of the Tasmanian Tiger; Tasmanian Devil: A Unique and Threatened Species.* Two icons of island wildlife (one extinct, one endangered); two books packed with fascinating facts and stories.

Tyrone T Thomas *120 Walks in Tasmania.* From thirty-minute strolls to extended hikes, most of these are circuit walks and all have trail profiles for easy comparison. The best overview of walks in the state.

Australian English

Australian English, or "strine" (which is how "Australian" is pronounced with a heavy Australian accent), is a vigorous, knockabout dialect with roots in Cockney convict argot, Irish and some Aboriginal languages. The language was Americanized during the gold mining boom of the 1850s – "bonzer", as Australian a word as you could wish for, is probably a corruption of the American "bonanza", for example – and spellings often follow the American '–or' rather than '–our' endings (though scholars argue the reason predates American immigration), though British words predominate. In fact the proliferation of Aussie soaps internationally has exported more words to the mother country than it has imported in recent decades. If one adjective defines Australian English it is informality. Australians have a tendency to abbreviate words to indicate familiarity, usually tacking on "o" or "ie" to produce sentences such as "We're having a barbie for the footy this arvo" – "We're having a barbecue for the (Australian Rules) football this afternoon". Informality is also reflected in the use of "bloody", "bastard" and "bugger" as terms of friendship, even affection, and a disregard for apostrophes in real names, which renders Kelly's Steps as Kellys Steps, for example. Other endearing quirks are the typically Irish use of litotes such as "You're not wrong" (ie "You're right") and a tendency to genderize objects: "She's buggered, mate" ("Your object is beyond repair").

Ankle biter Small child

Anzac Australia and New Zealand Army Corps; typically used in reference to an Anzac memorial.

Apples, she'll be It'll be OK

Arvo Afternoon

Avos Avocados

Aussie Rules Australian Rules football rather than jingoism

Barbie Barbecue (noun)

Barrack To support in sport, as in "Who do you barrack for?"

Beaut! or you beauty! Great, fantastic

Bloody oath! That's true

Bludger Lazy person or scrounger (as in "dole bludger")

Blundstone (or Blunnies) Brand name of an elastic-sided workboot close to Australian hearts

Bogan A slob who spends his days slacking and drinking heavily; also a derogatory term for suburban poor equivalent to American "white trash"

Bottleshop, bottle–o Off-licence, liquor shop

Brekky Breakfast

Budgie smugglers Men's bathing costume

BYO Bring Your Own, as in alcohol to a restaurant

Cellar door Wine sales or direct tastings from the estate

Chook A chicken

Cleanskin Bottle of wine without a label

Cobber Friend

Counter meal Pub meal

Cozzie/togs Swimming costume

Crook Sick (as in to feel) or badly made

Crow eater Someone from South Australia

Cut lunch Sandwiches

Dag Affectionate term for nerd or geek

Daks or strides Trousers

Damper Bread cooked in a pot on embers

Dekko Have a Look, as in "Have a dekko at..."

Digger Old-timer, especially a soldier

Dinkum, fair dinkum True, genuine. Also "Dinky-di", the real thing

Doco Documentary

Doona Duvet

Drongo Fool

Dunny Outside toilet, often buzzing with "dunny budgies" (blowflies)

Esky Large insulated food/drink container

Fair go A chance ("Give a bloke a fair go!")

Feral Abusive term for a hippie

Fossick To rummage or search for, or to prospect for gold, gems, etc

Galah Garrulous fool, named after the noisy native bird

Greenie Environmentalist

Grog Alcohol

Gutless wonder Coward

Hoon Yob, hooligan

Hotel Usually just a pub

Icy pole Popsicle, lollypop

Joey Baby kangaroo still in the pouch

Larrikin Mischievous but harmless youth

Mainland, mainlander The rest of Australia/any Australian not from Tasmania

Manchester Household linen

Mapatassie/map of Tassie Female pudenda (whose shape Tasmania is said to resemble)

Milk bar Corner shop that sells takeaway food

Ocker Unsophisticated Australian man

Oldies Parents

Op shop Opportunity shop – a charity/thrift store

Paddock Field

Piss Beer, hence "pissed" (drunk), "piss-head" (drunkard), "a piss-up" (drunken party) or "Let's hit the piss!" ('Let's get drunk!')

Pokies Gambling slot machines

Pommie/Pom English person, not always abusive despite the common "Pommy bastard"

Ratbag Mild insult

Raw prawn, to come the To bullshit

Reckon! You bet, definitely! As in "I…"

Rego Car registration

Rellie Family relative

Ridgy-didge The original article, genuine thing

Ripper! Rather old-fashioned term of enthusiasm

Root To have sex. Also as synonym: "I'm rooted" ("I'm tired") or "It's rooted" ("It seems to be beyond repair")

Ropable Angry to the point of needing restraint

Sandgroper Someone from Western Australia

Sanger Sandwich

Seppo American (from rhyming slang "septic tank" = "yank")

Servo Petrol station

Shackie Someone who lives in a remote shack, something close to the Tasmanian heart

Shark biscuit Novice surfer

She'll be right! It'll turn out OK

Shit house Poor quality. What you feel after a night on the piss

Slab Twenty-four pack of beer

Smokes Cigarettes, though "smoko" is a tea break

Snag Sausage

Sparrow's fart Dawn, as in "I was up at…"

Spewin' Furious

Spiffy Great, excellent

Spunk Attractive person of either sex

Sticky beak Nosy person or to be nosy ("Can I have a sticky beak?")

Stoked Very pleased

Stubby Small bottle of beer

Swag Bed roll, carried by a swagman (or "swaggie")

Tall poppy Successful people, so "tall people syndrome" is a tendency to criticize successful people

Taswegians Tasmanians, can be taken as derogatory

Thongs Flip-flops

Tinnie Aluminium fishing dinghy or a can of beer

Too easy! Generic approval when anything is completed quickly

True blue Patriotic

Tucker Food

U-ey, chuck/hang a Make a U-turn

Ute Utility vehicle or pickup truck

Weatherboard Wooden house

Wowser A prude or killjoy

Yabber To talk a lot

Yakka Work (noun) so "hard yakka"

Yobbo Uncouth person

Travel store

Great destinations, unique experiences

Want the Pure Tasmania experience? Come and explore deep into the World Heritage Area with Gordon River Cruises, ride a steam train into history on the West Coast Wilderness Railway, discover the heritage of the pioneers with Piners and Miners, paddle a sea kayak through perfect reflections on the Gordon River – and that's all from your base in Strahan Village!

From Freycinet Lodge, take a walk to Wineglass Bay, cruise offshore to spot dolphins and maybe a whale or two, rock climb and abseil on The Hazards – and at Cradle Mountain Chateau, take the circuit walk around Dove Lake, see the amazing collection of wilderness photography at the Wilderness Gallery and get close to local wildlife on an evening tour. In Hobart, experience the understated style, sophistication and cutting edge design of The Henry Jones Art Hotel on the city's picturesque waterfront.

It really is Pure Tasmania.

Phone (+61 3) 6225 7075
Freecall: 1800 084 620 (within Australia)
Email: bookings@puretasmania.com.au

Pure

puretasmania.com.au

The view from your bedroom

with Tasmania Campervan Rentals

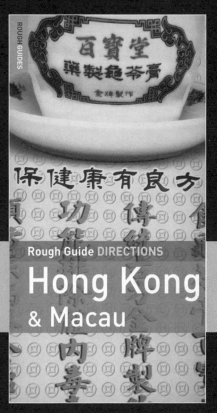

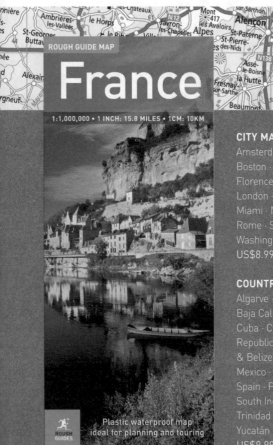

Small print and
Index

A Rough Guide to Rough Guides

Published in 1982, the first Rough Guide – to Greece – was a student scheme that became a publishing phenomenon. Mark Ellingham, a recent graduate in English from Bristol University, had been travelling in Greece the previous summer and couldn't find the right guidebook. With a small group of friends he wrote his own guide, combining a highly contemporary, journalistic style with a thoroughly practical approach to travellers' needs.

The immediate success of the book spawned a series that rapidly covered dozens of destinations. And, in addition to impecunious backpackers, Rough Guides soon acquired a much broader and older readership that relished the guides' wit and inquisitiveness as much as their enthusiastic, critical approach and value-for-money ethos.

These days, Rough Guides include recommendations from shoestring to luxury and cover more than 200 destinations around the globe, including almost every country in the Americas and Europe, more than half of Africa and most of Asia and Australasia. Our ever-growing team of authors and photographers is spread all over the world, particularly in Europe, the USA and Australia.

In the early 1990s, Rough Guides branched out of travel, with the publication of Rough Guides to World Music, Classical Music and the Internet. All three have become benchmark titles in their fields, spearheading the publication of a wide range of books under the Rough Guide name.

Including the travel series, Rough Guides now number more than 350 titles, covering: phrasebooks, waterproof maps, music guides from Opera to Heavy Metal, reference works as diverse as Conspiracy Theories and Shakespeare, and popular culture books from iPods to Poker. Rough Guides also produce a series of more than 120 World Music CDs in partnership with World Music Network.

Visit www.roughguides.com to see our latest publications.

Rough Guide travel images are available for commercial licensing at www.roughguidespictures.com

Rough Guide credits

Text editor: James Rice
Layout: Pradeep Thapliyal
Cartography: Miles Irving
Picture editor: Nicole Newman
Production: Rebecca Short
Proofreader: Helen Castell
Cover design: Chloë Roberts
Photographer: Rob Blakers
Editorial: London Ruth Blackmore, Alison
Murchie, Andy Turner, Keith Drew, Edward Aves,
Alice Park, Lucy White, Jo Kirby, James Smart,
Natasha Foges, Róisín Cameron, Emma Traynor,
Emma Gibbs, Kathryn Lane, Christina Valhouli,
Monica Woods, Mani Ramaswamy, Joe Staines,
Peter Buckley, Matthew Milton, Tracy Hopkins,
Ruth Tidball; **New York** Andrew Rosenberg,
Steven Horak, AnneLise Sorensen, April Isaacs,
Ella Steim, Anna Owens, Sean Mahoney, Paula
Neudorf, Courtney Miller; **Delhi** Madhavi Singh,
Karen D'Souza
Design & Pictures: London Scott Stickland,
Dan May, Diana Jarvis, Mark Thomas, Sarah
Cummins, Emily Taylor; **Delhi** Umesh Aggarwal,
Ajay Verma, Jessica Subramanian, Ankur Guha,
Sachin Tanwar, Anita Singh, Nikhil Agarwal

Production: Vicky Baldwin
Cartography: London Maxine Repath, Ed
Wright, Katie Lloyd-Jones; **Delhi** Jai Prakash
Mishra, Rajesh Chhibber, Ashutosh Bharti, Rajesh
Mishra, Animesh Pathak, Jasbir Sandhu, Karobi
Gogoi, Amod Singh, Alakananda Bhattacharya,
Swati Handoo
Online: Narender Kumar, Rakesh Kumar,
Amit Verma, Rahul Kumar, Ganesh Sharma,
Debojit Borah, Saurabh Sati, Ravi Yadav
Marketing & Publicity: London Liz Statham,
Niki Hanmer, Louise Maher, Jess Carter, Vanessa
Godden, Vivienne Watton, Anna Paynton, Rachel
Sprackett, Libby Jellie, Jayne McPherson, Holly
Dudley; **New York** Geoff Colquitt, Katy Ball; **Delhi**
Ragini Govind
Manager India: Punita Singh
Reference Director: Andrew Lockett
Operations Manager: Helen Phillips
PA to Publishing Director: Nicola Henderson
Publishing Director: Martin Dunford
Commercial Manager: Gino Magnotta
Managing Director: John Duhigg

Publishing information

This first edition published October 2008 by
Rough Guides Ltd,
80 Strand, London WC2R 0RL
345 Hudson St, 4th Floor,
New York, NY 10014, USA
14 Local Shopping Centre, Panchsheel Park,
New Delhi 110017, India
Distributed by the Penguin Group
Penguin Books Ltd,
80 Strand, London WC2R 0RL
Penguin Group (USA)
375 Hudson Street, NY 10014, USA
Penguin Group (Australia)
250 Camberwell Road, Camberwell,
Victoria 3124, Australia
Penguin Group (Canada)
195 Harry Walker Parkway N, Newmarket, ON,
L3Y 7B3 Canada
Penguin Group (NZ)
67 Apollo Drive, Mairangi Bay, Auckland 1310,
New Zealand

Cover concept by Peter Dyer.

Typeset in Bembo and Helvetica to an original
design by Henry Iles.

Printed and bound in China

© James Stewart and Margo Daly, 2008

No part of this book may be reproduced in any
form without permission from the publisher except
for the quotation of brief passages in reviews.

392pp includes index

A catalogue record for this book is available from
the British Library

ISBN: 978-1-85828-559-7

The publishers and authors have done their best
to ensure the accuracy and currency of all the
information in **The Rough Guide to Tasmania**,
however, they can accept no responsibility for
any loss, injury, or inconvenience sustained by
any traveller as a result of information or advice
contained in the guide.

1   3   5   7   9   8   6   4   2

Help us update

We've gone to a lot of effort to ensure that the
first edition of **The Rough Guide to Tasmania** is
accurate and up to date. However, things change
– places get "discovered", opening hours are
notoriously fickle, restaurants and rooms raise
prices or lower standards. If you feel we've got it
wrong or left something out, we'd like to know,
and if you can remember the address, the price,
the hours, the phone number, so much the better.

Please send your comments with the subject
line **"Rough Guide Tasmania Update"** to
✉ mail@roughguides.com. We'll credit all
contributions and send a copy of the next edition
(or any other Rough Guide if you prefer) for the
very best emails.

Have your questions answered and tell others
about your trip at
⊛ community.roughguides.com

Acknowledgements

James Stewart: Many thanks to Suzy De Carteret at Tasmania Tourism UK, and Ruth Dowty and Natalie Geard at Tourism Tasmania in Australia. Thanks also to Andy and Loretta Thompson, Paula Catchpole, Ian Ferrier, Jacinda Yeoman, Launceston Backpackers, Damo of Tasman Island Cruises, Jenny Willoughby and Nick Stranger, and to all at Rough Guides, especially James Rice.

James Rice: Thanks to James Stewart for making life easy, Pradeep Thapliyal for typesetting, Nicole Newman for picture research, Miles Irving for maps, Helen Castell for proofreading and Helena Smith for indexing.

Photo credits

All photos © Rough Guides except the following:

Cover
Front cover: Wineglass Bay, Freycinet
   © Profimedia International s.r.o./Alamy
Back cover: Cataract Bridge, Penny Royal,
   Launceston © Nicole Newman
Inside back cover: Colonial architecture, Ross
   © Rob Blakers/Rough Guides

Introduction
Painted cliffs, Maria Island © photolibrary
Bridestowe Estate lavender farm
   © Nicole Newman
Jansz Vineyards, Tamar Valley © photolibrary

Things not to miss
01 Trekkers on the Overland Track
   © Julian Love/Alamy
02 Coastal scene and Mount Strzelecki, Flinders
   Island © photolibrary
03 Weedy Sea Dragon and diver
   © WaterFrame/Alamy
04 Abseiling Gordon Dam © Mark Eveleigh/Alamy
05 The Neck sand spit, Bruny Island
   © Bill Bachman/Alamy
06 Surfer at Shipsterns © Tim Jones/Billabong
   XXL/Corbis
08 The penitentiary, Port Arthur © Fabian
   Gonzales Editorial/Alamy
09 Aerial View of Wineglass Bay © Yann
   Arthus-Bertrand/CORBIS
11 Sassafras tree, Tarkine wilderness
   © photolibrary
12 Bay at Bishop Mountain, Maria Island
   © imagebroker/Alamy
13 Rafting, western Tasmania © Rob Blakers
14 Tasmanian Devil © Ian Waldie/Getty Images
15 Coastline at Eaglehawk Neck, Tasman
   Peninsula © Bill Bachman/Alamy
16 Winter sunrise on Mount Anne, South West
   National Park © photolibrary
18 Sea kayaking in Coles Bay on the Freycinet
   Peninsula © Julian Love/Alamy
20 Bay of Fires © Rob Blakers

Great outdoors colour section
Pandani and deciduous beech, West Coast
   Range © photolibrary
Bay of Fires © photolibrary
Coastline, Tarkine wilderness © photolibrary
Pirates Bay, Eaglehawk Neck © photolibrary
Lake Oberon, Western Arthur Range
   © Auscape/Alamy
Pencil pine © Profimedia/Alamy
Myrtle tree and pandani, west coast
   © photolibrary
Bushcamping in the Franklin-Gordon Wild Rivers
   National Park © imagebroker/Alamy
Hiker on the summit of Cradle Mountain
   © John Warburton-Lee Photography/Alamy
Cradle Mountain © photolibrary

Black and whites
p.76 Salamanca Place, Hobart © Nicole Newman
p.115 Cliffs at Cape Raoul © LOOK Die
   Bildagentur der Fotografen/ Alamy
p.124 Peppermint Bay restaurant, Woodbridge
   © Julian Love/Alamy
p.144 Ross Bridge © Nicole Newman
p.174 View of Wineglass Bay from the Hazards,
   Freycinet © photolibrary
p.182 Cape Barren Goose, Maria Island
   © Dave Watts/Alamy
p.201 Bay of Fires © photolibrary
p.210 Alexandra Suspension Bridge, Cataract
   Gorge © Nicole Newman
p.292 Sign on the Overland Track © photolibrary
p.302 Tourists on cruise boat entering Hells
   Gates © David Noton Photography/Alamy
p.312 Dove Lake, Cradle Mountain-Lake St Clair
   National Park © JTB/drr.net
p.325 South West National Park © Hans Strand/
   CORBIS
p.346 Cape Wickham lighthouse, King Island
   © Graphic Science/Alamy

SMALL PRINT

ROUGH GUIDES

Index

Map entries are in colour.

A

Aboriginal art 49
Aborigines 188, 352, 355, 356, 362
abseiling 12, 329
accommodation 33
activities, Hobart 94
Adamsons Peak 138
Adventure Bay 131
air fares 19
airlines 22
alcohol 38
alcohol limit 27
Allendale Gardens 282
Alonnah 132
Alum Cliffs 168
Ann Bay 283
Ansons Bay 247
Antarctic 7
apartments 34
apples 7
Apsley Waterhole 197
Archers Knob 261
Arthur Pieman
    Conservation Area..... 286
Arthur River 16, 284
Arthur, George 146, 355
Arthurs Beach 284
Arthurs Lake 158
Arve Falls 138
ATMs 58
Aussie Rules 42
Australia Day 40
Australian English 372

B

B&Bs 34
backpacker
    accommodation 34
Bacon, Jim 362
Badger Beach 261
Bagdad 148
Bakers Beach 261
Balfour 287
Barnbougle Dunes 244
Barnes Bay 130
Bass Strait Islands
    333–348
Batman Bridge 235

Batman, John 230
Baudin, Nicolas 179, 188, 353
Bay of Fires 16, 204
Beaconsfield 232
Beaumaris 200
Beauty Point 233
beer .... 38 &
    Food and drink colour
    section
Ben Lomond
    National Park 238
Bernacchi, Diego, ... 181
Bicheno 192–197
Bicheno 194
Big Tree Reserve 326
Binalong Bay 204, 205
Bird River Walks 299
birdlife 178
bistros 37
black currawong 366
Black Line 357
Blackman's Bay 102
Bligh, William 352
Blue Tier, The 243
Bluff Hill 284
Boat Harbour Beach 274
boat travel 29
boats from Australia 24
Bonorong Wildlife
    Centre 147
books 369
Bothwell 156
Bowen,
    Lieutenant John 353
Brady, Matthew 231, 307
Brady's Lake 160
Brady's Lookout
    State Reserve 231
Break-Me Neck Hill 177
Bridestowe
    Lavender Farm 241
Bridport 244
Brighton 147
Bronte Park 161
Bruny Island 126–133
Bruny Island 127
Bryans Beach 191
Buckland 177
budgeting 52
Burke McHugo,
    Jonathan 214
Burnie 269–272
Burnie 270

buses, metropolitan 32
bushcamping 15, 35
bushwalking 16, 45, 46, 67, 112, 239, 315
Bust-Me-Gall Hill 177

C

cafés 37
Calcified Forest 347
Calverts Beach 106
Campbell Town 151
campervans 26
camping 35
Cape Grim 281
Cape Portland 245
Cape Tourville 192
Cape Wickham
    Lighthouse 343
car rental 25, 26
car, buying a 28
caravan parks 35
carbon offset schemes 21
Carrick 162
Cash, Martin 111
Cash's Gorge Walk 243
Catamaran 139
central highlands see
    The great outdoors colour
    section
Central Hobart 68–69
Central Plateau, The..... 155
Central Tasmania 146
Channel Highway 122
cheeses see *Food and
    drink* colour section
children,
    travelling with 51
Chinamans Bay 183
Chudleigh 167
Clarendon
    Homestead 153
Clarke, Marcus 306
climate 10
climbing 44
Cliton Beach 106
clothing sizes 50
coach travel 29
Coal Valley Vineyards
    104
Cockle Creek 140, 325
coffee 38

Coles Bay 190
Coles Bay.................... 187
Collins, Lieutenant-colonel
    David 353
conservation 8
Cook, James 352
Cooks Beach 191
Copping 108
Corinna 287
costs 52
Cosy Corner 205
cottages 34
Couta Rocks 287
Cradle Mountain
    .... 11, 312
**Cradle Mountain–Lake
    St Clare National
    Park** 311–320
crafts 50, 163
Creepy Crawly
    Nature Trail 328
crime 52
Crocketts Bay 192
Currie 345
cycling 31, 44, 88,
    95, 177, 224
Cygnet 125

D

D'Entrecasteaux,
    Bruni 140, 353
Darlington 182
Darwin, Charles 358
Deloraine 163–168
Deloraine...................... 164
Dempster Plains
    Lookout 282
Dennes Point 130
Derby 241
Derwent Bridge 319
Derwent Valley, The
    158–161
Devonport........... 253–258
Devonport 254
Dial Range
    State Forest 268
Dilston 235
discount cards 52
disabilities, Travellers with
    60
Dismal Swamp 282
diving 12, 274, 275
dolphins 367
**Douglas-Apsley
    National Park** 197, 362
Dove Lake 316

Dover 138
drink 38
driving 25
Duckhole Lake 138
Dunally 108

E

Eaglehawk Neck 110
eagles 366
east coast, The 176
Eastern Arthur Range
    330
eating .... 14 & *Food
    and drink* colour section
echidnas 365
Eddystone Bay 204
Eddystone Lighthouse... 247
electricity 53
Elephant Pass 198
Eliza Plateau 329
embassies 54
emergencies 52, 53
Emita 340
entry requirements 53
etiquette 49
eucalyptus .... 368 &
    The great outdoors colour
    section
Evandale 152–153
Exeter 231

F

Falmouth 200
farmstays 57
fauna 364
Federation Peak 330
ferries 24, 29
festivals 40, 227
fiction 369
Fingal 199
fish see *Food and drink*
    colour section
fishing 45, 157, 204
flights to Tasmania 19,
    20, 21
flights within Tasmania
    29
Flinders Island 337–342
Flinders Island 336
Flinders Trail 341
Flinders, Matthew
    .... 337, 353
flora 364

fly-drive packages 19
food .... 36 & *Food
    and drink* colour section
Forestier & Tasman
    Peninsulas 109
forestry 8
Fortescue Bay 112
Fossil Bluff 273
Fotheringate Bay 342
Four Mile Creek 200
Frankland Range 328
Franklin 135, 321
Franklin Blockade 311
Franklin dam 360
Franklin River 14
**Franklin–Gordon
    Wild Rivers
    National Park** 320–322
Frenchmans Cap Track
    322
Freycinet National Park
    186–193
Freycinet National Park
    187
Friendly Beaches 190
frogs 366
fruit-picking 56

G

Gandalf's Staff 326
Gardens, The 205
gay Hobart 93
gay travellers 54
Geeveston 135
George Town 236
Georges Bay 201
Ghost Rock Vineyard
    260
Gladstone 245
Goblin Forest Walk 244
Godfreys Beach 280
Gondwana 351
Gordon Dam 12
Gordon River 303, 320
Goulds Country 243
Governor Island Marine
    Nature Reserve 195
Gowrie Park 263
Granton 97
Grants Lagoon 205
Granville Harbour 309
Grassy 347
Gravelly Beach 232
Great Lake 158, 360
Great Oyster Bay 184
Green Point Beach 283

Greens Beach..............234
Grindelwald 231
Grove...........................134
Gulch, the...................195
gum trees see *The great
  outdoors* colour section
Gunns Plain.................266

H

Hadspen......................161
Hamilton 159
hang-gliding 44
**Hartz Mountains
  National Park** 137, 138
Hastings caves.............139
Haunted Bay................183
Hawley Beach 260
Hazards 190, 191
health............................54
Hells Gates.................306
Hellyer Gorge State
  Reserve.....................289
Henty Dunes................306
Highfield 280
Highland Lakes
  Highway....................157
hiking, Rocky Cape
  National Park.............275
history.........................351
HOBART 65–96
Hobart and around........66
Central Hobart.........68–69
Hobart suburbs.............83
Mount Wellington 87
  accommodation................70
  activities 94
  airport.............................67
  Allport Library and Museum
    of Fine Arts 82
  Alpenrail 84
  apartments.......................70
  B&Bs 70
  banks...............................95
  bars 92
  Battery Point 78
  beaches............................81
  Bellerive...........................85
  bike rental 95
  bookshops 95
  botanical gardens 82
  bus companies 95
  buses 70
  Cadbury's Factory.............84
  cafés................................89
  camping 95
  car rental 96
  Cascade Brewery..............86
  Cascade Gardens 86
  Centre for the Arts 74
  cinema 91, 93

classical music..................91
concerts 93
cruises.............................75
cycle tours 95
cycling, Mount Wellington
 88
diving................................96
docks 74
eating 89
Errol Flynn Reserve...........85
ferries 70
festivals 93
films.................................93
Franklin Square................79
gay Hobart 93
ghost tour.........................82
Glenorchy.........................82
Government House...........82
history 66
hostels.............................70
hotels 70
House-Museum Narryna....79
information 67
internet access................96
Knopwood,
  Reverend Robert 78
Lark Distillery 74
laundry 96
Maritime Museum of
  Tasmania.......................74
MONA 84
Moorilla Estate Winery.......84
Mount Wellington 86
nightlife............................91
parliament 77
Peacock Theatre...............91
Penitentiary Chapel and
  Criminal Courts..............81
pharmacy 96
Pinnacle Observatory
  Centre............................87
post office 96
pubs 91
Queens Domain 82
restaurants 89
Royal Showground 84
Royal Tasmanian Botanical
  Gardens 82
Runnymede........................84
Salamanca Arts Centre......77
Salamanca Market............77
Salamanca Place 75
Salamanca Square.............77
Sandy Bay.........................85
Sir James Plimsoll Gallery
 70
St David's Cathedral 80
surfing 96
swimming..........................96
Tasmanian Museum and
  Art Gallery......................80
taxis.................................96
theatre..............................93
Theatre Royal...............81, 91
tours..................................94
transport............................70
walking, Mount Wellington
 88

Wrest Point 85
yacht race 93
YHA..................................96
Hollybank Forest 240
honeyeaters.................366
Hope Beach 106
horses............................44
hostels............................34
hotels..............................33
Humboldt Divide...........328
Huon Highway..............132
Huon pine trees see *The
  great outdoors* colour
  section
Huonville......................133

I

Ida Bay Railway............139
Inglis River...................273
insurance................25, 55
internet 56
Iron Blow 299

J

Jacobs Ladder 238
Jericho..........................148
jobs................................56
Jordan River 148
Julius River Forest........282
Junne Cave 326

K

kangaroos....................365
kayaking 16
Kempton.......................148
Kettering.......................123
Killiecrankie 341
King Island 343–348
King Island...................344
King Solomons Cave....168
Kingston 102
kookaburras 366

L

Lady Barron..................342
Lagoons Beach
  Reserve......................200
Lake Barrington............264

Lake Big Jim.................160
Lake Burbury.................299
Lake Chisholm...............282
Lake Johnston Nature
  Reserve......................309
Lake Mackenzie 169
Lake Osbourne.............138
Lake Pedder 328
Lake Rhona 328
Lake St Clair.................317
Lake Tiberias 148
Lanne, William 356
Latrobe 258–260
LAUNCESTON..... 213–218
Launceston 215
  Aboriginal art...................221
  accommodation 216
  airport................................214
  Albert Hall 219
  Alexandra
    Suspension Bridge 223
  banks 228
  bars 227
  B&Bs 216
  Basin Walk 222
  bike rental 228
  Blacksmiths Shop 220
  Boag Centre for
    Beer Lovers 220
  bookshops 228
  Brisbane Street 217
  cafés 226
  car rental 228
  caravan parks 217
  Cataract Gorge 222
  Cataract Walk 222
  cinema 227
  City Park 219
  Civic Square....................219
  Cliff Grounds...................222
  clubs 227
  Customs House 220
  cycling..............................224
  Design Centre of
    Tasmania......................220
  Duck Reach Power Station
   223
  Duck Reach Track...........223
  Eagle Eyrie Lookout 222
  eating 225
  Eskmarket 221
  festivals 227
  First Basin 222
  Franklin House 225
  golf 228
  Heritage Forest 221
  hospital.............................228
  hostels..............................217
  hotels 216
  information 215
  internet access................228
  Inveresk Precinct 220
  John Hart Conservatory....219
  Kings Bridge 222
  Kiz Zag Track 222

Launceston Basin Chairlift
 222
Launceston Tramway
  Museum.........................220
markets 228
motels 216
National Automobile Museum
  of Tasmania 220
nightlife..............................226
Northbank Experience 221
Old Launceston Seaport
 222
pharmacy 228
Planetarium 221
post office 228
Princes Square.................219
pubs 227
Queen Victoria Museum
  and Art Gallery..............221
Railway Workshops..........220
restaurants 225
Ritchies Mill
  Arts Centre 222
Royal Park 221
Second Basin....................223
spas 228
swimming 222, 228
Tamar River 221
Tasmanian Wood Design
  Collection......................220
taxis 228
theatre...............................226
tours 224
Town Hall 219
transport............................216
Trevallyn 221
Trevallyn Dam...................224
Trevallyn State Recreation
  Centre............................224
volunteering 228
walking tour 219
laundry..............................56
Legerwood 242
Legges Tor.....................238
Leven Canyon 266
Lighthouse Point 283
Lilydale 240
Little Gravelly Beach 191
living in Tasmania 56
lizards 366
Longford 153
Lottah 243
Low Head 236
Lyell Highway 320
Lyons, Joseph 360

M

Macquarie, Governor
  Lachlan 146
mail 57
Mangalore....................148

Mango Bay 114
maps...............................57
Marakoopa Cave..........168
Margate 123
Maria Island 178–184
Maria Island 180
Marrawah......................283
Mawbanna 275
Maydena.......................325
Mayfield Bay Coastal
  Reserve......................184
Meander River 163
media.............................39
Medicare........................55
Melbourne,
  founding of 230
Mermaid's Pool 244
Miena.............................158
Milkshakes Hills Forest
  Reserve......................282
mobile phones...............59
Mole Creek 168
money.............................58
Montezuma Falls 309
Moorina 242
Moreys Bay 192
mosquitoes....................55
motels............................34
motorbikes 26
Mount Amos.................191
Mount Anne..................329
Mount Bischoff.............289
Mount Cameron West
 284
Mount Direction............235
Mount Field National Park
 99
Mount Jukes.................299
Mount Maria 183
Mount Michael Track....244
Mount Ossa..................318
Mount Parsons.............192
Mount Poimena............244
Mount Roland.......262, 263
Mount Strzelecki
  National Park.......12, 341
Mount Tanner 341
Mount Victoria
  Forest Reserve 243
Mount Wellington 86
Mount Wellington 87
Mount William National
  Park 246
mountain-biking 44, 88
Moutling Bay
  Lagoon.......................190
Musselroe Bay..............247
muttonbirds 340

N

Narawntapu
  National Park 261
national parks 46, 48
Nebraska Beach 131
Nettley's Bay 283
New Norfolk 97
newspapers 39
Nine Mile Beach 186
North Sister 198
northeast, The 212
northwest, The 252
Notley Fern Gorge 231
Nut State reserve 280

O

Oast House Hop Museum
  98
Oatlands 148
Ocean Beach 305
Orford 177
Ouse 160
Overland Track 11, 318

P

Pacoe Fawkner, John
  230
pademelons 365
painting 49
Palawa 356
Parks & Wildlife Service
  44
parrots 366
Patriarchs Wildlife
  Sanctuary 342
Pearce, Alexander 307
Penguin 268
penguins 238, 367
Peninsula Track 191
personal safety 52
Philosopher's Falls 289
phones 59
Picnic Rock Beach 247
Pipers Brook 241
platypus 365
Poimena 244
Pontville 147
Port Arthur 112–114
Port Davey Track 330
Port Esperance 138
Port Sorrell 260

possums 365
post 57
Preminghana Indigenous
  Protected Area 284
price codes 33
prison camps 355
prison settlement 112
public holidays 58, 59
pubs 35
Pyengana 243

Q

Queenstown 295–298
Queenstown 296

R

racism 53
radio 39
rafting the Franklin 321
Railton 263
rainfall 10
rainforest .... 367 &
  The great outdoors colour
  section
Ralphs falls 243
Ranelagh 134
Recherche Bay 140
Reidle Beach 183
restaurants 37
Richmond 102–105
riding 44
Robertson, George
  Augustus 357
Robigana 232
**Rocky Cape National
  Park** 274–275
Rosebury 309
Rosevears 231
Ross 149–151
round-the-world tickets
  22
Rubicon River estuary
  260
Russell falls 100

S

sailing 43
Salamanca Market 13,
  77, 89, 93
Sarah Island 306

Savage River 289
Scamander 200
Schouten Island 192
Scottsdale 241
scuba-diving 43
sea kayaking 43
seafood .... 36 &
  Food and drink colour
  section
seals 367
Settlement Point 341
Seven Mile Beach 107
Shadow Lake Circuit
  319
Shearwater 260
shearwaters 367
Sheffield 262–263
shellfish see *colour section*
Shelly Beach 177
shoe sizes 50
shopping 49
Sisters Beach 274
Skeleton Point 204
skiing 44
Skulduggery 147
Sleepy Bay
Smithton 281
snakes 55, 328, 366
snorkelling, Rocky Cape
  National Park 275
Snug 123
Sorell 108
Sorell, Thomas 354
South Arm 105, 106
South Coast Track 331
South Mile Beach 281
South Sister 198
Southwest Cape 331
Southwest National Park
  .... 15, 140, 323
southeast, The 122
speed limits 27
spiders 55
Spiky Bridge 184
sports 42
Spring Beach village 177
Springlawn
  Nature Park 261
St Columba Falls 243
St Helens 200–206
St Helens 202
St Marys 198
Stanley 276–280
Stanley 277
Staverton 264
steak see *Food and drink*
  colour section
Steppes Sculptures 157
Strahan 299–307

INDEX

389

Strahan........................300
Strathblane..................139
Strathgordon 329
Strzelecki National Park
........................341–342
Styx Valley 326
Sumac Lookout............282
Sundown Point.............287
surfing..............13, 42, 196
Swan Point 232
Swansea......................184
Swimcart Beach...........205
swimming 42, 196, 275

T

Table Cape 273
Tahune Forest Reserve
..................................136
Tamar Islands Wetlands
..................................230
Tamar Valley Point Mill
..................................234
Tamar Valley 228
Tamar Valley.................229
Taranna.......................110
Tarkine, The..........14, 282,
285, 286
Taroona.......................101
Tarraleah 160
Tasman Peninsula 15,
107, 114
Tasman, Abel Jansz 179,
188, 352
Tasmania Craft Fair 163
Tasmanian Devil
Conservation Park.....111
Tasmanian Devils...........15,
284, 364
Tasmanian Trail............258
Taylors Beach...............205
television 39
Temma.........................287
temperatures 10
Tiger Lookout 328
Timbs Track.................328
time...............................59
tipping 49
Tobias Furneaux Lookout
..................................342
Tolkein Track................326
Tomahawk 245
tour operators.....24, 31, 44
tourist information 59
tours
  Bicheno...........................197
  Bruny Island....................129
  Coles Bay.........................191

Cradle Mountain 314
Frenchmans
  Cap Track 322
Hobart.................................94
King Island 347
Launceston 224
Maria Island 183
Southwest
  National Park................324
St Helens...........................204
Tasman Peninsula 116
transport 25
travel agents...................23
traveller's cheques 58
Triabunna......................178
Trial Harbour.................309
Trousers Point 12, 342
trout fishing 157
Trowunna Wildlife Park
..................................168
Truganini 128, 356
Tullah 309

U

Ulverstone 267
Upper Florentine Valley
..................................326

V

Van Diemen's Land.......230
Van Diemen's Land
  Company 279
vineyards ....104, 237 &
  Food and drink colour
  section
visas 53

W

Waddamana Power Station
..................................157
walking 170, 206
walking, Cradle Mountain–
  Lake St Clare National
  Park 315, 319
walking, Deloraine 166
walking, Frenchmans
  Cap Track 322
walking, Maria Island....183
walking, Mount Wellington
..................................88
wallabies......................365

Walls of Jerusalem
  National Park ... 169–170
Waratah 289
Waratah Lookout..........138
Waterhouse 245
Waubs Bay 193
weather......................10, 55
websites 60
Weindorfer, Gustav 316
Weldborough 242
west and
  southwest, The 294
West Coast Wilderness
  Railways 298
Westbury 162
Western Arthurs Traverse
..................................330
Western Explorer 186
Westerway 99
whales 367
whaling 188
Whitemark 339
white-water rafting 43
Wielangta Forest Drive
..................................177
wildlife..........................364
Wilmot 265
wine 38, 104, 237
  & *Food and drink* colour
  section
Wineglass Bay..............191
Wing's Wildlife Park......267
wombats.......................365
Woodbridge..................124
woodcraft 49
Woolnorth 281
working...........................53
World Heritage Area 310
World Heritage Centre see
  The great outdoors colour
  section
Wybalenna............341, 357
Wynyard 273

Y

yacht race......................41
YHA 34
York Town 234
youth hostel
  associations................35

Z

Zeehan.........................307

Map symbols

maps are listed in the full index using coloured text

▪▫▬	State/territorial boundary	⊙	Statue
▫▬▬	Chapter division boundary	🏊	Swimming pool
══	Main road	🤿	Snorkelling
══	Minor road	🐟	Shipwreck
▭▭▭▭	Unpaved road	🌊	Surfing
▬▬	Pedestrianized street (town maps)	🍇	Vineyard
▥▥▥	Steps	开	Picnic area
▪▪▪▪	Path/track	★	Bus/taxi stop
··········	4WD	◆	Point of interest
══►══	Railway	@	Internet access
— —	Ferry route	ⓘ	Information office
••••••••••••	Chairlift	✉	Post office
——	River	⊞	Hospital
▲	Mountain peak	🅿	Parking
⚹	Viewpoint	⛽	Petrol station
⚘	Waterfall	⚠	Campsite
⚘	Spring	◉	Accommodation
⌂	Cave	◼	Restaurant
⚲	Lighthouse	⚱	Church (regional maps)
✈	Airport	▬	Building
✗	Domestic airport	⊢	Church
⚐	Fortress	▨	Park/forest
⛫	Stately home	▨	Beach
⛫	Monument	⊤	Cemetery